# Congress and the Presidency
## in U.S. Foreign Policymaking

# Westview Replica Editions

The concept of Westview Replica Editions is a response to the continuing crisis in academic and informational publishing. Library budgets for books have been severely curtailed. Ever larger portions of general library budgets are being diverted from the purchase of books and used for data banks, computers, micromedia, and other methods of information retrieval. Interlibrary loan structures further reduce the edition sizes required to satisfy the needs of the scholarly community. Economic pressures on the university presses and the few private scholarly publishing companies have severely limited the capacity of the industry to properly serve the academic and research communities. As a result, many manuscripts dealing with important subjects, often representing the highest level of scholarship, are no longer economically viable publishing projects--or, if accepted for publication, are typically subject to lead times ranging from one to three years.

Westview Replica Editions are our practical solution to the problem. We accept a manuscript in camera-ready form, typed according to our specifications, and move it immediately into the production process. As always, the selection criteria include the importance of the subject, the work's contribution to scholarship, and its insight, originality of thought, and excellence of exposition. The responsibility for editing and proofreading lies with the author or sponsoring institution. We prepare chapter headings and display pages, file for copyright, and obtain Library of Congress Cataloging in Publication Data. A detailed manual contains simple instructions for preparing the final typescript, and our editorial staff is always available to answer questions.

The end result is a book printed on acid-free paper and bound in sturdy library-quality soft covers. We manufacture these books ourselves using equipment that does not require a lengthy make-ready process and that allows us to publish first editions of 300 to 600 copies and to reprint even smaller quantities as needed. Thus, we can produce Replica Editions quickly and can keep even very specialized books in print as long as there is a demand for them.

# About the Book and Author

*Congress and the Presidency*
*in U.S. Foreign Policymaking: A Study*
*of Interaction and Influence, 1945-1982*

John Rourke

During the 1950s and 1960s, observers often dismissed Congress as a minor appendage of the foreign policymaking process. Later, in the aftermath of the Vietnam War and Watergate, politicians, the press, and scholars described a new era of codetermination of foreign policy involving a resurgent legislature and a weakened presidency. Arguing against both of these views, Dr. Rourke traces the interaction of the legislative and executive branches of government during the entire post-World War II period to demonstrate a regular pattern of influence in the policymaking process. His analysis shows that Congress was in fact more important during the days of the imperial presidency than often supposed, and that it is less influential now than many contend. Dr. Rourke bases his analysis on Lasswell and Kaplan's classic conceptualization of infuence and on interviews and extensive study of oral histories, congressional documents, and archives.

Dr. Rourke is an associate professor of political science at the University of Connecticut.

To my parents
for making me do my homework

# Congress and the Presidency in U.S. Foreign Policymaking
## A Study of Interaction and Influence, 1945-1982

John Rourke

Westview Press / Boulder, Colorado

*A Westview Replica Edition*

Copyright © 1983 by Westview Press, Inc.

Published in 1983 in the United States of America by
Westview Press, Inc.
5500 Central Avenue
Boulder, Colorado 80301
Frederick A. Praeger, President and Publisher

Library of Congress Cataloging in Publications Data
Rourke, John T.
Congress and the presidency in U.S. foreign policymaking.

(A Westview replica edition)
Bibliography:p.
1. United States--Foreign relations--1945-
2. Presidents--United States. 3. United States.
Congress. I. Title.
JK570.R68 1983        327.73        83-10171
ISBN 0-86531-989-8

Printed and bound in the United States of America.

10 9 8 7 6 5 4 3

# Acknowledgments

There was a time when I considered the title "author" a singular appellation. The experience of writing this manuscript has shown me how misleading that idea was. Part of any praise, but none of any criticism, that this study evokes belongs to an able cast of supporting characters. J. Garry Clifford, friend and colleague, read the manuscript several times, and I am indebted for his general intellectual leadership and his specific comments. Russell Farnen also read and thoughtfully critiqued the entire manuscript. Louis Gerson, W. Wayne Shannon, and Susan Koch also read and made helpful comments on parts of the manuscript.

There were also many "technical" supporters without whose help the task would have been virtually impossible. Kathie Holmes is an extraordinary typist who can read the unreadable and transcribe it accurately. Additionally, she has infinite patience for a multitude of changes and a fine diplomatic ability to point out where my usage was inconsistent or plain didn't make sense. Erni Hamlin also gave important help copy editing the manuscript.

I also owe a great deal to the archivists at the many manuscript collections listed in the bibliography. In perhaps two years of "on-the-road" research, I found them dedicated and helpful. They often stayed after hours and pointed to paths that I was not aware of. To paraphrase Will Rogers, I never met a manuscript librarian I didn't like. I would also like to thank the University of Connecticut Research Foundation and its head, Dean Hugh Clark, for the financial support of my research and typing.

For all these direct contributions, perhaps the greatest thanks go to Meredith and John Michael Rourke. They know of their contribution and of my caring, and that is enough.

Last I am grateful to the editors of Westview Press for their patience during the l-o-n-g gestation of the final manuscript.

J.T.R.
Hartford, Conn.

# Introduction

Commentary on the respective roles of Congress and the presidency in the formulation of foreign policy conjures up three literary allusions. One is a Dickensonian "A Tale of Two Presidencies" which refers to Aaron Wildavsky's concept of two areas of presidential power so decisively distinct that they must be considered separately. In foreign policy, Wildavsky tells us, the president reigns virtually supreme. Domestically, the president is but one among many. With apologies to Edgar Allen Poe, a second approach to the subject might be entitled, "The Policy and the Pendulum," in which the struggle between the first two branches of government cyclically swings the power pendulum to and fro while the captive corpus americanus watches from below. A third conceptualization of the process is Edward Corwin's "invitation to struggle" which brings to mind Shakespeare's soliloquy from Macbeth: "Tomorrow, and tomorrow, and tomorrow . . . to the last syllable of recorded time . . . full of sound and fury . . . ." Thus, as Corwin has it, the constitutional contest for power between the president and Congress is inevitable and unending.

At the risk of further muddying the waters, this study's view of the respective roles of the Congress and the Presidency in the field of foreign policy might be related to Jonathan Swift's classic Gulliver's Travels. Two scenes seem especially appropriate to this book's concept of reciprocal presidential and congressional influence. The first is when the shipwrecked Gulliver awakens on the shore of Lilliput to find himself bound by countless ropes. Although he is a giant among the Lilliputians, he is nonetheless their captive. A second apt analogy is suggested by Gulliver's description of the Emperor of Lilliput as "taller by almost a breath of my nail than any of his court, which alone is enough to strike awe into the beholders." Those two somewhat contradictory characterizations, a giant bound and an awesome emperor, tell us much about the American foreign policy process. The president's powers are awesome, even imperial, but Congress can cast a constricting web.

Scholarly interpretation of the balance of power in Washington has tended to portray the initial three quarters of the twentieth century as a period of long term decline of congressional

xiii

power and a concurrent increase in presidential power. The decrease of congressional initiative in policy formation has been particularly noted, with foreign policy cited as a pronounced example of Congress' failure or inability to play a significant policy-making role. Despite this seeming imbalance between the two institutions, many welcomed it. They argued that the speed and complexity of foreign affairs and need for decisive leadership precluded the ponderous, parochial, and fragmented Congress from any positive foreign policy role. The "imperial presidency" sparked a political dialectic that dispelled that prevailing thesis. In the aftermath of Vietnam and Watergate, scholars, journalists, and politicians found new virtues in Congress. From Capitol Hill and from along the sidelines, pundits proclaimed a new era of legislative influence on the foreign policy process. Assertions of equal influence with the Executive were made, and while the presidency stood abashed and hesitant in the 1970s, Congress armed itself with a series of assertive actions, statutes, and resolutions.

These analyses and proclamations leave a number of questions unanswered. Does the latter day sound and fury in Congress really constitute a policy process revolution? Even granting change, has there been a dramatic shift in the respective foreign policy roles of the legislative and executive branches? This study answers these questions in the negative. The basic thesis of the study is that Congress has long played a significant, if subtle, inconsistent, and secondary role in the foreign policy process. Further, the activism of recent years does not equate to a new era of dominant or even equal influence. Nor is it a long term or dramatic shift from the past. Congress was never as weak as it was usually portrayed in the past nor is it as powerful as contemporary commentary often pictures it.

To deal with these important differences of interpretation, we must consider the foreign policy roles of the President and Congress during the entire post-World War II period. One key concept used throughout is influence. Using the formulation of Harold D. Lasswell and Abraham Kaplan, influence is based on the interplay of "values" and "means." Basically the idea is that if one has the "means" to affect another's "values," then one has influence over that person. An example of a value would be "national unity," while means would include "dissent." Influence, then, is when an actor that values national unity acts, reacts, or stops acting in order to quiet real or potential dissent. A closely related concept is "scope," which refers to the kinds of issues over which influence is exercised.[1] In other words, it deals with issue-areas or policy typologies and the nature of reciprocal influence between the Executive and Congress in each area. One goal of this study is to identify the patterns of mutual influence based on values, means, and scope. That, in turn, will help explain why and how the president normally dominates foreign policy. It will also help delineate when Congress is likely to become active, how Congress acts, and why the Executive reacts.

This study divides the post-World War II period into three parts. The initial period covers the first term of President

Truman. These nearly four years are important because they marked a pivotal point in American foreign policy as the United States emerged as a world power, and also because extensive manuscript and archival source material are available to explore the influence of the respective branches. The second part of the study approximates Truman's second term through the early Nixon years. During these years both the pattern of the cold war and the foreign policy process generally continued as established in the 1945-1948 period. Therefore, by examining the 1949-1973 period it is possible to further identify and refine the values, means, and scope of legislative-executive influence. The passage of time and freedom of information have made substantial original source material for that period also available.

The final section which covers the post Watergate and Vietnam period deals with the much discussed surge of congressional activism. The conclusion of this study is that whatever changes have occurred have been both overestimated and are temporary in nature. The overestimation results from underestimating Congress' previous influence in the foreign policy process and also from making too much of what increased influence and activity there has been. Further, the values-means-scope patterns that were in evidence prior to Vietnam and Watergate have remained largely in force for nearly four decades and can explain the adjustments which have occurred. The persistence of these patterns also portends a return to the normalcy of marked executive dominance in the near future.

Past, present, and probable future presidential dominance of the foreign policy process has been and is supported by the dynamics of executive and legislative means and values. As will be detailed as this study unfolds, there are a number of congressional values which restrain that institution from exercising the full extent of its foreign policy powers. Parochialism is one such value. Normally there is scant connection between reelection and foreign policy. Therefore, members focus on constituency related domestic issues and leave foreign policy to the executive. Legitimacy is another restraining value. Congress is aware of both the tradition of executive dominance of foreign policy-making and also has severe self-doubt about its own ability to play a leading or equal role in that process. Congress thus views the president as legitimately in charge of foreign policy. Congress also values consensus. During times of international dispute, particularly during times of crisis, Congress is extremely reluctant to criticize the Executive and present "a house divided against itself" to the world. Party loyalty, for those of the president's party, is a value which largely keeps whatever dissent that might occur to the opposition party and also opens up the dissenters to the unwelcome charge of playing partisan politics with the national interest.

While these congressional values tend to work to make Congress acquiescent in the foreign policy process, most of them can have a reverse effect. They can activate Congress in some situations. These circumstances determine the scope, or areas of congressional interest. The electoral connection, for example, becomes operational when domestic resources or subcultural groups

become involved. Constituency considerations then occur and
Congress is much more attentive. Issues such as trade or those
involving ethnic groups often involve a struggle over their definition. Are they foreign or domestic in nature? How that issue
is resolved plays a substantial role in determining the level of
legislative activity and the likelihood of legislative influence.
A definitional struggle that results in a domestic focus also
breaks down Congress' value of executive legitimacy. No such
policy dominance legitimacy is extended to the president in
domestic policy, and Congress feels free and equal to contest the
issue. Similarly, the value of consensus has no relevance in the
domestic policy process.

When, contrary to the norm, issues become entangled with
partisan politics, Congress is again more likely to become
active. This can happen on a congressional level by the inter-
jection of narrow constituency interests such as economics or
ethnic group issues. On a broader level, it can also involve an
issue like Vietnam where many members of both parties sensed an
electoral stake in their stand on that issue. Presidential politics can also activate potential candidates who perceive a need
to build a foreign policy reputation.

The value of parochialism also works to the executive's dis-
advantage where innovative policy, rather than incremental
tactics, is at issue. Congress, along with its locally based
constituencies, is a part of the foreign policy periphery which
is disquieted by major changes in policy that break with the
existing consensus.

Issues or procedures which adversely reflect on Congress'
institutional pride or the egos of its individual members
constitute another area of legislative activity. When Congress
feels slighted by the lack of at least pro-forma consultation or
when it becomes sensitive to its own pattern of foreign policy
acquiescence, as happens after periods of prolonged crisis, then
it is much more likely to try to assert its institutional prerogatives.

Finally, in the delineation of scope, periods of executive
weakness also activate Congress in the foreign policy process.
This weakness can involve individual executive weakness where a
president is considered unskilled or unassertive or when there
are major divisions within the executive's ranks. Weakness can
also be a more institutional phenomenon. The damage done to the
stature of the presidency by Vietnam and Watergate is the most
recent example. Then it is the office, not just its occupant,
which is called into question and the congressionally held values
of legitimacy and consensus tend to break down. In such cases,
either individual or institutional, the executive branch is
deprived of a part of its consensus and/or its legitimacy to
conduct foreign policy.

In normal periods or even during times of marked congressional foreign policy activity, there are a variety of executive
means at the president's disposal. The chief executive can
invoke his office. As head of state as well as head of
government, the president can initiate action, emphasize the
quantitative information and expertise superiority of the

executive branch, dominate direct and indirect media communications to the nation, and wrap himself in the flag. Particularly in times of crisis, public and congressional opinion are then prone to swing strongly behind the president and national unity. It is a rare legislator who is willing to swim against the tide.

Political support is another means in the president's arsenal. There are a variety of benefits from dams to fund raising appearances that a president can bestow on cooperative congressmen. Sanctions are also occasionally employed. A closely related executive means is ego appeal. Presidents can work on Congress' institutional and individual prides through shows of access, consultation, praise, and even Oval Office trinkets. The White House is the center of the American political universe, and legislators love to bask in the sun.

When activated, there are also a range of congressional means which that institution can use to influence foreign policy. Congress possesses a number of formal powers including appropriations, ratification, confirmation, and general lawmaking authority. Beyond the direct impact of their application, Congress' formal means are potent because of the executive value of sanction avoidance. Legislative losses detract from the president's professional reputation and his domestic and foreign image as national leader. Faced with defeat, a president may choose to "switch" rather than "fight." Presidents are also mindful of the "carom effect." Even if the Executive can prevail on an issue, it may prove a pyrrhic victory which alienates powerful members of Congress and results in retaliation on other issues.

Criticism in the form of debate, dissent, investigation and the publicizing of alternate information is another informal congressional means. Presidents value consensus just as Congress does. In the face of vigorous congressional dissent, which the Executive tends to perceive as linked to public opinion, presidents often will move to compromise in order to achieve the national unity they feel is important to success on the international scene.

The scope of congressional influence over foreign policy, then, is a dynamic political process. It is determined in part by the formal, constitutional powers of the legislative and executive branches. But beyond these powers, it is also heavily dependent on an interacting series of congressional means and executive values and executive means and congressional values. Highlighting and defining that interactive process as it determines foreign policy is the task of the chapters that follow.

# 1
# Truman . . . Vandenberg . . . Byrnes:
# The Early Cold War Triumvirate

To say that the end of World War II marked the beginning of a new and distinct era of American foreign policy is an understatement. The world changed, United States foreign policy changed, and on April the 12th, 1945, the presidency changed. The vacuum left by the collapse of the old world and the void left by the death of Franklin Roosevelt changed policy and policy-making on both the global and national scene.

## A Most Unlikely President:  Harry S Truman

The man who stood necessarily at the vortex of American policy in the new era was the thirty-third President of the United States, Harry S Truman. Yet the new President was in many ways ill-suited to the difficult tasks before him. President Truman had little of the aura of power that Franklin Delano Roosevelt had possessed and everyone, including Truman, was well aware of his throttle bottom image as the "little man from Missouri." A popular quip of the day philosophized, "To err is Truman . . ." In particular, the new President lacked experience and expertise in the field of foreign policy. This was not only apparent to those in the Executive Branch, it was also a commonly shared view among members of Congress. Not long after Truman's accession to the presidency, Michigan's Republican Senator Arthur Vandenberg worried in his diary, "there is no longer any strong hand on our foreign policy rudder."(1) Republican Senator George Aiken of Vermont later recalled that the day Truman was sworn in he came to lunch with congressional leaders and "the tears ran right down his cheek. He kept saying, 'I'm not big enough for this job, I'm not big enough for this job.'" It was hardly a confidence building performance in front of the legislative barons who tended to agree with Truman's assessment of his ability. "And of course the people believed it too, that he wasn't," Aiken candidly concluded.(2)

Truman never really attained the reputation for foreign policy expertise that had been Roosevelt's. Soon after Truman entered office, nationally respected columnist Walter Lippmann wrote to John McCloy, "With Truman what he is, there is simply no

one to take a general view of our interests and our policy . . .
Since Truman can't conduct foreign policy as Roosevelt did . . .
we shall not succeed until we overcome this fundamental trouble
that there is no central command of foreign policy." McCloy
responded, "I do not think you could be more right about the lack
of coordinating direction in our foreign policy."(3)

In September 1946, Assistant Secretary of State Donald
Russell wrote to his boss, Secretary James F. Byrnes, "The overwhelming consensus here [in Washington] is that he [Truman]
really doesn't know what he is doing in the field of foreign
policy." The President, Russell continued, "is a man of good
will, but completely out of his depth . . . he still fails to see
. . . the implications of the policy he has been following."(4)
At the time of the Truman Doctrine in 1947, a friendly analyst
also has recalled:

> The authority of the executive branch of government was
> about as low as it was possible. President Truman had . . .
> inherited . . . a mantle that was ill fitting . . .
> Truman lacked confidence in his ability to perform accepta-
> bly the functions of his high office and freely admitted it.
> Moreover, his performance during the first year and a half
> . . . was not distinguished.(5)

## The Secretaries of State

Truman's first two Secretaries of State, Edward Stettinius
and James Byrnes, fared little better than the President in
Congress' estimation. Vandenberg believed that Truman needed a
strong Secretary of State, but found Stettinius more of a "general manager" of the State Department bureaucracy than a policy-
maker. As the ranking Republican on, and later chairman of, the
Senate Foreign Relations Committee, Vandenberg's opinions weighed
heavily. Congressional Republicans and even Democrats widely
followed his lead, and his confidence and cooperation was vital
to the success of the Administration's foreign policy programs.
There were other members of Congress who played an important
foreign policy role, but Vandenberg was the key to congressional cooperation.

Secretary of State Byrnes did even worse than Stettinius in
Vandenberg's initial view. Not only did the Senator consider
Byrnes ignorant on matters of foreign policy, he did not think
the new Secretary was Stettinius' equal as an administrator.(6)
In addition to thinking Byrnes inept, Vandenberg was dismayed by
his partisan background. "Our new Jimmy is not going to be so
strong for bipartisan cooperation," Vandenberg told his wife.(7)
Most importantly, Byrnes had made his reputation as Roosevelt's
broker of compromise, and Vandenberg feared that the Secretary
would follow his domestic political propensities when negotiating
with the Soviets. To the Senator, Byrnes' association with the
concessions made by Roosevelt to Stalin at the February 1945
Yalta Conference was a disturbing indication that he would continue to compromise with the communists. In letters to his wife,

Vandenberg voiced his apprehension about Byrnes as a man "who helped surrender Yalta" and a man "whose life has been a career of compromise."(8) Indeed, the entire State Department was suspect by conservatives of following appeasement with the Soviets in direct contradiction to the "obvious" lessons of Munich. It was not until the tenure of Secretary of State George C. Marshall that the Administration possessed a top ranking foreign policy official with both the personal and professional reputation needed to command respect and a degree of deference from Congress.(9)

Truman's and Byrnes' individual weaknesses were compounded by the fact that they did not work well together. It was not clear if Truman fully controlled foreign policy or if his Secretary of State was operating unchecked. It was common knowledge that Truman had been chosen over Byrnes for the Vice Presidency in 1944 after Truman had agreed to nominate Byrnes for that post. As a consolation prize, Truman had named Byrnes as Secretary of State in 1945, and the President's embarrassment and feeling of inadequacy combined to give Byrnes wide latitude. Also generally known was Byrnes' feeling that by right he, rather than Truman, should have been president. Ironically, it may have been the high regard accorded Truman by his fellow senators and Roosevelt's concern with the ratification of the United Nations Charter that led to Truman's selection by the President.(10) In any case, the Truman-Byrnes relationship was never the intimate one that should theoretically exist between a President and Secretary of State. As Truman later admitted, "More and more during the fall of 1945 . . . Secretary of State Byrnes was beginning to think of himself as an Assistant President in full charge of foreign policy."(11)

The tandem of an inexperienced President and a mistrusted Secretary of State working together poorly created an atmosphere in which Congress became much more willing and able to exert its will. The normal propensity of Congress to give way to the executive was mitigated by the appearance of disunity and weakness. This broke down the aura of executive expertise, and limited the ability of the President to invoke the prestige of his office.

## Congress: The White House View

Yet another factor which tended to increase congressional influence was executive apprehension about the mood of Congress. Truman feared that Congress would revert to its prewar isolationism and become a major stumbling block to the creation of peace. While it is true that at times Truman characterized the Capitol as a "cave of winds," in reality he did not dismiss Congress so lightly.(12) In his memoirs, Truman conceded, "I could never quite forget the strong hold which isolationism had gained over our country after World War I."(13) The President believed that there was a great flood of isolationist propaganda, much of it emanating from Congress, at work on public opinion. He was apprehensive that resurgent isolationist spirit would again become an important political factor.(14)

Although the Administration's concern with the rebirth of isolationism abated somewhat, it remained an issue throughout the period. As late as August 1947, Secretary of the Navy James V. Forrestal told the Cabinet that the country was facing a resurgence of "Let Europe Go" isolationism. If that sentiment prevailed, the result would be a vacuum in Europe which the Soviets would fill.(15) It was a judgment with which the President concurred.(16) Even with the European Recovery Program safely passed in 1948 and the United States strongly committed to Europe, internationalists could not feel secure. Arthur Vandenberg wrote that he had "no illusion that the Republican isolationists have surrendered." Rather, Vandenberg felt, "They will be back at the same old stand next January."(17)

The relationship that Truman and other executive officers saw between Congress, public opinion, and policy was nebulous but important. Administration figures clearly perceived that public support was vital to successful foreign policy. The repeated stress given this factor by the President and his supporting cast indicates that its invocation was more than a rhetorical gesture to democratic principles. Secretary Byrnes typically hastened to assure one correspondent that "the Department of State is fully conscious of the vital necessity of a fully informed American opinion."(18) Looking back on his long diplomatic career, Ambassador Charles E. (Chip) Bohlen expressed the typical conviction that "foreign policy in a democracy must take into account the emotions, beliefs, and goals of the people. The most carefully thought out plans of experts, even though 100 per cent correct in theory, will fail without public support."(19)

In the minds of administration officials, Congress and public opinion were related in two ways. First, Congress might be swayed by intense public opinion support of presidential policy. Second, public support might be upset by criticism from Congress. There was a constant concern, as we will see, that criticism from Congress would break down the appearance of national unity on which policy-makers felt their program must be based.

President Truman's concern that Congress would not support his policy also stemmed from his fear that the peace would also bring an upsurge of partisanship. His fear of partisan attack became even more pronounced with the victory of the Republicans in the 1946 elections that left the G.O.P. as the majority party in both houses of Congress. Under Roosevelt, Secretary of State Cordell Hull had established a system of periodic meetings with congressional leaders. With the war ending and with the change of administrations, this consultation lapsed. It quickly became obvious, however, that neglect of Congress would pay no dividends. Many in the Administration realized that no effective postwar foreign policy could be established amidst partisan controversy. Comparing the president's constitutional role to that of a frontier saloon piano player, Dean Acheson observed that the fundamental ideal of nonpartisan foreign policy is, as the classic saloon sign pleads, "Don't Shoot the Piano Player."(20)

Additionally, the Republicans were pressuring the Administration for a renewed foreign policy role. There was considerable disaffection among Republicans stemming from their exclusion from the policy formation process. Soon after the end of the war, Republican foreign policy expert John Foster Dulles, backed by Senate Republicans, spoke to several officials in the State Department, including Secretary Byrnes and Counselor Ben Cohen, regarding reestablishment of weekly meetings between a bipartisan Senate delegation and State Department officers. Byrnes quickly agreed—in theory.(21) Another precedent established by Hull, and adhered to by all Truman's Secretaries of State, was that State Department officials would avoid partisan activity. Although they received a number of requests for "political" appearances, both Byrnes and his successor George C. Marshall wisely declined to be drawn into such activity. As Secretary Byrnes responded to one such request, "Any political activity by me . . . would do great harm to our foreign policy . . ."(22)

The restraint exercised by the Secretaries of State was also reflected in the political activities of Senator Vandenberg. There was a tacit understanding that each side would avoid making foreign policy a political issue. In return for his support, Vandenberg also enjoyed de facto electoral immunity. Outraged that the Democratic National Committee had scheduled speakers in support of his 1946 opponent, Vandenberg wrote to Postmaster General and Democratic National Committee Chairman Robert Hannegan to protest. Arguing that he had spent most of the previous eighteen months cooperating with the Democrats on foreign policy, Vandenberg pointed out that his defeat would mean new Republican foreign policy leadership, and "Bang, 'Foreign policy' is back into politics." Even more pointedly, he advised Hannegan that unless efforts to unseat him ceased, he would make foreign policy a partisan issue himself. The key question, Vandenberg posed, was, "do I still keep still (which I am doing)? Or do I shove 'foreign policy' still further into politics—and probably for keeps?" Electoral pressure ceased.(23)

Still, the truce between Democrats and Republicans in the Michigan senatorial contest was an anomaly rather than the rule in 1946. Although foreign policy per se was not a major issue, communism was. Republican rhetoric was not aimed at the Soviet Union directly. Rather, it attempted to link international communism, the dislocations of conversion to a peacetime economy, and the fear of international conflict with the policies of the New Deal. Typifying the Republicans' 1946 campaign strategy, Ohio Representative John Vorys asked voters, "Got enough Meat? Got enough Houses? Got enough OPA? . . . Got enough inflation? . . . Got enough debt? . . . Got enough strikes? . . . Got enough Communism? . . . Had enough war?" Thus, much of anticommunism, with its concomitant anti-Sovietism, was connected with domestic New Dealism. After the Republican success in November 1946, the Administration faced a Congress that would loudly cry "New Deal appeasement" in response to conciliatory policies toward the Soviet Union, and, with equal gusto, condemn attempts to increase military or foreign aid spending as "New Deal extravagance." It was this domestically based schizophrenia, coupled along with isolationism, which did much to determine the level of rhetoric used by the Administration in "selling" their programs to Congress and the nation.(24)

The Republican victory in November 1946 heightened Truman's skepticism regarding congressional cooperation and his suspicions of the partisan motivations of Congress. Time proved Truman correct. In control of Congress for the first time in almost two decades and confidently looking forward to capturing the White House in 1948, Republican foreign policy activity became increasingly motivated by partisan considerations. Even prior to the election, Truman had been aware that Congress would be antagonistic toward the Soviet Union and hostile to any major aid program directed at the Soviet Union. Budget Director Harold Smith recorded the President as feeling that Congress was "generally obstreperous and recalcitrant and inclined to go out of its way to cause him all the trouble possible."(25) The Republican sweep reinforced these feelings. In a post-election meeting with Truman, Secretary of the Navy James Forrestal found the President pessimistic about the possibilities for future bipartisan cooperation. Truman believed that political maneuvering was inevitable and that little would come from Forrestal's desire to establish a cooperative relationship with the Republicans.(26) Truman's staff stressed the need for cooperation with Congress, but agreed with the President that conflict was almost certain. In late 1946, White House staff member James H. Rowe, Jr. prepared a memo for the President via presidential assistant Clark Clifford entitled "Cooperation or Conflict?--The President's Relationship with an Opposition Congress." This memorandum urged conciliatory language when dealing with Congress and a careful selection of issues to be pushed. Averell Harriman concurred, writing Clifford that in a period of serious domestic and international problems, partisan maneuvering would be injurious to both the Administration's program and the President's prestige.(27)

Elected on the themes of anti-New Dealism and anti-communism, the Republican Congress adopted a distinctly hostile posture toward both the Administration and the Soviet Union. The only bright spot from the White House's point of view was that Arthur Vandenberg became Chairman of the Committee on Foreign Relations. The overall complexion of Congress, though, was conservative and truculent, and threatened trouble if congressional sentiments were ignored.

## Arthur Vandenberg: The Key to Congress

The role of Senator Arthur H. Vandenberg, Sr., was pivotal in the events of this period. A mid-war convert from isolationism to internationalism, Vandenberg's influence became increasingly important during the period.(28) He was instrumental in spurring a hard line American policy toward the Soviet Union and was a chief architect of the Cold War. It can also be argued that the Senator was at times a dupe of the Administration--that through empty executive flattery he was totally co-opted and became a pawn manipulated to the President's advantage.

Vandenberg's strength stemmed from his seniority in Congress, his expertise in foreign policy, and his conservative reputation.

After the 1946 election, Vandenberg became Chairman of the Foreign Relations Committee and President Pro Tempore of the Senate.
By virtue of an informal division of power, the Republican Majority Leader, Robert A. Taft of Ohio, was left in charge of domestic policy and the Senator from Michigan had responsibility for
foreign policy. Vandenberg thus became the acknowledged foreign
policy leader in the Senate. Members sought his advice and
strove to win his endorsement.(29) His influence also spread to
the House of Representatives. Even the powerful House Appropriations Committee Chairman, John Taber, was willing to admit that,
to a point, he followed Vandenberg's lead in foreign affairs.(30)
For the Administration, Vandenberg's endorsement became the key
to congressional cooperation.

In many instances, Vandenberg used his influence in Congress
to help ease, or even save, the passage of administration programs. How much of substance he was able to extract in return
for his support is open to debate. Dean Acheson, for one, found
Vandenberg a vain man who when given careful and obvious attention and allowed superficial, but visible, concessions, could be
brought around. In Acheson's words, Vandenberg's method "was to
go through a period of public doubt and skepticism; then find a
comparatively minor flaw in the proposal, pounce upon it and make
much of it; in due course propose a change, always the Vandenberg
amendment. Then, and only then, could it be given to his followers as a doctrine worthy of all men to be received."(31) Particularly where international conferences preceded decisions, Vandenberg could be brought into line by including him in the delegation. The Senator himself recognized the potential clash of his
roles. Writing privately to Eleanor Roosevelt in 1947, he
pointed out that he "may act under instructions (with which I do
not agree) . . . and then I return to Congress under what seems
to me to be a moral obligation to support . . . something which I
did not and do not approve."(32)

Vandenberg's influence cannot be dismissed so lightly, however. He was the first major American political figure to push
consistently and publicly for a tough stand vis-à-vis the Soviet
Union. Vandenberg also played an important role in determining
the general tenor, if not the specific points, of the United
States' diplomatic attitude toward the Soviet Union.(33)

The motivations behind Vandenberg's anti-Soviet attitudes
were complex. The behavior of the Soviet Union deeply concerned
and disillusioned him. Beyond this, however, he also saw political advantage in a strong anti-Soviet stance. Cooperation with
the Administration resulted in the understanding that the Democrats would mount no serious opposition to his reelection. In
the same vein, his Michigan constituency included a large number
of Eastern Europeans, particularly Polish-Americans. In the
aftermath of Yalta and Potsdam, it behooved Vandenberg to be
properly outraged at the "betrayal" of Poland. As the details of
Yalta became known in the United States, Vandenberg faced a dilemma. In January 1945, the Senator had publicly embraced the basic
concepts of a world peace organization and Roosevelt had subsequently named him as a delegate to the San Francisco Conference
to organize the United Nations. Yet to participate in the

conference would imply his endorsement of the Yalta agreements which left Poland to Soviet domination. Not to participate, on the other hand, would serve to open the Republican party to charges of isolationism and would also endanger ratification of the United Nations Charter. Vandenberg's strategy was to attend the conference, but also to make a strong and obvious case on behalf of an independent Poland. It was a strategy destined to have considerable repercussions for the whole tenor of American policy toward the Soviet Union and Eastern Europe.(34)

## Congress and the Cold War

Arthur Vandenberg sincerely believed that he and his congressional allies were "the major influence in changing the American attitude from 'appeasement' to firm resistance."(35) As was often the case, the Senator was guilty of overstatement. It would be equally incorrect, however, to assume that he and Congress had no effect. The basic theme of American policy toward the Soviet Union from the death of President Roosevelt through early 1946 was ambivalence. With administration attitudes divided, Congress played an important role in tipping the balance toward a firm stance against the Russians.

Those scholars who argue that President Truman fostered a dramatic shift from Roosevelt's policy of cooperation with Russia to a policy of confrontation particularly stress two early events: Truman's volatile interview with Soviet Foreign Minister V.V. Molotov in April and the sudden cut-off of Lend-Lease to the Soviets in May. In fact, these two actions are actually more illustrative of Truman's inexperience in office than of any general reversal of Roosevelt's policy. Both incidents were also partly a result of congressional pressures.

The incident with Molotov occurred on April 23, less than two weeks after Truman became President. Within the Administration, a number of key advisors, including Ambassador to the Soviet Union Averell Harriman, already believed that firmness was the best approach to dealing with the Soviets. Only Secretary of War Henry L. Stimson and General Marshall strongly opposed a tough stance. Thus, the advice the new and uncertain President received was heavily one-sided, and the dressing down that Truman gave Molotov over Poland became inevitable.(36)

A major factor which influenced the Administration's concern over Soviet actions in Poland was the link between that issue and the success of the San Francisco conference. In the Golden Gate city, Vandenberg was voicing loud and continuous concern over the fate of Poland. Truman and his advisors were afraid that unless the Polish question was settled early, there might be adverse public and congressional reaction, making Senate ratification of the United Nations treaty uncertain. Stettinius recorded that "Truman felt that continued failure to settle this [Polish] question endangered the entire U.S. position in taking its place at the world council table . . . there would be little chance of a treaty on world organization approved by the Senate."(37) This point was stressed repeatedly in diplomatic conversations and in dispatches to the Soviets, including an early April message from Roosevelt to Soviet Premier Joseph Stalin and in Truman's abrasive lecture to Molotov.(38)

The actions of Truman in the Lend-Lease fiasco can also be attributed to a combination of Truman's inexperience, bad advice, and congressional pressure. Congress was determined to have a voice in the extension of postwar aid. Many members insisted that any move by the Administration to extend Lend-Lease agreements for postwar reconstruction had to be blocked. As early as May 1944, Vandenberg had warned the Administration that Lend-Lease must not be continued beyond the cessation of hostilities. Increasingly, other members of Congress issued similar warnings. By the fall of 1944, President Roosevelt's advisors were telling him that a failure to distinguish between Lend-Lease aid and postwar aid would lead to a serious dispute with Congress.(39)

The annual extension of the Lend-Lease bill which came before Congress in March 1945 was the occasion for a concerted attempt to block the use of appropriated funds for postwar aid. Led by Ohio's Representative John Vorys, Republican members of the Foreign Affairs Committee attempted during hearings to insert amendments which would have stringently limited the use of funds in the postwar period. Defeated in this attempt, they then filed a minority report urging Congress not to extend Lend-Lease to the postwar period. This March 8 report increased general congressional disquiet and was sufficient to bring the Administration to the bargaining table. The Vorys-led faction and Foreign Economic Administration officials agreed within a few days on the wording of a substitute amendment which according to Vorys would, "effectively prohibit the use of Lend-Lease as a postwar measure."(40) The Committee on Foreign Affairs then unanimously approved the compromise as did the House on March 23, 1945. Immediately, the Administration advised Ambassador Harriman to suspend Lend-Lease renewal talks with the Soviets in anticipation of the expected collapse of Germany and in view of the hostile congressional attitude. In place of Lend-Lease, the State Department suggested new negotiations on short term aid.(41) Although Harriman warned that the Soviets would not take the news graciously, he terminated the ongoing negotiations.(42) Under Secretary of State Joseph Grew and FEA Administrator Leo Crowley also recognized that Soviet officials would consider the limitations on Lend-Lease as a threat to their postwar recovery. Nevertheless, they warned Roosevelt that allowing the Soviets to procure capital goods, such as industrial equipment, even before hostilities ceased, might be considered by Congress as use of Lend-Lease for reconstruction and recovery. With the President's assent, Grew telegraphed Harriman that because of the congressional attitude the FEA was cutting off all delivery of industrial goods to the Soviet Union.(43)

When the Lend-Lease extension bill moved to the Senate, that chamber proved even less willing than the House to consider continuing the program after the war. Taft introduced an amendment to eliminate the compromise language from the House version of the bill. Although the Taft amendment was defeated, it was lost only after the Vice President broke a dramatic thirty-nine to thirty-nine vote. The Vice President who broke the tie was the same man, Harry S Truman, who having become President, signed the Lend-Lease extension into law on April 17, 1945. It was a vote that Truman would not forget as president.

Pressure from Congress did not abate with the signing of the compromise into law, and on May 11, the FEA suddenly cut off Lend-Lease shipments to Russia. Two explanations are possible, but both trace responsibility for the cut off to the Administration's reaction to a truculently watchful Congress. FEA Administrator Crowley claimed that Truman ordered the aid halt only seventy-two hours after the German surrender. Truman claims that Crowley acted beyond the spirit of his instructions.(44) Historian George Herring places the onus on Crowley's "excessive legalism," but given the Administration's unequivocal assurances during congressional hearings that Lend-Lease would end with the war, Crowley's strict compliance is understandable.(45)

Although Truman realized his mistake and soon countermanded his order, he remained cautious because of his desire to avoid getting into a wrangle with Congress so early in his term. In his memoirs, Truman explained that he understood that any attempt to use Lend-Lease funds would open his new administration "to a lot of trouble with the Senate."(46) The President took great pains to assure members of Congress that he intended to grant Lend-Lease within the spirit of the House amendment. A letter to Truman from five House Foreign Affairs Committee members demanded to know the Administration's intentions, and indicated that if Truman sought "loopholes in the Lend-Lease law to extend your power without consulting Congress . . . [it] would be disastrous." In reply, the President assured Congress that he was, "of course, in full agreement . . . that the Lend-Lease Act does not authorize aid for purposes of postwar relief, postwar rehabilitation, or postwar construction."(47) A week later, citing congressional pressure, Grew wired Harriman that deliveries of industrial equipment were being terminated.(48) Two months later, with V-J day, all but "pipe-line" deliveries were ended. Although it was legally possible to continue Lend-Lease if the President deemed it in the interest of the defense of the United States, Truman decided that, despite his preferences, the pledges made to Congress had to be honored.(49)

Despite appearances, neither the Lend-Lease cutoff nor Truman's confrontation with Molotov three weeks earlier signified established policy. In retrospect, Truman realized that he had accomplished little in his meeting with Molotov, but rather that he had tried to do too much too quickly. Less than two months later Truman was willing to accept the inevitability of Soviet domination of Poland if a "face-saver" could be arranged. The problem, he explained to Stalin, was that, "There are six million Poles in the United States," which, according to Admiral William Leahy, had the effect of "adding to the interest of America" in the Polish question.(50) While dining with Forrestal at Potsdam, the President went even further, observing that as a result of Hitler's egomania, "we shall have a Slav Europe for a long time to come. I don't think it is so bad."(51)

Similarly, the Lend-Lease cutoff was retrospectively viewed

as an error. In his memoirs, Truman claimed that Grew and Crowley had hurried him into signing the order without informing him of its contents.(52) The correctness of his recall of events not-withstanding, Truman's quick countermand of the order and his subsequent explanation indicate that the cut-off did not reflect firmly set policy toward the Soviet Union. As for the termination of aid in September, Dean Acheson, a staunch Truman loyalist, attributed the action to a "new and inexperienced" President getting "thoroughly bad advice." Far from supporting the move, Acheson indicated that if he or Assistant Secretary of State for Economic Affairs William Clayton had been present the decision would not have been made.(53)

Truman continued to vacillate in his approach to the Soviet Union through the fall of 1945 and into 1946. For all his occasionally tough language about standing up to the Soviets, the President had not given up hope of coming to some accommodation with the Kremlin. At Potsdam Truman wrote in his diary, "I can deal with Stalin. He is honest . . . ."(54) In September 1945 he described Stalin as a "fine man who wanted to do the right thing."(55) Although Truman was often angered by Soviet stubbornness, he considered postwar difficulties a part of normal readjustment after the cessation of hostilities, not an inevitable or enduring conflict. As he told one audience in October 1945, "We are having our own little troubles now . . .[but they are] just a blowup after the letdown from war."(56) Later he even remembered Stalin with a kind of gladiator's fondness. "I liked the little son of a bitch," the ex-president wrote to Dean Acheson in 1957. (57)

Secretary of State Byrnes did little to relieve the image of weakness and uncertainty projected by the President's inconsistency. Several of the President's advisors, including Forrestal, Leahy, and Harriman, favored a tough line with the Soviets. Others such as Wallace, Stimson, Harry Hopkins, and former Ambassador to Moscow Joseph Davies, favored a conciliatory approach. Byrnes vacillated between these poles. As discussed, Byrnes' reputation as a compromiser and his association with Yalta made his appointment initially unpopular with Vandenberg and many other members of Congress. His temporizing conduct, from his appointment until the end of February 1946, further outraged his hard line congressional watchdogs.

Byrnes' first chance to deal directly with the Russians came during the September 1945 London Conference. The Secretary's basic approach was to reach a compromise on the peace treaties for Finland, Hungary, Rumania, and Bulgaria which would at least gain a semblance of independence for those countries.(58) But Byrnes could not be too obvious in his willingness to compromise with Molotov. He realized that Congress was unlikely to accept peace treaties that seemed to give the Soviets license to control East Europe. Trying to explain the constraints of the American constitutional system to Molotov, Byrnes told the Russian Foreign Minister that he was sorry that he could not recommend recognition of the Rumanian and Bulgarian governments. Byrnes advised Molotov that if he presented treaties to the Senate and could not attest to the representativeness of the governments, ratification would be impossible.(59)

The presence at the conference of a Republican watchdog, John Foster Dulles, served to reinforce the Secretary's awareness that compromise would not necessarily win him accolades at home. A Dulles aide later recalled that Byrnes told Dulles, "Well, Pardner, I think that we've pushed these babies about as far as they will go, and I think we better start thinking compromise." Dulles replied that if Byrnes compromised, he, Dulles, would feel compelled to return to Washington on the first plane and publicly denounce the Secretary.(60) Dulles, backed by Vandenberg, clearly favored a stalled conference rather than compromise. The stand was indeed alien to Byrnes, but he could not afford to ignore the Dulles-Vandenberg position.

The Republicans were not happy, however, with Byrnes' reluctant consultation. Reporter James Reston, who had close contacts with Vandenberg, reported soon after the conference that leading Republicans were distressed with Byrnes' independence and lack of serious consultation.(61)

The Secretary's propensity only to consult seriously with members of Congress when forced was based on his personality as well as political considerations. In a less illustrious profession, Byrnes might have been known as a "wheeler-dealer." _Time_ magazine called Byrnes "a politician's politician,"(62) and even Truman referred to him as "my able and conniving Secretary of State" and a "country politician."(63) Byrnes was a true practitioner of the old saw that politics is the art of compromise. During his days with Roosevelt he was known as a man who could always effect an agreement between contending parties. He disliked being tied down by fixed positions and prided himself on his ability to negotiate on his feet. While the presence of Dulles in London indicates that Byrnes was willing to genuflect in the direction of bipartisanship, he had not really taken the concept to heart. Dulles' role at the conference cannot accurately be described as that of an advisor. Dulles found that Byrnes did not carefully plan his negotiating strategy with his delegation, but rather, "spoke freely and wholly 'off the cuff'."(64) Later, at the May 1946 Paris meeting of the Council of Foreign Ministers, Vandenberg gained the same impression. Byrnes' methods, the Senator wrote in his diary, were "exceedingly dangerous . . . He gives me the feeling that he improvises as he goes along."(65)

Byrnes was also a man with a distinctly partisan, New Deal background, and he and the Republicans were mutually suspicious. Vandenberg predicted to his wife soon after Byrnes' appointment that the Secretary would be receptive to partisan pressure to ease Vandenberg out of the foreign policy spotlight.(66) Byrnes reciprocated by doubting the true bipartisan spirit of the Michigan Senator. He chose Dulles, rather than Vandenberg, as his G.O.P. colleague at the London Conference because he believed the Senator was too partisan.(67) Although Dulles sought and obtained Vandenberg's approval, the failure to invite Vandenberg was an ill-conceived slight to the sensitive Senator.(68) Byrnes did not take a bipartisan delegation with him to Moscow, and when Vandenberg went to the first United Nations meeting in January

1946 it was at Truman's, not Byrnes', invitation. As late as the end of January 1946, Byrnes warned the Cabinet that Vandenberg, who was under pressure from his senatorial colleagues to disassociate himself from the "appeasement" policies of the Administration, could not be counted on for support. As Forrestal recorded, Byrnes said, "The fact had to be faced that Vandenberg's and for that matter Dulles' . . . activities . . . could be viewed as being conducted on a political basis."(69)

Ironically, it was Dulles who played a key role in trying to prevent an outright partisan split. Dulles worked with both administration and congressional figures to restore bipartisanship. In early October 1945, Dulles met with eight Republican senators, "of varying shades of belief." "None of them," he reported, "held the view that the Republican party should refuse to cooperate under proper circumstances nor did anyone suggest that cooperation should be made contingent upon getting a slice of patronage."(70) Dulles then telephoned State Department Counselor Ben Cohen to suggest reestablishment of the weekly meeting between members of Congress and the Secretary of State.(71) Dulles also put his suggestion to Byrnes directly on at least two occasions, and was informed by the Secretary in mid-November 1945 that contact had been made with Foreign Relations Committee Chairman Tom Connally regarding the proposed meeting.(72) Byrnes stalled, though, and the weekly meetings did not revive on a regular basis. When he did meet with members of Congress, he tended to tell the members what he was going to do rather than ask their advice. By the beginning of 1946, the bipartisan policy so carefully put together by Roosevelt and Hull and supported (in practice) by Acheson and (in thought) by Truman, was on the verge of collapse. Republicans felt shut out of the policy process. Vandenberg had "deep reservations" about Byrnes and his policies which he described as a "Truman-Byrnes appeasement policy which I cannot stomach."(73) By ignoring Congress, particularly Vandenberg, Byrnes both had appeared partisan and had injured legislative pride. In a little over six months, Byrnes' domestic partisan instincts had come close to destroying Byrnes' domestic support as a diplomat.

Byrnes' reputation continued to disquiet members of Congress as he flew to the Moscow Foreign Ministers' Conference in December 1945. As a man who had achieved success through the art of compromise, Byrnes considered the London Conference and its stalemate a failure by definition.(74) He was determined to approach the Soviets once more, deal in the conciliatory manner, and reach an agreement. Late in November, Byrnes had proposed Moscow as the site of the next foreign ministers meeting in hopes of dealing directly with Stalin and avoiding the obstinate Molotov. Even more significantly, Byrnes had decided not to take a watchdog Republican delegation. There would be no repeat of Dulles' threats at London. Byrnes seemed ready to grasp any favorable sign from the Soviets. He told British Foreign Secretary Ernest Bevin that the very willingness of the Soviets to discuss the Rumanian-Bulgarian issue indicated their willingness to reach some sort of compromise. When Bevin objected to the meeting, Byrnes went so far as to threaten to go without him.(75)

The Secretary was well aware that Soviet actions in Rumania and Bulgaria were designed to ensure their satellite status. In fact, he suppressed a report submitted to him on conditions in these countries because of its negative conclusions. He was determined that it would not cause a public outcry and restrict his negotiating position. On December 23, 1945, Byrnes reached an agreement with Stalin that, in effect, recognized the reality of the Soviet position in Eastern Europe, but included "face-savers." Stalin agreed to two non-communist ministers in Rumania and an unspecified, but Soviet-determined, broadening of the Bulgarian government.(76)

Byrnes' agreements illustrate his intense desire to reach agreement rather than any clear sighted recognition of the realities of Soviet power. George Kennan, American Counselor in Moscow, wrote that Byrnes' "main purpose is to achieve some sort of agreement, he doesn't much care what. The realities behind this agreement . . . do not concern him. He wants his agreement for its political effect at home."(77)

If Byrnes expected to reap accolades and political benefits at home for his efforts, he was sadly in error. On returning from Moscow, Byrnes found himself under attack from all sides. Republican Senator Homer Capehart of Indiana took up a favorite analogy of the day, proclaiming that Byrnes' concessions at Moscow reminded him "of Chamberlain and his umbrella appeasement of Hitler." Joseph Martin, House Minority Leader, put Republicans on record against "any betrayal of the small nations of the world in making peace."(78) Most importantly, Vandenberg agreed with his Republican colleagues, writing to magazine publisher Henry Luce that Moscow had been a "giveaway."(79) Byrnes also received a negative reaction to his Moscow maneuvering from the President and some of his advisors, which in turn may have been accentuated by Congress' ire.

These criticisms put Byrnes under tremendous pressure to adopt a hard negotiating position at the London meeting of the United Nations in January 1946. President Truman asked Vandenberg to go along, but the Republican was in a testy mood. Vandenberg was doubtful of his ability to work with Byrnes and refused to participate unless a hard position was taken on the issue of international control of atomic energy. When Truman and Acheson acquiesced to Vandenberg's demands, the Senator agreed to attend the conference. He felt that circumstances demanded that he be in London to assure compliance with his interpretation of atomic energy commitments.(80)

At London, Byrnes began to give way to the pressure. Vandenberg told a reporter at the conference, "Thank heavens Jimmy Byrnes hates disagreements, because I don't know where I would be if he decided to continue this fight."(81) Eleanor Roosevelt, who was also a delegate, wrote confidentially to Bernard Baruch that "Secy. Byrnes is afraid of his own delegation."(82)

Despite Byrnes' tougher stance at London, Vandenberg and Dulles returned from the conference in an unpleasant humor. They still felt Byrnes was being too soft in his approach to the Soviets. Their self-esteem was also hurt by Byrnes' continuing refusal to consult closely with his delegation. Then United

Nations Ambassador Edward Stettinius told Cordell Hull that "Van is pretty sore on not being taken into camp a little bit more, not only in London, but in Washington too. . . . Van . . . says collaboration at the present time is just being told about it the night before it goes into the newspapers."(83)

The combination of criticism after Moscow, pressure at London, domestic politics, and international events (particularly the Iranian situation) battered Byrnes.(84) Domestic compromise had made him a powerful Roosevelt ally, but international compromise threatened to destroy him as Truman's Secretary of State. Byrnes enlisted in the ranks of the cold warriors. The first indication of Byrnes' new anti-Soviet stance came in his speech to the Overseas Press Club in New York on February 28, 1946. In his address, Byrnes pledged the United States to resist the threat or actual use of force for ends contrary to the United Nations Charter. It was a speech clearly aimed at the Soviet Union.(85)

Preceding Byrnes' speech by one day, Vandenberg had made his strongest public statement on the Soviet Union, and had, in a left-handed fashion, openly criticized administration policy. Indeed, his speech on the floor of the Senate was the most virulent attack on the Soviet Union by a major American figure to that date. "What is Russia up to now?" asked Vandenberg. He asked it of Russia in Manchuria, Eastern Europe and the Dardanelles, the Baltic and the Balkans, Poland, and Japan—"What is Russia up to now?" Vandenberg called on the United States to abandon the "miserable fiction . . . that we somehow jeopardize the peace if our candor is as firm as Russia's always is; and if we assume a moral leadership which we have too frequently allowed to lapse." Vandenberg then praised Senator Tom Connally, Ambassador Edward Stettinius, British Foreign Secretary Ernest Bevin, French Foreign Minister Georges Bidault, and even the Soviet Diplomat Andrei Vishinsky for their performances at London. Damned by ignominious omission was James F. Byrnes.(86)

Coming so soon after Vandenberg's address, the Byrnes speech was seen by many as an echo of the Senator's remarks, the "Second Vandenberg Concerto." Vandenberg was pleased to take up the bestowed responsibility. Writing to Foreign Affairs editor Hamilton Fish Armstrong, Vandenberg gave Byrnes high marks for his "evangelical speech (for which I suspect I was partially responsible)."(87) In reality, Vandenberg's speech, per se, probably was not the motivation behind Byrnes' remarks the next night. It was, however, the apex of growing criticism—led by Republicans, who were in turn led by Vandenberg—which was a major force in bringing American policy to a position of confrontation with the Soviet Union. As New York Times columnist Arthur Krock noted, the address indicated that Republican criticism had had its effect.(88) Although there is no evidence to confirm the popular opinion of the day that Byrnes was reacting directly to Vandenberg's speech, there is little doubt that Byrnes was at least partly reacting to the criticism which the Senator's speech so dramatically represented. As one columnist concluded, Byrnes "thought it is what the country wanted and was waiting to hear."(89)

After the beginning of March, nearly all administration figures saw diplomatic events basically in terms of confrontation
with the Soviet Union. Truman continued to waver occasionally as
in the Wallace affair, but Byrnes became a convert to the "hard
line" camp. He also began to pay at least more lip-service to
bipartisanship and invited Vandenberg and Connally to the Paris
Peace Conference.(90) Vandenberg refused to attend, however, on
the grounds that the Peace Conference would only be a show piece
to ratify decisions made by the foreign ministers. Byrnes then
switched invitations and invited Vandenberg to the Council of
Foreign Ministers Conference in the same city. Still Vandenberg
sulked in his tent, suggesting to Byrnes that he might consider
Dulles instead. Byrnes was not about to make the Moscow mistake
again. He insisted that he would take only two official advisors, and both had to be senators. If Vandenberg declined, then
another Republican senator would be asked. Vandenberg then
agreed on the conditions that his concurrence be obtained on any
position and that a public "mandate" be sent to Warsaw criticizing the Lublin government for its failure to hold free elections.
Candidly citing pressure from his Polish-American constituency,
Vandenberg confessed, "I found myself saying that if he
[Byrnes] would 'play ball' at Warsaw, I would 'play ball' at
Paris."(91)

The exact impact of Vandenberg on the specifics of the United
State's negotiating position in Moscow is debatable. Senator
Connally felt that Byrnes ignored him, but worked hard to please
Vandenberg.(92) The Michigan Senator, conversely, complained
that Byrnes' negotiating methods were "exceedingly dangerous."
Vandenberg elaborated:

> He makes too many moves on the impulse of the moment. He
> gives me the feeling that he improvises as he goes along.
> He has no 'delegation meetings'. He consults Connally and
> me at the Council table on the spur of the moment.(93)

Generally, the Senator seems mostly to have acted as a stiffening
agent to Byrnes. At one point Vandenberg even threatened to
leave the conference unless differences with the Soviets were
brought to a head.

Although the negotiations in Paris in the spring and summer
of 1946 were not of paramount diplomatic importance, they served
to recast Byrnes as a non-appeaser in Vandenberg's eyes and to
establish a new relationship between Secretary and Senator.
Although Vandenberg continued to grumble about being in on more
"crash landings" than "take offs," he no longer felt embarrassing-
ly ignored as he had in 1945 and early 1946. Further, Byrnes'
policy had swung into line with the Senator's. Vandenberg was
flattered by the thought he was the architect of Byrnes' new
firmness and was responsive to the Secretary's show of attention
to his opinions. Writing privately, Vandenberg proudly related,
"When Byrnes phoned me his SOS from Paris last week he said that
inasmuch as he had now adopted a 'Republican foreign policy' he
is entitled to have the chief Republican conspirator sharing the
grief." At Paris, the man who Vandenberg had accused of

"loitering around Munich," had pulled off a "Munich in reverse" and had done "a magnificently courageous and constructive job." (94) Vandenberg's approval of Byrnes' new position was so complete that he was even willing to trust the Secretary to meet with the Soviets unattended. Writing to Byrnes, the Senator requested to be relieved of his delegation duties. "It seems to me that the pattern of our American attitude is now so clearly set," Vandenberg wrote, ". . . that you do not need your Senatorial advisors upon this particular occasion . . ."(95) James F. Byrnes had become a fully anointed cold warrior.

By mid 1946, then, the pattern was well established and the cold war joined. The role of Congress, particularly Vandenberg, in establishing this pattern cannot be denied. Members of Congress, particularly Vandenberg, were early critics of the Soviet Union. Plagued by the historical lessons of 1919 and the isolationism of the 1930s, lacking firm leadership, divided in its counsels, and concerned with domestic political repercussions, the Administration hardened its position against the Soviet Union more rapidly than would have otherwise been the case. It is true that changes in administration policy would have taken place without congressional pressure. Soviet actions in Eastern Europe, Germany, Iran, and other troubled areas were in themselves a cause for strained Soviet-American relations. A certain amount of conflict between the world's two new superpowers was almost inevitable. But the Republican-led cries of "Munich" at every attempt to compromise with the Soviets made negotiations difficult. The view, originally held by Byrnes, Stimson, and even, it seems, Truman, that the Soviet's domination of Eastern Europe was both inevitable and strategically justified became politically untenable. Any chance that Soviet expansion could be modified through the extension of aid rapidly waned as congressional hostility toward the Soviet Union increased.

# 2
# Early Postwar Policy

In addition to its impact on the general tenor of administration attitudes toward the Soviet Union, Congress played an important role in structuring specific policies during 1945 and early
1946. The important impact of Congress on Lend-Lease is one example. Congress also figured prominently in the formation of policy concerning the Soviet Union, atomic energy, trade, and the
United Nations, and in the negotiation of proposed loans to the
Soviet Union and Great Britain.

## United Nations

The first hurdle facing the Truman Administration was winning
Senate ratification of the United Nations Charter. The Administration was determined not to suffer a second League of Nations
fiasco and have the Senate reject United States membership in a
world peace organization. As it turned out, navigating the Charter through the Senate proved deceptively easy. Just a little
more than a week prior to the Charter's 89-2 ratification, Dean
Acheson described it as the "easiest of all" the State Department's pending legislative programs.(1)
The calm with which the Assistant Secretary viewed the pending vote resulted from the care that had already been taken to
avoid the errors associated with the League of Nations. It may
well be true that the death of Franklin Roosevelt ensured the
ratification of the United Nations Charter. That is clearer in
retrospect, though, than it was to the new president and his
advisors at the time. During his first meeting with the delegation to the San Francisco Conference, Truman candidly emphasized
that he "wanted to write a document that would pass the Senate,
and that would not arouse such opposition as faced Woodrow
Wilson." The President instructed Stettinius to consult with
Senators Connally and Vandenberg and to get their full agreement
on every issue. If an accord could not be reached, Truman
instructed Stettinius to call him so that he could directly
resolve matters with the Senators.(2)
Thus, the Senate's power of ratification was more influential
than the final vote would indicate. The Charter passed by a wide

margin because the Administration structured the document in accordance with senatorial wishes. Truman and his advisors were also careful to tout congressional contributions publicly in order to foster and appeal to legislative pride of authorship. Institutional considerations were also important in determining the degree to which the United States committed itself to collective security in the United Nations and the associated Western Hemisphere Defense Pact. In a number of areas regarding both the United Nations and hemispheric arrangements, division within the Administration enhanced the ability of Congress to exert influence. At times this influence was based on the Senate's power of ratification while at other times it resulted from either the presence of senators on delegations or the wish of the Administration to avoid congressional criticism. In the case of Vandenberg, the effect of domestic subcultural groups on senatorial attitudes was also well illustrated at the San Francisco Conference.

Preparations for submitting the United Nations Charter to the Senate began well before Truman became president. Once Secretary of State Cordell Hull had in 1943 secured Soviet agreement to the principle of establishing an international organization, intense efforts were undertaken to win the concurrence of the other potentially hostile power—the Senate. Bipartisan meetings were regularly scheduled between key senators and the Secretary of State. President Roosevelt made numerous statements on behalf of the proposed international organization. Following the Yalta Conference, James Byrnes led an intensive lobbying campaign in Congress and in public to emphasize Yalta's positive points, particularly the Big Three agreement to meet in San Francisco to form an international organization. Continuous efforts were made to monitor and counter congressional doubts about the proposed organization. The State Department even tried to persuade New York Times columnist James Reston to turn over his correspondence with members of the Senate on the subject.(3)

The Administration paid particular attention to Arthur Vandenberg. On January 10, 1945, Vandenberg had proclaimed himself in favor of "the basic idea of Dumbarton Oaks," as long as it was "consistent with legitimate American self-interest, with constitutional processes and with collateral events which warrant it."(4) Although this was a limited embrace of internationalism, such a statement coming from the Senate's leading isolationist was of great significance. Roosevelt astutely did not let his opportunity slip by. Along with other members of the Foreign Relations Committee, Vandenberg was invited to meet with the President the following day to discuss policy matters. Roosevelt let it be known he was taking fifty copies of the Senator's speech with him to Yalta. The speech made front page news; the New York Times carried it in its entirety. It was even beamed to American forces overseas. Vandenberg, although somewhat surprised, was obviously pleased with the splash.(5) Upon returning from Yalta, Roosevelt took a further step toward ensuring Vandenberg's cooperation on the United Nations and, hopefully, muting his Polish constituency-based criticism of the Yalta agreements. Vandenberg was named as a delegate to the San Francisco Conference.

Vandenberg's presence at San Francisco was also a matter of note to other delegates at the conference. The specter of the Senate, in this regard, had its beneficial side effects for the Administration. Leo Pasvolsky of the State Department told Vandenberg that he would be the key man on the delegation. He informed the Senator that "The big question in every foreign delegate's mind will still be the same one that has plagued them in the past: What will the Senate do?" This could be useful, Pasvolsky explained, because "when we are pressing for something we don't seem able to get, we'll send you in to tell them that it has to be done if they expect to get their Treaty past the Senate."(6) Vandenberg did not hesitate to use this concern. At various junctures he successfully invoked the Senate in disputes with his fellow American delegates, the Soviets, and the British.

The major factor that seemed to be on Vandenberg's mind at San Francisco was the Polish situation. He was determined that neither the United Nations nor, by implication, he be associated in any way with legitimizing the Soviet-dominated Lublin Polish government. He wished to appear tough on the issue for the benefit of his Polish-American constituents, yet he did not want the San Francisco negotiations to collapse. As he wrote to one ethnic leader, Frank Januszewski, "It would be a relatively simple matter to dynamite the new Peace League . . . . What would that do for Poland? . . . There would be no hope for justice."(7) Instead Vandenberg sought to have the proposed Charter revised so that "justice" would be an aim of the organization. He also wished to see the United Nations empowered to "recommend appropriate measures of adjustment which may include revision of treaties and of prior international decisions."(8) If these two points could be made, Vandenberg assured Stettinius, he would go along "100%" on the United Nations.(9)

Vandenberg's maneuvers were so patently motivated by domestic factors that he hardly bothered to try to disguise them. He was eager to inform Michigan's Polish-American leaders that he would link Poland and the concept of justice in the San Francisco discussions.(10) When he presented his points on justice and treaty revision to British Foreign Minister Anthony Eden and Ambassador Lord Halifax, he candidly admitted they were aimed squarely at Poland.(11)

In the main, Vandenberg's proposals were symbolic gestures. Where they might have caused difficulties (as in his suggestions to make Security Council consideration of disputes obligatory) he allowed himself to be persuaded that his revisions were either inherent in the Charter or would be injurious if added. If at all possible, though, every one from Harry Truman to Joseph Stalin gave way before Vandenberg's march to "justice." Both the President and Secretary of State recognized that the Polish question could jeopardize the conference and even decided to inform Molotov of the need to let Vandenberg have his way.(12) The Soviets accommodatingly gave in on issues to avoid irritating the Senator. Concerning one point, Pasvolsky related to Cordell Hull, "We have got the Vandenberg amendment though all right. . . I negotiated it with Molotov in Russian. He referred it to Moscow and they approved it." Hull was surprised that the

Russians "would go that far." As Pasvolsky explained, "They finally did. When I asked him if he had made up his mind about it he asked me if I advised him to accept it, and I told him I did." (13)

Vandenberg was not satisfied with merely obtaining provisions in the Charter which could allow the United Nations to deal with Soviet domination of Poland. He was further determined to block any attempt to seat the Lublin Government at the conference. It was over this question that, in his most dramatic display of influence, Vandenberg forced Stettinius into a public confrontation with the Soviet Union. In response to a Soviet prompted Czech proposal to seat the Lublin Government, Vandenberg, who was seated with Stettinius, demanded that the Secretary immediately and publicly kill the proposal. Vandenberg wrote out a quick statement, which Stettinius read verbatim, accusing the Soviets of failing to live up to the Yalta agreements and terming the thought of seating the Lublin Poles as a "sordid exhibition of bad faith."(14) Such public condemnations were supplemented by Vandenberg's attacks on the Soviet Union through the press. After Vandenberg appeared before 500 reporters at a "background" session, there was a spate of pessimistic articles on Soviet-American relations.(15) The Senator was not the only influential American operating from a basically anti-Soviet position, but he was clearly the most influential in determining the American position on Poland. He also contributed much to public concern over Soviet actions at the conference. At least one intimate observer depicted Vandenberg as the leader of an anti-Soviet faction contesting with the State Department for control of the delegation. Writing privately, Senator Warren Austin commented astutely:

> Such hostility to Russia, as appears in the San Francisco Conference, is not led by the State Department. It is led by those outside the State Department whose political office depends substantially upon the partisanship and votes of Poles.(16)

Beyond his activities on the Polish question, Vandenberg exercised influence on a number of other issues at San Francisco. The Administration saw the proposed Big Five veto on the Security Council as one potential trouble spot with Congress and the public. The Soviets took the position that the veto power included the ability to bar discussion of an issue. In this instance Vandenberg and Connally acted as allies in an intra-executive dispute over the American position. The White House proposed merely recording the differing Soviet and American interpretations in order to avoid a deadlocked conference. Stettinius did not support the compromise and dispatched a message to Harriman in Moscow to hold firm. There was tremendous pressure in Washington for compromise, though, lest the conference fail. Compromise was also supported within the delegation, specifically by Harold Stassen. Stettinius brought the matter before the two Senators, not so much to get their opinion, as to recruit them as allies against compromise. Vandenberg's reaction could hardly be doubted. Limiting debate meant that the Soviets could veto discussion about Poland. The Senator was unalterably opposed to that. Connally went along. With senatorial backing the Secretary's position prevailed over those of both the White House and the Kremlin. Talk of compromise from Washington ceased, and the next day Gromyko sought out Stettinius and accepted the American interpretation. Vandenberg was immensely pleased. Noting press reports that he had been crucial in upholding the adopted formula, Vandenberg modestly recorded, "I believe that's right."(17)

The congressional contingent was also influential on the "three vote" issue. At Yalta, Stalin had demanded six votes for the Soviet Union, equal to the number of British Commonwealth nations. Roosevelt's compromise allowed the Soviet Union three votes, with Byelorussia and the Ukraine being admitted to the United Nations. The United States was to receive three votes also. Roosevelt was inclined to take the three votes for the United States, but he was willing to let the delegation decide the matter. Vandenberg and some of the other delegates, however, were opposed to the multi-vote concept. The delegation issued a statement spurning the three votes for the United States in the hopes of "embarrassing" the Soviets into also dropping their claim. The ploy did not work. The Soviets held their position and received their three votes; the United States was left with one! But for congressional opposition, there might have also been three American votes. For cagey politicians, Senators Vandenberg and Connally inexplicably passed up the chance to have not only the United States, but perhaps Michigan and Texas also represented in the United Nations.(18)

## Regionalism

Regionalism was also an issue of particular interest to Vandenberg, and one on which he was able to exercise considerable influence. As on the veto and three vote questions, it was a division within the Executive that enhanced the impact of congressional opinion. Vandenberg became a prime mover in the early solidification of the Western Hemisphere as an anti-communist bloc. Under the leadership of Cordell Hull and his successor Edward Stettinius, the basic United States position on regionalism was to view the concept as a threat to the idea of international organization. At the Dumbarton Oaks Conference, the United States took the lead in proposing that regional agreements be subordinated to a universal international organization. The United States agreed with other powers that while regional organizations were valid, they could take no actions without authorization by the Security Council.(19)

There was a faction in Washington, however, led by Assistant Secretary of State Nelson Rockefeller and including the military, which desired to see closer inter-American ties, economically and militarily. Rockefeller testified before the Foreign Relations Committee, stressing the need for closer economic ties with Latin America to counter the threat of subversion of Latin America by non-hemispheric powers and ideologies. A military representative, Lieutenant General Stanley Embrick, stressed the need for vigil in Latin America, hinting that a possible communist take-over of a Latin country would put the Panama Canal, the Gulf Coast, and the Caribbean area within bomber range of potential enemies. At the early 1945 Inter-American Conference on the prob-lems of war and peace, the opponents of regionalism were largely successful in staving off attempts to create an inter-American defense organization. Colombia introduced a proposal binding all signatories to "defend by all means, including by arms, the terri-torial integrity and the political independence of all and each one of them, once it had been decided by an absolute majority of all the American States" that such action was necessary. The United States, led by Stettinius opposed Colombia's proposal, but agreed to a compromise "declaration of solidarity" in its place. (20)

While there is no evidence that Congress had any significant influence on American diplomatic positions at the Mexico City conference, Stettinius was careful to ensure the congressional opinions were sought. In addition to the pre-conference briefing given the Foreign Relations Committee by Rockefeller, the Com-mittee's Chairman Connally was invited to attend the conference as a delegate. Secretary Stettinius also asked Connally to review and comment on the Secretary's opening address to the dele-gates. Despite pressure from the other Latin American delega-tions, and his own desire to accede to them, Stettinius delayed approving the compromise Act of Chapultepec until Connally agreed. Once he did, the Act was signed.(21)

The defensive "Act of Chapultepec," which had only been reluc-tantly accepted by the Secretary of State, quickly became the focus of Congressional admiration. Rockefeller sought to strengthen the regional cause at the San Francisco Conference. Rockefeller's role at San Francisco as advisor to the American members of the committee on regional agreements put him in an advantageous position to gain the support of the chairman of the American contingent, Arthur Vandenberg. Vandenberg had initially displayed little interest in the concept of regionalism. His early suggestions on Charter revision made no mention of the issue. Rockefeller worked hard to ensure that the Charter in-cluded a provision allowing defensive regional pacts, an activity which did not meet with the approval of Stettinius and which put the Assistant Secretary in the considerable bad graces of his superior.(22)

The climax of Rockefeller's activities came on May 5. Al-ready concerned over exclusive reliance on the Security Council for action, Vandenberg was invited, in his words, "by a signifi-cant coincidence" to join Rockefeller at dinner. At their meet-ing, Rockefeller expressed fear that the Security Council could veto defensive action by the American Republics and effectively abrogate the Monroe Doctrine. The thought of the Soviets being able to nullify the Monroe Doctrine was just too much for the Senator. That very evening, Vandenberg, with Rockefeller's will-ing help, wrote a strong letter to Stettinius warning that if the United States did not honor its Pan American obligations or failed to preserve its rights under the Monroe Doctrine, ratification of the entire Charter by the Senate would be threatened. Vandenberg's letter caused a major split in the delegation.(23) Rockefeller was supported by Vandenberg, Representatives Sol Bloom and Doc Eaton and the military. Arrayed against them were most of the State Department people including the Secretary, Pasvolsky, and Stassen. The battle continued for more than a week, but with Vandenberg's strong position and Rockefeller's skill in lining up Latin American support for his position, the issue was resolved in favor of the "regionalists." On May 15, Vandenberg confronted Stettinius demanding that the Secretary make a firm decision on the question. Stettinius surrendered and announced that the United States would seek an amendment encompassing regional agreements and would also call a Latin American conference following San Francisco to implement the Act of Chapultepec.(24)

Having overcome delegation objections, the threat of the Senate was next used to defeat other delegations' objections. The British were unwilling to go along with regionalism, claiming it was an invitation to group domination. As Stettinius candidly admitted to Anthony Eden, the United States did not want it's regional amendment to impair the effectiveness of the United Nations. The United States delegation, however, was faced with a practical problem--trying to put the treaty through the Senate. Stettinius explained that unless some method was worked out by which the inter-American system could exist in conjunction with the United Nations, there was a good chance that the treaty would not be ratified by the Senate.(25) Vandenberg similarly warned Eden the following day. As Stettinius had, Eden gave way, agreeing to support general language if the specific reference to Latin America was dropped.(26)

Spurred by his anti-communism, Vandenberg's interest in Latin America also included the question of Argentina's representation at the San Francisco Conference. Formally neutral, but sympathetic with Germany during the war, Argentina was a hemispheric pariah. Excluded from the Mexico City Conference and facing exclusion from the San Francisco Conference, Argentina bravely declared war against the Axis powers on March 27, 1945. The belated declaration did little to resurrect Argentina in the eyes of most Americans. President Truman explicitly instructed the American delegation not to support Argentine admission to the conference. Rockefeller and Vandenberg were of a different mind, however. Rockefeller felt that the good will of the Latin American countries and the operation of the Western Hemisphere as a solid bloc in the United Nations was vital.(27) Vandenberg agreed with Rockefeller's argument. Specifically praising Rockefeller, Vandenberg wrote:

Now that we are going to an international organization where, as a practical matter, we shall need votes from time to time in the General Assembly . . . I think Rockefeller's work is indispensable.(28)

The Latin American nations were also anxious not to see one of their largest members excluded from the world organization, and the Assistant Secretary and the Senator were equally anxious not to disappoint them.

Vandenberg had visions of an anti-communist All-American front. The fact that the push for facist Argentina was an embarrassment for American diplomacy and was widely opposed in the United States did not deter Vandenberg. The point in Vandenberg's mind was that the Soviet Union opposed Argentine admission which made the Soviets look bad in the eyes of Latin America. On the day that Argentina was admitted to the U.N., the Senator wrote in his diary that Molotov's bitter opposition had "done more in four days to solidify Pan America against Russia than anything that ever happened."(29) In this case, even the President was forced to give way in the face of a divided Administration with Vandenberg supporting the opposition.

The admission of Argentina to the San Francisco Conference did not signal the end of the contest. Rather, it was round one of a prolonged struggle over United States relations with the South American nation and the price the United States was willing to pay to secure hemispheric organization. The Administration was caught between considerable public criticism of its pro-Argentine policies and pressures from various sources, particularly Vandenberg, to fulfill Stettinius' San Francisco commitment and convene a Pan American conference to establish a hemispheric defense agreement. In this, the second round, the Senator and his allies lost, but managed to give the United States a diplomatic bloody nose in the process. Bowing to public pressure, the President fired Rockefeller in August 1945, replacing him with ardently anti-facist Spruille Braden. The United States also decided to postpone the meeting scheduled for Rio de Janeiro to negotiate an inter-American defense treaty. The new Under Secretary of State, Dean Acheson, took on the task of telling Vandenberg and his colleagues of the postponement. Meeting with Senators Vandenberg, Connally, Wallace H. White, and Walter F. George, Acheson explained that the conference was being put off in favor of negotiating a treaty via diplomatic channels, thereby excluding Argentina without the necessity of a public fuss. The Senators and, two days later, the full Foreign Relations Committee refused to be persuaded. Partly annoyed by lack of prior consultation and unwilling to see the conference delayed, they thoroughly disagreed. Inasmuch as the United States had already communicated its desires to host-country Brazil, there could be no turning back. Acheson was forced, however, into a public statement justifying the United States position. Acheson resignedly described the situation: "Our position was logical but unwise . . . we had gotten ourselves at cross-purposes with the Senate and our Latin American friends."(30)

Vandenberg and others in Congress were neither pleased with Braden nor the anti-Argentine position he represented. For a time, the Foreign Relations Committee refused to consider his nomination as Rockefeller's replacement. Vandenberg was concerned that Braden's opposition to United States-Argentine cooperation carried with it the potential of destroying American solidarity against the communist menace.(31) The Senator's reasoning was simple. Vandenberg wanted an anti-communist front; Braden opposed a hemispheric defense pact which included Argentina; the Latin American countries opposed a pact without Argentina; and Vandenberg opposed Braden. Someone had to give, and it was Braden. In an early 1947 speech, the Senator called for quick convocation of the Rio Conference, and, by implication, for Braden's resignation. Senator Connally supported Vandenberg in private communications to Secretary of State George C. Marshall. Pressure from the Senators, the increasingly anti-communist senti-ment in the country, and Braden's own bureaucratic difficulties within the Department led to his dismissal in June 1947 and a decision to convene the long delayed conference in August. It was a round three victory for those, including Vandenberg and Connally, who cared little about the color of Argentine politics as long as it was not red.(32)

Under the watchful eye of the two Senators, the Rio Confer-ence became the capstone of the inter-American security struc-ture. Vandenberg was exceedingly pleased with his work, describ-ing the treaty as having, "Republican credentials written all over it."(33) Ironically, the single aspect on which the congres-sional delegation dissented was the strength of the American commitment. Jealously guarding the congressional power to declare war, Vandenberg and Bloom wanted specific language included in the treaty stating that a nation's voluntary contribu-tion of armed forces to hemispheric defense should be based on its "constitutional consent." Secretary Marshall persuaded them to drop the specific language, but only after agreeing to make the point clear to the American press.(34) Marshall was not pleased, but as he later explained to the Argentine Foreign Minis-ter, "in considering the treaty we were less concerned with the world situation than with problems arising out of our own govern-mental structure . . ."(35)

The question of the ability of the Administration to commit American material and forces to action without Congress' specific consent was not new to the Rio Conference. Just that year the House Foreign Affairs Committee had killed a proposed Inter-American Military Cooperation Act because of the open-ended and vague authority it granted the President. This question had also been at issue during the United Nations Charter ratification proceedings. As Senator Vandenberg explained to John Foster Dulles, the "latent opposition" to the Charter was "detouring into a flank attack" on the question of whether the American delegate to the Security Council would be empowered to commit the country to use of force. Vandenberg was of the opinion that if the opposition should take that tack, it would be an effective strategy, and the Charter's backers would find themselves "drawn into a far longer battle than . . . otherwise anticipated." Vandenberg was personally divided in his thoughts. He felt that the constitutional requirement that only Congress can declare war should not be ignored. On the other hand, he felt that Congress could not "ignore the precedents of one hundred and fifty years which give the President the primary right to decide whether the use of force falls within his own constitutional prerogatives . . ."(36) In the end, despite his reservations, Vandenberg joined with the Administration in defeating this line of attack.

Oddly enough, it was Dulles, supported by Connally, who brought
the matter to a head. In testimony before the Foreign Relations
Committee, Dulles observed that the special military agreement to
be negotiated between the United States and the United Nations
under Article 43 would be a treaty and thus subject to Senate
ratification. Dulles also said that the powers of the American
delegate would be defined in the agreement and that Congress
might include limitations of the disposition of American forces.
The State Department was put in a quandary by Dulles' statement.
On the one hand, Dulles' interpretation caused several Senators
to abandon their demand for a reservation restricting American
military obligations. On the other hand, the State Department
did not favor a separate military treaty, feeling that encumber-
ing restrictions might be attached by Congress. The Department
split on whether to oppose possible Senate reservations to the
Charter ratification. Pasvolsky felt the issue should not be
pressed. Acheson, on the contrary, felt it would be worth sacri-
ficing a few votes. It was agreed that the question should be
presented to Vandenberg and that the Department should be guided
by his advice. The appeal to Vandenberg worked and a compromise
followed. Acheson reported that Vandenberg had extricated the
State Department from Dulles' "trap."(37) Vandenberg and Connally, who reversed his position, told the Senate that they had
never insisted that the agreement be a treaty, but only that it
be submitted for congressional approval. In a letter to Senator
McKellar, the President agreed to make subsequent military commitments under the Charter only by statute. Those commitments were
never made, in part due to congressional restrictions.(38)

In the end, the careful attention given Vandenberg and the
rest of the Senate paid its dividends. Few rose to attack ratification of the United Nations Charter seriously. Where questions
arose, Vandenberg and Connally acted as Administration allies to
divert them. A week before the final vote, Dean Acheson could
confidently write his daughter that the push for ratification was
one of his easier tasks.(39) Even earlier, on July 3, President
Truman had written his wife predicting that the Charter would
pass with all but two votes.(40) It was an astute guess. On
July 28, the Charter was ratified by a vote of 89-2. Roosevelt
and Truman had learned the lessons of Wilsonian history well.

## Atomic Energy

On the morning of April 12, 1945, Harry S Truman did not know
of the atomic bomb. By that evening he was not only privy to the
great secret, he was responsible for establishing United States
policy on one of the most complex and important issues to face
the postwar world. More than any other single issue, the convoluted policy path followed by the Administration illustrates
the uncertainty, both substantively and procedurally, with which
foreign policy was formulated during the initial months of
Truman's presidency. With Truman's and Byrnes' leadership fitful, Congress exerted considerable influence. Congressional
interest and activity in the field of atomic energy was also

activated by the domestic question of civilian versus military control of nuclear power. The effect of this congressional influence was to force the Administration into a number of premature and unwise positions and, in the long run, to lessen the chances for international accord on atomic energy. Although Congress had little direct power over international negotiations, the Administration's desire to avoid congressional investigations, disabling domestic legislation, and general domestic criticism led it to pay heed to congressional objections to sharing atomic information except under the most rigid limitations. Congress' opposition to sharing was based primarily on its propensity to favor absolutist positions and not to accept the pragmatic arguments of the Administration in favor of limited cooperation. The congressional position was also partly in response to its being excluded from the policy-making process. Thus, Congress was able to exert its will even though the Executive neither asked for nor desired its opinion. Congressional means were largely indirect but effective. Truman had no wish to be publicly accused of giving away the nation's atomic secrets.

The President, as was so often true during his first year in office, was buffeted between the conflicting opinions of his advisors. Byrnes' duality sprang from his contradictory desires to use the bomb as an implicit diplomatic bargaining tool and his desire to reach an accord with the Soviets. The Administration never considered giving the Soviet Union the technical knowledge necessary to build the bomb, but there was widespread sentiment in the Administration in favor of sharing theoretical knowledge necessary as a background for the development of atomic energy. With the Administration uncertain and divided, Congress intervened and urged the hard line eventually adopted by the United States.

With the war at an end, the weapon developed specifically to achieve that purpose became a major focus of policy debate. The opening gun of the debate was fired by Secretary of War Stimson. About to retire and concerned with Byrnes' opposition to atomic energy cooperation with the Soviets, the Secretary of War wrote to Truman urging a positive approach to the Soviets. Failure to do so, the Secretary reasoned, would deepen Soviet suspicion and distrust of the United States and might lead to an atomic arms race. "The chief lesson I have learned in a long life" Stimson advised, "is the only way you can make a man trustworthy is to trust him; and the surest way you can make a man untrustworthy is a distrust him and show your distrust."(41) Meeting the next day, Truman and Stimson went over the Secretary's memorandum paragraph by paragraph, with the President endorsing each one and concluding that "we must take Russia into our confidence." Stimson also met with Acting Secretary of State Dean Acheson (Byrnes was in London) the next day, and found that Acheson was "strongly on our side in the treatment of Russia."(42)

Stimson's memorandum became the basis for a full scale debate in the Cabinet, which split fairly evenly. Acheson recalled that reactions in the meeting were principally "gut feelings." No one had had a chance to prepare for the subject's complexities, rendering, "the discussion . . . unworthy of the subject."(43)

Secretary of the Treasury Fred Vinson, Attorney General Tom Clark, Leo Crowley, James Forrestal, and Agriculture Secretary Clinton Anderson were all opposed to the premises of the Stimson memorandum. Supporting Stimson were his successor Robert P. Patterson, Henry Wallace, Labor Secretary Lewis Schwellenbach, Atomic Scientist Vannevar Bush, and Acheson.(44)

Although the question was in itself a momentous one, much of the President's immediate interest stemmed from the convergence of the domestic and international control issues. Acheson had briefed Truman on the Stimson plan, specifically concentrating on its relationship to domestic control of atomic energy and necessary congressional liaison. At the President's behest, Acheson agreed to draw up a memorandum on the entire question. The President hoped to delay consideration of the domestic military versus civilian control question because it raised still undecided international questions. A spate of bills being introduced in Congress on the domestic issue and the push for an investigation of atomic energy policy, however, forced the Administration's hand. The President's request to Acheson for a memorandum and his inclusion of the question in the Cabinet meeting resulted from his decision, on September 10, to try to preempt congressional initiatives by addressing a message to Congress dealing with both the domestic and international aspects of control.(45) The memorandum which Acheson sent to the President on September 25 was, according to Acheson, "deeply influenced by Colonel Stimson's paper." Acheson forecast that "Any long range understanding. . . seems to me impossible under a policy of Anglo-American exclusion of Russia from atomic development." He therefore recommended that the United States approach the Soviet Union and attempt to work out a program of mutual exchange of scientific information and collaboration on the peaceful development of atomic energy on the condition that the Soviets join in renouncing atomic weapons and agree to an adequate inspection of atomic facilities. Acheson also recommended to the President that a massive public relations drive be instituted to bring the country around to the Administration's point of view. He warned that "without the same informed and extensive public discussion that preceded the San Francisco Conference. . . the public and Congress will be unprepared to accept a policy involving substantial disclosures to the Soviet Union."(46) The President generally approved of Acheson's recommendations, and directed him to draft a message to Congress.(47) In his October 3 message to Congress, the President pointed to the fact that the theoretical knowledge behind atomic energy was widely known and committed himself to the principle of international control to avoid a desperate arms race. Truman also tried to head off negative congressional reaction by repeatedly emphasizing that proposed discussions with the British and Canadians and, by implication, possible talks with the Russians, would not reveal the bomb's manufacturing process, thus protecting the U.S. nuclear monopoly. The President further pledged to consult with Congress as talks proceeded and to submit any agreements to it.

Truman's message to Congress did not mean, however, that a clear policy had been finally formulated. Upon his return from

London, Byrnes moved away from a position favoring sharing nuclear information. Stung by the failure of the conference and Moscow's obstructive tactics, the Secretary resumed his former ambivalent stand and took no initiative to clarify policy. A still uncertain Truman did nothing to prod his Secretary of State into action, despite the rapidly approaching visit of Canadian Prime Minister Mackenzie King and British Prime Minister Clement Attlee to Washington to discuss atomic cooperation.(48) It was not until November 3, a mere week before the joint talks were to begin that planning was undertaken, and then it was at Vannevar Bush's initiative rather than Byrnes'. Writing to his former boss and longtime friend, Henry Stimson, Bush described his part in drawing up the American plan and the subsequent meeting in a letter which bears quoting at length:

> It has been a most extraordinary affair. I have never par-
> ticipated in anything that was so completely unorganized or
> so irregular . . . . The reason, I think, for the strange
> performance which has occurred is that the affair has been
> in the hands of amateurs, and I include . . . Mr. Byrnes and
> the President . . . .The result is that I have had experi-
> ences in the past week that would make a chapter in 'Alice
> in Wonderland'. . . . About ten days ago I became much
> disturbed at the lack of preparation and went to see Patter-
> son, and upon finding out that he was as completely in the
> dark as I, went directly to Byrnes. There I found there was
> no organization for the meeting, no agenda being prepared,
> and no American plan in form to present. Urging all of
> these things without success, I myself wrote a plan and put
> in Byrnes' hands . . . . Byrnes conferred with the President
> the next day, and they apparently resolved their discussion
> about this paper, as it appeared to be the only one they had
> that gave any plan . . . . It is somewhat appalling . . . to
> think of this country handling many matters in such an atmos-
> phere.(49)

Bush was also appalled by Byrnes' failure to consult with Congress, which predictably raised a storm of legislative ire. Bush had advised the Secretary to include influential senators in the policy planning process, but his advice had been ignored.(50) Senator Robert LaFollette, Jr. had also warned Admiral Leahy that congressional tempers were aroused over their exclusion from the talks.(51) In Bush's estimate, this needless incurring of senate wrath was the most dangerous mistake of the conference. Vandenberg and Connally were further aggravated by a last moment invitation to the White House to witness the signing of the Truman-Attlee-King accord. They refused to be photographed with the principals and left immediately after the signing. There was little the Senators could do about the immediate events, but they awaited their chance to retaliate, which rapidly came.

It was Byrnes who provided them with an opening. By early December, the Secretary had rallied from his pessimism after the London Conference and was determined to meet and deal with the Soviets. The draft proposal which Byrnes intended to use in his discussions with the Soviets was basically the same as the Truman-Attlee-King accord--with one significant difference. Whereas the tripartite agreement specified that an inspection and control system would be worked out before sharing was undertaken, Byrnes' working paper indicated that "successful international action with respect to any phase of the problem is not necessarily a prerequisite for undertaking affirmative action with respect to other phases." Meeting with key members of the Senate only two days before his scheduled departure for Moscow, Byrnes stepped squarely into a congressional beehive. The combination of the plan itself and being told rather than asked for advice was too much for the senators. Vandenberg huffed that the Foreign Relations Committee had been created to be consulted, not merely informed, by the Executive Branch. He and Connally also expressed opposition to sharing information, particularly without safeguards.(52)

There can be little doubt that Byrnes' intent was to be flexible on the question of atomic energy at Moscow, and that his differences with the senators was more than a misunderstanding, as the Administration claimed. Some members of the Administration were also distressed by the Secretary's intentions and told him so. Navy Secretary Forrestal wrote the Secretary of State on December 11, that he had just read the working paper, and felt "strongly that the proposed basis of discussion goes too far." (53) Major General Leslie R. Groves, Director of the Manhattan Project, sent a similar note to Byrnes on the same day.(54) Acheson, who had to meet the criticism at home while Byrnes was in Moscow, later conceded that the instructions the Secretary "had worked out for himself were somewhat more liberal" than those of the Truman-Attlee King accord.(55)

There is no indication that these protests in any way dissuaded Byrnes. Nor were the senators mollified by having lodged their protest. As Vandenberg wrote, they were of the "unanimous opinion that the Byrnes formula must be stopped."(56) On December 14, the two senators appealed directly to the President. Truman appears to have been caught unaware of the position Byrnes had taken. Truman indicated that he agreed with the senators' position and said he had instructed Byrnes to comply. Perhaps, Truman thought, the senators were mistaken in their interpretation of Byrnes' position. Apparently unsure of what his Secretary of State was doing, the President chose not to issue specific supplementary instructions to Byrnes.(57) Rather, he had Acheson report the conversation to Byrnes, adding that the President had assured the senatorial delegation that no disclosures were contemplated. Byrnes, seeming to pick up the broad hint, replied that he had never intended to agree on disclosures without proper safeguards.(58)

Vandenberg was unaware of this exchange, however, and on December 20 the senator utilized the New York Times column of his confidant James Reston to carry the issue to the public. Byrnes then proceeded to compound congressional alarm. The communiqué from Moscow paralleled the Truman-Attlee-King accord insofar as it required that each stage be completed before the next was begun, but it listed the security stage last.

Vandenberg was apoplectic. He immediately confronted Acheson, who in turn arranged a meeting between the Senator and the President. Truman assured Vandenberg that he had misread the communiqué, and agreed to issue a statement, drawn up by Vandenberg and Acheson, reflecting the Senator's views.(59) Once again, the Administration was forced to take a strong public stand when quiet negotiation might have furthered international accord. The possibility of a nuclear agreement with the Soviets declined in the face of congressional resistance to sharing atomic energy information.

The last serious attempt to reach an agreement on the international control of atomic energy came during the spring of 1946. With the general change of the Administration's attitude during this period, it is probable that this attempt, based on the Acheson-Lilienthal Report, was doomed from the beginning. Congress intervened, though, to seal its fate before it ever got to the international negotiation stage and by doing so made the United States' position seem threatening to the Soviet Union. The presidential committee, chaired by Acheson, and its board of consultants, chaired by David Lilienthal, tended to favor the Stimson-type approach. The report they submitted to Truman via Byrnes called for the establishment of an international Atomic Development Authority to assume control of all raw materials needed for atomic energy production. The United States would only slowly give up its own resources, weapons, and knowledge. While the plan would have probably been unacceptable to the Soviets, who were calling for complete and immediate nuclear disarmament, it was cast in terms of negotiation and cooperation by men who favored a serious attempt at accord.

Byrnes and Truman were well aware of congressional suspicion of anything that smacked of sharing atomic secrets or surrendering American atomic control, and they knew that they needed to have a man with both prestige and congressional acceptability to negotiate the plan if it was to have a chance of avoiding legislative opposition. The man they chose was Bernard Baruch. As Truman related, he chose Baruch for several reasons, "not the least of which was that Baruch enjoyed considerable esteem in the Senate."(60)

Baruch knew that his appointment was politically inspired, and used his position to modify the Acheson-Lilienthal report to his own views--which were considerably more cautious than those of the report. He began by giving assurances to Vandenberg, publicly and privately, that he would oppose disclosure of U.S. secrets without strong safeguards.(61) He also demanded the right to modify the Acheson-Lilienthal report, despite the fact that Byrnes had told Baruch that he was "favorably impressed." (62) The modifications Baruch made changed the basic nature of the document from a positive to a negative approach. Baruch further demanded that the Security Council inflict swift and sure punishment on any violator and that the veto power not apply to atomic energy questions. When supporters of the original position countered that such proposals could only lessen chances of Soviet acceptance, Baruch forced his point of view by threatening to resign. Having appointed him for political reasons, the

Administration realized that to fire him would be a political disaster. Thus, Baruch's uncompromising position prevailed. With
Vandenberg's support, it was introduced to the United Nations
where it was totally unacceptable to the Soviet Union. After six
months of futile debate it died in the Security Council.(63)
Whatever slim chances there were for international cooperation
instead of competition were in this instance, like the others
before it, doomed in part by the unwillingness of many in
Congress to give up what they incorrectly assumed would be a long-
term American atomic monopoly.


The Soviet Loan

     The failure of the American government to extend post-war aid
to the Soviet Union has been cited by revisionist scholars as a
primary factor in the estrangement of the Soviets and their
actions in Germany and Eastern Europe in 1945 and 1946. A great
deal of the story behind the abortive aid to Russia involves
Congress and its antipathy toward such a loan. In essence, the
Administration was unwilling to ask an unsympathetic Congress for
a loan to the Soviet Union. Proposals to fund a loan were abandoned on several occasions rather than run the risk of defeat and
face the certainty of anti-Soviet rhetoric in Congress. Thoughts
of trying to channel funds through Lend-Lease or UNRRA were similarly dropped rather than risk loss of those programs. Further,
in early 1946, the Administration had to pledge not to seek funds
for the Soviet Union in return for congressional passage of a
large loan to Great Britain. Congress opposed the Soviet Union,
was concerned about the proposed effect of Russian commodity
repayment on domestic economic sectors and used its power of
appropriation to structure United States policy.
     The first major moves toward a substantial postwar loan to
the Soviet Union occurred in January 1945. Molotov informed
Averell Harriman that the Soviet Union "would be willing to
accept" a six billion dollar loan at an interest rate of 2 1/4
percent. Simultaneously, but coincidentally, Treasury Secretary
Henry Morgenthau proposed to President Roosevelt that the United
States loan the Soviets ten billion dollars at two percent
interest. The proposals for a Soviet Loan met with little initial enthusiasm in the White House and State Department. Roosevelt hoped that the lure of loans and credits would be a useful
bargaining tool and considered discussion of a loan premature.
He wished to avoid the subject until after the Yalta Conference.
Ambassador Harriman supported this strategy. Commenting on the
Soviet request, the Ambassador advised the State Department that
the United States' attitude on such questions should be dependent
on the Soviet's behavior in international matters. It should be
noted, though, that neither the President nor the Ambassador ever
opposed the basic idea of a loan to the Soviets. Harriman, to
the contrary, expressed his support of a loan. He further
advised the Department that amicable postwar relations would be
tied, to a degree, with American aid to the Soviets in the solution of their reconstruction problems. Further, the sooner the

Soviet government could provide an acceptable standard of living for its people, the sooner it would become tractable.(64)

Domestic politics suggested to the State Department, however, that such a loan might fail. In background memoranda prepared for Secretary Stettinius, Emilio G. Collado, Chief of the Division of Financial and Monetary Affairs, argued that Congress was not likely to view such a loan favorably. Furthermore, he pointed out, the Treasury plan to allow the Soviets to repay the loan in the form of raw material would activate opposition from oil and mining interest supporters in Congress.(65) The Secretary concurred. Rather than risk congressional rejection, the issue was temporarily dropped.(66)

In the spring of 1945, the new President had to face the now reopened and still complex question of aid to the Soviet Union. Averell Harriman urged the Department to "make every effort to obtain from Congress the loan authorization."(67) Collado also recommended that, "if political considerations are favorable," preparations for obtaining legislative authority for an Export-Import Bank loan to the Soviet Union should begin.(68) The Administration was well aware of the anti-Soviet sentiment in Congress. Truman pointed it out to Molotov and noted that Congress had to approve any foreign economic measures. Intractable Soviet actions, the President added, would make passage of a loan through Congress difficult.(69)

To avoid running the legislative gauntlet the Administration settled on a "banker's" loan through the Export-Import Bank that would have a standard interest rate and would not require a specific congressional authorization. This, in effect, would save members of Congress from having to vote money for the Russians. Lend-Lease was not a viable alternative. Congress was particularly watchful of large sums going to the Soviets. Nor was relief through the United Nations Relief and Rehabilitation Administration (UNRRA) politically viable. An August 1945 Soviet request for $700 million from UNRRA was viewed in the State Department as a threat to the entire program. Acheson wired Assistant Secretary of State for Economic Affairs Will Clayton that he considered it unlikely that funds could be obtained from Congress. He suggested that if the entire UNRRA program was not to be jeopardized, the Russian request should be withdrawn. Acheson knew that UNRRA was already unpopular among members of Congress and believed that approval of the Soviet request would be a fatal stroke as far as future congressional appropriations. (70)

Unwilling to risk defeat or endanger other programs, the Administration chose the path of least resistance. In early June, Under Secretary of State Joseph Grew informed Harriman that Congress would soon be asked to authorize an extension of the Export-Import Bank's lending authority with one billion dollars at regular interest rates set aside for the Soviet Union.(71) With the Soviets still an ally and able to avoid a direct vote on a loan to the Soviets, Congress agreed to the Administration's request.

Congressional authorization of a billion dollar loan to the Soviet Union did not mean, however, that the loan would automatically follow. Aside from various historical speculation as to whether the Administration would have met a request, the fact is that the Soviets never asked for the money at a rate which the Bank was willing to grant. The highest interest rate the Soviets were willing to accept was 2 3/8 percent. The banks would go no lower than three percent. Operating under the assumption that the United States needed and wanted to make the loan for its own economic betterment, the Soviets were willing to wait for better terms.(72)

The Soviet's failure to ask the Export-Import Bank for funds puzzled American officials. Secretary of the Treasury Fred Vinson testified before a Senate committee in early 1946 that he expected the one billion dollars reserved for the Soviets to be utilized.(73) Byrnes was equally mystified and the only suggestion Bernard Baruch could make to him was that the Russians "must have some clever idea, and it is bound to develop very soon."(74) It was an odd picture of Soviet officialdom believing the Americans could not resist loaning the money and American officialdom believing the Soviets could not resist borrowing it.

It is obvious that the failure of the Soviets to apply for the available loan was not part of an aversion to American money. They tried to tap a number of alternative sources, but in each case were blocked by Congress. Their attempts to obtain substantial funds from UNRRA or Lend-Lease were vetoed in anticipation of congressional reaction. By elimination, the original Soviet proposal for a six billion dollar, 2 1/4 percent loan remained the focus of discussion. The loan and its interest rate were the main topic of conversation between Stalin and Representative William Colmer's Committee in September 1945. Despite the flattering attention given to them by the Soviet Premier, the Committee returned home suspicious of the Soviets.(75) Meeting first with Byrnes and then with Truman, Colmer stressed the importance of assuming a tougher stance vis-à-vis the Russians. Colmer made it clear that his committee would favor a loan only if the Soviets fulfilled a number of terms, including releasing vital economic data and loosening their control over Eastern Europe. Both demands were patently unacceptable to the Soviets. (76) Even if the Soviets had accepted these terms, it is uncertain whether Congress would have voted for a loan. Vandenberg, for one, doubted that it would.(77) The net result was, as Clayton wired Harriman in late November, that the subject of a loan to the Soviet Union was "dormant."(78)

Despite these political difficulties, the Administration decided to make yet another effort to negotiate a loan in February 1946. Harriman handed the Soviets a note suggesting that negotiations on the one billion dollar loan be renewed. Then early in March the State Department announced that it had found the Soviet loan request which had been "lost" since August. Concurrently, in a special message to Congress, President Truman indicted that he would ask for an additional $1.25 billion in lending authority for the Export-Import Bank. Although the terms attached to the loan offer were stringent and the contention that a billion dollar loan request had been misplaced was laughable, events show that the Administration was willing to consider a

loan. The United States and the Soviets could not agree, however, on the accompanying political conditions.(79) Asked at a
June press conference whether he was going to submit the $1.25
billion request to Congress, the President demurred, "I have not
yet got to the point where I can consider that."(80)

Congressional considerations now again intervened to choke
off the last hope of a loan to the Soviet Union. The problem was
simple. Not only had the Administration pledged not to seek new
funds for loans during the British loan debate, but Congress was
becoming increasingly antagonistic toward the Soviet Union. One
Department official wrote that not only was it unlikely that
Congress would approve a loan, but such a request was "almost
certain to lead to a free-for-all debate in Congress" with a
"needless airing of anti-Soviet opinion" that would both damage
relations with the Soviet Union and cause a strong public reaction against that country. His suggestion, which was followed,
was to accept the last Soviet refusal and bow out gracefully.(81)

Other communist countries faced similar difficulties when
attempting to obtain American aid. Although aid was given to
several Eastern European countries through UNRRA and directly to
Poland and Hungary in 1947, the Administration met increasing
opposition from Congress. As early as the fall of 1945, American
diplomats were complaining that Soviet policy in Eastern Europe
and the regimes' anti-democratic images were making it difficult
to sell Congress and the American people on the idea of aid to
these nations.(82) Congress was particularly outraged by restrictions placed on American journalists in the region. Preceding
the 1946 UNRRA appropriations, the State Department, in anticipation of congressional reaction, sent diplomatic notes to eight
countries requesting the admission and non-censorship of journalists.(83) Congressional interest in a free press had an anti-red
tinge to its high-mindedness. As Senator Alexander Smith explained to Warren Austin, if Russia was publicly challenged on
the issue of the free press, it

> would be compelled to let in our people or be convicted in
> the popular mind of the matters charged, and . . . . If this
> latter were the situation Communism might well be on the way
> to being defeated . . . if our men were let in they would
> probably substantiate the stories and the results would be
> the same.(84)

An added complication was Congress' dislike of UNRRA. This
well intentioned but poorly run agency became a favorite target
of fire from the Hill.(85) Criticism was so severe that the
organization's director, Fiorello LaGuardia, wrote Secretary
Byrnes that he was convinced that UNRRA should be terminated. In
a particularly candid paragraph, he explained:

> There is no doubt that Congress would not, at this time,
> appropriate another penny. The feeling up on the Hill is
> anything but good and the conduct is anything but conducive
> to international good will and harmony. Every gossip, every
> rumor is picked up and then sprung on the floor of either

House. I can't tell you how many man-hours and how much in
cable costs we spend every week checking on complaints,
rumors, gossip. To date, not a serious complaint has been
justified. What good we could have earned, I fear has been
partially lost by irresponsible statements and unjustified
accusations.(86)

Thus, with his staff harried, appropriations unlikely, and international discord rather than good-will being generated, LaGuardia
was willing to see his own organization die, even though, he
warned, "the termination of UNRRA does not mean that the need for
help will end this year."(87) There could be only one conclusion, and that was, as Acheson described it, " to clear away
another source of trouble with Congress, UNRRA would be wound up
. . ."(88)

Congress' paradoxical call for a tough foreign policy, while
simultaneously refusing to appropriate the dollars necessary to
support such a policy, constituted an important part of the background of American diplomacy in the early Cold War years. At
times, the Administration's efforts to persuade Congress to appropriate foreign aid almost reached comic-ridiculous. Washington,
for example, was forced to veto a gracious French proposal to pay
a bonus to American troops on the grounds that Congress would
misinterpret the gesture as evidence of French financial solvency
and proof that France did not need any more aid.(89) More seriously, congressional attitudes dissuaded the Administration from
taking a "stitch in time" by channeling sufficient aid to Europe
in 1945 and 1946. In the words of one senior State Department
official, "through 1946, Washington was not in any mood to
encourage any initiative . . . on measures to aid Europe. The
fear of Congress was very great and there was no chance that any
measure that would make it necessary to seek additional funds
from Congress would be approved by the State Department."(90)

The 1946 congressional election only compounded the problem.
A great majority of Republicans had opposed the creation of the
Export-Import Bank, the International Bank, and the International
Monetary Fund. Pledged to fiscal restraint, the newly empowered
Republicans were quick to demonstrate that they were men of their
word. One of their first actions, in February 1947, was to make
it clear to William McChesney Martin, Chairman of the Board of
Directors of the Export-Import Bank, and to Undersecretary of
State Acheson that Congress expected the bank to tighten up its
lending policies, restricting loans to gilt-edged, selfliquidat-
ing projects. In the words of one Department official, "the
world, the nation, and the administration . . . awaited with
great anxiety the answer to the question whether the Republican
Congress would accept the economic responsibilities of America's
new role in the world."(91) The omens did not augur well.


Trade

The setting of tariffs, quotas, and other controls on foreign
trade continued as a traditional area of congressional interest

and influence. More than any other aspect of foreign policy, trade had direct repercussions on domestic interest groups and rallied members of Congress to work in the interest of their industrial or agricultural constituents. Congress was also concerned about surrendering its prerogatives by giving the President discretionary authority to reduce tariffs. An aroused Congress at times effectively made use of their power of authorization to exact concessions, and in other instances, rather than risk defeat, the Executive did not submit some items for authorization or some agreements for ratification. Even where the Administration had the legal authority to restructure trade agreements, it sometimes hesitated for fear of retaliation against other parts of its program. The Administration had some success in invoking the prestige of the presidency and by causing a patriotic response, but these tactics were offset by a degree of divisiveness within the Administration which further enhanced congressional influence.

Perhaps the most difficult legislative task facing the State Department and its legislative liaison officer Dean Acheson was convincing Congress in 1945 to renew the Reciprocal Trade Agreements Act. This act, which had long been the subject of intense partisan debate, encountered trouble in the spring of 1945 with Congress maneuvering to regain its position vis-à-vis the Executive and varying interest groups seeking to benefit themselves in the new peace-time economy. The Administration was anxious to secure freer trade. The presumed lessons of the Great Depression and the long tenure of zealous liberalized trade advocate Cordell Hull as Secretary of State had left their mark on the State Department. Still the Administration was not unified in its advocacy of reducing trade barriers. The Department of Agriculture, in particular, favored policies designed to protect agriculture. That Department found widespread support for its policies in Congress, particularly from agrarian based Midwestern Republicans and Southern Democrats.(92)

Negotiations between the State Department and Congress on the renewal of the trade act began early, and brought storm warnings from Democratic leaders in Congress. Speaker of the House Sam Rayburn, Majority Leader John McCormack, and Ways and Means Committee Chairman Robert Doughton all warned the State Department that two sections of its proposed joint congressional resolution would bring particular trouble: Section 2 which granted the President the authority to cut tariffs up to fifty percent and Section 3 which approved a broad approach by the President toward removing barriers to international trade. The leadership stressed that unless the Administration pledged to be selective in its tariff reductions, Section 2 would become the focus of difficult and prolonged debate. The Administration's willingness to assure Congress that it would use its tariff reducing power judiciously allowed it to secure continued presidential authority to decree tariff reductions.(93) But the issue of discretionary presidential power was a contentious one that was destined to haunt the Administration throughout the period.

The battle was joined in Congress in May and seesawed back and forth with the Administration winning by the slimmest of margins. After squeaking through the Ways and Means Committee on a partisan 14 to 11 vote, the bill went to the House floor, where, Acheson feared, "We are in real trouble." The only way to save the bill was to obtain presidential intervention, and get him to "lay his political head on the block with ours." The President signed a supportive letter drafted by Acheson, and Rayburn used it, "with great dramatic effect . . . [and] stopped the Old Guard just short of victory."(94) The key vote had come on an amendment to strike out the authority given the president to reduce tariffs, and was defeated by only twenty-three votes.

The President was also busy in the Senate trying to line up support. Still, senators were also reluctant to give up their traditional prerogatives. As one friendly Democratic senator wrote the President, "when Congress delegates . . . the power to say what the tariff rates shall be, it is turning over its constitutional power . . . . If I judge the attitude of the American people correctly, they want Congress to assume and to discharge all of its functions . . . ."(95) The Senate Finance Committee reflected that attitude when it came out against the legislation. In the end, the bill passed, but only after all-out effort by the Administration and through repeated pledges to limit tariff reductions strictly.

Congressional action and opinion on trade were of almost as much interest and significance to foreign governments as they were to the American Administration. The British, whose economic relationship with the United States was crucial to their postwar recovery, were particularly concerned with Congress. As early as March, American diplomats in London were telling Washington that it was "indispensable" to sound out congressional leaders on future commercial policy.(96) At the same time, though, the British were hesitant about pursuing negotiations with the United States, fearing that possible leaks from Congress during preliminary negotiations would get dragged into British domestic politics during the upcoming parliamentary elections.(97) British concern over congressional restrictions on trade proved well founded. The very pledges that the Administration made to Congress in order to secure extension of the trade act made it impossible for American diplomats to negotiate broad trade incentives. The same restrictions also limited Canadian-American trade talks. As the Canadians were told, not only did the assurances given Congress preclude broad discussions, but, even if the pledges did not exist, it would be impossible to persuade the Senate to ratify such trade concessions. The Canadians proposed a prearranged breakdown of negotiations which they hoped, when combined with the lure of Canadian trade concessions, might bring Congress around. The suggestion was rejected, however, by Acheson and Assistant Secretary of State for Economic Affairs William Clayton as futile at that time.(98)

Neither congressional attitudes nor the Administration's prospects for broad trade powers improved during 1946. Despite pressing issues, the Administration delayed introducing new trade measures. The State Department had originally intended to begin negotiations for a general tariff reduction in October 1946, but political considerations intervened. Clayton delayed announcing

United States intentions until after the election to prevent tariffs from becoming a partisan issue in the campaign. The Administration's hope for a friendlier post-election Congress was sorely
disappointed. Clayton's November 9, 1946 announcement that the
United States and seventeen other nations would meet in Geneva
the following April to begin general trade talks brought swift
and angry reaction from Congress. Immediately after the Republican controlled 80th Congress convened in January 1947, Ohio's
Thomas A. Jenkins, a ranking Republican on the Ways and Means Committee, introduced a resolution designed to prevent American participation in the Geneva discussions. With the Jenkins resolution in the hopper and other similar measures being introduced,
the Administration launched a counteroffensive. Its strategy was
aimed at removing the tariff issue from the context of domestic
debate and presenting it as a foreign policy issue. In his first
appearance before the Foreign Relations Committee, Secretary of
State-designate General George C. Marshall contended that manifestations of economic isolationism would hurt the United States
negotiating position at the forthcoming foreign ministers talks
in Moscow. Outgoing Secretary Byrnes appeared with Senator
Vandenberg before the Cleveland Council on Foreign Relations on
January 11 to reaffirm bipartisan cooperation and discuss international economic affairs in international political terms.(99)

Vandenberg's support of the Administration on trade, however,
was not as unequivocal as it was on other issues. The Senator
recognized the pressing trade problems, but felt that the State
Department did not give sufficient consideration to possible
damage to domestic economic interests. Also, with members of
Congress prone to view trade from a domestic standpoint and with
trade legislation being considered in the House Ways and Means
Committee and the Senate Finance Committee, the ability of Vandenberg to bring his reputation for expertise or his power as Chairman of the Foreign Relations Committee to bear was considerably
dissipated. Nevertheless, Vandenberg acted as a key liaison
figure between Congress and the Administration. Vandenberg
brought Clayton and Acheson together with Senate Finance Committee Chairman Eugene Millikin to work out a compromise. The
Administration believed that a presidential veto would make it
impossible for Congress to modify the trade act of 1945. But it
had no desire to become involved in a long fight that would only
serve to make Congress more hostile and jeopardize other, more
immediate Administration efforts, such as the British loan.
Although negotiations were long and difficult, with at least one
proposed Administration statement being rejected by the senators,
on February 25, 1947, Truman issued an executive order incorporat-
ing most of Vandenberg's and Millikin's points regarding escape
clauses. He also called for a study and public recommendations
by the Tariff Commission on the domestic effect of tariff agreements.(100)

Truman's concessions did not end congressional opposition to
tariff reductions. Die-hards such as Representative Knutson
launched new attacks on the Administration's policy. In Dean
Acheson's words, "from the Imperial Box, thumbs were turned down
on the International Trade Organization."(101) Although the

United States was a principal sponsor of the organization, it never became a member. Conceived as an international body to encourage a liberalization of international trade, the ITO was an anathema to Congress. Not only did it represent a principle many legislators found abhorrent, but the organization was perceived as a threat to congressional control of trade. Proposals to submit the Charter to the Senate in May 1948 were killed by Under Secretary of State Patterson's contention that Congress had not been properly educated and that ratification would be subject to partisan fighting and probable defeat.(102)

Finally submitted to Congress in the spring of 1949, the Charter remained buried in committee as a continuing reminder of congressional opposition to the free trade concept it represented.(103) The Administration was concerned that the opposition would try to kill both the liberalized Trade Agreements Act and the ITO by linking the two measures.(104) The decision was to cut losses and let the ITO go. Acheson told Truman that pushing the ITO would not only endanger more general trade legislation, but would lead to "either rejection of the Charter outright or an indefinite delay . . . Either of these results would be damaging to our foreign policy."(105) Truman agreed, as did the Cabinet in the hope that "willingness to abandon the ITO [would] gain some concessions from some of the members of the House and Senate who might otherwise disapprove our Trade Agreements Program."(106)

Foreign oil also became an issue between Congress and the Executive. In this instance, the issue was public and involved a 1945 arrangement worked out with the British by Secretary of the Interior Harold Ickes and Dean Acheson for the joint sponsorship of a multilateral international petroleum production and distribution agreement. As with the ITO, the Anglo-American Petroleum Agreement suffered the ignominious fate of death by inaction. Still, hoping to see his creation given senatorial blessing, Ickes wrote Vandenberg in May 1948 asking for his support. Ickes felt that with the oil companies and their ally Tom Connally opposed to the treaty, only Vandenberg could help.(107) The Senator replied that although he favored the treaty, there was no chance of success. As he explained:

> The opposition of Senator Connally is of course important; but it is only one of the factors involved. Behind him are practically all of the Senators from the Midwestern oil States.(108)

Oil was seen as a domestic issue, not one of foreign policy. Ickes could only agree with Vandenberg's appraisal, sadly noting that, "When a man like Senator Connally can be scared within an inch of his political life, what is there to be expected?"(109)

Two other related State Department projects which were undertaken at approximately the same time as the Anglo-American treaty deserve brief mention. One of these, the establishment of national control over the resources of the continental shelf, was successful, while the other, the development of the St. Lawrence River into an international seaway and power supply, was blocked by Congress for nearly a decade. Both had to run the gauntlet of domestically inspired opposition in Congress. Even though the incorporation of the continental shelf into the national domain was to be accomplished by executive order, it was deemed judicious to secure the assent of Congress. It turned out to be a wise decision, for in his meeting with Connally, Acheson discovered that the proclamation would be viewed as a threat to the oil industry and bring the Senator into opposition. In this case, the difficulty was averted by the inclusion of the statement that the proclamation did not prejudice state claims to underseas resources in the affected area.(110) The obstacles to the Seaway could not so easily be overcome. A wide array of eastern seaboard interest groups, including railroads, labor, and the Atlantic ports were able to rally congressional support that prevented the Truman Administration from ever bringing the project to fruition.(111)

### The British Loan

From the end of the war until 1947, by far the largest and most significant economic measure submitted to Congress was the proposal for a 3.75 billion dollar loan to Great Britain. Although both the terms and amount were partially determined with Congress in mind, when the loan was sent up to the Hill in January 1946 its prospects were gloomy. Legislative opposition was aroused by the negative reaction of anti-British ethnic groups and a variety of economic interest groups. Further, the loan was presented as a pragmatic approach to economic betterment. Whatever the loan's merits, the argument left economy-minded members of Congress unmoved. In the end, the loan passed, but only by a legislative strategy that was to have important ramifications in the intensification of the cold war. Anti-communist justification succeeded where pragmatic economic argument failed.

With Assistant Secretary of State for Economic Affairs Will Clayton, as the chief American negotiator, there can be little doubt that much of the United States' position was determined by his desire to break up the British sterling trading bloc. By position and belief, Clayton was State's chief advocate of reducing barriers to international trade. Clayton was also aware, though, that Congress would need to be convinced that the United States was benefiting from the loan. Even though Clayton "loaded the negotiations with all the conditions that traffic would bear," Congress was still not satisfied.(112) Just prior to the loan's introduction in Congress, Vandenberg wrote, "the proposed loan agreement has too many side doors and back doors and escalators. The British _really_ agree to _very_ little."(113) The amount and financial terms of the loan were also concluded with Congress very much in mind. The British desired a $4 billion, interest free grant. Clayton favored giving the British the entire $4 billion, but was voted down by Secretary of the Treasury Fred Vinson and others on the grounds that Congress would not accept the figure. Reportedly, the British request for an interest free grant was also favored by the President, but, as Truman told the chief British negotiator, John Maynard Keynes, he dared not submit anything like that to Congress.(114)

The British were considerably disturbed by congressional attitudes. Not only were the British distressed by their failure to obtain the full amount with no interest, but they felt that Congress was responsible for interfering in their domestic affairs, for airing Anglophobic propaganda, and for requiring adherence to provisions of the loan even when they threatened to destroy the British economy. What the British considered interference in their domestic affairs sprang from congressional criticism of the socialist policies of the British Labor government. Chancellor of the Exchequer Hugh Dalton recorded in his diary, "Much of the criticism was . . . of the actual British Labour Government and its policies. There had been talk of 'putting England through the wringer,' by which was meant bringing heavy pressure on us to abandon our policy of nationalizing selected industries."(115)

Although the British informed American officials that they understood the difficulties of negotiating on the basis of hypotheses as to what Congress would accept, they were both angered and apprehensive. Economically, the British doubted their ability to service both the interest and amortization of the loan. They also feared that Congress was making it impossible for either the United Kingdom or the United States to follow sound economic policies. In the end, the British reluctantly accepted many of the terms in order to get the loan through Congress. Another British worry was over the requirement for the convertibility of sterling and foreign currencies. Although this had originally been a provision included by Clayton to encourage free trade, congressional opinion made it difficult for American officials to relax the provision even after it appeared to be damaging the British economy.(116) In January 1947, Secretary of the Treasury John Snyder had to warn Dalton that the "resistance that had to be overcome before we obtained Congressional ratification" (117) made it imperative that the British live up to their agreements. Despite their economic difficulties, the British reluctantly agreed. They were not, Dalton wrote, "inclined to risk further debate with Congress . . . repetition of this . . . would have been damaging to our credit and to Anglo-American cooperation in general . . . We decided to keep our word and face the consequences."(118)

Furthering British disaffection, Congress launched a vitriolic anglophobic attack. Although some members, such as Vandenberg, favored the loan "for the sake of some nebulous affinity which the English speaking world must maintain,"(119) many others, particularly those with Irish-American constituencies, voiced what Dalton described as "lengthy, ill-informed, unfriendly, and even spiteful criticisms of Britain."(120) Irish-American opposition to the loan aroused such concern for the British that at one point a prominent British banker suggested to Dalton that perhaps the Irish Premier, Eamon de Valera, could be persuaded to make a public statement in favor of the loan to relieve the pressure from Irish descendants in the United States. (121)

The net result of these varied channels of attack by Congress was to worsen British-American relations decidedly and to cause a number of important changes in British economic and financial policy. For the purposes of this study, the most important of these was to increase pressure within the British Cabinet to reduce overseas financial and man-power commitments sharply, a policy which led to the British withdrawal from Greece and the birth of the Truman Doctrine in the spring of 1947.(122)

In the United States, Clayton took intensive measures to ensure the passage of the loan. He arranged for speeches by a wide array of top government officials. Even Secretary Byrnes, who normally refused such tasks, thought the loan important enough to participate in the public relations effort.(123) Clayton also personally lobbied for the loan in Congress, sponsoring, among other efforts, a series of dinners at which he met with every member of the House. Like his boss, though, Clayton had not yet learned the lesson of careful consultation with Congress. There was no attempt to bring members of Congress into the negotiations with the British. Congress was left annoyed by its exclusion and unencumbered by the dual role which so often restricted Vandenberg and others.(124) Presaging Clayton's troubles, the Michigan Senator judged that the negotiations had been "badly handled."(125)

The basic argument presented by the Administration to justify the loan was economic in nature. During the course of debate, all official statements relied on economic arguments with no claim of security benefits.(126) Even during the loan's darker moments in the House during June 1946, correspondence from the President to the Chairman of the Banking Currency Committee continued to stress the economic benefits of the proposed loan. (127) Friendly congressional leaders followed the Administration's lead and also emphasized the loan's economic aspect in their addresses to Congress and in letters to their constituents.(128)

It soon became apparent that the cause was going badly. In addition to opposition springing from those with large anti-British ethnic groups in their constituency, from those who bridled at the lack of consultation, and from those committed to budget cuts, a number of adversely affected interest groups entered the fray. Mississippi's Senator James Eastland counseled the White House that the loan campaign was being handled very poorly in the Senate. His mail was running about 100 to 1 against the loan. He predicted that eight or ten Southern Democrats were going to vote against it unless the economic benefits of the loan could be made more obvious to their constituents. In particular, the Cotton Growers' Association had to be lined up in support of the loan.(129) Other opposition came from those whose partisanship and resistance to "New Deal give-aways" was heightened in a congressional election year, and by those who resented the attempt of the Administration first to commit the country and then argue that Congress should not break the moral commitment.(130)

With the loan in serious trouble in both the House and Senate, a new and portentous argument emerged. The loan suddenly became vital to shoring up the United Kingdom as a bulwark against the Soviet Union. Beginning in mid-April, and coinciding with the arrival in London of the new American Ambassador, Averell Harriman, the new line became a major theme. As Senator Edwin Johnson of Colorado put it, "it is whispered about that if we do not lend generously to Great Britain . . . [it] will go communistic."(131) The new strategy began to turn the tide in the Senate. "Every Senator on this floor knows that this legislation was doomed to defeat at the start," fumed Senator Burton Wheeler, "until the propaganda was spread that the passage of this bill was an utter necessity if we were going to save Britain from the clutches of Russia."(132) Johnson agreed that "A great many Senators are in favor of a loan being made because those Senators have a fear of Russia."(133) With the vote predicted to be close, Senate Majority Leader Barkley, who had opened the debate for the Administration, took the floor to present the closing arguments. His speech seemed almost to be on a different subject. Glossing over economics, Barkley hammered at the anti-communist aspects. The strategy paid off, and the bill squeaked through the Senate 46-34.(134)

Opposition in the House promised to be even tougher, and the anti-communist rhetoric that had begun to surface in the Senate reached a crescendo in the lower chamber. Majority leader John McCormack took the floor to make a strong anti-communist pitch for the loan.(135) "Doc" Eaton of the Foreign Affairs Committee did the same,(136) and John Dingell of Michigan called on members to vote for the, "premium payment on insurance against the encroachment of communism."(137) Just as Barkley had done, Sam Rayburn laid aside his gavel to present the closing argument. In his unusual and dramatic address from the floor, the Speaker declared that the loan must be made to stop the march of communism, to keep Western Europe from being, "pushed further into and toward an Ideology I despise."(138)

Again, the anti-communist rationale swung the tide in favor of the loan. Member after member confirmed that their vote was perceived as a blow against totalitarian expansion. Representative Wolcott, of the Banking and Currency Committee, attributed the favorable report of his committee to "the very important question of Communist expansion."(139) Even tight fisted and crusty John Taber had been brought around to favor the loan. Whereas in February he had opposed the loan, by April he was beginning to see it as "a bar to Russian aggression," and, on the day of the House vote, he wrote to Allen Dulles that "I have felt the loan was soundly based on just one thing, i.e., that of helping to build up a buffer state which would be friendly to us against Russian aggression . . ."(140) Representative Ralph Gwinn of New York summed up the general feeling of the House in his reasoning that, "I am going to cast my vote in favor of this agreement, not because it is a loan or a gift or something in between, but because it is a contribution like those we have been making in this war with tyranny which is still raging."(141) The British Loan was saved, but only by the use of anti-communist rhetoric. Congress, torn between its paradoxical stands for fiscal conservatism and against communism, had turned a deaf ear when approached on economic grounds. Only when the "red menace" had been raised, was the issue carried. It was the first use of a tactic which then became standard and which drove the Administration to increasingly tougher anti-communist arguments to justify its policies. Beginning from the contention that the loan would retard "creeping socialism" in England, many members expanded and confused this with communism, then creeping communism, and, thus, a Soviet threat.(142)

Legislative leaders, such as Barkley, Vandenberg, Rayburn, and McCormack, also certainly realized that the loan was in trouble and took up the anti-communist line on their own as a saving argument. But there is also evidence that the Administration helped plant the seed of anti-communist rationale. Senator Homer Capehart of Indiana noted that while the economic argument was the basic justification, Dean Acheson had said that to take the view that the loan was strictly business was incorrect.(143) At a later stage of the debate, Senator Wheeler revealed that the anti-Soviet argument was being pressed on him "not only by Senators, but by many people on the outside and by members of the Administration . . ." In specific, the Senator recalled that one "high government official" had "told him flatly that the loan had to be made or Britain would fall and Russia would take over." (144) Columnist Joseph Alsop later reported that Byrnes had made a trip to the Hill during debate "to make the House of Representatives' flesh creep with anti-Soviet horror tales."(145) The basic argument may very well have begun with the move of hard-line Averell Harriman from Moscow to London. Harriman was acutely aware of the political ramifications of the loan. He warned the Department that failure to pass the loan would force the British government to the left, and weaken British support of the United States' position vis-à-vis the Russians.(146)

Considering the events of the spring of 1946, the old attitudes of men like Harriman and Forrestal, the new attitudes of men like Byrnes, and the legislative difficulties the loan encountered, the indications that elements of the Administration engaged in "Bear-baiting" is readily believable. Although many in the Administration recognized the dangers of anti-communist rhetoric, they could not argue with success. The theme soon became the standard argument before Congress.

Throughout 1945 and into 1946, it was Congress that led the rhetorical attack on the Soviet Union, and pushed an ambivalent Administration toward an increasingly tougher international stance. Beginning quietly with the British Loan and continuing with increasing volume in 1947, the rhetorical leadership changed hands. The lesson that anti-communism was the one argument guaranteed to extract money from a parsimonious Congress became even more applicable with the election of the Republican 80th Congress. Where the Administration had previously been pushed somewhat hesitantly into confrontation with the Soviet Union, it now became a believer. There was still reluctance, nevertheless, to break openly with the former ally. The new Secretary of State, George C. Marshall, particularly advocated low key diplomacy and maintaining the fiction of postwar cooperation between East and West. The realities of the constitutional system would not allow the Administration, "to speak softly and carry a big stick," however, for Congress would not appropriate the stick unless the Administration spoke loudly of the threat. Thus, cold warriors in Congress helped launch the world into a new era of crisis diplomacy.

# 3

# The Declaration of the Cold War

There can be little doubt that the interaction between administration desires and congressional parsimony caused an overemphasis on the Communist "bogey-man" in securing the British Loan. With the Truman Doctrine the red threat became an essential element in persuading Congress to appropriate funds in support of Administration programs. The Administration certainly viewed Soviet ambitions and actions with suspicion and apprehension. Still, it exaggerated the terms in which the international situation was presented to Congress and the public and caused a reaction in Washington and the nation that intensified the cold war and made diplomatic flexibility difficult.

## Truman Doctrine

The political mood that prevailed in Washington during the winter of 1946-1947 has been discussed and need not be detailed again here except to reiterate that an opposition Republican Congress had been elected and Truman was already widely considered as a "lame-duck" President. It did not bode well for new initiatives or presidential leadership. Within this context a "crisis" occurred that marked a fundamental shift in United States foreign policy. In a diplomatic note handed to the Americans on February 21, 1947, the British declared that their military and economic support of Greece would end in six weeks. Although the immediacy of the British withdrawal surprised the State Department, the probability that Britain would withdraw had long been recognized in Washington. As early as October 1946, the withdrawal of British support from Greece, that country's importance to American national interests, and the probability of American aid to support Greek independence had been agreed to within the Administration.(1) At the same time, however, the Administration was concerned about getting such a program through Congress, and repeatedly warned the Greek government of the difficulties, particularly in the face of political repression.(2) Nevertheless, by the end of 1946 the Administration had determined to seek additional aid for Greece the following spring.(3)

Thus, the British demarche presented Washington with a problem of tactics rather than basic policy.

The short time factor argued for approaching Congress on a direct loan to Greece. Yet the slowness of regular appropriations procedures and the fact that the Administration had committed itself at the time of the British Loan to seek no new direct loans made a normal request for funds unacceptable. Further, the Democratic Congressional Conference had specifically warned the Administration against supporting British policies in the Mediterranean or supporting the Greek monarchy. The only way to secure the needed funds, Acheson advised Marshall, was to present a special bill "on an urgent basis" to Congress, emphasizing "the gravest consequences."(4)

While Congress eventually went along, the power of appropriation again proved a strong influence over the direction of United States policy. Facing a budget-minded Congress and bedeviled by its pledge not to seek new foreign aid funds, the Administration overemphasized the crisis in order to avoid internal dissent or even defeat of the program. The basic effect of the Administration's legislative strategy was to convert the issue from a pragmatic assumption of traditional British strategic responsibility to a moralistic stand against communism in a crisis atmosphere calculated to evoke a loyalty response. Given the context within which the issue was presented, Congress saw little choice but to give the President what he asked. Resentment arose, however, over the lack of consultation and the obvious stampeding of Congress. The next crisis found a wary Congress not so easily convinced.

From the initial discussions on how to present the aid request until the President's message to Congress on March 12, a basic issue was how "grave" to depict the "consequences." On all levels, there was a conscious and overriding attention to what was necessary to sell the aid to Congress, rather than how to present the problem accurately. Considering previous assurances to Congress and its general mood, the program might not even have been attempted had the issues been less crucial. As State Department speech writer Joseph Jones notes in his discussion of the crisis, "To a degree far greater than is healthy, each subordinate official in the State Department operates and makes recommendations on the basis of a personal estimate of what Congress or the American people will accept, and usually there are enough low estimates to keep policy and action flying low, if not grounded." (5) In the case of Greece, all agreed that action had to be taken, but there was despair at the thought of running the congressional gauntlet. The answer, lower level officials at State told their superiors, was to present the Greek situation in strong terms and as part of a global challenge. Jones wrote to Assistant Secretary William Benton that the world was approaching its greatest crisis since the dark days of World War II, but the Congress and the people were unaware of the gravity of the crisis. "The State Department knows," but, Jones lamented, "Congress and the people do not know." The result was "a powerlessness on the part of the Government to act because of Congressional or public unawareness of the danger or cost of inaction."

Therefore, Jones concluded, a "tremendous advance build-up," with "bold action at the top" should be launched prior to introducing legislation to Congress. Reflecting on the President's standing in Washington, Jones urged that the campaign be headed by Secretary Marshall, "who is the only one in the Government with the prestige to make a deep impression."(6) Others in the Department agreed with Jones. At the first meeting of the Department's special committee on the issue, Hubert Havlik of the Division of Economic Affairs urged that the program be presented on a global basis. John D. Hickerson of the Division of European Affairs concurred, saying he felt the program should be presented to Congress in such a fashion as to "electrify" the American people. (7)

The initial estimates of the Department on the necessity of an electrifying presentation were confirmed during preliminary contacts with congressional leaders. A meeting on February 28, between the top legislative and administration figures set the tone that was to dominate discussion of aid to Greece and Turkey. Leading off for the Administration, Marshall presented a reasoned and summarized case for the aid. The Secretary appealed for bipartisan support on the grounds that "internal division and delay might gravely imperil the success of the program we are planning." The members of Congress were unimpressed. The Secretary, Acheson notes in a rare criticism, had "flubbed his opening statement." Jumping into the fray, Acheson pitched his argument to appeal to the legislative leaders. Depicting Greece as in danger of communist takeover, Acheson compared it to the first rotten apple in a barrel with the inevitable result of spreading decay and a threat to the Middle East, Africa, and even Europe. Only the United States could avoid Armageddon. Delivering the benediction, Senator Vandenberg declared, "Mr. President, if you will say that to Congress and the country, I will support you, and I believe most of its members will do the same."(8)

Having rallied congressional support through an epochal argument, the basic line of Truman's address became foreordained. Meeting with Department officials the next morning, Acheson outlined his presentation of the previous day, the reaction it had received, and Vandenberg's "condition." The details of drafting the message need not be recounted here beyond the fact that its sharpness was disputed by many within the Department.(9) An initial draft of the message by Loy Henderson, Chief of the Division of Near Eastern and African Affairs, was rejected by Acheson on the grounds it was too weak with respect to the Vandenberg "condition."(10) George Kennan's objections to strong language were ignored,(11) as were presidential speechwriter George Elsey's.(12) Even Secretary Marshall, then in Moscow for the Council of Foreign Ministers meeting, was "startled" by the stress on anti-communism. Prior to leaving for the conference, Marshall had instructed Acheson that while he did not want his position at the Moscow Conference to mute the planned statement to such a degree that it would undermine the success of the request to Congress, neither did he want the message any stronger than necessary. Defining what was necessary in milder terms than Acheson, Marshall wired the President to question the propriety of the language in the message. Not even the General could prevail here, however, for, as he was told in Truman's reply, it was clear that use of such language was the only way the measure could pass.(13)

The strategy of adopting strong language to mobilize public and congressional opinion was supported by the Cabinet in its meeting of March 7. After Acheson's presentation of the issues, the main topic of discussion was not the program's merits, but rather the extent to which Congress could be persuaded to go along. Though considerable doubt about Congress was expressed by several Cabinet members, the consensus was to support Greece to the extent that Congress and the public could be persuaded to back the move.(14) The President would meet with congressional leaders on March 10, and depending on the outcome of that meeting, schedule his address to Congress for the 12th.(15)

The meeting on March 10 included a broader array of legislative leaders than had the meeting of February 27. According to Acheson, the reception given the President's "matter-of-fact" presentation was "cool and silent." The President evidently made a mistake somewhat akin to that made by Marshall and kept his presentation low key. Vandenberg found it necessary to reiterate and emphasize his previous conditions: the crisis had to be put before Congress in its broadest setting.(16)

The Senator's advice was taken. Dramatically appearing before a broadcast joint session of Congress, the President told the legislators and the nation:

> The gravity of the situation which confronts the world necessitates my appearance before a joint session of Congress. The foreign policy and national security are involved . . . . I believe it must be the policy of the United States to support free peoples who are resisting attempted subjugation by armed minorities or by outside pressures . . . . It is necessary only to glance at a map to realize that the survival and integrity of the Greek nation are of grave importance in a much wider situation . . . . Collapse of free institutions and loss of independence would be disastrous . . . for the world . . . . Should we fail to aid Greece and Turkey in this fateful hour, the effect will be far-reaching to the West as well as to the East . . . .(17)

With the actual enabling legislation introduced in Congress in conjunction with the President's address, the task of winning approval began. Although many in Congress were disturbed by the implications of Truman's address, the crisis atmosphere persuaded member after member to rally around the flag.(18) Prior to the speech H. Alexander Smith of New Jersey was concerned over the possibility of "building antagonisms with Russia;" early April found him sure that communism was "divisive and . . . not the protagonist of freedom;" by the day of the passage of the aid bill he was resolutely determined that "Russia must be told that she has obstructed long enough."(19) Senators from the normally conservative Midwest were convinced that the program was necessary to stem "the onward march of communism," and the Chairman of the Foreign Affairs Committee wrote the Secretary of War condemning the "ignorance, prejudice and stupidity [of those] 'Thinkers' --who shrink from confronting Russia with any equipment more formidable than a perfumed feather-duster."(20) Even the restraint that the Administration was showing by not directly naming the Soviet Union as a threat was criticized. John Vorys found it "exasperating . . . to have the President and all of our cabinet officials and Generals mince words on all of this."(21)

Ironically, a major aspect of the request which rankled many members was the very crisis atmosphere with which it was presented. The general feeling in Congress was one of entrapment by the Administration. They felt they had been told, not consulted. There were implications and factors which they did not like, yet they had to support the measure or repudiate the President in time of crisis. Vandenberg could privately complain that "the trouble is that these 'crises' never reach Congress until they have developed to a point at which congressional discretion is pathetically restricted. When things finally reach a point where a President asks us to 'declare war' there usually is nothing left except to 'declare war'."(22) Vermont's Senator Ralph Flanders could write his colleagues that "it does not seem to me proper that the Senate should follow the foreign policy of the Chief Executive with submissiveness."(23) But neither man could bring himself to say "no" to a presidential request during a crisis. In the last analysis, as Representative Francis Case of South Dakota explained to President Truman, the "argument was not 'We like to do this' but rather 'We have to do this'." Case estimated that at least seventy-five members would have voted against final passage "had it not been that we thought it would be like pulling the rug out from under you and Secretary of State Marshall."(24) The same was true in the Senate. Although he had reservations, Senator Charles Tobey wrote constituents that he would vote for the measure. To reject it "would hurt our standing in international affairs tremendously," and would require the disregard of General Marshall's good counsel.(25) The tandem of a presidential call in crisis backed by the heroic George C. Marshall was more than most members could bring themselves to oppose. The votes of 67 to 23 in the Senate and 287 to 107 in the House testify to the effectiveness of the legislative campaign.

The impact of anti-communist rhetoric used to sell the Truman Doctrine to Congress and the public should not be underestimated. What began with the British Loan and blossomed in the spring of 1947 became a vital ingredient. Francis Wilcox, then chief of the Foreign Relations Committee staff, relates that from the Truman Doctrine on, "policies were sold to a receptive Congress as essential steps that would enable the United States and its Western allies to meet the challenge of Communist expansion. Indeed, whenever the executive branch ran short of logic it used the anti-Communist argument which rarely failed to generate support on Capitol Hill."(26) The effect of the campaign for passage of the Truman Doctrine and the subsequent use of the anti-communist argument is an area that has afforded common ground for both traditionalist and revisionist historians. Testifying before a House subcommittee on the origins of the Cold War,

Arthur Schlesinger expressed his belief that the "philosophical escalation" of the cold war began when, "President Truman felt it necessary, evidently in order to carry the Congress with him, to present a defensible and limited program of aid to Greece and Turkey in sweeping and crusading language." Following Schlesinger to the stand, William Appleman Williams found himself in rare agreement with his colleague. "Professor Schlesinger is absolutely correct," Williams testified, "and I think it is hard to overestimate the importance of . . . the massive overkill in selling . . . these policies to Americans. I think they exaggerated the fear, they exaggerated the urgency, and they created a psychological situation which became terribly difficult to deal with."(27) A number of scholars have also found connections between the rhetoric of the Truman Doctrine and the development of McCarthyism in the United States in the 1950's.(28)

That the Administration believed that the Soviet Union and its communist allies posed a threat to the West cannot be denied. The Administration generally saw the issue, however, in terms of Realpolitik, not ideology. Truman was especially fond of comparing the Soviet-American confrontation to the struggles of Greece and Persia or Rome and Carthage, and saw the Russian interest in the Dardanelles as a traditional policy dating from Peter the Great.(29) Even some in Congress realized the stress on communism was misplaced. "We make too much of Communism," Senator Flanders chided his colleagues, "and not enough of this third attempt to a totalitarian power at world domination."(30) Having narrowly passed the British Loan and having been repeatedly warned by Vandenberg to assume the rhetorical high road, however, the Administration felt that there were few in Congress or the public who would accept power politics or economic arguments. The strategic considerations of the Greek-Turkey situation were played down, Jones recalls, because "The American people were not accustomed to thinking . . . in strategic-military terms."(31) Although it was another year before the President specifically named the Soviet Union as the threat to international peace, the cold war had become a permanent and frightening reality in the minds of Americans.


## The Marshall Plan

Even as the aid request for Greece and Turkey was being debated in Congress, the State Department was beginning to work toward a new and vastly larger aid program that would encompass all of Europe. This program, which became known as the Marshall Plan, was in many ways an extension of the Truman Doctrine and the British Loan. Reasoned, pragmatic arguments failed to arouse either Congress or the public. In the last analysis it was by placing the issue in the context of halting communism and by capitalizing on an international crisis that the Executive was able to carry its program.

The struggle over passage of the Marshall Plan richly illustrates many of the points of congressional influence being discussed in this study. The power of authorization proved extremely potent, not so much through denial, but by extracting concessions in return for passage. Many of the aspects of the Marshall Plan which have been cited as contributing to the Cold War were the result of the Executive anticipating congressional objections. The Administration also took great pains to consult with Congress and to counter domestic economic group objections. Despite these efforts, a number of factors inhibited the progress of the program. The Administration was in a poor position to exercise decisive leadership. The President's professional reputation remained low and Marshall's personal prestige was offset by his low-key presentations to Congress. Further, as the 1948 election approached, partisanship became increasingly important. It was not until a crisis atmosphere resulted from the communist coup in Czechoslovakia that domestic objections were overcome by appeals to national solidarity and the Marshall Plan was assured of passage.

The complex reasoning behind the formulative aid program varied somewhat from decision-maker to decision-maker. The initial impetus came from Dean Acheson on March 5, 1947, and was apparently based on international political considerations more than any other single factor. In letters to Secretary of War Patterson and Secretary of the Navy Forrestal, Acheson noted that the Greek-Turkish problem was only one aspect of a larger situation which resulted from the change in British strength and other world circumstances. At Acheson's direction, the State-War-Navy Coordinating Committee began to prepare a report covering all nations that might need long-term aid. Military aid, as well as economic assistance was to be considered. Further, the committee was to consider a number of factors, including to what extent countries were threatened by internal or external pressures, and what considerations of national security or interest should govern the decision of the United States on the extension of aid. (32) Secretary Marshall's early interest in such a program was also largely based on diplomatic considerations. He had returned from the Moscow Conference disillusioned and discouraged, feeling that the Soviets had little interest in serious negotiations and could not be induced to cooperate in achieving European recovery. (33)

Economic factors also urged American support of the European recovery effort. Although Clayton was in Geneva during most of the early planning stages, there was considerable input from his subordinates in the economic sections of the Department. As Acheson's initial public address in May reflects, the impact of a potential European economic collapse was clearly on the minds of Acheson and those around him. In the atmosphere of the time, though, even the Department's economic specialists tended to be highly conscious of the political ramifications of Europe's economic distress. Enroute on March 5 to Geneva from Washington, where he had testified on the Truman Doctrine, Clayton wrote Acheson that he was deeply disturbed by the world situation and its implications for the United States. Clayton saw a systematic campaign underway to destroy the integrity and independence of many nations in Western Europe. Only if the President and Secretary of State shocked the nation into action could the necessary

aid be given and the peril to our national security be averted.
(34) The major document emanating from the economic section of
the Department during the planning stage, and forwarded to George
Kennan's Policy Planning Staff on May 9, emphasized that the
primary objective of United States policy toward Europe should be
designed to convince the Soviets that it was to their advantage
to collaborate with the United States on Europe as a whole.  The
"carrot" was immediate material benefits that would accrue to the
Soviet Union and Eastern Europe.  Secondarily, economic policy
should be constructed to strengthen Western Europe and increase
its orientation toward American leadership so that effective
resistance could be made to the Soviet Union should it continue
on a program of expansionism.  Uncertain about the attainability
of the primary objective, the report recommended concentration on
the secondary objective.(35)

Congress was an important factor in both the timing and
specifics of General Marshall's address launching the program at
Harvard on June 5.  For all of Acheson's initiative, it was
Marshall who was primarily responsible for the speed with which
the idea of a European Recovery Program was launched.  Convinced
during his trip to Moscow that something had to be done, the
General did not want to be placed in a defensive position vis-à-
vis Congress.  On April 29, the day after his return, he summoned
Kennan to his office and directed him to set up the Policy Planning Staff with an initial assignment of dealing with the
European situation.  Giving Kennan a maximum of two weeks to
develop his recommendations, Marshall explained that "I don't
want to wait for Congress to beat me over the head."  The Secretary felt that considering Congress' attitude toward foreign aid,
it was necessary to "spring the plan with explosive force."(36)
Unless he acted quickly, Marshall was afraid that others, particularly people in Congress, would begin to make their own suggestions on what ought to be done for Europe and that premature
political debate would lessen chances of congressional and popular acceptance of his plan.  For the same reasons, Marshall stern-
ly cautioned his own advisors against any leaks about the plan
prior to his address.(37)  Thus, Marshall's selection of the
first available platform, even though Acheson objected to a
commencement speech to launch the plan on the grounds no one ever
listened to them, and the extraordinary lack of build-up or even
notification of foreign governments, was predicated to a large
extent on Marshall's strong desire to launch the program quickly
and suddenly in order to avoid being pre-empted or pre-condemned
by congressional ideas and criticisms.(38)

The content of Marshall's address also reflected congressional influence.  Marshall called on Europe to join together and
initiate a coordinated plan, which the United States would directly fund and which would hold the promise of returning Europe to
self-sustained economic solvency.  The European initiative was
important, Acheson told an interviewer, because the Administration had "oversold" its case on the Truman Doctrine and couldn't
return to Congress so soon.(39)  If Europe, in effect, asked for
funds, that would lift some of the onus from the Administration
and, hopefully, excite Congress' imagination.  The European

initiative also had to be coordinated. The reaction of Congress to the Greek-Turkish program indicated to the State Department that a piecemeal approach would be rejected by Congress.(40) The Department's reluctance to approach Congress with individual requests was so strong that it withdrew at least one priority aid request (for Korea).(41) The program would also have to be administered by the United States. Clayton was the prime advocate of this aspect. His remark that "the United States must run this show," which is so often quoted to indicate his intention to manipulate aid in order to win trade concessions beneficial to the United States, was immediately preceded by the clause ". . . we must avoid getting into another UNRRA."(42) In other words, he was attempting to avoid the mismanagement and constant congressional criticism that had marked UNRRA's existence. Having just agreed under congressional pressure to end one internationally administered aid project, the Administration was not foolish enough to suggest another. Still another requirement was that the program be designed and presented as a cure rather than another stop-gap. Kennan recalls that "It was clear that we could not . . . recommend to the Congress another interim program."(43) Another observer, Ernest Van Der Beugel, found Clayton particularly emphatic on this point. In his discussion with the Dutch diplomat, Clayton stressed the need to "sell" the plan to the United States Congress and to public opinion and the importance of demonstrating that the proposal would put Europe back on its feet again.(44)

In fact, Van Der Beugel discovered, the existence of Congress influenced much of the supposedly European-conceived plan. In the initial contacts with European diplomats on the plan, Van Der Beugel has recalled, Clayton and American Ambassador to Great Britain Lewis Douglas "laid much emphasis on the importance of Congressional reactions and opinions. Much of what was said or suggested by the United States Administration was openly motivated by the necessity of getting something done which would be acceptable to Congress." It was a revelation to Van Der Beugel and some of his colleagues, who were "for the first time fully exposed to a basic problem in the conduct of the foreign policy of the United States, caused by the very special relation between the executive and legislative branches of the Federal Government."(45) Beyond the format of the European request, Clayton and other "advisors" also played a primary role in determining the size of the request, drastically scaling down the European estimate to a level they deemed acceptable to Congress. (46) At a later date, British and French objections to conditions written into the program by Congress, were bluntly dismissed by the State Department with the advice to those governments that "if they had any idea, as participants, that they could tell the Congress what they would or would not accept as conditions, they had better give up the idea of ERP."(47) In the estimation of the American Ambassador to Moscow, Congress also became a factor in Russian diplomatic maneuvers. Reporting on Soviet tactics in the United Nations and Europe, Walter Bedell Smith indicated that one of the motivations behind Soviet desire to create unrest was to "make Congress wary of voting credits

which would be regarded as hopeless in view of fear of war and
general unrest in Europe." Smith noted that, in particular, the
public statements of House Appropriations Committee Chairman John
Taber, then in Athens, were encouraging the Soviets in this view.
(48) Perhaps most importantly, the European knowledge of the
limited funds available from Congress and its attitude toward
Russia played a role in British and French treatment of Molotov
at the Paris Conference and the subsequent Soviet withdrawal from
participation in the plan.

The question of Soviet participation in the European Recovery
Program was the most dangerous issue faced by General Marshall
and his advisors. Many in the State Department had been shocked
by the militaristic popular conceptions of the Truman Doctrine
caused by the interaction of Congress and the Administration.
Kennan urged that "steps should be taken to clarify what the
press has unfortunately come to identify as the Truman Doctrine."
Kennan and his staff believed that the "root of the difficulty"
was "the disruptive effect of war on the economic, political, and
social structure of Europe." Kennan urged the Department to
adopt a positive approach with the emphasis "directed not at
communism as such, but to the restoration of the economic health
and vigor of European society."(49) Clayton, in an independent
memorandum, sought a similar course. "It will be necessary for
the President and Secretary of State, " he wrote departmental
officers, "to make a strong spiritual appeal to the American
people to sacrifice a little themselves . . . in order to save
Europe from starvation and chaos (not from the Russians)."(50)
Marshall, whose Harvard address was extensively based on the
Kennan and Clayton memoranda, was disposed to follow this view
that a positive emphasis should be placed on humanitarian and
enlightened self-interest support for European revitalization
rather than a negative emphasis on the communist threat. Although very discouraged by his first attempt at negotiating with
the Soviets, he quickly reverted to his basic position of wishing
to deal moderately and unemotionally with the Kremlin. As he had
in regard to Truman's speech to Congress on the Greek-Turkish
crisis, Marshall continued to counsel against antagonizing the
Soviets. On at least two occasions closely following his Harvard
address, Marshall spoke out in the Cabinet for moderation vis-à-
vis the Russians. On June 27, the Secretary objected to a
proposed embargo of West Coast oil shipments to the Soviet Union
on the grounds that the action would be provocative. On July 18,
during a discussion on Soviet reparations policy in Germany,
Marshall reminded the Cabinet that international pressures on the
Soviet government caused by the war's devastation were responsible for part of the Soviet course.(51) Specifically regarding
the extension of the aid offer to Europe, Marshall decided that
the Soviet Union had to be included. Agreeing with Kennan and
Clayton, the Secretary did not want the program to be characterized as anti-Soviet. Not only did he not want to bear the
responsibility for dividing Europe, he also felt that an overtly
anti-Soviet program would make it difficult for some nations to
join.(52)

The decision to include the Soviet Union was, as Bohlen put

it, "a hell of a big gamble."(53) Marshall realized that Soviet participation might be fatal to the program. Congress was not likely to react favorably to a request for a loan to the Soviet Union or to vote sufficient funds to sponsor an effective program if the Soviets' astronomical needs were included.(54)

Warnings that Congress would not vote a loan for the Soviet Union were abundant. The Administration had just undergone a difficult fight to persuade Congress to allow even the continuation of Lend-Lease pipeline transfers to the Soviet Union in the spring of 1947. Faced with an intense congressional effort to cut off these shipments, Acheson used the ploy that congressional refusal would be injurious to the American negotiation position at an international conference. The Under Secretary cabled Marshall in Moscow asking for an "emphatic affirmative self-contained answer" to the proposition that "your position in dealing with Soviet Union may be weakened if Department does not obtain authority to complete . . . shipments." The Secretary quickly responded by sending the required message to Acheson and by informing Molotov that unless the Soviets cooperated on negotiations, the political situation in Washington would force him to declare the Soviet Union in default with a resulting termination of the Lend-Lease agreements.(55)

Marshall's use of Congress to press Molotov paid off, but his attempt to use Molotov to pressure Congress did not. Just having heard the Soviets vilified on the Truman Doctrine presentation, Congress not only continued to resist, but Senator Flanders, Representative Colmer, and others also began to introduce legislation designed to prevent all shipments, including commercial, to the Soviet Union. As the situation deteriorated, only the most strenuous efforts by Marshall and Vandenberg headed off the congressional onslaught. Under strong attack in the Senate for his support of the Administration position, Vandenberg sent word to the Department that he needed a statement, attributable to the Department, that strongly excluded any chance of a major loan to the Soviet Union. Vandenberg also hand-delivered a conciliatory letter to one of the strongest of his attackers, Senate Appropriations Committee Chairman Styles Bridges.(56) Marshall responded to Vandenberg's request by approving a "no loan" statement, and also wrote Vandenberg strongly disapproving of Flanders' resolution.(57) Considering the strategy being used to push the Greece-Turkey aid legislation, the wonder is not that Congress reacted the way that it did, but that the Department was able to persuade Congress to relent. In the last analysis it was only through Vandenberg's efforts and Marshall's tremendous prestige that Congress was swayed. After having to wage an intensive lobbying campaign to avoid a congressional cut-off of minor pipeline shipments to the Soviet Union and having pledged not to propose a loan to Russia, Department officers were rightfully chary of including the Soviets in the Marshall Plan.

Thus, the rhetoric used to sell the Truman Doctrine to Congress came back to haunt the Administration on Lend-Lease and continued to bedevil it throughout the Marshall Plan campaign. After widespread conversations with members of Congress, Dulles found that there was, "the fear in many quarters here that any economic relief which we give to Russia would be used by them to build up a military establishment which might later be used against us."(58)  Supporting Dulles' estimate, Vandenberg expressed "great skepticism" over the inclusion of Russia in the plan.(59)  John Vorys was even more blunt.  "One thing ought to be made clear," he wrote, "what we are doing in Europe two years after the war is not war relief, but anti-communist spending." (60)  In particular, any chance that the Administration might have had to reverse their rhetorical field in the early summer of 1947 was eliminated by the necessity of obtaining funding for the Truman Doctrine.  The authorizations had easily passed the House and Senate in May, but obtaining funds from the Taber-dominated House Appropriations Committee was still at issue as the British, French, and Russians met in Paris to discuss Marshall's offer. As Bernard Baruch wrote to Josephus Daniels, Taber's desire to bring in an appropriations bill markedly lower than the authorization was not only a threat to the Truman Doctrine, but also to the Marshall Plan.  If Taber was successful, Baruch wrote, "that will be the last you will hear of the Marshall Plan, for the President has already agreed to that."(61)

With the cards so obviously stacked against a Marshall Plan which included the Soviet Union, it is difficult to believe that the offer to the Soviets was made in good faith.  Yet apparently it was--after a fashion.  Kennan, probably more than anyone else, was aware that chances for Soviet participation in any coordinated plan dominated by the United States ranged from slim to non-existent.  Kennan's advice to Marshall to "play it straight," though, probably meant different things to the giver and to the receiver.  Albeit a bit ingenuously, Marshall still did want to play it straight with the Soviets.  He was sincere in his desire not to provoke already strained relations through an overtly anti-Soviet program.  Marshall's struggle throughout the legislative battle for passage of the ERP is particularly reflective of the Administration's attempt to avoid the extremes of rhetoric which had so alarmed the country in April while dealing with the mutually exclusive necessity of selling a program to Congress, which would only buy it if stampeded. Truman was also apparently sincere in his support of the offer to the Soviets.  Although he was concerned about Soviet intentions, he saw a potential confrontation between the United States and Soviet Union rivaling the classic contests between Rome and Carthage, Athens and Sparta, and Greece and Persia.  He told the Cabinet that the willingness of Russia to join with France and Britain in Paris in response to Marshall's speech was a ray of hope.(62)

Of course, the sincerity of Truman and Marshall and, certainly, of men such as Kennan and Acheson, was bolstered by the knowledge that the Soviets probably would not participate.  There is no evidence, however, that the specifics of the American conditions which worked against Soviet participation were deliberately designed for that purpose.  In fact, as shown above, two of the main factors, the requirement for a coordinated plan and thus, Soviet economic disclosures, and the requirement for American control and administration of funds, partly sprang from congressional pressures on the Administration. It would be interesting, but futile, to speculate what would have happened had the Soviets participated in the plan. Probably the Marshall Plan would have died a premature death at the hands of Congress or been rendered ineffective by an overly thin dispersement of funds. Officials were careful to withhold comment on the Soviet withdrawal from the tripartite conference, but at least one later admitted breathing "a sigh of relief" when Molotov went home.(63)

Aside from American foreign policy-makers' views on Soviet participation in the plan, important European statesmen were against it. Neither British Foreign Minister Ernest Bevin nor French Foreign Minister Georges Bidault wanted Russia involved. In conversations with Bevin and Bidault, American Ambassador to Paris Jefferson Caffery gained the impression that the two foreign ministers, particularly Bevin, felt it necessary to invite the Russians, but hoped they would refuse the invitation.(64) Bidault later explained the thinking at the time:

> If the USSR accepted Marshall's offer, everything would become more difficult. Besides, America was rich, but its wealth was not unlimited, and if the Communist countries joined in, then obviously there would be much less to go round. The American Congress would also be far less well-disposed or even interested if the Communist countries were included.(65)

If Van Der Beugel was unacquainted with the exigencies of the American legislative system, Bidault and Bevin were not; if Marshall was willing to risk congressional antipathy over Soviet participation, Bidault and Bevin were not. The British, backed up by the French, were distinctly cool to the Soviets. They summarily rejected Molotov's demands for modification of a coordinated approach and speeded Molotov's withdrawal from Paris.-(66)

The withdrawal of the Soviets from the Paris planning session far from ended the difficulties of the ERP in Congress. The contention that Marshall quickly introduced his ideas in order to preempt discussion rather than in response to the immediacy of the European situation is supported by the fact that, having introduced the idea, the Administration proceeded to wait nearly six months before seriously approaching Congress with the plan. The delay was principally occasioned by the necessity of mounting an informational and pressure campaign on Congress and the public. The chief responsibility for selling the ERP to Congress fell to Dean Acheson and, upon his resignation, to his successor as Under Secretary, Robert A. Lovett. Six months later, with the Marshall Plan before Congress, Ambassador Lewis Douglas was brought to Washington to serve as a special liaison with the Hill during consideration. Congress', or more specifically, Vandenberg's reaction to the idea of the massive aid plan for Europe was less than encouraging. The Administration had pledged during the fight for the Truman Doctrine and post-UNRRA aid bills not to seek more aid during the session. Even then, Vandenberg had had a difficult time maintaining the Administration's $350 million

figure for general aid legislation. Amid general and rising speculation about the need for a billion dollar program for Europe,
two events--Acheson's Delta Council speech and an article by
James Reston reporting that the Administration was contemplating
a five-year, $20 billion program, set the Senator off. Vanden-
berg's immediate reaction, as he expressed it to Reston, was:
"Either you are wrong or this government is out of its mind. Any
plan of that size is out of the question."(67) Vandenberg also
communicated his worries to Marshall who, meeting with the Senator and Acheson, was able to convince his agitated legislative
ally that while a program might be needed at some time in the
future, only a small amount, if anything, would be required prior
to the second session of the Eightieth Congress.(68)

Another meeting between Acheson and a larger group of senators on May 27, the day of the key meeting between Marshall and
his advisors on the ERP, lent further support to the conviction
that Congress could not be hurried into a aid program for Europe.
Lunching with a dozen senators, Acheson found himself under pressure to disclose the meaning of the rumors abounding in the Capital. Having just received Marshall's caution against any leaks,
Acheson was reluctant to discuss planning, and was told in return
that any attempt to replicate the passage of the Greek-Turkey aid
bill by presenting Congress with a _fait_ _accompli_ would be
fatal to the program.(69)

Faced with warning flags flying from the Capitol's cupola,
the Administration proceeded slowly toward introducing an aid
program in Congress. Press speculation began in late May that a
special session of Congress would be called for the fall. The
Administration, however, was uncertain. Presidential Press Secretary Charles Ross wrote to the Editor-in-Chief of the _Boston_
_Herald_, John H. Crider, that he just did not know if there would
be a special session, nobody knew. It was possible, Ross admitted, "but if I had to pin myself down, I should say that it is
not probable."(70) Efforts to win congressional support lagged
throughout the summer and into the fall. The major difficulty
sprang from the lack of leadership exercised by either the President or Secretary of State in publicly or privately touting the
plan. Truman's position was an unenviable one of "damned if you
do, damned if you don't." Although the President's prestige had
risen dramatically in March from the rally 'round syndrome connected with the Greek-Turkey crisis, and stayed over fifty percent through autumn, it was still considered politically damaging
to identify his name too closely with the proposed aid plan.
Thus, the President's public attitude toward the ERP was muted.
Even the sobriquet Marshall Plan was derived from Truman's unpopularity in Congress. Clifford had suggested to the President
that the ERP be termed, "The Truman Plan." "Are you crazy?" the
President had admonished. "If we sent it up to that Republican
Congress with my name on it, they'd tear it apart. We're going
to call it the Marshall Plan."(71)

With presidential leadership blocked, the burden fell to
Marshall to arouse public clamor and congressional support for
his project. Yet the Secretary was ill-suited for the task. He
was a colorless speaker, who, Acheson remembered, "read bad-

ly."(72)  He tended to rely on reasoned, dispassionate arguments which usually failed to sway Congress.  Bohlen has commented, "Politicians were a race that [Marshall] . . . did not really understand.  Their motivations mystified him."  For example, when he was urged by Lovett and others to cultivate Vandenberg, Marshall replied that he assumed the Senator was animated by the national interest and therefore required no cultivation by any-one.(73)  He also fared poorly in press conferences, and avoided them.  British correspondent Leonard Miall has explained that not only was the Secretary unused to the give-and-take of a press conference, but he was slightly hard of hearing.(74)  On the high-est level, then, there was a lack of leadership.  There were vigorous efforts in the lower levels of the State Department and by sectors of the "elite" public, but they could not make up for the absence of top level leadership.

It was Acheson, then Lovett, as Under Secretary that carried the burden of bringing Congress around to support a massive aid program with Europe.  The first congressional challenge fielded by Acheson after Marshall's address involved a suggestion by Vandenberg that a high level, non-partisan commission be created to deal with the European aid question.  Fearing "a tripartite monstrosity . . . appointed by the House, the Senate, and the President," Acheson hastened to prod Marshall and Truman to go along with the Senator's idea, but take the initiative for making the appointments.  It was a point well taken.  Vandenberg's sug-gestion was for committees that would examine the relationship between aid requirements and the impact of such a program on the domestic economy.  The committees that were subsequently ap-pointed, headed by Secretary of the Interior Julius Krug, Harri-man, then Secretary of Commerce, and Edwin G. Nourse, Chairman of the Council of Economic Advisors, compiled impressive documenta-tion minimizing the disruptions and enhancing the benefits of the program to the American economy.  These reports did much to dis-sipate the domestic economic argument by the program opponents in Congress which Vandenberg had so accurately anticipated.(75)

Taking up where Acheson left off, Robert Lovett continued to work closely with Vandenberg.  He also brought Marshall and the Senator together frequently and kept key members of Congress informed of the progress of the sixteen nation Committee of Euro-pean Economic Cooperation (CEEC).  To spread the faith to the congressional rank-and-file, the Administration encouraged a wide variety of committees and individual members to travel to Europe, view the devastation, and hear about the red menace.(76)  During the period between the end of the regular session in July 1947 and the special session in December, more than two hundred mem-bers made the pilgrimage across the Atlantic.  Once in Europe, American diplomatic personnel ensured that congressional eyes were filled with destruction and that congressional ears were filled with Europe's peril from the East.  After lunching with Ambassadors Caffery and Douglas, Senator H. Alexander Smith was left breathless by the revelation that, "the alternative to our giving economic aid under the Marshall Plan is chaos and an ab-sorption of Europe."(77)  Smith received similar anti-Soviet expositions from embassy personnel in Hungary, Rumania, and

Bulgaria. Even after he had returned to the United States, the Senator continued to receive reinforcing communications from American diplomatic personnel in Europe including a biography of a Bulgarian Agrarian Party member, Nikola D. Petrov, who was executed by the Bulgarian Communists in September 1947 and examples of Communist propaganda in anti-American press clippings.(78) Duplicates were also sent via Department dispatch to all members of the Smith-Mundt Committee who had toured Europe. Taber got much the same treatment in Europe, including a memorandum from the Embassy in Athens that was decidedly anti-communist in tone and included a six page report by Apostolos Alexanres, a "reformed" communist who claimed Russia was still hoping to conquer Greece in order to, "break up the contiguous bloc formed by Italy, Greece, and Turkey and overcome the bastion of western democracy."(79) Most members returned home appropriately distressed.

Despite these efforts, some members of Congress remained skeptical about the extent of the European crisis.(80) Public and congressional enthusiasm was slow to develop, and the program's future seemed uncertain. The most important cause was the continuing lack of top level leadership. Marshall had neither the temperament nor the flair to galvanize the public, and Truman continued to worry that his pronounced support would be a kiss of death for the program. As the next presidential election became ever more present in the minds of Washingtonians, the chances of an enthusiastic Republican reception of any program too closely identified with the President declined. Both the President and his advisors displayed considerable apprehension at this time about relations with Congress. Truman worried about increasing partisanship, and felt it endangered his foreign program.(81) This opinion was backed up by political allies who felt that the Republicans were attempting to catch Truman in a political snare over Europe and the special session. "The brethren of the opposition," Senator Carl Hatch (D-N.M.) wrote the President, "are laying a trap." Urging the President to call a special session, Hatch advised:

> They do want very much to be in a position of saying that if the emergency relief is not granted soon enough, the responsibility rests upon the Executive . . . . If funds are taken by the President and used for emergency relief purposes without the authority of Congress, there is going to be plenty of criticism piled upon the head of the Chief Executive for doing so. If such is not done, however, and Congress is not called into session, then again the Chief Executive is going to be damned because he did not follow either course.(82)

Forrestal was also concerned by the decline of relations. Dining with Congressman John Lodge in late June, Forrestal was told that progressive Republican members of the Foreign Affairs Committee were having increasing difficulty dealing with the charge that they were helping carry out New Deal policies in foreign affairs. Forrestal asked Lodge's cooperation in ensuring

that as little as possible occur in Congress which would
embarrass Marshall and Lovett.(83) Two weeks later, a worried
Forrestal presented the President with several paragraphs dealing
with the diminishing power of the Executive vis-à-vis Congress
from Woodrow Wilson's classic, Congressional Government.(84)

Truman came under increasing pressure from the State Department and the White House staff to call a special session. In
August, the Ambassadors to Great Britain, France, and Italy met
with Clayton in Paris and called for immediate emergency aid. On
September 9, Marshall publicly stated that emergency aid for
Europe was necessary before the end of the year. Still, Truman
delayed. Two scenarios are available to explain why Truman
waited until October 23 to inform congressional leaders that he
would ask Congress to reconvene on November 17. The first has
Truman as a master political tactician, waiting until his committees reported, members of Congress toured devastated Europe, and
public pressure for action reached the breaking point. This is
exemplified by one columnist's description:

> Truman's delay was agonizing. He didn't cry 'Fire,' till
> the flames were almost singeing the hairs of the Congress-
> men's heads and till the exasperated public was yelling at
> him almost as much as at Congress. Now it is all yelling at
> Congress.(85)

Alternately, and closer to the truth as the author sees it,
Truman was far from in command of the situation. Beset by low
prestige and a target for partisan attack, the President was
unable to exercise effective leadership. His subordinates, both
at State and in the White House were dismayed by his hesitation.
In a press conference in mid-August, Truman indirectly repudiated
Clayton and the three ambassadors by telling the press he saw no
need of calling a special session. After talking with Speaker
Martin, one reporter recorded in early September that the Administration had not made any contact with Democratic or Republican
leaders about a special session.(86) Compounding the situation,
there was confusion in the Administration as to exactly what was
going on. At the same time State Department officials were vigorously urging a special session on the grounds that Europe could
not survive the winter, Treasury officials were expressing the
view that "this problem should be handled exclusively by the
administrative solution and that no special session of Congress
should be called . . ."(87) George Elsey, who headed the White
House working group on the Marshall Plan, wrote despairingly that
his group was concerned by the "lag between the preparation of
the estimates of European needs and the preparation of a plan for
administration of our relief assistance to Europe." The memorandum also urged an increased public affairs effort and expressed
alarm "at the apparent lack of attention being given by the White
House and the State Department to men such as Speaker Joe Martin,
Sam Rayburn, John McCormack, Vandenberg, and Barkley."(88) Obviously the White House staff was not in on the State Department's
assiduous courting of Congress. The explanation, Marshall later
disclosed, was that the State Department had felt it necessary to

keep the close contacts between the Secretary and Senator from the White House because "some in the President's entourage were suspicious of Vandenberg—or perhaps jealous."(89)

Finally, Truman made a tentative move toward a special session. Meeting with congressional leaders on September 29, Truman, Marshall, and Lovett "officially" presented the European problem to Congress. Lovett presented a general picture, and was followed by Marshall who concentrated on the communist threat, particularly to France and Italy. Truman then declared that there was no alternative but to summon the appropriate committees to begin considering emergency legislation. Congress, he felt, should accept the responsibility of reconvening. Truman's proposals met with opposition. The leaders felt that the program was not supported in the public and would be vulnerable to charges that it was fueling inflation. They predicted a tremendous fight in Congress lasting many weeks. If the President wanted a special session, it was his responsibility to call it. The most they would agree to was a meeting of the Foreign Relations/ Affairs and Appropriations Committees in early November. If these committees made progress and agreed to recommend aid, then, and only then would they agree to a special session.(90) Lovett was despondent over the inability of Truman to move Congress toward consideration of the program. Forrestal found Lovett:

> extremely depressed at the outcome of the President's conference with Congressional leaders. He said that he had the feeling that the stage was set for the President to exercise strong and vigorous leadership, that he allowed the lead to slip from his grasp.(91)

The motivations behind Vandenberg's opposition to the special session are somewhat unclear. Although the Senator harbored presidential ambitions, it is unlikely that partisan politics was a factor. His consultation with Marshall, Acheson, and Lovett and his later invaluable role in moving the ERP through Congress tend to discount this. More likely, his reasoning was based on the theory that introducing the legislation prematurely would endanger it. Writing to Senator Taft, Vandenberg expressed a preference for letting the foreign situation "jell a bit."(92) Among other inauspicious signs, the Senator may well have been thinking of the opinion of the Chairman of the Select Committee on Foreign Aid Christian Herter. Representative Herter had just returned from Europe and had publicly announced that no special session was required. Vandenberg was also temporarily annoyed by what he considered an attempt to stampede Congress. In letters to congressional leaders on September 21, only a week before Truman proposed a special session, Lovett had indicated only that Marshall would discuss the European situation with Truman in the near future.(93)

The role that Vandenberg was to play in passage of the ERP through Congress was pivotal. In the crusade against Godless communism, which he had originally joined partly in deference to his Polish constituents, Vandenberg was not only a true believer, but a gospel preacher. With the conversion of the Administration to the true faith, he moved from critic to ally. His willingness to cooperate with the Administration and the counsel he gave on waging legislative battles probably saved the Administration from defeat in its foreign programs. He recognized that Congress could play its most effective role by normally using the informal methods of criticism and prodding, combined with a thinly veiled threat of legislative sanction. In response to a suggestion that his Republican majority assume national leadership in foreign affairs, Vandenberg replied:

> As a _literal_ proposition this is impossible--not only because the Constitution gives the President exclusive priorities in international negotiations, but also because there is no practical way for us to take this priority away from him. On the other hand, we Republicans very definitely hold a "veto power" on foreign policy in the Senate.(94)

As the weeks after Truman's initial dismal meeting with congressional leaders passed, however, the domestic and international pressure reached the point that not even Vandenberg's opposition could block the calling of a special session. In a memorandum to the President in early October, Clifford argued strongly that "this is a critical problem . . . of such importance as to take precedence over all other questions." He urged Truman to make "full use of his Constitutional powers," in order to " . . . put up to [Congress] squarely this responsibility for taking action." Beyond the gravity of the situation, Clifford was disturbed by the decision to place a veto power in the hands of the committees that were to hold preliminary discussions. This was particularly dangerous with regard to the House Appropriations Committee; failure of that normally antagonistic committee to approve aid would lead to "an impossible situation." Dismissing congressional objections, Clifford predicted that based on "the recent history and present composition of the Congress," it would continue to delay "no matter how tragic the consequences of postponement," but that "when the issue is forced to a decision, the Congress is likely to give a favorable response."(95) Truman took the advice of Clifford, Hatch and his other diplomatic and political advisers. On October 23, he met with the legislative leaders, significantly not including Vandenberg, and announced that he would call Congress back into session on November 17.

The emergency relief bill during the special session and the subsequent full scale fight over the ERP during the regular session which convened in January 1948 can be considered together. Two factors combined to ensure that the interim aid bill would pass with relative ease. The first was the cataclysmic terms with which the Administration presented its aid request. Congress was told that Europe could not survive the winter without immediate aid; people would starve, governments would fall, chaos would reign, communism would triumph. The second was the dual relationship established between interim aid and the ERP. The emergency aid was indispensable to the ERP; without it European countries would not survive long enough to be aided by the Marshall Plan. Or, as Marshall testified, "to put it bluntly

. . . we are buying an option on time in which to consider whether or not a long-range program is going to be acceptable to the
Congress and, of course, to the people."(96) Vandenberg stressed
that support for the interim measure could not be construed as a
commitment to support the ERP. This tactic put opponents in the
position of throwing Europe to the Communists and letting Europeans starve without giving Congress a chance to decide on the
larger question. It was an untenable position. Vandenberg had
routed the opposition and was able to predict that not more than
a dozen Senators would dare vote against the measure. Under
"Doc" Eaton the foreign policy leadership was much weaker in the
House than in the Senate, but the blitz proved too effective to
allow serious opposition in the lower chamber. After some grumbling about administration tactics and minor skirmishing over the
size of the authorization and aid to China, the interim aid
passed in mid-December by an overwhelming margin of 83 to 6 in
the Senate and by voice vote in the House.

The rush with which the interim aid bill was pushed through
Congress did not mean that significant opposition to aid to
Europe was not present, nor did it mean that the opposition to
the ERP would be so easily swept away. Optimism within the Administration and on Vandenberg's part was not high. Marshall felt
the odds of success had declined from two-to-one to fifty-fifty.
(97) Vandenberg wrote his wife that if the opposition developing
to the interim bill was any indication of the future for the ERP,
there would be a tremendous fight. The Senator mentioned politics as a primary motivation behind the opposition.(98) Under
Vandenberg's leadership, a pincer movement was launched, composed
of both a defensive and an offensive strategy. The first was
designed to ward off attacks based on partisan politics and domestic economic considerations. The second was designed to nullify
the opposition by the use of the anti-communist theme.

In the winter of 1947-48, electoral politics and the economy
were the domestic issues of the day. President Truman's political advisors were urging him to reassert foreign policy leadership which had been taken over by Marshall and Vandenberg.
Bipartisanship was unlikely to stand up against the pressures of
election year politics; a renewal of confidence in presidential
leadership was vital to Truman's reelection chances. Congress
was also in a partisan mood. House Appropriations Committee
member Frederic Coudert wrote to his chairman, John Taber, that
it was time to "get off the boat of bipartisanship and proceed to
paddle our own canoe." Coudert's concern for Europe was more
than matched by his concern for the domestic economy and his
party. "Will not a great foreign-aid program, like a tidal wave,
submerge all domestic issues and the Republican Party with it?"
Coudert asked.(99) In the Senate, Taft and his allies viewed the
question of large-scale aid for Europe largely from the perspective of its impact on the American economy. Elected on a platform of fiscal conservatism, they saw the ERP as either forcing
heavy tax increases or inducing rampant inflation.(100)

Vandenberg and the Administration recognized these issues and
acted early to head them off. The Harriman, Krug, and Nourse
Committees were appointed. The Committee for the Marshall Plan

was also formed with Administration encouragement. Its members included many leading financial, industrial, business, and former government officials, and it played a large role in generating favorable press coverage and in gathering group endorsements, fifty-two in all, for the Marshall Plan. Groups of businessmen were brought to the White House for top level briefings, and presidential committee reports were released to dispel economic reservations.(101) Anticipating the appearance of business spokesmen in opposition to the ERP, Vandenberg wrote Lovett that it was "vitally important" that a number of top-level business-men be available as witnesses. Vandenberg specifically suggested that Stimson and Patterson recruit the witnesses from the Commit-tee for the Marshall Plan. Lovett immediately replied that he agreed with the Senator and had taken his suggestion.(102) Dur-ing the hearings, both for interim aid and on the ERP, the Admin-istration sent its top economic officials including the Secre-taries of Agriculture, Interior, Treasury, and Commerce to testify for the plan and deny that it would injure the domestic economy.(103)

Closely related to the domestic economy and political ques-tions was the issue of the American administrative structure which would handle the aid program. Remembering the early New Deal, Vandenberg and other Republicans were reluctant to give the Administration control over the billions to be channeled through the ERP for fear that the money would give the Administration the power to decide the 1948 election. Initially, the State Depart-ment fought Vandenberg's suggestion for an independent admin-istrator. Vandenberg's reaction to Marshall's resistance was quick and pointed. "My final request to you," the Senator told Marshall at the conclusion of his Senate testimony, "is, most prayerfully, that you continue to study this question of adminis-tration . . . because I contemplate that it is the question, finally, which involves our greatest controversy, not only here but over in the House of Representatives."(104) The Department reluctantly gave in, and agreed to an independent administration and also pledged not to try to interfere with the administrator's judgement as they related to the domestic economy. Congress even played a pivotal role in the selection of the administrator. The Administration would have preferred to place a "loyalist" in the position. A Washington Post story, probably launched as a trial balloon, named Will Clayton as the President's choice for ERP administrator. The article brought a quick reaction from Vandenberg who immediately wrote Marshall that the story had caused, "very unhappy repercussions" on the Hill. "I want to sound this warning . . . now and hereafter . . . . It is simply a reflection of the overriding Congressional desire that the ERP Administrator shall come from the outside business world with strong industrial credentials and not via the State Department." Marshall responded the next day, indicating that the balloon had been properly deflated.(105) Truman also tried to persuade Dean Acheson to allow his name to be offered. Acheson declined on the grounds that his association with the President and Marshall was too close. He told Truman that it would be difficult enough to obtain money from Congress, and his nomination would hinder that

process. He knew Vandenberg supported Studebaker President Paul
Hoffman for the job. On Acheson's advice, Truman submitted both
his and Hoffman's names to Vandenberg. Hoffman became the ERP
Administrator.(106)

Countering domestic objections was important in avoiding
defeat or dismemberment of the ERP, but it was not sufficient to
sell the program to Congress. The interest of the Administration
in European reconstruction was many-faceted, and varied in emphasis from official to official. Clayton, undoubtedly, saw the
Marshall Plan in terms of economics. Marshall and Acheson were
aware of these considerations and believed that an economically
sound Europe was essential to an economically sound United
States. All also shared a certain degree of humanitarian concern
with Europe's distress. There can be little doubt, however, that
those principally responsible for the development of the Marshall
Plan saw it primarily in political terms. Both Marshall's and
Acheson's initial interest had been spurred by the potential
political collapse of Europe. The basic cause in the minds of
these men, though, was an economic one. Europe's economic difficulties were fostering conditions that enhanced the chances for
communist takeover of various Western European governments.
Marshall, in particular, wished to present the program in this
context. As evidenced in his Harvard address, Marshall favored a
low-key approach, utilizing a variety of arguments, but de-empha-
sizing the anti-communist aspect of the program in order to avoid
the negativism of the Truman Doctrine. Others in the Department,
however, realized that while Marshall's approach might be diplo-
matically desirable, it was not politically feasible. Acheson
rightly has observed that if the General thought "that the American people would be moved to so great an effort as he contemplated by as Platonic a purpose as combating 'hunger, poverty,
desperation, and chaos,' he was mistaken." Rather, Acheson
found, "what citizens and the representatives in Congress alike
always wanted to learn in the last analysis was how Marshall aid
operated to block the extension of Soviet power." (107) Taking
Acheson's side, Vandenberg told Marshall that if he wanted his
plan, he would have to fight it out on an anti-communist line.
Marshall later recalled that he would have preferred to keep it
more constructive, but that he could not ignore the advice of
Vandenberg, who was his principal advisor on American political
problems.(108)

While accepting Vandenberg's point, Marshall still hoped to
avoid the necessity of publicly emphasizing the anti-communist
aspects of the aid program. Through January 1948 the major
public emphasis continued to be on the economic plight of Europe,
usually relating this to the national interest only vaguely or in
terms such as the maintenance of European democratic institutions. Specific security interests were discussed only infre-
quently, with American economic interests receiving the least
attention.(109)

The subtle approach proved ineffective. Marshall and the
State Department were, in the last analysis, trapped between two
alternatives which they wished to avoid--loss of their program
and use of hysteria tactics to get the ERP program through.

Marshall's testimony clearly shows his reluctance to overstate his case. Although he starkly pictured the threat that a Europe dominated by an antagonistic power would pose to the United States, he spent much more time on humanitarian and economic motivations. He also showed great restraint in avoiding the pointed questions of committee members trying to draw him into attacking the Soviet Union.(110) The net result was something of an ambivalent case which failed to dramatize the issue. The Alsop brothers noted that the Administration had failed to arouse the public, that it had put forward its case dressed in humanitarian and economic rationale while disguising the real motivations. (111)

Whatever Marshall's desires, Vandenberg and many other members of Congress were ready, even demanding, to be frightened. Vandenberg was admittedly structuring his hearing along an anti-communist theme.(112)  Attempts to downplay the anti-communist theme by Administration witnesses in public testimony were countered by committee questions continually pushing for more explicit statements about the anti-communist impact of the program. Although the pressure to inveigh against the Soviet Union was of concern to the State Department, witnesses often felt compelled to follow the committee members' lead.(113) Kennan has recalled that Lovett, in particular, was much more concerned with congressional reaction than objective analysis. Once Congress had taken up the subject of the ERP, they went in their own direction and there was little the Department could do about it.(114)

The State Department's reluctance to emphasize publicly the communist threat to Western Europe did not extend to private statements. On that level, the red menace became the Department's principal point, even being exploited by Marshall. After an October White House meeting between businessmen and administration officials, including Marshall, Lovett, and Bohlen, one participant came away profoundly disturbed by the centrally directed threat of communism to Western Europe--and the United States. Marshall put a clear choice to the business leaders: the United States could either aid Europe or risk a Soviet police-state control of Western Europe that would affect the security of the United States and the whole world.(115)  Similar arguments were made to Congress.  With the interim aid bill being considered in Congress, Ambassador Douglas wired a message via Lovett to Congressmen Vorys, Eaton, Herter, and Martin to tell them of the grave situation in France.  "There is in France a very real struggle for power," the congressmen were told.  The situation had deteriorated rapidly in the preceding two weeks, the wire continued, "If we are not to run the serious risk of losing France, we should act promptly . . . . Hardly a day can be lost."  If the potential fall of France was not enough to stir Congress, the telegram concluded that such an event would have "far-reaching significance to Germany, Italy, the Mediterranean, North Africa, and to other areas."(116)  Such a cataclysmic assessment was substantially motivated by the situation in Congress rather than the situation in Europe.  At the same time this dire warning on the French political situation was being issued, the American ambassador in Paris, Jefferson Caffery, was reporting his own optimism and the optimism of French leaders on their ability to contain the communists. On November 3 Caffery reported that the Communist Party was on the defensive. Later in the month, Caffery was told by Leon Blum that opposition to the communists was growing daily, and that for the first time since 1945 there was a good chance of eliminating communist control of the trade unions. Just a day after the warning to the House leaders, Caffery wired the State Department that the majority of the French working class was now opposed to the French Communist Party, and events in recent weeks had been "most desirable and satisfactory."(117)

During the hearings on the ERP, Administration witnesses balanced their public restraint by punctuating the communist threat much more vividly in executive session testimony. As one leading figure recalled these sessions, witnesses felt freer to voice their concerns about the European political situation, and at times some even over-emphasized the threat to win congressional support.(118)

These confidential efforts to utilize the anti-communist argument proved insufficient. The public and many members of Congress who were not privy to the executive sessions were unstirred by great concern over the political consequences of failure to aid Europe. As the ERP legislation moved to House and Senate floor consideration in late January, there were doubts expressed in both Congress and the press as to the bill's future. The Administration engaged in a high level debate over how to create a sense of urgency in the public. The outcome was obvious. Beginning in February and reaching a crescendo in March, the emphasis in public discussion of the Marshall Plan shifted to the threat to Europe, and indirectly to the United States, of the Soviet Union and its fifth-column supporters in Western Europe. Some continued to resist such an emphasis.(119) Kennan did not see a Soviet threat, as such, to Europe. He told one journalist, who had reproached him for failing to expose adequately the strategic realities underlying the Marshall Plan, that he had never understood that part of his job was "to represent the U.S. government vis-à-vis Congress," and that he had no sympathy with the allegation that Congress had not been given the facts.(120) Marshall also attempted to keep the rhetoric in hand, but with declining luck.

A number of pressures converged to ensure that the oratorical castigation of the Soviet Union as a sinister plotter against European freedom would reach an all-time high. The most relevant to this study was the desire of Marshall's subordinates to give Congress what it wanted in order to get the ERP through. They had been doing it privately and were now willing to do it publicly. Kennan, in an oblique way, has charged Lovett with this practice. Discussing the mood in Washington in early 1948, Kennan found that the Under Secretary was prone to "catering to senatorial opinion in instances where one might have better attempted to educate one's protagonists to a more enlightened and effective view."(121) Beyond concern with the ERP, Truman was also being counseled by his political advisors that a very strong speech would be the best vehicle for the reassertion of his foreign policy leadership. Lastly, and perhaps most importantly, the Soviets stepped in, as if on cue, to demonstrate the threat in Europe. On February 25, 1948, the Czechoslovakian government was overthrown by a communist coup. On March 10, it was reported that the Czech's patriot hero, Jan Mazaryk, had been killed under mysterious circumstances. The United States was gripped by a war scare. Marshall was genuinely alarmed. On March 5, General Lucius Clay, American Governor General in Germany, wired the warning that war with the Soviet Union, "may come with dramatic suddenness."(122) Marshall publicly evaluated events as, "very, very serious," and depicted Czechoslovakia as existing under a "reign of terror."(123)

The war scare neatly brought together the State Department's desire to push the ERP through Congress and the White House's desire to have Truman make a strong foreign policy speech. The Department, in conjunction with the White House, began to draft a presidential address. Marshall urged Truman to be moderate, advising the President that the world was a keg of dynamite, and inflammatory language on the part of Truman might set it off. The Secretary found the State Department drafts too tough and appealed for a more moderate message. As a last alternative he submitted his own draft. The combination of the need to push the legislation, the political motives of Clifford, and the President's determination to appear decisive overruled Marshall's objections. On March 15, Truman read Marshall's draft and the State Department's draft to Clark Clifford, Press Secretary Charlie Ross, and other White House staffers. The unanimous opinion was that the Marshall draft was too weak. If the President was to ask Congress for legislation, the address would have to be blunt.(124) On March 16, five days past the first anniversary of the Truman Doctrine speech, the White House announced that the President would again address Congress and the nation on a matter of vital national interest. The atmosphere is captured by the New York Times headline, "TENSE CAPITAL AWAITS TRUMAN SPEECH," and the Washington Times Herald banner, "TRUMAN WILL ASK VAST WAR PREPARATION." Confirming fears, the President told Congress and his national radio audience that the Soviet Union presented an "increasing threat to nations which are striving to maintain a form of government which grants freedom to its citizens." Stressing that "at no time in our history has unity among our people been so vital," Truman alarmingly called for the speedy passage of the Marshall Plan, universal military training, and a reinstitution of the draft. The speech had its intended effect. The House, which had not expected to vote on the ERP until June, passed legislation through two weeks later.(125)

Once again, the Administration had been forced to "electrify" Congress in order to carry its legislative program. Under the influence of Marshall, the State Department had kept the communist bogey as much in the background as possible--and had endangered the program. Under persistent pressure from Vandenberg and, finally, facing serious trouble in the House, the communist issue became ever more important. This is not to say that Marshall and others in the foreign policy apparatus did not see a communist threat, but their concerns became magnified out of proportion in the process of selling the Marshall Plan to Congress and the public. The Administration had its program, but at the cost of intensifying the Cold War.

## China

The path of United States' relations with China during the first Truman Administration was heavily influenced by congressional attitudes. Hemmed in by the nature of their appeal for foreign aid and by legislative insistence on tying the questions of aid for Europe and aid for China together, the Administration had little choice but to go against its own better judgment and submit to congressional demands for a China aid program.

The background of the China tangle has been well told in a number of studies, and need not be repeated here. What is important, picking the skein up in mid-1946, is that the Administration had concluded that the Chinese Nationalists under Generalissimo Chiang Kai-Shek could not defeat the Communists and dominate all of China by force of arms. General Marshall, then a special presidential envoy was in China attempting to bring the Kuomintang and Communist Parties together in a coalition government. Marshall's most potent diplomatic weapon in dealing with Chiang was a potential American aid termination. His use of this lever, however, was considerably hampered by Congress' open sympathy with Chiang. Although Marshall was able to prevent a China aid proposal from being brought to the floor of the House, the pressures in Congress for aid to China were well known to Chiang and helped persuade the Generalissimo to seek a military solution on the assumption that American aid would be forthcoming if China were faced with a communist defeat.(126)

With the collapse of the Marshall Mission in late 1946 and intensified fighting between the Nationalists and Communists, congressional criticism of Administration policy and calls for aid to China increased. On January 11, 1947, Vandenberg demanded that the Administration shift its emphasis away from supporting Communist Chinese representation in a coalition government and toward helping Chiang re-establish Nationalist control of all China. Other Republicans in Congress also took up this call. A number of reasons account for the upsurge of Republican criticism of the Administration's China policy in early 1947 and the increasing volume of the attack throughout that year and 1948. The first of these was General Marshall's tremendous prestige. The presence of Marshall in China during 1946 served to keep criticism at a low level. With his withdrawal, though, this inhibition ceased to be a factor, and other forces pushing for congressional activity came to the fore. A background factor was the total failure of the Administration to bring Congress into consultation on its China policy. A second factor which became increasingly important was domestic politics. Republicans increasingly saw the deteriorating China situation as a potential political issue and avenue of attack of Truman's foreign policy. Vandenberg clearly saw China as a partisan issue and Governor Thomas Dewey, leading contender for the 1948 Republican presidential nomination, took up the demand for a "two ocean" foreign policy in the fall of 1947. Perhaps the most important factor motivating Congress was anti-communism. As evidenced by the House's attempt to include Spain in the ERP, Congress was more interested in what a foreign government wasn't than what it was. This feeling was intensified by the Administration's rhetoric in support of the Truman Doctrine and, later, the Marshall Plan. In addition to focusing congressional attention on anti-communism, the rhetoric also made it extremely difficult for the Administration to justify cutting off millions to Chiang while asking for billions to stave off communism in Europe.(127)

Unwilling to risk its European program, the Administration steadily gave way before demands for support of Chiang. On May 26, 1947, a ten-month-old embargo on the shipments of arms and munitions to China was lifted. In July, at the behest of Representative Walter Judd, powerful member of the House Foreign Affairs Committee and a former missionary in China, General Albert Wedemeyer, former commander of American forces in China, was sent on a fact finding mission (his subsequent report recommended aid to China). During the summer, withdrawing American Marines "abandoned" sixty-five hundred tons of ammunition to the Nationalists. And in September, John Carter Vincent, who had originally advocated a coalition government, was relieved as Chief of the Office of Far Eastern Affairs in order, Acheson has written, "both to appease Republican critics and to remove him from the direct path of Republican vengeance."(128)

The introduction of the interim aid bill and then the ERP in Congress gave Congress an even' greater chance to force China aid on the Administration. It is unnecessary to go into the complicated legislative details of the congressional drive to tie aid for Europe and China together. The crux of the matter is that Congress was publicly and privately insisting that aid be extended. Marshall had promised Vandenberg in October 1947 to submit a separate aid package for China. By January, though, the Administration was trying to avoid honoring its commitment, but Congress would not let the issue drop. Senate Appropriations Chairman Styles Bridges sent Marshall a public letter demanding the immediate submission of a China aid bill. In the House, China aid was legislatively tied to European aid in an omnibus authorization package. Members of Congress were in close contact with China's representatives, including Madame Chiang, and were even advising them on the best way to run their lobby.(129) The Administration had little choice but to concede. Lewis Douglas advised General Marshall that although neither of them liked it, unless China aid was granted, the ERP would be lost; if the aid were granted, he could almost guarantee success for the ERP. The issue was settled.(130)

In the last analysis, the China aid program of 1948 was a political disaster. With the military situation deteriorating rapidly, it was already too late for it to save the Chiang regime. It only served to prolong the war, thereby not only earning increased emnity from the communists, but also alienating the opinion of a large segment of China that supported neither the communists nor the Kuomintang.(131) More significantly, the aid was the first step in a pattern of American policy toward

China that led to the non-recognition of the world's most populous nation. The aid also signified the first extension of the principles of the Truman Doctrine outside the European sphere, not because the Administration wanted it so, but because they were afraid to repudiate the logic of anti-communism at a time when their European program rested on it. It would take a quarter century for diplomats to extricate the United States China policy from the pitfall of domestic necessity.

As will be seen in succeeding chapters, the psychological cold war that was, to a degree, created and intensified by the legislative strategy of the Administration became the basic context of diplomacy for the next quarter century. To a substantial extent, the course of American foreign policy in the immediate postwar period was not based on diplomatic desirability, but on domestic political necessity. To be sure, conflict with the Soviet Union would have occurred. American diplomatic and economic objectives in many cases ran squarely counter to those of the Soviet Union. Ideologically, the capitalist American and communist Soviet systems were inevitably conflictive, or so it seemed to the statesmen of the time. Perhaps by some systemic law of international political behavior, the power vacuum in Europe and the rush of the two new superpowers to fill it preordained a struggle, no one can be certain. What is certain is that history has witnessed no contest, short of open warfare, equal to that between the United States and the Soviet Union. On the American side, it became not only governmental policy, but also a basic public belief that the policies and, indeed, the very existence of the Soviet Union was inimical to the United States. Congress, parochial and parsimonious in its outlook, can be directly linked to this viewpoint. If Truman had possessed dictatorial powers or if Congress had been dominated by enlightened internationalists, the cold war, at least in its intensity, might never have occurred.

These things were not so, however. The President was not a dictator. To the contrary, a part of Truman's difficulty in selling his international program to Congress can be traced to his real or perceived weaknesses as President. Any Vice President succeeding Franklin Delano Roosevelt would have suffered from a comparative image problem. Truman, though, was particularly vulnerable. Vice President for only three months, product of Missouri machine politics, and a self-acknowledged novice in foreign affairs, Truman was handicapped in his dealing with Congress. Few including Truman himself, were confident of his ability to "measure up." Through ill-conceived attempts to appear decisive mixed with naiveté, Truman further detracted from his image during his first year in office. The result was that Congress was less willing to accept presidential leadership than it would have been if Roosevelt had continued in office.

Many other factors also intervened to spur congressional interest and activity in foreign affairs. Most of these stemmed from Congress' parochial and conservative orientation. Congress viewed issues predominantly through a localized, domestic prism. Where foreign programs were perceived as affecting the domestic economy (and almost all appropriations were seen as such), where ethnic constituents were aroused, where electoral politics became involved, where the prerogatives of the Legislative Branch came into question, Congress became decidedly less willing to follow the Executive lead.

Thus, Congress played an important part in the formulation and conduct of American foreign policy from 1945 through 1948. Most importantly, it was a prime factor in establishing the general context of United States policy. On the specific level, Congress also strongly influenced policy in a number of instances. The Soviet loan was never made, partially as a result of congressional resistance. Many of the specifics of the Marshall Plan which have been cited as contributing to the emergence of the cold war were also necessitated by the presence of Congress in the governmental process. At times, Congress acted alone in forcing policy decisions. More often, Congress was able to tip the scales when there was division within the government over policy direction. Isolating the exact impact of Congress in these policy debates is difficult if not impossible, but it was undeniably there. The Administration got most of its program, but it had to pay the price.

# Part II

# 4

# Consensus, Dissent and Foreign Policy

The initial phase of this study lends support to a series of observations about the pattern of executive-legislative influence in foreign policy. These can be organized within Lasswell and Kaplan's conceptualization of influence. The value that the Administration placed on bipartisan unity was an important factor in enhancing legislative influence. Other general factors which added to Congress' impact was the weakness, on a number of fronts, of the Executive, and Congress' attempt to reassert its institutional prerogatives after the submissive World War II years.

The increased activism of Congress did not signal any attempt to supplant presidential power. Even Vandenberg continued basically to look for executive leadership, and in times of crisis Congress rallied strongly to the "chief." Beyond playing off Congress' own values of national unity and loyalty, the Executive was able to utilize a number of other means which interacted with legislative values such as party loyalty, parochialism, and personal and institutional ego to persuade Congress not to contest the Executive's lead.

Yet at times, administration tactics were not successful and Congress asserted itself. Beyond the more general explanations of executive strength and institutional ego, such factors as domestic economics, domestic ethnic groups, and domestic politics, were particularly evident as causes of legislative activity. The key word is domestic. When an issue remained purely foreign in its perceptual focus, the president normally prevailed. The more domestic considerations intervened, the more Congress became involved. When it did, Congress' sporadic use of formal means combined with its informal power of dissent, proved to be powerful tools in delaying, modifying, or even occasionally defeating executive initiatives. Valuing his program and professional reputation, the president often chose to go along in order to get along.

The second part of this study continues to focus on the means, values, and scope of influence in the foreign policy process. The basic attitudes of presidents and legislators from 1949 through 1972 are examined first. The value of bipartisanship held by both institutions continued as a strong factor shaping both presidential concern with Congress and also congressional deference to presidents. Variations in executive strength also continued to be an important factor, building to strong dominance in the 1960s and then collapsing in the mid-1970s. Congress' post World War II institutional ego anxiety was assuaged by late in the Vandenberg era, and thus that factor tapered off, thereby enhancing executive influence in the Eisenhower era and after.

A variety of issues continued to command congressional attention, though, even in this more acquiescent period. Again, the domestic connection was a key consideration. And again, like any sleeping giant, when Congress stirred, the Executive could not ignore its influence. The latter chapters of this second part examine policy in a number of areas such as Europe, Asia, economics, and personnel in order to specifically identify the scope of congressional influence and the means and values of both institutions.

## Truman's Second Term

The attention to Congress evident during Truman's first term remained a factor during his second administration. Even though Truman's 1948 reelection also brought a return to a Democratic Congress, his concern with consensus continued. Truman's appointment of Dean Acheson as Secretary of State in 1949 brought a statesman to that office whose wary regard of Congress had been honed as Assistant Secretary of State for Congressional Relations and, later, through the uncertain legislative odyssey of the British Loan, Truman Doctrine, and other important initiatives. Symbolic of the continuing bipartisan emphasis, Truman invited the ranking Republicans, as well as the Democratic chairmen of the respective foreign policy committees of Congress, to Acheson's swearing in ceremony on January 21, 1949.

Ronald Stupak and David McClellen, in separate studies of Acheson's "operational code" found that one of his fundamental beliefs as Secretary was that "policy in a democratic society must rest upon popular knowledge and understanding." Acheson did not believe that public opinion should govern policy formation. Rather he believed that opinion should be educated and brought to support policy. A primary method of building support and displaying unity was to obtain advance congressional approval of policy. (1)

One of the best single expositions of Acheson's thinking can be found in a July 1950 letter to Senator Homer Ferguson. Artfully interweaving quotations from Republican foreign policy leaders John Foster Dulles, Thomas Dewey, and Arthur Vandenberg with his own ideas, Acheson defined the purpose of bipartisan foreign policy as reaching "agreement . . . [that] will have the support of the American public and thus lift foreign policy issues from the arena of partisan consideration." Acheson saw bipartisanship as a two-way street. It required the Administration to consult with Republicans, particularly those on the Foreign Relations and Affairs Committees. The payoff for Acheson was that bipartisanship also required the consulted "members of the opposition to

cooperate loyally to get support in the Congress and in the country for policies that have been worked out together."(2)

Acheson's concern was more pragmatic than philosophic. He
elevated bipartisanship to a level of patriotic necessity in
order to give himself and Truman the support they considered an
essential element of successful foreign policy. As Acheson
observed from the safety of retirement:

> Bipartisanship in foreign policy is the ideal for the Execu-
> tive because you cannot run this damned country any other
> way except by fixing the whole organization so it doesn't
> work the way it's supposed to work. Now the way to do that
> is to say politics stops at the seaboard--and anyone who
> denies that postulate is a son-of-a-bitch or a crook and not
> a true patriot. Now, if people will swallow that then
> you're off to the races.(3)

Unfortunately, from Acheson's point of view, not every
blankety-blank bought his argument, and the bipartisan baton was
often dropped during the race.

The question of Asia and the (Senator Robert A.) Taft wing of
the Republican party were particular sources of discord. In
early 1950 long existing rumblings broke into the open with Taft
minimizing bipartisanship as having "never covered a very large
area" and in any case being a policy that "hasn't existed at all
for a whole year."(4) The Administration's reaction to such
criticism took two tracks. At times Acheson encouraged Democrats
such as Senate Majority Leader Scott Lucas to counter-attack and
offered State Department resources to provide ammunition.(5) In
addition to the natural propensity to self-defense and smiting
one's opponents, three factors argued for verbal retaliation.
First, as Under Secretary of State James Webb wrote to President
Truman, defending the Democratic position was necessary because
"dangerous confusion has been created in the public mind by persistent Republican attacks."(6) Second, spirited counter thrusts
also helped assuage Democrats in Congress. Acheson found Connecticut's Democratic Senator William Benton, for one, "quite
critical" of the Secretary for spending "too much time and effort
conciliating . . . opponents and not enough time working with
. . . friends."(7) Third, it was not beyond the President's
White House political advisors to attempt to use breaches of the
bipartisan spirit to belabor the Republicans. In late 1951, for
example, a team under Kenneth Hechler put together a very partisan pamphlet on foreign policy. It was, according to Hechler,
designed to "concentrate on constructive achievements" and "to
pull together one section on Republican and isolationist opposition with a clear indication of what might have happened had we
followed the advice of certain leading Republicans . . ."(8) The
resulting effort was, in fact, so slanted that Hechler's attempt
to have it released by Foreign Relations Committee Chairman Connally was rejected, and Hechler had to settle for Connecticut's
Democratic Senator Brian McMahon as its supposed sponsor.(9)

The aggressive track, however, was not the norm under Acheson. More commonly, the Secretary's advice was to be concilia-

tory. In December 1950, Senator Lucas told the Secretary that it
"was apparent that the Republicans did not want unity at all" and
that "the time had come to take the gloves off." Acheson demurred, however, telling the Senator "it would be disastrous if
we followed such a course."(10)

As he had been during Truman's first term, Arthur Vandenberg
was the focal point of Acheson's bipartisan efforts. China, however, proved to be the issue on which the bipartisan ship found-
ered, despite Acheson's and Vandenberg's attempts to deep it
afloat. In late June 1949 Vandenberg made a speech on the floor
which offered cooperation in return for consultation on China.
Acheson quickly sought to take up the offer and received the concurrence of both the President and Senator Connally, who agreed
it was a good idea "to get the Republicans in."(11)

Despite these good intentions cooperation scarcely lasted six
months. Truman's January 5, 1950, State of the Union address
which essentially declared noninterference in the fate of Taiwan
was followed by what Acheson subsequently termed "The Attack of
the Primatives . . ."(12) Arguing that the Republicans had not
been consulted and demanding American protection of Chiang Kai-
shek, Senator William Knowland condemned the Administration for
the "bankrupt policy which now stands revealed in all its sorry
detail." Even Vandenberg joined in the criticism.(13)

Vandenberg's comments may have been motivated more by his
desire to maintain credibility within his own party than by real
distress over the supposed lack of consultation. A mere two
weeks after attacking Acheson publicly, Vandenberg privately told
him that

> There was more nonsense talked about bipartisan foreign pol-
> icy than any single subject, and that the attacks which had
> been made on me to the effect that bipartisan foreign had
> ended in my [Acheson's] administration were grossly unfair.
> [Vandenberg] said I had discussed all important matters with
> him and sought him out . . . .(14)

Whether the "consultation gap" was real or politically perceived, the virulent attacks caused grave concern within the
State Department.(15) Acheson moved to shore up his right flank.
From Vandenberg he sought a nomination for a Republican roving
ambassador to the Far East and Japan and also suggestions on how
to reestablish relations with the Senate Republicans.(16) Vandenberg suggested that the appointment of John Foster Dulles to a
foreign policy post was "acutely advisable . . . if we seriously
hope to restore some semblance of unpartisan unity at the water's
edge."(17) Within weeks Dulles was appointed to head the Japanese Peace Treaty negotiations, both to ensure the smooth passage
of that pact and to begin work on a bipartisan approach to foreign policy.(18)

Vandenberg's health was failing, however, and Acheson also
had to deal with Alexander Wiley, the next ranking Republican on
the Foreign Relations Committee. With Vandenberg convalescing
from surgery and not to return to the Senate, Acheson met with
Wiley to explore establishing a new consultive process. Although

Wiley did not reject Acheson's advance, neither did he have Vandenberg's deep commitment to bipartisanship. Further, Wiley's ego was more secure than Vandenberg's. Acheson reported that Wiley said that "while he was very flattered by my calling on him, he did not expect any consultation individually . . ."(19)

In fact, despite continued approaches to the Republicans and sporadic reciprocal cooperation, true bipartisan spirit was not to be restored during the balance of Truman's term. With Vandenberg the spiritual leader gone, with China policy remaining a decisive issue, with McCarthyism beginning to brew, and with the 1952 contest for the White House growing always closer, the two parties perceived it to be increasingly in their interest to stake out their respective positions. Bipartisanship had to wait for a new president and a new Congress.

## Eisenhower—-Constitutional Conservative

If Truman and Acheson were pragmatically bipartisan, President Dwight Eisenhower was philosophically bipartisan. One factor behind Eisenhower's desire to include Congress in the foreign policy-making process was his view of the Constitution. Meeting with the Foreign Relations Committee during the 1956-57 Middle East crisis, John Foster Dulles captured the President's orientation. Dulles pointed out that Eisenhower

> takes a more conservative view of the power of the Executive than some other Presidents have taken. Possibly because he comes to the office as a general, he feels the responsibility . . . to share responsibility with the Congress more than perhaps a civilian president would . . . . [He] leans over backwards in his unwillingness to use the Armed Forces of the United States in ways which Congress has not indicated it wants.(20)

The President told his Cabinet, "I believe it was proper to set up the intermittent strains between the branches of government . . . I will have no part in upsetting that balance . . ." (21) On another occasion Eisenhower even refused to rein in one of his subordinates who was offering critical testimony before Congress. Army Chief-of-Staff Matthew Ridgeway had openly opposed the President's desire to reduce military manpower. Yet even though Eisenhower complained that he was getting "tired of having to defend myself against charges of being out to wreck the army," he also believed that "anyone testifying, if asked, must state his personal opinions."(22) As will be further discussed below, Eisenhower's constitutional scruples also caused him to reject a subordinate's advice to take a stronger stand against Senator Joseph McCarthy's attacks on the grounds that Congress' power of investigation should not be denied.(23)

As Dulles noted, Eisenhower's views on the proper balance of power within the government were particularly pronounced when there was a question of military action. During his eight years in office, Eisenhower faced a number of crises in Asia, the

Middle East, and in Europe which involved the potential or actual use of American armed force. In each of these instances he not only sought congressional support, in his subsequent actions he seemed to take account of the advise and consent process.

The first crisis occurred in early 1954. Through the first three months of that year the United States watched the situation in Indochina with increasing concern as the communist Viet Minh troops fought French forces to a standstill and seized the initiative. In February several French regiments occupied the valley outpost of Dien Bien Phu in an attempt to threaten the Viet Minh's supply lines, thereby drawing the insurgents into a major battle. In was an ill-advised move. By mid-March more than thirty thousand communist troops had surrounded and were steadily closing in on the heavily outnumbered French garrison.

The Indochina situation intensely concerned Washington, and the threatened fall of Dien Bien Phu created a crisis condition in that capital as well as in Paris. The impact that surrender would have on the French government of Premier Joseph Laniel was the most immediate concern. Washington feared that the fall of the beleagured outpost would cause the collapse of Laniel's coalition government with disastrous ramifications. Newsweek publisher Harry Kern had passed along to Dulles an extract of remarks made by French Defense Minister Rene Pleven in which the minister predicted that, in Kern's words, "If [Laniel] falls for any reason, the next . . . government will be elected by Communist votes . . . It will accept any settlement offered by [the communists]. It will be the last French government oriented toward America for some time."(24) It was an evaluation with which Washington agreed.(25) A French collapse, many also feared, might not just be confined to Vietnam. Chairman of the Joint Chiefs-of-Staff Admiral Arthur Radford predicted to the President that a French defeat could "lead to the loss of all of S.E. Asia to Communist domination."(26) The Administration also saw a link between the future of the French position at Dien Bein Phu and European defense plans. The United States was supporting the formation of a European Defense Community and believed that Laniel's government offered the best prospects for French membership.

Pressure to intervene steadily increased on Eisenhower. Dulles, Radford, and Vice President Nixon all favored action.(27) Radford suggested to the President that "the U.S. . . . be prepared to act promptly and in force."(28) Indeed both Dulles and Radford slyly suggested to the French that the United States would in fact act. On April 3 Dulles told French ambassador Henri Bonnet that resistance to communism in Vietnam required a strong coalition "prepared to fight if necessary" and that the United States "would play its full part."(29) Even more pointedly, the American Embassy in Paris reported that Radford had given personal assurances to French Chief-of-Staff Paul Ely that he would do his best to get naval support if needed.(30) It was an assurance that, in private, the President rejected.(31)

The mood in the White House itself was reflected in Press Secretary James Hagerty's March 29 diary entry that the "Indo-China problem is getting graver" and occasioning daily top level

meetings(32) and the President's March 24 public characterization
of the crisis as "transcendent" among American concerns.(33)

Despite these pressures, Eisenhower was reluctant to act. A
primary consideration was Congress. In mid-March, Eisenhower
stated emphatically that the United States would not enter the
war without the consent of the "constitutional process that is
placed in Congress."(34) In private conversations that same morning, Dulles had argued that in emergency situations the president
could act unilaterally. But Eisenhower had insisted, "We are
following Constitutional rule. Retaliation or instant stopping
of [an] attack is one thing; actual mobilization of [the] country
in war, that is [for] Congress."(35)

The President's instance on congressional concurrence with
any military move proved to be the immovable stumbling block.
Rumors of a possible American intervention had been circulating
for some time and had brought an early resistance from a number
of congressmen. Senate Appropriations Committee Chairman Leverett Saltonstall spoke to the President at least twice about avoiding an Indochina entanglement and warned Eisenhower that appropriations for the area might be endangered by precipitous action.
(36) Mississippi's Senator John Stennis also wrote to the Secretary of Defense objecting to the possibility of using U.S. troops
in Indochina,(37) and when Eisenhower floated the idea at a meeting with congressional leaders in mid-February, it was not enthusiastically received.(38)

The crucial point came on April 3 when eight congressional
leaders met with Dulles, Radford, and Deputy Secretary of Defense
Roger Kyes. Dulles opened the meeting by telling the legislative
delegation that Indochina was the key to Southeast Asia, and
"that if the communists gained Indochina and nothing was done
about it, it was only a question of time until all of Southeast
Asia fell along with Indonesia, thus imperiling our western
island of defense."(39) Radford also urged intervention, and
Knowland raised the specter of "appeasement" of the communists.
(40) The majority of the congressional delegation objected,
however, to U.S. action without the cooperation of allies. When
Dulles and Radford pointed out that no commitment of ground
forces was contemplated, the delegation held fast, sagely arguing
that once the flag was committed, the use of land forces would
inevitably follow.(41) The stance of the congressional leaders
essentially ended the intervention option. Dulles had to call
Eisenhower and inform him that unilateral action was not possible
(42) and to cable the French that "Congressional action would be
required" before he could act.(43) Although Dulles tried to put
an allied action together, his best efforts failed.(44) Britain
refused to cooperate and, given congressional sentiments, Eisenhower told Dulles that a unilateral American move was "impossible" and would be "in the absence of some kind of arrangement
getting support of Congress . . . completely unconstitutional and
indefensible."(45)

Eisenhower's response to later crises closely parallelled his
action during the spring of 1954. In each case he sought a
supportive resolution. During the 1955 confrontation with mainland China over the Nationalist held islands of Quemoy and Matsu,

Eisenhower went to Congress in order "to make clear the unified and serious intent of the United States."(46) The resolution request was also partly motivated by domestic legal considerations. Eisenhower told Speaker of the House Sam Rayburn and House Minority Leader Joseph Martin, "We want to be very careful to move within the constitutional processes."(47) Although many, including members of Congress, argued that the president's powers as Commander in-Chief were sufficient to permit a presidential action, Eisenhower resisted that interpretation. Instead he insisted to Dulles that "unless we get the backing of Congress, [we] can't make . . . assurances,"(48) and that he had the "right to defend Formosa only so long as Congress agrees to it."(49)

As in Indochina, Congress' role in the Quemoy-Matsu crisis seems to have been one of restraint. Even more than in early 1954, Eisenhower seemed determined not to go to war, and congressional Democratic "doves" provided a counterbalance to the "hawks" within his own administration and within his own party in Congress. There was general agreement that the United States should defend Formosa and the close-by Pescadores from attack. There was no such agreement on the desirability of defending Quemoy and Matsu. Small and within artillery range of the mainland, the two islands were considered by many to be neither defensible nor vital to the preservation of Nationalist China. Secretary Dulles, Admiral Radford, and Republican Senate Minority Leader William Knowland, however, all favored both defense of the islands and action against the mainland.

By contrast, Senate Majority Leader Lyndon Johnson and Armed Services Committee Chairman Richard Russell both opposed defending the offshore islands. Senator Hubert Humphrey and Senator Herbert Lehman offered language to specifically exclude Quemoy and Matsu from the congressional resolution authorizing the President to defend the general Formosa area.

The resolution Eisenhower sought passed easily, but the lopsided vote did not accurately reflect the wooing of Congress that had been necessary. The Administration wanted not only to get the measure through, they wanted to get it through without embarrassing opposition. A key to avoiding serious opposition was Senate Foreign Relations Committee Chairman Walter George. Dulles approached George, in part, through former Secretary of State James Byrnes. Dulles' Democratic predecessor was able to assure the Secretary that "George has undertaken to talk with those fellows who are playing politics, and after his talking with them, there will be no trouble." George, Byrnes confidently added, "will be a Vandenberg to the Secretary."(50) The support of George, Johnson, and Russell for the resolution assured overwhelming passage, but did not still criticism. Resolution opponent Senator Wayne Morse complained, "It made me most unhappy to find out that so many members of the Senate were willing to admit in cloakroom discussion that they would have liked to have joined in opposing the Resolution . . ., but they simply had to go along with the Democratic leadership."(51) Thus, an eruption of opposition awaited a wrong move and urged caution on the Administration. Dulles also appealed to Asian specialist Senator Mike Mansfield. "It is a critical situation," he told Mansfield, and "any show of division by anyone as well known as you in that area would not be good." When Mansfield demurred that he had not made up his mind, Dulles promised restraint, and assured the Senator that the President would "lay down the law that he [rather than the Joint Chiefs of Staff] will make the decision" about action in the Formosa area. Mansfield replied, "That helps," and said he would discreetly see to it that word got to the right quarters.(52) Even some of Dulles' normal congressional allies began to urge caution. New Jersey's Republican H. Alexander Smith wrote the Secretary, "These islands are of no real important military value to the Nationalists." "This line of reasoning," Smith continued, "seems to reduce the matter to a question of 'face' and the danger of demoralization of Chiang Kai-shek's . . . forces should Quemoy and Matsu be lost to the Reds . . ."(53) Smith suggested the matter be transferred to the United Nations.

Although no single point can be identified as decisive in the debate within the United States, the uproar in Congress helped tip the balance in favor of those who opposed a firm commitment to defend the offshore islands. According to one report, a warning from Senator George that there was growing Senate opposition to the defense of Quemoy and Matsu helped persuade the President to send Assistant Secretary of State Walter Robertson and Chief of Naval Operations Admiral Robert Carney to Chiang to persuade him to reduce his commitment to the islands.(54) The choice of that twosome was an interesting one given the fact that both were noted hawks on the issue and, in Eisenhower's own estimation, it was clear that "Radford and Robertson . . . could not grasp the concept" of a tactical diplomatic withdrawal.(55) Inasmuch as the mission failed in its overt goal, a fact that surprised the President not at all, it would seem that the message on restraint was aimed not so much at the hawks in Taipei as at the birds of that feather in Washington.(56) The ultimate result was that restraint carried the day in all the capitals involved and war was avoided. In the view of one expert observer:

> Eisenhower . . . maintained a superb sense of proportion and managed . . . to retain control of the United States government, including those powerful factors within it who did not share, . . . the President's peaceful purposes.(57)

Thus, the starring role was certainly Eisenhower's, but credit is also due the able supporting cast of Mansfield, Morse, Humphrey, et al. Congress, as in 1954, was a force on the side of restraint.

President Eisenhower returned to Congress for support once again during the 1956-1957 Middle East crisis. Faced with the possibility of using force to defeat supposed communist backed aggression, the President successfully sought congressional ratification of the "Eisenhower Doctrine." In meeting with congressional leaders, the President stressed the desirability of issuing a policy declaration subscribed to by both the Executive and Congress. Arguing that consultation or even a request for a declaration of war would be undertaken if time permitted, he worried about what would happen if a crisis occurred and Congress was not in session. In that case the first twenty-four hours of combat might be decisive. Therefore, prior legislative authorization was vital. In response to the contention of House Majority Leader John McCormack that the president already had the power to act, Eisenhower insisted that both the Constitution and the immediate situation argued for prior congressional authorization.(58) The 1959 Berlin crisis brought still another repetition of the familiar pattern. In a joint meeting of legislative and administration leaders, Secretary of State Christian Herter pointed to charges by Wayne Morse that the President might take unauthorized action. To the contrary, Eisenhower flatly asserted, he would "not take action to go to war without first contacting Congress."(59) Thus, consultation was a continuing theme of the Eisenhower years, and was a significant factor in keeping Congress cooperative, if not always in total agreement.(60)

## Eisenhower, Dulles and Pragmatic Consensus

President Eisenhower's desire to work with, rather than around, Congress stemmed from more than his strict constitutionalist views. He also desired consensus as a requirement of an effective foreign policy. Working with the records of Eisenhower's administration, the researcher finds repeated evidence of his concern with presenting a united domestic front to the world. Assuring that support, however, was not an easy task. Eisenhower faced potential opposition from both the Democrats, who controlled Congress for six of his eight-year tenure, and from the conservative wing of his own Republican party. Maintaining the support of both groups required a difficult balancing act which Eisenhower negotiated with considerable skill.

Even though Eisenhower soundly defeated his Democratic rival, Adlai E. Stevenson and returned the Republicans to power for only the second time in two decades, the new president's legislative margins were thin in both houses of Congress. During his first week in office the President met with Republican legislative leaders, canvassed them about bringing Democrats into foreign policy and national defense discussions, and emphasized his desire to work toward bipartisan cooperation.(61) As Eisenhower explained later in the year to Speaker Martin, "because of the thinness of our party margins, we will more than once in the days ahead be dependent upon some Democratic voting strength."(62) Even less optimistically, he predicted to House Majority Leader Charles Halleck that he would "obviously require Democratic support in almost every tough vote." That being so, the President advised, "we must by all means quickly show our readiness to cooperate in every decent way."(63)

When the Republicans lost control of Congress to the Democrats in the 1954, Eisenhower's bipartisan spirit realistically intensified even more. Soon after the election the President opened a bipartisan meeting with legislative leaders by letting them know that in the field of foreign policy and national security he was "without reservation, anxious to establish new and even better patterns of bipartisanship, [and] . . . to consult in advance on policy matters."(64) The President also wrote a circular letter to his top department and agency heads in the foreign/ defense policy area. He told them that "under the changed circumstances brought about by the last election" the Administration's normal policy of bipartisan cooperation "will require renewed and even greater effort on our part" with "consultation prior to the crystallization of policies and programs," in order to obtain "cooperation in the effort to get approved plans enacted into law."(65) When the Republicans failed to regain control of Congress in 1956 despite Eisenhower's personal landslide victory, the President had to face up to the probability that he would have an opposition Congress for the rest of his tenure. The day after the election, and in reference to the Suez crisis, Eisenhower told British Prime Minister Anthony Eden, ". . . although I had a landslide victory last night, we are not like you, and we lost both Houses of Congress. Therefore I have to have the Senate and House leaders in . . . I have to get them to back up whatever we agree to."(66)

Secretary of State Dulles did not share the President's constitutional scruples, but he did share the pragmatic evaluation of bipartisan foreign policy. Several factors seem to have had a particular impact on Dulles. The first was the defeat of President Woodrow Wilson and The Treaty of Versailles by the Senate in 1920. Dulles served on the American delegation in Paris. His uncle, Robert Lansing, was Secretary of State, thus making the Senate's rejection a personal as well as a political blow. "From the collapse of Wilson's tower of hopes" one biographer concluded, "Dulles . . . drew the conclusion that policy makers must respect and accommodate to domestic political realities, however unpalatable they may be . . ."(67)

More immediate to his own tenure as Secretary, Dulles took warning from the acrimonious partisan attacks that had marked his predecessor's term. In the words of one subordinate, Dulles "had a lively sense of the difficulties which Mr. Acheson had had with the press and Congress."(68) A third specific cause of Dulles' concern with Congress was his own experience during his short Senate term and subsequent loss to Herbert Lehman. According to Richard Nixon, Dulles' defeat taught the Secretary that being right was only half the battle. You also "had to win politically in order to have your policies go through."(69)

Less personally, Dulles was also convinced that presenting a united domestic front to ally and antagonist alike was the most effective strategy. It was a theme that he repeatedly preached to Republicans as well as Democrats. In office less than two months, he wrote James Richards, ranking Democrat on the Foreign Affairs Committee, "I have long believed that only through true bipartisan cooperation can we accomplish our objectives, and I am determined to seek the greatest measure of bipartisan participation in the formulation of foreign policy that is possible."(70) Shortly before his resignation and death and at the time of the 1959 Berlin crisis, Dulles met with members of the Foreign Relations Committee who were slated to have lunch with Soviet Deputy Premier Anastas Mikoyan. Senator Wiley asked for recommendations as to the senators' proper stance in their meeting with the

Soviet leader. In his reply Dulles stressed that the most important impression which Mikoyan had expressed was doubt as to the
workability of American foreign policy with a partisan division
between the Executive and congressional branches of government.-
(71) Dulles urged the senators to show the Soviets that the American government was unified. Summarizing Dulles' attitude toward
Congress, Nixon remembered that

> . . . he knew he could only do what he could get the public,
> the Congress, the Senate, his own party, and enough of the
> opposition party to support . . . . He knew the worst thing
> he could do . . . would be to get the President and himself
> to advocate a policy that the Congress . . . would reject or
> that public opinion would not support.(72)

The records of the Administration indicate that both the President and Secretary worked diligently to keep Congress assuaged.
For a president who supposedly lacked sharp political instincts,
Eisenhower understood the sensitivity of congressmen and stressed
meeting regularly with the leadership of both parties and as
frequently as possible with rank-and-file members. As he told
House Majority Leader John McCormack during the 1959 Berlin
crisis, he did not "think all Democrats had tails and horns just
because they were so mistaken as to be Democrats."(73) He also
pressed Dulles to keep in contact with Congress(74) and urged
Republican House leaders to keep junior members better informed
on policy matters.(75)

Dulles also attempted to keep open channels with Congress,
although his records and the recollection of his staff indicate
that preference and the limitations of time focused his attention
on the leadership, Foreign Relations Committee members, Foreign
Affairs Committee members, and other members in that general
descending order of priority.(76) At least as remembered by
Republican legislators of the day, Dulles' efforts were effective. Speaker Martin recalled that Dulles "went out of his way"
to help members.(77) Bourke Hickenlooper found that Dulles had
"less conflict" and "enjoyed about as near . . . universal respect" of the Foreign Relations Committee as any Secretary he
knew.(78) The key factor, according to Senator George Aiken, was
that more than usual Dulles tried to take the committee into his
confidence,(79) and, recalled Senator Dirksen,"he always had an
appropriate respect for the Senate and its members and he didn't
take an axe and whittle them down to size."(80)

Eisenhower and Dulles also took account of congressional
sensitivities in a variety of other ways. Preparing for a 1955
speech in South Carolina, Dulles and his staff worked over several redrafts, exorcising any comments that might be construed as
partisanly Republican and worrying over the order and magnitude
of verbal accolades to be given House Foreign Relations Committee
Chairman James Richards, who was to be on the platform with
Dulles, and Senate Foreign Relations Chairman Walter George who
would not be present but who, by tradition, was senior to Richards.(81) In the same spirit, the President and his key foreign
policy advisors avoided, at least on the surface, partisan

sniping at the Democrats on foreign policy.

During the 1958 campaign, for example, Eisenhower called Dulles to suggest the possibility of making at least one partisan presidential speech on behalf of Republican congressional candidates. Dulles demurred that he did not want the President "to get foreign policy in politics." After some discussion, Eisenhower agreed that "maybe [I] should not do it," and said he would review the speech to ensure "it would be the least partisan."(82) Other prominent figures also routinely rejected invitations to make partisan speeches. United Nations Ambassador Henry Cabot Lodge, Jr., explained to the Newton, Massachusetts Woman's Republican Club, "If a person in my position were to make partisan speeches during the campaign, it would be inescapably construed as an act of partisan politics, and this in turn would have a bad effect on the President's efforts to have America present a united front before the world."(83)

The Administration also took great care to bring Democrats on board to give a bipartisan flavor to the foreign policy agencies. There were at least two attempts to bring defeated Democratic presidential candidate Adlai Stevenson into the Administration. In 1953, with the concurrence of Lyndon Johnson, Walter George, and Sam Rayburn as well as G.O.P. leaders, Dulles offered Stevenson a spot in the United Nations delegation.(84) In 1955, Dulles again tried to appoint Stevenson, this time as a consultant on the Middle East. The idea, the Secretary explained to Vice President Nixon, was patterned on his own service in Asian affairs during the Truman Administration. In Dulles' estimation, the Middle East situation "was filled with danger," and, he said, "we could lose the whole Arab world if we play this on a partisan basis. It could be as dangerous as the loss of China was."(85) With Stevenson on the road to another Democratic presidential nomination and somewhat critical of the Democratic congressional cooperation with the President,(86) the appointment never occurred. Both Representative Richards and Senator George, however, who simultaneously retired in 1956, were appointed as special presidential representatives in the foreign policy field. George, physically ailing and facing a possible primary challenge in his native Georgia, had been seeking an appointment as a graceful way of retiring and had tacitly been trading cooperation toward that end.(87) An administrative spot for George was also being sought by Majority Leader Johnson who suggested, Dulles told Eisenhower, that "we try to keep George in some working relationship with us as far as possible, as he would still have considerable influence with the Democrats."(88) Richards was also offered a position more than a year before he retired and responded by assuring Dulles that "partisan politics will have no part in my outlook."(89) Although it died in the talking stage, the strength of the bipartisan appointment urge can best be seen in Eisenhower's toying with the Lincolnesque idea of running on a national unity ticket in 1956 with a Democratic Vice Presidential running mate. He was particularly intrigued with the idea of a Southern Democrat, such as Florida's Senator George Smathers, although he also considered such northern possibilities as Ohio's Senator Frank Lauche.(90)

## Bipartisanship and the G.O.P.--A Tightrope

For all that Eisenhower needed and courted Democratic support
and despite the nearly obligatory universal acclaim of the concept of bipartisanship, putting the policy into practice required
considerable delicacy. Out of power for two decades, the Republicans were hungry for political power and the appointments that
went with it. Eisenhower and Dulles had to sail a narrow course,
being bipartisan enough to please the Democrats and at the same
time being partisan enough to please their fellow Republicans.

At first, G.O.P. congressional leaders encouraged bipartisanship, with Republican Senate Minority Leader William Knowland
even chastising the State Department for not appointing enough
Democrats.(91) Knowland's position, however, was both a minority
view and short-lived. More commonly, the newly empowered G.O.P.
congressional majority wanted patronage and attention. As Dulles
commiserated with his predecessor James F. Byrnes at one point,
every time he "managed to get the Democrats behind him, that
annoyed the Republicans . . ."(92) When, in one case, Democrat
David Bruce was appointed a special representative to the European Defense Community, Senator Bourke B. Hickenlooper called
Dulles to object, saying, "We have suffered too much, and they
have cut our throats . . . . The Democrats' purpose is to destroy
the Republican party."(93) Dulles defended his bipartisan appointments to Hickenlooper and in the Cabinet on the basis of the
need to keep Democratic support to offset a core of persistent
Republican opposition.(94) He also protested to Republican
National Party Chairman Leonard Hall that he had "appointed 125
leading Republicans" to the Department and felt as senior Cabinet
officer he was "entitled to some protection."(95) Dulles wanted
to know if Hall wanted "policy or patronage," a clear distinction
in the Secretary's mind, but one in the same in the estimation of
many Republican stalwarts. As Senator Karl Mundt explained it to
Undersecretary of State for Administration Donald Lourie:

> It is not so much that we are concerned especially about the
> ugly rumors of disloyalty and sexual perversion which have
> influenced the State Department for so long a time, as it is
> the basic fact that human nature being what it is, there is
> little likelihood of our having any great change in foreign
> policy so long as the people who were architects of our
> foreign policy in the past continue to be the architects of
> the policy of the present and the future.(96)

In fact, Dulles and Eisenhower tried to assuage the Republican right through a number of appointments. Senate Majority
Leader Robert Taft's law partner, John B. Hollister, was named to
head the foreign aid program, and Taft's son, William Howard Taft
III, was dispatched as Ambassador to Ireland. In a different
field, a cousin, Ezra Taft Benson, became Secretary of Agriculture. Others, such as Scott McLeod, who was suggested by Senator
Styles Bridges and who headed the State Department's Bureau of
(Internal) Security, also represented the conservative wing of
the party.(97) Even McLeod, however, who Dulles called "a

shining example of Republicanism"(98) and who Mundt thought was "a sure shot,"(99) had limits to his partisanship. With regard to one appointee, McLeod wrote to Mundt that the subordinate had been disciplined because "Unfortunately, there is no indication this fellow has done anything except be a Republican . . . I am sure you know I want to promote and foster Republicans in the Department, but I feel it is only reasonable to expect that they will do something more than just be Republicans."(100)

Republicans also exhibited a good deal of testiness over real or imagined slights vis-à-vis administration attention to the Democrats. Despite the fact that Eisenhower met with the Republican leadership every Tuesday, Knowland was sensitive to White House meetings with the Democrats unless he received equal time. (101) He would press Dulles for special Republican briefings on international problems, regardless of the Secretary's concern that such meetings would raise a "storm of Democratic protests." (102) House leaders also showed partisan jealousy. When Democrat John Rooney publicized a Department document that evidently had not been passed to the Republicans first, powerful Appropriations Chairman John Taber sarcastically wrote Dulles, "It would be interesting to the Republicans to know just what the Department thinks and what its attitude is. If they are relying on the Democrats we might just as well know it and know on which side of the fence they stand."(103)

Eisenhower and Dulles also received their share of sniping from the Democratic side of the aisle, despite their attempts to placate that group. Relations with the opposition leadership such as Johnson, George, Rayburn, and McCormack were at least reasonable. It was the middle ranking members who were more likely to take the Administration to task. Senator J. William Fulbright, for one, felt Dulles was in a "complete funk" and "unable to articulate any ideas or policies appropriate to present circumstances."(104) Another middle range Democratic senator, Hubert Humphrey, presents a particularly interesting study of relations with the Administration. Privately he could be extremely critical. As early as 1950, when Truman appointed Dulles as a special representative, Humphrey found him "far overrated . . . If Dulles is the best the Republican Party has to offer in foreign policy then indeed it has little to offer."(105) Later, with the Republicans in office he wrote, "Our foreign policy is even becoming foreign to those of us who are supposed to know something about it. It is no longer a policy, it is a crossword puzzle and I was never good at that particular game."(106)

One of Dulles' principal aides, William Macomber, remembered that Humphrey was a "favorite--somewhat surprisingly--of Dulles." According to Macomber, "The only trouble was that every now and then Senator Humphrey would call on Dulles to resign." Dulles did not like that the first few times because "behind the scenes there was a pretty close relationship," but he also "knew the way politics worked" and so, said little. The third or fourth time, however, Dulles "was pretty teed off." The next time Macomber saw Humphrey, he told the Senator, "Boy, the boss is really irritated at you." Humphrey professed surprise. "You're kidding. He can't really be" the Assistant Secretary remembers Humphrey protesting. "For God's sake, he knows I don't mean it. It's politics."(107)

The reaction of the Administration to potential and active criticism from the several camps ranged from conciliation though counter-attack to despair. Eisenhower's basic instinct was to try to play the diplomat, as he had in Europe during World War II, and to try to avoid antagonizing any of the various factions. Even during partisan campaigns, the President was reluctant to attack on foreign affairs issues. During the 1954 campaign, for example, Eisenhower called his Vice President into the Oval Office to talk with him about Nixon's "castigation" of the Democrats on foreign policy. Eisenhower pointed out that he and Dulles were trying to get bipartisan support, but that the Democrats were "smarting" over recent Nixon attacks. In response to the Vice President's defense that he had criticized Dean Acheson, not congressional Democrats, the President pointed out that while many Democrats had not supported Acheson's policies, they still felt that Nixon's remarks reflected on them. The Vice President agreed to delete future anti-Democratic references from his speeches.(108)

Eisenhower's bipartisan bent should not be taken to mean that he was incapable of asserting himself for partisan advantage or protecting what he deemed proper presidential prerogative. Particularly in the 1953-1954 period, Eisenhower repeatedly stressed to Republican congressional leaders that party solidarity and establishing a good record were keys to retaining control in 1954. Press Secretary James Hagerty recorded in his diary that he and the President agreed to tell G.O.P. leaders that "if they didn't get off their cans" and stop "wasting time" on McCarthy, the Bricker Amendment, and other things, "they weren't coming back." Eisenhower told his press secretary to draft up the remarks, and as Hagerty left the office called after him, "Jim, make it tough," to which Hagerty appended, "Hurray!!!!"(109)

Bipartisanship also presented itself as a useful tack to avoid electoral criticism of foreign policy and to club any Democrat who failed to adhere to the maxim of halting politics at the water's edge. The Republicans, in fact, wanted to emphasize their self-perceived foreign policy successes, but had to be careful not to violate the niceties of bipartisan restraint. Almost a year before the 1956 elections, Secretary Dulles and Ambassador Lodge agreed that foreign policy was "a big Republican asset" and that there was no doubt that foreign policy would be debated on a partisan basis. Dulles wanted to be sure, however, "that since the country likes bipartisanship . . . [we] can tag the Democrats as the first to break it."(110) Bipartisanship also had its advantages relating to the presidential contest. Referring to an Eisenhower speech, Lodge wrote the President:

> The sentence: "The big fight is not between Republicans and Democrats, etc." is not only smart politics and good for national unity; it is also a good attitude toward the Democratically controlled Congress. The Democratic presidential aspirants won't like it because it tends to put them out of business. But they can't say anything.(111)

After the 1956 elections, Eisenhower became somewhat less concerned with close congressional cooperation. As a norm, he still sought consensus, but he was somewhat more willing to respond in kind to attacks and to assert his authority. Part of his combativeness was caused by the increasing antagonism of congressional Democrats. The retirement of Walter George and the succession of Theodore Francis Green to the chairmanship of the Senate Foreign Relations Committee was of particular importance. Whereas George was seen as both strong and cooperative, Green was perceived as weak and at least potentially hostile.(112) Eisenhower was stung when Green publicly accused the Administration of only giving lip service to bipartisanship and asked Dulles to work up a comparative study of his own and other administrations' contacts with Congress. Dulles agreed to the idea, but warned that "Congress itself is not well organized--they are jealous among themselves . . . . Cooperating with Senator Green is impossible."(113)

More than Green, William Fulbright, who was to succeed the aging Rhode Island Senator to the chair of the Foreign Relations Committee in 1958, was the leader of an increasingly antagonistic opposition. Just as Republican bipartisan cooperation had broken down over Asia in the late 1940s, the veneer of accord with the Democrats became unstuck in the mid-1950s over United States policy toward the Middle East, in general, and toward Israel, in particular.

The assumption generally found in the Administration was that the Democrats were playing politics with the Middle East and that the bipartisan breach was more attributable to such senators as Fulbright, Humphrey, and Morse than to such leaders as Johnson, Russell, and George, before his retirement.(114) The Republican estimate of the Democratic line-up was essentially correct. In the interest of not appearing co-opted, Johnson and George made some disparaging sounds, but did so quietly and privately. George wrote the very partisan Chester Bowles that he was "greatly disturbed" by foreign policy,(115) and Johnson wrote that United States foreign policy shortcomings were "particularly apparent in the situation in the Middle East where we have been unprepared for every major development."(116) Such comments, however, were exceedingly mild when compared to the scathing evaluations others aired to Bowles. Fulbright wrote that "It is truly tragic that we have such an inadequate President and Secretary of State during these difficult times."(117) Humphrey described himself as "heartsick" over the way things were going and characterized the President as "plain lazy" and "unaware of what is going on." Dulles, according to the Senator, was "worn out" and had lost "any usefulness that he might have had."(118)

Even though such criticism stung the Administration and, in the estimation of some officials, warranted counterattack, relations with the Democrats usually precluded a sharp response. In calls by Dulles to Nixon and Brownell, both of whom served as political point men for the Administration, it was agreed that the charges by Fulbright and others could not go unanswered. The response, however, would have to be moderate and indirect to avoid rallying the Democrats behind the dissidents. Too aggres-

sive an attack, it was feared, might injure relations with the
likes of Senators Johnson and Russell who, according to Nixon,
were not "gunning" for Dulles and had "gone out of their way to
speak in a friendly way."(119)

Eisenhower's emphasis on getting along with Congress certainly did not stem from admiration. Quite the reverse, the President's attitude toward Congress often ranged between contempt and
despair. Early in his second term, and after a particularly divisive time over Middle East policy, Eisenhower wrote to a confidant:

> Concerning my present situation, I think it best described
> by merely saying "the grind goes on." I am repeatedly aston-
> ished, even astounded, by the apparent ignorance of members
> of Congress on the general subject of foreign affairs and
> relationships. I realize that by this time I should accept,
> as a matter of course, Congressional reaction that seemingly
> reflects either this abysmal ignorance or a far greater
> concern for local political sentiment than for the welfare
> of the United States . . . . In the general case each of
> them thinks of himself as intensely patriotic; but it does
> not take the average member long to conclude that his first
> duty to his country is to get himself reelected. This sub-
> conscious conviction leads to a capacity for rationalization
> that is almost unbelievable.(120)

The frustration and even anger of the President and his advisors over Congress was heightened when it came to dealing with
resisting right wing Republicans. Surprisingly, Robert Taft,
Sr., who was called "Mr. Republican," who had been Eisenhower's
rival for the 1952 Republican nomination, and who epitomized
conservative Republicanism, fared well in Eisenhower's estimation. For his part, Taft was careful to assure the President and
the Secretary of State that he supported them, even when he gave
isolationist speeches which seemed at odds with Administration
policy.(121) Taft's stroking was effective. After the Senator's
death, Eisenhower recalled, "Before Taft died I talked to him
frequently and I found to my amazement that in most things he was
more liberal than I was." The President wistfully remembered
that in their last talk Taft had told him "anything I can do to
help you, that is my job and that is what I want to do."(122)

By contrast, Taft's successor, William Knowland, who was not
a personal rival of Eisenhower's and who presidential advisor
Bryce Harlow remembered having generally been supportive,(123)
was regarded by the President and Dulles as an antagonist. James
Hagerty's diary records that "Dulles [was] particularly bitter
against Knowland and [other GOP] Senators for failing to back
[the] Administration on foreign policy." The diary quotes Dulles
as railing,

> We have the greatest President since Washington--a military
> genius and a statesman who is trying to guide our country
> through a very difficult situation with war on both sides of
> the road we are taking . . . that is a tough job. Why those

people on the Hill cannot understand that and cannot back us
up is more than I can understand. They are interested only
in themselves and their own seat and apparently care nothing
or less than nothing for our country.(124)

Similarly, and just a short time later, Eisenhower told Attorney General Brownell, "Knowland is the biggest disappointment I
have found since I have been in politics."(125) And when Knowl-
and was not reelected in 1958, Hagerty's disappointment over the
continued decline of Republican congressional representation was
offset by the thought that many of the "old mossbacks" had gone
down to defeat and that, "To be frank about it--in the Senate,
Knowland's defeat gives the Republican party a chance to change
its leadership."(126)

While conciliation was Eisenhower's basic thrust, he was
often urged to react by more combative subordinates. Hagerty,
for example, wrote to the President that foreign policy was
"exclusively" the responsibility of the Chief Executive, but that
"some politicians--particularly in Congress, and more particularly in the Senate" were trying to "muscle their way" into the area
and "give the public the impression they are great statesmen and
diplomats." Hagerty's recommendation: "They should be slapped
down hard."(127) Henry Cabot Lodge was also prone to recommend-
ing greater assertiveness. At one point he urged Eisenhower to
conspire to purge Republican congressmen "who are hopeless moss
backs, beyond persuasion or redemption."(128) Even Eisenhower
occasionally turned combative, especially against uncooperative
Republicans. He directed at one juncture that when any Republican asked for a favor that the member's voting record should be
attached to the request when it reached the President's desk.
(129)

Eisenhower could also assert his presidential prerogatives,
and became more likely to so so during his second term. Earlier
in his tenure, he was prone to be a bit apologetic about his
unilateral powers and to explain them in terms of unfortunate and
burdensome necessities. In a 1954 meeting with Senator Knowland,
the President typically explained:

Now there is one thing as long as you are here that I have
been thinking about, one thing that you apparently don't
know that you should know and that is this. In the conduct
of foreign affairs, we do so many things that we can't
explain . . . . I know so many things that I am almost
afraid to speak to my wife . . . . I have never tried to
make a rubber stamp out of any Congress or anyone, and I do
realize that there must be a close understanding between us,
but I do try to spare other people some of the things I do.
(130)

As time went on Eisenhower became more positive and protective of presidential power and prerogatives. One Republican
member of Congress remembered that when he asked Eisenhower
whether to seek assignment to the Ways and Means Committee or
Foreign Affairs Committee, the President told him to opt for the

former because on taxes the Ways and Means Committee was king, but on foreign affairs he, Eisenhower, was supreme.(131) In another instance midway through his second term, Eisenhower demonstrated a punctilious concern for his prerogatives when he squelched a meeting between British Prime Minister Harold Macmillan and the Senate Foreign Relations Committee. Eisenhower let it be known that he strongly objected. If Macmillan met with Fulbright and the Committee before meeting with the President, it would be a breach of etiquette. If the British Prime Minister and the senators met after the presidential meeting, it might seem as if the Prime Minister was reporting to the Committee or being quizzed about his discussions with the President. Neither alternative was acceptable to the White House. Abashed, the British Ambassador withdrew the suggestion.(132)

Eisenhower also changed his views about Congress' power of investigation. Early in his terms the President was reluctant to intervene, even in the excesses of the McCarthy investigations. He believed, as noted, that "it was proper to set up the intermittent strains between branches of government" and refused to have "any part in upsetting that balance."(133) By 1959, however, the President had changed that attitude sufficiently to act vigorously to constrain a move to investigate the operations of the National Security Council. Eisenhower told Senate leaders that the proposed probe sponsored by Henry Jackson would "inescapably thrust Congressional investigative activities deeply into the Nation's highest national security and foreign policy deliberative process which traditionally as well as Constitutionally have remained within the province of the Chief Executive."(134) With the cooperation of Senators Johnson and Russell, a compromise was reached on a set of guidelines which termed the procedure a study rather than an investigation. Jackson also agreed not to attempt by legislation or otherwise to infringe on the constitutional powers of the president, to receive all National Security Council officials in executive session, and to limit his inquiry to procedural rather than substantive matters. It was a clear victory for the assertive president.(135)


## Eisenhower and Dulles--Reaction to the Right

Eisenhower, like Truman and Roosevelt before him, was an internationalist who often feared that congressional isolationists would try to reverse the new era of American globalism. The records of the period show a concern throughout Eisenhower's presidency for the potential of a dangerous return to the foreign policy attitudes of the 1920s and 1930s. Decision-makers were aware that, even though it was a minority view, isolationist sentiment still strongly existed within elements of the public and Congress. Typical of the type of public opinion letter often found in the constituent correspondence during that era, one South Dakotan wrote that "Secretary Dulles is totally incompetent for his job . . . [and] his thinking is dominated by the ultra-internationalism viewpoint that is eager to spill the blood of American boys anywhere on the globe."(136) Another domestic related theme of the isolationists can be seen in the warning of a midwestern senator that "There are enough bloody traps laid down . . . in Japan, in South East Asia, in India, in Africa, in Europe, so that if the Fair Dealers won again, they could quickly complete the World Welfare State . . . "(137) The result of such a reactionary policy, Eisenhower once told Senator Eugene Milikin would be analogous to Dien Bien Phu with "The Reds surrounding it and crowding the French into a position where they have to surrender or die." "If we ever come back to the fortress idea of America," Eisenhower worried, "we would have . . . one simple, dreadful alternative--we would have to explore an attack with everything we have. What a terrible decision that would be to make."(138)

Paradoxically, Eisenhower was also periodically pressed by the somewhat schizophrenic right to attack when he favored moderation. During the Korean War negotiations the President was concerned that "some reactionaries" wanted full scale war, but resolved that he would make Congress opt for all out war and take the responsibility before he would do it himself.(139) As noted, Eisenhower also had to fend off right wing congressional pressure which demanded military action in Indochina, the Quemoy-Matsu area, and other spots in the Asian theater.

Underlying the substantive foreign policy issue was the question of who was going to control the Republican party. Eisenhower had defeated Taft for the presidential nomination in 1952 and beneath the usual veneer of public harmony, there was considerable suspicion on the part of the Taft forces that the latter-day Republican Eisenhower and his apostate, internationalist followers were going to try to take over the party. One of Taft's principle aides wrote to the Senator that "by skillful maneuvering, a minority of our party now controls the Party's presidential machinery." If Eisenhower won, the aide worried, there would be an attempt by his group which had "little claim to basic Party principles" to use the "patronage, privilege, and other favors" available to the president to ensure the control of the "internationalist-New Deal wing of our Party."(140) Other Republicans were suspicious also. Indiana's Republican Senator William Jenner wrote to former President Herbert Hoover that the Fair Dealers were using Eisenhower's forces as "monkey paws" in an "attempt to break up the Mid-western Republican party, which is the best hard core of Republicanism . . ." Jenner suspected the divisive thrust would come in some "beautifully staged drama of foreign policy . . . peace in our time, or perhaps mock anti-Communism . . .following the path so carefully laid down by John Foster Dulles at the suggestion, I believe, of Mr. Acheson."(141)

To mollify the right wing of their own party Eisenhower and Dulles took a variety of administrative and policy actions. A number of appointments were made at the behest of such senators as Taft and Bridges. The Administration also took several symbolic positions to assuage the Republicans. In the opinion of one Dulles biographer, at least part of Dulles' hard-line anticommunist public stance was a response to the Taft wing of the party.(142) Exemplifying his willingness to go along with tough public talk, Dulles supported repeated Republican resolutions in

Congress to "liberate Eastern Europe." As evidenced by the (non)-
reaction to turmoil in East Germany, Poland, and Hungary, his
commitment was more rhetorical than practical.(143) As George
Kennan commented, "He was terribly concerned for his image . . .
vis-à-vis the Republican majority in the Senate and he would go
very far, indeed, to please these people by what he said."(144)

An illuminating case study of the early interaction between
the moderate and the conservative Republican factions is the
maneuvering over the so called Bricker Amendment. The issues the
amendment addressed were the related questions of the president's
power to conclude executive agreements and the legality of the
domestic application of treaties. Bricker's constitutional amendment:

1. Specified that treaties which conflicted with the Constitution would have no effect;

2. Specified that treaties could only become domestic law
through additional legislation that would be valid in the absence
of the treaty; and

3. Gave Congress the power to regulate executive agreements
and to subject them to points one and two above.(145)

Bricker's amendment, in part, was reaction to such pending
international agreements as the United Nations Covenant on Human
Rights and the Genocide Treaty. Elements within the United
States felt that adherence to those treaties could be used by
political and judicial liberals to upset states rights and under-
write non-legislated liberal policies, particularly in the area
of civil rights. It was quickly agreed by Nixon, Dulles and
others within the Administration not to press those matters in
the hopes of defusing Bricker.(146) In particular, Dulles feared
that any attempt to adhere to the Genocide Convention would alienate Southern Democrats, especially Senators George and Russell,
and move them to support Bricker.(147) Support of Bricker was
also symptomatic of a wider move to assert congressional prerogative and limit the presidency. Assistant Secretary of State John
Hickerson, for one, was concerned that "allegations of our intent
to use the treaty power to amend or circumvent the Constitution
can no longer be dismissed." There was, he concluded, an attack
on "the treaty-making power generally."(148)

In general terms, Dulles was worried about a head-on colli-
sion with the Bricker forces. Soon after assuming office the
Secretary told the Cabinet that the amendment was "impossible,
even if revised."(149) Nevertheless, Dulles sought compromise
because, in the words of one observer, the Bricker amendment was
"very dear to the Republican leadership."(150) Eisenhower also
wished to avoid a fight. He worried that a compromise would only
delay the issue, but outright defeat would be a Pyrrhic victory
that would split the Republican party.(151) More importantly,
the President believed that public opinion shared the concerns
behind the Bricker Amendment and that outright defeat of the
amendment would not defeat that opinion.(152) The upshot, Eisenhower warned, was that the amendment would be a continuing electoral issue.(153) Even as late as 1956, after the Bricker amendment movement had spent most of its energy, Eisenhower continued
to fret about its electoral impact. Relating to his own office,

Eisenhower worried that the "Old Guard wing of the party might challenge his party control or even his renomination at the 1956 convention. He believed, for one, that the retirement of Governor Dewey of New York might lead to conservative inroads into the convention delegation, and he worked with that state's Attorney General, Jacob Javits, to forestall that possibility.(154) As the convention drew nearer, concern continued that the Bricker forces might take their cause to the floor. New Jersey's Senator Smith cautioned Dulles that he had "a hunch that the Bricker Amendment crowd may be noisy at the Republican convention and may try to get a Bricker Amendment recommendation passed which might be embarrassing to you and the President. This is a suggestion that we be forearmed."(155)

Eisenhower's reluctance to mount a frontal attack on the Bricker Amendment was also motivated by his constitutional scruples. The President pointed out on numerous occasions that the president has no formal role in the constitutional amendment process. Therefore, he told Walter Bedell Smith, "We cannot say what the Senate should say or not say; the Executive is without a role in this case."(156) The net result was the Eisenhower spoke more forcefully in private than in public. To individuals he would increasingly complain that the senators "want to tear down the Constitution, brick by brick, by Bricker,"(157) or proclaim he was "beginning to like Bricker for an enemy."(158) He also told his Cabinet, "We'll fight in every state if necessary(159) and wrote his brother he intended to "fight them--to the bitter end."(160)

His public stand, though, was more moderate despite advice from nearly all sides to stand firm. Dulles urged a strong early stand.(161) Knowland repeatedly asked for a definitive presidential statement,(162) and even the Democrats indirectly signalled for an executive pronouncement.(163) But Eisenhower refused, beyond one open letter to Knowland, to make the fight public. Frustrated by Eisenhower's equivocating, Dulles took the wholly uncharacteristic step of challenging his boss openly, urging him on one occasion to stop being fuzzy on the issue.(164) In another, later conversation, Dulles told Eisenhower that his public stand on the amendment was seen as "weasel-worded" and that Dulles was getting letters from senators asking "Are you for it or against it?"(165)

The lack of a strong message from Eisenhower was also based on a substantive hesitancy. He had a level of visceral sympathy with the Bricker concept and also did not fully understand the implications of the proposal and all its modifications and counter proposals. The result was ambivalence on Eisenhower's part which, along with his reluctance to speak out, generated uncertainty in Congress among those looking for a signal of presidential leadership. This lack of decisiveness was particularly complicated by the fact that the Administration seems to have reached out to Democratic Senator Walter George to help sponsor a mild alternative, then found that the move had alienated some of the Republicans, and finally reversed its field by moving to block the George amendment as unacceptable. On January 10, 1954, Eisenhower told Dulles that he had asked George to work on the

Bricker Amendment on a non-partisan basis.(166) Knowland called
several times on January 25 indicating he was appealing to
George's bipartisanship, but that George was favoring language
Dulles might find unacceptable.(167) On the 28th, Eisenhower
discussed the George amendment with Walter Bedell Smith. The
President had no objection to the language, and even expressed
some enthusiasm. Smith, by contrast, thought the George text was
"worse" than Bricker's, prompting the President to promise to
"play it close to the vest." Attorney General Brownell also
called to urge caution and dampened the President's initial positive attitude.(168) Within twenty-four hours Smith again called
Eisenhower to tell him, "Republicans now feel they cannot accept
the George amendment and have it said that the Democrats had to
save the GOP from a fight on the Bricker Amendment." Smith was
also worried by yet another alternative amendment, this one
sponsored by Knowland. Smith believed Knowland was going ahead
without Eisenhower's acquiescence. Yet a subsequent call by
Eisenhower to Knowland indicates that the Knowland language was
"along the lines I believe." Eisenhower told the Majority
Leader, "as a non-lawyer things don't look to me too dangerous,"
but indicated "people are trying to open my eyes to them." Adding to the confusion, Smith later called Eisenhower to tell him
of Dulles' approval of the George language. Despite what seemed
to be indications that Eisenhower and Dulles were willing to go
along with the George amendment and George's statement on the
Senate floor that there was nothing in his language to impinge on
the President's powers, the legal advisors of the Justice and
State Departments objected and the Administration wavered and
finally opposed both the Bricker original and the George and
Knowland alternatives. The result of the Administration's ambivalence, Eisenhower's propensity to tell senators he couldn't
personally understand what the fuss was all about, but that his
legal advisors insisted on language changes, and Eisenhower's
reluctance to go strongly public was confusion on Capitol hill.
In the end the Bricker and Knowland efforts were defeated handily, but George's, which had started out as something of a cooperative effort, almost carried the day. In the February 16, 1954
vote it appeared the George Amendment had actually passed the
Senate by the required two-thirds before Senator Harley Kilgore
reversed the decision with a dramatic last second "no" vote which
left the tally 60 for, 31 against.

Beyond demonstrating Eisenhower's reluctance to challenge the
right directly, the specter of the Bricker Amendment had a variety of policy impacts. There is some evidence that Eisenhower's
refusal to take unilateral action in Indochina during winter-
spring 1954 was based in part on concern that precipitous executive action might tip the balance in favor of Bricker or George.
Also, the Bricker Amendment, as it had in 1953 and 1954, continued to frustrate any possible American adherence to the Genocide Convention and other international conventions. Even after
Bricker's defeat for reelection in 1958, the Ohio Senator's
presence continued to be felt. In February 1959, Dulles recommended to Eisenhower that the Administration seek repeal of the
so-called Connally reservation which prohibited United States

acceptance of the compulsory jurisdiction of the International Court of Justice.(169) Presidential staff member David Kendell warned Eisenhower, "A lot of the same people or same thinking that went into the Connally Reservation are still present . . . and John Bricker has only just gone. It would seem unfortunate to stir things up . . ."(170) Kendell's argument carried the day. Despite indications that the move would have cleared the Senate Foreign Relations Committee substantially,(171) and a thinly veiled plea from Fulbright to the Secretary of to make the Administration's stance clear, the repeal remained unsupported and died an early death.(172)


## John F. Kennedy and Consensus

The election of John Fitzgerald Kennedy to the presidency and the partisan reuniting of the White House and Congress did not substantially lessen the Executive's emphasis on bipartisanship. Having received less than fifty percent of the popular vote in November 1960, Kennedy was conscious of the fact that he was a "minority" president. One tack Kennedy took was appointing or offering foreign policy positions to a large number of Republicans. Just days after his election, Kennedy contacted outgoing Vice President Nixon and, by extension, President Eisenhower about the possibility of appointing Henry Cabot Lodge, Jr., and C. Douglas Dillon, to high foreign policy posts.(173) There are also reports that Kennedy offered the State Department Post to Republican Robert Lovett,(174) but Dean Acheson recalls that Kennedy rejected his suggestion to appoint a Republican because "it would be too bad for a Democratic President to take the attitude that there was no one in his own party who was good enough to be Secretary of State."(175) It is sure, though, that Kennedy did offer Lovett the post of Secretary of the Treasury and, when Lovett declined, appointed Republican Dillon.(176) Other top spots also went to Republicans. Robert McNamara was appointed Secretary of Defense, McGeorge Bundy became National Security Advisor, John J. McCloy and William C. Foster coordinated disarmament activities, and Allen Dulles then John McCone directed the Central Intelligence Agency. Indeed, Kennedy appointed so many Republicans to foreign/defense policy posts that it caused a negative reaction among some Democrats. The President-elect had originally intended to appoint William Foster as Undersecretary of for Economic Affairs. When word of the impending nomination surfaced, Adlai Stevenson and William Fulbright protested, blocking Foster's appointment and sending him to the disarmament staff instead.(177) The basic idea according to Theodore Sorenson was that "the President felt that the country was narrowly divided, that it was terribly important to have as much national unity as possible in foreign policy questions, and that Republicans in and out of Congress would be much less likely to attack a McCloy, or a McCone, McNamara or Dillon than they would a [liberal Democrat]."(178)

Kennedy's concern with maintaining bipartisanship extended beyond his principal advisors and also focused directly on his relations with Congress. As with Truman and Eisenhower before him, President Kennedy felt primarily threatened by the anticommunist, fitfully isolationist conservative coalition. The opposition of the Republican right which had bedeviled Eisenhower was strengthened by normal partisan instincts. The administration was particularly sensitive to Republican charges of being "soft on communism" and acted both publicly and privately to refute "the charges that we are appeasers . . . unwilling to use nuclear weapons . . . unwilling to follow tough words with tough actions."(179) Also like Eisenhower, Kennedy had to deal with a disgruntled conservative element within his own party. Senator Richard Russell, for one, saw

> very little difference between the foreign policy of the Republican and Democratic parties, except that this administration has taken a much softer line toward the Soviets than did Eisenhower and Dulles. I hope that this will contribute to the permanent peace we all so prayerfully crave, but I doubt it. I do not think that fear inspires those in charge of your foreign relations as much as an erroneous belief that they can placate Soviet authorities.(180)

Kennedy's concern with maintaining congressional support extended to his principal foreign policy advisors and led to the careful monitoring and nurturing of ties with the Hill. Testifying before the Jackson subcommittee on national security affairs, Secretary Rusk observed that he considered it important to consult with Congress on matters which did not require formal legislative action as well as those which did.(181) Even the Republicans, such as Bourke Hickenlooper, recall that Rusk was "meticulous" about "almost continuous contact" with the Foreign Relations Committee.(182) McGeorge Bundy, Kennedy's and then Lyndon Johnson's National Security Advisor, similarly testified to the presidential concern with legislative opinion. Before the Foreign Relations Committee, Bundy noted, "It has never been my observation that presidents pay no attention to Congress. They may not agree with Congress, but they are concerned about its position." In response to Chairman Fulbright's somewhat incredulous reaction to his observation, Bundy chided, "The Chairman underestimates the degree to which his views were watched closely, certainly in the years I was there."(183)

Kennedy's careful courting of Republican Senate Minority Leader Everett Dirksen typifies his concern for maintaining bipartisan support in Congress. A Dirksen biographer found that the Illinois senator was especially beguiled by the careful attention Kennedy paid to him.(184) Dirksen continued to call the President "Jack" in contravention of normal protocol. Once, when Dirksen had been scolded by his wife for this breech of form, Kennedy even came to his rescue. "Why Ev," he said, "who more than you has the right?" Kennedy took particular pains to call Dirksen every few weeks, to extend such public courtesies as trips on the presidential jet and helicopter, limousine rides, and frequent intimate meetings at the White House. Dirksen told an audience in Illinois that Kennedy "calls me to the White

House. He sits in the rocker. I tell him what I think from the bottom of my heart, and I think that's why he keeps asking me back." At one point Dirksen even bought and proudly displayed a twenty-five cent drugstore key inscribed "The White House - Back Door."(185)

Congressional critics impinged on the foreign policy process on several occasions during Kennedy's three years in office. During both the Laotian crisis of 1962 and the Vietnamese Buddhist crisis of 1963 Kennedy found his policies opposed by congressional hawks as too soft and by congressional doves as too risky.(186) In the case of Laos, on the day before Kennedy's inauguration, Dwight Eisenhower had told the incoming President to put troops into Laos.(187) In a scenario akin to the Dien Bien Phu 1954 Vietnam crisis, Kennedy was able to avoid armed intervention in part because of the resistance of members of Congress. In a memo to Secretary of State Rusk, Asian specialist Senator Mike Mansfield made a direct analogy with the situation on the Loatian Plaines des Jares which he termed "strikingly similar to the one which was considered and rejected with fortuitous results at the time of Dien Bien Phu."(188) Direct or indirect intervention, Mansfield counseled, would alienate important neutrals like India, might prove indecisive, and might bog the United States down with the third string (Pathet Lao and Viet Minh) communist powers. Mansfield argued that even given a communist victory, "the grimmest result is not without some compensations." Such an occurrence, he predicted "would further stiffen the attitudes of neighboring countries . . . toward communism." Also, "Laos would become a fiscal drain on the communist nations as it has been on us." Calculating the domestic political impact of a Laotian collapse, Mansfield suggested the damage could be mitigated by blaming events on the Eisenhower Administration, but, in any case, loss of Laos would be less painful than a prolonged involvement which would certainly be a financial strain and, if American casualties occurred, would be "politically disastrous for the Administration."

Mansfield's objections were seconded by congressional leaders in an April 27, 1961 meeting that Walt Rostow characterized as one of the toughest White House meetings he had attended in the entire Kennedy administration.(189) While the specifics of that session are not entirely clear, it seems to have been reminiscent of the April 3, 1954 meeting in which the legislative delegation required international cooperation as a minimum condition of congressional support. When Kennedy probed the support of the S.E.A.T.O. allies he found France strongly opposed to intervention, the British reluctant, and others willing to make a token contribution at most.(190) As with the Indochinese events seven years earlier, congressional conditions dovetailed with presidential preferences and allowed Kennedy to withstand the pressure from the administration, congressional and military hawks.(191) Following the analogy through, the Laotian struggle was finally played out at the bargaining table in Geneva with a temporary modus vivendi which gained time but did not prevent an ultimate communist takeover.

Kennedy's "failure" to intervene in Laos arguably had the

unintended effect of forcing him into a harder stand on Vietnam. As with Laos, Kennedy was caught between the congressional doves and hawks, both of whom contributed to the increased American commitment in Vietnam. Kennedy was reluctant to intervene militarily in Vietnam for many of the same reasons he had avoided action in Laos. Yet he was also reluctant to disavow intervention for fear that it would set off a political storm on the domestic right. Therefore he followed the worst possible course; he equivocated. A controversy has occurred over Kennedy's ultimate intentions in Vietnam. Some of the President's advisors have contended that he intended to withdraw from Vietnam during his second term. If that is true, then it certainly demonstrates Kennedy's sensitivity to the right's potential charge that Democrats were soft on communism and its potential impact on the 1964 congressional and presidential election. Others, notably Dean Rusk, have emphatically stated that Kennedy never discussed such a maneuver; it was unthinkable in human terms and potentially disastrous politically to sacrifice American lives for electoral ends.(192) A possible resolution may have been offered by Ted Sorenson. In <u>Kennedy</u> he points out that the President steadily increased the size of the military assistance mission from 2,000 advisors in 1961 to 15,500 at the time of his assassination, while at the same time deciding against an American commitment of ground combat troops. Thus, in effect, Kennedy sought simultaneously to avoid an extended commitment and to avoid criticism from hawkish elements in Congress and elsewhere by giving the impression of continued resolve. In Sorenson's own words:

> Formally, Kennedy never made a final negative decision on troops. In typical Kennedy fashion he made it difficult for any of the pro-interventionist advocates to charge him . . . with weakness.(193)

The anti-interventionist elements may have also contributed to the continued American commitment in Vietnam. When South Vietnamese President Ngo Dinh Diem's autocratic policies finally led to open opposition, including the horrifying spectacle of Buddhist monks publicly burning themselves, Sorenson related that Kennedy, while deeply disturbed, at first "paid too little attention to those members of Congress and the American press . . . who complained that we were aiding a dictator."(194) Later, as the situation became intolerable, Kennedy wrote Diem that unless there were important domestic reforms, public and congressional opinion would make it impossible to continue American support. Finally, Kennedy was forced to publicly disavow the Diem regime and to cable, in late August 1963, that the United States would not oppose a military overthrow of Diem.(195) The predictable coup occurred on November 1, and the point might well be made that Kennedy and his successor, Johnson, were forced to support the existence of the "reform" government which American policy had certainly helped create. It was a commitment which led the United States into an increasing involvement that eventually cost more than 50,000 American lives.

Of all the various foreign policy questions during the

Kennedy years, none so dramatically illustrates the ability of
Congress to exercise indirect influence than the Cuban missile
crisis. Although President Kennedy refused to allow overt discussion of domestic political considerations during the week of meetings that culminated in the decision to "quarantine" Cuba, there
are numerous indications that the President and his advisors were
well aware of the impact of the crisis on domestic politics and
the vulnerability of the Administration and the Democratic Party
on the issue of Cuba. As Robert Kennedy has noted while setting
the scene in his Thirteen Days, "It was election time."(196)
Led by Senators Kenneth Keating, Barry Goldwater, and Homer Capehart, the Republicans specifically concentrated on rumors that
offensive weapons were being introduced into that country and the
Republican Senatorial and Congressional Campaign Committees
announced that Cuba would be the dominant issue of the 1962 campaign. Even the Soviets were aware of the pressure on Kennedy
and the Democrats. In a move perhaps calculated to lull the
President, Ambassador Anatoly Dobrynin relayed a message (September 6, 1962) from Chairman Nikita Krushchev to Kennedy which
pledged "nothing will be undertaken before the American Congressional elections that could complicate the international situation . . . . The Chairman does not wish to become involved in
your internal political affairs."(197)

The effects of Republican attacks on the thinking of the
Administration and on the resulting policy decisions during the
crisis have been underlined by State Department official Roger
Hilsman:

> These political pressures--and the administration's response
> to them--had already foreclosed some of the policy alterna-
> tives . . . . In trying to meet the opposition's charges and
> to reassure the public . . . Kennedy had been forced not
> only to deny that "offensive" weapons were in Cuba but to
> put himself on public record that his administration would
> not tolerate their being put there . . . . If the missiles
> were not important enough strategically to justify a confron-
> tation with the Soviet Union, as McNamara thought, yet were
> "offensive," then the United States might not be in mortal
> danger but the administration certainly was.(198)

The Republican attacks and the Administration's response,
then, made a confrontation between the United States and the
Soviet Union inevitable once the missiles were discovered.
Defense Secretary McNamara's argument that "a missile is just a
missile," and that the introduction of offensive missiles into
Cuba had little military significance was dismissed out-of-hand.
(199) The question was never whether the missiles should be
removed, but how.

There was also considerable evidence that the President's
advisors incorporated the congressional attack and its domestic
implications in their considerations. Presidential advisors widely shared a feeling which is summed up by Sorenson's observation
that Cuba was the President's "political Achilles heel." At one
point during a decisional meeting, Secretary Dillon passed a note

to Sorenson that read, "Have you considered the very real possibility that if we allow Cuba to complete installation and operational readiness of missile bases, the next House of Representatives is likely to have a Republican majority?"(200) The President was also aware of the implications. Presidential Assistant Kenneth O'Donnell has related that when Kennedy showed him the photographs of the missile sights the President predicted, "We've just elected Capehart in Indiana and Ken Keating will probably be the next President of the United States."(201) Sorenson has also recalled that on another occasion Kennedy, worrying that he would be seen as an appeaser, ruefully commented, "Well, I guess Homer Capehart is the Winston Churchill of our generation."(202) Kennedy was also aware that there could be little compromise with removal of the missiles. Although overt criticism by others during the crisis was restrained, it threatened to erupt if the missiles remained. Even among the Democrats, what private criticism there was tended toward advocacy of a quick military solution. When Kennedy briefed legislative leaders prior to his national address, Senate Armed Services Committee Chairman Richard Russell and Foreign Relations Committee Chairman William Fulbright both argued for immediate military action to directly remove or eliminate the missiles.(203) An exasperated Kennedy muttered to his aide Sorenson that if Russell or Fulbright thought they could do a better job they could have it. Thus, in domestic political terms more than in diplomatic terms Kennedy had his options closed.(204) Doing nothing was a non-choice, and, as nearly happened, had the Soviets persisted in resisting the blockade, military action would have been inevitable. After it was all over the President wondered aloud to his brother if there was any way by which he could have escaped the crisis. Robert Kennedy replied, "I just don't think there was any other choice, and not only that, if you hadn't acted, you would have been impeached." "That's what I think," agreed the President, "I would have been impeached."(205)

## Lyndon B. Johnson and Consensus

Like most modern presidents, only perhaps more so, Lyndon Baines Johnson was torn between his desire to be an independent and decisive leader and his need to gain congressional cooperation in his quest for consensus. He could, on the one hand, proclaim "There are many, many who can recommend, advise and sometimes a few of them consent. But there is only one who has been chosen by the American people to decide."(206) He could also recount—with a wistful glee a conversation he had with President Truman, "one of the few comforts I had all during the war." Johnson had been complaining of the difficulties he was having with Fulbright and other legislative dissenters to which Truman advised, "Why, I'd just go ahead and smack them, just pay no attention to these over-educated Senators, that's all there is to it." At another time Johnson recalled, when he had again been bemoaning Fulbright's attack, Truman had interrupted, "But you are the President. You make policy, not him."(207)

Such announced or adopted bravado did not, however, accurately reflect Johnson's basic orientation. Instead he was very much concerned with consensus and, like his predecessors, was especially apprehensive about the conservative elements in the country. Johnson's orientation resulted from a number of factors. Part of the emphasis sprang from Johnson's basic approach to politics. His congressional career, particularly his tenure as Senate Majority Leader, emphasized compromise and consensus. His strength lay not in proposing bold new programs, but in spanning the seemingly unbridgeable gap between the conservative southern and liberal northern/western elements of the Democratic party. More than any other phrase, Johnson's "Come, let us reason together" symbolizes his approach to politics. More specifically, history and his success as majority leader taught him lessons which he carried over to the White House. Once in the Oval Office his fascination with Congress continued as did his belief that the techniques he had applied in the Capitol corridors could be used with equal success as president. His favorite reading material was the Congressional Record, and his aide Jake Jacobson's job was to peruse and mark up the journal before dawn each day so it would be ready for Johnson to read while he ate breakfast.(208)

He would also ask for summaries of the voting records of key legislators,(209) and assigned an aide the specific job of following congressional foreign policy statements.(210) Johnson also believed that he could resolve conflict much as he had in the Senate, by communicating, cajoling, and perhaps coercing. As political counselor Larry O'Brien explained, "Johnson tended to think that if any Democrat criticized him, it was simply a failure of communication, and that if we would just explain our position better the problem would be solved."(211) Even when continued explanation failed, Johnson never really understood why the technique had not translated from one office to the other. Meeting with his foreign policy staff in December 1965, Johnson complained, "You have no idea how much I have talked to Fulbright [and others] . . . . They are not coming around, but we must listen to what they are saying."(212) And just a short time later he angrily despaired, "It rankles me that we have to prove again to Congress that we are striving for peace. We've done it again and again."(213)

The President also carried the infamous "Johnson technique" with him to the White House. He assumed that everyone had a "price," that their opposition to his program would be subject to the elbow squeezing, chest thumping, nose-to-nose intimidating rushes by the six foot plus president. Senator Frank Church has recalled the typical approach:

> There was a time when Lyndon Johnson thought that he might win back some of the dissidents by giving them the famous Johnson treatment, and he attempted that . . . . To keep Congress placated, he held a series of elaborate orientations at the White House . . . . Then he proceeded to answer questions, sometimes allowing Mr. Rusk a few minutes, sometimes Mr. McNamara, but usually jumping up and sitting

> them down and answering the questions himself. He was very
> excited . . . and really acted almost like a carnival
> barker, using all his persuasive powers which were always
> impressive and calling upon many a folk tale to fortify his
> argument . . . . He [looked] to me like a lightbulb about
> ready to go out.(214)

Church then relates that the President got him in a corner and
for a half hour was "very determined to show me my error" while a
room full of senators waited for the meeting to adjourn. Afterwards fellow dissident Senator Eugene McCarthy half-seriously
groused that "If Frank Church had just surrendered, we could have
all gone home thirty minutes ago." Church did not, and Johnson
probably never really understood why.

When persuasion and cajolery failed, Johnson was not above
retaliating or seeming to. An illustrative story again involves
Church and his dissent on Vietnam. In the above encounter,
Church had told the President that he (Church) agreed with Walter
Lippmann's opposition to the war and Johnson had said little in
response. The next day, however, Johnson had floated the story
through a press interview that he had told Church, "The next time
you want a dam in Idaho, Frank, go to Walter for it." The message was clear, be careful and calculate the price of opposing
Lyndon Johnson.(215) Even more than Church, Fulbright earned
Johnson's particular approbation. Fulbright had been excluded
once from the White House after a dissenting speech on the 1965
Dominican Republic action,(216) but Vietnam was the final wedge
between the President and the man who Johnson, as Vice President-
elect, had heavily promoted for Secretary of State. Johnson
could deal with some opponents, like Oregon's Senator Wayne Morse
who was known as an irascible maverick and who, having been one
of two Senators to have voted against the Tonkin Gulf Resolution,
was at least consistent. Fulbright, on the other hand, was a
traitor who had turned on his former supporter and who tried to
refute his earlier support of the Resolution.(217) Johnson could
not imagine it was a matter of conscience for Fulbright. Rather
it must be a move for political self-aggrandizement, a cowardly
opportunity to beset an already beleaguered president. "Even a
blind hog could find an acorn once in a while," Johnson thought.
(218) The end result was a severing of relations. Fulbright was
cut off from White House social functions and virtually excluded
from business matters. It was, in a way, the worst possible
retribution Johnson could imagine, to cast the sinners into the
darkness, away from the light of political power that emanated
from the Oval Office.

Johnson's concern with congressional cooperation also stemmed
from his experience as Senate Majority Leader vis-à-vis the
presidency of Dwight Eisenhower. The impact of those years were
especially evident in Johnson's desire for the Tonkin Gulf Resolution to support his military move into Vietnam. Presidential
intimate Jack Valenti recalls that Johnson "fretted" over congressional support, and that "all the past mistakes of other presidents neglecting the key and crucial embrace of Congress paraded
before the Johnson memory."(219) The President could remember

Truman's intervention in Korea without congressional support and the later attacks of Taft and others which turned the conflict into "Truman's War" and ended his presidency.(220)  In contrast, Johnson was well aware of Eisenhower's careful inclusion of Congress and the political insulation that move afforded the president.  Johnson aide Erv Duggan relates that:

> Johnson said that the reason he got the Gulf of Tonkin Resolution was that he remembered how passionate Eisenhower was about not making a move without the full cooperation of Congress, not doing anything that he could get in trouble with Congress about.  And Johnson thought that was extremely shrewd of Eisenhower politically.  And the reason he was so careful to get a piece of paper in his pocket on the Tonkin Gulf was that he was following Eisenhower's example.(221)

The essential idea Johnson told a leadership meeting in early 1965, was the same as the Vandenberg formulation of nearly twenty years before.  The President wanted the Congress, and the Republicans in particular, in on "all the take-offs and not just the crash landings."(222)

Johnson's orientation toward Congress also reflected the role he had played as majority leader in the 1950's.  "We junked the old Taft practice that the duty of the opposition is to oppose," Johnson announced when Eisenhower entered office in 1953.(223)  Instead, Johnson felt it was important to support the president in foreign policy.  It was not, he explained, that he was "petticoatin' around with Eisenhower."  Rather he wanted to make sure "that the Communists don't play one branch of government against the other . . . .  The danger is they'll think we're fat, fifty, and fighting among ourselves . . . .  If you're in an airplane . . . you don't run up to the cockpit and attack the pilot.  Mr. Eisenhower is the only President we've got."(224)  Based on that philosophy, Johnson had served as the loyal opposition.  When he disagreed, he did so privately and before the decision was finalized.  Once the decision was announced and in his public statements he supported the President.  He believed that was the proper way to conduct foreign policy in 1955 and he still believed it in 1965.  Unfortunately, in Johnson's eyes, Fulbright, Church, and others did not agree.

A last and intriguing source of President Johnson's concern with Congress was based on his suspicion of public passions and the impact he feared Congress might have.  "The smaller the area of conflict shown to the American public," he cautioned, "the less I worried about the public's tendency to go off on a jag, paralyzing itself in endless debate or stampeding."(225)  The more the parties and the legislative and executive branches agreed, the less likely it would be that divisive, dangerous debates would occur to stir the public's darker impulses.  The power of the political right, particularly as evidenced in McCarthyism was especially fearful to Johnson.  He saw the public as apathetic, but with the potential for "a violent overreaction to fear, a violent explosion of panic."(226)  McCarthy was long dead by the time Johnson came to the Oval Office, but he was afraid that the "ism" was merely dormant, not deceased.  He was also

afraid that if the question of Israel became a major issue in the
United States that anti-Semitism would erupt.(227) He also
feared that the right might demand a military solution to
Vietnam, an invasion of the North possibly provoking Chinese or
Soviet countermoves, and raising the specter of World War III.
(228)

This concern with the right caused Johnson to adopt two somewhat antithetical policies in the early days of Vietnam.(229)
One was to downplay the military task involved. He refused to
declare war, call up the reserves, or in other ways put the country on a war footing that might have helped rally political opinion to this side and might have avoided some of the later economic misery his guns and butter policy provoked. Johnson feared
that congressional conservatives might use the resource requirements of a major military confrontation as an excuse to wreck his
Great Society domestic programs.(230) Therefore, in the words of
one biographer, "dissembling" was the way "to keep the stampede
from beginning." "By pretending there was no major conflict
. . . Johnson believed he could keep the levers of control in his
hands."(231)

While concerned that beating the drums too loudly would start
a McCarthyistic anti-communist, anti-Great Society crusade, Johnson was also paradoxically swayed to be more aggressive than
might have otherwise been the case for fear of being labeled as
soft on communism. In part his early toughness was related to
the 1964 Republican presidential candidate Senator Barry Goldwater. If Johnson appeared firm, Goldwater would be left with
only the nuclear-nut right. Johnson also wanted to maintain his
popularity as a source of ego and domestic policy strength. He
worried that his landslide over Goldwater "might be more of a
loophole than a mandate."(232) Vietnam threatened to destroy his
popularity and mandate. He remembered how Harry Truman, a staunch
anti-communist, had been accused of losing China. Truman had not
really lost China, but he did lose Congress and eventually the
country. That wasn't going to happen to Lyndon Johnson, no sir!
He would be tough enough in Vietnam so that the right could never
accuse him of losing anything to the communists.(233)

The image of Lyndon Johnson ignoring Congress to pursue a
universally unpopular war in Vietnam projects a false image, both
as far as the specific example and the general stance of the
President with regard to Congress. As discussed above and as
will be further considered below, Johnson's Vietnam policy was,
to a degree, responsive to Congress. Or, at least, it was fitfully responsive to the eddying currents of hawk and dove opinion. Nor does the unresponsive image accurately reflect Johnson's general posture vis-à-vis Congress. More than any other
modern president, Johnson was a creature of Congress who thought
he understood that body, courted it, and reacted to it even when
he constitutionally might have ignored it. As Nicholas de B.
Katzenback, Under Secretary of State, in the Johnson Administration testified, "Whatever the powers of the President to act
alone . . . every President seeks in various ways--formal and
informal--the support of Congress for the policies which the
United States pursues in its foreign relations."(234) Many

members of Congress have recalled that Johnson paid close attention to Congress, meeting with and personally briefing members on
foreign policy and insisting that Cabinet departments, the Central Intelligence Agency, and other units also keep Congress
informed.(235)

Congressional impact can further be seen in a number of Johnson's policy decisions, several of which will be discussed in
greater detail at a later point in the text. Lack of congressional enthusiasm helped abort the European-American Multilateral
Force (MLF). Congressional opposition that arose after the 1965
intervention in the Dominican Republic was also a factor in the
relatively rapid withdrawal of American forces and the restraint
practiced thereafter. Assistant Secretary of State Charles
Frankel has reported that a Senate speech by William Fulbright
condemning the Administration for its military move caused a reaction "like a bomb falling."(236) Johnson told Dwight Eisenhower
that Fulbright's remarks had "injured us badly."(237) It also
resulted in Fulbright's first exile from the White House social
list.(238) During the 1967 Arab-Israeli Six Day War Johnson
initially favored United States sponsorship and participation in
an international naval force to keep the blockaded Straits of
Tiran open. Before committing American forces, however, Johnson
felt it necessary to obtain congressional support. That, he
found, would be difficult. With a dim prospect for winning quick
support and wishing to avoid damaging domestic dissent, Johnson
dropped the idea of an allied intervention. In yet another incident, Johnson was again restrained from extended intervention in
another crisis. In this case, the President dispatched military
transport aircraft to the Congo (Zaire) to help quell a threatened recurrence of the violence of the early 1960's. Johnson
wanted to be ready to aid the possible evacuation of Americans
and Europeans and also to lend tangible support to the Congolese
government in its struggle with the mercenary backed Kataganese
rebels. Initially, there was some hope that opposition would not
break out. The Defense Department reported that the Senate and
House Armed Services Committee Chairmen, Richard Russell and
Mendell Rivers, would go along.(239) In an early briefing with
Secretary Rusk, Senator Fulbright did not object.(240) Congressional quiescence was short lived, however. Objections sprang
from a number of sources. Lack of consultation with Congress
offended institutional pride. Fear of increased American involvement and counter-Soviet or Chinese intervention also surfaced.
Reports of brutal behavior, including cannibalism, on the part of
Congolese troops, added to congressional qualms. As Walt Rostow
predicted to the President, the fact that such reports were
unfounded would not "keep our brethren on the Hill from using the
news against us."(241) Rostow was right. Russell told Rusk that
he strongly objected, and other legislators quickly joined the
chorus publicly and privately.(242) Senators Fulbright, Stennis,
and Case openly opposed the move. Mike Mansfield pronounced himself "shocked, surprised, and dismayed."(243) Eighteen Republican senators joined in a letter to the President describing themselves as "utterly dismayed," objecting "strenuously," and "most
strongly" urging Johnson to recall the aircraft.(244) Because of

the ambivalence within the Administration, the exact impact on Congress is not totally clear. Rusk claimed that no intervention beyond the C-130 mission was planned and that Congress had used the incident as political chance to "beat the ears off [a] president" who was increasingly unpopular.(245) There are other indications, however, that more aid was contemplated. A State Department report to the Cabinet said a main problem in the situation was how the help the Congolese government of President Joseph Mobutu given the Senate opposition to the C-130 missions.(246) Whatever the specific policy of the Administration, further aid was contemplated and advocated by some, but the opposition of Congress helped tip the balance against action.

## Richard Nixon and Consensus

In stark contrast to his predecessor Lyndon Johnson and his former chief Dwight Eisenhower, President Richard Nixon was contemptuous of Congress and, it indeed seems, the entire democratic process. Even as Vice President he chafed under the "inefficiencies" of the American political process and compared it unfavorably with the "smooth, quick action" of the Soviets. A major cause of American lack of decisiveness, according to Nixon, was the necessity of coordination between the executive and legislative branches.(247) Nixon's attitude became even more pronounced as president, and it acted to alienate both Democrats and Republicans. William Safire reports, for example, that during the briefing on the mining of Haiphong harbor in May 1972, Nixon incensed Mike Mansfield and several other senators by essentially presenting them with a take-it-or-leave-it proposition. He would appreciate their support, of course, but he could and would go ahead without it if necessary.(248) He treated Republicans little better. Maine GOP Senator Margaret Chase Smith complained as early as 1969 that she had no idea what Nixon's Vietnam plan was; he had asked the Republican leadership to take him on faith. (249) Even Senate Minority Leader Hugh Scott was left in the dark and angry. After a syndicated column was published in May 1970 detailing repeated instances when Scott was kept uninformed or was even misled by the White House, the President's party chief in the Senate wrote to Henry Kissinger and other White House aides that "I must have substantive evidence of support of my leadership . . . close consultation, which will erase the steady drum beat of criticism I am receiving.(250) Even more outrageous to members of Congress were comments by Nixon and his entourage that implied congressional critics were un-American. Senator Stuart Symington wrote to Mansfield and a dozen other Senate colleagues protesting White House chief-of-staff H. R. Haldeman's "infamous" remarks on national television which charged, according to Symington, that "those in public life who criticized the President's recently proposed peace plan were consciously aiding and abetting the enemy for partisan reasons." Such remarks, Symington worried were in "complete disregard of the freedom of speech, posed a grave threat to the American political process," and were "a powerful whip to still even the most reasoned voices of dissent, for it means that anyone who voices opposition. . . may be greeted with the accusation that he is betraying his country."(251)

Hubert Humphrey offered a classically colorful and only slightly caricatured characterization of the Nixon technique. Comparing President Johnson with the incumbent, Humphrey observed:

> Now Johnson used to rob the Senate, but when he wanted to take something from you, he'd invite you to lunch. He'd put his arms around you and talk to you while he picked your pocket . . . . But Nixon stuck you up in the night. You didn't even see him. It was like rape without any personal contact. I mean, the Senators are used to being had, but not being ignored. That drives them mad . . . .(252)

Yet for all his propensity for an "imperial" attitude, Nixon could not be completely contemptuous of Congress. Like all his predecessors from Truman on, Nixon both sought bipartisan support and was more concerned with potential conservative opposition than with liberal dissent. In his memoirs, Nixon claims he had a bipartisan foreign policy supported by Republicans and by conservative southern Democrats such as Thad Montgomery of Mississippi and Joel Waggonner, F. Edward Hébert, and Otto Passman of Louisiana in the House, and Richard Russell of Georgia, John Stennis of Mississippi and John McClellen of Arkansas in the Senate.(253) Nixon also sought the support of Washington Democratic Senator Henry "Scoop" Jackson. Nixon reportedly offered Jackson the posts of Secretary of Defense and later, perhaps, Secretary of State. Nixon also acted to support Jackson electorally. Washington Republican State Chairman Montgomery Johnson related that he was pressured by Nixon, Erlichman, and Senator John Tower, Chairman of the Republican Senate Campaign Committee, not to actively oppose Jackson's reelection in 1979. "Well, Gummie," Nixon said, "I hope you're not going to defeat Scoop." It was, in the Chairman's estimate, "an illicit love affair." (254)

Although he was continually besieged by liberals over Vietnam, Nixon ironically seems to have worried more about potential conservative opposition. Nixon was concerned that his approach to mainland China would spark criticism from his conservative supporters and hastened to assure them he would not abandon Taiwan.(255) Nixon was also apprehensive about crumbling support for his policy in Vietnam. Kissinger recalls that after a 1970 conversation with conservative Senators Harry Byrd, Jr., and Gordon Allot the President was "shaken." "We've got the left where we want it now," Nixon gloated. "All they've got to argue for is a bug out, and that's their problem" but, he worried, "when the right starts wanting to get out, for whatever reason, that's our problem."(256)

Actually, the record shows that dissent from both wings was his problem. As will be discussed in detail below, the Nixon Administration was bothered and to a degree manipulated by congressional criticism and the potential for formal legislative action. A constant theme in the speeches and writings of Nixon and Kissinger is that congressional criticism played into the hands of the North Vietnamese. Dissent also sapped the morale of administration officials. Under public and congressional attack, Kissinger dramatically relates, "The very fabric of government was falling apart. The Executive Branch was shell shocked."(257) "We were caught," Kissinger said at another point, "between officials seeking to protect the American [military] forces for which they felt responsibility and a merciless congressional onslaught that rattled these officials in their deliberations." (258) Nixon and Kissinger were also pushed by the knowledge that eventually Congress would legislatively end United States involvement in Vietnam. A Kissinger aide remembers that time and again Kissinger would mutter, "We'll never get through another session of Congress without their giving the farm away."(259) And Kissinger himself has concurred that the final decision to push for a Vietnam settlement in 1972 was based on the fact the Administration was "pushed against the grindstone of Congressional pressure."(260)

## Presidents, Congress, Public Opinion and Consensus

Thus, presidents do seek congressional support and do react to real or potential criticism. The key is not constitutional requirement, but a feeling in the Executive that in order to be effective foreign policy must have united domestic backing. In the case of Dwight Eisenhower, there was also a feeling that the governmental balance of powers should be maintained, that Congress properly had a place in the foreign policy process. Within the context of the modern presidency, however, Eisenhower's strict constructionist views on the legislative role were singular, and even he became less concerned with tenets of constitutionalism as time passed. Nevertheless, Congress remained a strong factor. Each president reviewed in this study sought congressional support—some, surely, to a lesser degree than others, but even a Richard Nixon felt obligated to try to maintain a semblance of bipartisan support. That requirement, whether real or imagined, has given Congress influence beyond its often latent constitutional powers. While it is impossible to separate completely formal and informal powers, it is clear that presidents seek accommodation with Congress in order to avoid the political damage they believe dissent will cause both at home and abroad.

It is significant to note that presidents do not normally consult Congress willingly. They only do so with reluctance. That reluctance, however, coupled with the frequency of interaction is impressive testimony to the fact that despite the lack of constitutional necessity, the White House does not feel it can ignore Congress—even if it would like to. And it would like to. It is not difficult to uncover the generally contemptuous attitude of presidents toward Capitol Hill. Chip Bohlen has recalled that he was shocked to find out how bitterly Roosevelt perceived the Senate. On board the USS Quincy returning from Yalta in

1945, Roosevelt denounced the Senate as "a bunch of incompetent obstructionists," and declared, "the only way to do anything in the American government [is] to bypass the Senate."(261) In strikingly similar terms, Lyndon Johnson's Press Secretary, George Reedy, testified before the Senate that during his experience in the White House there was a "feeling that Congress is merely a problem to be grappled with . . . and resisted. And some things must be run around Congress."(262) Even those in the Eisenhower Administration came to regard Congress as a burden. Eisenhower's son wrote his father that "It can be taken as a starter that selling the program to the Congress cannot be based on any concept of a mature, balanced, nationally minded group which will take the recommendations of what is good for the country and duly enact the same."(263) Indeed, Eisenhower became so wearied and discouraged after six years of dealing with an opposition Congress that he privately mused about the idea of having an American prime minister or first secretary.(264)

Executive officials not only believe that congressional criticism will signal division and weakness to foreign capitals, they believe that congressional opinion interacts with public opinion which in turn affects both the president's diplomatic strength and his domestic political standing. As seen from the Executive Branch, congressional/public opinion influence is perceived as reciprocal in nature. Congress is both reflective of public opinion and can also influence public opinion. Typically, a Dulles assistant observed that the Secretary had a very strong sense of public relations. "He felt that a great mistake Acheson had made was to lose Congress and the country--or the country and the Congress. You could take it in either order you want."(265) From a more scholarly perspective, one survey found that 70% of all State Department officials explicitly saw Congress as having a public opinion role. Fifty-six percent believed Congress manifested public opinion and 44% saw Congress as a shaper of public opinion.(266)

While no president could or would admit that he is controlled by public opinion, the most elementary archival research demonstrates a high interest in polls, mail counts, and other indices of public opinion. These indices are also used internally to support arguments among executive officials. For example, Chester Bowles, a liberal State Department official, used a Gallup poll to try to persuade Secretary of State Rusk to increase foreign economic assistance. "Contrary to a widespread assumption here in Washington," Bowles contended, "the foreign aid program commands an extraordinary amount of public support." The poll result Bowles forwarded showed 58% in favor of foreign aid. Bowles further observed that aid opponents were mostly Republican anyway and even indicated he had personally consulted with George Gallup who added his "puzzlement" at the misreading of public opinion.(267) Bowles was also willing to argue on the other side of the question when polls went the other way. On China he contended, "It's our clear responsibility to look beyond . . . what it is assumed that Congress or the public will accept . . . to the stark question of what is required."(268)

Vice President Hubert Humphrey's people used public opinion

to try to keep Humphrey liberal on Vietnam, and Humphrey in turn used the same arguments on President Johnson. William Connell wrote Humphrey numerous memos marshalling public opinion on the side of restraint in Vietnam. Bombing of North Vietnam, Connell reported, had brought in 700 letters, 90% of which could be summarized as objecting that, based on the bombing policy, "I might as well have voted for Goldwater."(269) Connell also dismissed conservative opinion, telling the Vice President that polls indicated a four to one majority among Democrats in favor of the President's policy. The greatest disapproval was from the right. "We can afford that," Connell counseled.(270) The aide even passed on the advice of arch critic Barry Goldwater. The defeated presidential candidate, Connell reported, had told Ronald Reagan not to be fooled "by the same little old ladies in tennis shoes that used to cheer and clap for him and did the same thing for Bob Taft and Tom Dewey." In other words, do not be fooled by the enthusiastic response of a handful of hard core conservatives.(271) Humphrey responded by using the same type of argument with the President. Within a month of the inauguration the Vice President warned of the danger of increased military action, advising that some were attacking the Administration for following the Goldwater line and following a program "remarkably similar to Republican policy."(272) In explicit domestic terms, the Vice President advised that 1965 was a year of "minimum political risk." "It is the first year we can face the Vietnam problem without being preoccupied with the political repercussions from the Republican right . . . . Political problems are likely to come from new and different sources if we pursue an enlarged military policy very long." The new opposition would be Democratic liberals, independents, labor, church groups, et al.-- the President's natural constituency.

The estimated value of political strength vis-à-vis Congress that presidents credit to popular opinion makes that factor an important calculation. The reputedly non-political Dwight Eisenhower was convinced that once in his lame duck term "my influence in the next four years . . . is going to be determined by . . . how popular I am with the multitudes . . . . Strength can be marshalled on both sides of the aisle only if it is generally believed that I am in a position to go to the people over their heads."(273) The very political Lyndon Johnson agreed that "Presidential popularity is a major source of strength in gaining cooperation from Congress."(274) The Johnson team kept in regular contact with pollsters. Richard Scammon was an official with the Bureau of the Census, but Johnson sought his estimates of opinion on foreign policy questions.(275) The Administration also attempted to plant questions with national polls to bolster the chances of international legislation before Congress.(276) But Johnson realized that popularity was the most fragile of commodities. Even his record 1964 landslide, the president worried, "might be more of a loophole than a mandate."(277)

To a degree, Congress is seen as a reflection of public opinion. Averill Harriman, for instance, testified before Congress that foreign policy officials "must . . . know what the people are thinking, and for this information Congress is a prime source of knowledge."(278)  H. Schuyler Foster, Assistant Secretary of State under Eisenhower, also observed that "The impact of public opinion is felt directly by the State Department and also through the people's representative in Congress."(279)  Also important is the belief that Congress can affect public opinion. In an early example, Under Secretary of State James Webb wrote President Truman that "Although the Administration policies are sound and are consistent with the natural inclination of most Americans, dangerous confusion has been created in the public mind by persistent Republican attacks."(280)  Robert Bowie, Assistant Secretary of State in the Eisenhower Administration, similarly testified that a prime prerequisite of successful foreign policy is favorably shaping "the popular attitudes or frame of mind of the citizenry which is partly a function of the way congressional members try to educate opinion."(281)  In a still later example, Senator Church recalled that President Johnson had not taken Senate Foreign Relations committee opposition seriously until the committee had begun public hearings.  "It was," said Church, "the klieg lights the President feared, not my misgivings concerning policy expressed behind closed doors . . . ."(282)

This issue here is not whether presidents should react to public opinion or if, in fact, domestic dissent damages foreign policy.  Nor is the issue whether Congress can impact public opinion or whether it reflects citizen sentiment.  The point is that presidents and other executive actors are concerned with public opinion, value national unity, and believe that congressional attitudes are both a cause and effect of public attitudes.  These beliefs and the efforts of executive policy-makers to avoid or mute criticism gives Congress considerable potential for influence.  Referring to congressional criticisms of administration policies in Cuba and the Congo, Assistant Secretary of State Robert Hilsman has aptly focused on the executive view of members of Congress:

> . . . their activities were always a factor to be taken account of in the policy discussions--and policy was at times either adjusted to accommodate some element of their view so as to disarm them or presented in such a way as to forestall them.  For even though . . . [they] did not become the rallying points for an alternative policy, they had the potential for doing so.(283)

While Congress has often failed to utilize its potential influence, it has on other occasions effectively influenced policy either by actual criticism or by anticipated reaction by the Executive to potential dissent.  Although the degree of responsiveness varies between administrations based on personality and political circumstance, no president can remain completely insensitive given their belief in the foreign and domestic impact of congressional dissent.  The fact that this aspect of congressional influence is indirect, that it cannot be counted in votes cast, treaties defeated, or appropriations withheld does not detract from its importance.

# 5
# Congressional Means and Presidential Values: Europe, Asia and the Middle East Policy

The value that presidents place on consensus and the impact of congressional dissent discussed in Chapter Four are only two of the pieces in the interlocking puzzle that determines presidential and congressional foreign policy power. A variety of other factors also make up the picture. The following two chapters focus on these other aspects of legislative and executive values and means during the 1948 to 1972 period. The scope, or areas of interest, that Congress has in foreign policy is also discussed. By examining the years between Truman's second and Nixon's first term, we can utilize the United States' foreign policy-making process toward Europe, Asia, the Middle East, trade, aid, and other subjects to further confirm, refine, or deny the means and values that were identified in Chapters One through Three.

## Congress and Europe

The impact of Congress on the formation and conduct of United States foreign policy toward Europe has been limited. What influence Congress has exercised has generally been in the form of limiting commitments to the defense of Europe. In 1948 two major foreign policy events in Europe demonstrated the solidifying American commitment to the defense of that continent. The first was the Berlin Blockade which began in June and lasted until May 1949. During that crisis, and in subsequent intermittent crises over Berlin, Congress played a supportive role with virtually no influence over American policy. The other event, which began in mid-1948, centered on negotiations for the formation of the North Atlantic Treaty Organization. When Britain, France, the Netherlands, and Luxemburg entered into an agreement for economic cooperation and mutual defense in March 1948, the Administration quietly informed European leaders that it supported the move and would attempt to bring the United States into the concept. The first step was to persuade Congress to declare its support in theory for the concept of United States participation in a regional agreement with Europe. Under the leadership of Under Secretary of State Robert Lovett the idea was first presented to Senate Foreign Relations Committee Chairman Arthur Vandenberg.(1)

Although Vandenberg favored such a move, he used the question to push two ideas which Congress had tended to support throughout the post-war period. One was allied cooperation. Vandenberg felt Congress would respond much better to a Europe which was helping itself. He therefore urged the Administration to continue to push for a Western European Union (WEU), a concept in the genesis of the European Economic Community. Aside from the leverage of the formulating NATO pact, Vandenberg also tied the future of aid to the continued development of the WEU.(2) Vandenberg also stressed the concept of a limited commitment to Europe --no permanent troops, no involvement in war without a congressional declaration.(3) After the proper amount of coaxing and assurance, Vandenberg was persuaded to sponsor a resolution which, popularly bearing his own name, passed the Senate 64 to 4.

The ease with which the Vandenberg Resolution passed did not mean, however, that American negotiators could proceed with confidence that the Senate would ratify any agreement they concluded. Dean Acheson, who became Secretary of State in January 1949 upon Marshall's retirement (Lovett also stepped down), continued assiduously to court Vandenberg and Tom Connally who had, once again, reversed their roles as chairman and ranking member of the Senate Foreign Relations Committee when the Democrats assumed control of Congress in January 1949. At his first meeting with European negotiators in February 1949, Acheson cautioned that he could not move any faster with the treaty text than he could move in his discussions with Senators Connally and Vandenberg "since agreement would mean little unless it carried senatorial opinion with it." Acheson has described his task of simultaneously negotiating with those two sovereign constellations, Europe and the Senate, as being like "a circus performer riding two horses-- for one to move ahead of the other would mean a nasty fall. Safety required the use of ambassadors to urge on the senators, and the senators to hold back the ambassadors."(4)

Two issues particularly concerned the senators, and both were related to domestic implications of the treaty. The first was whether the treaty should deal with cultural, economic, and social cooperation as well as military security. Many senators opposed such an extension, and the Administration was reluctant to contest the matter. Acheson had just been through a "punishing experience" on the same subject in regard to the treaty resulting from the March 1948 Bogota Conference. This accord, which also established the defensive Organization of American States, announced a sweeping commitment to the right to education, health, welfare, and other such social concepts. Claiming that such a treaty pledge posed serious constitutional complications in federal-state relationships, numerous senators, led by Senators Walter George of Georgia and Tom Connally of Texas, forced the deletion of such agreements from the treaties founding both the OAS and NATO.

The second sticking-point with the senators was the question of "automatic involvement." This issue, which Acheson has described as the "most difficult" of the treaty, centered on the nature of America's response to an attack on the European signatories. The Europeans favored an unequivocal commitment to mutual military support in case of attack. The Administration was prone to agree. The Senate objected. Senators Vandenberg and Connally worried that unless the treaty's provisions recognized the constitutional power of Congress to declare war (or not to) the treaty would face difficulties in the Senate.(5) Also adding to the treaty's peril was administration concern that the early stages of negotiation would be interjected into the congressional and presidential campaigns of 1948.(6) The upshot of this controversy was a provision which declared that while an attack on one signatory was to be considered an attack on all, each nation would have to determine its response in accordance with its respective constitutional processes.

The "constitutional processes" language which Congress insisted on in the NATO Treaty proved to be more of a compromise of form than substance. Even during the negotiations/ratification process, State Department officials told the Europeans that while only Congress could declare war, the President as Commander-in-Chief could order military assistance required to meet United States commitments.(7) The introduction of a multi-division American force into Europe in the early 1950s and various later military actions connected with the OAS and the Southeast Asia Treaty Organization (SEATO) illustrate that the President was able to by-pass the language. In the case of NATO, the 1950 Administration decision to station four to six divisions in Europe and cooperate in a Joint European Command was easily moved through (or around) the Senate in the midst of the Korean Conflict. A resolution supporting the introduction of troops and a joint command, but expressing the sense of the Senate that not more than four divisions be sent without congressional approval, passed the Senate by a vote of 69 to 21. With American forces in Europe and certain to be engaged by any Soviet attack, the issue of automatic involvement became an academic point.

It may also be argued, however, that legislative dissent on automatic involvement signaled a continuing congressional stance against too close an integration of the United States and Europe on a military, economic, and social level. There is some evidence that Congress' posture throughout the post-World War II period both warned the Administration against over-ambition in Europe and helped convince Europeans that it would be unwise to rely too heavily on Washington. Specifically referring to NATO, Acheson has commented that European uncertainty about the American commitment "grew out of a particular American situation: . . . the division of powers, and what is the government of the United States and who speaks when what is called 'The United States' speaks."(8)

In addition to the automatic involvement clause, congressional suspicion of the European involvement was expressed in a number of other ways during the period. Resistance to economic and social cooperation envisioned in early treaty negotiations has already been mentioned. The question of NATO membership also came under congressional restriction. There was a question of including Italy among the original members, and initial Administration opposition was withdrawn only after determining that Connally and Vandenberg would not raise a fuss.(9) Congressional

pressure also resulted in a public acknowledgement by Acheson
that new members would be admitted to NATO only with the advice
and consent of the Senate.(10)

With the ink on the NATO treaty barely dry, heavy congressional opposition next arose to the extension of military aid to
Europe as contemplated (according to the Administration) in the
treaty. At first the President considered sending an aid request
to Congress even before the NATO Treaty ratification. Warnings
from the Hill that such a move would complicate the ratification
procedure persuaded Truman to delay.(11) When the $1,161,000,000
presidential request was sent to Congress on the day after ratification, the Administration battened down for the expected storm
of opposition.(12) Opposition to the Military Aid Program (MAP)
sprang from a number of sources. Conservatives objected to the
amount and its impact on the hope for a balanced budget. Isolationists found a new vehicle for opposing the extension of the
U.S. commitment. The "China bloc" sought to use the measure to
force a partial redirection of military aid to Korea. Acheson
also attributes resistance to "bitter resentment of the Republicans to the President's wholly unexpected victory in 1948."(13)
Interest in the House also seems to have partially resulted from
frustration at being shut out of the NATO Treaty process.(14)
More than any other single issue, however, there was the question
of presidential authority. As with the NATO Treaty itself, the
question of the constitutional position of the President and
Congress was the center of dispute. In part this was based on
policy implications, but it was also a "pure" matter of constitutional authority.

At issue was the latitude the bill would grant the president
to extend aid to new countries, to move money between categories,
and to take other discretionary measures. The provisions were,
Walter Lippmann wrote Vandenberg, a "shocking example of utter
disrespect for our constitutional traditions and for the very
process of law." Lippmann contended the measures smacked of
"sharp practice" and suggested that the Senator give the President a "stern lecture . . . on the need for a return to recognized standards of conduct in dealing with Congress . . . ."(15)
With such outside commentary adding to his own predilection to
defend congressional prerogative, Vandenberg roared to the
attack. Referring to the MAP measure as the "War Lord Bill," the
Senator led a revolt that included most of his Republican colleagues in both houses plus such influential Democrats as Harry
Byrd, Richard Russell, and Walter George in the Senate and James
Richards in the House.(16) Caught between the Senate's constitutional prerogative attack and House led moves to cut the amount,
which at one point reduced the appropriation to half, the Administration capitulated on the theoretical issue to get the money.
On September 22, 1949 the compromise bill easily passed the
Senate. The bill still faced potential trouble in the House, but
announcement of the Soviets' first atomic test on September 23
ensured passage in the alarmed lower chamber. "Once again,"
Acheson must have chuckled inwardly, "the Russians had come to
the aid of an imperiled nonpartisan foreign policy."(17)

The next round between Congress and the Administration over

the military commitment came in early 1951. The question was the authority of the President to station troops in Europe. In addition to international events, primarily the Korean War, which increased anxieties about communist intentions, considerations of European allied relations also argued for an additional United States commitment. The British were disquieted by the American refusal to admit Britain to participation on the use of atomic weapons. Prime Minister Clement Attlee visited Washington to press the issue. His purpose inevitably leaked, resulting in the introduction and vigorous debate by two dozen Republican senators of a resolution requiring Senate ratification of any agreement. The congressional mood was no surprise. In earlier conversations, Acheson had told the British that talks on British-American atomic cooperation were restricted by the McMahon Act, would get into the papers, and, in an election season, would cause trouble in Congress.(18) Again in Washington, Acheson reminded Attlee that the Republican resolution had given fair warning of the legislative mood and a reopening of the issue would occasion a vicious attack.(19)

France was also a consideration. The French were pressing for close cooperation, particularly in the event of German rearmament and participation in NATO. Although Congress favored European cooperation, that support stopped well short of American integration into the political, military, economic, and financial institutions supporting NATO as the French proposed. Acheson recalled that he "paled at the thought of bringing so vague, unexplored, and enormous an idea before the Congress."(20)

Thus, in part to reassure its allies, the Administration proposed to introduce American forces to Europe, the first permanent stationing of combat forces abroad in peace time. The move brought the expected outburst from Congress. As in previous rounds, isolationism and constitutionalism were significant objections. Senate Minority Leader Robert Taft called on Congress to assert its right to participate in the foreign policy-process. "No divisions should be committed to an international army until . . . approved by Congress," he argued.(21) Others agreed. Senator Karl Mundt worried about an international army commanded by a European general and the prospect of "American boys . . . being ordered into combat . . . by a foreign personality." He predicted "staggering" consequences if Congress "divests itself of the powers imposed on Congress by the Constitution."(22) Representative Frederick Coudert wrote to former President Hoover that "there should be an irresistible storm of demand from the 'grass roots' that Congress act to tie down the proposition that the President may not so use the armed forces as to incur the risk of war without full congressional action as a matter of right - not mere grace."(23) Coudert also wrote to Carl Vinson of the House Armed Service Committee, calling on the Chairman to "show up this hoax upon the public by demanding that the House take action to reassert the historic constitutional role of Congress."(24) The debate also had its partisan overtone. Indiana's Republican Senator William Jenner later reflected, "We should never have been able to elect a Republican administration . . . if it had not been for the Great Debate on troops for

Europe."(25)

Once again the Administration won the battle. A sense of the Senate resolution was introduced at bipartisan urging.(26) The resolution had, said Acheson, "a present for everyone."(27) It supported sending troops to Europe, but no more than four divisions without congressional approval. At first Truman even opposed that, but was persuaded by advisors that it allowed Congress to retain some semblance of its institutional pride.(28) The resolution passed easily 69–21.

As indicated, it is difficult to define precisely the toll these skirmishes had on European faith in the American commitment to Europe. It did raise doubts, however. General Marshall hastened to assure the Belgian Prime Minister not to worry about the restrictive resolution, it did not legally limit American support.(29) The resolution also did not reassure the nervous French who viewed American talk of congressional politics as "pure legal formalisms."(30) France was never sure of American intentions, and they eventually created their own independent nuclear force and withdrew from full membership in NATO. Certainly Congress was not the only source of these qualms, but just as certainly it added to the uncertainty. It was a pattern that did not cease in 1951.

Throughout the balance of the 1950's Congress did not mount any major assault on the basic issue of American participation in the defense of Europe, but constant pressure to cut the budget in both defense and military aid kept the sanctity of the United States commitment in doubt for European allies. In the election year of 1952, for example, President Truman's Military Security Appropriation Act was cut for Western Europe by 1.5 billion dollars and continued to decline after that. During the Eisenhower Administration, the defense doctrine of "massive retaliation" can also be partly attributed to budget pressure in Congress. As discussed above, Eisenhower had to mollify the conservative wing of his party which favored budget cutting and greater reliance on air power and which still harbored the strains of isolationism, by then converted to the nondiscredited term "unilateralism."(31) No less a keen observer than Dean Acheson attributed the budget problems and massive retaliation as a significant factor in French alienation from NATO, the development of the force de frappe, and the collapse of the proposed European Defense Community. Other congressional related factors also contributed to French estrangement. They were distressed by commentary in Congress about policy in North Africa(32) and by the role of Congress in blocking American support at the time of Dien Bien Phu.

In the 1960s and 1970s Congress continued to resist increased commitment to Europe and nuclear sharing and to press for a greater European contribution to their own defense. The proposed Multilateral Force (MLF) of the mid-1960s, which would have been comprised of nuclear armed, NATO controlled ships manned by international crews, fell afoul of Congress and exemplifies that body's continuing attitude. The concept of MLF was favored by important decision makers such as McGeorge Bundy, George Ball, and Walt Rostow, and the new President Lyndon Johnson was reasonably disposed to follow the lead of his supporting cast. An early and too optimistic State Department report on Congress found "a substantial degree of interest and some enthusiasm with no opposition" to the MLF idea.(33) The State Department estimate found Hubert Humphrey "very favorable." In fact, Humphrey was not. His close advisor, John Reilly cautioned him about speaking out, however. To do so, he advised Humphrey, would "infuriate some influential people including those who see the President regularly, if not daily," and would tell Johnson "every other day for the next month, 'why did that damn fool Humphrey . . . stir up trouble?'"(34)

Others, not interested in the Vice Presidency, were less reticent than Humphrey and expressed antagonism based on a variety of issues. Institutional pride was involved, with eight senators and forty representatives sending letters to Johnson warning against presenting Congress with a _fait_ _accompli_.(35) Presidential advisor Frederick Dutton also warned that "Congressional resistance to MLF has been sharply aggravated . . . by the feeling that the Hill should be consulted at a much higher level . . . ."(36) Senator Fulbright was reluctant based on concern over Vietnam, Agency for International Development funds, and having his "nose out of joint" by an imagined slight by the Administration. Bundy suggested that the President might want "to give Fulbright a coat of butter."(37) Opposition was also stirred by objections in the American Jewish Community to the prospects of Germany having even partial access to nuclear weapons.(38) More importantly, the administration's position was weakened by intra-executive dissent at home and allied reluctance abroad. Senior Defense Department and military officers were privately advising members of Congress that they were skeptical and others, such as Ambassador to India Chester Bowles, were also confidentially opposing the force.(39) European qualms did the most damage of all. After a trip to Europe, influential Representative Chet HoliSield, Vice Chairman of the Joint Committee on Atomic Energy, found that German participation "and the latent fears of its resurgent power is a matter of deep concern in Europe." The British Labour Party and many Tories were also opposed, according to Holifield, as were Italy and France. Even the Germans had said that they were only going along with the MLF because they thought the United States wanted them to and because they saw it as a "step toward sovereign custody and control of nuclear weapons." The overall impact, Holifield concluded, was that the MLF carried "the seed of division . . . that . . . will split NATO."(40) With Holifield and others such as Senate Majority Leader Mike Mansfield increasingly in opposition in late 1964 and early 1965 to the MLF publicly as well as privately, the President rethought his support.(41) Johnson was unwilling to engage in a protracted battle with Congress to gain support for nuclear sharing. Faced with the continuing pressure from Congress which felt that the United States was doing more than its share in NATO, the President concluded that he did not want to be "a Woodrow Wilson, right on principle and fighting for a principle, and unable to achieve it."(42) As with the EDC, the MLF was aborted, and the gap between ideal and real in the NATO military structure remained wide.

Congress was not satisfied just to limit the growth of the United States' NATO commitment. It soon moved to reduce the American troop contingent in Europe. Although there had been periodic calls for force reductions,(43) the move gained real strength in the late 1960s when Senate Majority Leader Mike Mansfield took up leadership of the drive. A number of resolutions sponsored or encouraged by Mansfield pressured the Johnson and Nixon Administrations to cut troops and also pressured European governments to increase their defense efforts. In 1967-1968 after Mansfield threatened legislative action, part of one Army division and a number of Air Force units, totalling nearly 60,000 personnel, were withdrawn from Europe.(44) Congress was motivated by a variety of factors, many of which dated to the original NATO commitment. Henry Kissinger argues that neo-isolationism was again made respectable by the Vietnam War. He characterized Mansfield as "reflecting the historical nostalgia that sought to maintain America's moral values uncontaminated by exposure to calculations of power and petty quarrels of shortsighted foreigners."(45) Kissinger's evaluation is almost certainly overdrawn, but there can be little doubt Vietnam inspired a retreat from internationalism, and the NATO troop reductions were a part of that withdrawal. Congress' long standing feelings that Europe was relying on the United States to make sacrifices while they concentrated on domestic development also contributed to the legislative mood. A significant related factor was the injection of domestic economic issues into the dispute. Concern about the gold outflow and the general drain of defense expenditures on the United States worried senators.(46) There were also a number of short term forces which added to the mood of Mansfield and his allies in the 1965-1975 decade. Vietnam not only exacerbated the feelings already noted, it created new concerns. Congress became increasingly concerned with its status, not with the specific focus on the automatic involvement clause of the NATO treaty, but in more general terms. Kissinger portrays Congress as spurred on by the "Liberal Establishment" which had abandoned its traditional adulation of a strong executive in favor of pressing on Congress "its obligation to control tightly an allegedly power-mad and war-obsessed Administration."(47) More precisely, Senator Charles Mathais noted during debate that the object of the Mansfield resolution was domestic, "a constitutional objective within the United States to restore to the Senate the powers . . . which the Senate had gradually delegated to the President."(48)

The most immediate impact of the series of resolutions was the troop reduction of 1967-1968. The Administration was concerned that extended debate would unfavorably affect scheduled Trilateral talks. There was also concern that the troop level question would serve to enhance a drive being led by Stuart Symington to cut the defense budget.(49) President Johnson was also worried that the issue would be interjected by the Republicans into the 1968 campaign. He was further swayed by the fact that many of the conservatives, such as Richard Russell, who were worried about the cost of the commitment were those whose support of his Vietnam policy he considered vital.(50) Finally, the

Administration's position was weakened by the fact that there was internal disunity. Secretary of the Treasury Henry Fowler quietly favored some reduction.(51) The result was presidential action withdrawing 60,000 troops in anticipation of and to forestall even stronger legislative dissent and action.

The drive continued through President Nixon's tenure. In September 1969 Defense Secretary Melvin Laird proposed, and later partially instituted, reducing naval force commitments to NATO by some 55 ships, lowering ready reserve commitments to Europe, and withdrawing elements of an Army infantry division. Laird's Byzantine strategy, as described by Kissinger, was to forestall pressure from the Budget Bureau and Congress to cut defense expenditures by making reductions as painful as possible and threatening others. In some ways Laird's maneuvers were successful. He was able to preserve most of his budget, and NATO allies were persuaded to form the "Eurogroup" to study programs to augment their contribution to NATO. But there were other less tangible drawbacks. Kissinger cites allied concern over the lack of consultation, renewed fears about the strength of the United States commitment, and encouragement of the Soviet Union as problems which, Kissinger predicted to Nixon, would lead to "the gradual 'neutralization' of Europe."(52)

Laird's reductions provided a hiatus of congressional pressure for only a year, however. In early May 1971 Mansfield introduced a draft law amendment that would cut United States forces in Europe by fifty percent, 150,000 troops. Kissinger described the Mansfield proposal as a "serious threat to our entire foreign policy," which Senate leaders on both side of the aisle predicted would pass. It would amount, Kissinger said, to "Vietnamizing Europe." Believing that it would be easier to defeat the drastic Mansfield amendment than a more palatable compromise, the Administration chose to go to the mats. A conference of old guard establishment luminaries, including Democrats such as Dean Acheson was convened and branded the Mansfield amendment "asinine." Lyndon Johnson concurred. The New York Times reacted with an editorial, "Senator Mansfield's Folly." West German Chancellor Willie Brandt said adoption would leave the "irradicable impression that the United States is on its way out of Europe," and NATO Secretary General Manlio Brosio warned the reduction would "withdraw all creditability" and destroy the alliance. Still, the issue remained in doubt. Senate generated compromises surfaced as members responded to institutional loyalty and tried to avoid inflicting "a clear cut defeat on a revered colleague."

Ironically, it was again the Soviets who saved the day. In a speech on May 15, 1971, Soviet party chief Leonid Brezhnev proposed mutual-reduction-of-force talks. Everyone seized on his remarks as reason not to reduce forces unilaterally and thus negate the quid pro quo. In a vote that Kissinger recalls "came none too soon for our sanity," the Mansfield Amendment was defeated handily.(53)

With NATO still in existence and Europe at peace, it is difficult to assess the impact of congressional attitudes and actions on European-American relations. There can be little doubt that

Congress has served to keep the United States commitment to
Europe limited both in terms of certainty of reaction and numerical strength. Those limits have not escaped European leaders
either. The statements of Brandt, Bosorio and others before
them, while partly staged to sway Congress, also reflect real
concerns. NATO has long been a troubled alliance, and Congress,
justifiably or not, has added to that distress. There is also
evidence that the Soviets have monitored congressional attitudes
toward NATO with great interest,(54) and that, among other
things, these interests in mutual troop reduction have been
cooled in the hope that Congress might legislate what they would
have to negotiate.(55)


## Congress and Asia

The role which Congress has played in the formulation of
policy toward Asia has been more significant than its European
role. Europe is arguably more vital to the immediate interests
of the United States, but Asia has been more volatile. It has
been the scene of two American wars, in Korea and Vietnam, major
nationalist and ideological movements, and the economic resurrec-
tion of Japan. Asia has also been the focus of shifts in American foreign policy which mirror the evolution of the cold war.
Policy toward China has, in turn, been a microcosm of the
policy orientation toward Asia and the world. Congress effectively utilized its formal, as well as informal, powers throughout
the 1950s to influence policy, primarily to the end of inhibiting
any thought of normalizing relations with the People's Republic
of China--or Red China, to better capture the mood of the day.
Policy toward China during Truman's first term has been discussed
above. Suffice it to recapitulate that Washington received Generalissimo Chiang Kai-Shek and the Kuomintang Nationalists with
shrinking sympathy. As a special envoy, George Marshall attempted to promote a coalition government with the Communists.
Republican pressure from Congress continually frustrated administration attempts to assume a neutral position. Partisan politics
and rabid anti-communism brought even that pillar of bipartisanship, Arthur Vandenberg, to the attack. Using the Administration's European program as hostage, the congressional G.O.P.
contingent was able to force continued aid to the Nationalists.
The result of such policies, according to Acheson, was to negate
the admittedly slim prospects of a negotiated settlement of the
civil war. "Die-hard Kuomintang members . . . [urged] the Generalissimo to renew the war against the Communists, since American
help would be forthcoming . . . . The Communists, reaching the
same conclusion, used the proposed legislation as proof that concessions . . . were useless."(56)
That pattern persisted during the pivotal last throes of
Chiang's mainland regime and the consolidation of communist
control. By early 1949 the collapse of Chiang had changed from
probable to imminently inevitable. To avoid continuing China's
agony, the fall of more equipment to Mao's armies, and aggravat-
ing the already hostile victors, the Administration sought ways

to embargo the flow of arms procured under the China Aid Act (1948). Acheson claims that before China became an electoral issue, the Senate Foreign Relations Committee, including Republicans Henry Cabot Lodge, Jr., and Bourke Hickenhooper, "expressly considered and expressly rejected" increased military aid to Chiang.(57) But by 1949 the Republican mood had changed. Acheson's attitude was clearly that Chiang was a disaster, that support should end, and that the United States should adopt a wait-and-see attitude toward the rapidly approaching communist ascendency.(58) The National Security Council recommended to the President that aid be suspended. Consultations with congressional leaders, however, brought unanimous opposition to the NSC's recommendation. In response, Truman temporized. He ordered that aid formally continue, but also that it be delayed where informally possible.(59) Acheson has recalled that he was left with the "unenviable authority" to coordinate interpretation of that instruction.(60)

Administration ambivalence did not extend to Congress. Senator Pat McCarran of Nevada introduced a 1.5 billion dollar aid bill for China which was supported by 50 senators, half of them Democrats. Fifty-one Republican congressmen also asked for a presidential commission on China. Trying to head off the move, Acheson suggested waiting "until the dust settles." It was an unfortunate phrase which haunted Acheson for the balance of his tenure. As he explained, "any stick is good enough to beat a dog, but this was an example of my unhappy ability--if I may mix a metaphor--to coin a stick."(61)

With the movement of the Nationalist capital to Formosa on December 8, 1949, the communist victory was ratified. Two principle and related questions faced the United States. What would relations be with Chiang? What would relations be with Mao? Both the State Department and the Joint Chiefs of Staff agreed that Formosa would probably fall to Mao in 1950. Evidence abounds that the Administration was willing to adopt a cautious, perhaps even conciliatory, attitude toward the mainland's new masters. In private discussions with congressional leaders, Acheson argued that the defense of Formosa was not vital to American interest, the Chinese Communists were not irretrievably dominated by the Soviets, and that it was possible to foster nationalistic independence for Peking.(62) Acheson also outlined the alternatives to Truman. One was "to oppose the Communists' regime, harass it, needle it, and if the opportunity appeared, attempt to overthrow it." The other alternative, which Acheson favored, was "to attempt to detach it from subservience to Moscow and over a period of time encourage those vigorous influences which might modify it." Truman cautiously concurred.(63) Acheson made the same points publicly in an address before the National Press Club on January 12, 1950. Also publicly, Truman announced on January 5, "The United States Government will not provide military aid or advice to Chinese forces on Formosa" and "will not pursue a course which will lead to an involvement in the civil conflict in China." Clearly, the Administration both expected and was willing to accept the fall of Formosa and was at least contemplating the establishment of some form of <u>modus</u>

vivendi with the communist government of a reunited China.

Whatever the course of policy might have been, it did not develop in a vacuum. Events, in which Congress played an important role, soon foreclosed moderate options. The Administration had worked to engender bipartisan support of its policy,(64) and there is some evidence that at least in private some Republicans were not violent in their opposition.(65) Bipartisanship was not to be however. Vandenberg was dying and his influence was lost. Republicans were pressing the Administration to dispatch an Ambassador to Taipei, to aid Chiang, and even to consider using American forces to occupy Formosa and defend other outlying Nationalist held islands.(66) Acheson's National Press Club speech set off a torrent of criticism in Congress which Acheson describes in his chapter, "The Attack of the Primitives Begins."(67) Senator Taft charged that the State Department was being "guided by a left-wing group who obviously had wanted to get rid of Chiang and were willing to turn China over to the Communists for the purpose." Senator Styles Bridges demanded a vote of censure against the Administration, and William Knowland called for Acheson's resignation.(68)

Congress also acted to force aid to Chiang. The vehicle the Republicans chose was a Korean aid measure. In June 1949 President Truman had requested Congress to authorize $150 million in economic aid for Korea. Hearings were quickly begun in the House where Foreign Affairs Committee Republicans were highly critical. Representatives John Vorys, Walter Judd, and others branded the measure a cover up which would not save Korea. They insisted that without accompanying military aid the $150 million would be wasted and the progress of the bill bogged down in acrimony. The problem, as Acheson characterized it in a dispirited letter to Ambassador David Bruce, was that "the all-or-nothing boys refuse to do what is possible in Korea, because we will not attempt what is impossible in Korea."(69) With unfortunate mistiming the bill was brought to a vote in the House on January 19, 1950, seven days after Acheson's National Press Club speech and amid the tremendous turmoil that followed that address. House Republicans chose to risk losing Korea in order to save Formosa. Joined by Southern Democrats they defeated H.R. 5330 by one vote, 192 to 191. The Administration was shocked by its loss. "This has been a tough day," Acheson wrote his daughter. He described the defeat as a "bitter and unexpected blow."(70) It was a risky move by the House Republicans which even perturbed their Senate colleagues. Vandenberg, temporarily back at the Senate, described the defeat as shocking. The move was undeniably successful, however, in terms of House G.O.P. goals. The Administration was forced to give way. A new bill retitled the "Far Eastern Economic Assistance Act of 1950" was quickly introduced. The primary change was to extend assistance to the non-communist areas of China, namely Formosa. Acheson also agreed to include 75 million dollars in Chinese military aid in the then pending general foreign aid bill.(71)

Two results, one sure, one speculative, can be attributed to the skirmishing over Korean aid. The first, indisputable outcome was that despite the public and private pronouncements of the

President and Secretary of State, Nationalist China continued to receive aid. Whatever the chances for accommodation between Washington and Peking might have been, they were rapidly fading. Any such move would have sparked not just dissent, but charges of treason in the United States. Peking was also surely aware that the United States would continue to support its domestic enemies despite Truman's protestations to the contrary. Less certainly, Acheson suggests the aid maneuvering may have led to the Korean War. In turn, Acheson has been similarly accused. His National Press Club speech drew a defense perimeter which excluded Korea, leading some to argue that it signalled a green light for invasion to North Korea and its supporters to the north. As an alternative, Acheson responded that if the communists were indeed watching the United States for signals of its intentions, they would have been more impressed with the defeat of the aid package and other arguably isolationist congressional actions.(72)

Beyond the din of criticism coming from Congress, backed up by that body's appropriations power, legislators were also influential in stirring domestic forces to oppose the "fellow traveler" tendencies within the Truman Administration. One was the Committee of One Million. This organization, in part organized and later headed by Representative Walter Judd, a former missionary in China, was dedicated to preventing mainland China's admission to the United Nations. Also by extension it acted as a lobby for the Nationalist Chinese cause.(73) Initially it included two dozen senators and nearly one hundred representatives. It quickly became such a thorn in the side of the Administration that Truman wanted an investigation of the organization "from hell to breakfast."(74) The hope was that, among other things, the investigation "would be highly embarrassing to a sizable group of Republicans in and out of Congress, and that it would reveal interesting information on the financial backers of Senator McCarthy, Senator Knowland, and a number of others."(75) Yet, despite the intense interest of the White House, the investigation never materialized. The State Department resisted the move, fearing it would be difficult to find a committee in Congress that could overcome "senatorial courtesy," and also because Acheson was unsure of the outcome of such an investigation.(76) Among other factors, this was the time of General of the Army Douglas MacArthur's relief and the subsequent congressional investigation, loss of support for the United Nations, and increasing attacks by Joseph McCarthy, all of which, according to Acheson, "increased [the] energy spent on unwise proposals . . . [which] added to our difficulties and by doing so diminished our effectiveness."(77) Thus, the Committee's effectiveness continued unchallenged. Its campaign and effect on Congress was clearly demonstrated by the inclusion of anti-Chinese communist statements in the 1956, 1960, and 1964 national platforms of both the Republican and Democratic parties. By 1966, a total of 334 members of Congress were on the roles of the Committee of One Million. As will be discussed below, the organization retained a powerful influence over American policy toward China until, ironically, its crusade was defeated by its early supporter, Richard Nixon.(78)

A second congressionally inspired, domestically oriented force originating at the turn of the decade was McCarthyism. In a malevolent way, the hearings conducted by Senator Joseph McCarthy to explore possible communist influence in the State Department and other segments of American official and private life may have been the most effective use of Congress' investigatory power in history. Its impact was felt for decades, both directly and through its progeny such as the House Un-American Affairs Committee (HUAC). Although McCarthy was eventually censured by the Senate and rejected by the public, his tactics virtually destroyed the State Department's expertise on mainland China and inhibited normalization of relations for two decades. While details will be provided below in the discussion of Congress' impact on foreign policy personnel, the point here is that more than twenty foreign service officers, representing nearly all the Department's "China hands," were fired, forced to resign, or transferred to posts in less "sensitive" areas.

McCarthy's attacks devastated the Truman Administration. Acheson characterized their intensity and impact on tate Department personnel as a "mad massacre . . . [a] night of the long knives from 1950 through 1953." He described its impact on the public as "toxic . . . like air pollution, one did not have to believe in it to be poisoned by it."(79) A subcommittee chaired by Senator Millard Tydings to investigate McCarthy's accusations found them groundless and serving only to "inflame the American people with a wave of hysteria and fear of an unbelievable scale in this free nation."(80) Even many Republicans dissented. Senator Margaret Chase Smith criticized her own party for allowing the Senate to be "debased to a level of a forum of hate and character assassination sheltered by the shield of congressional immunity." She saw four apocalyptic raiders loose in America, ". . . four horsemen of Calumny--fear, ignorance, bigotry, and smear."(81)

Such rebukes did little to halt McCarthy. Beset by the cold war, Korea, China's loss, and a host of other seemingly malevolently inspired travails, the public was ready to believe McCarthy's attacks. If anything, McCarthy's influence increased with the election of the Republican Administration in 1952. Vice Presidential candidate Richard Nixon focused on communist conspiracy charges as the main campaign theme. Eisenhower also deferred to the supposed impact of McCarthy. During the campaign he declined to defend his long time associate George Marshall who had been defamed by McCarthy. Once in office, Eisenhower continued to show reluctance to challenge the Wisconsin senator whose position was elevated by the new majority status of Republicans in Congress. Secretary of State Dulles also buckled before the attack on the State Department. Given his sensitivity to Congress and his horror of the calumny heaped on his predecessor Acheson, Dulles did little to defend his official charge. One observer has accused Dulles of creating an "atmosphere in the Department that amounted to . . . appeasement . . . of McCarthy's attacks on the Department."(82) Even as sympathetic a source as Dulles' sister (and diplomat), Eleanor Lansing Dulles, has recalled her brother refusing to defend a subordinate. "This would be an almost impossible thing for me to do," she quoted him. "I'm under fire, the administration is under fire, and I've got to handle this thing with great care."(83) Even pleas from within the Department fell on largely deaf ears. Early in 1954 Deputy Under Secretary of State Robert Murphy wrote to Dulles characterizing the Department's state of affairs. He described morale as "shaken and disturbed," with uneasiness based on "fear and uncertainty" stemming from the fact that "officers are not assured the understanding support in political matters" by the upper echelons of the Department.(84) The unstated plea in the letter was for Dulles to come to the Department's defense. He did not.

The impact of McCarthy's vendetta continued long after the Senator's censure and disgrace in 1954 and his death soon thereafter. As Francis Wilcox explained in 1971:

> Americans who are now in the upper ranks of the Foreign Service were junior officers during the McCarthy era . . ., and they still bear the marks of that traumatic experience. Some of them tend to grossly mis-estimate political forces in this country and particularly the influence in Congress of the elements with foreign interests . . . . They tend to be influenced by those voices on Capitol Hill which are the loudest instead of those which are the most powerful or sensible.(85)

Executive Branch concern over congressional investigations can be seen throughout the postwar period. While it is unlikely that a determined administration will be deterred by the threat of an investigation, there is no doubt that the power to probe can affect policy. Illustrated by the McCarthy hearings, which most people eventually rejected, and the Vietnam hearings, which most people eventually supported, investigations can both provide information and arouse Congress and the public. A testimonial to the importance of congressional query is the reluctant amount of time executive officials give to appearances before committees. Dean Acheson, for one, quoted Woodrow Wilson's comment that while Congress often cannot fathom what it sees, "the special, irksome, ungracious investigations which it from time to time institutes . . . can violently disturb . . . the waters of the sea in which bigger fish of the civil service swim and feed. Its dragnet stirs without cleansing the bottom."(86) All in all, Acheson estimated that he spent one-sixth of this time meeting with 214 congressional groups during his four years as Secretary.(87)

The warily respectful attention that John Foster Dulles rendered to Congress has already been documented. President Eisenhower recalled that Dulles was "constantly" and "explosively" irritated by committee hearings.(88) At one point, Dulles railed, "I spend at least one-fourth of my time testifying before Congressional committees, and the galling thing is that much of the time there is wasted at the very moment I have so many other things to do."(89) At a later juncture (1958), Dulles poignantly complained, for he was only months from his cancer-caused death, "You know, I have testified [many times] up on the Hill during this session of Congress, and I'm supposed to run the State Department in the meantime . . . . If I weren't a strong man, I wouldn't be able to do it."(90) Indeed, the constant summonses by Congress of the Departments of State, Defense, and others, became such a concern that the problem was discussed by the Cabinet. It was wisely decided that developing closer personal relations with, rather than resisting, Congress was the best tack.(91)

Dean Rusk similarly spent twenty percent of his time on the Hill and invested countless other hours in mock hearings prior to testimony. During one of his myriad appearances, Rusk discreetly labeled committee hearings as "beneficial," but did admit that the schedule of appearances was "a bit strenuous at times."(92)

Even when investigations have been conducted behind closed doors, they carry the potential of upsetting administration policy. The problem is the ever-present leak. In his study of Congress and foreign policy, John Lehmann has focused on the results of leaks from just one investigation, that of the Senate Foreign Relations Committee's Subcommittee on United States Security Agreements and Commitments Abroad (understandably, the "Symington Committee") established in February 1969. Numerous leaks of classified information from that subcommittee distressed America's Asian allies. Intimations of corruption led the Philippines to withdraw a battalion from Vietnam. Four years later a former Ambassador to Manila said relations had still not recovered. Disclosure that the United States had paid Thailand one billion dollars to send troops to Vietnam left the Thai prime minister convinced that the Americans were on the "verge of a mental breakdown," that it could no longer be relied on as an ally, and that U.S.-Thai relations must evolve toward a more "selective basis."(93)

Congress was also aware of the leaks. In the case of the Symington Committee, staff members blamed the leaks on executive officials and confirmed, "The premature release of [information] can only hurt the Subcommittee and perhaps do real damage to the national security."(94) Whether or not in this particular case the subcommittee was the source of the leak, Congress is certainly part of the sieve that for good or ill feeds the media. As Hubert Humphrey put it, "When you go before too many members of Congress with anything that is highly sensitive you might just as well put it right out in the New York Times. And that's a fact!"(95)

Returning to the mainstream of Asia policy, Congress continued to exert heavy influence throughout the 1950s. The Korean War, particularly the Chinese intervention, served to confirm the right's suspicions and to drive any thought of moderation beyond the pale. The decision-making process that occurred during the first few weeks of Korea is not important in terms of Congress' impact on policy. It does, however, illustrate many of the causes and effects of the Executive's and Congress' mutual perceptions and the nonsalutary impact of the jealous protection of the separation of powers.

Once it was determined that North Korea had launched a full scale attack against its southern scion, Truman and his advisors moved quickly and decisively to interject American arms. The role of Congress was minimal, and therein lay the problem.(96) From the Administration's point of view, Congress was consulted. Legislative leaders met with Truman on June 27, two days after the invasion. An even larger bipartisan group was consulted on June 20. According to Acheson, and there is nothing to refute his account, the President received virtual unanimous support. Senator Connally advised the President not to seek a declaration of war.(97) Only Senator Kenneth Wherry questioned the authority of the President to take action unilaterally. Senator H. Alexander Smith did not object, but suggested a congressional resolution to support action already taken.

Despite this private acquiescence, opposition to the intervention quickly arose in the Senate in the person of Robert Taft. It was not the action per se to which he objected. Indeed, Taft said on July 28, he would have voted to approve a resolution supporting the move. The problem was that the President had done the right thing the wrong way. Truman's unilateral action was unconstitutional. That charge was picked up by Wherry and others and became the basis for dumping the responsibility for what was to become the very unpopular "Truman's War" squarely on the President. Within weeks the Republicans were at work on a white paper designed to lay responsibility for losing China and perhaps Korea at the Democrats' door. The political exposé also painted a picture of resolute Republicans opposing defeatist policies in Asia and established a "reference book" for the Fall 1950 congressional campaign.(98)

Acheson dismissed Taft's position with his usual hauteur in his 1969 memoirs as legalistic quibbling. In terms of domestic tranquility, it was an unwise position then as it is now. It is also interesting to note that soon after leaving office Acheson was less assured. In a July 1953 interview Acheson admitted he had not given "adequate attention to Senator Smith's suggestion of a congressional resolution. "I think it would have been a good thing if we had done it," Acheson admitted.(99) Perhaps the wounds were fresher in 1953 than in 1969.

Actually it appears that Smith's suggestion was given full consideration. At a White House meeting late in the afternoon of July 3, 1950, the main topic of discussion was the wisdom of seeking a supportive congressional resolution. Both in his memoirs and in his 1953 interview, Acheson takes the position that he opposed going to Congress. As he explained in his earlier recollection it would have been "very dangerous to guild a lily . . . everybody was in enthusiastic support of what we were doing and if you try putting it in words, you might get into some trouble, get yourself tangled up . . . might better leave it alone."(100) The record of that meeting differs with Acheson's recollection. The Secretary opened the meeting by presenting the recommendation of the State Department that the President go before a joint session of Congress to report on the Korean situation.(101) That would be followed by a congressionally "initiated" resolution he had helpfully drafted for Congress. Several State Department officials supported the idea. Averell Harriman, newly returned from Europe, commented on Atlantic alliance reaction and stressed the need for a close relation between the President and Congress. "While things are going well now," he accurately cautioned, "there may be trouble ahead." Assistant Secretary of State for Far Eastern Affairs Dean Rusk also argued that congressional support would help abroad. The attacks of Taft and Wherry might raise questions of American solidarity. Secretary of the Army Frank Pace felt something should be done to assuage Congress' strong desire for participation. Almost everyone else disagreed with the State Department. Senate Majority Leader Scott Lucas said the President had acted properly without consulting Congress and many of the members were "sick" of the Taft-Wherry position. He added that to go to Congress might sound as if the President were asking for a declaration of war. Further, many members had suggested that the President keep away from Congress and avoid debate. A row in Congress would not be helpful abroad. Finally, he erroneously predicted, "Congress would not stir things up." Others joined in to support Lucas. Postmaster General Jesse Donaldson contended that once he went to Congress, the President would be called back again and again to answer more questions. Chairman of the Joint Chiefs of Staff Omar Bradley expressed concern over protracted debate, and Secretary of Defense Louis Johnson worried about everyone in Congress posing as a constitutional expert. Truman, while making no final decision, tended to agree with Lucas. He made the interesting distinction that he had taken action as Commander-in-Chief, not as President, and that while he did not want to appear to be getting around Congress, he had talked to the leaders. Although the option remained open, the idea quickly faded, and the domestic cold war over Asia continued.

In the latter days of the Truman Administration and the early days of the Eisenhower Administration the pro-Chiang element in Congress, which became know as the "China Lobby," kept up pressure on a number of fronts. One of these involved the Japanese Peace Treaty. Given Republican criticism of Far East policy, the Truman Administration moved cautiously toward a treaty. As will be discussed in fuller detail at a later point, an initial step was the appointment of Republican John Foster Dulles as the chief American negotiator. Dulles' charge was to not only negotiate with the international parties but to also win Senate cooperation. In discussions with that body, two concerns arose. One was that adherence to any Pacific defense treaty had to be left somewhat vague. Congress' right to decide on war must be preserved.(102) The other, more important, issue was the future relationship between Japan and the two Chinas. The short of the matter was that the Senate was opposed to Japanese recognition of Peking.(103) To ensure adherence to the Senate's wishes, Republican H. Alexander Smith and Democrat John Sparkman were attached to the American delegation. A complication was that Japan had to deal with other powers, particularly the British who had already recognized China and preferred to see Tokyo follow suit. Also Japanese Prime Minister Shigeru Yoshida had little enthusiasm for following the unrealistic American attitude. The result was that Yoshida adopted an attitude of ambiguity. This ploy was encouraged by Acheson, apparently with at least the passive support of

Dulles. At a September 1951 meeting between Acheson and Yoshida, the Secretary suggested that the Japanese take the position that the China issue was "under study and that no decision has yet been reached, but that it is hoped to arrive at some conclusion after the treaty had been signed."(104) If Dulles had any objections, they went either unvoiced or unrecorded. The Japanese, British, and American governments may have agreed that the question of recognition was a matter of Japan's sovereignty, but the Senate did not. In mid-September, 56 senators wrote Truman a warning that they would consider formal Sino-Japanese ties "adverse to the best interests" of the United States.(105) In December Senators Smith and Sparkman traveled with Dulles to Tokyo to press the Senate's view on the Japanese government. It was an unequal contest. The Senate won. On December 24, Prime Minister Yoshida issued a letter agreeing to recognize Nationalist China and expressing "no intention to conclude a bilateral treaty with the Communist regime of China."(106)

Another convenient target for the China Lobby's anti-Communist China campaign was the United Nations. To the China Lobby the thought of Peking entering the world body was almost as heretical as the idea of American recognition. China's entry (and Formosa's expulsion or demotion from permanent Security Council status) was favored by many countries, including Britain, and the American Administration could have made the decision to acquiesce to that development without reference to Congress. Such a course, however, would have risked retaliation on the U.N. Conservative elements of Congress were already suspicious of the United Nations. They had blocked mandatory acceptance of International Court of Justice jurisdiction in 1947. As part of the McCarthyistic binge, the loyalty of Americans working for the U.N. had been questioned. There were congressional hearings, resort to Fifth Amendment rights by the "accused," and a generally unfortunate spate of publicity which resulted, according to Acheson, in "a highly unfavorable opinion of the United Nations in the United States and the United States in the United Nations."(107)

Unable to directly control China's status in the United Nations, Congress employed its appropriation power to threaten to cut off all United States financial support if Peking was seated. In May 1953 the Senate Appropriations Committee initiated threatened retaliation by attaching an amendment to a foreign aid bill directing the termination of financial support if China was admitted to the United Nations. It took President Eisenhower's personal intervention to head off the move. It would, Eisenhower told Republican congressional leaders, wreck the United Nations and seriously hamper his ability to conduct foreign policy. More ominously, he added, destruction of the United Nations would result in a break-up of NATO and threaten American security. In exchange for withdrawal of the binding amendment, Eisenhower agreed to a sense-of-Congress resolution and to communicating Congress' views to other governments.(108) Eisenhower instructed Dulles to transmit the warnings, and the indications are that Dulles warned foreign leaders of Congress' reaction.(109) Eisenhower's victory did not end the war. Congressional pressure persisted. In a 1957 meeting with British Prime Minister Macmillan, Eisenhower and Dulles rejected any thought of Chinese admission to the United Nations, citing congressional sentiment and arguing the entry of China might lead to the withdrawal of the United States from membership.(110)

Congressional concern over United States-United Nations-China relations also surfaced in a number of other guises. Conservative disquietude over peace talks in Korea were partly based on the suspicion that a package deal to end the war would include China's membership.(111) Attacks on United Nations personnel policies also continued with the added threat of a funding cut off. Senator William Jenner, for instance, had written to Ambassador Henry Cabot Lodge that Congress might reconsider American ties with and contributions to "an agency whose staff includes secret collaborators with the Soviet attack on free nations." (112) Such threats were taken seriously by the Administration. (113) Congress also demanded anti-Chinese statements from Dulles in return for passage of the general foreign aid budget.(114)

This accounting of Congress' opposition to dealing with mainland China does not imply that in the absence of Congress the United States would have embraced Mao Tse-tung's government with open arms. Certainly that would not have been the case. It is difficult to escape the conclusion, however, that things would have been different. The gulf might not have been so wide; the road to reconciliation might have been shorter. The early moderation of Truman and Acheson toward China and the subsequent impact of congressional assaults has been detailed. Something of the same picture emerges with Eisenhower and Dulles. Even against the background of China's intervention in Korea, the new President and Secretary of State seemed inclined to adopt at least limited flexibility in dealing with China. External factors, of which Congress was one, conspired to preclude that option. There is some fairly clear evidence that Dulles was not quite the consummate cold warrior he has often been pictured. In a 1939 book, War, Peace, and Change, Dulles had argued against the futility of not recognizing existing governments. More pointedly, his 1950 War or Peace recommended recognition of China once Mao's government overcame serious domestic opposition.(115) He was not opposed to Japan recognizing Peking. Dulles' aides have also recalled that he mentioned on numerous occasions that eventually the United States would have to deal with China.(116) Eisenhower's attitude is less clear, but he did oppose retaliation against the United Nations if China were admitted and at one point termed following the Wilsonian policy of implying approval through recognition as "unfortunate."(117)

There is also evidence that there was some consideration of a reorientation of policy toward China during the 1955-57 period. In discussions with Prime Minister Macmillan, Dulles noted that public opinion favored remaining in the United Nations even after China's admission. Henry Cabot Lodge wrote the President that if any policy change was in the offing it should be postponed until after the election. Eisenhower termed the suggestion "shrewd." (118) An internal discussion paper written by an outside observer and passed to presidential assistant Bryce Harlow suggested that "the vital interests of the U.S. are not served by the pro-longed non-recognition of Communist China" and predicted both admission to the United Nations and recognition by the United States of China.(119) Assistant Secretary of State and China hard-liner Walter Robertson also worried to Dulles that "off-the-cuff statements by the President in his press statements have also been interpreted to indicate a pending shift in policy." Robertson also worried that certain language in the Secretary's speech that he was reviewing "would be disturbing . . . for the implication that we may already have in mind broadening our nego-tiations with the Chinese."(120) How disturbing those remarks were was a matter of perspective. Some of Dulles' staff did not feel the address went far enough and urged the Secretary to be more forthcoming. Andrew Berding wrote Dulles that the draft "gives an impression of rigidity of policy toward Communist China." By contrast Berding pointed to some language toward the end of the speech which gave "some indication to the contrary," and suggested, "I would like to see several pages in this direc-tion."(121) Clearly, the Administration was going through a period of questioning its China policy. Perhaps there was no fire, but there was surely smoke. There were also those within the Administration to which anti-communism was virtually a relig-ion and their position was enhanced by their support in Congress. Chief among these was Assistant Secretary of State for Far Eastern Affairs Walter Robertson. Illustrative of Robertson's rather basic approach to the eastern evil was his reaction to reports of growing Chinese steel production. It had to be wrong: "No regime as malevolent as the Chinese Communists could ever produce five million tons of steel."(122) Robertson had been suggested for his position by Walter Judd and served as a watch-dog on the purity of the Administration's anti-mainland policy. (123) In that capacity Robertson was both a shield and a burden. His position helped protect the Department from criticism from the China Lobby, but it also meant that the Secretary could not stray too far. Aides recall that while Dulles respected Robert-son, "Walter annoyed him terribly occasionally." Dulles "felt that we were getting nailed [to the China Lobby position], and he didn't like getting nailed."(124) The bottom line is that Dulles was ambiguous in his own mind, "fishing," according to Rod O'Conner. In the face of his own uncertainty, and concerned by congressional grumblings from both the liberals and conservatives about his stewardship at State, Dulles was unwilling to move to an exposed position. When asked if Dulles considered his Assis-tant Secretary too much in the China Lobby camp, O'Connor observed

Yes, I think so. I think he felt Robertson's position was absolutely firm . . . . He . . . defended the flank in Con-gress, which in those days, to the administration, was very important. You remember that Knowland was really shooting us out of the sky . . . . And so I think he felt, until he could find something better that he was sure of, that that was a good situation.(125)

Even among liberal Democrats, the China question was considered too hot to handle. Hubert Humphrey commented that the "tragic" part of China policy was that it had become involved in domestic politics. "The political division in the Republican party over our China policy . . . compels the Administration to make concessions to the Knowland wing of the party even at the expense of a sensible and practical foreign policy."(126)  Yet, under the electoral pressure, even a Humphrey was unwilling to take the plunge for recognition. Running for the Democratic presidential nomination in 1960 he stressed his opposition to Red China. "Remember I am under the political gun," he told his staff and ordered conservative material distributed "just in case any of the right wingers . . . get to working me over on the communist issue."(127)  There was also interest in the Foreign Relations Committee, particularly amid the administration's mixed signals in 1957. Carl Marcy, Committee Chief of Staff, advocated a comprehensive review of Far Eastern, particularly China, policy. Fulbright suggested "quiet executive sessions." Robertson would be called because of protocol, even if he was "rabid" on China, but afterwards the Committee could call "anyone we like." (128)  The hearings were held, but were inconclusive. Fulbright and a few others made tentative public statements, but were careful, as Marcy warned Fulbright, "not to get too far out in front on this issue."(129)  Thus, the decade ended much as it had begun. A policy of no admission and no recognition for China truculently guarded by the congressionally based China Lobby.

China policy through the Kennedy and Johnson Administrations remained essentially unchanged. Kennedy had given some indication of favoring a change in policy in the mid-1950s, and there were a few of his advisors who also advocated revision. Undersecretary Chester Bowles was the most outspoken. Mixing advice on domestic and international politics, Bowles urged President Kennedy to reduce commitments to the Nationalists as an opening gambit to improving relations with the mainland. "I understand and respect your desire to avoid a political Donnybrook in regard to China policy with the congressional elections only five months away . . . ," Bowles wrote in 1962. Nevertheless, support of Chiang, who was looking to increase operations against the coast, involved "grave political risks at home" and abroad. Bowles called for a bold presidential initiative. "Once we have broken the unwritten rule that it is impossible to change a bankrupt China policy we have inherited from our predecessors" the Undersecretary predicted, flexibility would be possible."(130)  Bowles was a lonely prophet, and already suspect in Congress for his views on China.(131)

Repeatedly, Congress short-circuited any attempt to deal with China. In 1961, faced with increasing pressure from the newly admitted Afro-Asian bloc in the United Nations, the Kennedy Administration attempted to opt for a year's study by a special United Nations committee on the question of seating China and enlarging the Security Council to accommodate a two-China policy. The decision immediately encountered intense opposition from the Committee of One Million and its supporters in Congress. Despite Administration attempts to block it, the Senate passed a dissenting resolution in July, and the House followed suit in September by a vote of 395 to 0.(132)

The strength and effectiveness of congressional opposition to any diplomatic move which even tangentially approached relations with China is also aptly illustrated by the defeat of an administration move to recognize Outer Mongolia in 1961. Originally encouraged by Under Secretary of State Chester Bowles and tacitly supported by the President, a State Department announcement in June that it would hold discussions with Mongolia provoked a storm of criticism. Members of Congress feared that recognition of Mongolia would be a mere preliminary to establishing relations with Peking, and dismissed State Department arguments that representation in Ulan Baton would be valuable as a listening post near Communist China. Senator Styles Bridges proclaimed his belief that the only thing such a listening post would hear was "the bleating of sheep, the whinnying of vast herds of wild Mongolian ponies, the lowing of cattle, and whatever musical notes yaks may emit." Perhaps encouraged by those in the Administration, such as Dean Rusk, who did not support the move, Congress mounted an overwhelming attack on the proposed policy and threatened to destroy the Administration's foreign aid program if it persisted. Within a few weeks the campaign was over; the Administration beat a hasty retreat, and the question of relations with Mongolia was again relegated to the depths of Foggy Bottom.(133)

Bowles' daring on the China question was not generally shared within the Administration. George McGhee, head of the State Department's Policy Planning office, directed his staff to refrain from fielding any new ideas on improving relations with mainland China. Specifically referring to the McCarthy hearings, McGhee told his staff that the subject of Red China was sacrosanct; he had never been investigated by Congress, and he did not want to undergo the ordeal of his predecessors.(134)

During the Johnson years the opposition to China began to slowly moderate. The Sino-Soviet split became more obvious. Senators such as Robert Kennedy, Jacob Javits, and William Fulbright went public. Fulbright held nationally televised hearings on the issue in March 1966. Yet the conservatives, which Johnson feared, were still strong and reevaluation in the face of Vietnam was impossible.(135)

McGeorge Bundy has explained that Johnson was "flexible" on the issue and even "inclined to take a flyer now and then." But in the face of Congress those "fliers" never got far. Bundy recalls that Rusk "was _very_ careful" on the issue. Whenever any minor move was made it "would just not be backed" in Congress, "It would come back with static levels on the Hill." Nobody, said Bundy, was willing to tell the President "Damn the torpedoes! Go Ahead! . . . Congressional reaction was always . . . [assumed] to be high, you couldn't do it."(136)

The fact that the beginning of rationalizing policy toward China came during the Nixon presidency is one of those exquisite turns of history that contributed to the axiom about politics and bedfellows becoming so tritely true. Richard Nixon and Henry Kissinger take, as they are due, a great deal of credit for the

China opening. But events had also eased the way. Liberals had become more vocal, as the 1966 Fulbright hearings illustrate. Disillusionment over Vietnam had strengthened the hand of those who argued the United States needed to seek accommodation rather than confrontation in Asia. The rapid downturn in the troop commitment in Vietnam also lessened the direct adversary role between China and America. The increasing hostility between the Chinese and Soviets, which included significant border conflicts by 1969, also meant that even many conservatives could comfortably condone dealing with China. In their respective memoirs Nixon and Kissinger both explain their moves in terms of real politik, dealing with the new "triangular" politics. Other conservatives came to see an advantage in playing the "China card" against the Soviets.

Still, Nixon and his advisors worried about conservative reaction. Nixon's political genesis was in part connected to the China Lobby. In a sense that was an advantage since no one could accuse him of being soft on communism; yet it also meant that seriously alienating that element would cost him part of his political base. He also needed congressional conservatives to support his policies in Vietnam. The State Department was ambivalent. Facing inevitable Chinese entry into the United Nations, the Department was advocating a Two Chinas Policy. Kissinger attributes this to the Department's attempt to walk the line between the China Lobby, in which it placed Nixon, and the liberal wing of Congress "which was tormenting us on Vietnam." Kissinger implies that he never really considered Two Chinas a viable alternative, but the Administration continued to issue false signals to Congress. In September, Assistant Secretary of State Marshal Green told the Foreign Relations Committee that Two Chinas was the official policy.(137) That deception continued up to he last minute of China's October admission to the U.N. House Foreign Affairs Committee Chairman Clement Zablocki saw Nixon to discuss rumors that the United States was going to go along with Formosa's expulsion and China's admission. "He received us graciously," Zablocki recalled. "He gave each of us a set of cuff links. After we left, we read in the evening paper that the United States had abstained on the vote."(138) Kissinger remembers that "reaction in Congress was bitter and surprisingly widespread." (139) Reaction, however, was also superficial. Conservative attempts to reduce support of the United Nations was stalled in the Senate. A snap vote engineered by liberal senators who were appalled by the glee of Afro-Asian nations over Formosa expulsion killed the entire foreign aid authorization bill, but it was later restored. Congressional reaction was mostly media oriented, designed to protect political flanks.

Still, Nixon fretted, mostly about the conservatives. One of his earliest contemplated gestures toward China, allowing grain shipments, was abandoned when conservative senators objected. Attempting to get Congress in on the "take off," Nixon encouraged Senator Mike Mansfield to apply openly for a visa to visit China, (140) a move which had been decisively rejected by the White House only three years earlier.(141) When Nixon finally decided to go to China without consulting Congress, Kissinger observes the President "left himself quite naked should anything go wrong."(142) At the end of the China trip, when wrangles over the final communiqué came up, Kissinger describes Nixon as "beside himself." He did not want to press the Chinese, but could not ignore State Department objections which would leak to domestic opponents. "He recognized his political dilemma." Not to sign might end the trip in discord, but "he was already edgy about the reaction of his conservative supporters to the trip; he dreaded a right wing assault on the communiqué."(143) Discussions were reopened. Chinese anger was less forbidding the conservative vitriol. To the Americans' great relief, China agreed to change much of the "objectionable" language. Nixon left China in self-defined triumph, but he worried about how he would be received in Washington. On the flight back Nixon "stewed in his cabin." His worry was ill founded. Congress, even most of the conservative wing, was ready to accept reality. He was met by a large bipartisan delegation at the airport. Within five minutes of arriving at his office, Kissinger checked with arch-conservatives Senator Barry Goldwater and Governor Ronald Reagan. Both promised support as long as American support of Formosa's defense continued. Kissinger pledged that it would.(144) Nixon was out of the ideological fire. For a brief while he was a hero at home as well as abroad.

Vietnam was a crucial chapter in the saga of the United States Asian policy. American involvement in Indochina spanned a quarter century, the last decade of which included large scale military action. It represented the height, and perhaps the end, of unfettered American penetration into Asia. It also resulted in rethinking the containment doctrine, domestic turmoil, and internal and external pressure on Congress to assert its will in foreign policy.

Some of the Vietnam story has been related above. The Dien Bien Phu crisis might have resulted in American involvement, but Congress had intervened and allied itself successfully with President Eisenhower to prevent conflict. As has often been the case, however, Congress, while unwilling to fight, would brook no attempt to moderate relations with the communists. Even with his tremendous prestige, President Eisenhower felt compelled to call in congressional leaders prior to his first summit conference in 1955 in order to assure them that no decisions would be made without prior legislative consultation and there would be no appeasement.(145) With specific reference to Indochina, Congress acted to block involvement, but then detracted from the American negotiating position by insisting that no concessions be made to the communists at the bargaining table. While it was to be expected that Senator Knowland would warn against a "Far Eastern Munich," liberals such as John F. Kennedy also equated partition or coalition with appeasement. As Senator Estes Kefauver summed up the situation, "Congress sent Dulles to Geneva with his hands tied." (146)

The conservative pressure on Presidents Kennedy and Johnson has also been discussed. Johnson in particular was concerned with Congress, especially the right. He remembered the pounding Truman had taken over Korea, and how Eisenhower had avoided that by asking for supportive resolution. Johnson was also afraid of a rebirth of McCarthyism and was concerned that the war would be used by conservatives as an excuse to dismantle his Great Society programs.

The August 1964 incidents in the Tonkin Gulf in which North Vietnamese torpedo boats reportedly fired on American destroyers precipitated the beginning of full-scale involvement in Vietnam. Mindful of the contrast between Truman's and Eisenhower's techniques and the differing results, Johnson resolved to get Congress in on the take off. There are indications that the Administration was moving toward a hard line in Vietnam in the Spring of 1964. Support of a South Vietnamese invasion of the North was contemplated and hefty increases in aid were programmed. Despite this and the acknowledged fact that the war was primarily being waged by indigenous Viet Cong, the President still estimated that "the prospect in South Vietnam is not bright."(147) McNamara was particularly aggressive and was already alarming members of Congress by what one characterized as commitment to "all out war in Vietnam."(148) A congressional resolution supporting American involvement was also drafted and ready. Whether Johnson was deferring making a decision on whether to intervene farther in Vietnam or whether the decision existed and its execution was being deferred, Johnson's partisan calculations were a major source of the delay. But the reported attacks on the USS Maddox and USS Turner Joy could not be ignored.

Johnson had to tread the line between being the "nuclear nut" he was portraying Senator Goldwater as, and being subjected to the "soft on communism" charge that has bedeviled Democratic presidents. Records of National Security Council meetings in the immediate aftermath of the Tonkin Gulf incidents indicate decision-makers believed an actual attack had occurred. It is also clear, as CIA Director John McCone observed, that the Council members knew "the North Vietnamese are reacting defensively to our attacks on their off shore islands." It was also decided, in Rusk's words, that "an immediate and direct reaction by us is necessary."(149)

It was also decided to ask congressional leaders if they thought a resolution should be sought along the lines of Eisenhower's Middle East support measure. Predictably, Johnson was able to move the Tonkin Gulf Resolution through Congress virtually unopposed. Later squabbles over whether Johnson had misled Congress are not terribly important to the events of the Vietnam era. Both administration and legislative sources recall that early in the war Johnson carefully consulted with or informed Congress prior to each major move.(150) In each case, Congress supported intervention. Many members, however, patriotically followed the President's leadership rather than enthusiastically endorsing his policy. During the debate on the resolution, Senator George Aiken summed up the feeling of many: "I am still apprehensive [but] . . . as a citizen I feel I must support our President whether his decision is right or wrong."(151) Later, Mike Mansfield, who had time-and-again publicly stood by presidents despite his private doubts, reminded Johnson that "what has been done in the way of resolutions, however one-sided the votes,

has been done with great trepidation on the part of many Senators. It has been done largely on faith, out of loyalty to you
and on the basis of the general view that when the President has
the responsibility and when he requests legislative support in a
crisis, he should have it."(152)

Mansfield's views were undoubtedly accurate and the Administration realized it. Secretary McNamara warned that "in both the
Senate and House Committees there is broad support, but this
support is thin. There is a feeling of uneasiness and frustration."(153) Senators Wayne Morse and Ernest Gruening had been
the only two members of either house to oppose the Tonkin Gulf
Resolution, but others soon joined in. After Johnson began bombing North Vietnam in February 1965, at which time he considered
and rejected asking Congress for yet another resolution,(154) and
after the introduction of ground combat forces in summer 1965, a
dozen liberal senators became increasingly critical of United
States involvement.

For most of Johnson's term, however, the doves were a minority. The majority actively or passively supported the war. After
one early visit to Congress, Ambassador to South Vietnam Maxwell
Taylor reported to the President that there was no trouble in the
House and that the Senate was concerned but not opposed. Rusk
supported Taylor's characterization of Congress' mood.(155) Aide
Charles Roche sent the President a number of memoranda indicating
hawk sentiment in Congress. Roche and others found various members feeling "that there is a far greater need at this point to
counter the demands of the far right hawks for more aggressive
bombing and full utilization of military potential," discounting
"the effect of peaceniks," favoring "maximum bombing efforts,"
adamant that "we should go all out," equating "the same people
who are anti-Vietnam now" with "the ones who were peaceniks in
regard to German aggression," and believing that "the vast majority of the American people support the bombing program and want
more bombing."(156) Further while the Senate Foreign Relations
Committee was a source of opposition, other committees, such as
the Senate Armed Services Committee, were distinctly hawkish and
pressured Johnson to unleash the Joint Chiefs and win the war
militarily. That Committee in a 1967 report urged, "It is high
time, we believe, to allow the military voice to be heard in connection with the tactical details of military operations."(157)
Thus, the President received mixed signals from Congress. Perhaps because they coincided with his own views and reflected the
normal presidential concern with the right rather than left elements, Johnson long discounted the power and intensity of his
liberal critics. They were a minority and, he told the National
Security Council, he could not let the views of "a few senators
. . . control his actions."(158)

In time, President Johnson learned that he had underestimated the opposition. The Democrats would, and did, destroy his
presidency over the war. Beyond simple opposition to the war
per se, congressional opposition among Democrats was strongly
based in concerns about domestic politics and fear of the partisan advantage the unpopular war would give the Republicans. A
constant theme throughout Johnson's and into Nixon's terms was

the negative impact on domestic programs. Senator Stuart Symington told Johnson aide Jack Valenti that Robert Kennedy and
William Fulbright were arguing the war's cost in domestic terms.
Symington agreed, contending, "the tragedy of Vietnam right now
is that it causes the American people to worry visibly and vocal-
ly about the race problem, ghettos, crime, the cities - with the
public complaint being: If we didn't have the war and its cost,
we could solve all these other things." Symington's basic question, Vanenti reported, was "Why are we spending $30 billion a
year in Vietnam?"(159) Four years later in a Foreign Relations
Committee mark-up of Southeast Asian foreign aid, Symington put
the issue more pithily and parochially. "I think," he complained, "we should express less interest in South Asia and more
in South St. Louis."(160) The same type of message was also
clear in a report to President Johnson by Mike Mansfield after a
series of meetings the Majority Leader held with Democratic
members of the Senate. Some of the comments Mansfield forwarded
to Johnson included:

- The war is hampering domestic programs of the Administration.
- There is a deep concern and a great deal of confusion which
  could explode at any time; in addition, racial factors at
  home could become involved.
- The cost will soon reach $2 billion a month. We should
  . . . get out as best we can; and sooner rather than later,
  because it is a very expensive war.(161)

Perhaps the ultimate fear of domestic ramifications was
voiced by Senator Vance Hartke, who predicted at one point that
"the American people are going to suffer bomb casualties for the
first time in history . . . . Washington, D.C., will be bombed
by election day."(162)
Democratic senators were even more concerned with the electoral implications of the war. In Mansfield's reports comments
on this issue included:

- There is a strong conviction that candidates of the Democra-
  tic party will be hurt by the war.
- If the war drags on, the party will suffer badly.
- Vietnam is worse than Korea and remember what [candidate]
  Eisenhower did with the latter.
- The war in the long run is a heavy liability for the Democratic Party.
- Polls have been correct in showing over-all support of
  [the] President. Much of the support, however, comes from
  Republicans who will not support [the] President or Democrats in elections. It is among Democrats that the principal uneasiness exists over Vietnam. If 6% or 7% are unhappy enough to vote Republican in protest in November,
  think what it will do to Democratic candidates for Congress.(163)

From within the Administration, President Johnson was receiv-

ing a great deal of mixed advice about support of the war.
Johnson recognized that early support of the war was broad but
shallow and that escalation would cause greater public discontent.(164)  Vice President Humphrey, for one, tried to persuade
Johnson of the disastrous domestic policy and partisan consequences to Vietnam.  "There is danger of shifting emphasis away
from Great Society programs to military outlays," Humphrey wrote.
He also argued that "from a political point of view, U.S. people
find it hard to understand why we risk World War III by engaging
in a war under terms we found unacceptable in Korea twelve years
ago."  Humphrey concluded by dismissing the danger from the
Republican right and warning of the potential alienation of traditionally Democratic groups like liberals and labor.(165)

Such advice was in the minority however.  Most of Johnson's
advisors were hawks, and even Humphrey had to be cautious in his
dissent.  An aide, John Reilly, warned Humphrey that even though
"the whole U.S. establishment [may be] wrong--McNamara, Taylor,
Rusk, Alex Johnson, the Bundy's, Lodge . . . it is highly dubious
for you to take on the whole U.S. establishment . . . ."(166)
The reports from presidential aides also tended to reassure
Johnson.  The finding and reporting of hawk sentiment in Congress
by Charles Roche has already been cited.  Roche also wrote
Johnson memoranda such as "The Political Impotence of the 'Peaceniks' and the Latent Strength of Isolationism."  Roche pointed to
a New York primary victory of a war supporter as significant.
Describing the incumbent and victorious Democrat Leonard Farber-
stein as "a sitting duck . . . who has been living on borrowed
time," Roche characterized the primary as having "repulsed . . .
a brilliantly mounted peacenik raid . . . under virtually the
worst set of conditions imaginable."  Rather than be concerned
with the peaceniks, Roche counseled, "what is serious politically
is the revival of isolationism . . . which is nourished by Fulbright and others, and can play into the hands of the Republicans."(167)  Roche also warned the President that while the
Republicans had been less critical of Vietnam than elements of
the Democratic Party, the G.O.P. "cannot afford to remain quiet
on the only cutting political issue they now have."  A solution
according to Roche would be a highly publicized meeting between
Johnson and legislative leaders on both sides of the aisle.  That
would "demonstrate the Executive and Legislative Branches working
together . . . tend to lock the Republican party into a position
of support, . . . force from the peace element an explanation of
their real motives . . . [and] would bolster the Democratic candidates for Congress."(168)

As it turned out, the Republicans continued to be less troublesome to Johnson than liberal Democrats.  The "bomb 'em back
into the stone age" crusade that Johnson and his aides feared
never seriously materialized.  Further while that sentiment was
present in Congress among a few conservatives, particularly
centered around the Armed Services Committees, it was those conservative members who were most reluctant to violate the "water's
edge" dictum against criticizing presidential foreign policy.
Conservative Senator Karl Mundt, for one, would write privately,
"I am completely disillusioned by the disregard for manifest

truth by the Johnson Administration," express dismay that the war was being left to "military amateurs like McNamara and Johnson," and advocate that "we must rely on the trained, experienced, and dedicated professional military leaders . . . if we are to avoid defeat or disaster."(169)  But men like Mundt would not go public.  "It it my studied conviction," he wrote Senator Javits, "that we Republicans can best serve the national interest . . . by trying to allay rather than accelerate the divisive debate which is so frequently misunderstood and misinterpreted abroad by Communist propagandists . . . ."(170)  Among Democratic conservatives, Senator Richard Russell would similarly write: "In frankness, I was opposed to our entering Asia to fight a land war in the jungles there, but it is too late to debate this question now.  We are in Vietnam - our flag is there - and, above all, American boys are under fire, and I am supporting all of the President's efforts there to the hilt."(171)

More moderate Republicans also tended to support Johnson's war effort and the President cultivated them.  Jack Valenti reported that Senator Hugh Scott was tremendously pleased by a presidential telephone call of appreciation for Scott's support.  Scott's opinion of the President:  "What a man!"(172)  Johnson's care and handling of Everett Dirksen also paid off.  The Republican Senate leader relayed his support to Johnson, but asked "for sympathy if to keep his own forces in line he was compelled from time to time to make 'Republican' noises."(173)  Even crusty George Aiken was careful not to be too critical.  After his comment that the Administration should declare a victory in Vietnam then get out, he passed the word that it was a "silly" remark in which "I really went further than I should have."(174)  Johnson also tried to forestall possible criticism from the right by lining up military support.  Valeti recommended to Johnson, "Before you make final decisions on . . . Viet Nam, you 'sign on' the Joint Chiefs . . . .  If . . . something should go wrong later and investigations begin in Congress . . . there can be no recriminations."(175)  The President also "signed on" former President Eisenhower and invoked his support in discussion with members of Congress.  "I give much credit . . . to members and leaders of the Republican party . . . especially in Congress. [They] are standing up magnificently," he wrote Eisenhower.  Johnson even suggested partisan benefits for the opposition G.O.P.  "As I have told members of your Party myself, I am confident that this stand they are taking will mean new strength in Congress for them at the next election."(176)

What pressure that did come from congressional Republicans came mostly on domestic programs.  In 1968, when Johnson urged an income surtax to relieve the deepening dollar problems, the President suspected Republicans of stalling the tax so they could campaign against "Johnson's inflation" as well as "Johnson's war." (177)  Democratic members of Congress urged Johnson to wrap the flag around the tax bill.  But Johnson was afraid of stirring up the American public in that fashion.  The specter of McCarthyism haunted him and he refused to do it.(178)  By withdrawing from candidacy for reelection he could therefore negate the Republican ploy, and heroically save the domestic economy as well as negotiate for peace, free of intra and inter party bickering.(179)

In the end it was his own Democrats, heavily centered in the Senate, who brought Johnson down. The reports from the likes of Humphrey and Mansfield of growing Democratic discontent, rather than the internal reports of support, more accurately reflected reality. At first Johnson tried to use the successful techniques from his Senate days on Fulbright, Church, and other dissenters. Flattery, appeals to partisan unity, patronage and other support given and withheld, careful consultation—all meant to find a way to reason together—were tried. The President wanted to cooperate. So did the senators, particularly Fulbright who was distressed at the rift with his former friend and mentor. On more than one occasion in the early going the Senator signaled his concern. "I make no secret of the fact that I think you were the best Majority Leader the Senate has ever had, and that I think you are and will continue to be a great President," Fulbright wrote. "I sense from various sources that you were displeased by my recent speech. I regret this," he worried.(180) He was disturbed by stories that he and the President had a falling out. Fulbright told Arthur Goldberg he was anxious to "make up."(181)

Johnson and Fulbright wanted cooperation—but in form, not substance. Johnson felt compelled to pursue the war, Fulbright and others to dissent. In the end Johnson shut his detractors out. Fulbright and Church were banned from the White House. Johnson even spread the word that Fulbright's opposition was racially inspired. "They're just not our kind of people," Johnson quoted Fulbright as telling him.(182) Senate Democrats began to threaten Johnson's presidency directly, and the suspicions of evil mounted on both sides. On November 30, 1967, Senator Eugene McCarthy announced his candidacy for the Democratic nomination. The White House considered it a "joke,"(183) but moved quickly to defuse "McCarthy's Catholic grandstanding" by arranging Johnson's personal appearance along with the military's chief chaplain at the funeral of Francis Cardinal Spellman.(184) But McCarthy's good showing in the New Hampshire primary was a blow. More than McCarthy, the President and his aides feared Senator Robert Kennedy. White House insiders had long tried to either win Kennedy's cooperation(185) or disparage his disloyalty to the Democratic cause.(186) John Roche told the President that Kennedy was the biggest threat: "Bobby . . . has a vested interest in the defeat of the national ticket in 1968." The solution: "The Kennedy Corporation must be convinced that if we go down in bankruptcy they will go down with us . . . . It might even be insinuated that if they shaft the ticket in 1968, a number of us will be on world tours in 1972. . . . [As for the Republicans] we can beat [them]—if we find the time to go after them"(187) Kennedy did shaft the Johnson candidacy in 1968, but not by sitting it out. He announced his own candidacy.

Many factors went into Lyndon Johnson's decision not to seek reelection. His support in the public and the establishment had evaporated. He felt pressured by the judgement of history to make a grand gesture to salvage the shambles of the Great Society and Vietnam. Certainly he must have also been simply discouraged and tired. But the humiliation of defeat or pyrrhic victory over his Senate based challengers also attacked his self-image. It might be argued that the McCarthy or Kennedy candidacies, or the impact of Goldwater's in 1964, on Vietnam were not manifestations of congressional influence. Such an interpretation would be too narrow. The existence of the Senate and the status it gives its members gave them the platform necessary to make their voices heard and their candidacies taken seriously. The Senate has increasingly become a route to the presidency, and members seek assignments on the Foreign Relations and Armed Services Committees to further that ambition.(188) In short, Johnson did not withdraw exclusively because of Congress. But if Congress had not existed, he might well have been reelected. Fulbright, Church, McCarthy, Kennedy and others helped create and then feed on a climate of disillusionment and dissent which resulted in the decision by Lyndon Johnson that he would be more at ease in the Perdenales country of Texas rather than at work in the White House in Washington.(189)


Nixon and Vietnam

The flow of events in Vietnam during Richard Nixon's first term were in many ways a continuation of the political/diplomatic course set during the waning Johnson tenure. The main focus was no longer on how or whether to win in South Vietnam. The debate was over immediate withdrawal vs. "peace with honor." Whatever the outcome of the presidential election in November 1968, the concluding pages of the Americanization chapter of Vietnamese history were already being written. No American president, except at extreme electoral risk, could have departed from the pre-determined goal of an end to what Henry Kissinger describes as "The Agony of Vietnam."(190)

That America's involvement in Vietnam would end does not mean that by January 20, 1969 it was over. More than 14,000 more Americans would die on the battle field. Others would die in the streets and campuses at home. Cambodia would be mercilessly bombed then invaded; on a lesser scale Laos would suffer the same fate. North Vietnam was not only bombed anew, but the mining of Haiphong harbor and other actions which had previously been rejected as risking Chinese and/or Soviet intervention were dared.

Discussion of Congress' role in these events will focus on the impact of that institution on the pace and terms of the American withdrawal. That was primarily determined by domestic political pressure. As will be seen, the pressure exerted by Congress, both in direct legislative terms and as part of the public opinion process, was important in molding the shape if not the inevitability of the withdrawal. A related secondary point that must be considered is the impact of Congress on the diplomacy of North Vietnam. A constant Nixon-Kissinger theme is that domestic dissent aided and abetted the enemy.

In his memoirs, Kissinger accurately reflects the domestic political shifts that the change of presidents and parties in the White House brought. While the main opposition to the war had been Democratic, many members of that party had been restrained by the presence of a Democrat in the Oval Office or by the hope of a continuation of Democratic control of that office. The theme, as Speaker of the House John McCormack wrote his colleagues, was that "no matter how anyone feels on the Vietnam situation, there is no reason why they should vote against Humphrey-Muskie or any Democratic candidate."(191) With a Republican in office the party considerations that had constrained many Democrats—say a Mike Mansfield—were gone. On the Republican side, Nixon's presence made it easier to reconcile the Republican right to withdrawal. But the "fight-it-out" option had already lost any real standing. Kissinger correctly concludes: "Thus there was no conservative counterweight to the increasingly strident protests . . . . The center of gravity of American politics shifted decisively to the anti-war side."(192) It is not necessary to detail more than briefly the pressures brought by Congress against continuation of the war. They took three forms—direct and indirect legislative action against involvement and the reciprocal swelling of public and congressional protest.

Indirect legislative pressure in the form of threats to the defense budget persuaded supposedly the most militaristic elements of the foreign policy bureaucracy, the Defense Department and eventually even the Chiefs-of-Staff, to become withdrawal advocates. Kissinger has detailed the stand of Secretary of Defense Melvin Laird. Laird and Kissinger disagreed on the size and timing of troop withdrawals in 1970 and 1971. Kissinger was concerned about stability in Vietnam. Laird, by contrast, "saw Vietnam as an obstacle to his plans to modernize our armed forces; congressional pressures to cut his defense budget could be reduced," he thought, "if he was identified with troop pull-outs."(193) Laird, a former congressman and political expert also told the President that he had better increase the withdrawal rate before the November 1970 congressional election or "you might just as well forget the election."(194) After an intricate political skirmish between the National Security Advisor and the Defense Secretary, Laird's "amazing tours de force" won out and withdrawals increased.(195)

More directly, Congress exerted pressure through numerous direct legislative proposals or actions against the war. Here again, an exact chronicle of legislative actions is not as important as an assessment of their impact. Heavy pressure began in September 1969 when Congress returned from its summer recess. The honeymoon ended. Between September 24 and October 15, eleven anti-war resolutions were introduced in Congress. Senate hearings on the war resumed under Fulbright's strident antiwar guidance. A sensitivity to legislative reaction surfaced as early as March 1969 in the Nixon Administration. In response to North Vietnamese offensives Nixon was disposed to bomb the North. Laird objected, however. Kissinger recalls that Laird's "instincts were rather on the bellicose side," but that "he was also a careful student of the public and congressional mood."(196) As an alternative Nixon ordered B-52 strikes against sanctuaries in Cambodia. This time Secretary of State William Rogers objected. According to Kissinger, "Rogers objected not on foreign policy, but on domestic grounds . . . . Rogers feared that we would run into a buzz saw in Congress just when things were calming down." The end result was a compromise--a single raid on March 18, a far cry from the initially envisioned massive strike against the North.

Such episodes did not finally deter American action in Cambodia or the North, but the congressional factor reinforced opposition, particularly Secretary Rogers', within the Administration and helped deflect military pressures and the predilections of Nixon and Kissinger for even more aggressive military action.

Another illustration revolves around the ground invasion of Cambodia in April 1970.(197) Nixon clearly favored actions in Cambodia, but was opposed by Laird's and Rogers' "fear of domestic consequences." Although Nixon insisted on the move, "the various agencies [began] to position themselves so as to deflect on to somebody else the public uproar certain to ensue. Leaks began to occur in "a clear attempt to generate congressional and public pressures against any assistance to Cambodia." Nixon reacted by largely excluding his Secretaries of Defense and State from the decision-making process. Congress was to be consulted, but only in the form of Senators Stennis and Russell whose support was predictable.

The explosion of domestic reaction to the American ground entry into Cambodia exceeded even the gloomy projections of Rogers and Laird. Kissinger describes it as "The Domestic Travail." Kissinger cites polls to show that the silent majority was overwhelmed by outraged protests of a minority in Congress and the public symbolized by campus riots and the death of four students at Kent State University on May 13. Senators Frank Church and John Sherman Cooper introduced an amendment banning all military aid and activity in Cambodia after June 30. George McGovern and Mark Hatfield introduced language to cut off all funds for conducting war in Indochina by the end of 1970. Although both moves were eventually defeated, the votes were close and the impact felt. "The enemy was being told by the Senate that Cambodia was on its own."

Even Nixon could not stand scornfully apart from the fray. At a congressional briefing Nixon projected a June 30 deadline for the end of the excursion. It was an off-the-cuff remark, but "it was soon sacrosanct." At another session with members, the President improvised a thirty kilometer limit to the area of operation. That too became policy. In a sense the Cambodia intervention was not so important as a single event. Rather it was crucial as a catalyst that accelerated protest during, rather than after, action and mobilized critics to legislatively end the war. Whether he realized it at the time, in retrospect Kissinger saw

> . . . the pattern was clear. Senate opponents of the war
> would introduce one amendment after another, forcing the
> Administration into unending rear-guard actions to preserve
> a minimum of flexibility for negotiations. Hanoi could only
> be encouraged to stall, waiting to harvest the results of
> our domestic dissent.(198)

At least in the first part of his analysis, Kissinger was correct. Congressional pressure was relentless. Frustrated by the inability to win, even the conservatives began to desert Nixon. Defections by the likes of Senators Harry Byrd and Gordon Allot left Nixon "shaken."(199) Even a loyalist like Republican Senate Leader Hugh Scott began to waiver. Kept uninformed by the White House, urged on by staff to help "restore some balance to our constitutional system of checks and balances,"(200) and personally rebuked by some colleagues,(201) Scott said he would not support reentry into Cambodia and would not tolerate the long term continuance of a major American presence there.(202)

An American backed South Vietnamese operation into Laos in early 1972 sparked introduction of five congressional resolutions to ban operations in that country. On February 22 the Senate Democratic Policy Committee unanimously endorsed a call for the withdrawal of all American forces from Indochina prior to 1973. Supporting that call were many Southern conservatives on whose support Nixon had relied for his self-styled "bipartisan" coalition. On February 25 Senator Walter Mondale and conservative Senator William Saxbe (who later became Nixon's Attorney-General) cosponsored legislation to bar American support of an invasion of North Vietnam without prior and explicit legislative permission. (203)

The deluge continued. April through July saw 17 "end-the-war" votes in Congress. In late June a sense of the Senate resolution was adopted calling for the "prompt and early withdrawal of all forces." After a late summer recess, new measures were introduced. On October 13 the Foreign Relations Committee voted to limit aid to Cambodia to $250 million and restrict American personnel in that country to 200. On November 5 a congressional conference committee adopted language calling for a prompt withdrawal. Kissinger notes the implications: "The day when Congress would legislate a deadline was clearly approaching." (204)

The day was not at hand, though. There yet remained one last dramatic military confrontation.(205) It was the most dangerous of the war internationally. Domestically it brought new explosions of outrage, tinged with fear. In April 1972 the North Vietnamese launched an offensive south of the DMZ (demilitarized zone). New bombing raids were launched against North Vietnam. They did not stem the tide in the South, and in early May Nixon decided to mine Haiphong harbor and increase the interdiction of supply routes between Hanoi and the Chinese border. Direct confrontation with China and the Soviet Union loomed. Kissinger describes Nixon's announcement of the mining as "overwhelmed by Congressional and media outrage."(206) Whatever the diplomatic dividends of the mining, and Kissinger and Nixon claim substantial success, the move opened the floodgates of domestic criticism even wider.

By the late summer and fall Nixon and Kissinger both realized they had to settle the war. They reasoned that North Vietnam would be most pliant before the November 1972 presidential election. Hanoi would not want to deal with a Nixon who had a new

found political lease on life after November 4. The President
and his National Security Advisor also felt that Congress would
certainly legislate the end of the war when it returned in January 1973.(207) A Kissinger aide remembers him continually mutter-
ing, "We'll never get through another session of Congress without
their giving the farm away."(208) Nixon told South Vietnamese
President Nguyen Van Thieu that if he did not end the war Congress would.(209) Kissinger refers in his memoirs to "the grindstone of congressional pressures."(210) The breakthrough came in
early October. Both sides were exhausted by military losses and
various forms of domestic destruction and were under pressure
from their allies. The terms were not all the Administration
hoped for, but they substantially met earlier American proposals.
To have rejected them, says Kissinger, would have left him negotiating under "the clamor of Congress" and media attacks. Final
details had to be worked out, but Kissinger realized the Administration was "being inexorably pushed toward a congressional cut-
off of funds." Laird informed Kissinger and Nixon that meetings
with congressional leaders indicated an aid cut-off would occur
within two weeks of its return. Nixon agreed. Although he had
been reelected by a huge margin, three pro-war votes had been
lost in the Senate. Kissinger describes the situation as a diplomatic "nightmare" he "dreaded." Congress would end the war;
there was no leverage on the North Vietnamese. Then, on the
brink of peace, negotiations once again stumbled. Once more
North Vietnam was bombed. "New Madness in Vietnam" headlined the
St. Louis Post. "Stone Age tactics," "outrage," "disastrous"
chorused Democratic senators.(211) Many conservatives agreed.
Ohio's Senator Saxbe was quoted as saying Nixon had taken leave
of his senses. The exact quote, corrected Saxbe, was that Nixon
"was out of his f------ mind."(212) Negotiations in Paris
dragged into January. Congress convened in Washington. The
domestic din continued. The final breakthrough came on January
9, 1972--Nixon's birthday. Kissinger wired greetings and his
admiration of the President for having withstood congressional
and public pressure.(213) In a tactical sense, Kissinger's accolades were well founded. The mining, the Christmas bombing, and
other escalations in the face of frenzied domestic criticism took
a certain political courage, well placed or not. They may have
also been also been justified in the warped logic of war diplomacy. But as both Nixon and Kissinger attested, in a strategic
sense Congress was very much a part of ending of the American
phase of Vietnam's struggle. The details of the truce were
Nixon's and Kissinger's, but the fact of peace was in part
Congress'. Congress would not let the war go on. The President
knew that. And so it ended.


## Congress and the Middle East

As in Asia, Congress has been fairly active in Middle Eastern
affairs. One of the legislative themes in Asia was the preservation of the relatively small outpost of Formosa. In the Middle
East, congressional sympathy has similarly focused on a small,

embattled Jewish island in an Arab sea, Israel.

The domestic impact of Israel has already been touched on in a number of instances. Concern with Democratic congressional electoral fortunes helped prompt Truman's support of massive Jewish immigration to Israel in 1946. Congressional pressure and pronouncements during this period generally served to frustrate State Department attempts to strike an even handed policy between Jews and Arabs.(214) Acheson denies parochial influence, but Truman's own statement that "we could have settled this Palestine thing if U.S. politics had been kept out of it," is more persuasive.(215) Truman's quick recognition of Israel in 1948 was at least partly tied to his own electoral plans. He received considerable pressure from his White House staff to recognize Israel, although the move was so blatantly partisan that Secretary of State Marshall heatedly declared it "downright politics" and fumed at his boss, "You wouldn't get my vote."(216) Powerful congressional figures were also urging Truman to extend recognition.(217)

Congress also soon began to pressure the White House to give generous economic and military aid to Israel. As early as 1951 Congress was exceeding administration requests for aid to Israel and distressing State Department officials who were attempting to maintain cordial relations with the Arab states.(218) During the Truman years, however, Congress was just one force among the many within the contest of partisan politics that argued for favorable treatment of Israel.

During the Republican Eisenhower Administration the role of Congress became more definitive. Because Jewish votes and campaign contributions normally have benefitted the Democratic Party, Republican presidents, including Eisenhower, have felt freer to pursue a somewhat more balanced policy in the Middle East.(219) Pro-Arab or anti-Israel politics met strong resistance in Congress, however. The two crucial and related issues the Administration faced occurred midway through Eisenhower's eight years. The first concerned possible American aid to Egypt for building the Aswan Dam. The second concerned United States reaction to Israel's attack on Egypt in late 1956.

Secretary of State Dulles believed that the Truman Administration had gone overboard in its support of Israel for purely domestic political purposes. He felt that policy had not followed the State Department's point of view, had dangerously weakened relations with the Arabs, and had to be readjusted. He also knew that would make him "damned unpopular" with the Jewish community.(220) That quickly proved true. Dulles moved early to cut back military aid to Israel and met heavy opposition. Senator Jacob Javits described Dulles as at his "nadir" over the aid issue and recalled the "most dramatic confrontations" which he and Representative Emmanuel Celler had with Dulles on the issue. (221) The other New York Senator, Republican Irving Ives, also pressured Dulles, citing among other things the impact of Dulles' action on New York State politics.(222) Javits, Ives and others also helped organize Jewish community leaders and arranged meetings between them and Dulles.

A far more serious clash with Congress over Middle East pol-

icy occurred over the Administration's offer to help Egypt
finance the Aswan Dam. Arab anti-western feeling was abating,
and the President and Secretary felt that the proposed $156 mil-
lion loan would further gain Arab favor and keep oil moving
through the Suez Canal. By late 1955 Dulles was afraid that
Middle East policy would, like China, become a partisan battle
ground and, he told the Attorney General, "We might lose the
whole Arab world and maybe Africa." Dulles even contemplated
asking Adlai Stevenson to play the same kind of bipartisan role
the Secretary had played in the Far East during the Truman Administration.(223) Dulles also wanted to aid Egypt as part of his
backing of the British sponsored anti-communist Arab security
organization (which became the Bagdad Pact), although he was careful not to become too closely associated with the British designs
because "Congress would go through the roof if they ever thought
we had surrendered our independence of action."(224)

Two factors intervened to block the loan. Egypt was uncertain of western reliability because of the continuing Anglo-
Egyptian dispute over the status of the Canal, and let it be
known that the Soviet Union had also offered to help fund the
dam. This, plus an Egyptian arms deal with the Communist Bloc,
angered many Americans, including Dulles. Still, Egyptian President Gamal Abdel Nassar's neutralist position and his flirtation
with the communist world did not deter Dulles' plan to aid Egypt.
It did, however, cool his enthusiasm.

Congress, however, did not share the Administration's desire
to aid Egypt. Sympathy for Israel, Jewish constituent pressure,
Southern concern over increased Egyptian cotton competition, and
anger over Nasser's dealings with the communists all combined to
bring most of Congress into firm opposition to the loan. An
early meeting with Senator Walter George and Representative James
Richards, respective chairmen of the Foreign Relations and
Affairs Committees, had left Dulles confident that "we don't need
to feel any concern about going through with it." Dulles had
passed assurances on to Nasser.(225) However, at a later meeting
with congressional leaders on the subject of the loan, Dulles'
argument that aid would keep the Egyptians from going into the
communist camp for at least a decade met with little success.
Senate Majority Leader Johnson and Speaker Rayburn both opposed
the loan on the grounds of Egypt's past dealings with the Communist Bloc. Further evidence of congressional sentiments came in
July 1956 when the Senate Appropriations Committee's report on
that year's Mutual Security Act directed that "no funds provided
under this act shall be used for assistance in construction of
the Aswan Dam without approval of the Committee." Although the
President and Secretary argued the report had no standing in law,
it did have a decided political standing. In the hierarchy of
parlance in committee reports, "direct" is the strongest term.
Administrators can ignore such language only at the risk of
retaliation when the next appropriations request is submitted.
(226) Dulles agreed that pragmatically the language had "binding" effect and agreed not to move without further committee
action.(227) The Secretary had little choice. Senate Republican
Leader Knowland warned him that if he ignored the Committee

report the Department "would proceed at its peril because it would have to come up sometime or other." Also, if the Secretary did not agree to abide by the informal injunction of the report, the Committee members "would feel sufficiently strongly so they would write one into the bill . . ."(228)

Congress' opposition stemmed from more than the normal opposition to aiding Israel's enemies and anger over Egyptian relations with the Soviets. Construction of the dam would have considerably expanded Egypt's agricultural land, much of which was devoted to cotton. That would have directly entered into competition with southern grown American cotton. Cotton was already at issue between the Departments of State and Agriculture. Representatives of the latter agency intimated to Congress that State cared more for foreign than American interests, and Dulles appealed to the President for support.(229) That brought some Southern senators, such as Mississippi's John Stennis, who normally supported Eisenhower on foreign policy, in opposition. As Thomas Dewey noted after discussing the issue with Dulles, "Certainly the cotton situation is so heavily fraught with domestic-political pressures that it seems to be almost an impossible situation."(230)

As is most often the case, Congress was not the only factor in a decision. Rather, it was one of several considerations. Eisenhower and Dulles had to incorporate the fact that Congress was not inclined to appropriate funds for the Aswan project. Any attempt to make the loan would have at best occasioned a time-, energy-, and political credit-consuming struggle with Congress. Given the facts that 1) the Administration itself was divided (with Treasury Secretary George Humphrey and Agriculture Secretary Ezra Taft Benson opposed to the loan), 2) the loan would not be supported by cotton state Democrats, 3) the loan became an institutional status issue (whether the committee report could bind Dulles), all in addition to 4) the normal anti-Arab/anti-communist opposition, Dulles faced probable defeat if he pushed the loan. Concerned with a losing struggle that might also make the Middle East the focus of a bitter bipartisan struggle, the Administration withdrew. "The Aswan Dam was not a popular project in this country, especially in Congress;" Eisenhower recalled, "it would take all the pressure Foster and I could bring to bear to obtain congressional approval for our contribution, and we had little zest for an all out legislative fight." (231) By July 17, Dulles was passing word to Congress that he was "pretty sure" the loan would not be offered.(232) On July 19 Dulles informed Egyptian Ambassador Ahmed Hussein that the United States would not be able to proceed with the loan.

In his explanation to Ambassador Hussein, British Ambassador Roger Makin, and his brother Allen Dulles, the Secretary explained the withdrawal primarily in terms of Congress.(233) Writing later to the President, Dulles further explained his withdrawal of the loan offer. "There had for some time been mounting congressional opposition . . . if I had not announced our withdrawal when I did, the Congress certainly would have imposed it on us, almost unanimously."(234)

Either because of the loan cut-off or by way of using it as

an excuse, Egypt's President Nasser nationalized the Suez Canal on July 26 with the avowed intention of using the Canal's profits to finance the Aswan Dam. This action led to consternation both in Western Europe over the transit of oil and in Israel whose ships were totally denied transit by the canal's new Arab masters. In late October, Britain, France, and Israel attacked Egypt.

Once again the Eisenhower Administration found itself caught between diplomatic wisdom and domestic political reality. At first, in the midst of acute international tension in the Middle East and in Hungary, the Administration was able to follow its diplomatic instincts. Eisenhower was caught largely by surprise and was not pleased. That France and Great Britain would take action without consulting with the western alliance's senior partner boggled the President. Israel's aggression also outraged him. "All right, Foster," the President directed his Secretary of State, "you tell 'em [the Israelis] that, goddamn it, we're going to apply sanctions, we're going to the United Nations, we're going to do everything that there is so we can stop this thing." (235)

Beyond the portentous international implications, the Middle East crisis also intruded into the middle of the 1956 presidential and congressional campaigns. As noted, Dulles was deeply concerned about the Middle East becoming mixed in partisan debate. There was evidence of even the Administration's most loyal foreign policy Democratic supporters wavering. Lyndon Johnson felt that "we have been unprepared for every major development" in the area,(236) and Walter George described himself "greatly concerned" over Middle East policy.(237)

Republicans felt the heat. Dulles' aide John Hanes passed to Dulles the recommendation of the Republican National Committee's "Jewish Consultant," Bernard Katzen, that Eisenhower make some form of gesture toward Israel. Hanes agreed that some Democrats would make a partisan issue of Middle East policy. He was concerned, though, that responding would alienate those Democrats still trying to be bipartisan. "I also confess," Hanes gloomily added, "that I have never had the slightest confidence that anything we might do would gain the Republicans much political advantage among Bernie's constituents."(238) Dulles agreed with Hanes but felt it was a "close decision."(239)

As the election drew closer, "close" was enough to keep Jewish support a Republican concern. Maxwell Rabb, who also served as a Jewish liaison for the Administration, reported that of his speeches on behalf of House and Senate candidates, "at least 50% and at least two in every State are directed to handling the Israel question. This is, as you know, of vital concern to a large bloc of our population . . ."(240) Republican candidates also pressed for a gesture toward Israel. Robert Cutler, for example, wrote Dulles on behalf of Representative Curtis Laurence who was in a "tremendous fight" in a district "if not predominantly, [then] very strongly Jewish."(241)

For Dulles and others in the Administration, the crucial issue, however, was the presidential election. There, Eisenhower's long lead and the Democratic leanings of the Jewish community worked against Israel's supporters. Vice President Nixon and Dulles agreed that calling Congress back into session and giving the Democrats an enhanced platform would be a mistake, but discounted the electoral impact. Some pro-Israel votes would be lost, but not many would vote Republican anyway. Also, Nixon reasoned, Eisenhower would gain from the crisis because "at such a time you don't want a pipsqueak for President." Dulles agreed, adding that the President was firm that he would not sacrifice foreign policy for political expediency.(242) Eisenhower's position was as Dulles portrayed it. Townsend Hoopes describes the President's attitude as even "cavalier" about the election. "I don't give a goddamn" was Eisenhower's reaction to warnings about the New York election.(243) Later, Eisenhower took pride in his stand. Not only had he won, carrying New York by 1,600,000 votes in his landslide, he had done so while putting the interests of the United Nations and United States above his own.(244)

Thus, despite the domestic pressures, on October 30 the United States sponsored a United Nations resolution calling for a cease fire and a withdrawal of British, French, and Israeli troops. The Soviets sponsored a similar resolution, and the United States found itself voting with the Communist Bloc and the Arabs against its NATO allies and Israel. The United States also supported a Canadian resolution to introduce United Nations troops to supervise a cease fire. Under intense diplomatic pressure Britain and France withdrew and Israel began to fall back across the Sinai.

In early 1957 the crisis threatened to flare anew. Israel halted its withdrawal at the twenty-five mile wide Gaza Strip and refused to comply further with United Nations demands for a complete evacuation of Egyptian territory. Demands for economic sanctions against Israel arose in the General Assembly. Eisenhower was initially inclined to support sanctions, but realized that all the options harbored international or domestic dangers. Supporting Nassar would be unpopular in the nation and Congress. Supporting Israel, Dulles told _Time_ publisher Henry Luce "is the end of any hope for us in the Middle East."(245)

The pressure in the United States by the Jewish community on Congress and the Administration was intense. "It is almost impossible . . . in this country to carry out foreign policy not approved by the Jews," Dulles told Luce.(246) The Secretary also complained to Protestant laity leader Roswell Barnes that "Jewish influence here is completely dominating the scene and [it is] almost impossible to get Congress to do anything they don't approve of. The Israeli embassy is practically dictating to the Congress through influential Jewish people in the country."(247) United Nations Ambassador Lodge also attested to the religious influence. Writing to Dulles, Lodge recalled:

> Thirty years ago when I first became a newspaperman in Washington, I observed the extent to which minority groups could paralyze Congress and then get Congress to paralyze the Executive Branch. As a Senator for thirteen years I saw exactly how it was done--and how very _little_ it took to

create a wave of fear in Congress and in the Executive
Branch.(248)

Hemmed in by Jewish pressure, Dulles and others tried to
rally Christian counter pressure. Dulles enlisted Congressman
John Vorys to tell the Methodist bishop of Ohio that by trying to
lean over too far not to be anti-Semitic, one ran the risk of
being anti-American.(249) Dulles directly contacted Edward Elson
of the National Presbyterian Church, Roswell Barnes, and other
religious leaders. He told Elson that if the Jews had a veto on
American policy, the United Nations might collapse and asked if
something could be said from the pulpit. Elson agreed. Barnes
was told the non-Jewish elements had to become more active to
avoid a diplomatic disaster. The goal, Barnes concurred, was to
convince the Israelis that "they may be losing the sympathy and
patience of the Protestant and Catholic community in this country
which they can ill-afford to do."(250)
  If Dulles' exhortations to the Christian community had any
significant impact on public or congressional opinion, it was not
obvious. A few members such as Representative John Vorys sided
with Dulles,(251) but most either avoided the issue or strongly
opposed any move to have the United States join in voting sanctions against Israel. Both the Senate Majority and Minority
Leaders opposed sanctions. Johnson wrote Dulles to tell him
"most frankly, how disturbed" he was over stories of sanctions.
"Justice" and "morality" weighed against such a move, Johnson
argued.(252) Johnson's letter was leaked to the press. Knowland
called Dulles and told him that deciding on sanctions would bring
a "parting of the ways" between the President and his party's
Senate leader. Knowland further threatened to resign his seat on
the United Nations delegation if sanctions were voted. Senators
who tried to support Dulles complained to the Secretary about the
"great deal of heat in the past few weeks on the subject of . . .
Israel,(253) and even senators from states with negligible Jewish
constituencies received a heavy volume of mail urging support of
Israel.(254)
  Dulles leveled arguments that would have normally brought
Congress quickly behind Administration policy or at least si-
lenced dissent. He told a bipartisan leadership meeting that
Israeli intransigence would lead to guerrilla warfare, the stop-
page of oil supplies, and the growth of Soviet influence in the
Middle East.(255) In individual conversations with with members,
he made even more dire predictions. Vorys was told, "We face a
critical situation as far as the Arab world is concerned because
they are watching closely to decide . . . if a Republican Administration finds it impossible to have a foreign policy the Jews
don't approve of, and if that is their conclusion, they will line
up with the Soviets."(256) Knowland was warned that if the
United States would not force Israel to withdraw, the Soviets
would and that probably meant general war and the loss of the
Middle East.(257)
  Such apocalyptic predictions certainly alarmed members, but
it did not change their opposition to sanctions. Growing partisanship among the Democrats encouraged their resistance. The

new Chairman of the Senate Foreign Relations Committee Theodore Francis Green accused the Administration of only giving "lip service" to bipartisanship. Dulles, in turn, pronounced "coopera- ting with Senator Green . . . impossible."(258) Dulles had to concede, however, that "with the Democrats and now half the Republicans playing partisan politics, there was not much left in Congress."(259) Dulles' estimation was that there probably would be a unanimous vote for a resolution against sanctions in both houses and the Administration might lose its authority to impose sanctions.(260) Implications of the portentous confrontation with Congress also extended beyond the immediate issue. Johnson warned Dulles that Congress' support of the entire international- ist position of the United States was in danger. "The Southern group is lost," he said, "and if you lose the Israeli group and throw in a couple of Republican isolationists," the situation would revert to 1936 and 1937.(261)

The pivotal meeting between administration and congressional leaders occurred on February 20, 1957. Eisenhower acknowledged Congress' opposition, but warned that inaction might bring on collapse of the United Nations, communist domination of the Arabs, and war. Senator Fulbright, never a particular friend of Israel, suggested a Senate resolution calling on Israel to with- draw might strengthen Dulles' hand. Vorys argued for an immedi- ate bipartisan leadership statement calling on Israel to with- draw. Eisenhower and Dulles favored Vorys' idea but others quickly dissented. Speaker Rayburn asserted flatly that he would not be a party to a congressional resolution, and both Rayburn and House Majority Leader John McCormack believed it would be impossible to agree on the language of a statement. Senator Russell agreed with his House colleagues, and the meeting ended in a stalemate. Eisenhower's and Dulles' hope for some expres- sion of congressional support did not come to fruition. It is worth noting that many of the same members who gave Eisenhower virtual war power in the Middle East and Formosa resolutions of 1957 and 1954 respectively, who acquiesced to Truman's War in 1950, and who would later vote for the Tonkin Gulf Resolution, refused to stand behind the President where the Jewish state was involved. At most, the meeting brought a respite in congression- al criticism. Members such as Senator Russell urged the Presi- dent to make an address to the nation to "crystallize public opinion." Senator Smith asked Eisenhower for guidance as to what statements could be given to the press after the meeting. Eisen- hower asked only moderation. Speaking last for the legislative delegation, the Speaker of the House told Eisenhower, "America has either one voice or none," and that was the President's, even if everyone did not agree with him.(262)

The result of all this maneuvering was delaying action by all parties. The Administration worked to put off a vote against Israel in the United Nations. Israel delayed its withdrawal, Henry Cabot Lodge suspected, in order to allow congressional pres- sure to grow. And members of Congress delayed individual or collective action so they would not have to make a public choice between the interests of Israel as defined by David Ben Gurion and the interests of the United States as defined by Dwight David

Eisenhower.

The reluctance of the members to oppose Eisenhower openly did, however, give the Administration some leverage to keep pressure on Israel. By late February time was also running out on the inevitable date of United Nations action. Israel slowly made concessions. Dulles theorized that Israel did not want to antagonize a newly elected Eisenhower for four years.(263) By February 24 Israel had agreed to withdraw from the occupied territories if a United Nations peace keeping force was substituted as a buffer. The United States had also added assurances which were to become an issue a decade later. On February 11 Dulles had handed Israel's Ambassador Abba Eban an aide-mémorie calling for Israel to withdraw from Gaza and Sharm al-Sheikh, which guarded the Red Sea approach to the Israeli port of Elath. Dulles declared the sea lane international waters open to all shipping and pledged that the United States would join with others to ensure free and innocent passage. During the following two weeks much of Israel's effort focused on getting the Administration to clarify the vague assurances of the eleventh. Facing a stubborn Israel and Congress, there is evidence that American officials reluctantly gave additional guarantees with regard to Gaza. Dulles told Lodge that the President felt he could assure Ben Gurion that Egypt would not be allowed to militarily reoccupy the area, but that Israel "could not go about shouting about it."-(264) Dulles also authorized Lodge to say the United States would back Israel up if it was attacked.(265) Finally on Sharm al-Sheikh, there is some evidence that the Administration made a commitment to Israel to keep the approach to Elath open to both Israeli and international shipping.(266) This last commitment, in particular, was to resurface during the 1967 Mid East War.


War Again - 1967

During the next decade, Congress' role in Middle East policy settled into two main themes. One, discussed both above and below, was to defer to the president in the containment of communism. In early 1957, Eisenhower asked Congress for a resolution to extend aid to friendly countries in the area and pledged armed assistance by the United States to any country subjected to "overt armed aggression from any nation controlled by international Communism." The proposal met resistance from a number of Senate Democrats based on factors including growing partisanship, disenchantment with Dulles, reaction to the Aswan Dam-Suez War fiasco, and institutional qualms over surrendering the war power, but in the end deference to the president in the face of external threat overwhelmed the opposition and the resolution passed by a wide margin. Eisenhower soon utilized his authority to support the regimes of Jordan and Lebanon. From April through the summer of 1957 the Jordanian government of King Hussein was threatened by Nassarite-leftist internal elements backed by Syria. To avert a coup and/or invasion by Syria, the Sixth Fleet steamed on several occasions into the eastern Mediterranean. Even more serious events occurred in early 1958. The overthrow

of Iraq's King Fisal on July 14 by pro-Nassarite elements of the
army renewed concern over the threat to other pro-western governments by "radical" Pan-Arab (and presumably pro-Soviet) forces.
On July 15 the United States landed 14,300 troops in Lebanon.
Simultaneously, the British moved 3,000 paratroops into Jordan.
Most of these actions in 1957-1958 closely fit the provisions of
the Middle East Resolution. Although there was some congressional grumbling, especially over Lebanon, few were willing to oppose
the President in time of crisis, and executive authority went
unchallenged.

Congress also continued to support Israel heavily. Atypical
of the usual fight to get the foreign aid program passed, Congress lavished aid on Israel, at times even exceeding administration requests. Congress also was responsible, in any number of
other small ways, for demonstrating bias on behalf of Israel. At
one point and in a typical vignette, Special Ambassador to the
Middle East James Richards planned a trip to the area which did
not include a stop in Israel. Under Secretary of State Herter
advised him to stop in Tel Aviv to avoid raising the ire of Congress and perhaps endangering the pending Mutual Security Program.(267) On another occasion sentiment arose in the Senate to
pass a resolution extending tenth birthday greetings to Israel.
The State Department objected on the grounds that it would not
only alienate Arab nations by displaying obvious favoritism, but
that it would also insult other nations whose anniversaries were
not similarly honored. When administration protests headed off
the resolution in the Foreign Relations Committee, the Senate
bypassed the committee, brought the resolution directly to the
floor, and passed it without even a quorum call.(268)

The impact of Congress on policy-making at the time of the
1967 Arab-Israeli Six Day War illustrates another common pattern
of legislative influence. As in the Indochinese and Quemoy-Matsu
crises of the mid-1950s, Congress had been strongly supporting
pro-western elements. As the crisis reached the stage where
American intervention threatened, however, Congress was reluctant
to condone action. American arms were one thing, an American
army was an entirely different matter. In a repeat of its position in 1954 at the time of Dien Bien Phu, legislative leaders
demanded, at a minimum, allied action. In both cases congressional reluctance and conditions were important elements in restraining United States military action.

The immediate focus of the crisis was the Strait of Tiran.
In May 1967 the Egyptians closed the Strait to shipping bound for
Israel. This altered the decade old understanding of 1957 which
had kept open the access to Elath on the Gulf of Aqaba. The Egyptian blockade was seen as a causus belli by Israel and also
raised the question of whether the United States would honor its
1957 commitment to keep the Strait open to international shipping. Israel also became convinced that Egypt was about to
launch an attack across the Sinai Desert. Israel resolved to
strike first, but hesitated under American pressure generated in
part by Congress.

Although the formal assurances given to Israel by the Eisenhower Administration were somewhat ambiguous, there is evidence

that informal clarifications were much stronger. The Israelis called on President Johnson to honor that commitment, and Johnson was disposed to intervene. At one juncture, Israel's Foreign Minister Abba Eban pointedly asked Johnson, "Can I take it that I can convey to my Prime Minister that you have decided to make every possible effort to assure that the Strait and the Gulf would be open to free and innocent passage? The President's reply was an unequivocal "Yes."(269)

In reality, Johnson's position was not nearly so decisive. There were numerous signals from Congress cautioning against action. Secretary of State Rusk met with the Senate Foreign Relations Committee on May 23 and reported back to the President that the Committee backed Israel, but would oppose unilateral United States action.(270) A meeting of Vice President Humphrey and Secretaries Rusk and McNamara with bipartisan leaders and members of the Senate Armed Services and Foreign Relations Committees yielded the same result. Without European allies, Senator John McClellen told the Administration's representatives, action would be "unacceptable to the Congress and the American people would not support it."(271) The President was also carefully monitoring commentary on the floor of Congress which confirmed the opposition of many members to unilateral action.(272)

The President's normal concern with Congress and his reliance on the Eisenhower model of securing a covering congressional resolution prior to action was sharpened by his difficulties in Vietnam. He was already under strong attack for his "adventurism" in Asia and was not about to become similarly involved and accused in the Middle East. Also, Johnson heavily relied on such conservative Democrats as Senators John Stennis and John McClellen for support of his Vietnam policy. They opposed unilateral action in the crisis, and Johnson could not afford to alienate them and have them join forces with the likes of Fulbright, Morse, and Gruening who were opposing intervention in Israel as well as Vietnam.(273)

These domestic considerations determined the basic American stance. During late May and early June administration officials told the Israelis repeatedly that the United States could not act without congressional support. Israel was also warned that favorable congressional and public opinion was dependent on that country being beleaguered. If Israel took action alone, it could not expect support. Johnson favored a two front approach. One was utilization of the United Nations. He told Minister Evron that he did not have much hope that the United Nations could resolve the crisis, but felt that the effort was important to gain support in Congress and in domestic and world opinion.(274) Given congressional attitudes, Johnson also resolved to seek the creation of an international naval force, soon dubbed the Red Sea Regatta, to break the Egyptian blockade.

At a meeting at 5:00 p.m. on June 25 between Israeli and American officials, Eban was told that before an international force could become reality "an American decision on the proposal . . . would require consultations in Congress and perhaps a joint resolution of both Houses."(275) After a quick consultation with the President, Secretary Rusk returned to tell Eban that "the

President would not act without full congressional approval . . . the President was convinced that it was essential for him to be able to carry the Congress with him."(276) The next day President Johnson personally delivered the message. Meeting with Evron, Johnson told the Israeli diplomat that "any American involvement would require congressional support of the President. Without this there would be no value whatever in the intentions and decisions of the President . . . anything involving even a possibility of force would be impractical and would boomerang unless the proper congressional basis were laid in advance."(277) An hour later Johnson reiterated to Eban in an aide-mémoire that "the United States has its own constitutional process," and promised vigorous but unspecific action. At a noon meeting with his advisors, Johnson decided to continue to try to restrain Israel while preparing the groundwork for possible action. He could not, he told his staff, make a clear commitment to use force because of congressional opposition. Yet, Johnson realized, his inability to give Israel specific commitments might not be enough. Faced with increasing evidence of Egyptian, Syrian, and Jordanian preparations, Israel might feel compelled to act first. (278) After his discussion with Eban, Johnson realized he was right. As Eban left, he told his advisors, "I failed. They're going to go."(279)

Johnson was correct. Israel went. War erupted. There is ample evidence that Israel delayed the decision for war for two weeks.(280) They wanted American support and Johnson both wanted and felt obligated to give support. He would not move without Congress, though, and congressional conditions proved a stumbling block. The proposal for an international naval force proved elusively difficult to orchestrate. The Defense Department objected and resisted. Secretary of Defense McNamara feared a new "McNamara's War." The military chiefs hesitated over the "too political" concept of a hastily gathered force, with confusing lines of command and insufficient power to overcome any possible opposition.(281) Eugene Rostow recalled that "we wanted to get this thing into motion; and we were held up by naval planning. The Defense Department people were planning it as if they were going to open up the second front in Normandy."(282)

Adding to the Defense Department's reluctance, was the possibility of serious legislative opposition to any movement. By May 31 Rusk was publicly assuring Congress that any action would come only in conjunction with other countries and through the United Nations. Leaks from the White House began to suggest that Israel accept Nassar's fait accompli in the Straits of Tiran. The Administration had concluded that obtaining a congressional resolution, even in the framework of joint United Nations action, would be difficult or impossible. In a joint memorandum to the President, Rusk and McNamara reported that "while it is true that many congressional doves may be in the process of conversion to [Israeli] hawks . . . an effort to get a meaningful resolution runs the risk of becoming bogged down in acrimonious dispute." (283) Johnson was unwilling to pay the political price necessary to launch the Red Sea Regatta. It never sailed and the Middle East was engulfed in war for the third time in two decades.

Ironically, Congress, Israel's staunch supporter, was not willing
to acquiesce tamely to a Gulf of Aqaba Resolution. Johnson felt
he needed Congress, but Congress was not going to repeat its
Tonkin Gulf licensing mistake. War might have been avoided, but
it was not.

For the balance of Johnson's term and into President Nixon's
first term, American policy in the Middle East remained heavily
pro-Israel. The impact of the approaching 1968 presidential-
congressional elections were lost on no one. Johnson had been
under pressure from the domestic Jewish community during the 1967
crisis,(284) and after Israel's spectacular victory the Administration hastened to make domestic political capital. Presidential aide Mike Manatos happily reported to his chief that "the
goodwill that has accrued to the President as a result of his
handling of the Middle East crisis . . . is reflected in conversations which I have had with many members of the Senate—from
Mansfield and Dirksen on down."(285) Another aide recommended
both public and private touting of the President's support of
Israel. Hopefully that might offset the opposition to the
Vietnam war that was widespread in that constituency. Be subtle
the aide advised, "Minimize the impression of playing politics
with Israel."(286)

Israeli politics, however, was being lustily played. Foreign
Minister Eban told an American Jewish audience that Israel's
victory had come with "the great help of your President." When
asked about the 1968 election he responded, "You can help Israel
by returning LBJ to the White House."(287) Although Johnson
later withdrew from a second term, Israel's electoral connection
remained strong. Prime Minister Yitzak Rabin openly discussed
the pressure on Democratic candidate Humphrey, Democratic Party
leaders, and others that led to a letter by seventy senators to
Johnson and to the subsequent sale of fifty F-4 Phantom jets to
Israel less than a month before the election. Senate pressure
even included a threat to the entire Military Sales Bill if
Israel was not granted virtual carte blanche to buy weapons
on easy terms.(288)

Strong congressional support of Israel continued unabated
during Nixon's first term. In 1970 Congress gave the President
unlimited authority to sell arms to Israel despite the fact that
the Administration had made no such request. Elements in the
Administration, particularly the State Department, favored taking
a somewhat less pro-Israel approach and even applying some pressure on Israel to moderate its adamant refusal to return any of
the Arab land seized during the 1967 war. Nixon was prone to
agree with the the approach. When Nixon moved toward four power
(U.S.-U.K.-U.S.S.R.-France) talks on the Middle East, he and
Kissinger found themselves at cross purposes with Israel's
insistence that negotiations be based on direct talks between
them and the Arabs. Fear of an "imposed" settlement arose. A
bipartisan House delegation headed by Emmanuel Celler visited
Kissinger, then Nixon to object. As Kissinger remembers their
oppositon, "If there was already concern in Congress over the
negotiating form, I could imagine the outcry once we turned to
substance." Continued discussions of such possible talks next

brought a resolution in Congress supporting Israel's rather than the Administration's position. As Kissinger succinctly put it:

> At home, a majority of both Houses of Congress rallied to support Israel's position in a public declaration: direct negotiations, a contractual peace, and no pressure on Israel to withdraw prematurely. As in Vietnam, we would wind up negotiating with ourselves.

That, added to the normal difficulties of Mid East diplomacy, soon led Kissinger to conclude that "the time was not ripe for active negotiation." The Administration's initiative was put in limbo.(289)

An interesting, if perhaps overdrawn, perspective on the influence of Israel on Congress during the period can be gained from the comments of William Fulbright, one of the few members of Congress not staunchly pro-Israel. Writing to a West German diplomat, the Senate Foreign Relations Committee Chairman observed:

> I really believe that the President and the Secretary of State have desired to follow a more even-handed and balanced policy, but that the Congress . . . [has] undermined the Administration's position.(290)

To another correspondent, Fulbright wrote:

> I am unable to find any substantial support in the Senate for a balanced attitude toward the contending forces in the Middle East. When I moved to delete Senator Javits' open-ended authorization for Israel I obtained all of seven votes, [which] is a fair sample, apparently, of the strength of the zionists in the Senate. As you know they are now in the process of appropriating $500 million more for Israel, and there is no power that I know of that can prevent it. (291)

To a religious leader, Fulbright lamented:

> I have in the past urged what I believe to be a sensible settlement in the Middle East, but to no avail--other than to be accused of anti-semitism . . . . The influence of the zionists in the Congress and in our government is so great that our policies are subject to the direction of officials in Israel.(292)

Finally, Fulbright told former World Bank President Eugene Black that "It seems to be that the Senate of the United States is as subservient to the Israeli officials as is the Knesset [Israel's parliament]."(293) If Fulbright was even partially correct, and he was, it spelled a pervasive pattern to foreign influence, through a domestic interest group and via Congress on American foreign policy.

# 6
# Congressional Means and Presidential Values: Trade, Aid and Personnel

## Congress and Trade Relations

For an area where it traditionally reigned supreme, Congress' influence on trade policy during the post World War II era has been surprisingly limited. Spurred by the economic interests of their constituents, members of Congress still evidenced considerable interest in such matters as tariffs and quotas, but much of Congress' authority was surrendered to the Executive Branch. An important factor responsible for this transfer of power was the increasing complexity of the international trade structure. By 1945 the task of adjusting individual tariffs had become so contentious and so complicated that rate setting became burdensome and a political liability to Congress. Congress was averse to giving up its power over foreign economic relations, but gradually its inability to deal with the massive skein of regulations overwhelmed its reluctance.(1)

A second factor in the transfer of trade barrier control to the Executive was the general agreement in Congress with free trade philosophy. Few members disagreed with the premise that trade restrictions had helped precipitate the Great Depression and that free trade was important to domestic and international prosperity.(2) Finally, in an era of executive dominance of foreign policy, vigorous presidential leadership was able to carry the day for trade liberalization. Because of its parochial base, Congress has been prone to view trade questions in domestic terms. The President and State Department have been prone to view trade from a foreign policy perspective. The extent of executive control has, to a degree, depended on whether the foreign policy or domestic definition prevailed. Added to the other factors favoring liberalized trade and executive control, the ability of the Executive to portray foreign trade as important in waging the cold war struggle against communism usually ensured that the president's programs would carry the day.

That does not mean that Congress played no role. As an alternative to specific control, protectionist, domestic oriented members of Congress sought to restrain the Executive from making radical changes and from manipulating tariffs exclusively as a foreign policy instrument to the detriment of domestic economic interests. The methods utilized by Congress were usually akin to those employed in the tariff fight of 1945--insert escape clauses, limit the percentage of possible tariff adjustments, put time restrictions on executive authority, seek informal executive pledges to act marginally, protect industry where possible, and mandate consultation with Congress if major changes were contemplated.

Conservative congressional influence was most potent during the Eisenhower Administration. In 1953 conservatives were able to secure the nomination of Joseph E. Talbot, a strong protectionist, to the Tariff Commission. His addition to the protectionist strength already on the Commission arguably was as effective in protecting domestic economic interests as formal tariff restrictions.(3)  The Administration also had to settle for a one-year extension of its tariff setting authority.

In 1954 Congress again limited the extension of authority to one year. Eisenhower had appointed the Commission on Foreign Economic Policy chaired by Clarence Randall. As expected the Commission recommended wider presidential latitude and greater cuts in tariff policy. Its report, however, was not as strong as some administration elements hoped it would be and the cause was traced in part to Congress. Presidential Special Assistant C. D. Jackson wrote to Dulles to complain that Randall's recommendations had been watered down to what was "politically possible . . . a fairly low common denominator." The cause, Jackson theorized, was that:

> The intellectual, emotional, and political limitations are such that men in government, even the best, will tend to water down their ideas, work out interdepartmental compromises, and look over their shoulders at Congress, with the result that their end product is already diluted. By the time it emerges from the political hopper, most of the imaginative juice has been squeezed out of it.(4)

If the anticipated reaction of the Randall Commission was not enough, Congress also gave very direct warning signals to Eisenhower and other executive officials. Members were worried about the domestic economic impact of various aspects of the report; they were concerned about the possibility of greater trade with communist countries; and the domestic political implications worried the Republican legislators. Any attempt to push the bill through Congress, Republican leaders of both houses warned, would cause a pitched battle which would be divisive for the President's party. Eisenhower called for party unity so that a good record could be put before the voters and the leaders agreed, but the respective solutions differed. Eisenhower meant achieve unity by voting for a strong tariff reduction bill. The leaders meant achieve unity by muting or ignoring the Randall Commission. (5)  Eisenhower also did not help his cause by telling members that the Randall report did not completely represent his views, but that he could not bring down a "bunch of smart fellows" then impose his own views completely.(6)  The legislature prevailed. The Ways and Means Committee, which handles trade measures, threatened to hold up a social security package if the trade issue was pressed. As the fall election drew closer, Republican leaders pressed the point that they did not want the trade issue interjected into the election. Eisenhower railed against Congress' failing to live up to its responsibility in a matter important to the national interest, but in the end he had to settle again for a simple one-year extension of his tariff setting authority.(7)

Eisenhower was finally able to secure a three-year extension in 1955, but only after asserting himself vigorously. At a pre-legislative session with Republican leaders he was told that Congress was reluctant to surrender its authority over trade to either the Executive or to any supra-national authority (an expanded GATT-General Agreement on Trades and Tariffs). At the end of the meeting Senator Eugene Millikin urged Chairman Randall to leave Congress some elbow room to which Randall responded with a remark about the big elbows of Congress.(8) The Democratic congressional victory in November 1954 actually brightened the chance of Eisenhower's trade program, although an economic recession, much of it in Democratic areas, had a negative impact. Southern Democrats, traditionally free traders, reversed their usual stand out of concern with southern textile interests. It was only after a series of compromises which strengthened escape clause provisions and after promises by the Administration to guard against trade abuses and domestic damage that Eisenhower finally got his three-year extension.(9)

The next major change in trade policy came when President Kennedy won passage of the Trade Expansion Act of 1962. The President gained broad new powers to reduce tariffs up to 50%. A strong presidential commitment to passage of the act and an intensive White House lobbying effort were the keys to success. Even though the 1962 Act was a significant victory for the Administration and expanded its power, Congress made a number of adjustments. The Act mandated that the United States multilateral trade negotiating team include two members each from the House and Senate. The vote by which Congress could override a presidential decision on an escape clause issue was reduced from two-thirds to a simple majority, and restrictions were imposed on trade concessions to communist countries. Further presidential promises were given for special (protectionist) consideration to textiles and timber. Most importantly, Congress created the new office of Special Trade Representative in the Executive Office of the President. This action removed trade negotiations from the State Department where, Congress suspected, tariffs were manipulated for foreign policy gains with little attention to domestic economic impact. Congress also prohibited tariff cuts on those products where domestic injury had been found by the Tariff Commission.(10)

In the area of tariffs and other economically oriented trade barriers, Congress has generally acquiesced to expanded executive authority to make tariff cutting reciprocal trade agreements. But Congress has been torn in its attitudes toward trade regulation. On the one hand it supports the basic concept of free trade and recognizes the difficulties of handling complex tariff reductions in a burdened and parochial Congress. Therefore it was willing to pass off responsibility to the Executive, knowing full well that meant substantially lower trade barriers. On the other hand, there are several countervailing motives. For philosophical and parochial reasons, protectionism has persisted. Institutionally, Congress has been reluctant to give up a sphere of authority. Numerous informal executive pledges to protect industries have been gained. Escape clauses and legislative vetoes have been inserted. Trade matters have been largely removed from the State Department.

Pastor has concluded that "if the Congress is obsessed with any facet of trade policy, it is certainly not to assist special groups, but to see that the International Trade Commission [Tariff Commission until 1975] is free from all--including congressional--distorting influence."(11) That characterization is not quite the entire picture. It is true that Congress has worked to ensure that if it did not make decisions, at least they would be made on an equitable basis. But it is also true that on numerous occasions Congress has used its powers to intervene. Presidents have honored numerous pledges of restraint given to win passage of various trade measures. Congress has also utilized its legislative veto to thwart executive decision. That branch has also used its general legislative powers to manipulate policy on individual items. Referring to Latin America, Pastor contends that "the existence of Congress means we . . . are more dilatory and niggardly in giving . . . economic/trade concessions." He points out the fact that the domestically oriented Ways and Means and Finance Committees handle trade legislation in Congress. Pastor even cites instances where the supposedly foreign policy oriented Foreign Affairs Committee has had a protectionist impact. One illustration he gives is the influence of Dade County, Florida's Representative Dante Fascell, Chairman of the Subcommittee on Inter-American Affairs, and his successful pressure on the Departments of State and Agriculture to limit the importation of Mexican tomatoes.(12) In another instance, presidential candidate Richard Nixon reportedly promised South Carolina Senator Strom Thurmond that in return for support of his electoral bid, he would negotiate a reduction of textile imports from Japan.(13)

The two examples also illustrate the common, informal legislative process. Congress has not so much tried to restrict executive negotiating authority. Indeed, it has regularly expanded it. Rather it has tried to ensure a judicious, even somewhat sympathetic executive response to domestic disruption caused by tariff reductions. Pastor points out that "Congress has only moved to deny the Executive negotiating flexibility when the Executive has failed to demonstrate sufficient responsiveness to the legislative mandate."(14)

In a variation of Freidrich's classic "anticipated reaction" formulation, Pastor picturesquely describes the legislative-executive interaction in the trade policy as a "cry and sigh" process. The essentials are if domestic sectors are hurt by foreign competition they cry for relief--first to the Executive and, if frustrated there, to Congress. Congress begins to consider relief legislation, which brings <u>cries</u> of protectionism from free traders and foreign governments. As debate proceeds, safety valves open. Foreign governments and economic interests back off to avoid legislation. The executive also responds by pressuring foreign interests and taking short-term relief action, again to avoid more permanent and extensive legislative remedies. Thus pressure is eased and a <u>sigh</u> of relief is heard. It is the threat, then, rather than the actual passage of legislation which is Congress' most common weapon. As long as the escape clause valves remain open, Congress supports free trade. When they close it threatens to revert to the Smoot-Hawly days. No one really wants that, and so, by a subtle process, Congress acts to alter the trade process even though the bill fails and people who count votes and numbers of acts passed conclude Congress has surrendered all its authority.(15)

## Trade with Communist Countries

An area in which the White House was less successful in liberalizing international economic relations was in the extension of trading privileges with communist nations. In the early cold war period Congress acted in numerous ways to limit severely trade with communist countries. Legislation was even passed designed to cut off foreign aid to other countries that sent strategic materials behind the iron curtain. In the spirit of the times, successive administrations had realistically if not enthusiastically acquiesced to such restrictions. By the 1960s, the changes in East-West relationships and the increased attractiveness of trade with the communists for purely economic reasons found the Kennedy and Johnson Administrations increasingly interested in significantly expanding trade with the Soviet Union and its East European dependencies.

Growing executive enthusiasm was not matched in Congress. President Johnson's first clash with Congress over trade with communist countries came only four days after his assumption of the Presidency. The issue was the sale of wheat to the Soviet Union and, in particular, an attached amendment by Senator Karl Mundt prohibiting the Export-Import Bank or any other agency from guaranteeing loans to Communist countries to finance trade. Only by working throughout the night of November 26 was Johnson able to defeat the amendment 57 to 36. On December 12, however, the House passed a foreign aid bill with an amendment that was identical to Mundt's. The conference committee's compromise version did not include the controversial amendment. Holding fast, the House rejected the compromise bill and adjourned. Again, Johnson, riding his prestige as a new President and fighting hard, was able to prevail by calling the House back into session and threatening to hold it through Christmas.(16)

The 89th Congress, which convened in January 1965, also spelled trouble for Johnson's attempts to liberalize trade with the Soviet bloc. In 1964 the United States and Soviet Union had signed a Consular Convention to allow the establishment of trade offices in cities other than the nations' capitals on a recipro-

cal basis. The convention required two-thirds Senate ratification to take effect. Following a classic tactic, the President
appointed a Special Commission on United States Trade Relations
with Eastern European Countries and the Soviet Union. On April
29, 1965 the Commission filed its expected favorable report.
Several of Johnson's advisors and some in Congress pushed for a
quick submission of the convention to the Senate.(17) Fulbright
argued that by not taking the convention up "we are strengthening
the hand of a small, irresponsible group of the radical right.
(18) He also contended that 1965, a nonelection year, would be
more favorable than the following year. Other signals to the
White House were considerably less optimistic. Foreign Relations
Committee Chief-of-Staff Carl Marcy told an aide to Hubert Humphrey that congressional leaders did not think the treaty could
pass.(19) Johnson cautiously agreed with the pessimists. Based
on negative signals from Congress, troubles over Vietnam and the
Dominican Republic, and the fact that he did not want to further
dilute his strength to push for Great Society legislation,
Johnson chose to delay.(20) Without White House support, Fulbright backed off his advocacy.

True to predictions, 1966 proved to be an even more difficult
year. Fulbright and other liberal senators such as Joseph Clark
again pushed for action.(21) Both Fulbright and Clark felt that
a strong presidential effort could secure passage. "What bothers
me most," Fulbright complained to Mike Mansfield, "is that I do
not believe the possibility of action has been explored fully
. . . . My fear is that this important measure may be lost simply because the Government has not focused its energies on getting something done."(22) The Senate Majority Leader disagreed.
He told Assistant Secretary of State Douglas MacArthur II that
action could not be considered in 1966. With the election
approaching, "there would be certain members of the Senate who
would be tempted to take a demagogic attitude on the Convention,"
and other "Senators who were up for reelection that had extreme
right-wing opposition would be placed in a difficult position if
they were obliged to vote for it before the election in November."(23) Although Johnson dabbled with the idea of submitting
the treaty throughout 1966, in the end he delayed. In response
to Fulbright's pressure, presidential aide Francis Bator advised
Johnson, "the truth is that it would be bad foreign policy, as
well as bad domestic politics, to take a chance, go for broke--
and lose." Bator's conclusion was that "our entire East-West
posture would be tarnished if, after a nasty fight, we lost--we
can't take a chance if its going to be close."(24) Johnson
agreed, and the Consular Convention languished for another year.

Nineteen sixty-seven was the year to push the issue. With
the election behind and East-West relations relatively placid,
Johnson submitted the Consular Convention. In a separate but
related action he also called on Congress to pass legislation
removing special tariff barriers to East-West trade. The Administration's joining of the battle did not, however, come with
enthusiasm. As the new Congress met in January, there was considerable doubt as to what Johnson would do. A Humphrey aide
advised the Vice President that, in view of Republican gains in

Congress, it would be difficult to pass the convention and East-West trade act. "The real question," the aide wrote, "is how much of a fight is the White House willing to make to get them through?"(25) The key to successful passage, in both the estimation of the White House and Mike Mansfield, was Minority Leader Everett Dirksen. Faced with statements of opposition by Dirksen as late as January 23, 1967, the President and Majority Leader hesitated. They wanted to move, but not to lose. Others were less cautious. The likes of Senators Fulbright and Clark were joined by Republican Thurston Morton of Kentucky. Morton, a former Assistant Secretary of State for Congressional Relations, was frustrated with Dirksen's leadership. He approached White House officials. "I can straighten [Dirksen] out . . . . If you guys go, I'll go."(26) The White House remained reluctant, but Morton went anyway. On January 31 Morton took the Senate floor to urge immediate consideration and adoption of the treaty.

Johnson still had his doubts, but the prospect of losing the initiative on a foreign policy issue to the antithetical Fulbright, much less the Republican Morton, was even less inviting. Victory required a strong presidential effort focused on Dirksen and, secondarily but still importantly, on conservative Southern Democrats to whom Richard Russell was the key.

Congressional opposition was based on a number of issues. The most general was opposition to increasing economic relations with the communists, especially at a time when American troops were fighting the communists in Vietnam. There was also concern that Soviet consular offices in the United States would serve as platforms for Soviet espionage. Federal Bureau of Investigation Director J. Edgar Hoover had testified in 1967 that consular offices would increase the potential for subversive activity and make the Bureau's job more difficult. Despite protests by Hoover that "the FBI is not a policy-making agency and we do not express opinions," and "Since 1924 when I became Director the FBI has refrained from interjecting itself into the area of legislation," Hoover supplied ammunition to the conservatives. Writing Senator Karl Mundt, he prompted:

> You asked whether these efforts by communist diplomatic personnel still continue. They most certainly do. Representatives of the KGB (Soviet Committee of State Security) and the GRU (Soviet Military Intelligence Service), comprising a large segment of the Soviet diplomatic corps in the United States, are conducting an intensive campaign aimed at the most sensitive data regarding our scientific and technical developments, our military and defense programs, and the future plans of our government.(27)

Others pitched in with similar scare scenarios. A former official with the State Department's security office wrote Dirksen that Soviet consulates (prior to their 1948 closing) had been bases for atomic spying. Word was spread that Soviet officials were personally lobbying Senator Dirksen,(28) and, indeed, the Soviets were active in probing Congress' probable course.(29) The Consular Convention was also attacked as part of the commu-

nist coddling "bridge building" of Johnson and the liberals.
Senator Roman Hruska wrote his party leader that the treaty was
just the first of many such measures culminating with the "bomb-
shell" East-West Trade Bill. The idea, Hruska warned, was to
gain momentum to "force the Congress into going 'all the way'"
(30)

The Administration countered these arguments by trying to
contend that the convention was primarily a treaty to protect
American citizens travelling in the Soviet Union.(31) Richard
Russell was plied with the convoluted argument that by easing
tensions with the West via the treaty, the Soviets could concentrate on their rivalry with China, thereby loosening China's grip
on North Vietnam, with the end result that less Americans would
be killed in Vietnam.(32)

More than on any single argument, the issue rested on the
position of Everett Dirksen and on the persuasive abilities of
Lyndon Johnson. The President also had an unlikely and valuable
ally in Thurston Morton who campaigned hard among fellow Republicans to win their support of the treaty. Dirksen was caught in
the middle. He found himself too far out in front, or perhaps
behind, a substantial number of moderate Republicans who threatened to break with his leadership.(33) He was also at odds with
a president whose patronage was important to his political and
ego standing. The result was a personal pilgrimage from opposition to support that was reminiscent of Arthur Vandenberg.

The Administration helped him in his journey. Assurances
were wrung from J. Edgar Hoover that Soviet consulates would not
pose an insuperable security threat. Dirksen dramatically
confided the "top secret" information to Barry Goldwater that
Walt Rostow had said that American consulates in the Soviet Union
would provide a much greater intelligence source than Soviet
consulates in America. (34) The Administration also worked with
Dirksen to supply the Senator with a letter from Dean Rusk that
would answer conservative qualms and justify Dirksen's support.
Among other balms, Rusk's letter agreed to consult with the
Senate and with local officials before allowing a Soviet consulate in a specific city. Further, no consulate would be established in the immediate future.(35) Rusk also pointed out that
President Eisenhower had advocated a consulate exchange in 1959,
and the former President was persuaded to endorse the convention
as in the national interest. All this added to Lyndon Johnson's
patented persuasive techniques and turned the tide. Opponents
fought on. Mundt explained that they felt there was an "outside"
chance of blocking the treaty, but more importantly,

> even if we fail . . . we have compelled the Administration
> to exert so much pressure on those it is able to influence
> that I believe that they are exhausting most of their ammuni-
> tion and dissipating the powers of influence sufficiently so
> that when the really big battle begins over the approval of
> _increased . . . East-West trade with Communist countries,
> the Administration is going to have much more difficulty
> convincing the Senate to vote against the desires of their
> constituents and the best interests of our fighting men in
> Vietnam.(36)

By early March Mundt was predicting the vote would come soon
after the Administration had "twisted enough arms and broken the
backs of enough would-be Senatorial resistors so that they can
win the battle."(37) Mundt was right. On March 16, the Senate
ratified the Consular Convention by a vote of 66 to 28, a scant
three votes above the necessary two-thirds.

Mundt was also correct in his assessment of the inability of
White House and congressional liberals to move the Consular Convention and East-West Trade Bill in tandem. The opposition
heavily attacked the latter bill as virtually "trading with the
enemy" during the Vietnam War. Republican conservatives dubbed
the measure the "kiss and kill" bill. They also began to see
possible partisan advantage. "All in all," Mundt wrote, "I
believe this is setting the stage for a landslide defeat of
President Johnson if he dares run for reelection next year . . .
No American president before him has ever followed a 'kiss and
kill' formula as Commander in Chief in time of war by which he
kisses the hand of our enemy economically by sending them supplies which they fabricate and transship to Hanoi to kill our
brave and gallant American fighters there."(38)

The Administration tried to sell the bill as a step toward
peace, as economically advantageous to the domestic economy, and
as threatening to communist control in the East. Johnson described "the daily contact with American businessmen . . . [as] a
real challenge to those in the Communist world who try to paint a
false picture of what America really is." Further, Johnson
argued trade would stimulate the eastern block appetite for
consumer goods, "an appetite that [its] leaders cannot ignore,"
thus diverting communist industrial activity from heavy to light
industry.(39) Administration officials also tried to reach opposition senators through the domestic economic connection. Vice
President Humphrey tried to organize a committee of economic
interests. He believed that Dirksen could be influenced by organizations such as the Soy Bean Council, International Harvester,
and John Deere. North Dakota's Senator Milton Young could be
approached by the food and meat industry in the Midwest. Representative Wilber Mills of Arkansas could be pressured by the
tobacco people.(40)

What had been successful for the Consular Convention failed
in the battle for the East-West Trade Bill. Many did not buy the
economic argument. "It must be remembered," Mundt wrote, that
the communists do not desire "greater and larger purchases of
wheat, corn, and other American farm products for their own
usage, but rather they are seeking advanced technology and techniques which relate primarily to the expansion of their potential
military-industrial complex."(41) The opposition in Congress was
also strengthened by resistance from within the Executive including the Commerce Department and Assistant Secretary of State
Thomas Mann. As summer became fall and the aid bill remained
bottled up in Congress, Administration enthusiasm waned.
Congress placed new restrictions on the private extension of
credit to the Soviet Union. As popular and congressional support

of Vietnam eroded, the President became increasingly dependent on the very elements that were most opposed to the trade bill. In the end the President and his leaders in Congress decided it was better to cut their losses. The bill never came to a vote.(42)


## Congress and Foreign Aid

The impact of Congress on foreign aid policy has resembled its effect on trade policy. On the surface, the Executive has pretty much controlled policy, getting most of what it wanted and limiting formal congressional changes, mandates, and restrictions to marginal areas. Also like trade, though, Congress' impact in the sum of the marginal alterations, plus the informal promises and tactics needed to move aid programs through Congress, had a noteworthy effect on foreign policy.

Several examples of congressional influence on aid policy have already been discussed. The refusal to fund the Aswan Dam is perhaps the most far-reaching example of legislative influence through aid appropriations. Congressional insistence on substantial aid to Nationalist China and Israel are also important examples of aid influence. The maneuvering over the 1950 Korean aid bill and Acheson's charge that it may have tempted North Korea to attack the South is yet another notable instance where Congress played an important role.

On a less dramatic, but still significant level, Congress also acted to preserve the cold war atmosphere through the medium of foreign aid. Foreign aid has been one of the most difficult overseas programs for the Executive to defend. To a substantial degree the problem boils down to how to convince Congress to give domestic resources, taxpayers' dollars, to foreigners. Lacking a consistent political rationale or supportive domestic groups, aid has been vulnerable to sharp legislative attacks. Stemming from their parochial orientation, many congressmen tended to translate the issue into domestic terms. Opponents of foreign aid consistently based their arguments on domestic considerations--that charity should begin at home, that government spending is inflationary, that the taxpayer is sorely overburdened. The problem for successive administrations was how to overcome these objections and to shift Congress' perceptual focus to foreign policy where the president has a psychological advantage.

The mental slight of hand required to present aid as a foreign rather than domestic policy question was often accomplished through a reliance on cold war rhetoric. As in the examples of the 1946 British loan, the 1947 Truman Doctrine, and the 1948 Marshall Plan, the Executive was forced to rely on the communist bogy-man to convince the Congress to fund otherwise unpopular aid programs. When international tensions were high and aid pictured as a stop communism measure, Congress gave the president most of what he asked. In 1958, for example, Secretary of State Dulles worked to ease cuts in the aid request by arguing that no areas had been lost to communism during the Eisenhower Administration, "but that happy situation could well change if the House Committee cuts were allowed to stand." If the United States could not put funds into critical areas "it would almost serve as notice that we would have to take some losses."(43) Similarly, military aid programs were consciously sold to Congress as critical to the defense of the United States proper rather than merely as bolstering the capability of foreign countries.(44) Senator Dirksen, for one, was converted after an administration-sponsored trip to Asia. Dirksen was moved to proclaim that foreign aid was not an international "welfare program." Rather, "this is the most selfish program I know of . . . . We are not undertaking it out of charity . . . . We are doing it for our own skins . . . . I used to attack the program . . . . I take it back."(45) The importance of the USIA was similarly touted on its anti-communist value.(46)

That line of argument generally continued to dominate during the Kennedy and Johnson Administrations. When it did not, disaster was invited. Kennedy's 1963 foreign aid request was cut nearly 34 percent, for one, partly because of the fact that rather than stress anti-communism the Administration relied on other arguments. It stressed humanitarian concerns and also contended foreign aid increased American exports and opened new and expanded markets for the future. Congress was more comfortable dealing with domestic economic implications, felt at liberty to disagree, and made a record reduction.(47)

More typically, even a figure such as Chet Bowles, the leading soft-liner in the Kennedy and Johnson Administrations was prone to utilize the anti-communism theme to sell aid. As Ambassador to India, Bowles wrote to members of Congress pointing to India as a counter-weight to China in Asia.(48) Bowles was not really comfortable with that line of reasoning; yet it was realistic. Replying to a letter from the Ambassador, Senator Fulbright agreed, commenting, "I find myself in agreement with your observation that there has been a fallacy in presenting foreign aid as an anti-Communist weapon. However, it has not only been presented in that format in the past but still is being presented in that format."(49) President Johnson, in his presentation of foreign aid, argued strongly from the anti-communist perspective. That tendency was enhanced by the war in Vietnam. Writing to Senate Finance Committee Chairman Carl Hayden, Johnson typically stressed:

A candid look at the situation in Asia, Africa, and Latin America reveals no diminution in the continuing intensive thrust of Communist penetration and subversion. The interests of the United States are deeply engaged in the effort to establish freedom and progress in those areas. In my judgment, as in the judgment of Presidents Kennedy, Eisenhower and Truman before me, the future welfare and security of the American people requires us to support the struggle of the peoples in the developing countries to achieve and maintain their freedom.(50)

The anti-communist rationale has had its drawbacks. Congress has inserted numerous restrictions, many of an anti-communist nature, in aid bills which have angered foreign governments and

restricted executive flexibility. The Mutual Defense Assistance
Control Act of 1951, popularly known as the Battle Act, barred
aid to countries which shipped strategic material to Soviet bloc
countries. Congress also attempted to include a requirement that
aid recipients declare their alignment with the "free world."
The Administration managed to have this softened so that only
recipients of military aid would have to pledge their allegiance.
Congress insisted, however, that all nations receiving aid reaffirm their adherence to the principles of the United Nations.
(51) The finer points of the wording compromise escaped most
people at home and abroad. Within the next few years ten nations
refused American aid rather than submit to what they felt was
blatant political pressure. One government, the Indonesian,
actually collapsed because of internal dissention caused by the
requirement. Five years later, in 1956, Congress refused to
grant aid to Yugoslavia unless the President found that assistance was in the national interest. Although President Eisenhower quickly found such to be the case, the incident proved
unsettling to Yugoslavia's delicate position between the two
superpowers. Former Ambassador to Yugoslavia, George Kennan,
specifically mentioned the incident while telling the Jackson subcommittee that congressional limitations, "were the main impedi-
ments I experienced to the full deployment of my usefulness at my
post.(52)

Another theme in congressional concern with foreign aid has
been promoting free enterprise and defending American economic
interests. In 1961 Iowa's Senator Bourke Hickenlooper successfully sponsored an amendment which enjoined giving aid to states
that expropriated American- owned property without compensation.
Evaluation of the impact of the Hickenlooper Amendment has varied
significantly. The Kennedy and successive administrations
opposed it because it restricted executive flexibility. Yet, it
was evaluated by Dean Rusk as working out "pretty well in a
number of situations."(53) Although company and government valuations of expropriated property have differed greatly, the amendment encouraged various countries to make at least partial repay-
ments. It encouraged Brazil to compensate American communications companies after expropriations in 1962. In 1963 aid to
Ceylon was suspended after that country seized oil company property. Ceylon's immediate reaction was understandably negative.
More property was taken over, but in 1965 a settlement of the
dispute was negotiated. The amendment also worked in more subtle
ways than by application. Pastor notes that the State Department
gained added resolve in pressuring Latin American governments on
compensation. Although the amendment was actually invoked only
in the Ceylon case, Pastor finds "its 'spirit' continues to rever-
berate through the halls of Foggy Bottom.(54) That author also
notes that the amendment gave business elements greater access to
the State Department. He quotes one of the State Department's
country directors as admitting, "If I don't spend five minutes
with a businessman, then I may have to spend three hours with his
Congressman."(55)

Others are less positive in their evaluations of the Hickenlooper Amendment. W. E. Kuhn found that the amendment's benefits

fall "woefully short" of its sponsor's intent. He contends that "probably it has not enhanced respect for U.S.property by host country governments." He also finds it has "soured" relations with governments which expropriated American property under pressure from their own domestic constituencies.(56) Kuhn's evaluation does not take into account some of the more subtle processes noted by Pastor, however. Nor does it distinguish between the potential of the amendment's usefulness and its actual application. Because of natural executive resistance to congressional restrictions and because the State Department is normally more interested in good foreign relations than in recovering assets for American companies, the main shortfall of the amendment arguably was in executive application rather than in congressional intent. In the case of Peru's 1969 expropriation of $200 million (company valuation) in property of the International Petroleum Company, a Standard Oil of New Jersey subsidiary, the Nixon Administration was reluctant to pressure the military regime which the President saw as a counter-weight to the evolving communist government of Salvador Allende in Chile. In Henry Kissinger's words,

> The Nixon Administration stretched our legislation almost to the breaking point to reach an equitable settlement . . . without having to invoke restrictive legislation. We repeatedly sought pretexts to postpone application of the Hickenlooper Amendment and made clear that we were prepared to accept . . . less than full value, so as to maintain friendly relations with an important country.(57)

Still, the amendment's existence served as a "club in the closet," and a settlement was eventually negotiated. As one Peruvian government leader told an interviewer in 1970, "You should understand that the principal political leaders of the military government for almost eighteen months have been almost exclusively preoccupied with whether or not the United States would apply the Hickenlooper Amendment."(58)

The concept of the Hickenlooper Amendment also led to several clones. In 1972 Representative Henry Gonzales successfully sponsored an amendment which required the President to instruct the (American) Executive Director of the Inter-American Development Bank to oppose loans to any government which did not compensate for expropriated property. Congress also amended the Sugar Act in 1972 to cancel an offending government's entire annual quota of sugar exports to the United States. The 1967 Fisherman's Protective Act also extended the concept to apply to the uncompensated seizure of assets of that industry by Peru, Ecuador and others. Finally, in 1973 Congress amended the original amendment to give the president authority to waive its application "in the national interest." A survey of its members by the Council of the Americas, which represents 90 percent of all American corporate investments in Latin America, found that 76 percent of these members thought the amendment had "outlived its usefulness."(59) Congress' action also brought the legislative language into accord with actual execution by the Executive. The conclusion of one scholar that the 1973 charge "defused, if not actually re-pealed the amendment" is overdrawn, however.(60) Its intent still stands, and in the dynamics of executive-legislative rela-tions it serves notice to both the American and foreign adminis-trations that wantonly uncompensated expropriations will occasion congressional displeasure and possible action.

Also related to the encouragement of free enterprise and the protection of the domestic economy, Congress, in 1963, amended the Foreign Assistance Act of 1961 to require that all projects of $100 million or more be specifically approved by Congress. This clause was quickly used by Congress to veto a contribution of $500 million to finance India's Bokaro Steel Mill. While aid to the project might have been politically advantageous, with India's steel mills operating below capacity, utility of the grant was dubious. Congress also had a long-standing aversion, encouraged by domestic steel interests, to funding foreign steel mills which might compete with American mills.(61) Additionally, the steel mill was to be an enterprise of the Indian government, and, according to Senator Fulbright, "there is a great deal of opposition to the Bokaro steel program . . . [because] it social-izes the Indian economy." Fulbright also cited resentment against Indian leaders Jawaharlal Nehru and Krishna Menon, concern over the American balance of payments deficit, and voter opposition to foreign aid as contributing to the congressional veto of the project.(62)

Congress has also been substantially responsible for such foreign aid innovations as the use of agricultural surpluses to augment foreign aid under Public Law 480. While this was basi-cally conceived of as a way to relieve surpluses and support prices in the United States, by extension it brought billions of dollars of food to agriculturally poor countries.(63) Congress was also responsible for the establishment of other worthwhile innovations such as the Development Loan Fund. This fund was urged by Senator A. S. Mike Monroney through Senate Resolution 264 in 1958 over the initial objections of the State Department. (64)

If any one area can be singled out for an accusing finger against Congress, it is that of aid organization. Some of Congress' activities, such as the establishment of the Office of Inspector General and Comptroller of Mutual Security, added to the integrity of the aid program. But overall, constant congres-sional shifting of bureaucratic boxes in aid administration has certainly done more harm than good. From 1948 to 1966 the admin-istration of foreign aid was restructured six different times and came under ten directors. The President and Secretary of State usually gave in to these organizational changes to save the program. As Robert Lovett once starkly put it to Harry Truman, "We must make a deal sooner or later—either a separate [aid] agency or a big cut."(65) The result of the almost yearly experi-ence of congressional harassment has been in the words of one scholar, "disorganization, constant reorganization, caution, timidity, and uncertain purpose."(66) Although administrative reorganizations have often had the helpful by-product of resur-gence of congressional confidence and support of the aid program, they have also resulted in a decrease in employee morale, a decline in efficiency, and a lessening of foreign recipient confidence in the program.(67)

Congress has also regularly employed the "carom effect," using foreign aid to win concessions in other areas or register dismay over executive controlled areas of policy. Senate Republican Minority Leader Everett Dirksen in just one example, submitted a disabling amendment to the 1964 foreign aid bill in an attempt to force the Democratic Administration to agree to changes in a bill governing court action on legislative reapportionment. Dirksen's ploy was successful.(68) The tactic may have annoyed, but should not have surprised, President Johnson. He was a past master himself. President Eisenhower's congressional liaison, Bryce Harlow, has recalled that, as Senate Majority Leader, "Lyndon loved to use, just loved to use, Eisenhower's pet, foreign aid, as a shillelagh on Ike. He would hold it up deliberately to be the last item in a session of Congress and use it as leverage for making Ike do what he wanted [him] to do on other things." When asked if the maneuver worked, Bryce replied, "Oh yes, yes [he made] all kinds of trades. [He] just used muscle, just muscle."(69)

The overall impact of Congress on foreign aid was an occasional help and an occasional hindrance, but never influence in proportion to its potential power. Congress undoubtedly caused a degree of inefficiency by harassment of the organizations of aid administration and through the year to year uncertainty of funding. In a few cases, congressional refusal to appropriate aid has strained, or, in the case of Egypt, contributed to a serious deterioration in relations. Thus, Congress was able to gain a stronger voice in foreign policy formation through foreign aid appropriations. When one considers the tremendous potential inherent in the power of the purse, however, it also becomes obvious that congressional influence fell far short of what it might be. The history of foreign aid during the period was primarily one of initiatives by the president and his advisors. There is little or no evidence that Congress crippled the aid program or frustrated its major goals. Even the most strident opponents of foreign aid came to accept it much as protectionists accept executive discretion in tariff and quota regulation. As Otto Passman, long-time foe of foreign aid put it, "I am opposed to foreign aid; it has been, in my opinion, one of the greatest foreign policy failures in history. But as a realist, I recognize that it is, however distasteful, a political 'fact of life' today."(70) In short, foreign aid appropriations were used only sporadically by Congress and have been limited in their impact.(71)

## Foreign Policy Personnel

An area of congressional influence which has been tangentially discussed, but not specifically focused on, is the impact of Congress on the "hiring and firing" of foreign policy officials. At the most overt level, Senate confirmation of presidential

appointments, Congress has seldom formally rejected a nominee.
Between 1945 and 1974 only one of 425 ambassadorial nominations
and one of 182 nominations as representative to an international
organization was turned down. In the area of major military
posts, which also involve foreign policy, presidents had sixty-
four successes and no defeats. Overall in the area the presidential batting average was .998.(72)

Presidential success in gaining confirmation is based primarily on the feeling in Congress that presidents should be able to
pick their own team. Senator Arthur Vandenberg wrote a Senate
colleague: "I am frank to say that Mr. Acheson would not have
been my choice for Secretary of State . . . [But] as a general
rule, I would let [Truman] have his own way in choosing his
personal advisors . . . and then hold him to strict accountabil-
ity for the ultimate results."(73) At another juncture Styles
Bridges, a staunch conservative, wrote to Henry Kissinger who had
commented on the nomination of Chester Bowles, an equally staunch
liberal, as Under Secretary of State: "As you know, with rare
exception presidential appointments of this type are confirmed by
the Senate in accordance with the belief that the Chief Executive
should be entitled to his own chief associate."(74)

It would be a mistake, however, to view Congress' influence
from the narrow perspective of Senate confirmation votes. The
personnel process is a very political undertaking in which Congress possesses some potent tools. Beyond simple confirmation,
appointments at times are made at the behest of members or are
made, not made or withdrawn, in anticipation of congressional
reaction. Congress also can influence the relief, resignation,
or reassignment of incumbent officials. In this period, as was
true during the earlier period, Congress was able to exert
considerable influence over personnel policy, although its application was sporadic and generally confined to second level officials.

Congressional interest in foreign policy personnel at times
is a function of policy issues beyond the individual per se.
The single most important foray of Congress in the field occurred
in the late 1940's and early 1950's. Numerous officials came
under legislative fire because of their supposed sympathy or
connection with Yalta, the "loss" of China, or communist/leftist
causes in general. Before the McCarthy hysteria died out, over
twenty of the State Department's experts on China had either
cashiered or had been exiled to obscurity outside their area of
expertise. The fate of John Carter Vincent provides one striking
example. Vincent was one of the "China hands" in the Department
of State. He had warned of the fatal corruption of Chiang's
Nationalist government and advocated bringing Mao's communists
into a coalition Chinese government. Once China fell to Mao,
rather than being praised for accurate diplomatic forecasting, he
was attacked for sympathizing with the communists and undermining
Chiang. In September 1949 Vincent was removed from his post as
Chief of the Office of Near Eastern Affairs and transferred
(demoted) to Minister to Switzerland in order, according to
Acheson, "both to appease Republican critics and to remove him
from the direct path of Republican vengeance."(75) Under con-

tinued attack, Vincent's odyssey outward to beyond the pale found him further transferred to become Minister to Morocco and Diplomatic Agent at Tangier. Even that remote corner was not safe. In December 1952 Vincent was suspended from his post under charges of disloyalty based, in Acheson's words, "upon policies that he had recommended and the valuations of situations he had made and that largely I had accepted."(76) Acheson stood behind his subordinate, but with the change of administrations in January 1953 Vincent lost his last vestige of protection. The new Secretary, Dulles, concluded Vincent's judgments were deficient and accepted his "voluntary" retirement on March 31, 1953.

Others in the Acheson State Department came under attack simply because of their liberalism. The Secretary's valued assistant Lucius Battle was transferred to an overseas post in mid-1952. "Looking toward the day my enemies might be in a position to wreak vengeance on anyone who had long been associated with me," Acheson recalled, "Luke's friends, with my sad concurrence, had concluded that he would be less conspicuous if he were assigned to a foreign post." It was a good thought, but Battle was eventually forced out of the Department anyway.(77) Others, such as Francis Biddle who had served as Attorney General, were denied appointments. Biddle was considered for appointment as Representative to the United Nations Economic and Social Council. Acheson declined to go forward with the nomination, however, telling Biddle that the Foreign Relations Committee "was strongly of the opinion that the . . . Council might turn into a do-good and spending organization and that they felt that [he] was too sympathetic with what they regarded as New Deal ideas along these lines."(78)

The advent of the Republican Eisenhower Administration in 1953 enhanced the influence of McCarthy and his sympathizers. As discussed, Dulles was especially sensitive to Congress and anxious to avoid what he saw as Acheson's mistake of incurring legislative wrath. The result, both friends and foes agreed, was to pander to McCarthyistic attacks. Officials were dismissed or demoted and, at the urging of Senator Styles Bridges, Scott McLeod was brought in as Department security chief to pass on the purity of officials and appointees.(79) George Kennan left the Department because, according to Kennan, "further assignment would run into difficulty in the Senate."(80) China hands like John Service were dismissed because Dulles was unwilling to come under Senate fire. The impact according to John Emmet Hughes was to create "an atmosphere in the Department that amounted to . . . appeasement . . . of McCarthy's attacks."(81) Even Dulles' associates were appalled. Under Secretary Robert Murphy wrote to his chief that Department morale was "shaken and disturbed,"(82) and five distinguished American diplomats wrote to the New York Times in early 1954 that the nation's foreign service was being destroyed, and "accuracy and initiative have been sacrificed to acceptability and conformity."(83) Even Dulles' own brother Allen, serving as Central Intelligence Agency Director, decried McCarthy's attacks and investigative techniques, claiming: "The mere disclosure that a particular person is working for us may destroy an entire operation. This has already happened to us in connection with congressional investigations."(84)

Perhaps the most spirited contest over any of Eisenhower's early appointments occurred over the nomination of Charles Bohlen as Ambassador to Moscow. The bruising confirmation fight that followed in the Senate stemmed from a variety of factors. At the most general level, Republicans wanted to ensure that after twenty years of minority status key posts were filled with party loyalists.(85) This left Eisenhower in something of a bind-- trying to balance between the normal "requirement" to make bipartisan appointments in foreign policy and Republican pressure to satisfy their long pent up hunger for patronage positions and power. Bohlen was a career diplomat, but was considered Democrat by philosophy and association if not by formal affiliation.(86)

Bohlen had also been tainted, in McCarthyite terms, by association with Yalta. He had served as President Roosevelt's Russian language interpreter at the conference, but in the minds of many Republicans, Bohlen "without doubt . . . was much more than simply an interpreter in connection with the meetings at the end of World War II which were so catastrophic to world peace."(87)

Beyond these concerns of policy substance, a gaggle of other matters clouded Bohlen's nomination. The most irrelevant was a rumor that the ambassador-designate was a homosexual. Everyone involved denied giving the gossip any credence, but Dulles did advise Bohlen to travel with his family to avoid fueling the whisper campaign.(88) Opposition was also voiced as a sop to home town voters. Senator Homer Ferguson was worried about pleasing the large contingent of Polish-American voters in Michigan. (89) Styles Bridges also felt it would help in New Hampshire to be against Bohlen.(90) Finally, Bohlen got caught in a jurisdictional dispute. Senator Smith was moved to oppose Bowles not so much on substance "as the way this thing was done." Smith fumed that his Foreign Relations subcommittee had not been consulted. "I think its an important principle, and I am voting no on this . . ." Smith's stand on principle brought mixed reaction. Fulbright agreed, but Senator Brien McMahon called it a "unique and strange theory." John Sparkman said the only question was whether Bohlen was competent and a good man. Guy Gillette went to the other extreme contending there was "no obligation whatsoever on the part of the Executive to consult with the Senate prior to nominations." Gillette was mostly correct in theory and Smith in practice, but it was Bohlen who lost points through the debate.(91)

If it had been up to Dulles, he would probably never have made the nomination. Bohlen, however, was a personal Eisenhower selection. The President had met Bohlen during World War II and had gained "admiration and respect" for the diplomat.(92) Once the nomination had been made, Dulles was caught between two unfortunate options as he saw them. To campaign for a withdrawal of the nomination would anger Eisenhower. Retreating on Bohlen would also mean, he agreed with his predecessor James Byrnes, that "if we lost this one we would never be able to get anybody we really wanted confirmed again."(93) On the other hand, Dulles did not want his new secretaryship scarred by the _affaire d'Bohlen_. Dulles refused to be photographed with Bohlen(94) and downgraded the diplomat, telling senators that Bohlen might only be in Moscow for a few months before being recalled(95) and that the ambassador would be "simply a reporter--out of a policy-making role."(96)

The catalyst of the ideological opposition to Bohlen was Scott McLeod. He had been appointed security chief because of congressional pressure and as a right wing Republican purity filter in the Department. He had recommended to Dulles that Bohlen not be appointed. When the nomination proceeded, McLeod took his case outside, first to the White House and ultimately to his Senate mentor, Styles Bridges.(97) Dulles was outraged, and it is a testimony to the strength of the McCarthyites and Dulles' fear of them that McLeod was not summarily fired. Bohlen's record was clear. Even McLeod had found no "technical" faults, but policy barred sending Bohlen's file en toto to the Senate. Dulles finally hit on the idea of asking the respected and conservative bipartisan duo of Robert Taft and John Sparkman to come to the Department and examine Bohlen's record. The Senators cleared Bohlen, and given their stature, one Dulles aid recalled, not even McCarthy "dared open his yap on the thing." (98) Thus, Bohlen was confirmed, but there was a postscript. Taft reportedly told Eisenhower that one intraparty squabble of that magnitude was enough, he wanted "no more Bohlens." There were no more. When Secretary of Defense Wilson, for example, tried to get Paul Nitze appointed as Assistant Secretary of Defense for Foreign Affairs, the nomination was blackballed by Senator Knowland because of Nitze's connection with the policies of Acheson.(99)

Dulles was certainly familiar with the ability of Congress to influence diplomatic appointments. Earlier he had himself been appointed Japanese Peace Treaty negotiator as a result of legislative intervention. Dulles had served a short stint in the Senate, being appointed by New York's Thomas Dewey on the resignation of Robert F. Wagner. In a special election in November of that year, Dulles was defeated by Herbert Lehman.

Soon after his defeat, Dulles acted to reinsert himself in the foreign policy process. He signaled his wish to join the State Department as a bipartisan advisor. The reaction of Under Secretary James Webb, Secretary Acheson, and President Truman was negative. Dulles, after all, had forfeited his neutrality, especially during the campaign and its incumbent attacks on administration policy. Indeed, the rejection was so strong that the matter lay fallow for some months. Gradually, under pressure from Vandenberg to rejuvenate bipartisanship, Webb then Acheson changed their minds. It is interesting to note, however, that the feeling against Dulles was so strong that in a March 29, 1950 letter to Acheson discussing the possibility of appointing a Republican consultant on the Far East, Vandenberg did not even mention Dulles.(100) On the following day, however, Dulles met with Vandenberg to press his case.(101) The following day the Senator wrote Acheson pressing Dulles' name. "I deeply feel that it is acutely advisable to bring [Dulles] back into active service, and important cooperation with the State Department," Vandenberg wrote, "if we seriously hope to restore some semblance of unpartisan unity at the water's edge . . . I owe you the frank statement that from a Republican viewpoint . . . [nothing] can approach in importance the renewed association of Mr. Dulles with active foreign policy."(102)

On April 4 Acheson telephoned President Truman to urge Dulles' appointment on the grounds he was Vandenberg's top choice. Truman was still reluctant based on Dulles' campaign criticisms of the Administration's domestic policy. Perhaps, Truman grumbled, he would appoint Dulles, but certainly not as anything so august as Ambassador-at-Large.(103) That left Dulles somewhat short of his hoped for title. After some sharp dickering between Dulles and Acheson they agreed that the Secretary would publicly portray Dulles as one of his "top" advisors, thus implying a direct line from Dulles to Acheson.(104) One other piece of business which had to be cleared up involved Dulles' possible future "political" career. Truman and Acheson were not interested in appeasing Vandenberg at the cost of promoting Dulles for a reelection try against Lehman. In their March 30 conversation, Vandenberg had gained and passed on Dulles' pledge not to run for the New York seat. With Vandenberg's assurances and those elicited from Dulles in a conversation with Assistant Secretary Dean Rusk and a note to Acheson,(105) Acheson called Senator Lehman to assure him that Dulles "was not in the frame of mind to go ahead with a political career," and that the President thought the arrangement "will be advantageous, both for bipartisan foreign policy and to [Lehman] in the campaign next fall. (106) Dulles had to raise his hand on the Senate race one more time. In his appointment interview with Truman he implied that if he had earlier been appointed to the United Nations, as he and Vandenberg had wanted, he would not have run for the Senate in the first place. Now, with his new responsibilities he could assure the President the electoral episode in his career was over.(107)

In a rough sense, congressional influence can be divided between positive impact, where people are appointed or retained because of Congress, and negative impact where appointments are blocked or where incumbent personnel are removed at the behest of Congress. The most numerous actions fall in the former, positive category. Dulles' appointment is but one example.

Particularly when there is a change of administrations, there is considerable pressure over possible appointments. In just one compilation, Under Secretary of State Chester Bowles received twenty-eight calls from members in the first month of the Kennedy Administration. Positions sought on the behalf of constituents, friends, and political allies ranged from Assistant Secretaryships to the head of the Furnishings and Decorations unit of the Foreign Building Operations.(108)

The receptiveness of executive officials to using personnel appointments to gain political points varies greatly. Many express dismay, although few refuse to participate and reap the benefits. Eisenhower, for example, could write Dulles complaining that he was signing too many political nominations. "Are we running out of qualified career men?" he asked. "As you know, I much prefer career men to others for most posts."(109) Eisenhower's reaction may have been partly based on public and private criticism he was getting from Congress for being overly political in his appointments.(110)    He could also become angry at senators of both parties for "trying to make . . . appointments." (111)   Yet Eisenhower, when it suited him, could also pass the word to House Majority Leader Charles Halleck that he appreciated his support, and that if he had any candidates for ambassadorships or other jobs, to let Eisenhower know.(112)

In part, the high political content of Eisenhower's nominations stemmed from the fact that Dulles and Henry Cabot Lodge were both quite partisan minded.   One aide recalled that Dulles

> In terms of appointments and internal dickerings and so forth . . . was keenly aware of the political.  I don't say he was an expert.  I think he was an enthusiastic amateur . . .  We spent a lot of time on appointments and thinking about what kind of partisan advantage there might be, and who on the Hill might react to which kind of appointment. (113)

Lodges' personnel advice was similarly full of political considerations.  Typically in one recommendation, Lodge wrote Eisenhower: "It naturally would also be well if [the appointee] could come from some state in which a friendly Senator could be pleased or a hostile Senator might be moderated."(114)

One category of legislatively inspired appointment is the inclusion of members of Congress in diplomatic positions.  Although such a practice violates at least the letter of the Constitution which prohibits simultaneous service in two branches of government, the legal niceties are either ignored or circumvented by terming the member a "consultant," "observer," or other such ambiguity.   Presidents are loathe to repeat Woodrow Wilson's reputed mistake in leaving Senator Henry Cabot Lodge, Sr. at home.   The service of Senators Vandenberg and Connally on numerous negotiating delegations, Sparkman's and Smith's roles in the Japanese Peace Treaty, and others have already been mentioned. Others, such as Senator Walter George and Representative James Richards, were appointed special envoys immediately after their retirement from office.   There is ample evidence that such moves not only won accolades from and improved access to Congress, but that knowledge of the appointments enhanced the members' cooperation in their waning days.(115)   Members of Congress also have frequently been attached to the United Nations delegation and to disarmament negotiating teams.(116)

Usually there is not an explicit "swap" characteristic to appointments, i.e. they are not connected directly to other aspects of policy or other appointments.  Everett Dirksen seems to have been one of the more avid appointment hounds in recent decades, and was particularly proud of his ability to wangle appointments out of Republican and Democratic presidents alike. Dirksen recalled that Eisenhower, "on my recommendation . . . appointed several ambassadors whom he did not know before."(117) One such appointment was Howard Donovan who Dirksen sponsored and who, within a month, was dispatched to become Consul General in

Zurich, Switzerland.(118)  As he gained stature and leadership of
the Senate Republicans, Dirksen's clout increased.  In an instance late in his career, Dirksen rejected a list of assistant
secretaries submitted as a courtesy by Secretary of Defense
Melvin Laird.  Laird's offense was to have omitted the name of
James D. Hittle, a retired Marine brigadier whom Dirksen knew and
liked.  "I told Mel Laird to send down another list," Dirksen
ruffled, "and if this man's name wasn't on it, don't bother to
send down any names."  Hittle became Assistant Secretary of the
the Navy.(119)  Perhaps more than at any other time, Dirksen's
appointment bargaining reached its height with another old horse
trader, Lyndon Johnson, in the White House.  Dirksen influenced
so many appointments that even Johnson was a bit aghast, exclaim-
ing at one point, "Dammit Everett, if I am not careful you'll
have a marker on every appointee to every agency in town."(120)

Examinations of the archival records reveals many such
appointments.  Chester Bowles' diplomatic career was launched by
Connecticut's Senator William Benton who argued, "We spend too
much of our time and effort conciliating our opponents and not
enough time working with our friends," and pointing out that
Bowles would be "particularly effective" in the 1952 campaign.
(121)  Bowles was appointed Ambassador to India and Nepal.  When
Lyndon Johnson wanted Robert McKinney appointed as Representative
to the International Atomic Energy Agency, he was, despite the
fact that Eisenhower's Chief-of-Staff Sherman Adams reported
strong Republican hostility because of McKinney's "attitude of
hostility toward the President personally and the Administration
as a whole."(122)  When Styles Bridges wanted Robert Hill to
receive a diplomatic post in Latin America, Hill was dispatched
as Ambassador to El Salvador.(123)  Bridges was also able to
secure the post of Assistant Secretary of State for Administration for former New Hampshire Governor Lane Dwinell(124) as well
as the Department's security job for Scott McLeod.  In another
key Eisenhower appointment, Walter Robertson, a doctrinaire anti-
communist, was appointed as Assistant Secretary of State for Far
Eastern Affairs at the suggestion of two China Lobby leaders,
Walter Judd and William Knowland.(125)

Such types of direct congressional intervention on appointments were not limited to the Eisenhower Administration.  The
appointment of Charles Frankel as Assistant Secretary of State
under President Johnson can also partly be attributed to congressional influence.  Before the White House would send Frankel's
name up for confirmation he was required to meet with Foreign
Relations Committee Chairman J. William Fulbright.  Subsequently
the White House began to cool on Frankel's nomination, largely
because of his dissident views on Vietnam, but Fulbright had
decided he liked Frankel and the appointment went through.  As
one State Department official told Frankel, "Bill Fulbright wants
this appointment.  And what Bill Fulbright wants, Bill Fulbright
gets."(126)  Similarly during the Johnson Administration the
support of George Feldman, a Democratic fund raiser, by Speaker
McCormack for a diplomatic post led to Feldman's appointment as
Ambassador to Malta.(127)

Other appointments are made not as a result of direct congressional recommendation, but rather in anticipation of reaction on the Hill. One version of Dulles' appointment as Secretary of State has it that Eisenhower initially favored John J. McCloy for the post, but changed his mind when advisors convinced him that only Dulles, among leading contenders, would be acceptable to the Taft wing of the party.(128) Several other appointments, discussed above, including a son, cousin, and law partner, were also made to win Taft's pleasure. Francis Wilcox, a former Democratic chief-of-staff of the Foreign Relations Committee became Assistant Secretary of State for International Organization, in part, based on Henry Cabot Lodge's recommendations that Wilcox "would be helpful from the standpoint of congressional relations."(129) A Dulles aide has also recalled that, in part, Dulles selected Herbert Hoover, Jr., as Under Secretary because "the Secretary thought Hoover was a great help insofar as the Hill was concerned."(130) President Nixon has said that he appointed William Rogers as Secretary of State, in part, because he could help "thaw [the] freeze between the White House and Foreign Relations Committee. Melvin Laird was similarly appointed Secretary of Defense partly because of his high standing in and knowledge of Congress.(131)

Still other appointments are made in more of an explicit trading atmosphere. At times this can be quite general as when Speaker Sam Rayburn and President Eisenhower discussed Rayburn's support of mutual security legislation and Eisenhower's level of bipartisan appointments over breakfast.(132) In other instances the deals can be much more defined. When Senator William Langer asked Dulles how to ensure that Thomas Whalen would retain his post in Nicaragua, the Secretary wasted no words: "Vote for some of our men."(133) Eisenhower struck a deal with Senator Bricker that, in exchange for modification of the annual push for the Bricker Amendment, Bricker could fill the next vacancy in the District Court of Iowa. Uping the ante, Bricker reminded the President that he had recommended Potter Stewart for the vacancy on the Supreme Court. Eisenhower replied that he had great respect for Stewart, but had come to the conclusion that Stewart did not have enough experience for the high court. The Senator and President parted agreeing to think things over. Soon thereafter Potter Stewart was named to the Supreme Court and the Bricker Amendment became a historical footnote.(134)

In another instance, an Eisenhower bipartisan appointment, that of Ellsworth Bunker as Ambassador to India, encountered opposition from Vermont's Republic Senator George Aiken. Aiken finally withdrew his objection in exchange for an appointment to the Small Business Administration.(135) Another variation is foreign policy support in exchange for a domestic appointment. Foreign Affairs Committee Chairman Doc Morgan traded an appointment for Francis Urbany in a high position with the Office of Emergency Planning for support of the 1964 foreign aid bill. As one White House congressional liaison officer bluntly put it, Morgan "wanted you to know that he would get a good report on the Foreign Aid bill, but that . . . Urbany is a must."(136)

Congress can also be a negative factor in the appointment process, rejecting nominations or causing dismissal, demotion, or

transfer.  A number of McCarthy era instances have already been
discussed above and others occurred.  Dr. Wilson Compton, the
first Administrator of the International Information Agency
resigned from office under McCarthyite pressure.  His particular
crime was not burning all books on McCarthy's list of subversive
literature from IIA overseas libraries.  Ironically, Compton had
been appointed by Truman largely because of his good standing
with Congress.  While he had no government or communications
experience, he was a Republican and knew many members well from
his twenty-six years as a lobbyist for the National Lumber Manu-
facturers' Association.  Compton's successor, Robert Johnson,
followed suit by quickly resigning under McCarthy's pressure.
(137)

Although it has been less common, liberal members of Congress
have also blocked nominees based on philosophical differences.
One instance which resulted from the Indochina conflicts involved
G. McMurtrie Godley.  Godley had served in the post of Ambassador
to Laos and was identified with unpopular administration policy
and tactics there.  He had also been part of a controversy in
1970 when the Administration forbade his testimony before an
executive session of the Foreign Relations Committee unless there
was only one transcript and that was in the exclusive control of
the State Department.  The Executive's position, declared Mike
Mansfield, "was just too much to swallow."(138)  When Godley was
nominated as Assistant Secretary of State for Far Eastern Affairs
in 1973 the Foreign Relations Committee took its revenge.  Godley
was rejected in an action that Chairman Fulbright said he hoped
would "lead the President to give more serious attention to the
Committee's views on the selection of officers to hold policy-
making positions."(139)

Many other negative legislative actions were the result of
less lofty motives than policy disagreement.  Criticism of
Congress has often been a fatal mistake.  In 1957 United States
Information Agency chief Arthur Larson lost his job after declaring in a public speech: "Throughout the New and Fair Deal, this
country was in the grip of a somewhat alien philosophy from
Europe."  This indiscreet attack on the Democrats who controlled
Congress plus a later clash with Lyndon Johnson earned Larson a
budget slash of thirty-three percent and a new job well away from
congressional view.(140)  The case of Clare Booth Luce presents
even a more direct example.  Eisenhower had nominated Luce as
Ambassador to Brazil, in part, at the urging of Republicans such
as former Speaker Joseph Martin.(141)  During confirmation hearings, the outspoken Ambassador designate had clashed with the
equally outspoken Wayne Morse who had, among other things, called
her New York physician demanding to know the name of her psychia-
trist and other personal details.  The matter might have abated
after Luce's seventy-nine to eleven confirmation had not the
Ambassador issued a statement saying that her troubles with the
Senate had begun "when Senator Morse was kicked in the head by a
horse."  The "slur" on the distinguished chairman of the Subcommittee on Latin America infuriated a number of senators, both
opponents and (previous) proponents.  There followed a tempest in
Congress, in the White House, and in the Luce household.  Ambassa-

dor Luce's husband, Harry, the publisher of Time-Life, urged his wife to resign in the face of a political vendetta. Several senators concurred for assorted reasons. Lyndon Johnson told the President he still supported Luce, but was being charged with backing her in an attempt to gain her husband's editorial support for a 1960 presidential bid. White House officials such as Bryce Harlow worked feverishly on the phone with Everett Dirksen to arrive at a "line" to defend her, and in the turmoil Dirksen got his metaphors mixed on the floor and referred to the Ambassador as an "old bag of bones." To his everlasting credit, Eisenhower remained calm and amused, recording in his diary, "All in all a great hassel. The amusing thing to me was that everyone was very excited, cluttering around in my office as if, at the very least, war had been declared!" The upshot was that Ambassador Luce resigned without ever reaching Brazil.(142)

In 1961 Paul Hoffman, who had long experience in international affairs, was blocked from a United Nations delegation appointment because of an article he had written criticizing some senators.(143)

A last example of senatorial pique saw Gordon Scherer of Ohio vetoed as an Alternative Representative to the United Nations. Ohio Democratic Senator Stephen Young wrote to Fulbright that he "violently" objected to Scherer's appointment, claiming that Scherer had questioned the senator's "loyalty and patriotism" in 1959. Like elephants, senators seem never to forget, and Scherer remained in Ohio.(144)

The "electoral connection" is another cause of a substantial number of senatorial objections to diplomatic nominees. In 1953 Eisenhower moved to nominate Indiana's Governor Craig to the United Nations delegation. Both of Indiana's senators, Homer Capehart and William Jenner, objected that not only had they not been consulted, but that Craig had announced that he was going to run against Capehart in the next election. Capehart called Dulles to tell him that if the nomination went forward Jenner "will really jump up and down," and that the two would have to "teach them a lesson and make an example of the case." Craig remained at the Capitol in Indianapolis.(145)

Eisenhower and Dulles also encountered partisan objections to nominations from the Democratic side of the aisle. Wright Morrow fell afoul of Congress twice. In 1954 his name was withdrawn from the United Nations delegation list after political objections arose. Eisenhower angrily called Dulles, upset over retreating as in the Craig case and wondering why Dulles had turned the matter over to the politicians.(146) In 1957 Eisenhower tried again, this time moving to appoint Morrow as Ambassador to Mexico. Again trouble arose. Lyndon Johnson objected. Morrow, it seems, was a Texas Democrat, but had supported Eisenhower both in 1952 and in 1956, a stand which had resulted in his being ousted as Democratic National Committeeman from Texas. In addition to that, Morrow's cousin had made a primary bid to unseat Johnson. It was more than the Majority Leader could tolerate. Johnson not only threatened to block Morrow's confirmation, but told Dulles that he would take a billion dollars out of the foreign aid bill if the Secretary did not "behave." Dulles and Adams did a lot of growling between them that Johnson was "throwing his weight around," that they shouldn't take the Johnson "dictatorship," and asking "What did Johnson do for us?" But in the end they faced the inevitable and Morrow's name was withdrawn.(147)

Another potential envoy to fall before constituency considerations was General Mark Clark. President Truman's desire to nominate Clark as representative to the Vatican was vetoed by Texas Senator Tom Connally. Connally was angered because he had not been consulted and because Clark had been in command of the World War II landing at Salerno where a Texas division, due to alleged miscalculation, had taken severe casualties. Opposition was also based on Protestant opposition, especially centered in the South, to relations with the Catholic Papacy.(148)

Race, unfortunately, has also been a question on occasion. When Lyndon Johnson appointed Carl Rowan as head of the USIA he felt constrained to call Arkansas' Senator John McClellen and ask him not "to cut [Rowan's] guts out because he's a Negro." Happily, McClellen was feeling charitable: "I know you have problems and you're going to do a lot of things I wouldn't do—unless I was President."(149) Less fortunate was George Carter, a black, slated in 1961 to be ambassador to Niger. The "hang up," Bowles wrote Kennedy, was that Carter had a white wife and might draw criticism from Capitol Hill. Carter was not posted to Niger. (150) Another African specialist, who fell at that time to congressional opposition, though not racial, was John Emmerson. Senate Republicans such as Bourke Hichenlooper had prevented Emmerson from moving in title from Consul General to Ambassador to Nigeria when that country became independent in 1960. When Kennedy assumed office, Emmerson, then Counsel General in Rhodesia, was again tapped for an ambassadorship—this time to Tanganyika. Again he was blocked by potential objections and "exiled" to the second seat at the embassy in Tokyo, well away from his area of expertise.(151)

Another handy vehicle for control of appointments has been the State Department's administrative budget. For most of the period that came under the sway of House Appropriations subcommittee chairman John Rooney, something of a terror. Wilber K. Carr, who spent 47 years in the Department, much of it as principal executive officer, was relieved of his duties and dispatched as Minister to Czechoslavakia when Rooney refused to deal with him. (152) Democratic appointees fared no better than career officers. Chester Bowles has recalled that he recruited Philip Coombs to head the Bureau of Educational and Cultural Affairs. Coombs, however, soon crossed swords with Representative Rooney over Coombs' budget. Bowles has related what followed:

> Rooney got mad. Rooney went to the White House. Phil was called in by George Ball, who says, "You're fired." Phil said, "What for?" And George said, "I don't know. I was asked to do this." And so Phil asked, of course, to see Rusk. Rusk was very composed. He said, "I don't really know, its something in the White House. I don't know."(153)

Indeed it was considered remarkable when, in 1969, William Macomber's appointment as Deputy Under Secretary of State of Administration survived Rooney's opposition. As one observer put it, "No one could remember when State's top administrative official had either been appointed or survived in office without Rooney's approval." Actually Rooney was not so much beaten as bought off. In return for Macomber, Secretary Rogers agreed to accept a Rooney choice as Macomber's assistant.(154)

Members of Congress can also protect those in office from the displeasure of their executive superiors. Already mentioned was the survival of Scott McLeod despite his attempt to undermine the Bohlen nomination. The head of the passport office proved to be another sensitive job because of the favors that could be done for members and their constituents. Recalling the long time head of that office, Mrs. Shipley, Dean Acheson remarked, "Now, there were always areas like Mrs. Shipley's which were not within any rule, and there you had to move very carefully because if you got into trouble with Mrs. Shipley, you were really in trouble!"(155) When Shipley retired in 1955 a struggle broke out over the nomination of Francis Knight who was accused of being a McCarthy witch hunter by the Democrats and defended by Republicans. Like Mrs. Shipley, Mrs. Knight went on to become unchallenged chief of her fiefdom.(156) Putting the phenomenon of bureaucratic immunity in general terms, Acheson observed: "Over a period of time you develop people down in the administration—in the Department—who are not really subject to discipline of the Department itself because they have accumulated powerful congressional backing.(157)

The overall picture of congressional influence on foreign policy personnel is, as with most of the areas of formal power, a fitful one. Legislative authority through the confirmation power and, somewhat less often, through the purse strings is indeed potent. Yet its use has been occasional at best and usually not based on policy considerations, but rather on a variety of other factors such as institutional pride and electoral advantage. The one major example of policy impact through the manipulation of personnel was the result of the McCarthy era, universally acknowledged to be one of the most unfortunate chapters in American history. Generally, barring direct insult, electoral threat, or other such tangential issues, Congress was willing to defer to the Executive on appointments. Yet the examples of legislative influence cited above are only illustrative. Scores of diplomats and administrative officers have been appointed, or not appointed, at least in part, as a function of congressional influence. The impact is difficult to measure in an overall sense, but, as Lyndon Johnson complained to Everett Dirksen, with "markers . . . all over town," Congress certainly gained significant influence over China policy and also some influence over other areas by personnel manipulation.

## Foreign Perceptions of Congress

A fascinating, but difficult to document, aspect of Congress' impact on foreign policy centers on the reaction of foreign governments to the presence of Congress in the process.

There is ample evidence that foreign governments are aware of and concerned with Congress' role in the foreign policy process. Stephen Gilbert in his work on Soviet perception of American politics has said that prior to 1973 Soviet analysts tended to dismiss the ability of Congress to limit presidential power. After 1973, according to Gilbert, the Soviet view changed, with two analysts describing the War Powers Resolution as "both an epilogue and a prologue to many other important events . . . it is almost the equivalent of a constitutional amendment in importance."(158) Gilbert's finding of increased congressional credibility after 1973 is almost certainly correct, but there is also ample evidence of strong Soviet interest in legislative attitudes before that date. Soviet diplomats have been recorded as "aggressively seeking to establish social contacts" with legislators.(159) More importantly, Soviet Embassy officials often met with congressional members and staff. First Secretary Igor Bubnov met with Foreign Relations Committee Chief-of-Staff Carl Marcy to probe reaction to a speech by Premier Alexi Kosygin and to discuss the settlement of the Arab-Israeli war. Bubnov and Marcy also discussed a summit meeting between Premier Kosygin and President Johnson. In the course of the conversation, Bubnov mentioned that he had "been seeing a good many staff assistants on the Hill," and that Senator Robert Kennedy was seeking to see Kosygin during his visit.(160) Just a week earlier Viktor Kopytin of Tass had "dropped in to ask about the mood of Congress during the Middle East crisis." Meeting with staff member Bill Bader, Kopytin had referred to Egyptian President Abdul Gamel Nasser as "irresponsible," and asked about possible peace terms. He also wanted to know whether Bader "thought the Soviet Union had used restraint during the crisis and whether Congress felt Russia had suffered a great diplomatic defeat."(161)

The Kopytin-Bader conversation was not an isolated event. In April 1968 they met for lunch at Kopytin's invitation to discuss Senate floor action on the defense appropriations bill as it related to anti-ballistic missiles. Kopytin also was interested in Bader's projections for post-Vietnam defense spending and the American's views on the Middle East.(162) Bader and his Soviet lunch partner met again in July to discuss the Soviet intervention in Czechoslovakia and that event's possible impact on ratification of the Non-Proliferation Treaty. Kopytin also wanted to discuss the anti-ballistic missile system, congressional willingness to accept nuclear parity, and the Soviet view that Arab radicalism which had toppled the Iraqi government might spread to Egypt and Jordan.(163) In a somewhat later conversation, Soviet attache Victor Degtyar called Foreign Relations Committee Chief-of-Staff Pat Holt to discuss Latin American policy. Among other points, Degtyar indicated he had attended committee hearings and wondered about party differences on Latin American.(164) The Soviets have also shown interest in legislative elections, even probing the Vice President's office for interpretations of the 1966 elections and the likely role of Vietnam as a campaign issue in 1968.(165)

The Soviets were not the only ones to monitor Congress. In 1952, Senator Wayne Morse published a memo dated June 24, 1949, purportedly from the Counselor of the Chinese Embassy to Chiang Kai-shek urging that they "should especially strive for a closer relationship" with Congress. Other documents in Morse's possession went into procedures for dealing with Congress, making contact with Senator Taft, and obtaining restricted information from Representative Judd.(166)

Instances of Congress influencing another country's foreign policy can also be glimpsed, but for obvious reasons are hard to conclusively document. The impact on British and European negotiating positions during the British Loan and European Recovery Plan were discussed earlier. So was the issue of which China the Japanese would recognize. During 1960 Senate hearings on national security policy, Karl Mundt commented on the necessity of other governments negotiating with the Senate in mind, to which Robert Lovett responded "That is true, I think most of the countries overseas have come to accept the U.S. Senate as an act of God."(167)

One role of Congress comes when the Executive uses the need of ratification or other legal process as a bargaining tool. American negotiators will argue that because of Congress they must insist on some particular point. At times this may be a ploy. Or it may represent reality. In 1967 negotiations with Panama over the Canal, for instance, American negotiators warned the Panamanians that they had gone as far as possible and increased demands would strengthen congressional opposition.(168) In still other situations the Executive may utilize legislators to make some diplomatic gesture. In 1969, for example, the White House encouraged Senator Mansfield not only to seek a visa to visit mainland China, but to do so publicly, thus signalling to China the Administration's wish to ease the two decade long diplomatic freeze.(169)

More often the Executive is annoyed by congressional involvement in the diplomatic process. Kissinger records with obvious dismay the 1971 visit of Senator Edmund Muskie to Moscow amid SALT and ABM negotiations. Muskie told Premier Kosygin that there was great pressure in the United States. With scorn, Kissinger noted, "The Senator did not consider it harmful to our foreign policy . . . to tell the Soviet Premier that influential members of Congress were seeking to reduce our defenses."(170)

Kissinger and his chief, Nixon, are even more critical of Congress' "meddling" in the Vietnam negotiations. The pressure that the Administration felt from Congress to reach a peace settlement has already been detailed. Kissinger and Nixon also complain that legislative activity played into the hands of the North Vietnamese. Kissinger argues that Vietnamese negotiators "threw out tantalizing public hints" about the release of American prisoners to egg on congressional pressure to fix a deadline. (171) President Nixon wrote Senator Hugh Scott that anti-war "resolutions [not only] cannot help the negotiations . . . They could seriously jeopardize them by removing the incentives for the other side to negotiate."(172) In the face of a congressional ban on action in Cambodia, the President wrote to Mike Mansfield, "I can only hope that the North Vietnamese will not draw the erroneous conclusion from this Congressional action that they are free to launch a military offensive in other areas of Indochina."(173)

Such comments, of course, reflect frustration as much as fact, but there is evidence that foreign negotiators react or take Congress into account in their positions. With regard to Indochina, Kissinger records a conversation with North Vietnam's Le Duc Tho who was quoting statements of congressional and other war critics:

Kissinger:   I won't listen to statements by American domestic figures . . .

Le Duc Tho: I would like to quote a sentence from Senator Fulbright . . .

Kissinger:   Our domestic discussions are of no concern of yours, and I understand what the Senator said.(174)

Whatever the merits of the exchange, Kissinger was wrong on his last point. The domestic discussion was very much of concern to the North Vietnamese.

President Nixon supports the evidence for foreign reaction to Congress. According to Nixon, after the cut-off of funds for action in Cambodia, Kissinger protested violations to Soviet Ambassador Anatoly Dobrynin. The Soviet diplomat rejoined that the Americans had no leverage because of the legislative ban on action. Kissinger huffed, "There should be no illusion that we will forget who put us in this uncomfortable position." Dobrynin's squelching reply: "You should go after Senator Fulbright, not us."(175) It was an idea which certainly must have appealed to the National Security Advisor.

There is also evidence that Fulbright's position was followed and even reported in the Soviet press(176) and of reaction to his and other legislator's positions. As early as 1949, Soviet expert Chip Bohlen was reporting that a Soviet peace offensive was designed to influence public opinion and thereby congressional reaction to the pending NATO treaty.(177) There is also interesting speculation that congressional considerations may have been a factor in the Soviet's placement of missiles in Cuba in 1962. Presidential advisor Theodore Sorenson noted that during the 1961 Kennedy-Khrushchev summit, "It was clear he [Khrushchev] had read--or had been briefed on . . . a good many obscure Congressional debates . . ."(178) Scholar David Detzer speculates that one reason the Soviets placed the missiles was the hope that the United States would do nothing. He quotes a June 1961 Fulbright speech in which the Senator said "I suppose we would all be less comfortable if the Soviets did install missile bases in Cuba, but I am not sure that our national existence would be substantially in danger." That, and other such congressional comments, Detzer says, may have misled the Soviets.(179)

A last illustration or two on Soviet appreciation of Congress can be drawn from arms limitation talks. During test ban negotiations in 1962, Khrushchev told author Norman Cousins that the Soviets would allow on-sight inspections. "Congress has convinced itself that on-sight inspection is necessary and the President cannot get a treaty through the Senate without it," the Soviet party chairman explained. "Very well then, let us accommodate the President."(180)

Kissinger further records that during SALT I discussions, the Soviets were skillful in exploiting differences between Congress and the Administration. Referring to ABM, Kissinger relates, "the Soviets accepted our proposal with amazing and totally unprecedented speed . . . The Soviets knew a good thing when they saw it. They did not mind keeping what they had while nailing us to what Congress would never approve."(181)

The Soviets of course were not the only ones aware of the American Congress. Spanish Generalissimo Francisco Franco had a strong ally in Congress in the restoration of that facist dictator to world good-standing.(182) Paul Culbertson, American Chargé in Madrid, wrote Secretary of State Acheson that visits of friendly members and speeches in Congress had convinced Franco, who was "the kind of Spaniard who likes to get into the movies without buying a ticket," that he could gain acceptability without concessions. "As a result," Culbertson concluded, "Franco leans back with complacency and anticipates that the world will come to him on his terms."(183) After Congress voted $62.5 million to Spain over Administration opposition, an exasperated Culbertson cabled:

> Congress has by its action rather effectively taken out of our hands the conduct of one of the most important political factors in our relations with Spain . . . The Congress has certainly made a first class liar out of me [as I had predicted the aid] did not have the chance of a proverbial snowball.(184)

Congress' impact may also be more general. The theme of a Theodore Lowi article entitled "Making Democracy Safe for the World" was the uncertainty other governments face when estimating the future path of America's multi-voiced foreign policy.(185) The danger aspect is somewhat speculative, but a case can and has been made that the North Korean invasion of the South in 1950 and the Soviet stationing of missiles in Cuba in 1962 were partly based on erroneous signals from Congress. More certain is the uncertainty congressional activity can cause at times. During the turbulent early 1950's, as an illustration, a State Department paper on relations with Great Britain contended that "Full British cooperation with us is inhibited by their doubts that U.S. policy is consistent or persistent." The paper went on that in part because of Congress, "when the Executive preaches the removal of trade barriers, specific Congressional actions often seem to be in the reverse direction."(186) The contention over the firing of General Douglas MacArthur was another source of uncertainty during these years, with Canadian Ambassador Hume Wrong telling Secretary Acheson that "one of the most unfortunate results of the hearings would be a distinct loss of flexibility in the future conduct of our foreign affairs stemming from the many statements on foreign policy which those testifying are being called on to make during the hearings."(187) Even more distressful to foreign observers were the antics of Senator McCarthy. NATO Commander, General Alfred Greuenther told Senator H. Alexander Smith that one of his greatest problems resulted from McCarthyism. The challenge to President Eisenhower's leadership was being "misunderstood and misinterpreted . . . it is not a question of whether Senator McCarthy is wrong or right—the point is that he has encouraged doubt and uncertainty with respect to our leadership abroad and we can ill afford the luxury of such divisiveness . . ."(188)

Congress' impact on foreign policy, then, is not confined to the domestic process. It extends into the diplomatic process. The Executive may utilize Congress to win a negotiating point or to signal intentions abroad. Congress may also become a more direct factor through its own initiative. Members travel abroad frequently and, as Senator Muskie did, meet with foreign leaders. Those same leaders are also aware, although perhaps imperfectly, of the diversity and occasional divisiveness of the American policy system. Congress may not be an "act of God," but certainly they must consider the potential of an "Act of Congress" in their negotiations.

# 7
# Congressional Values and the Scope of Congressional Influence

## Congressional Deference

The quarter century (1948-1972) that this second phase of the study examines was characterized by an assumption in Congress as well as in the Executive, Courts, and public that the formulation and conduct of foreign policy was essentially a presidential function. As in the initial period of the Truman presidency, Congress was prone to defer to the Executive in matters of "pure" foreign policy. Even when individual members disagreed, presidential invocations of office usually sufficed to bring dissident legislators into line or to render them isolated and impotent voices.

Congress' Support of Presidential Authority. Much of what was later to be described as presidential usurpation of Congress' proper constitutional authority actually resulted from a willing congressional concession of authority. Numerous scholars have found that a key cause of legislative diffidence in foreign policy is the widespread belief that the president legitimately occupies a preeminent place in the foreign policy process. This results from a variety of factors. In the instant communications, supersonic, atomic post-World War II era, the speed, complexity, and often critical nature of foreign policy have left Congress with what John Manley termed an "inferiority complex," agreeing that legislative bodies are inherently ill-suited to deal with foreign policy in the modern age.(1)

A survey of the important leaders of Congress during this era finds a marked similarity in their willingness to grant presidents wide discretion. The attitudes of Senators Vandenberg and Connally, who dominated congressional consideration of foreign policy during the second Truman term as they had during the first, has already been discussed in detail. With the passing of those two, and Truman as well, from the political scene, new senators became important voices for their institution. Lyndon Johnson, as Democratic Majority Leader, might have vigorously opposed Republican President Eisenhower, but chose instead to accede to his authority. Johnson believed that Congress ordinarily had little stake or interest in foreign policy and that legislative initiative was inappropriate. Reaction to presidential initiative rather than congressional inspired action was the

proper legislative role.(2)   William Macomber, legislative liaison for the State Department, has recalled that Johnson once told
Speaker Sam Rayburn to oppose a restrictive clause in one piece
of legislation.   "Sam, I hope you'll try to head this thing off,
because it's a bad thing . . .  You know, Sam, we might just as
well impeach the fellow [Eisenhower] as put this kind of thing in
there."(3)   Johnson could even be deterred on those occasions
when he took the initiative.   In May 1960, the Senate Majority
Leader and others of his party authored a telegram to Soviet
Premier Nikita Khrushchev.   When the State Department was reluctant to deliver the message, Johnson was, according to Christian
Herter, "in a very irascible frame of mind."   After a short time,
however, Johnson calmed down and, Herter recalled, "indicated
that, of course, the President, in his constitutional role, was
solely responsible for our foreign policy and that, if the President felt the delivery of the telegram would be injurious to our
foreign policy that he, as a Senator, might not like it but he
would be forced to agree."(4)

During the Democratic Kennedy and Johnson Administrations,
Senate opposition might reasonably have been led by Everett
Dirksen, but he, too, believed in congressional deference.   At
one point the leader of the loyal opposition defined his role by
observing

> When you're in the field of foreign affairs and an issue or
> a policy or a course of action is firmly resolved by the
> President as the conductor of foreign relations, then, of
> course, we believe, and I think all like-minded Americans
> believe, that the President merits support.   It simply
> wouldn't do under the fevers that beset the world today to
> have any differences of opinion . . .  We'll take no action
> and make no statement or indulge in any expressions that
> will add difficulty and obstacles to the course the Presi-
> dent may pursue.(5)

As Dirksen's comments reflect, legislators value national
unity in foreign policy.   A primary fear is that congressional
dissent will be mistaken for weakness by international antagon-
ists.   Senator Bourke Hickenlooper told an interviewer, "The
Foreign Relations Committee, when it indulges in divisive and
diverse sharp criticism, can be harmful to American foreign policy, because it indicates to any opponent a lack of unity.   So it
can have . . . a very adverse effect on the best interests of the
United States".(6)   Another key senator who later became a leader
of congressional reassertion, William Fulbright, argued in 1964
that "a vital distinction must be made between offering broad
policy directions and interfering in the conduct of policy by the
executive branch.   Our history is strewn with examples, which
have invariably had unhappy results, of congressional efforts to
exercise executive functions . . . [and] either forcing or binding the hands of the executive."(7)

That kind of attitude was particularly prevalent when dealing
with any policy involved with military action.   Samuel Huntington
in his study of military affairs quotes one senator, probably

Richard Russell, as reacting with a "God help the American people if Congress starts legislating military strategy."(8) Dirksen's attitude was the same. Congress," he said, "has the job of raising and supporting the Army, but the direction of the military is the business of the President."(9)

In an era of perceived continuous confrontation with communism these attitudes precluded an aggressive congressional role in most circumstances. As Arthur Schlesinger, Jr. observed, the cold war enabled, perhaps required, even a "Whig" president such as Eisenhower to enlarge the power of the Executive in foreign affairs. "Mesmerized by the need for instant response . . .," Congress really accepted, "the high flying theories of presidential prerogative."(10)

The Information and Expertise Gap. The normal submissiveness of Congress also resulted from a perceived information and expertise gap between the two branches. Roger Hilsman has noted that the command of both the channels of communications and the services of foreign affairs experts has given the Executive an "intellectual" initiative in establishing and carrying out policy.(11) This feeling of inadequacy is widely noted among academic observers,(12) and has also been recognized and labeled in Congress as "the cult of expertise."(13)

During most of the period, Congress' professional foreign policy staff was extremely limited. It has also been said, only half jokingly, that Congress' primary independent source of information was the New York Times. These shortcomings became increasingly apparent and disturbing to many members in the late 1960s. Hubert Humphrey termed Congress "its own worst enemy," and Senator Sam Ervin lamented, "The Executive branch has seized power brazenly because Congress has . . . failed to equip itself physically to carry out its legislative duties independent of the Executive branch."(14) In a typical example of the period, one member of the Foreign Affairs Committee noted that members often do not know "what is really really going on . . . What do you say when they say the Dominican Republic is being taken over by Communists? I looked at fifty-eight names too, but they meant nothing to me."(15)

The concern over lack of information and expertise was particularly evident in the Foreign Relations Committee toward the end of the 1948-1972 period. As one former White House official pointed out:

> My frank reaction is that you have been much too cautious about emphasizing the idea of sending a few staff people abroad for reporting purposes. Congress cannot begin to cope with the Executive Branch, much less the mushrooming problems of the world, until it has far more adequate continuing staff resources.(16)

Fulbright and key committee staff people like Carl Marcy tended to agree with that evaluation,(17) but reacted with caution. Marcy was concerned that staff observers abroad "could raise serious questions about who conducts foreign policy," and

that other committees might follow the example and post staff
abroad "thus usurping this Committee's jurisdiction."(18)
Fulbright interestingly also acted, at least at one point, to
restrict his own sources of information. It is plain when examining Fulbright's papers that he received considerable amounts of
information outside formal channels from American diplomatic
personnel. Yet at one point, Fulbright complained to the White
House of "time consuming" ambassadorial contacts and asked if
they could be limited.(19)

Indeed Congress was not only prone to give way to the Executive, it expected leadership and complained when it was not provided. Commenting on what he saw as a lack of presidential leadership on the 1965 foreign aid program, Senator Wayne Morse
chided President Johnson for not wanting "to tell the country the
form in which he, as Commander-in-Chief and President of the
United States, thinks foreign legislation ought to be passed,
which might I say, is just elementary in this system of government. The country has the right to look to the President for
recommendations as to the form it ought to take instead of passing the buck to Congress."

## Congress and Crisis

Congress' deferential attitude was magnified many fold in
times of crisis. Except during protracted conflicts where there
was no immediate threat to national safety, as in Korea and Vietnam, criticism of executive initiated policy was rare. There was
no instance of Congress reversing presidential short-term crisis
policy. Even criticism during consultation prior to announcing a
decision or taking action was unusual and virtually vanished once
a public commitment was made.

Don't Call Us. President Eisenhower often found that his
belief that Congress should be consulted seriously was not shared
by the members of that body. Congress should certainly be
credited with helping the President exercise restraint in the
1954 crises in Indochina and the Formosa Straits area, but in
those instances the majority in Congress was allied with Eisenhower in opposition to hawkish views in the bureaucracy and among
a minority in the legislature. If on those occasions Eisenhower
had been hell-bent to take action, it is doubtful whether Congress would have tried or been able to stop him.

Throughout Eisenhower's eight years in office, Congress was
somewhat taken aback by the President's willingness to share
power. When the Southeast Asian Treaty Organization treaty was
before the Senate in 1955, that body rejected attempts to limit
presidential authority to react to aggression under the pact's
provisions. Fulbright opposed the restrictions on the grounds
that "we can only rely on our good sense not to elect Presidents
who are so unwise or arbitrary or uncivilized as to exercise arbitrary powers."(20) The venerable Alben Barkley said he also
would vote for the SEATO treaty. "I do so with some trepidation
and hesitation," he said. "But we have got to take some chances

here, and I think if we had waited until Congress passed a declaration of war in 1950 there would have been no occasion for a declaration of war because the Communists would have had all of Korea before we ever got action or got a vote on it in the Senate."(21)  William Knowland echoed their concern with Congress' ability to respond quickly.  It is "not inconceivable," Knowland theorized, "that the Nation's Capitol itself could be wiped out."  In time the Senate could be reconstituted, he thought, but in the meantime the president's hands would be tied and the country left "paralyzed and impotent . . . The next war might not last more than ten days or two weeks conceivably, and we might lose the ball game before it ever began."  When Eisenhower went to Congress for the even more speculative and loosely worded Formosa Resolution, he encountered similar sentiments. Minority Leader Joseph Martin told Eisenhower that the resolution would get through the House in forty-five minutes, but that Eisenhower already had the necessary authority.  Both Martin and Rayburn pledged to stand by the President and guaranteed that no one in the House would criticize or oppose Eisenhower.(22)

In the Senate there were more qualms about the resolution, but little movement to defeat the grant of authority outright. The comments of Hubert Humphrey, one of those most concerned about possible military action, underline the Senate's quandary. Writing to Democratic National Chairman Paul Butler, Humphrey observed, "The simple truth is that . . . [we were] trapped by the President on this Formosa Resolution.  Once he had announced the policy, there wasn't much else we could do but go along."(23) Expanding on that theme to a constituent, Humphrey explained:

> This Formosa Resolution was not an easy one for us.  To be quite frank about it, . . . once the President announced his Formosa policy and had revealed to the world the nature of the resolution he was submitting to Congress there was very little else we could do but support it.  If we rejected [it] . . . we would have had the same President and the same policy, but the policy repudiated by the elected representatives of the people in Congress.  Personally, I thought that was too big a risk to take in view of the situation that prevails in the Far East.(24)

Not only were most members more than willing to give the President broad authority, many voiced concern that the request was constitutionally improper.  In words that must have rung tinnily a little more than a decade later, Mike Mansfield said he was glad the President was asking Congress'advice and consent, but what "perturbs me is that I don't like to see the President reducing the power he has under the Constitution.  And I don't like to see Congress taking power which normally should be in the hands of the Executive."(25)  The President, Mansfield worried, was "abdicating" his power.  Instead he should "retain his full power as Commander-in-Chief and retain freedom of action accordingly."(26)  Senator Thomas Hennings agreed and expressed misgivings lest "the great historical powers of the Presidency . . . be limited for future generations."(27)  More sharply and perhaps more accurately reflecting the crux of congressional concern, Wayne Morse charged, "Eisenhower is passing the buck."(28) Somewhat the same story can be told about the 1956-1957 Middle East crisis. The Eisenhower Doctrine did bring more opposition than the Formosa Resolution had, but the tried and true executive methods of winning overall support proved effective. Eisenhower and Dulles appealed for unity at the water's edge by citing the menace of Soviet expansionism to the Middle East and, by extension, to the United States, by forecasting the possible need for quick response, and by playing on the danger of having to wait for a congressional authorization to act.(29) The possibility of partisan sniping was further reduced by gaining President Truman's endorsement.(30)

Any serious opposition which might have been mounted by Fulbright, Morse, and the like was overshadowed by the nearly solid support of senior Democrats. Attempts by Hubert Humphrey to initiate a Foreign Relations Committee investigation were quashed by the outgoing Chairman Walter George and the incoming Chairman Theodore Green on the grounds they would heighten tension and show division within the United States.(31) Given that level of opposition, Humphrey found it prudent to give way to the Chairman's "wise and prudent" caution as well as his "greater expertise and experience."(32) Lyndon Johnson and Richard Russell also cooperated in moving the resolution as quickly as possible through Congress.(33)

As in the Formosa Resolution debate, legislators expressed concerns that Eisenhower was diluting the presidency's constitutional powers. Senator Smith wanted the resolution to "approve" rather than "authorize" presidential action.(34) House Majority Leader John McCormack asked Eisenhower why he wanted a congressional resolution authorizing him to act when he already possessed the necessary constitutional power,(35) and even Humphrey argued that the President could act without legislative authorization.(36)

Eisenhower's attempts to consult with Congress during the 1959 Berlin crisis once again encountered a level of incredulity. In response to the President's assertion that he would not take military action without conferring with Congress, Representative McCormack hastened to assure Eisenhower of Democratic support, (37) and Senator Russell told Eisenhower, "If you have to act, Mr. President, go ahead and act. Don't come to us."(38) Recalling Russell's largesse, Eisenhower later sardonically remembered:

> Several times I said I would consult with the Congress insofar as possible if the Berlin situation seemed to intensify. And several times Senator Russell assured me that consultation was appreciated but not necessary—the initiative was mine and Congress would support me. There was almost an amusing quality of "Don't call us" about it.(39)

Rally 'Round the Flag. Two facts stand out when considering congressional reaction to international crisis situations. The first is that Congress often shied away from a willingness to recommend or support the use of force. During the crises in Indochina, the Middle East in 1956 and 1967, and the Formosa Straits, congressional leaders were hesitant about the use of force. Only during the Cuban missile crisis was there any significant feeling that more force should be used. The second tendency, however, was that once a policy was announced or Congress was called upon to support potential presidential action, it inevitably gave its assent. No presidential call during this period for national unity in time of crisis was seriously disputed by Congress. The Formosa Straits crisis is a typical example. Many members of Congress were doubtful, but few were ready to deny the President their support. Despite his own reservations, Senator Hubert Humphrey voted for the resolution on the grounds that to deny it, "would be to undermine the President's authority completely and totally."(40) Commenting on the resolution which passed by 410 to 3 in the House and 83 to 3 in the Senate, another member observed, "We gave the President authority that we are by no means agreed we want to do. And we did it all in the name of national unity."(41)

Even military actions which were later subjected to considerable congressional criticism initially received strong legislative support. Truman's intervention in Korea not only received strong support, but he was advised by many members not to seek legislative approval for his action. The 1965 intervention in the Dominican Republic was also given early support by congressional leaders, including Fulbright who was later a vocal critic. (42) Senator George Aiken later related, "Well, I don't think anybody believed there was any large number of Communists in the Dominican Republic at that time," but still he could not recall "any opposition at all" to Johnson's dispatching of the Marines. (43)

The Tonkin Gulf Resolution similarly sailed through Congress, again with Fulbright's support. That resolution continued to be supported by a majority in Congress despite a minority's increasingly discordant dissent. In July 1965, when Johnson decided to introduce American combat forces into Vietnam, he met with the legislative leaders and received almost unanimous support. Only Senator Mansfield expressed doubt, and he finally agreed to support the President because he felt it his duty as Majority Leader to do so in the name of national unity.(44)

By 1966, an increasing number of members were openly opposing the Vietnam involvement, but most agreed with the sentiment expressed by Karl Mundt:

> If Congress gets into the decision-making process in these areas through too much open debate and too great a confusion of counsel, I am afraid we not only would set back the steps required to produce an enduring and enforceable peace, but in the meantime we would also create an era of indecision and uncertainty which may well prolong the war and which would certainly increase the loss of American lives overseas.(45)

Jacob Javits, later an opponent of the war, expressed a similar sentiment, saying "Despite the disagreements and reservations

which many have concerning Vietnam policy, few would wish to
repudiate our President in time of war."(46) Summing up the
early congressional support of involvement in Vietnam and the
later unwillingness to use the power of the purse to end the
Americanization of the conflict, Fulbright depicted Congress as a
"legislature which does not hesitate to defeat or override the
executive on domestic legislation . . . but which reverts to a
kind of tribal loyalty to the 'chief' when war is involved. . . .
It is not lack of power which has prevented Congress from ending
the war in Indochina, but lack of will."(47) In a less charitable mood, the Chairman also attributed the problem to Congress
having "so many trained seals."(48)

## Executive Strength

The Imposing President. Another key factor in the determination of the Executive's ability to sway Congress, particularly
in the absence of crisis, is executive strength. The President
is the key, although other factors, such as the standing and
efforts of the Secretary of State and his department and the
presence or absence of intra-branch dissent, may also play a
role. If the president is reluctant to try to force his views on
Congress, as Eisenhower often was, then Executive strength
suffers. When the president vigorously asserts his authority and
status, it is difficult for Congress to resist. A veteran like
William Fulbright has pointed to the "psychological barrier" of
contesting foreign policy with the president at the White House.
It is difficult to "contradict kings in their palaces," the
Senator ruefully observed.(49) A decline in the president's
personal/political prestige will limit his ability to exercise
influence. This was certainly true for Truman, and extended to
his first two Secretaries of State, Edward Stettinius and James
Byrnes. Lyndon Johnson's standing also seriously declined in the
latter part of his tenure. Although he persisted in Vietnam, he
was limited in other areas. One Assistant Secretary of State
wrote in early 1967, "The change in the Congressional mood. . .
is remarkable. It doesn't do much good now, and it can often do
harm, to say the President is personally interested in a piece of
legislation."(50) It is also the case that when the standing of
the presidency itself is diminished, executive influence will
decline. While this was not a factor during either the intensive
or extensive study periods, it is visible at the time of this
writing in the aftermath of Watergate, tax scandals, vice presidential corruption, and intra-executive spying.

If We Don't All Hang Together . . .. A last aspect of
Executive strength is unity. Unity is important for two reasons.
When there is disagreement within the Executive, the contending
sides will often seek congressional allies in the policy struggle. Lack of unity also breaks down the image of expertise. Not
only is Congress often supplied with information which contra-
dicts the official executive stand, but it may receive opinions
from dissenting "experts" which vary from the official rationale.

While defense issues, _per se_, do not fall within the scope of this study, the military is often involved in foreign policy-making where, for example, military action is contemplated or undertaken or where arms negotiations are conducted with foreign governments. In the research for this work the author was struck by the repeated evidence of the independent positions of the Defense Department, the Joint Chiefs of Staff, and the respective services and the alliances they formed with Congress. The interaction of General Douglas MacArthur and elements of Congress, particularly Representative Joseph Martin, in trying to expand the Korean War to mainland China is an example already touched upon. Admiral Arthur Radford's bellicosity in alliance with various civilian figures over Indochina and again in the Formosa Straits crisis are yet other examples which have been discussed.

In an excellent short study of the defense policy process, Edward Laurance has theorized that in part the Executive dominates foreign policy because of its virtual monopoly of military expertise, and that Congress' participation in defense policy-making is enhanced when there is a lack of executive consensus on policy options.(51) The primary manifestation of lack of consensus are alliances between the uniformed military and its supporters in Congress in opposition to the President, Secretary of Defense, and other supporting civilian officials.(52) Secretary of Defense Robert McNamara who earned the particular opposition of the military and its congressional allies for his attempts to control the Pentagon warned that "It's not the military-industrial complex that represents danger. That only involves money. I worry more about the military-congressional complex. That involves the security of the country."(53)

When it came to basic matters of defense posture or military utilization during the Truman through Nixon years, many members of Congress valued the opinions of the uniformed military over its theoretical civilian masters. Representative Leslie Arends once accused, "I-know-all-the-answers-McNamara" of "substituting civilian for military expertise."(54) Senator Dennis Chavez, Chairman of the Defense Appropriation Subcommittee, similarly told Army Chief-of-Staff Lyman Lemnitzer, "I prefer your judgment over that of civilian personnel in the Pentagon."(55)

Congress has insisted on its right to continue to hear formally, as well as sub-rosa, from the uniformed military. One congressional staff member related that "A general comes over here and they pat him on the shoulder and say 'How are things going, General?' If the general says 'OK,' then they are relaxed."(56) If not, Congress is agitated. Periodic attempts to keep the military across the Potomac and away from Congress failed during the period. A 1958 defense reorganization act contained specific provision that Congress have direct access to the Joint Chiefs-of-Staff. Congress has thereby served as a conduit for airing dissenting military views, often prearranging for certain questions to be asked at hearings to bring out the "personal" views of the military chiefs.(57) Chairman of the Joint Chiefs Earle Wheeler, for instance, contended that "In answer to direct questions the military leader has no moral alternative to giving Congress the same candid professional judgment that he previously stated within the JCS, to the Secretary of Defense, or the President."(58)

Two points should be noted. First, much of the military-congressional liaison is related to arms and manpower levels rather than foreign policy issues. Secondly, the military is not in continuous and open insubordination of the President and Secretary of Defense. Arnold Kanter found that the civilian authorities have the upper hand and can gain "acquiesence of the military services by making no more than modest concessions."(59) Henry Kissinger has also noted that

> High military officers must always strike a balance between their convictions and their knowledge, that to be effective they must survive to fight another day. Their innate awe of the Commander-in-Chief tempts them to find a military reason for what they consider barely tolerable. Contrary to some of the public mythology, they rarely challenge the Commander-in-Chief; they seek excuses to support, not to oppose him. (60)

Yet studies also conclude that the military is a definite factor. Kanter points out that Defense Department policy stands are affected by the ability of the Joint Chiefs to go to Congress, thereby making it politic for the Secretary of Defense to bargain and compromise with his subordinates in order to gain their endorsement.(61) Also, Kissinger gives repeated testimony in his memoirs to the role of the defense establishment in determining Strategic Arms Limitations Talks (SALT) and other policy. In choosing his recommendations for the basic American negotiating position on SALT, Kissinger confesses, "I regret to admit that in doing so I was swayed by bureaucratic and political considerations. . ." One choice for instance was rejected because "all hell would have broken loose both in Congress and the bureaucracy."(62)

It is the anticipated reaction, demonstrated by Kissinger, perhaps more than direct dissent, that gives power to the military-congressional complex. General Wheeler, for example gained access to President Johnson's Tuesday luncheon meetings on Vietnam policy due to pressure from Congress to include the military in the decision-making process.(63) Senator Karl Mundt reflected that feeling, telling a South Dakota radio station president, "I have lost most of the respect which I ever had for McNamara. . . Rusk and LBJ are getting far too much counsel urging them to continue to make certain decisions and determinations which I believe should be left in the hands of responsible and respectable trained professional officers. . ."(64) That kind of sentiment from conservative legislators, whose support Johnson needed, led Jack Valenti to recommend to the President, "before you make final decisions on the problems in Vietnam, you 'sign on' the Joint Chiefs in that decision." Valenti recommended bringing General Wheeler in on the Tuesday luncheon. Johnson's margin note reply was that he had already talked to Wheeler who thus became a member of the Vietnam policy process. (65)

Executive Strength and Foreign Aid. The various factors such as professional reputation, popular standing, and executive unity, that affect executive strength, can all be seen in the ongoing saga of foreign aid policy.

During fiscal years 1949 through 1965, Congress reduced Administration foreign aid requests by an average of 17.5 percent. In six of of those years, the Administration was relatively successful in getting its proposals adopted and funded. Losses of less than 13 percent were achieved in fiscal years 1949 (-12.5%), 1950 (-11.3%), 1951 (-8.4%), 1959 (-12.4%), 1961 (-9.2%), 1965 (-7.7%), and 1966 (-6.9%). In five other fiscal years, foreign aid requests were cut by more than 20 percent: 1953 (-24.0%), 1956 (-23.5%), 1958 (-22.4%), 1957 (-28.2%), 1964 (-33.8%), 1968 (-22.8%), and 1969 (-39.7%). Examining and comparing these years of relative success and failure gives some insights into the ebb and flow of executive-legislative relations.

The ability of the Truman Administration to prevail in FY 1949 and FY 1950 was based on the initial ability to obtain Marshall Plan funds, the obligation of Congress to continue the program, and in the former year, the President's reelection and renewed political strength. The crisis that occurred in the aftermath of the Czech coupe and the Administration's utilization of the tense atmosphere contributed greatly to the passage of the Marshall Plan for FY 1949. The following year, the Administration reduced its request by nearly one-and-one-half billion dollars and was extensively directed toward the continuation of the ERP to which Congress had morally, if not legally, committed itself. Furthermore, Truman had won a stunning reelection victory in November 1948 and the Democrats had recaptured both houses of Congress, thereby sending the President's political stock soaring. The low 8.4 percent reduction in FY 1951 can again be explained by the continuing ERP obligations and by the increase in military funding for Europe and the Far East in the aftermath of the downfall of the Nationalist Chinese on the mainland and the outbreak of the Korean Conflict in June 1950. During these years, the Administration suffered only one major setback. In January 1950 the Korean aid bill was temporarily defeated. This was a result of its being used as a hostage by Congress to force the Administration to extend aid to Chiang Kai-shek. Also, Acheson has admitted, it failed because, in the midst of other concerns, he was "complacent and inactive." Conceding aid to China and mounting an active campaign, the Secretary saw aid to Korea reinstated during February. The FY 1953 reduction of 24.0 percent can be attributed to a number of factors. The President's political standing was in deep decline due to frustration over the Korean stalemate, McCarthyism was running rampant, the Bricker Amendment to restrict the treaty-making power was being strongly pushed, and a national election was impending. In Acheson's words, "The mood of Congress in this spring and summer of political turmoil was a curious and unpredictable one." Military aid took the major slash, while civilian foreign assistance remained stable. Even though the war in Korea

was still being fought, it had become domestically unpopular.
Congress reacted against the increases in military aid which the
Administration had been able to push through earlier. It cut the
Western European section of mutual security funding by $1.5 bil-
lion, which accounted for nearly 75 percent of the total reduc-
tion.(66)

In the years since World War II, the Eisenhower Administration compiled the worst record in obtaining its foreign aid
requests from Congress. In FY's 1956, 1957, and 1958, the Executive's aid figure was slashed by a total of nearly three billion
dollars. Reductions were kept under 15 percent in only two
years, FY 1959 and FY 1961. The principal shortcoming centered
on the President. His normal inclination to avoid heavily pressuring Congress was complicated by division within his Administration. The Executive Branch was beset by internal conflicts. In
the mid-fifties, a group known as the "4-H Club," comprised of
Treasury Secretary Humphrey, Under Secretary of State Herbert
Hoover, Jr., ICA Director John B. Hollister, and Bureau of the
Budget Director Rowland Hughes consistently opposed expansion of
the foreign aid program.

Typically, for FY 1956 to FY 1958, the Administration proposed a three year, lump sum authorization which caused considerable opposition on the grounds Congress would lose its control of
the foreign aid program. The President did not enter the fray
until late, and then did so clumsily. Signing the authorization
bill, which had only reduced the Administration request by 11
percent, the President called on Congress to appropriate the full
amount or face a special session in the fall. The majority of
Democrats rebelled at this public attempt to exert political
blackmail. Speaker Rayburn, who usually supported the President
on such matters, was particularly annoyed, and the appropriations
committees proceeded to cut another $620 million, leaving the FY
1958 appropriation a full one billion dollars lower than the preceding year.(67)

Eisenhower's difficulties in securing his aid requests can
also be traced to a slow rise in general dissatisfaction with the
Administration. Dulles, in particular, became a partisan target.
By 1955 Hubert Humphrey was comparing the Administration to "a
ship without a rudder," and asserting that "the Democratic Party
must outline in detail its differences with the Administration
. . ."(68) Later he described Eisenhower as "plain lazy" and
Dulles as "worn out." The Secretary "Even when he was vigorous
. . . lacked imagination and flexibility," Humphrey scathingly
went on. "Now that he is older and tired and sick, he has lost
any usefulness that he might have ever had."(69) William Fulbright was equally caustic, writing Arthur Krock of the New York
Times that "the feeling that we have no intelligent and understanding leadership is almost overwhelming."(70) To Bowles,
Fulbright lamented, "It is truly tragic that we have had such an
inadequate President and Secretary of State during these difficult times."(71) The attacks on Dulles grew so strident by early
1958 that President Eisenhower felt compelled to defend Dulles.
"Foster has now, as always before," he wrote Representative
Walter Judd, "my total support and confidence. I cannot imagine

how anyone, anywhere, could doubt that fact."(72)

Eisenhower gained some respite in FY 1959 and FY 1961 which can largely be attributed to an increase in cold war tensions and a decrease of dissension within the Executive Branch. The Berlin Crisis, the U-2 incident, the collapse of the May 1960 summit conference, and leftist riots in Japan all tended to put foreign aid in more of a cold war context. Although Eisenhower did not exert strong leadership, the fortunes of foreign aid were further enhanced by the fact that all of the 4-H Club had departed from government service.(73)

John Fitzgerald Kennedy's first two years as President saw cuts of 18.0% and 18.4%, and his request for FY 1964 ended in a disaster. Congress reduced the recommendation by $1.53 billion or 33.8%. The Administration's troubles arose chiefly from political mismanagement. Kennedy had alienated many potentially supportive Republicans by a strong campaign effort in 1962. The appearance of the President on the behalf of the Democratic opponent of Walter Judd, who had generally backed Kennedy's proposals in the Foreign Affairs Committee, was particularly damaging. More importantly, Kennedy made a disastrous mistake in his appointment of a commission headed by General Lucius Clay to study the aid program. Faced with rising congressional discontent over the aid program, Kennedy appointed a commission of generally conservative businessmen that was designed to appeal to Congress. While the use of a presidential commission is a tested political ploy, the selection of its membership was ill-conceived. Instead of turning in the expected favorable report, the commission's findings were critical of many aspects of the program. The Administration wavered, cutting nearly $400 million from its own request. This admission that the request was "fat" plus the collapse of expertise caused by the Clay report upset the delicate balance with which the foreign aid battle is fought each year. The result was a massive cut which the Administration, even using belated cries that national security was being threatened, could not stave off.(74)

President Johnson's first two years of success in FY 1965 and FY 1966 can be explained by a mixture of the license which a new president is often given, his paring of the requests to near the appropriations level in FY 1964, and a turn of political fate which elevated a fellow Texan to the chairmanship of the House Appropriations Committee. In FY 1968 and FY 1969, Johnson's earlier success was completely reversed, with the Administration suffering successive reductions of 28.8% and 39.7%. Inflation, a negative trade balance, the tax surcharge, and the opposition of some aid recipients to American policy all played a role. More importantly, many members of Congress were frustrated by the Vietnam War and used foreign aid to lash out at the President. William Fulbright wrote that the "war in Vietnam is having a very deleterious effect" on foreign aid and other programs.(75) To another correspondent he lamented that because of "disillusionment with the thrust of American foreign policy .... some of us are becoming negative even on good programs, simply because we believe this Administration will distort good programs for the accomplishment of some misguided objectives. I have always supported foreign aid, but if it is to be used to blackmail and bribe others to support a tragically wrong policy in Vietnam, I cannot bring myself to vote for it."(76)

Fulbright also conveyed that attitude to the White House. After one visit to discuss aid, Agency for International Development Director David Bell reported to Johnson that there was "virtually no progress," and that "the Chairman was plainly in a gloomy and unhappy mood" over Vietnam.(77) Perhaps the clearest exposition of the impact of Vietnam on foreign aid can be found in a letter from Fulbright to Bowles:

> On the subject of aid, this year this Committee is pretty negative—not so much out of vindictiveness. . . but largely I believe because the liberals on the Committee, of both parties, have lost confidence in this Administration. It is a strange phenomenon, only partially explained by Vietnam. The criticism runs much deeper than that based on the inevitable misadventures of administration. It goes to a feeling that the Administration is committed to the concept of the importance of an "aid presence" everywhere, tends to proliferate economic programs, ignores balance of payments problems, proliferates military assistance programs, is self-righteous, tends to permit aid to mushroom into commitments, etc.(78)

Thus, Vietnam became a kind of political cancer that spread to attack the Administration's credibility and all its programs. As the prestige of the President steadily declined, he was proportionally less able to use the aura and power of the office to carry the aid program. By FY 1970 foreign aid stood at $1.76 billion, the lowest since the inception of the Marshall Plan.

Deference—A Summary. Based on the events during these years, it is apparent that Congress voluntarily relinquished much of the control it might have exercised over foreign policy. Adding to the traditional view of Presidential primacy in foreign affairs, Congress felt that the increased complexity and stakes of international affairs and the Executive's superiority of information and expertise mandated executive dominance. Taxed by their parochial interests and responsibilities, members of Congress were ordinarily willing to let the Executive determine policy.

In times of international stress, Congress displayed a particular willingness to support presidential action—even when there were considerable legislative misgivings. Congress and the nation have traditionally rallied behind the President in times of crisis. The speed and violence of atomic age international politics has intensified this tendency. One can hardly imagine a response similar to Senator William Borah's in May 1939 when he was told by President Roosevelt and Secretary of State Cordell Hull that legislation was needed in light of approaching war in Europe. "I do not believe there is going to be a war in Europe," declared Borah. When Hull pleaded with the Senator to look at State Department dispatches, Borah, claiming his own sources of information, roared back, "I don't give a damn about your dispatches."(79)

When the president sought true consultation in time of stress, Congress was often reticent. Eisenhower's views on constitutional processes gave the legislature an open opportunity to exert itself in the conduct of even crisis diplomacy. Each time it was asked, Congress demurred. One has to believe that even in Indochina, had the President acted, Congress would have followed. Restricting the Executive in times of international tension became such an anathema to Congress that the cold war was effectively overplayed to sway recalcitrant legislators. The tactic of stressing cold war consequences to carry unpopular policies is particularly evident in the area of foreign aid. Although such methods were successful in passing legislation, they also served to continue the cold war mentality which gripped the United States.

The ability of the Executive to invoke a right to predominance in the foreign policy process was not constant, however. Presidents and the presidency varied in strength. When the personal and/or political prestige of executive actors was low, when unity of purpose was missing, or when activism was absent, then Congress' influence rose. The Eisenhower Administration's troubles often sprang from the President's unwillingness to exert his authority. Presidents Truman and Johnson suffered declines in personal and political prestige during their terms in office. In other cases, even where prestige was high and a vigorous effort was waged, division within the Executive broke down the actual or perceptual information and expertise gaps and dissipated administration efforts.

## The President as Politician

A second group of factors that promote presidential power in the foreign policy process involve the president's ability to utilize certain skills as a "politician" as well as a "world leader." Part of this occurs because the president can gain influence by invoking his position as party leader and because members of his party in Congress are often willing to accept that leadership. The president can also gain influence by bestowing political benefits. These can range from public support of a member to tangible rewards, such as federal spending in a member's district, and are generally related to members' reelectoral ambitions. Partisan considerations are not, however, an undisguised benefit for presidential power. Just as they can at times work to enhance executive authority, they can also be a factor in making members resist presidential direction.

Presidential Patronage and Pork. Contrary to what is often popularly imagined, there is little evidence of overt swapping of patronage or other political perks by presidents for support on specific foreign policy measures. As one recent study found, executive-legislative liaison on these matters is more often nonspecific in nature, with reciprocal, non-bargaining support build-

ing up. Patronage has already extensively been discussed. While
there is substantial evidence of foreign policy personnel being
appointed on the initiative of members of Congress, there were
relatively few instances of overt deals being made. Apart from
any philosophical qualms, there were practical reasons for the
general absence of direct swaps. As Johnson's presidential aide
Henry Hull Wilson explained, if word got around that the president was trading for votes, "then every one would want to trade
and all other efforts at persuasion would automatically fail."
(80)
    That is not to say that deals were never made. The struggle
over the Trade Expansion Act of 1962 was the scene of a rare
example of overt swaps and arm twisting by White House lobbyists.
Concessions were not only made on the substance of the legislation, but on outside matters. The pressuring and dealing became
so blatant that even members of Congress were appalled.(81)
Senator Robert Kerr, for example, made an overt deal with President Kennedy for an Arkansas River project in exchange for
support of the trade act.(82)  Ted Sorenson has also recalled
that to secure foreign aid support Kennedy would agree to help
members with the pet projects in their districts.(83)  A somewhat
more widespread pattern of horse-trading can also be found in the
related area of defense. The fate of the ABM, for one, brought
on considerable negotiations with Congress. Senator Charles
Mathias was told by a regulatory agency official whom he called
about a problem, "We might give more attention to your ideas if
you would get on the team" with regard to the ABM.(84)  A committee chairman hinted to President Nixon that he could secure
support on ABM in return for a major federal installation in his
district.(85)  Nixon also made concessions on desegregation
enforcement in Mississippi to gain Senator John Stennis' vote on
ABM,(86) and threatened Republican Senator James Pearson that
defense contracts might not be made with Kansas industry if he
did not reverse his opposition to ABM.(87)
    Bargaining, or attempts to, can also rebound negatively.
Representative D. S. Saund tried to swap the retention of a Veteran's Administration hospital in his district for foreign aid support, but Kennedy rejected the deal and later snubbed Saund by
excluding him from the platform while speaking in the Representative's district.(88)  On the same bill, Sorenson also remembered
that "another recalcitrant member found the new federal office
building scheduled for his district suddenly missing from the
budget."(89)  There is also the story, related above, of President Johnson circulating the rumor that he had cut off dams, et
al. to Frank Church's Idaho. Based on his own legislative experience, Johnson saw that as at least a creditable threat. Even
the supposedly apolitical Dwight Eisenhower became so distressed
at Republicans who voted against him that he asked that when any
favor was asked of the White House, the member's voting record be
attached to the request when it reached him for decision.(90)
Presidents also can occasionally become involved in manipulating
committee assignments in Congress. While that process is generally a legislative process, there is some evidence that the White
House is interested in, monitors, and at times tries to influence

committee assignments.(91)  Members also occasionally ask executive officials to help them gain seats on the Foreign Relations
or other desired committee(92) and legislative leaders also discuss committee assignments with the Executive.(93)

   The Electoral Connection.  Presidential support or opposition in the electoral process is a somewhat more common tool
utilized by the Executive.  Yet it still cannot be characterized
as widespread.  In part this stems from a realization that members
enjoy a level of immunity from direct presidential intervention.
In 1962 John Kennedy correctly pointed out that members "take
care of themselves first . . . I don't and I couldn't hurt most
of them if I wanted to."(94)  Kennedy not only believed that he
couldn't electorally threaten Congress, but that any attempt to
do so might well rebound negatively.  Theodore Sorenson observed
that Kennedy felt that he was faced with "a Democratic Congress
with which he had to get along and that there was no advantage to
be served by opening a cold war with Congress by appealing over
their heads to their constituents."(95)

   What is generally true, however, is not, by definition, always true, and there are a number of examples of presidential
electoral intervention.  The most interesting of these involves
"non-aggression" against friendly members of the opposition
party.  The respite given Senator Vandenberg has already been
discussed as have the signals Nixon sent to Washington state
Republicans not to strongly oppose the reelection of Scoop
Jackson.  The Democratic opponents of Everett Dirksen also received little support from the White House.  In 1970 Nixon directed leading Republicans not to aid the campaign against
Senator Gale McGee, a supporter on Vietnam.(96)

   Attempts at negative electoral pressure on individual members
can also be occasionally found.  Despite his reservations, President Kennedy made a pointed personal appearance on behalf of
Representative Walter Judd's opponent.  Surprisingly, President
Eisenhower seems to have been fairly "purge-minded."  He conspired with Henry Cabot Lodge, Jr., and Sherman Adams to work to
defeat Republican "hopeless mossbacks, beyond persuasion or redemption . . . who persistently and consistently oppose Administration policies."(97)  In 1956 Eisenhower also attempted to push
United States membership in the Organization for Trade Cooperation by threatening not to support Republicans who opposed the
measure.  The effort was to no avail, though, and the United
States remained outside the organization.(98)  By contrast,
support of Eisenhower on foreign policy could help win his
support.  Eisenhower aides recommended in 1956, for example, that
the President not support Senator Alexander Wiley because of his
lack of support on domestic issues such as agriculture.  A memo
of the discussion notes that Eisenhower "quarreled violently"
with the idea, citing Wiley's support on the Bricker Amendment
and on foreign aid, and insisting "It is the foreign problems
which really create all our other problems."(99)

   Richard Nixon also was not above a purge and successfully
aided in the defeat of New York Republican Senator Charles
Goodell in 1970 because of his opposition to Vietnam.  William

Safire quotes Nixon as telling a meeting of political operatives, "We are not out for a Republican Senate. We are out to get rid of the radicals . . . We are dropping Goodell over the side." (100)

More commonly, foreign policy concerns are reflected in general concern for the composition of Congress. Activity in the congressional campaigns, however, carries with it the danger of alienating the bipartisan support presidents value. The Eisenhower Administration made the connection between elections and foreign policy more clearly than any of the others which occupied the White House during the period. Besides supporting friendly or considering purges of unfriendly members, Eisenhower constantly reiterated that the way for the Republicans to maintain, or later regain, control of Congress was to cooperate with the President and show the public a united and progressive Republican Party.(101) Unusually for a Secretary of State, Dulles was also fairly active in campaigns from the sidelines. Like all Secretaries of State, he tended to stay formally neutral, giving lip service to bipartisanship, but behind the scenes and, when possible, in public he was an active partisan. New York's Kenneth Keating, for one, who was gearing up for a Senate run, asked Dulles to appear on a television show Keating hosted. Dulles' Assistant Secretary for Public Affairs, Carl McCardle, advised his boss not to appear on Keating's show. "The political atmosphere is super-charged now," McCardle warned. "I am afraid that . . . however sanitized your remarks, you would be regarded as partisan . . ." Dulles accepted the invitation anyway.(102) Dulles was also in regular contact with partisan figures such as Republican National Chairman Leonard Hall(103) and Senate Campaign Committee Chairman Barry Goldwater who sent the Secretary a handkerchief embroidered with the initials YCERBSOYA. They meant, wrote Senator Goldwater "'You can't elect Republicans by sitting on your ---,' and I will leave the last letter to your interpretation. It could be either anatomy or ankle."(104) Generally, however, and even though Dulles worried that if the Democrats became too strong it would result in "an appeasement that will leave the Soviets in control of practically all of Asian, African, and the Middle East," he realized that he depended on bipartisanship and had to be careful not to become too partisan.(105)

Beyond overt or covert campaign assistance, presidents have occasionally used foreign policy to try to influence congressional elections or have made foreign policy decisions based on the pressure generated by a mid-term campaign. In 1970, for example, Richard Nixon took a number of steps related to the November elections. Nixon explored the possibility of a Fall 1970 summit meeting in Moscow in part because of the beneficial effect it might have on House and Senate races.(106) When that move failed he travelled to Europe in September and October. According to Kissinger, "To say that Nixon in deciding on his . . . European trip was unaware of the glow it might cast on the forthcoming Congressional elections would be to deny him the qualities that led him to the Presidency."(107) In another area, Secretary of Defense Laird persuaded the President to increase the troop withdrawal rate from Vietnam because of the imminent elections. The President's estimate was that the "elections would make congressional demands for more troop withdrawals impossible to stop and difficult to ignore.(108) Nixon also imposed an oil import quota on Canada in 1970. He was concerned with over seventy congressional races in seven oil states. Six of these states had cast Republican electoral ballots in 1968, and Nixon hoped to increase Republican representation from them in 1970.(109) Finally, when the question of a Soviet naval base in Cuba arose in September 1970, Nixon sought to suppress the issue until after the elections. Kissinger urged action because "to delay the showdown for two months greatly increased the danger," but Nixon refused because "He did not . . . want some 'clown Senator' asking for a Cuban blockade in the middle of an election."(110)

## Congress and Partisan Opposition

President Nixon's mischaracterization of members of the Senate should not detract from the truth of his underlying assumption that legislative foreign policy activity is often spurred by partisan considerations. If the general tenets of party unity and the manipulative partisan tools available to the president can enhance executive influence, the reverse can also be true. Concern with their party's and their own individual electoral fates may motivate members of Congress to oppose presidential policy. This is most often true for opposition party members, but may also hold for members of the president's own party.

The White House or Bust. Presidential electoral politics is once source of legislative maneuvering in foreign policy. The increase of the Senate as a path to the White House has led senators to seek assignments to the Foreign Relations and Armed Services Committees and, even if not on those bodies, to increase their foreign policy activities.(111) Hopefuls such as John Kennedy, Hubert Humphrey, Frank Church, Edmund Muskie and Stuart Symington all were members of the committee. George McGovern was also a member, but not until after several frustrating tries. In both 1968 and 1970, McGovern requested that he be assigned to the Foreign Relations Committee, agreeing to give up his seat on the Interior Committee which was an important assignment given his South Dakota constituency.(112) It was not until 1973 that McGovern finally gained the coveted, although belated seat. The allure of the committee has also attracted Republicans. Karl Mundt had an opportunity to join the committee beginning in 1963. To do so, however, he would have to surrender his seat on the Agriculture Committee which was an immeasurably more important assignment to South Dakota voters. Advice from constituents included, "it would be very unwise politically to make this exchange. From the standpoint of the people of South Dakota the committee on agriculture is the most important committee in the Senate."(113) Mundt made the switch anyway.

The presence in the Senate of presidential hopefuls increases both their interest in foreign policy and their desire to stake out independent positions and establish politically enhancing reputations. In 1960, during discussion with the President on the military budget, Representative Leslie Arends contrasted the difficulties in the Senate hearings with the smooth sailing in the House and speculated that in the latter chamber things were easier "because there are no Presidential candidates on that committee."(114)

Eisenhower also lost support to Lyndon Johnson's ambitions. Johnson became piqued when at a stag dinner for press people Eisenhower omitted Johnson's name from his discussion of possible presidential candidates for 1960. At the next White House meeting with Democratic leaders, Johnson virtually refused to speak to the President, offering nothing and replying to questions in monosyllables. After the meeting Johnson grabbed Navy Secretary Robert Anderson aside and brandished a press clipping of the President's snub, telling Anderson, "I have had about all I can have of this." Eisenhower brushed the incident aside, but congressional liaison Bryce Harlow was "deeply worried" about the effect in the Senate."(115)

Other Ambitions. Not all the maneuvering in the Senate could be laid at the Democrats' doorstep however. Some of it resulted from attempts by the Republicans to derail potential Democratic nominees. Harlow, for one, did not think Eisenhower's omission of Johnson's name was inadvertent, but rather the result of "General Persons and Jim Hagerty . . . poisoning the President's mind."(116) In the Senate itself, the Republicans plotted with the White House to sponsor amendments to the foreign aid bill designed to force votes that would discomfit Johnson and John Kennedy.(117) On occasion, maneuvering can also be related to the attainment of some other political office or goal. When House Foreign Affairs Committee Chairman Thomas "Doc" Morgan decided to run for governor of Pennsylvania he picked fights with Fulbright's committee to gain publicity. As part of the same chain, Wayne Hayes vowed to vote against administration policy in an attempt to gain the chairmanship Morgan was vacating.(118)

To Win a Majority. Congress can also be activated by a more general party-oriented concern with electoral politics. Control of Congress and the White House are powerful motivational factors. The Republicans' feeling that they would win the presidency and regain a majority in Congress after their "near miss" in 1948 led to a distinct rise in partisanship in the 1950-1952 period. The Washington Star noted at the time that "there has been a restless stirring in the Republican ranks, a rising revolt against the 'me-tooism' which some hold responsible for the succession of G.O.P. disasters at the polls."(119) Senator Robert Taft, the leading Republican presidential possibility in the early-going, led the attack on a broad front against the Truman Administration. The Democrats were accused of abandoning bipartisanship, and losing China, caving in at Yalta, and a host of other sins.(120) Even Senator Vandenberg, the champion of bipartisanship, cautiously joined the melee, writing to journalist Edward R. Morrow that Truman had thrown away inter-party cooperation by castigating the Republicans.(121)

A similar rise in Democratic partisanship occurred in the mid-1950s. Most of Eisenhower's first term was marked by foreign policy cooperation. But by 1955 the Democrats, spurred by electoral considerations, frustrated by feeling shut out of consultation, and disagreeing with presidential policy, began to rebel. A center of the agitation was Adlai Stevenson, Democratic presidential nominee in 1956 and a hopeful for 1960.(122) Chester Bowles, a strong Stevenson supporter, was particularly active in urging congressional Democrats to take a strong, critical stand on foreign policy. Bowles made his case in strongly partisan terms. To Lyndon Johnson he wrote, "As the opposition party, we will want to do everything we can . . . to improve our political position vis-à-vis the 1958 and 1960 elections."(123) Bowles wrote similarly to Hubert Humphrey that if the Democrats' lack of a defined foreign policy continued, "the President will not only win easily in 1956, but he will win by enough to pull a Republican Senate in with him . . . Personally," Bowles concluded, "I am convinced that if we want to hold our position even on Capitol Hill in 1956, it would be folly to allow this situation to develop further."(124)

Bowles' admonitions struck a responsive note in the more liberal Democrats in the Senate. Humphrey, who was himself to vie for the Democratic presidential nomination in 1960, wrote Bowles, "There is no doubt . . the Democratic leadership must join the issue on foreign policy."(125) Humphrey felt the "concession the Eisenhower Administration makes is to the neo-isolationist wing of his own party."(126) He told a colleague that "The American people know we won a majority in Congress, therefore [they] are going to expect we have some ideas of our own,"(127) and he wrote others that it was time to call on the President to be "alert to his responsibilities instead of his personal comfort at a trout stream."(128) As noted, the Democratic leadership in the two houses remained more or less cooperative and acted to restrain an all out attack on the Administration, but in the late 1950s bipartisanship was distinctly on the wane.(129)

A decade later it was Lyndon Johnson's turn to be on the losing end of growing congressional concern about the electoral impact of the war in Vietnam. Many members certainly were in sincere, substantive opposition to American involvement, but that concern was strengthened by worry about the electoral consequences. A series of memos written by Mike Mansfield to Johnson in mid 1966 illustrate that dual view. After meeting with his Democratic Senate colleagues, Mansfield distilled the comments for Johnson. One point which Mansfield found "so constantly reiterated and so unchallenged as to suggest . . . heavy agreement," among senior members was that "there is a strong conviction that candidates of the Democratic Party will be hurt by the war."(130) Junior Senate Democrats seconded that sentiment. They argued that in the long run the war was a "heavy liability" for the Party, that much of the popular support came from Republican voters, and that "it is among Democrats that the principal unhappiness exists over Vietnam. If 6% or 7% are unhappy enough

to vote Republican in protest in November, think what it will do
to Democratic candidates for Congress."(131)

Johnson was also sampling congressional opinion through Larry
O'Brien. The liaison officer found that many Democratic critics
"wanted to support the President, but they had elections coming
up and they knew their constituents were disturbed by rising
draft calls and rising battlefield casualties."(132)

After the 1966 elections which resulted in the Democrat's
losing forty-seven House seats, four Senate seats, and eight
governorships, partisan concern became even more acute. O'Brien
recounts that at a meeting between President Johnson and Senate
Democratic leaders in January 1967, William Fulbright characterized Vietnam as the "strongest undercurrent" which had swept away
so many Democratic officeholders. John Pastore later told
O'Brien "Our problem is Vietnam-[coffin] boxes coming back,
casualties going up. Back home not a good word from anyone for
us . . . We are losing Democrats in droves . . . ." O'Brien's
summary opinion was that by 1967 the war was "a disaster politically."(133)

The Republicans were not oblivious to the political opportunity the war presented. In July 1966 Charles Percy, campaigning
for the Senate in Illinois, called for an all Asian peace conference to settle Vietnam. Republican strategist Senator Thurston
Morton picked up the idea and persuaded a number of Republican
senators and even Richard Nixon to endorse the idea.(134) In
1968 with the presidential election upcoming, Percy also acted to
establish a Republican initiative on the USS Pueblo seizure.
(135) When Nixon became president, many Democrats felt less
restrained in their criticism, but that did not necessarily mean
the Republicans fully rallied to support the new President's war
policy. Some, such as the new Republican Senate leader, Hugh
Clark, did feel constrained to do so. Michigan Republican (later
Democratic) Representative Donald Riegle wrote to Scott protesting his strong support of Nixon and predicting that "such a
course will propel the Republican Party toward an election
disaster in 1972." In reply, Scott derided "those Democratic
hopefuls who for so many years stood mute when, first, President
Kennedy, then President Johnson committed us deeper and deeper
into Vietnam." Also, Scott reminded Riegle, "I have added responsibilities to my Party . . ., which on occasion requires me to go
to the defense of [the] President."(136) Rank-and-file Republicans did not feel Scott's responsibilities. Speaking as a fresh-
man, Republican William Saxbe, a relatively conservative Ohio
Senator and later Nixon's Attorney General, pointed out, "We come
to the Senate with the attitude that . . . the War wrecked
Johnson and that it will wreck Nixon unless he responds . . . our
election was largely responsive to the national attitude."(137)


## Congress and Public Opinion--A Reciprocal Relationship

Saxbe's comment is reflective of the concern in Congress for
public opinion and its link to the electoral process. The reality may be that foreign policy has little impact on legislative

elections. A study by Glenn Parker found a lack of substantial relationships between war and the unpopularity of Congress, leading to the conclusion that "Congress, unlike presidents . . ., is not held responsible for . . . involvement in foreign wars."(138) Another study found that in the 1950s and 1960s voters were generally unconcerned about foreign policy, with only approximately twenty-five percent listing foreign issues in an open-ended survey.(139)

   Public Opinion Counts. Be that as it may, members of Congress tend to believe that public opinion does respond to foreign policy questions and that, in turn, affects their electoral chances. Often this can enhance presidents' influence. A president can dominate the news(140) and public opinion tends to support executive foreign policy, particularly in time of crisis. (141) The partisan urge to differ with a president can also be restrained by the knowledge that a legislator is the likely loser in such a contest. Arthur Vandenberg warned his fellow Republican Michigan Senator Homer Ferguson in 1950 that attacking Truman might boomerang. "We may not successfully ask the American people to elect a Republican Congress in 1950 . . . if we notify them in advance that there can be no bipartisan foreign policy . . ."(142) The attempt in the mid 1950s by liberal Democrats to generate attacks on the popular Eisenhower also fell short in part due to the potential backlash. Soon after the President's landslide victory in 1956, a dispirited William Fulbright wrote, "It is extremely difficult to arouse any interest among the Democrats in a critical attack on the policies of the President." (143) Even Hubert Humphrey, one of the critics of that time, recognized the danger. In an insightful letter fifteen years later, Humphrey wrote to Dean Rusk

> It is very difficult for the opposition party to gain the initiative on the President when it comes to foreign affairs, and surely it is even more difficult for a member of Congress--unless he wants to be totally irresponsible. To me, it seems the best politics for Democrats is to support the President in these diplomatic initiatives when they seem basically right . . . This does not deny the right of constructive criticism and alternative proposals, but I do believe the American people are fed up with nitpicking and cheap party partisan politics just for the sake of trying to make headlines. It is my view that the Democrats cannot . . . really win against Mr. Nixon on foreign policy.(144)

   Congress can turn on a president, however, when public opinion flows away from the chief executive. Vietnam was certainly one such instance. Paul Burnstein and William Freudenburg found that Senate voting on anti-war motions was positively related to shifts in public opinion against the war.(145) Both supporters and opponents of the war showed a strong interest in opinion on the conflict.
   Henry Kissinger and Richard Nixon believed that Congress reacted to public opinion and tried to demonstrate opinion sup-

port to members of Congress.(146) They were also urged on by supportive members to mount a counter attack on the public opinion-driven drift of Congress into increasing opposition to the war and to put "the monkey . . . on the backs of the McGoverns and the Fulbrights and the other doves."(147) In addition to various strategies to win or keep public support, poll results were dispatched to Congress. On one occasion, Special Counsel Charles Colson wrote to Hugh Scott, sending new polls and congratulating the Senator on his use of the previous day's public opinion sampling. "The proof of the pudding is the fact that very few Democrats spoke up in Congress today," Colson crowed. "I think you put their heads in the trenches but good."(148) Public opinion samples were also sent to supportive members to keep their morale up. Presidential Counsel Clark MacGregor hastened to let Karl Mundt know that the mail from South Dakota favored Nixon's Vietnam policy by nearly a twenty to one margin.(149) Bryce Harlow even tried to influence Fulbright, sending him a Gallup poll and adding, hopefully, "I am sure that you were impressed as I am with the overwhelming public support [Nixon is receiving]."(150) Fulbright, of course, was getting his own "friendlier" reports, which showed reaction to his antiwar stands as high as fifteen to one.(151)

The Danger of Foreign Policy Leadership. Another aspect of perceived public opinion which has affected congressional attitudes toward foreign policy is the widely held belief that foreign policy activity and support carry danger at election time. This is especially true in the case of support of foreign aid. Dean Acheson related the instance of Foreign Affairs Chairman James Richards' near defeat in 1950 primary by a challenger who accused Richards of getting more aid for Yugoslavia than South Carolina. Richards survived, but, according to Acheson, "The primary proved to be a close call for the chairman and a damper on his enthusiasm for foreign aid."(152) It is not lost on members that most of the post-World War II chairmen of the Foreign Relations Committee have been involuntarily retired by homefront challenges partly based on their internationalist sympathies. Walter George, for example, was attacked by his successor Herman Talmadge for being concerned with the world rather than Georgia.(153) Eisenhower found his request for foreign aid support rejected, in part, because of George's fate and the similarly inspired end to Tom Connally's congressional career.(154)

At another juncture, Lyndon Johnson told Eisenhower that everywhere he went in Texas he heard people complain about dollars being spent overseas when there was no money being spent for a particular dam they felt was necessary.(155) Dulles and Eisenhower worked to try to make foreign aid more popular and to support members in their districts,(156) but the program was seen as so unpopular at home that Charles Halleck even suggested finding a new label to replace "foreign aid."(157)

That situation persisted into the sixties and seventies. Fulbright wrote Bowles in 1964, "You and the Administration are whistling past the graveyard if you think the American people are in favor of the present foreign aid program."(158) Carl Marcy put the problem succinctly in a letter to Mike Mansfield. Marcy recommended a continuing resolution on aid, saying it would "take a lot of members off a very hot seat." After all, Marcy asked, "How can one vote for aid to foreigners and against public works for his district?"(159) Another Foreign Relations committee member told Richard Fenno that service on the Committee is "a political liability . . . You have no constituency." The senator went on to explain: "In my election campaign last fall, the main thing they used against me was my interest in foreign relations. [They said] I was more interested in what happened to the people of Abyssinia and Afghanistan than in what happened to the good people of my state."(160) As a last point, it should be noted that just as Connally and George had been, Fulbright was defeated in a primary in 1974, and his successor as chairman was, in turn, defeated in the 1980 election, thus continuing the real or mythical electoral vulnerability of internationalist, foreign aid supporters.

## Partisan Pull of the White House

In addition to examining the more specific causes and effects of the partisan relationships between the White House and Congress, the role of party can be seen in the more generalized attitudes exhibited by members of the two parties toward the president and his programs. The role of the president as "party leader" has been long recognized, although the exact impact of partisan presidential leadership has never been definitively explained. The fact remains that the program of the president has a "centripetal effect" on what David B. Truman terms the "congressional party."(161) The majority party in Congress works, to a degree, as a group because of and in response to the initiatives of the Executive.

The effect of party loyalty on the actions of members of Congress in relation to foreign policy has also received attention. James N. Rosenau, in his study of the attitudes of senators toward Secretries of State Dean Acheson and John Foster Dulles, found that senators from both parties generally reversed themselves and behaved differently toward Dulles than they had toward Acheson.(162) In a broader study of presidential partisan leadership, Stuart Gerry Brown reached a conclusion paralleling Rosenau's.(163) A number of studies have demonstrated that members of both the House and Senate alter their voting patterns in accordance with the party which controls the White House. Mark Kesselman, in his studies of voting shifts from the Truman to the Eisenhower presidency and from the Eisenhower to the Kennedy term, has shown that party-related variations did occur. Surveying House members who served in both the 81st (1949-50) and the 86th (1959-60) Congresses, Kesselman found that sixteen Republicans became more internationalist, while only two became more isolationist. Of the Democrats, only seven became more internationalist, while twenty-five became more isolationist. During the 87th Congress (1961-62) the trend was reversed. Twenty-one Democrats became more internationalist in their voting; just five moved toward isolationism.(164)

Using the 86th-87th Congresses and the 90th-91st Congresses (1967-68, 1969-70, respectively) to extend and review Kesselman's studies, Charles Tedmarch and Charles Sabatt did much to reaffirm the original findings. Using the Senate, Tedmarch and Sabatt found similar shifts. Only in the 90th-91st Congresses was the pattern broken, with 7.7 percent of the Democrats becoming internationalist, while only 5.8 percent moved in the opposite direction. Surveying the 86th-87th Congresses, in the specific field of foreign aid, Michael O'Leary reached a similar conclusion. He found that shifts in voting patterns could be attributed largely to the partisan attraction of the White House incumbent.(165) The effect of party in these studies should not be overstated, however. Each of the studies found that a significant percentage of senators and representatives were unaffected by which party controlled the White House. In Kesselman's first study, 198 (82%) of 353 members did not shift. Kesselman's second study showed 109 (68%) of 159 representatives remaining consistent. Similarly, Tedmarch's and Sabatt's statistics revealed that 73 percent and 84 percent of senators voted consistently before and after the shifts in party control of the White House which occurred in 1961 and 1969. Only O'Leary's study showed predominant movement, with only 17 percent of the senators and 28 percent of the representatives having the same support level for foreign aid.(166)

George Edwards, in a more recent examination of presidential party affiliation, found similar evidence of party attraction. For Democratic Presidents Kennedy and Johnson, the House Democrats' support score was 70 percent; the Republicans' support score was only 40 percent. For Republican Presidents Eisenhower and Nixon (through 1970), the Republicans' support score rose to 57 percent, while the Democrats' support score dropped to 62 percent. The pattern was similar in the Senate. For the two Democratic presidents, the Democrats' support score was 62 percent; the Republican support score was only 52 percent. For the two Republican presidents, the Republicans' support score jumped to 72 percent, while the Democrats' support score fell to 53 percent.(167) Aage Clausen's single study, his work with Carl Van Horn, and a study by Herbert Weisberg and Herbert Asher found similar presidential influence on party members.(168) Finally, a recent study by Barbara Sinclair further confirms the tidal pull of the Oval Office on the congressional sea. Measuring support of international involvement, Sinclair found that, under Truman, the Democrats scored 84.9 percent, the Republicans 33.2 percent. Under Eisenhower, Republican support almost doubled to 60.8 percent; Democrat support declined to 69.0 percent. In the Kennedy-Johnson years, Democrat support increased to 77.1 percent; the Republican score ebbed to 39.6 percent. With Nixon and Ford in the White House, the tide again turned, with Democratic support down to 63.9 percent and Republican support up to 51.8 percent. (169)

The extensive evidence of individually- and general party-motivated responsiveness on the part of members of Congress should not be taken to mean that legislators are an unpatriotic, self-centered, partisan lot who would derail the nation's foreign policy in order to gain political office, influence, or other benefits. They are not by and large, as Eisenhower once characterized them, a bunch of people "trying to make political capital out of something they don't know anything about."(170) They are political actors who respond to political stimuli, but the partisan maneuvering is heavily restrained by loyalty and deferential ethics. The "rally 'round the flag" response and belief in bipartisanship have normally limited sharp partisan divisions to more marginal and incremental issues such as trade and aid. As Fenno quotes a State Department official, "Sometimes, of course, the members get partisan, butthey'll never admit it. Partisanship is a dirty word. . ."(171)

The evidence of the 1948 to 1972 period, then, largely confirms that of the 1945-1948 period. Partisanship is present, but it is limited by both the numbers of congressmen who are swayed by such considerations and by the issues in which partisanship is a factor. Even in those rare instances of international tension, such as Cuba, where partisanship was a factor, it dissipated once the tension reached the crisis stage. Thus, while the propositions that members of Congress will tend to accept the foreign policy leadership of a President of the same party and that partisan considerations will activate Congress are confirmed, their impact was not a primary factor. Indeed, the limited role of partisanship in determining congressional disposition made it perilous for a president to attempt to gain influence by invoking his position as party leader. For Democratic presidents, on questions of trade and aid, this tactic has had some effect. Eisenhower also met with some success in mitigating the opposition of his party to liberalized aid and trade. But whether Democratic or Republican, whether faced with an opposition Congress or not, presidents have had consistently better luck by avoiding partisan emphasis and concentrating on the relationship of their proposals to the cold war and national security.

## Institutional and Personal Ego

To a degree, governmental processes are a matter of form as well as substance. A rule of conduct that executive actors have had to learn, and occasionally relearn, is that Congress ordinarily should be formally "consulted" at least. This does not necessarily mean that congressional advice need be heeded. Often the mere gesture is sufficient. Legend has it that Foreign Affairs Committee Chairman Sol Bloom cared little what the president decided, so long as he was informed fifteen minutes before the announcement.

The essence here is whether the Executive observes the minimum etiquette of at least pro forma congressional participation in foreign policy-making. If the institutional or personal pride of members is slighted, the Executive risks an upsurge of legislative activity. Thus, it is wise for the president to pay, at a minimum, symbolic attention to Congress.

As a related note, intrainstitutional relationships can also play a part in determining Congress' interest and stance on foreign policy. Committee jurisdiction, individual relationships, and the role of institutional leaders can have a significant effect on policy.

Addressing this last point first, the 1945-1972 period was marked, for most of its span, by a limited, generally clear, and formally defined foreign policy hierarchy. Through the mid 1960s, if the Executive could gain the support of this leadership nucleus, it was extremely unlikely that significant opposition would develop in Congress. Into the early 1950s, the pivotal roles were played by the alternating chairmen of the Foreign Relations Committee, Senators Vandenberg and Connally. Toward the end of his career, Vandenberg wrote to Walter Lippmann denying, but obviously flattered by, a comparison the journalist had written between the Senator's position and that of British Prime Minister Winston Churchill. With a good deal of ingenuousness, Vandenberg clucked, "I feel certain embarrassment with my Republican colleagues who must be persistently irked by reading in the newspapers that I am their 'spokesman on foreign policy'."(172) It was only late in his tenure, in failing health and with Republicans increasingly frustrated with electoral reverses and seemingly fruitless bipartisanship, that Vandenberg's dominance began to wane. When Robert Taft, the Republican leader on domestic issues, began to move into the foreign policy domain, Vandenberg worried to his wife, "The Taft speech [against NATO] will lengthen the battle because it lends a certain respectability to the opposition, and some who wouldn't have dared stand up on their own will now join the anti parade."(173)

By the mid 1950s with the Democrats back into control of Congress, the leadership focus shifted to that side of the aisle. There were still important Republicans. Bryce Harlow engineered a private breakfast between President Eisenhower and Senator Styles Bridges on the grounds that "Bridges is susceptible to flattery, he is a walking 25 votes in the Senate."(174) But the really important members were the likes of Walter George, Lyndon Johnson, and Richard Russell in the Senate and Sam Rayburn in the House. Executive officials from both the Eisenhower and Kennedy Administrations have contrasted the relative ease and certainty of dealing with what Dean Rusk has referred to as the "whales" of Congress to the later difficulty of dealing with a decentralized Congress, which Rusk characterized as 535 "minnows."(175) William Macomber dates the decline in centralized leadership from the retirement of Walter George in 1957.(176) Certainly by the middle 1960s, with the less dynamic Mike Mansfield as Senate Majority Leader and John McCormack and Carl Albert as House Speaker and Majority Leader, and with Fulbright distinctly less influential than a Vandenberg or a George, the ability of the president to consult with a limited circle on the Hill and to be reasonably assured of congressional cooperation had largely disappeared. This phenomenon will be dealt with more fully in the commentary on the post-1972 role of Congress.

There were also a number of non-leadership members who were able to utilize expertise or institutional position early in the period to influence limited areas of foreign policy. The role of individual specialists, such as Representative Walter Judd on China, has already received some attention. In the appropriations area, John Rooney ruled over the State Department budget and was the bane of a long line of Secretaries of State.(177) Otto Passman was the terror of foreign aid legislation for years. The importance of centralized leadership was that, internally, Congress looked to committees, specialists, and formal leaders for guidance on foreign policy. In most cases that made Congress easier to deal with, made "democracy safer for the world," and, given the nature of the leadership, made Congress more compliant. On the other hand, it made the leaders more powerful, and when they did disagree with executive policy, the period saw numerous adjustments and compromises to win their support.

    Personal Prerogatives. Whether it is accomplished with a few "whales" or whether it is more general, consultation can be an effective executive tool with Congress in both a personal and an institutional sense. Personally, congressmen are flattered when they receive unexpected presidential attention and insulted when they feel unjustly ignored. Vandenberg, of course, was a prime example of an ego in need of sustenance. His counterpart, Senator Connally, was also a man of considerable ego--an ego which could be especially wounded by too much attention to Vandenberg. In these two men, it is difficult to separate the factors of personal and institutional pride. It may be, and this was certainly true of Vandenberg, that many members have such a unified sense of identity between themselves, Congress, and their formal committee or leadership roles, that a slight to one is automatically a slight to all.

    Everett Dirksen was another legislator who particularly enjoyed basking in the warmth of public presidential attention. Eisenhower, Kennedy, and Johnson all made a special effort to flatter Dirksen and were rewarded with his unswerving support on crucial foreign policy issues. "I may not always approve of what you do," he told Lyndon Johnson in 1965, "but once I have had my day in court, I support you."(178) Dirksen's association with the two Democratic presidents became so open that it occasioned some criticism among other Republicans. "That fellow [Kennedy] down in the White House," said Representative William Miller, who was to be the Vice Presidential nominee in 1964, "has certainly got Dirksen's number. Ev goes down there to a foreign policy briefing, and he comes out with stars in his eyes, and there's nothing you can do with him."(179) Such criticism did not overly bother the Republican leader. Even when he felt compelled to engage in partisan criticism, he was careful to tell the White House not to take the broadsides too seriously. He had to make a show for the Republican ranks, he explained. "I have to throw them a piece of raw meat now and then."(180)

    While Vandenberg and Dirksen may have had particularly susceptible egos, even in inflated congressional terms, the roles of consultation and other forms of ego massage are evident on a wide scale throughout each of the five administrations covered in this period.

    When Senator Clinton Anderson told Dean Acheson he ought to

make more calls to supportive congressmen, the Secretary's records show calls that day to Senator Connally to congratulate him on a speech, to Senator McFarland to praise him for his leadership, and to Senator Tobey to express delight on his assignment to the Foreign Relations Committee.(181)

In the Eisenhower Administration United Nations Ambassador Henry Cabot Lodge, Jr., who also had a long record of congressional service, was especially insistent on the need to work with Congress. He worried whether "all members of the Cabinet and other high ranking executive officials cultivate Congress as they should," and advised, "There is no group of men in the world who . . . respond to courtesy more gladly."(182) He urged Cabinet officers to ensure that "members of Congress . . . never feel that any agency or department head is saying to himself: 'Why should I, a big shot, . . . waste my time with these tin-horn politicians'." Lodge also counseled: "It is vital to have social contacts with . . . Congressmen" and stressed careful attention to legislative mail so that "whenever a Congressman asks a small favor . . . he gets it quickly and politely. . . You can," Lodge advised, "rise or fall on these relationships." (183) Eisenhower also heard such recommendations from congressional leaders. Bryce Harlow reported, at one point, that Lyndon Johnson had suggested that after the Senate passed the 1957 mutual security bill that Eisenhower "issue a statement to the effect that the Senate has acted patriotically [and] that it heartens you a great deal and you commend Johnson and Knowland and other Senators who led this battle. . ."(184) Eisenhower agreed with the advice he received from Lodge, Harlow, and others (185) and frequently urged his ranking subordinates to make a special effort to establish good personal relations on the Hill. (186) The tactics worked well, too. Lyndon Johnson, in a typical response at one point, expansively thanked Eisenhower for taking him into his confidence and promised to do whatever he could do to help the President.(187)

The same pattern was followed during the Kennedy Administration. Under Secretary of State Bowles, in one illustrative memo, wrote the President of his consultation with Fulbright on the foreign aid bill. Fulbright had stressed the need for a number of private presidential talks with pivotal senators. According to Bowles' recounting, "Dick Russell . . . would be so flattered if you paid him some special attention that he might become a powerful and perhaps decisive force in support of your efforts." John McClellen, "too, would be flattered by any attention you might give him, and that would have a great influence." The key to Bourke Hickenlooper in Fulbright's estimation would be to get him to "picture himself as Vandenberg," and "Jerry Ford. . . might be persuaded to see himself in the role that Chris Herter took in the House during the Marshall Plan." Bowles said that Fulbright made a strong suggestion that, if the Foreign Relations Committee was invited to the White House, it would "pay very great dividends." As for Fulbright himself, Bowles said, "he feels slightly left out . . . His itchiness grows from the belief that his opinions have not adequately been sought out." The answer, Bowles advised, was to let the Senator "stop by the

White House and have a drink with you every week or two."(188)

The personal attention given to Congress increased even more under President Johnson. Reflecting his boss' attitude, Jack Valenti observed, "Too much care and emphasis cannot be given to the care and feeding of key members of Congress. The leadership must be consulted often, warmly, carefully . . . One surly, offended subcommittee chairman can give a president hives."(189) The courtesies ranged from the kind of attention and prerequisites Johnson extended to Everett Dirksen to much more mundane matters. Presidential aides worried, for instance, when Senator Hickenlooper left the White House in a huff after he could not find a parking place.(190) Wayne Hayes of the Foreign Affairs Committee complained to more than one president about lack of attention.(191) According to one report to President Johnson, Hayes was so angry at being ignored by the Executive that "he told Rusk he didn't know peanuts from turds about politics," and complained that he never got to talk to the President or his principal aides. "If you're not a Texan, forget it," Hayes fumed. "I talk to Marvin Watson and he says, 'Well, we're pretty busy down here.' Well, I'm not going to kiss Marvin's ass."(192) Johnson occasionally even catered to Republicans, openly praising, for instance, Silvio Conte for his assistance in passing the 1964 foreign aid appropriation."(193)

In his initial period as president, even Richard Nixon apparently was careful to consult with Congress. Hubert Humphrey pointed out that the Foreign Relations Committee was treating Nixon deferentially because the President had "systematically and assiduously . . . consulted with the leaders of Congress . . . One thing I have learned about Senators is that they're all prima donnas. They all like to be individually consulted."(194)

Institutional Prerogatives. On a more institutional level, Congress has similarly reacted against any policy or oversight construed as a threat to its constitutional prerogatives. Lyndon Johnson has observed that, "the greatest threat to the Chief Executive's 'right to govern' comes traditionally from Congress . . . jealous of its prerogatives. All too often jealousy turns into a stubborn refusal to cooperate in any . . . way . . ."(195)

Institutional prerogative has two facets. The first is the "right" to be consulted. Stated negatively, members of Congress will tend to react adversely if at least the form of consultation is not practiced. Treaty ratification, for example, has been smoother in those instances when Congress was allowed to advise as well as consent. The potentially controversial Japanese Peace Treaty was ratified with few problems, due to the care given to the Senate. Senators were regularly consulted and their contributions publicly acknowledged. The resulting identification with and acclaim for the treaty disposed the Senate to agree on its attractiveness. The Administration similarly eased the path of the 1963 nuclear test ban treaty through arms negotiator Gerald Foster's attention to the Senate during negotiations and by President Kennedy's personal attention to Everett Dirksen.(196)

When Congress has been ignored, the Executive's programs have often run afoul of legislative pique. Although President Tru-

man's failure to consult Congress before intervening in Korea did
not detract from initial support, as the war dragged on, he came
under considerable criticism for waging an "unconstitutional conflict." Remembering the charges of "Truman's War," President
Eisenhower was careful not to repeat his predecessor's mistake in
time of crisis. Even Eisenhower, though, neglected at times to
pay deference to congressional specialists in non-crisis decisions. Senator Mansfield's criticism of policy in Vietnam began
in 1955 when he, as the Senate's expert on the area, began to
feel shut out of the policy process.(197) Part of the reason the
Eisenhower Doctrine program received an unusually negative
response in the Senate was that it was leaked to the press before
congressional leaders were briefed, leaving them appearing uninformed and unimportant.(198) Summing up the attitude in Congress, particularly among the minority party, Senator Hickenlooper responded to charges that Republican members of Congress
were shattering bipartisan unity by countering, "Republicans have
never been consulted in advance of decisions . . . If you have no
voice in or consultation about foreign policy, you certainly are
not bound to accept Administration policy."(199)

Whenever Congress has felt slighted, it has not been reticent
about voicing or acting on its displeasure. At the leadership
level, that might involve Hugh Scott writing to Bryce Harlow to
complain about being sidestepped and to issue the thinly dis-
guised warning that "bypassing the Leadership makes it extremely
difficult for me as the Republican Leader to help the Administration secure Senate passage of desired legislation."(200) On a
more general level, slights to the institution can lead to direct
counter attack or, where that is impossible, to a carom effect.
When the Johnson Administration resisted Foreign Relations Committee jurisdiction over the Central Intelligence Agency, a presidential assistant reported that a multi-year foreign aid authorization had been eliminated because the committee was "furious," and
"this vote was the only convenient stick at the moment."(201) In
another example, the committee cut $45 million from the United
States Information Agency budget in 1972 because the agency
refused to supply certain documents to Congress. "The issue in
this case," Fulbright told his colleagues, "is . . . will the
Senate assert its right to information so that it can properly
discharge its responsibilities, or will it bow to the will of the
Executive?"(202)

Along with injuring its pride by ignoring it, nothing was
quite so likely to spur Congress' indignation as an Executive
attempt to "usurp" one of the legislature's powers. As with
consultation, the question at issue was often one of form rather
than substance. In the quarter century after World War II,
Congress legislatively or by default gave the Executive extremely
wide latitude in determining foreign policy. In trade, for example, Congress no longer set specific tariffs or quotas. Instead,
it gave the President multi-year authority to regulate trade
within broad boundaries. At the same time, though, Congress took
care to keep up the facade of control. This was done by escape
clauses, time and substantive limits on Executive discretion,
legislative vetoes, and other such qualifiers. In some cases,

these restrictions proved effective. In others they were not. The power to declare war is the most pointed example of Congress' trying to maintain the fiction of legislative authority. Beginning with the Rio Treaty of 1948 and the 1949 NATO Treaty, Congress insisted that in all such pacts the United States' response be governed by its "constitutional processes." Twenty-five years and several wars later, such clauses are obviously meaningless.

In other instances, presidents had to agree to consult Congress prior to any radical use of their power. This has been especially true for trade. In 1963 a $100 million project discretion-limitation was instituted as such a consultation requirement for aid. With increased usage of Executive agreements, senators also pressed for presidential promises that treaties would only be revised with the advice and consent of the Senate. Such a promise by Kennedy was an important factor in winning ratification of the nuclear test ban treaty.(203) Heavy senatorial pressure was also brought to bear on Lyndon Johnson to prevent an executive agreement revision of the treaty governing the use of the Panama Canal.(204)

Congress has been particularly reluctant to give up its power over the purse. Clashes in this area have been ones of substance rather than form. Administration requests for multi-year appropriations, lump-sum appropriations, authority to switch funds from one recipient or project to another, "back-door financing," and other such discretionary authority have more often been denied than granted.

In the broadest terms, Congress will also respond to a general sense that it has lost its authority in foreign policy vis-à-vis the Executive Branch. Part of the upsurge of legislative activity in the years immediately following World War II can be attributed to that feeling. After years of being dominated by not only an overpowering president, but one further armed as a commander-in-chief in wartime, Congress by 1946 felt compelled to reassert its perceived proper place in the constitutional balance.

That same sense began to work on Congress by the mid-1960s and in the last section of this study will be seen working very strongly in the 1970s. The Mansfield European troop reduction resolutions picked up support for this reason. As Senator Charles Mathias put it, "the objective is a domestic one, a constitutional objective within the United States to restore to the Senate the powers . . . which [it] has gradually delegated to the President."(205) Even conservatives such as Senator Harry Byrd began to support action to "reverse a trend and reestablish the Senate's traditional role in foreign policy."(206) The discussion around the 1969 National Commitments resolution centered on the same theme. This sense-of-the-Senate resolution urged that all significant future foreign agreements be submitted to Congress. It "may be the most significant measure the Senate will consider during the current session of Congress," Frank Church wrote to Richard Russell, because:

During my 12 years in the Senate, nothing has disturbed me more than the steady decline of Congress within the structure of our Constitutional system. The abdication of Congress—and the consequent erosion of the intended separation of powers—has been particularly apparent with respect to our foreign commitments . . . The erosion of Congressional power in foreign relations has gone so far that a full return of the pendulum cannot be expected in the passage of a single . . . resolution. But here, I submit, we must make our start."(207)

The change in Congress' mood in the late 1960s and 1970s, as will be discussed, can be strongly traced to this issue of institutional ego. Coupled with a variety of other factors, the sense in Congress that the institution had slipped to second class status in the policy process embarrassed members and urged them to reassert their body's "rightful" place. Whether or to what extent there had been an objective decline in legislative authority was ture of our Constitutional system. The abdication of Congress—and the consequent erosion of the intended separation of powers—has been particularly apparent with respect to our foreign commitments . . . The erosion of Congressional power in foreign relations has gone so far that a full return of the pendulum cannot be expected in the passage of a single . . . resolution. But here, I submit, we must make our start."(207)

The change in Congress' mood in the late 1960s and 1970s, as will be discussed, can be strongly traced to this issue of institutional ego. Coupled with a variety of other factors, the sense in Congress that the institution had slipped to second class status in the policy process embarrassed members and urged them to reassert their body's "rightful" place. Whether or to what extent there had been an objective decline in legislative authority was secondary. The point was that members felt impotent and ignored. Pride, then, came before the rise.

## Foreign Policy as a Domestic Resource Issue

The questions of the commitment of domestic economic resources to foreign policy and the impact of foreign policy on domestic economics are issues which have consistently aroused congressional interest. First of all, domestic economics is an area with which members of Congress feel familiar. To the extent that the Executive receives deference in foreign policy, that advantage is lost in the area of domestic affairs. In fact, stemming from their general parochial orientation, members will tend to translate issues into domestic terms. In many instances executive success has depended on how well it was able to keep the issue focused in the foreign policy sphere.

A good deal of work relevant to this domestic/foreign policy perceptual struggle has been done by political scientists. No single definition of policy typologies has gained general acceptance in the discipline, but they do make some valuable observations. "The point," noted James Rosenau, "is that the functioning of political systems does depend on the nature of the issue." (208)

Within the context of foreign policy, both James Rosenau and Theodore Lowi have found that the involvement of domestic resources affect the foreign policy process. Lowi found that resource involvement changed the process characteristics from centralized and cooperative to conflictive.(209) Rosenau has argued that "the more an issue encompasses a society's resources and relationships, the more it will be drawn into a society's domestic political system."(210) Commenting on the work of Rosenau and Lowi, Stephen Cimbala also has found that domestic issues may be important in the determination of the nature of the foreign policy process. Where Rosenau and Lowi are basically striving for objective typologies, though, Cimbala placed more stress on subjective factors. He found that Congress is often bewildered by the complexity of foreign policy and, therefore, members of Congress, latently if not manifestly, tend to translate foreign issues into terms by which they orient themselves on domestic issues. In other words, where there is any potential connection with foreign policy and domestic forces, Congress will be prone to view the policy through a domestic prism.

The matter of perspective is Cimbala's principal dispute with the work of Rosenau and Lowi, and one which is of importance to all attempts to form policy typologies. It is Cimbala's basic contention that not all actors in a national political system will perceive the same substantive issues as falling within the same process typologies.(211) To understand the process variations, then, it is necessary to understand the varying, and at times conflicting, perceptions of the substantive issues. In the estimation of some scholars, such as Robert H. Salisbury, usage of perceptual material is the keystone to building policy typologies. Salisbury has observed, "Policy typologies may be based on data that are composed of perceptions of the actors . . . I suggest that any hypothesis we might advance relating process variables to policy types would, in fact, assume that policy types were so derived." He concludes it would be "odd" if actors "behaved in systematically variable ways without perceiving some parallel variations in the substance of their actions."(212) In a somewhat different, but related context, Snyder, Bruck, and Sapin focused on the importance of perceptions in determining decision-makers' actions. "The definition of the situation," according to these authors, "is a key intervening variable in the decisional context, and is built around the projected action as well as the reasons for action. That is, the situation is conceived of in light of the projected policy response as well as the causal force that prompted activation of the policy process."(213)

This fits into the work of Lowi and Rosenau as well as Cimbala. If, for example, the United States is having some difficulties with a foreign government and decides to break relations or seek censure in the United Nations, few resources are involved, and the issue will theoretically remain in the foreign policy arena, attracting little popular or congressional interest. If the decision is to try the proverbial carrot rather than the stick and offer foreign aid, then resources will be involved, and the public and Congress may become much more interested and active. Foreign aid is an excellent example of the impact of differing perceptions. The 1954 passage of PL 480 to distribute surplus food overseas was accomplished over mild administration objections primarily because it was seen in Congress as a way of supporting domestic prices by disposing of surpluses.(214) Many members who were foreign aid supporters even sold the program to their constituents on the grounds of its favorable impact on American agriculture.(215) Within a few years, however, the program was much less popular in Congress and receiving major cuts. The reversal in legislative sympathy resulted from testimony by Department of Agriculture officials that the program was interrupting normal foreign markets and from a general struggle with the State Department which wanted to distribute food to enhance foreign policy rather than support domestic prices.

Other types of foreign aid were often also tied to domestic resource considerations. There were attempts to argue that foreign aid was good for domestic economics. Trying to defend the Nixon Administration's aid request in 1971, Hugh Scott told his colleagues that more than three-forths of aid money eventually went to support American jobs.(216) The Kennedy Administration tried in 1963 to stress aid's favorable impact on increased exports and the development of new markets. Such tactics have not been successful. The more common belief in Congress, as Senator George Aiken put it, is that "other countries which we have aided have gone into the world market and taken some of our business away; . . . foreign aid has resulted in hundreds of thousands of jobs . . . leaving this country for other parts of the world."(217) The Administration request was cut in 1963 by 33.8 percent. As these illustrations indicate, domestic considerations have generally proven to be a negative factor. The norm, as Christian Herter wrote Dwight Eisenhower in 1959, was that congressional opposition was often for "purely domestic, political reasons having to do with such things as the overall Administration position on domestic programs. . ."(218)

The common pattern, then, has been for aid opponents to base their arguments on domestic factors. Supporters have tried to pitch aid in terms of national security. As major programs such as the Truman Doctrine, British Loan, and Marshall Plan, and a host of annual aid battles demonstrate, Administrations have been most successful when picturing aid as a bulwark against communism. Reviewing the entire aid process, Michael O'Leary has highlighted this phenomenon of perceptual differences in his conclusion that:

> Part of the difficulty facing the executive branch in attempting to win congressional support for foreign aid arises from a problem of definitions. The executive has been unable to win full acceptance of its definition of foreign aid as a policy question, which would imply a high degree of congressional compliance with executive requests. Congress tends to react to foreign aid in terms of domestic standards and expectations.(219)

Domestic economic factors have also inspired congressional opposition to a number of other executive initiatives. The building of the St. Lawrence Seaway which, as discussed earlier, was blocked early in Truman's presidency by Congress, continued for almost another decade to run afoul of domestic economic interests. A push for the Seaway in 1952 ran aground on opposition ranging from Senator Fulbright's concern about construction costs increasing the budget deficit(220) to Senator McMahon's concern that attempts to develop a steel industry in New London, Connecticut, would be damaged by the proposed waterway.(221) President Eisenhower renewed the Executive's campaign. In his memoirs he listed the United Mine Workers, most of the ports on the Atlantic seaboard and Gulf Coast, Pennsylvania and West Virginia coal operators, and eastern railroads as all opposing the Seaway. Only by appeasing some of the domestic groups and emphasizing the national defense aspects of the waterway was Eisenhower finally able to push it through Congress.(222)

The opposition in Congress to Vietnam provides an even more striking example of the role of domestic resources in legislative activity. In their study, Burnstein and Freudenberg found that, along with public opinion, increased commitment of resources was positively correlated with rising congressional opposition.(223) Several senators personally told President Johnson in early 1967 that they were disturbed by the negative impact of Vietnam on Great Society programs.(224) Fulbright wrote to Chester Bowles that "the pressure on our budget is becoming quite acute,"(225) and to a constituent observed, "I am convinced . . . that we have given too much attention to Vietnam . . . and too little attention to serious problems at home."(226) Stuart Symington put it a bit more pithily: "I think we should express less interest in South Asia and more in South St. Louis."(227) Senator George Aiken in his oral history contribution at the Johnson Library captured the widespread feeling in his observation that the war "probably resulted in an increase of crime in the streets in the United States. It. . . resulted in dissatisfaction among advocates of domestic programs who [felt] that money [was] all going into the war and that they [were] all being left short in their own programs."(228)

The extent of congressional activity, then, is partly determined by a definitional struggle. Policies involving the reallocation of funds away from domestic programs or impacting domestic economic interest groups are often perceived by Congress in domestic terms. In such cases the Executive loses many of the psychological advantages it has in foreign affairs.


## Hyphenate Americans and Congress

Economic interest groups and factors are only one of those to which Congress pays heed. Any issue of foreign policy which causes reaction in a segment or among a cross-section of a congressman's political base is apt to stimulate interest and activity on his part. In these cases, just as with domestic resources or partisan politics, the issue typology shifts from the international to the domestic sphere.

If the United States is a melting pot, it is an imperfect one. Numerous groups based on ethnicity, race, and religion abound. Concentrations of such groups of Polish-, Italian-, Jewish-, Greek-, Black-, and Whatever-Americans—the Hyphenate Americans, as Louis Gerson has called them—in various states and electoral districts, have led members of Congress to be aware of and responsive to their sympathies.(229)

The impact of Irish-Americans on the British Loan, Jewish-Americans on Palestine, and Italian-Americans on the Italian Peace treaty were in evidence during Truman's first term. The balance of the years from Truman's second term through Nixon's first term also saw social group influence on Congress. The single most influential group was undoubtedly the "Jewish lobby." In the previous discussion of United States policy toward the Middle East, especially in 1956-1957, the role of the ethnic connection in influencing American policy was readily seen.

Although large concentrations of Jewish-Americans are limited to a relatively few geographic areas, their lobby effort is well organized and financed. It is impressive for a researcher to note during archival searches the amount of mail generated by questions relating to Israel. Even in the files of senators from the very un-Jewish states demonstrate that issues involving Israel generate far more correspondence than any other single foreign policy question.

Senators and representatives of both parties hastened to endear themselves to Jewish constituents and supporters. Hugh Scott, for one, was willing to respond to a suggestion from the American-Israel Public Affairs Committee to co-sponsor legislation to aid the development of a desalinization plant in Israel. (230) Scott's cooperativeness was returned by Jewish organizations such as B'nai Brith, which published a book containing favorable references to Scott and produced a thirty-minute movie on Israel featuring Scott commenting on Israeli-American relations. The value, a Scott aide wrote, was "to serve the purpose of alerting the Jewish community that Senator Scott is up for reelection next year."(231) Hubert Humphrey, on the Democratic side, also had a lively interest in Israeli affairs. In Minnesota, according to Humphrey, "the Jewish constituency represents some of my best friends."(232) Humphrey found trips to the Middle East the source of good speech material to bring back to Jewish constituents.(233) Humphrey also was aware of his standing among national Jewish supporters and its relationship to his quest for the Vice Presidency, Presidency, and Senate Democratic Leader posts. While seeking the latter spot, for example, an aide directed the staff to play to Humphrey's strength among Jews, to point out that Humphrey would be more helpful to the survival of Israel than his competition, Robert Byrd, and to have Jewish leaders contact their senators. "The Jewish community in this country is very well organized and can be mobilized on Humphrey's behalf. . .," the memorandum concluded. "Virtually every Senator has Jewish friends who are major and long term supporters . . . Now there is a favor [we need] and it affects the future of Israel more than any arms shipment or resolution."(234)

Most of the "Jewish lobby" activity in Congress relates to Israel _per_ _se_, but there are examples of activity in other areas. The Multilateral Force, discussed above, is one such example. Representative Chet Holifield wrote to the President that West German participation on the MLF and "latent fears of [Germany's] resurgent power is a matter of deep concern . . . among many of our own people, especially those groups who were victims of the Nazi tyranny of the recent past."(235) A Humphrey aide advised the senator that if he supported the MLF, he would alienate "good friends, supporters, people in the communications world--to be blunt, MLF . . . is not very popular among American Jews."(236)

Congress' concern with the ethnic connection can further be seen in relation to East Europeans, Irish, Greeks, and other groups. A member's ethnic heritage is considered an important electoral factor, and leaders try to arrange trips for members to the "old country" to enhance their electoral prospects.(237) East Europeans were an important group during the early cold war years. The kind of concern that Vandenberg had for that group and his truculence toward the Soviet Union based on that factor is one example. In the fifties, Congress continually passed liberation resolutions calling for freedom of East Europe,(238) and the Administration joined in cautious posturing for ethnic groups.(239) These statements of principle did not put the United States in the position of intervening in the region, as Hungary in 1956 clearly shows, but it did add to the rhetorical excesses of the era, almost certainly increased Soviet anxieties, and may have been misunderstood and helped encourage the abortive uprisings in Hungary and elsewhere.(240) Irish constituency considerations led, in part, to the Irish president being invited to make a state visit in 1959. Senators Saltonstall in Massachusetts and Keating and Javits in New York were especially interested, and considerable attention was given to ensuring that the Irish President remained in Republican hands, rather than being "taken in tow by Democratic politicians."(241) German-American constituents helped convince Congress that charity was a wise policy in the post war treatment of Germany.(242) Later in the period, Greek-Americans exerted influence on American policy toward Greece and Turkey. Politicians such as Hubert Humphrey were anxious to have themselves photographed with the Greek Prime Minister when he visited Washington and to have pictures distributed to the Greek community and publications.(243) When the question of the status of Cyprus brought Greece and Turkey to the brink of war, many Senators, such as Connecticut's Thomas Dodd, who had Greek communities in the state and/or were up for re-election, became active on Greece's behalf while Turkey, which has virtually no ethnic representation in the United States, was proportionally friendless in Congress.

Ethnic groups were not the only types of societal groups to play a role in affecting congressional attitudes toward foreign policy. Already mentioned was the pressure by some Protestant groups not to appoint, and counter pressure by Catholics to appoint, a full-scale diplomatic representative to the Vatican. (244)

Race has also been a factor, primarily in a negative sense. During the period, Southern members of Congress became distinctly less internationalist and were less likely to support even a Democratic president's initiative than their other Democratic colleagues.(245) Some of this trend can be traced to the racial implications of dealing with the largely non-caucasian countries which have gained independence since 1945. Aid is the most obvious manifestation of the South's retreat from internationalism. Many Southern congressmen who supported the British Loan and European Recovery Program became increasingly critical of aid in the 1960's. Members whose districts included the largest percentage of blacks became the most isolationist. In 1953, with a Republican president in office, 74.1 percent of Southern Democrats in the House voted for foreign aid. That figure declined to 54.6 percent in 1956 and stood at 41.9 percent in 1962, even with a fellow Democrat in the Oval Office.(246)

Immigration is another foreign policy related issue seemingly affected by racial/ethnic considerations. Western Europe ethnic groups have tended to oppose increased immigration or revision of quotas. Eastern and Southern Europeans have been on the opposite side of those questions. Southern Democrats steadily opposed the liberalization of immigration laws and quotas for non-caucasians, particularly blacks, and they remain virtually non-existent.(247)

Another victim of racial pressures has been the United States' (non)adherence to a variety of international agreements which might be interpreted as subjecting domestic racial problems to international debate. In 1948, for example, Congress blocked United States support for an ECOSOC attempt to draw up a Covenant on Human Rights.(248) For much of the same reason, Congress refused to ratify the Genocide Treaty of 1949 and continued to block that multinational pact throughout the period.

Secretary of State Acheson termed the failure of Congress to act on the Genocide Convention "a matter of great embarrassment," but was unable to secure ratification.(249) Some groups such as Polish-Americans favored the pact and brought pressure on their representatives.(250) Others were in the negative column. Put in the most formal terms, the main objections centered on the belief that the convention would "result in an invasion of domestic law" and that "it defines genocide so broadly . . . as to make the killing of one individual an international crime."(251) On a baser level, that translated to racial concern. One point involved the treatment of Native Americans. Senator Smith worried, "I think the first charge they [the Soviets] would make is that we genocided the American Indians, and it is pretty nearly true too."(252) The treatment of blacks, however, was the main issue. Would, for instance, the lynching of blacks qualify as genocide? Would adherence to the convention stir up blacks and lead to racial strife?(253) The result of ratification, Tom Connolly predicted, would be that "every country will be clawing us whenever there is a little local row."(254)

During the Eisenhower Administration, opposition in Congress to the Genocide Convention continued. Senator Walter George opposed ratification because he feared the pact might bring anti-lynching legislation within the realm of federal authority.(255)

The controversy over the Bricker Amendment also dampened administration enthusiasm for pushing for ratification. Secretary of
State Dulles feared that any attempt to ratify the convention
might tip the congressional balance in favor of passing Bricker's
proposal.(256) During the 1960s, the convention was stalled by a
chicken-egg scenario, with the administration reluctant to risk
failure and international embarrassment by pushing for ratification,(257) and congressional supporters blaming the Executive for
being "slow to announce their support," and giving "largely <u>pro
forma</u> . . . support when it did come."(258) A number of
related treaties, including conventions on the political rights
of women, forced labor, slavery, and racial discrimination, were
also submitted to the Senate during this period, but with the
tacit acceptance of the Executive, they lay dormant in the Foreign Relations Committee. Only the Slavery Convention was
finally ratified in 1967, after four years, largely because of
embarrassment that the United States had not ratified any of the
United Nations human rights conventions.(259)

Race, Congress, and foreign policy also intersected at a
number of other junctures. William Fulbright was considered for
Secretary of State in 1960, but was rejected, at least in part,
by President-elect Kennedy because the Arkansan had signed the
"Southern Manifesto" supporting segregation. Walter Lippmann,
for one, had "the distinct impression that [Kennedy] was inclined
to appoint Fulbright as Secretary of State," but finally concluded, "I don't think I can take Fulbright because of his positions with the Negroes and civil rights in the South."(260)
Indeed, Fulbright's foreign policy position and his Southern
political base came into conflict on more than one occasion.
Fulbright felt vulnerable to attack at home because of his chairmanship, and tried to soften civil rights legislation to ease
pressures in Arkansas.(261) In 1966, Black leader A. Philip
Randolph asked Fulbright to join in sponsoring a campaign to get
American banks to stop supporting South Africa. The problems
such support would have caused were so acute that an aide suggested of the letter, "Why don't we just lose it?" "O.K. File
it," Fulbright wrote in the margin.(262) It is ironic that
Lyndon Johnson, who as Vice President-elect had strongly supported Fulbright for Secretary of State only to be frustrated by
charges of the Senator's racism,(263) in turn, charged that Fulbright was a racist over Vietnam. Angered by Fulbright's criticism of the war, Johnson implied that the Senator opposed risking
White lives to protect Orientals and quoted Fulbright as saying,
"They're just not our kind of people."(264)

Whether President Johnson was right or libelous, the point is
that ethnic, racial, and religious factors strike a responsive
cord in Congress. Urged on by constituency groups, what is perceived as a foreign policy issue at the White House and State
Department, takes on domestic ramifications for members of Congress and engenders increased activity.

## Innovation and Pragmatism

In addition to policy typologies which concentrate on resource allocation or domestic group involvement, there have been
a number of other suggested categories of foreign policy issues.
Salisbury has suggested that an "innovative incremental" typology
might be helpful.(265)  John Lovell has gone so far as to formulate the hypothesis that:

> Changes in foreign policy sufficient to produce a sustained
> change in orientation of the nation-state toward its world
> environment will occur only after a period of dissension
> among national leaders in terms of their images of the na-
> tional identity and the national interest and after a formu-
> lation of a new consensus.(266)

According to this view, then, Congress will normally be more
active and critical at times of foreign policy innovation.  This
pattern is also supported by Westerfield and Manley in their discussions of Congress' foreign policy role since World War II.
Both see Congress as important early in the period when the basic
anti-communist consensus and "free world" structure were being
established.  Congress then faded into the background during the
prolonged execution of consensus policies.  In the midst of a
national anti-communist consensus, as Manley sees it, the state
of congressional participation in foreign policy-making was not
so much a question of loss of power, as one of change in role
from critic to supporter.(267)  Westerfield has termed this consensual period an "era of routinization" during which Congress
played a ceremonial legitimizing function.(268)
Extending this line of thought, it can also be said that
Congress will be particularly opposed to innovative policies
which are perceived as reversing moralist/absolutist policies.
Johan Galtung has found that the more moralistic and absolutist
an issue is, the more likely it will be accepted at the periphery
(or mass).(269)  Without getting into a long exposition of American political culture, the point is that a combination of lack of
mass interest in foreign affairs, a reservoir of dated and sim-
plistic ideas on the periphery, and a tendency to crusade black-
white imagery when aroused, has made public opinion a restraint
on American policies which are innovative and pragmatic.  Most
members of Congress have peripheral rather than elitist views on
foreign policy.  One scholar found that, while members of the
Senate Foreign Relations Committee stressed realism, Congress as
a whole had an ideological orientation.(270)  This ties in with
the proposition that there is a direct relationship between
distance from a decision-making role and orientation toward ideology.(271)  Thus, in what has been referred to as a "thermos-
bottle effect," Congress has an attachment to policies that were
successful in an earlier period, and will almost automatically be
skeptical of innovative policies.(272)  This is especially so
where the old policy is of a moralist/absolutist nature, and the
innovative policy is presented as pragmatic and gradualist.
The theory is supported by the events of the post World War

II period. The early years of the cold war were ones of innovation for United States foreign policy. Congress was also active during these years. Although many factors spurred legislative activity, one must conclude that the very nature of the policy reorientation was an important factor in stirring congressional interest. Being an out-and-out isolationist had lost most of its prewar respectability, but many members of Congress had been isolationists before the war and, in fact if not in name, remained committed to those principles. While the majority of those suspicious of international involvement were Republicans, not all were. Some Democrats, such as Senator Harry Byrd of Virginia and Senator Kenneth McKeller of Tennessee, also leaned in that direction. Furthermore, criticism of Truman's policies was not limited to the right. Several Democrats, including Senator Claude Pepper of Florida and Senator Glen Taylor of Idaho, objected that the United States was adopting an overly hostile attitude toward the Soviet Union. The debate on the basic direction of the United States' foreign policy, then, was bipartisan. Republicans were probably less restrained than they would have been if Thomas Dewey had occupied the White House, but their objections went deeper than mere partisanship.

Attempts to present programs in a pragmatic light as opposed to a moralist/absolutist manner encountered a greater degree of congressional opposition. During the British Loan debate, administration arguments as to the economic benefits of the loan were a disaster, but claiming the loan was a donation to the crusade against communism saved the program. Similarly, when Truman and Marshall first presented the Greek-Turkey loan proposal to congressional leaders, they argued on pragmatic realpolitik terms. Sensing that Vandenberg and his colleagues were unimpressed, Dean Acheson intervened and firmly interjected anti-communism. Only then did Vandenberg agree to support the proposal, provided that the President agree to galvanize Congress and the nation using Acheson's rationale. Thus, even in a crisis, it is more effective for the president to present the issue in black/white terms rather than indulge in the nuances of international politics.

By the late 1940s, the country had settled on an anti-communist theme as a basis of its foreign policy. This helps account for the "decline" in legislative activity. Because of the high level of consensus, less activity in the general direction of policy was needed or possible. On a micro scale, though, Malcolm Jewell found that new programs, particularly those involving basic commitments (and thus innovative), tended to spark bipartisan debate.(273) Partisanship, by contrast, was more likely to come to the fore during consideration of continuing, incremental programs. This coordinates well with the finding that aid policy is subject to considerably stronger partisan movement than foreign policy in general.

Congress' varying reactions to innovative and incremental policies are modified by the relative pragmatism or morality/absolutism of the program. As we have seen, the Executive has been relatively more successful when presenting incremental foreign aid programs in cold war, moralist/absolutist terms than

it has been when presenting aid in developmental, pragmatic
terms. The effectiveness in Congress of the Executive's periodic
calls to unify against the communist world has been partly based
on the fact that they not only helped move the policy focus from
domestic to foreign, but they also tend to focus debate on the
morality and absolutism of the cold war rather than the incremen-
talism of an ongoing policy.

On the other hand, Congress usually opposed any move away
from a moralist/absolutist stand against communism and toward
pragmatic cooperation. This was true on incremental issues such
as trade. Even more strikingly, it was true for innovative pragmatic ideas. Congress' absolutist opposition to pragmatic compromise in the Far East, at least through the late 1960s, is the
strongest and most consistent example of congressional influence
in the post World War II period.

# Part III

# 8
# The Old Order Changes—A Little

The decade that followed 1972 has been characterized by considerable uncertainty and fluidity in the foreign policy process. Bludgeoned by the twin traumas of Vietnam and Watergate, not to mention Koreagate, Abscam, and other political debacles, the American public began to question the essential soundness of the political system. With specific reference to the foreign policy process, dismay with a corrupt and imperial presidency brought both internal and external pressures on Congress to reassert its power. Those urgings have certainly had their effect on foreign policy-making. Congress in recent years has been the scene of increased foreign policy activity and influence. Many political analysts have contended that fundamental changes in the policy process have occurred, with Congress joining the Executive Branch as a codeterminer of foreign policy.

## Policy-Making Changes:   Small and Temporary

That interpretation is understandable given short-term events and attitudes, but it is not valid in the long run. First, as the preceding chapters document, the role of Congress in the post World War II era has often been underestimated. The presidency maintained preeminence in the foreign policy process, but Congress often exercised significant influence on the tone and direction of such policy. The role of Congress as an initiator and conservator of the cold war is but one example. Thus, by underestimating Congress' previous role, it is easy to overestimate Congress' current influence. There have been changes, but the relative movement is not as great as is sometimes supposed.

Furthermore, the foreign policy process during the second Nixon Administration and beyond can be explained substantially in terms of the basic patterns that have existed, at least since 1945. Some factors, such as Congress' institutional pride and presidential weakness, became accentuated and led to an upsurge of legislative activism. Such considerations have long played a role in determining the distribution of power, although not in recent history has such a concentrated juxtaposition of the two occurred simultaneously. Other factors such as domestic

economics, partisan politics, and ethnic group pressures have
continued to operate much as before. Most of the ongoing process, then, is a continuation of long-term patterns rather than a
break with the past.

The past decade should also be treated partly as an aberra-
tion. The sense of institutional ego which helped activate
Congress is cyclical in nature. Having risen up, Congress will
be satisfied that it has performed its constitutional responsibilities, and the urging of that motivation will weaken.
Congress will revert to accepting executive leadership without
suffering acute pangs of embarrassment.

Another aberrational characteristic of the last decade has
been the pronounced weakness of both the institution of the presidency and some of the individuals of that office. The White
House's loss of stature began with the Vietnam-related alienation
that afflicted Lyndon Johnson's presidency. The hauteur with
which Johnson and, even more, Richard Nixon and his entourage
conducted themselves in office further increased public and
congressional dissatisfaction with the chief magistry. Gerald
Ford suffered from that general malaise and also because of the
unique, non-elective path that brought him to the White House.
Jimmy Carter's election brought the hope of a break with the
past, but his poor legislative liaison skills and his lack of
public opinion support combined to prevent a pronounced reestablishment of the presidency's previously preeminant power in
the foreign policy process. Ronald Reagan's brief tenure to date
has given some evidence of a "return to normalcy," but after only
one year, it is impossible to judge confidently. Sooner more
probably than later, however, the memories of the late 1960s and
early 1970s will fade, and systemic weakness of the presidency
will dissipate. Whether it be Reagan or a successor, a strong
figure will occupy the Oval Office and reestablish the institution's normal grandeur.


## Continuing Themes

If congressional pride and executive embarrassment have been
sources of presidential weakness during the last decade, other
factors have continued to work for presidential strength as they
did in the past. The long tradition of executive foreign policy
leadership remains. Also the factors which especially enhanced
presidential power after World War II continue unabated. The
world-wide, complex scope of American involvement, the supersonic, instant communications nature of conflict and diplomacy,
and the ultimate stakes of the game all continue to inhibit
Congress. The Executive retains the ability to take action (the
instrumental initiative) and, despite some legislative advances,
continues to hold quantitatively superior foreign policy information and expertise. In particular, Congress' response to recent
crises, as in the Mayaguez or Iranian hostage affairs, has not
significantly differed from its response to earlier confrontations.

These and other factors are all now working together to swing executive, legislative, public, academic, and press expectations in favor of a more assertive presidency. Voices are now more frequently heard which argue that Congress has not proven itself equal to codeterminance in foreign policy. Congress continues to be highly disorganized. A multitude of committees and individuals address pieces of the puzzle, but no legislative entity has the entire picture. Indeed, Congress has become even more disorganized in the last, decade with a devolution of internal authority from the two chambers' leadership and committee structures to the subcommittee and individual level. To many observers the imperial presidency no longer seems so threatening, particularly when contrasted with government by a chaotic Congress.

## Congressional Activism

The pendulum is a much used metaphor in the discussion of the executive-legislative struggle over foreign policy control. There is no doubt that it swung in Congress' direction in the immediate post Vietnam and Watergate periods. Whether it crossed into the congressional sector is another, more doubtful, proposition. Thomas Frank and Edward Weisband argue that there has been a "revolution" that has "radically redistributed the power of government" and that "among the booty" is "control over U.S. foreign policy."(1) Others are more cautious. Cecil Crabb and Pat Holt contend that, "although recent years have witnessed a new congressional militancy in foreign relations, the fact remains that the president is still in charge of American foreign policy."(2) The current position of the pendulum is a key question, but before that can be addressed, we must examine the reasons why this swing began in the first place.

## Institutional Ego

The role of institutional ego and related individual legislative egos was evident throughout the pre-1972 period. Vandenberg, of course, provided a clear example of the effect of individual ego. On a higher level, numerous examples of negative reactions to lack of consultation reflected Congress' institutional concerns. On an even more general plane, Congress reacted to a marked deferential period during World War II by attempting to reassert itself after 1945 when the danger had passed. This phenomenon led one analyst to the term "the cycle of Congressional reassertion after wars . . . historic and reliable."(3)

Post war congressional assertiveness was again evident in the aftermath of Vietnam. Not only was the struggle in Southeast Asia over, but by the mid-1970s the long-term cold war crisis also seemed to be passing into history. The Nixon-Kissinger era of "detante" in Soviet-American relations yielded SALT I, friendly summit meetings in Washington and Moscow, and a growth in trade and cultural exchanges. In short, communism seemed less threatening. Diplomatic relations were even opened with Peking, and that fearful multitude gradually evolved from the "Chicoms"

to the "Chinese Communists" to the "Peoples Republic of China."
There seemed to be less need to rally 'round the flag than there
had been in decades.

At the same time, the feeling grew in Congress that it was a
poor relative to the Executive in foreign policy-making. Of
eighty-two members who responded to a 1969 survey, only five
percent believed that Congress should strive for either predominance or equality in the field of foreign affairs. Indeed, only
slightly more than half of the respondents even thought Congress
should exercise a strong voice in the determination of foreign
policy.(4) Seven years later, by contrast, another survey showed
191 (84%) of 228 members contending that Congress should assume a
more active role than it had in the past.(5) Supporting that
finding, still another questionnaire found 79.1 percent (73 of
92) of responding members dissatisfied with Congress' role.(6)
Senator William Fulbright typified the mood change. In 1961 he
had worried that Congress had "hobbled the President by too niggardly a grant of power." By 1974 he was describing the presidency as a "dangerously powerful office."(7)

The War Powers Resolution and Indochina. The first major
congressional push for greater power centered on foreclosing
American action in Indochina and on the related passage of the
1973 War Powers Resolution which attempted to define and to limit
presidential authority to wage an undeclared war. Debates surrounding those congressional actions were based not only on
substantive issues, but also were spurred by institutional pride.

Congressional opponents to continued American military action
in Indochina extensively used the institutional prestige argument. Proponents of one stop-the-war measure wrote to colleagues, "Our bill would resolve doubts about the source of
authority . . . In the process it would restore a proper balance
between Executive and Congressional responsibilities on issues of
war and peace."(8) Hubert Humphrey echoed this feeling, editor-
ializing that Congress must exercise "its constitutional responsibilities and powers . . . Congress is a co-equal branch and
policy discussions in the field of national security are not the
sole prerogative of the Executive . . ."(9) Republican Jacob
Javits utilized the same line. Attempts to end the bombing of
Cambodia, Javits said, involved "the question of legal and constitutional authority and not a question of the correctness of
policy."(10)

Even supporters of the war and the Administration recognized
the power of the argument and were swayed by it. Republican Hugh
Scott was told by his staff that policy in Cambodia per se
was "almost . . . a peripheral issue to what is emerging as the
overriding concern, the Constitutional questions of the balance
of power between Congress and the Presidency."(11) This argument
helped bring the Senator around to support the Cooper-Church
Amendment to end the war.(12)

Debate in Congress over the War Powers Resolution evidenced
even stronger elements of institutional pride than the Cooper-
Church genre amendments.(13) Sponsor Jacob Javits summarized the
widespread feeling when he told the Senate, "What we are trying

to do is . . . to bring about an end to the guerilla warfare
between Congress and the President in which Congress has been
constantly bested."(14)   When Nixon vetoed the Resolution, the
House Foreign Affairs Committee Chairman drafted a statement
which asserted that "the great majority of Congress wants and
expects its rightful role in the decisions of war and peace."(15)
Congress clearly demonstrated the depth of that feeling by overriding the presidential veto by 284 to 135 in the House and 75 to
18 in the Senate.

## The Territorial Imperative

Congressional activism was also fostered by any number of
internal congressional contests for status, turf, and power.
Commentators on Congress agree that the 1970s brought profound
shifts in the legislative process, with accompanying significant
internal shifts in the locus of power.   Those shifts increased
members' uncertainty and promoted legislative conflict.   The
result was that individuals and committees often had to assert
their authority in order to keep it.   On the individual level,
administration supporters began to worry about their prestige.
Senate Armed Services Committee Chairman John Stennis worried,
for example, that he might appear to be simply a mouthpiece for
the Executive.(16)   An aide to Hugh Scott warned the Minority
Leader, "my fear is that you will become . . . the focal point
for the opposition . . . which looks to the Senate Leadership
to restore the Constitutional balance."(17)   The diffusion of
power in Congress also meant that individual members no longer
accepted the authority of "whales," be they leadership or committee whales, to speak for the institution.   When, in one characteristic instance, Senate Armed Service Committee members assured
colleagues they would watch over the level of U.S. troops in
Korea, Alabama Democrat James Allen retorted, "It would not be a
decision of Congress if the President has a breakfast meeting
with a couple of committees . . . I do not feel Congress is
speaking when committees meet with the President."(18)
Numerous inter- and intra-committee battles further spurred
legislative foreign policy activity.   The House and Senate Appropriations committees were galvanized by Nixon's 1973 shift of
funds to pay for the bombing of Cambodia.(19)   The authority of
the Senate Appropriations Committee was also contested by the
Foreign Relations Committee which, as a result of the 1972 passage of the Foreign Relations Authorization Act, captured new
control over the budgets of the State Department and other foreign affairs agencies.(20)   The House Foreign Affairs Committee
also sought a place in the sun.   Fenno's 1973 study found its
members with little to do and complaining they were only a foreign aid committee.(21)   A more recent study, by comparison,
pointed to the expanded authority of the Foreign Affairs Committee and the committee's aggressive desire to improve its status
versus the Executive and its counterpart in the Senate.(22)
The Foreign Relations Committee was also the scene of frequent power plays.   The Committee had long operated with few

subcommittees and a unified staff. It also usually worked in bi-partisan concert. Those patterns began to break down in 1969 with the creation of Stuart Symington's autonomous Subcommittee on U.S. Security Agreements and Commitments Abroad. The Commit-tee's atomization accelerated in 1973 when Republican members demanded and won a separate minority staff. The upshot, in one staff member's estimation, was that "the Committee . . . became the site of attempts at individual power."(23)

The fragmentation of power within the Committee, combined with the restrained style of John Sparkman who chaired it from 1975 to 1979, weakened the Committee's previous preeminant inter-nal position on foreign policy. In the most recent years, Sparkman's successors, Frank Church (1979-81) and Charles Percy (1981- ), have attempted to restore the prestige of the Committee by adding to its activity. As one State Department official noted, "The committee isn't significant in foreign policy--won't be seen as such--unless there is a major issue to contest with the executive branch."(24)


## Presidential Weakness

Presidential weakness was a second major factor which stirred congressional activism during Nixon's second term and during the subsequent tenures of Ford and Carter. Periods of perceived weak-ness, as in Truman's first term, had limited presidential leader-ship before, but the distrust engendered by Vietnam and Watergate brought the office to its lowest ebb in many decades.

The Presidency in Disrepute. It hardly seems necessary to recount the devastation that Watergate visited on the already Vietnam-weakened White House. Remembering the war's impact, Kissinger has described the Administration as "shell shocked" with the "very fabric of government . . . falling apart."(25) From that low point, things got even worse. Watergate toppled Nixon from office, and the government--or at least Nixon's govern-ment--did fall apart. People like Senator Fulbright had previous-ly attacked "the capacity of people in high places to do stupid things,"(26) but Watergate changed those perceptions of presiden-tial power from simply inept to dangerous. By 1974 Fulbright was arguing for greater congressional power on the grounds that, even if Congress was "slow, obstreperous, [and] behind the times," at least it posed "no threat to the liberties of the American people."(27)

Gerald Ford inherited Nixon's unhappy legacy. By 1976 public confidence in the Executive had sunk to eleven percent. Ford also suffered from being the first president elected neither to that office nor to the Vice Presidency. He also faced an over-whelmingly Democratic Congress and was burdened from the wide-spread expectation that he was a caretaker who would be replaced in 1976.(28)

The repute of the presidency was so low that when Ford asked Congress for flexibility in Asia to evacuate anti-communist leaders, Representative Donald Fraser sadly noted, "the distrust of the executive branch runs so deep in this chamber that members are afraid [to give] any discretion, any grant of authority to the executive branch."(29) Even liberal critics began to worry about the decline in presidential authority. "The leadership on this side of the Atlantic is in total disarray," Hubert Humphrey wrote British Prime Minister Harold Wilson; ". . . the President . . . is incapable of leadership."(30)

The election of Jimmy Carter carried with it the possibility of restored executive strength, but the new president did not fulfill that potential. Carter's problems stemmed in part from the residual onus of the office. Even more, they were caused by his poor relations with Washington's inner circle, Congress in particular. His anti-Washington campaign rhetoric alienated those he would later need, and once in office, he continued to dismay those who should have been his allies. "They don't know anything about Congress, and they don't like Congress," one Democratic member lamented.(31) Congressional Quarterly reported in 1978 that there was "near unanimity in Congress that Carter and his staff had blundered repeatedly in pushing their proposals."(32) The causes of Carter's travails need not be belabored. The point here is that a combination of the President's disdainful attitude and his staff's ineptitude, followed by policy reversals and plummeting popularity ratings that sank even lower than Nixon's, left Carter the third successive occupant of a debilitated presidency instead of the initiator of a rejuvenated chief magistracy.(33)

The Galleries. Dismay with legislative weakness and condemnation of the imperial presidency was not confined to Congress. In 1959, sixty-one percent of the respondents to a public opinion survey felt the president should be the prime force in government; only seventeen percent chose Congress. A similar questionnaire in 1977 found fifty-eight percent choosing Congress and only twenty-six percent in favor of strong presidential leadership.(34)

Academic and media commentary agreed with the tone of these surveys. A decade earlier there had been widespread concern with the restraints put on the presidency by a supposedly anachronous and cumbersome Congress. In the 1970s scholars, symbolized by Schlesinger's The Imperial Presidency, decried executive authority.(35) Others focused on Congress' positive points in foreign policy(36) or fielded suggestions for implementation of the new legislative role.(37)

By the mid-1970s the rout of executive forces was extensive. Even those executive actors with the most to lose were compelled to pay homage to the new order. Henry Kissinger, hardly an earnest advocate of power sharing, told the American Society of Newspaper Editors that:

The decade-long struggle in this country over executive dominance in foreign affairs is over. The recognition that Congress is a coequal branch of government is the dominant fact of national politics today. The executive accepts that the Congress must have both the sense and the reality of

participation; foreign policy must be a shared enterprise.
(38)

Presidents Ford and Carter also made formal kowtows to Congress. Ford promised legislators that his approach to them would
be characterized by "communication, conciliation, compromises,
and cooperation."(39)  Carter followed that theme in an early
interview with the New York Times.  He noted that the War
Powers Resolution was "a reduction obviously in the authority
that the President had prior to Vietnam," but conceded, "I think
it is an appropriate reduction."(40)


## Consensus

A third factor of the 1970s was the breakdown of the anti-
communist consensus that had guided American policy for thirty
years.  Nixon-Kissinger foreign policy emphasized realpolitik,
the opening to Communist China, and détante with the Soviet
Union.  The catharsis of the American retreat from Vietnam and
its abandonment to the communists required a psychological shift
to at least not seeing the struggle with communism as a mono-
lithic zero-sum game.  Carter's early humanitarian emphasis
differed considerably from his predecessors, but his foreign policy also failed to establish a unifying theme.  It continued the
trend, begun formally by the Nixon Doctrine, of wounded and uncertain isolationism.  The country agreed it was no longer responsible for all the world.  It could not agree, however, for what
part, if any, it was responsible.  Carter emphasized the complexity of problems and at the same time called for a moral humanitarian approach to foreign policy.  One observer dubbed it the
evangelist-engineer approach.(41)  As a theme, humanitarianism
largely failed as a consensual theme at home, while rudderless
pragmatism continued to foster uncertainty in the policy process.
Just as had happened after World War II when the country strug-
gled to find its international bearings, uncertainty spurred
congressional activity.(42)
It is likely that the massive surge of Congress' institutional ego gratification, combined with the personal and institutional presidential weakness that characterized 1970s, will fade in
the 1980s.  Indeed, there is considerable evidence which will be
discussed later which demonstrates that.  The nation's ability to
achieve a new foreign policy consensus is much more doubtful.
Writing in 1978, James Chance saw the possibility that "in the
end, we may have to do something we are not used to doing and
thus may not be very good at.  We may simply have to learn to
conduct foreign policy for a very long time without a single
unifying theme on which to base a broad national consensus."(43)
Chance may be correct, but the invasion of Afghanistan, the American boycott of the 1980 Olympics, reaction to events in Poland,
the "window of vulnerability" and resulting arms buildup, the
scuttling of SALT II, and a host of other factors may preview a
consensus based on nationalist assertiveness and anti-Sovietism,
if not anti-communism.

## Congress Unchained

Through the seventies, Congress took a number of initiatives to constrain executive authority, to enhance congressional authority, and to change executive policy preferences. In discussing those actions, the emphasis here is not so much what happened, but rather why change took place. Part of the causation can be traced to the general factors of institutional ego, presidential weakness, and lack of consensus. In many cases, though, factors were involved which would have motivated Congress in any era. These factors are highlighted here to help establish the long-term continuity of the policy process.

## Indochina and the War Powers Resolution

Apart from the substance of the war, congressional action to end it was heavily influenced by the desire to recapture the vaguely defined equality in the policy process that legislators presumed had previously existed. As the earlier discussions of Indochina and the War Powers Resolution demonstrate, congressional limits on military action in Indochina and its attempt to define the powers of the Commander-in-Chief were matters of inter-branch power as well as substantive policy.

## National Commitment Resolution

Another early initiative by Congress was its attempt to limit the scope and secrecy of executive agreements. In the period between 1946 and 1977, the United States signed more than 7,300 executive agreements with foreign governments. By contrast, only 451 treaties were submitted to the Senate. Most executive agreements are technical in nature, but some have had important policy ramifications. It was over that issue that the Bricker Amendment contest was waged and narrowly won by the Executive in the 1950s.

Congress again moved in the early 1970's to address that issue. Senator Clifford Case was the prime sponsor of a measure which required that Congress be informed of all agreements entered into by the Executive. The principal motivating factor was institutional pride. Case expressed this underlying urge in a letter to Richard Russell that argued it was "demeaning for the Senate to be dependent on news leaks or on the initiative of journalists and outside organizations for a full understanding" of foreign events and policy.(44)

Congress enacted the measure requiring the President to notify it of executive agreements, and thus having soothed itself, largely gave up pressing the matter. In 1976 the General Accounting Office found numerous instances of executive failure to transmit the details of executive agreements made after adoption of the Resolution. These included such significant actions as offering post-war aid to North Vietnam (1973), agreeing to utilize American personnel as monitors in the Sinai (1975), and the Helsinki Accords (1975). Even in the face of these disclosures,

Congress refused to take action to rebuke the Executive or strengthen its own position. Earlier bills in 1972 and 1973 by Senator Sam Ervin, which would have made executive agreements subject to congressional veto, died in the House. A 1976 bill by Senator Dick Clark suffered a similar fate.(45) The result of Congress' lack of perseverance is that the National Commitment Resolution has served as little more than a balm.

## Legislative Veto - Arms Sales

Congress also acted to give itself a legislative veto over arms sales, an area previously in the executive domain. Amendments in 1974 and 1976 to the Foreign Military Sales Act obligated the president to give Congress thirty days' notice of intent for any foreign sale of arms over seven million dollars. Congress may, during that period, block the sale by concurrent resolution.(46)

AWACS. The legislative veto over arms sales has played a role in foreign policy primarily by causing delay, encouraging public debate, and promoting compromise. The most fortunate example concerned the proposed sale of Airborne Warning and Control System (AWACS) aircraft to Iran. In July 1977 President Carter notified Congress of his intent to sell seven AWACS aircraft to Iran. Negative reaction in Congress, led by Iowa's John Culver, focused on the security risks of selling the super-secret system. The House International Relations (Foreign Affairs) Committee agreed with Culver and voted to recommend veto of the sale. President Carter responded by temporarily withdrawing sale notification, then resubmitting it to Congress in September with strengthened security provisions. On the second try, the sale cleared Congress, but the revolution in Iran occurred before the planes could be delivered. Whether the revised provisions would have prevented Khomeini-controlled AWACS is problematic. What is certain is that congressional concern was well founded and, along with considerable luck, did safeguard AWACS' security.

The other examples of legislative-executive interaction on arms sales fall more within the classic pattern. In the last analysis, Congress has not blocked any sale, but the potential use of its tool has caused compromise. The strength of Congress in this area can also be traced to a traditional motivation: ethnic influence.

Arms, Arabs, and Israel. Throughout the entire period of this study, the question of Israel and the involvement of the Jewish-American community has proven to be a compelling motivation behind congressional assertions of power in the policy process. Arms sales controversies have clearly reflected this factor's force.

In 1977 Congress was able to modify the terms of sale of Hawk surface-to-air missiles (SAMs) to Jordan to include assurances that the SAM's would be placed in fixed, rather than mobile, sites well away from Israel's borders. In 1977 congressional

opposition also led to a reduction from 1,500 to 650 in the number of Maverick television-guided surface-to-ground missiles sold
to Saudi Arabia.   During a 1978 dispute over the sale of advanced
combat aircraft to Israel, Saudi Arabia, and Egypt, Congress was
able to force the Administration to sell more aircraft to Israel,
to deny sidewinder missiles, bomb racks and extended range fuel
tanks to the Arab aircraft, and to gain assurances that the Saudi
aircraft would not be stationed within striking range of the
Israeli border.

Two arms sale initiatives by Carter in 1980 met with mixed
success.   Despite strong criticism from such long-time Israel
supporters as Representatives Benjamin Rosenthal, Stephen Rosenthal, and Jonathan Bingham, all of New York and all with a significant number of Jewish constituents, the Administration was
able to proceed with the sale of 100 M-60 tanks to Jordan.
Jordan, however, was forced to sell older tanks on a one-to-one
basis to keep its armor force at the existing level.(47)   The
Administration was less successful on a second sale.   In June,
Saudi Arabia asked for the missiles, fuel tanks, and bomb racks
precluded in the 1978 sale compromise, in order to enhance the
capabilities of its F-15 aircraft.   The Administration reportedly
told the Saudis that submission of the request to Congress, especially given the 1978 agreement and the prevailing election-year
political climate, would provoke a firestorm of opposition and
would probably end in defeat.(48)   In October, Carter announced
that the Saudis would not be given offensive capabilities, and,
in effect, the decision was deferred until the battle was rejoined under the Reagan Administration.

AWACS - Again.   The first major test of foreign policy
power with Congress faced by the Reagan Administration came over
Middle East arms sales.   Some of the elements of the sale (F-15
fuel tanks and Sidewinder missiles) were essentially an extension
of the controversy from which the Carter Administration had re-
treated some months before.   Complicating, and soon dominating,
the debate, the Administration also proposed to sell Saudi Arabia
five AWACS aircraft.

Within days of the April announcement, an Associated Press
survey found forty-five senators inclined to veto the sale.
Oregon's Republican Senator Robert Packwood predicted the bill
would be defeated and led the opposition in his chamber.   House
members also quickly lined up in opposition.   Representative
William Green of New York pronounced himself "outraged and flab-
bergasted," and nearly one hundred House members expressed concern.(49)

Opposition to the sale resulted from a number of factors.
The most important was unusually strong and open condemnation of
the sale by the Israeli government, Jewish-American groups, and
their supporters in Congress.   Prime Minister Menachem Begin
voiced "profound regret" and "unreserved opposition" to the sale.
The intensity of the Jewish lobby effort was so strong that some
members, but only a few, reacted negatively to the pressure.
Representative Pete McCloskey publicly urged, "We've got to overcome the tendency of the Jewish community in America to control

the actions of Congress." He pronounced the lobbying against the sale "some of the heaviest I have ever seen."(50)

Other factors, also traditional motivators, compounded the situation. One was executive weakness caused by internal division. Secretary of State Alexander Haig and other key officials were widely reported as wishing to defer the decision on AWACS. (51) Some members of Congress were also irritated by slights to their institutional egos. They charged that the Administration failed to answer questions on the impact of the arms deal and had failed to adequately consult with Congress.(52) Still other members contended, as they had during the Iranian AWACS dispute, that the aircraft would be in danger of falling into hostile hands if sold to the Saudis. After less than two weeks of negative commentary and wishing to concentrate its efforts on its domestic economic package, the Administration withdrew notification of the sale. According to Senate Majority Leader Howard Baker, it was a tactical retreat designed to give Congress the opportunity "to give advice on the final shape and form of the package to be submitted."(53) Baker admitted that the delay was also related to the approaching Israeli parliamentary elections, which Washington hoped would result in the defeat of Begin and the election of a new government whose opposition to AWACS would be more moderate.

Begin, however, was reelected and the next phase of the AWACS battle was joined in September. Although the Administration had unified itself internally, with Haig speaking out strongly in favor of the sale, the other negative factors remained. Congress still did not feel sufficiently consulted. Security provisions also remained unsatisfactory to a number of senators. Senator Packwood complained, "Nobody on either side of the aisle was consulted . . . Consultation would definitely make a difference," and Robert Byrd added, "I've never seen anything more badly botched than this one."(54) The impact on Israel, however, remained the crucial issue. Packwood again led the opposition in the Senate, gathering forty-six names on a disapproval resolution and claiming five additional supporters. Saudi Arabia, Packwood said, was the "principal bagman" for the Palestine Liberation Organization and an enemy of Israel. Even more conclusively, Representative Clarence Long, Chairman of the House Foreign Operations Subcommittee, released a list of 253 House members, thirty-five more than a majority, pledged to reject the sale.(55)

The Administration was defeated in the initial skirmishes. Almost simultaneously in mid-September, the House voted 301 to 111 to block the sale, and by a vote of nine to eight, the Senate Foreign Relations Committee recommended to its parent body that it also vote to block the sale.

The real battle, however, was waged in the main body of the Senate and provided President Reagan with a dramatic 52 to 48 victory. The analysis of the President's ability to prevail provides a panoply of the forces that act on Congress.

One key to Reagan success was the changing nature of the debate. Opposition forces stressed two issues: the threat to Israel and the possibility of AWACS falling into hostile hands if the "unstable" Saudi monarchy suffered the same fate as Iran's

Shah. The Administration was able both to counter these substantive arguments and to also change the focus of the debate to include presidential prestige, his ability to carry on foreign affairs, and the ability of foreign leaders to rely on a steady American foreign policy.

Regarding the substantive issues, Reagan's most effective tool was a last-minute letter in which he promised that before the AWACS were transferred, he would "certify" that he had obtained agreements from the Saudis aimed at preventing either the use of the aircraft against Israel or the compromise of AWACS technology. The President's letter also implied that the Saudis would mute their antagonism toward Israel and that the Administration would support continued Israeli military superiority in the region. Reagan also gave several senators what Roger Jepsen termed "highly classified" information that "lessened their concerns" about the sale. Those assurances were rumored to have included tacit Saudi agreement to allow continued joint control of the aircraft, at least until 1990.

The President's prospects were also enhanced, perhaps decisively, by his ability to change the focus of the debate. As the vote drew closer, the issue increasingly became one of presidential and national prestige. Presidential Assistant James Baker said that what was at stake was the "President's ability to make foreign policy."(56) Reagan told a news conference that the institution of the legislative veto over arms had gone "too far in weakening the President's powers." If the sale did not go through, he asked, "How do I then go forward with this quiet diplomacy of trying to bring the Arab states into the peacemaking process [when] they can sit there and say, 'Well, we don't know whether you can deliver or not. You're not the fellow that's in charge. Congress is.'"(57) Stirred by their common perspective, past presidents joined the chorus. "Defeat on AWACS," Richard Nixon said, "would be a serious embarrassment to Reagan . . . If he loses . . . everyone loses . . . [People] ought to trust the President." Jimmy Carter agreed that "once a President makes a commitment, it's important that it be fulfilled." From his corner, Henry Kissinger cautioned that rejection of AWACS would "jeopardize the entire design of our foreign policy" and warned that "Congress must not undermine the President's authority in international affairs."(58)

Such rhetoric has always struck a deferential chord in Congress, and it did so again. Senator Jepsen noted that the controversy over the sale had "changed the stakes involved" and put the President's prestige on the line. An early opponent of the sale, Jepsen changed his position.(59) Russell Long, the last uncommitted senator, supported the sale because, he said, "I concluded that it was most imperative that Congress support the President." As sale opponent John Glenn ruefully concluded, "When the President says 'I need your help,' that's a rather potent argument."(60)

The President's efforts also reversed the ego considerations that had been bruised by earlier lack of consultation. Glenn spoke of the aura of "sitting down with the most powerful person in the free world, maybe the whole world," and opposition leader

Packwood conceded that the turning point in the debate had been "when the President started calling up senators and inviting them down to the White House. They came back converted."(61)

There were also widespread reports that the White House offered senators constituency-oriented "incentives," although Reagan claimed, "There have been no deals made. None were offered."(62) Perhaps literally true, but there may have been "understandings." Senator Dale Bumpers said, "It often works with a wink or a nod. They don't have to make overt promises. They know the way things work around here."(63) Among the rumored "winks and nods" was an agreement by the President not to campaign in Colorado against Dennis DeConcini in 1982. Iowa's Republican Charles Grassley found the White House suddenly willing to speed up his request for a patronage appointment. Washington's Slade Gorton received White House support for 2.6 million dollars to renovate a public health hospital in Seattle, and Montana's John Melcher was reportedly offered funding for an experimental coal plant in Butte. The gravy train could also run in the other direction. Fifteen minutes after Minnesota's Rudy Boschwitz became the only Republican to vote against the AWACS sale in the Foreign Relations Committee, he was notified that an Air Force facility in Duluth would be closed. Boschwitz termed the timing of the announcement "symbolic . . . They would like people to think you must pay a price for opposing them."(64)

Still another factor that affected the vote was partisanship. The Democratic National Chairman opposed the sale, and Democratic presidential hopeful Walter Mondale also spoke against it in clearly partisan terms. "Party loyalty" was the obvious explanation Senator Glenn offered in partial explanation of the final vote that saw Republicans vote with the President by a forty-one to eleven margin and Democrats vote in opposition by thirty-six to twelve.(65)

The intense lobbying effort on both sides was also important. In addition to the President and his administration's cast, the pro-AWACS forces included business concerns such as Boeing and Westinghouse, which individually lobbied senators and hired a public relations firm to tout the sale. Arab-American groups also were active and represented by such insiders as former presidential assistant Frederick Dutton. The Saudis were also directly active. Prince Bandar bin Sultan visited Senate offices, and the Saudis spent $470,000 on the services of publicist Crawford Cooke.

A final and unfortunate element working against the sale was anti-Semitism. Senator Mark Hatfield said he feared the debate had fueled a "resurgence of anti-semitism," and John Tower agreed, saying "It shouldn't be raised to the level of public debate, but unfortunately I'm afraid it has been." Joseph Bidden said, "American Jews are being made a scapegoat," and several senators expressed dismay over the surge of anti-Semitic mail. "I have never experienced anything like this in my life, in terms of basic prejudice," David Durenberger sadly commented.(66)

The anti-AWACS forces also mounted a strong effort. The American Israel Political Affairs Committee (AIPAC) and other Jewish-American groups were active. Menachem Begin personally lobbied

Congress during a Washington visit. Many senators felt the pressure. "There's a big Jewish community in this country," observed
Dale Bumpers, "and nationally they are the big hitters in the
Democratic Party." Another senator was quoted as estimating that
half his campaign contributions came from Jewish sources. "Any
time its close . . .," he said, "you're going to go their way."
(67)

The activities of AIPAC and others which had usually prevailed were to no avail in the case of AWACS. It was a close
vote and in doubt until the end, but the President proved a
master of persuasion. The deal was finalized.

## Congress--The Ethnic Connection

As it did from 1945 through 1972, Congress in the recent period has been repeatedly activated by ethnic considerations. The
contentiousness of Congress concerning numerous arms agreements
with the Arabs is but one set of examples.

The Jewish Lobby. Jewish-Americans have also heavily lobbied against periodic administration attempts to force Israeli
concessions in the Middle East. Because of the normal pro-
Democrat character of the Jewish vote, Republican administrations
have more often tried to "balance" policy and have been beset by
pro-Israel elements in Congress. The events surrounding Eisenhower's pressure on Israel in 1957 were but the first example.
More recently, Republican Gerald Ford and, ironically, his Jewish
Secretary of State Henry Kissinger were the target of the pro-
Israel congressional-interest group combination. In 1975 Kissinger vaguely speculated on a "reassessment" of policy after the
breakdown of talks designed to restore Egyptian control of the
Sinai. Congress immediately sprang to Israel's defense. In May,
seventy-six senators signed a letter to President Ford endorsing
Israel's demand for defensible borders. Senator John Culver
reportedly admitted, "The pressure was just too great. I caved."
Senator Daniel Inouye pragmatically philosophized, "Its easier
to sign one letter than to answer five hundred."(68) The letter,
issued amid Kissinger's shuttle diplomacy, made the Secretary,
according to columnist Tom Brader, "nothing more than an errand
boy . . . powerless to arrange a deal . . . [He] might as well
stay home."(69) The letter and its derailing of the administration initiative was, according to Senator Charles Mathias, "perhaps the most spectacular . . . success of AIPAC [American Israel
Public Affairs Committee], the group that works most directly for
Israeli interests in Congress."(70)

The question of Jewish influence on Congress has proven to be
an elusive phenomenon. Some deny the ethnic connection, arguing
that Congress supports Israel for moral and realpolitik reasons. "Jewish Lobby? There is no such thing. I have no time to
discuss anything like that" an aid to Jacob Javits recently ex-
claimed. Senator Howard Metzenbaum concurred, terming Jewish
Lobby "an inappropriate term that almost smacks of anti-
Semitism."(71) Less emotionally, a recent academic study found

that numbers of Jewish constituents and honoraria from Jewish groups did not correlate with pro-Israel voting in Congress.(72)

Others disagree. William Fulbright told a correspondent, "We intervene and do everything possible to support Israel because we have an extremely active and powerful Zionist group in this country."(73) The impact, Fulbright argued, was that "Prime Minister [Golda Meir] of Israel is so sure of her support in Congress that she is not disposed to make any concessions—so we have the Secretary of State pursuing one policy and Congress . . . pursuing another."(74) Supporting Fulbright's view, an envious lobbyist from another organization termed the Jewish lobby "an impressive operation. I just wish we had something like that."(75)

Few argue that the success of AIPAC and other Jewish organizations is based purely on domestic electoral politics. Senator Mathias strikes the right balance in his observation:

> [I do] not suggest that Congress supports Israel for no better reason than fear of the Israel lobby; on the contrary, I know of few members of either house of Congress who do not believe deeply and strongly that support of Israel is both a moral duty and in the national interest of the United States. It is rather to suggest that, as a result of the activities of the lobby, congressional conviction has been measurably reinforced by the knowledge that political sanctions will be applied to any who fail to deliver.(76)

The electoral/constituent connections are many. One study estimated that in 1974 a majority of contributions over $10,000 to Democratic congressional candidates were from Jewish donors and that sixty percent of all Democratic funds and forty percent of all Republican funds came from Jewish sources.(77) When Alaska's Senator Mike Gravel finally voted for the 1978 sale of jets to the Egyptians and Saudis, he ruefully commented that this "kisses away all kinds of financial support."(78)

Constituent protest is another effective tool. Representative Toby Moffett observed, "The twisting of arms doesn't go on [in Washington]. It really goes on back in the district."(79) When Charles Percy refused to sign the 1975 "defensible borders" letter, the senator had to face irate Jewish constituents in Illinois. An aide remembered, "There were some meetings in Chicago, I wondered if we'd get out unharmed."(80)

The size of the Jewish constituency is not necessarily the key factor in voting decision. One midwestern Republican pointed out, "Everyone loves to be loved. You don't want to displease any group of constituents if you don't have to. It's not likely that Jews could affect my reelection chances, but I sure don't want to experiment. Jews are a bloc, vocal and well informed." A border state Democrat agreed that while Jews were a small percentage of his constituency, they were "influential . . . active in all areas of political life." "Though they couldn't cause me any real election problems," the member continued, "you like to have them on your side."(81)

The skein of mutual interest is also not limited to district considerations. A House member explained that he was thinking of running for the Senate, and "my Jewish friends here in Washington want to do some fund raising for me."(82) Presidential ambitions are also a factor.   In a 1976 debate over the sale of aircraft to Egypt, George McGovern, who was in a position to know, noted, "This is an election year, and I think it is a foregone conclusion that the candidates are going to be positioning themselves for maximum votes."(83)

   Other  Ethnic  Lobbies.   The  coalition  of  Jewish-American interest groups may be the juggernaut of ethnic-based interest groups, but it certainly is not alone in the field.  The impact of East European groups was evident in the earlier period.  Over 130 members of the 96th Congress were members of the Ad Hoc Committee for Irish Affairs, supporting the end to British rule in Northern Ireland.   Greek-Americans also formed a potent interest coalition spearheaded by the American Hellenic Institute (AHI). Senator Mathias has compared the Greek lobby to its Jewish counterpart:

> There are only three million Greek-Americans, compared to
> six million Jewish-Americans, but, like the Jews, the Greeks
> are concentrated in a relatively few urban states where they
> represent sizeable and important voting blocs.  In addition,
> like the American Jewish community, the Greek community in
> the United States is generally well organized, internally
> cohesive and motivated, well represented in business and the
> professions, and politically active in both parties.(84)

   The influence of the group was clearly demonstrated in the imbroglio between Greece and Turkey over Cyprus.  When, in 1974, Turkey occupied a substantial section of northern Cyprus (in response to Greek provocation, Turkey claimed), Congress moved decisively to cut off arms aid and sales to Turkey.  A number of motivational factors were involved.  One was presidential weakness.  The events in the eastern Mediterranean occurred amid the resignation of President Nixon, and neither he nor President Ford was in a position to exert strong executive influence.  Attempts by Secretary Kissinger to equivocate on enforcement of an existing law that forbade the offensive use of American-supplied arms further alienated Congress.(85)  It might be added parenthetically, though, that what constitutes "offensive" is a matter of interpretation.  When Israel destroyed an Iraqi nuclear reactor, few in Congress called for an arms embargo on Israel.  Indeed, many members objected to the Administration's flaccid, short delay in the delivery of combat aircraft to Israel.
   Members were also upset by a perceived lack of consultation in the Cyprus affair.  Frank and Weisband observe that "what was at stake was the integrity of procedure; and, as every old hand on Capitol Hill knows, even legislators who agree on nothing else usually close ranks to protect The Process.(86)
   The influence of the Greek lobby, however, outweighed any of the other factors.  Representatives John Brademas, Paul Sarbanes, Gus Yarton, and L. A. Bafadis became known as the "Greek mafia" on the Hill.   They were supported by a strong ethnic lobby

effort. An aide to Michigan's Robert Griffin recalled the Senator spent forty to fifty hours on the phone talking to irate
Greek constituents and received 300 pro-Greek telegrams a day.
An aide to Representative Donald Clancy remembers Greek constituents as "hysterical" and recalled his boss commenting, "Maybe I
wouldn't have lost my seat over this, but who wants the hassle."
(87)

Numerous bills and resolutions were introduced to embargo
arms sales to Turkey. One member pleaded, "It is time we quit
voting on the basis of our ethnic, color, or religious beliefs,"
but his words were to no avail. Congress exercised its power
and, in return, Turkey withdrew from most NATO functions and took
over American installations in the country. Advocates on both
sides of the issue characterized the lobby effort as the key
factor. Representative Brademas said, "Without the kind of
support we got from the Greek community, our case might have not
been sufficient to win."(88) A House aide who had tried to block
the embargo observed, "The main reason we lost was the Greek
lobby," and another explained, "Without the lobby it never would
have happened." For the Administration, Assistant Secretary of
State for Congressional Relations Robert McCloskey agreed: "The
Greek lobby is not as big as the Israeli lobby, but it has many
of the same characteristics. It is emotional, ruthless and effective."(89)

Racial Groups - Black and White. The question of race, or
perhaps Afro-American ethnicity, has also continued to be a
factor in determining congressional attitudes. As noted, race
has projected itself negatively, with, for example, white southern congressmen becoming less supportive of foreign aid as the
recipients of that aid became increasingly non-caucasian. Unfortunately, at least tangential evidence indicates that bias continued into the most recent period. One indication was the (Senator Harry) Byrd Amendment which became law in 1966 and blocked
American adherence to United Nations-sponsored sanction against
trade with the white racist regime in Rhodesia (now Zimbabwe).
The main trade connection was chrome, and the Byrd amendment
specified that imports of chrome from non-communist countries
could not be cut off unless imports from communist countries were
also embargoed. Inasmuch as the only other major chrome exporter
was the Soviet Union, the Administration could not stop importation of Rhodesian chrome without also embargoing Soviet chrome.
That would have left the United States with no source of the
vital ore.(90)

Support for the Byrd Amendment came from several sources,
including certain industrial interests concerned with chrome
imports. Members of Congress who could not vote against the
clever anti-communist connection and some who were concerned with
a steady supply of the militarily important resource also supported Byrd. Additionally, race was a factor. Mississippi's
Representative Joe D. Waggonner said of Rhodesia, "Three generations ago a group of resourceful white men went into the jungle
of what is now Rhodesia . . . The lesson of history was crystal
clear then as it is now: the natives were not capable of produc-

ing any semblance of what we call civilization."(91) Periodic attempts, sponsored in part by the black congressional caucus, were made to repeal the amendment, but the combination of corporate pressure, conservative congressional strength, and administration ambivalence defeated them. A major repeal attempt failed in 1974, due to lack of Administration support. Senators Hubert Humphrey, Gale McGee, and others tried to get the Administration to intervene in favor of repeal, but, in Humphrey's estimation, because of the fear of "alienating conservatives so vital to Nixon's support," the Executive refused to act.(92) It was not until 1977, with the humanitarian-oriented Jimmy Carter in the White House that the amendment was repealed.

In addition to the Rhodesian issue, racially related factors also probably motivated some southern senators to lead the resistance to ratification of the Genocide Treaty.(93) While their arguments avoided open racial connotations, many observers agree it was partly based on the fear that the Genocide pact "could be used to pillory the United States for its treatment of Indians, blacks, and other minorities."(94) On the reverse side of that pressure group battle, blacks have not generally played a cohesive or strong role to influence policy toward Africa, human rights, or other areas. That reality may be changing, though, and there are some observers who contend that black interest and influence on these questions is rising.(95)

The Ethnic Connection Evaluated. Just what the long-term influence of ethnic groups will be is uncertain. In the recent period of presidential weakness and congressional assertiveness, they have exerted a strong force. More than at other points in time, concern is now high over their impact. Vice President Rockefeller told an investigating commission in 1975 that, in several major issues, "foreign lobbies . . . are guiding U.S. policy." (96) With reference to AWACS, President Reagan became so nettled at Israeli and AIPAC lobbying that he publicly warned that "American security interests must remain our internal interests. It is not the business of other nations to make American foreign policy."(97)

Even members of Congress have become uneasy. During 1978 hearings on the Middle East, Israel supporter Senator Clifford Case worried that "in some quarters . . . there is talk about it being time we had a confrontation with the American-Jewish Community."(98) A senior Senate staff member, referring to the Jackson-Vanik Amendment, picked up the same vibrations. "Some bona fide supporters of Israel," he said, "feel that they [AIPAC] are on the verge of overdoing it."(99) Other members are not so much worried that AIPAC will damage itself or its cause, but that it will damage Congress or foreign policy. House Foreign Affairs Committee Chairman Clement Zablocki charged that "Congress is too responsive to the lobbies of ethnic and special interests in the U.S. to be able to take the lead in foreign policy without endangering the national interest."(100) Senator Mathias has agreed that "ethnic politics, carried as they often have been to excess, have proven harmful to the national interest.(101)

It is unlikely that ethnic politics will disappear or even

become unimportant. Congress' constituency base and the propensity of Americans to define themselves in hyphenated terms preclude that. It is more likely that the recent surge of ethnic influence will recede. If Americans continue to become more nationalistically concerned with their self interests, and if the Executive continues to regain strength, then these factors will produce counter pressures to ethnic appeals and will also reduce the role of Congress, which is perhaps the most fertile field for ethnic group lobbyists to till.

## "Intermestic" Affairs - Trade

A number of analysts have, in recent years, highlighted the increasing intertwining of domestic and international affairs. This trend has progressed to the point that John Manning has suggested the label "intermestic" to symbolize the progressive merger.(102) The policy debates of the entire post-World War II era demonstrate that the interrelationship has been an important issue. On trade policy and a variety of other issues, such as the European Recovery Program, the fate of proposals have often depended on the definitional struggle between domestic (favoring congressional influence) versus international (favoring executive influence). The intermestic connection continued to spur legislative interest during the recent period discussed in this chapter.

A Matter of Definition. A major definitional debate occurred during the Trade Act of 1974. Analytically, that act can be separated into two parts. The first deals with the more traditional aspects of trade legislation, such as tariff levels and escape clauses. The second issue revolves around the question of granting most-favored-nation (MFN) status to the Soviet Union.

Congress, as is normal, tended to view the traditional trade issues more in terms of domestic resource allocation than foreign policy per se.(103) Congress was further activated by the factor of executive weakness, with the debate occurring at the height of Watergate. Legislative egos were also antagonized by scant consultation that I. M. Destler has characterized as "more formal than substantive . . . [with] no major substantive changes" resulting. (104)

With these motivational factors working, Congress moved to revise the bill presented to it by the Nixon Administration. Indeed, the bill as submitted already evidenced congressional influence. Pastor points out:

> The major changes in the trade bill occurred as a result of interbranch politics. Even in the debates within the executive branch, the major determinant was the "law of anticipated reactions." Because the Executive knew it had to write a bill that would not be rejected out-of-hand by the Congress, it included a section on adjustment assistance, some loosening of escape valves, and some congressional participation in the negotiating process. Without a Congress, the Executive would probably have omitted these provisions.(105)

The specifics of the changes inserted by the Executive and subsequent modifications by Congress are not as important as their domestic orientation. Opening the Senate hearings, Finance Committee Chairman Russell Long declared himself "tired of the United States being the least-favored nation in the world . . . We can no longer expose our markets, while the rest of the world hides behind [protective trade barriers]."(106) Highlighting the differing perceptions of the Executive and Congress, Long observed that "trade policy has been the orphan of U.S. foreign policy," and that the Executive had "granted trade concessions to accomplish political objectives."(107)

Although in many ways the final act enhanced presidential power to negotiate trade questions, it also possessed many congressional provisions that were domestically aimed. The Special Trade Representative was statutorally placed in the Executive Office of the President, where it would be "safe" from the State Department. Numerous provisions were also added to allow congressional veto of certain trade barrier reductions, to provide for assistance for workers displaced by imports, to provide protection to certain industries (footwear was a major example), to provide escape valves and other relief to adversely impacted industry, and to prevent unfair trade practices such as dumping. (108)

Thus, the interactive pattern of the Trade Act of 1974 had significant similarities with the trade reforms under Truman and Kennedy and also with lesser interim adjustments, such as the increased authority granted Eisenhower in 1955 and 1958. In each case, Congress granted the president significant power, acceding to the president-dominant foreign policy aspect of trade. But Congress also responded to the domestic impact of trade and, to that extent, placed restrictions on and extracted concessions from the Executive.

It may be that the growing intermestic nature of the issue is one of the long-term factors that will spur even greater legislative control in the area. Destler, for one, thinks so, arguing that "economic pressures seem to be gaining force; the standard postwar counterargument . . . that domestic economic interests [should] be subordinated to the exigencies of the cold war . . . carries far less weight."(109) The rising importance of intermestic economics is further demonstrated by the presence of an increasing number of economic interest lobbyists in Washington. Corporate lobbies have increased from one hundred to five hundred in the last decade, and 1,500 national trade and professional associations and fifty unions are represented in Capitol corridors. Many of these follow and attempt to influence foreign policy, especially when their economic interests are involved.

In a related area, Congress has also been heavily involved in attempting to monitor foreign investing. Pastor identifies a host of actions regarding foreign investment in the United States that resulted from "congressional prodding."(110) It is significant that foreign investment rose from twenty to thirty billion dollars between 1973 and 1976 alone, and that the number of lobbyists registered as representing other governments rose from 481 to 631 (+ 30%) between 1973 and 1978. Thus, Congress has become the target of not only domestic economic interest groups, but foreign lobbies as well. The resulting pressure may well serve to keep Congress active and influential in international economic relations.(111)

The Jackson-Vanik Amendment. A second aspect of the Trade Act of 1974 which merits attention here is the issue of most-favored-nation status for the Soviet Union. In addition to the issues affecting trade legislation, as such, the MFN issue activated Congress on the grounds of anti-communism, domestic electoral politics (i.e., Senator Henry Jackson's presidential ambitions), and ethnic considerations.

In October 1972 a trade agreement was signed with the Soviet Union granting them MFN status, but implementation required legislative action, which was included in the proposal for the 1974 Trade Act. Almost simultaneously, resolutions were introduced in the Senate by Henry Jackson and in the House by Charles Vanik that denied MFN status to countries which restricted emigration. These resolutions were aimed squarely at the Soviet Union and its restrictions on Jewish emigration. By early 1973, a majority of House members and thirty-two senators had signed on as co-sponsors. This surge of legislative support sprang from the same anti-Soviet feeling that had frustrated Lyndon Johnson's attempt to grant the Soviets MFN status in the mid-sixties. Proponents also appealed to institutional pride by charging the Administration with no prior consultation.(112)

Additionally, and more importantly, electoral politics and ethnic group considerations joined to promote the Jackson-Vanik amendment. Paula Stern has argued that "without understanding the election imperative of would-be president Henry Jackson . . . one cannot understand the history of the Jackson amendment."(113) Two important groups to Jackson's electoral coalition were the labor unions and Jewish-Americans. Therefore, the strategy behind the amendment was based, in part, on appealing to AFL-CIO President George Meany who was strongly anti-communist. It was also partly based on appealing to domestic Jews by championing the cause of Jewish emigration from the Soviet Union. In contrast to policy in the Middle East, the Jewish lobby was, at least initially, manipulated by Jackson rather than being a prime mover. In the view of potential rival Gerald Ford, "Jackson had a strong constituency among American Jews. He was about to launch his presidential campaign, and he was playing politics to the hilt."(114) A Jewish aide to a senior Republican senator took the same view: "Jackson is . . . going to milk the Jewish bloc for everything its got." Rather than coming from Jewish-American groups, then, the MFN-emigration link was an "anticipatory" stand originated in the Capitol offices of Jackson and others.

Considerable "credit" must also be given to an array of congressional staff members. Jackson's Richard Perle, Ribicoff's Morris Amitay (who later was to head AIPAC), and Vanik's Mark Talisman are all Jewish and were all principally involved in pushing the amendment. Electoral and constituency connections motivated many members to sign on as co-sponsors. Vanik had no presidential ambitions, but his Cleveland district was eleven percent Jewish. Once the ethnic lobby was organized, others signed on because, as one senator explained, "There is no political advantage in not signing. If you do sign, you don't offend anyone. If you don't sign, you might offend some Jews in your State."(115) A House member expressed a similar sentiment, saying, "I just got on the bandwagon and it didn't hurt among my constituents."(116) Even those without significant Jewish constituencies were often persuaded. Georgia's Senator Herman Talmadge's law partner was president of the Atlantic Chapter of the American Jewish Committee.(117) Russell Long was persuaded to be a co-sponsor through a Jewish supporter from Alexandria, Louisiana, who served as treasurer of Long's campaign committee.(118)

The pressure was sufficient to cause a trilateral negotiations among the Soviet Union, the Executive, and Congress. The Soviets were no match for an aroused Congress, and they agreed to give assurances that they would increase emigration. They argued, however, that the issue was a matter of an internal affair and therefore refused to give written statements on the grounds such an action would abridge their sovereignty. The question was whether Congress would accept substance without form.

There were numerous compliant signals from the Soviets. Minister of the Interior Nikolai Shekelokov, who oversaw emigration, asked Senator James Buckley to assure the Senate that restrictions would ease and that "Soviet leaders are as good as their words."(119) Communist Party chief Leonid Brezhnev met personally with Secretary of the Treasury George Shultz in Moscow, promised easier emigration, and called the exit tax a "bureaucratic bungle."(120) During a visit to Washington, Brezhnev personally brought the message to Congress, assuring seventeen members of the Foreign Relations Committee that the Soviets would not back away from liberalized emigration.(121) Secretary Kissinger sent Jackson a letter assuring him of Soviet good faith pledges, and Soviet Ambassador Dobrynin told President Ford that the Soviets would allow an annual minimum of 55,000 Jews to emigrate.(122)

The pledges were good enough for such major amendment supporters as Senators Ribicoff and Javits, but not good enough for Jackson.(123) He insisted on a formal certification of at least 60,000, the Soviets balked, and both MFN status and Jewish emigration collapsed. Both Nixon, who was president when negotiations began, and Ford, who was president when they ended, blame the Jackson-Vanik Amendment for not only disrupting relations with the Soviet Union, but also for harming Jewish emigration which stood at 35,000 in 1973 but dropped to 13,200 in 1975.(124)

In a bitter-sweet irony, Jackson was caught between Meany's desire to block MFN status and AIPAC's desire to use MFN status as bait for increases in exit visas. When compromise loomed, Jackson had to choose between labor and Jewish-Americans. His ambitions to build support had outrun his ability to manage the coalition. In the end, although he ultimately supported labor and abandoned Soviet Jewry, Jackson's waffling alienated Meany.

He did, however, earn considerable American-Jewish support from
those who saw the surface, but not the details, of his maneuvering. In his 1976 presidential bid, he received 104 delegates in
the New York primary, with sixty-one percent of his vote and
forty to seventy percent of his contributions coming from Jews.
It was not enough, though. He remained Senator Jackson.

## Congress and Foreign Aid

Like trade policy, Congress' attitude toward foreign aid was
governed by a variety of domestic as well as international considerations. Aid remained within the domain of the Executive,
but Congress acted on a number of fronts to use aid packages as a
vehicle for legislative influence.

Domestic Minuses. Part of Congress' most recent approach,
as has been traditionally so, was to reduce executive requests.
President Carter pledged during his 1976 election campaign to
double foreign aid during his term. He soon had to deal with the
reality that it is difficult to get Congress to pass any foreign
aid bill, much less a significantly expanded one. During his
four years, Carter's requests suffered cuts as high as twenty-one
percent, and appropriations rose only one billion dollars, which
meant a fourteen percent loss to inflation in real dollars. In
Carter's last two fiscal years, 1980 and 1981, Congress did not
even pass a regular foreign aid appropriations bill and funded
aid under continuing resolutions.
Foreign aid bills suffered from the general antipathy that
the public has toward aid. This was reflected in Congress, particularly toward multilateral aid, which actually decreased from
2.2 billion dollars in FY 1978 to 1.8 billion dollars in FY 1981.
A typical legislative explanation for the anti-foreign aid posture was, "I voted against this bill because my district is
against it." Another representative argued, "Ninety percent of
my constituency is against foreign aid." Yet another, getting to
the heart of the matter, admitted that voting against foreign aid
was based on electoral politics: "You don't score any points
. . . by voting for a foreign aid bill."(125) Other than, perhaps, aid to Israel, without which Congressional Quarterly has
suggested, "the annual foreign aid bills would have little chance
of passage,"(126) voting for aid carries few electoral pluses.
To the contrary, members tend to remember examples, such as Representative Frank Smith, who was unseated by Jamie Whitten in
Mississippi amid charges that the incumbent had supported "communist" programs like foreign aid.(127)
The fate of foreign aid requests during the Carter years was
also hurt by the Administration's poor relations with Congress
and the Executive's, only sporadic, lobbying attempts.(128)
Carter's general refusal to engage in horse trading may also have
hurt. President Ford, for instance, had salvaged a close vote by
letting Republicans know that their vote on the Foreign Assistance Act of 1974 would be considered in making patronage appointments. Many who had never voted for aid before suddenly found

virtue in helping others overseas.(129)

   Congress, Humanitarianism, and Foreign Aid. Somewhat countering the reductions in multilateral aid, Congress' influence in
recent years helped interject humanitarian considerations as a
criterion for foreign aid. Congress was important in establishing a human rights bureaucracy within the Executive. Especially
with the election of President Carter, who shared that concern,
Congress was able to restrict aid to countries deemed serious
violators of human rights. A number of former recipients such as
Argentina and Chile were cut off from military aid because of
their internal policies.(130)
   The early days of the Reagan Administration has seen a continuation of anti-aid feeling, but a relaxation of human rights standards. Amid drastic budget cuts, legislators found it difficult
to justify foreign aid and were also persuaded by heavy constituent opposition.(131) Administration proposals were also damaged
by internal divisions. It as generally known that Budget Director David Stockman and Secretary of State Alexander Haig disagreed over the level of the requests. The result was that, for
the first time ever, the State Department authorization bill was
defeated in the House with 131 Republicans voting against it.
   On the human rights front, the change in administrations weakened the forces favoring that standard to judge aid recipients.
Reagan took several administrative actions, such as instructing
American delegates to international funding agencies to vote for
aid to previously proscribed countries. He also asked for and
got a relaxation of restrictions on direct aid to some countries,
although for others, notably Chile, the ban was continued.


## Angola

   Congress' prohibition in January 1975 of the use of funds to
intervene in the Angolan civil war provides an interesting study
of the impact of both new, short term and traditional motivational factors to legislative activism. As typical of this period,
the general climate of executive weakness and congressional assertiveness formed a backdrop. The characterization of the struggle
as an African Vietnam, with all the negative connotations, was
particularly damaging to the prospects for American involvement.
Concern about CIA abuses was also a negative factor in that purga-
tive period. Also, the automatic anti-communist consensus had
been destroyed, at least temporarily, by the frustrations in Indochina, and Congress was unwilling to accept the Executive's call
to containment.
   The Angola issue, however, also reveals that many of the key
elements leading to the cutoff of U.S. activity were based on
traditional congressional motivations. Lack of consultation,
executive disarray, and electoral considerations all provided a
powerful impetus to congressional interest and activity.
   The facts of the matter are simple. A struggle for power
occurred in Angola between a faction increasingly backed by the
Soviets and Cubans and one backed by the United States, South

Africa and others. In early 1975, some thirty-one million dollars in CIA funds were earmarked for Angola. Throughout the year, CIA covert support of the "pro-west" faction grew.

Congress' interest in Angola was initially marginal. A few members involved in CIA oversight were briefed in mid-1975, but they either agreed with the action or were boxed in by secrecy requirements. Senator Dick Clark and a few other liberals voiced concern over a possible American role in Angola earlier in 1975, but they aroused little interest among their colleagues. Most members were ignorant on African affairs and could see little reason to expend their energy on the issue. One member, on first being told there would be hearings on the country, greeted the news with the query, "Where the - - - - is Angola?" Another senator noted that it was difficult "getting our colleagues to distinguish between Angola and Mongolia."(132)

As American involvement grew, however, so did congressional interest. Congress' concern over an African Vietnam was also exacerbated by doubts and divisions within the Executive. John Stockwell, the CIA Angola task force head, felt that "Angola had little plausible importance to American national security."(133) Nathaniel Davis, the Assistant Secretary of State for African Affairs, resigned in protest over the Administration's determination to intervene.(134) Numerous leaks of information to Congress sprang from those who either opposed any action or who felt that administration options would deliver "too little, too late" to decisively alter the balance. The absence of Secretary Kissinger from Washington during congressional debate also weakened the executive's strength. In the estimate of two analysts, "the Secretary of State was the only Administration figure with enough prestige and persuasiveness to have swayed votes on Capitol Hill."(135)

Congress was also annoyed at being initially ignored. A few members were briefed, but the general body was much less willing to accept that in lieu of personal contact. In fact, a number of senators, such as McClellen, Case, and Sparkman, were criticized by their colleagues for failing to inform more of the membership about the situation in Angola. Secretary Kissinger claimed two dozen senators, one hundred House members, and another hundred staffers were briefed, but this was done in the most ambiguous, even misleading terms. Indeed, one nail was driven into Angolan aid when the CIA Deputy Director of Operations told the Foreign Relations Committee that arms were being sent directly to Angola. That afternoon the Deputy Assistant Secretary of State denied direct transfers; then, when confronted with the contradiction in testimony, he reversed his statement. Outraged, the Committee denounced the hapless diplomat and unanimously forwarded the aid cutoff legislation. Commenting later, a key Senate staff member noted, "If the CIA and State had been relatively frank with us, we might not have gone all the way."(136) Surveying the Senate action, two other observers noted that, "the chief complaint voiced by several senators was not that the U.S. was giving aid . . . but that Congress had not been consulted by the Administration . . ."(137)

The spark that set off the tinder of congressional resentment was the political ambitions of Senator John Tunney. Up for re-election in 1976 and faced with a lackluster, playboy image, a tough primary, and a tougher general election, Tunney was in need of a cause to enhance his recognition. His committee assignments had nothing to do with foreign or defense affairs, but under his staff's prodding, with the support of California colleague Alan Cranston, and finally with the acquiescence of the Democratic leadership, Tunney spearheaded the anti-administration drive. (138) Tunney won the battle and aid was terminated, but he lost the war and was defeated in November 1976.

There may be "forevers" in politics, but the end to Angolan aid is probably not one of them. The Reagan Administration re-opened the issue in 1981, and met with success, when the Senate voted to repeal the ban. "If we're a world power," Barry Gold-water advised, "we need muscle in the President's office to act like a world power."(139) Administration efforts in the House, however, were less successful, and the Foreign Affairs Committee refused to recommend repeal by a nineteen to five vote.(140) The issue remained unresolved into early 1982, but analysis in the press has argued that, given Reagan's strength and the renewed cold war concerns, the Senate will probably prevail in confer-ence.

## Making and Breaking Treaties

During his four years in office, President Carter dealt with three treaties, the fates of which give insights into the ongoing foreign policy process. The Panama Treaty provided the President a victory over a reluctant Congress. Carter's abrogation of the Mutual Defense Treaty with Taiwan, again, decisively demonstrated presidential strength. SALT II was a set-back for Carter, but an ambiguous one.

Panama. The negotiation stage of the Panama Canal Treaties extended for thirteen years and included several near agreements that were aborted in the face of strong congressional opposition. The first preliminary agreement was reached in 1977, but leaks to the American press sparked a negative reaction. Many members of the Senate had been regularly briefed on the negotiations from their inception and knew of the agreement, but they expected the documents to be kept secret until submitted to the Senate.(141) The sudden disclosure and resulting political backlash temporar-ily ended any chance for the treaties. In the words of opponent Karl Mundt, the Administration had "pulled back its horns . . . realizing that they would probably get clobbered in the Senate." (142)

The Ford Administration appeared nearly ready to move forward with a treaty, but was beset by division within its own ranks. The Pentagon was the principal dissenter. It pressed for strong-er protection clauses and undercut the State Department on Capi-tol Hill. Bureaucratic infighting became so severe that Senators McGee and Humphrey called on President Ford to resolve differ-ences between the Departments of State and Defense:

We realize the differences within the Executive Branch are
properly questions for you to resolve, however, in this case
the various obvious conflicts between two key Executive
departments have caused serious difficulties with efforts in
the Congress to support the general position of your administration for negotiations. The divisive and harmful bureaucratic maneuvering has already had a detrimental effect on
congressional attitudes towards the treaty.(143)

The treaty was finally signed and submitted to the Senate in
1977. The difficult ratification process illustrates the salience of a variety of legislative motivational factors and also
the ability of an organized, flexible, and determined president
to prevail. An early poll of the Senate found (with sixty-seven
votes needed to ratify) thirty-six for and twenty-seven against
the Treaty and thirty-seven uncommitted. Beyond the substantive
issues of the treaty--and many were strong proponents and opponents on that basis--a number of other factors played on senatorial preferences. Given the closeness of the vote, these turned
out to be crucial.

The electoral connection was the most important. At times
mail against the treaties ran 300:1. Kansas Senator Robert Dole
observed, "I guess everyone here had a very difficult time deciding what to do, how to posture himself, and how to vote, because
there are political implications to the votes on these treaties."
(144) And Majority Leader Robert Byrd, reflecting on the negative public opinion, cogently concluded that not only was there
"no political mileage in voting for the treaty," but any senator
who did so "will have some of the political skin taken off his
political nose."(145) Some, such as Edward Zorinsky, decided to
follow their constituents' mandate despite their personal convic-
tions. Others wavered. Jennings Randolph worried in an interview that seventy-five percent of his constituents opposed the
treaty, but bravely added, "I must not evaluate the ultimate vote
on whether it weakens my candidacy for reelection." The comment,
the listener added, seemed "as much for his own benefit as for
the interviewer's." (He finally voted no.)(146) Still other
senators defiantly announced they would follow the Burkean example and follow their own views over those of their constituents.
Thomas McIntyre announced that he would vote for the treaties.
"My political fate is not my concern here today," he resolutely
proclaimed.(147) The electoral concern was not spurious, either.
Whether it is objectively true or not, the perceptual truth that
will not be lost on senators in later struggles is that, in 1978,
almost fifty percent (7 of 15) of the senators who voted for the
treaty were defeated for reelection (including McIntyre), while
nearly ninety percent (8 of 9) who voted against the treaty were
returned to office.(148)

The electoral connection also motivated amendments by members
who wanted to support the treaties but who needed to show the
voters they had "toughened" them. Forty-two senators visited
Panama, and there were direct Senate-Panama negotiations in that
country and in Washington. What the future impact of the changes
to the treaties adopted by the Senate will be is unclear. Look-

ing at the key DeConcini change, one scholar argues that, in accepting it, the President had learned "the lessons of Versailles too well," and made a deal which was good for domestic politics but bad for international relations.(149) It is also possible to argue that the change--which migrated from amendment through reservation to condition status--has no legality and caused only temporary dismay in Panama, and that a decision to militarily intervene after the year 2000 in the Panama Canal area would not be affected by the existence or non-existence of the DeConcini condition. Perhaps even DeConcini recognized that. One set of observers have commented

> DeConcini's motivation was fairly straightforward. He was convinced . . . that his state's voters were overwhelmingly opposed to the treaties. His own inclination was to vote for them, but only if, along the way, he could demonstrate a canny talent for driving a tough bargain.(150)

That view is supported by a DeConcini aide who later recalled, "We were just looking for a reason to vote for it."(151) That view also is in agreement with Crabb and Holt's observation that the amendment process "allows the Senate to skirt an issue rather than meeting it head on," and on the Panama question "enabled a senator to avoid coming out foursquare for the treaties as negotiated."(152)

Congressional egos seem to have been generally sated in the ratification process. Members felt "consulted," and the trips and the 145 amendments, 26 reservations, 18 understandings, and 3 declarations they offered allowed them to, at least, assert their views. Changes to the treaty made it a product of the Senate as well as of the Executive, winning increased sympathy in that body, and individual successful changes tacitly meant that sponsors would support the treaty they had now helped to formulate. (153)

The Administration's strong liaison effort massaged egos effectively. Senator Zorinsky wangled 250 invitations for Nebraskans to visit the White House; the President called several times; Mrs. Carter called Mrs. Zorinsky; Sol Linowitz (the chief negotiator), Vice President Mondale, Zbigniew Brzezinski, Cyrus Vance, Defense Secretary Harold Brown, and Henry Kissinger all visited his office. (In the end, Zorinsky voted no, but was reported ready to vote yes, if needed.) All in all, President Carter made eighty-seven phone calls to senators within a two-week period, met with or spoke to each senator at least once, and had a phalanx of administration figures in constant contact with members.

The White House also orchestrated an intense campaign to sway "informed" public opinion. Cabinet members drew up a list of mutual acquaintances with senators who could be contacted. The Democratic National Committee sponsored a phone drive to have 5,000 prominent Democrats in twelve states call wavering legislators. Hundreds of opinion leaders were briefed at the White House. Ranking executive officials made appearances and barnstormed the country, and the President made a national television appeal.

Contrary to the White House's prideful assertion that it did not trade political goodies for votes, there is ample circumstantial evidence that such tactics were also used. Early on, the White House announced it would buy 250 million dollars worth of surplus copper, much of it from DeConcini's Arizona, to help support the metal's prices. Senator Herman Talmadge became a treaty supporter, and the Administration withdrew its opposition to a Talmadge-sponsored farm bill it previously had denounced as inflationary. Kansas Senator Robert Dole, an opponent, joked that he was holding out for a naval base in his state; New York's Patrick Moynihan grumbled that, if he had wavered, he could have solved New York City's financial problems; and a ranking administration official added, "I just hope the Panamanians get as much out of this thing as some U.S. Senators."(154)

The legislative effort was one of the best in Carter's years. In the end, the Senate passed both treaties by identical votes of 68-32, a vote to spare and without the need of calling on Senators Randolph's or Zorinsky's "only-if-needed" votes. The key element was intensive presidential involvement and skillful use of the variety of persuasive tools available to the White House. An apt tribute to Carter's effort was later paid by Senator Paul Laxault, a treaty opponent. Four years later while supporting a Republican president's sale of AWACS to Saudi Arabia, Laxault predicted victory and pointed to the Panama Canal Treaty fight as an example of what intensive presidential lobbying could accomplish.(155)

Treaty Termination--Taiwan. The events surrounding termination of the Mutual Defense Treaty (1955) with Taiwan also illustrates continued presidential power in the treaty process, albeit from a different perspective. On December 15, 1978, President Carter announced that, as part of his uncontested power to switch diplomatic recognition from Taipei to Peking, he was also terminating the mutual defense pact with Taiwan. The action was taken without consultation with Congress and in contravention of language in the 1978 foreign aid bill directing prior consultation. It also came only three months after President Carter had said that "there should be prior consultation between Congress and the executive branch on any proposed policy changes affecting . . . the Mutual Defense Treaty . . . ."(156)

Congress was stung by the action. Many were appalled by what they interpreted as an abandonment of a long-standing, pro-Western ally to assuage the communist, normally virulently anti-American, Peking government. On a less substantive basis, members of the Senate were especially distressed by the lack of consultation and by the Executive's rejection of the proposition that, if the Senate has a role in making treaties, it also has a role in breaking treaties. John Glenn said members were determined to show that "Congress is an equal partner in this thing." (157) The Senate resolved 59-35 that "approval of the United States Senate is required to terminate any mutual defense treaty between the United States and another nation." A number of senators, led by Barry Goldwater, filed suit in federal courts to overturn Carter's action. Congress also extensively rewrote the Taiwan Relations Act, strengthening ties beyond the executive version and inserting language promising to support Taiwan in the event of a military attempt by the Mainland to incorporate it. In a separate action, Congress also authorized extensive military aid to Taiwan.(158)

Congress' efforts did not, however, alter the main thrust of Carter's policy. On December 13, 1979, the Supreme Court by 7-2 dismissed the Goldwater suit. Four justices held the issue "a political question," beyond the Court's jurisdiction; Lewis Powell found the issue not ripe for judicial review because Congress had not officially taken a position (ignoring the one-house Senate action); one justice agreed with Carter substantively; and one other concurred without comment.(159)

Formal action in Congress was forestalled by a number of factors. One of these was the reluctant acceptance of the action by Taiwan, which did not want to alienate the White House further. "You can't be more Catholic than the Pope," one conservative glumly noted.(160)   Assurance from both Washington and Peking were also helpful. Chinese Vice Premier Teng Hsiao-ping had met in Peking in July 1978 with a delegation from Congress and assured them Taiwan would not be repatriated by force. When Teng visited the United States in early 1978, he again spent considerable time meeting with members and assuring them of China's peaceful intentions.  Finally, Congress' alterations of the Taiwan Relations Act were largely symbolic, with its most important point, military support, being of dubious constitutionality. (161) In short, despite some predictable resistance, partly based on institutional ego, the President clearly dominated the process and also won an important, if somewhat ambiguous, victory in the Supreme Court.

SALT II. The saga of the second Strategic Arms Limitation Treaty provides a curious picture of congressional power and impotency. From one perspective, Congress played a marginal role in SALT II. It was negotiated without senatorial advice and achieved defacto implementation without senatorial consent. Yet, despite that, it can also be correctly pointed out that SALT II was never ratified, having fallen victim to a combination of congressional objections, executive ineptitude, and aggressive Soviet foreign policy.

During the negotiation process, which stretched through the Nixon, Ford, and Carter Administrations, the Senate's role was limited. The detailed studies of Alan Platt and of Strobe Talbott both conclude that the Senate had little substantive impact on the treaty that was signed by President Carter in June 1979.(162) The information that was given Congress was limited. Further, most senators viewed the negotiating process as an executive function, believed that the legislative body was ill-suited to participate in the negotiating process and might jeopardize it, and felt that they and their staffs lacked the expertise to make a useful contribution.(163)

What changes in the American negotiating stance that did occur were generally made by the Administration in anticipation of possible congressional objectives rather than as a result of actual legislative dissent. Suspicions of the Soviets were deeper in Congress than in the White House and were reflected, in part, by legislative attempts to "toughen" the negotiating team. Paul Warnke, Carter's nominee as chief SALT negotiator, received spirited opposition from hard-line Senator Jackson and others who considered Warnke "soft." Warnke's relatively narrow 58-40 confirmation was widely considered a notice to be tough and was, in part, saved by Carter's pledge to keep the Joint Chiefs of Staff informed and consulted on arms negotiations.(164)

Jackson also worked to ensure that the military delegate to the negotiations was sufficiently strong. At his behest, General Royal Allison was removed from the delegation, and Lieutenant General Edward Rowny," a Jackson man," became the chief military representative" (165) As a result of these pressures on the staff and under repeated public criticism from Jackson and others, there is some evidence that the Administration hardened some of its negotiating positions. There were also several changes adopted in direct response to specific legislative opinions. Examples of these include language to allow the sharing of cruise missile information with allies and to prohibit encrypted telemetry.(166) These modifications were peripheral, however, and the basic negotiating strategy remained firmly in the hands of the Executive.

Maneuvering began in the Senate months before the President signed the treaty or submitted it to the upper house. As the treaty approached the signature and ratification stages, legislative and executive movement, individually and interactively, increased. An early survey found forty senators for SALT, twenty against it, and forty uncommitted. Immediately after Carter signed the treaty in Vienna, the Senate count stood at fifty-eight for, thirty against, twelve uncommitted. It was clearly a close contest, with sixty-seven needed to ratify.

Those in favor of the treaty stressed the need to control the arms race. Proponents tended to picture the treaty as a "best possible deal in a real world" and as a necessary interim step toward a more comprehensive, arms-reducing SALT III. Treaty advocates also argued that failure of the Senate to ratify the treaty would brand the United States as a war monger.(167) Soviet expert Averell Harriman hinted that failure to ratify might bring about the overthrow of Communist Party Chairman Leonid Brezhnev and the installation of hard-liners in his place.(168)

The Soviets helpfully joined in on this and other themes to help sell the treaty to the Senate. Americanologist George Arbator told an ABC-TV audience that rejection would ruin détente.(169) Brezhnev and Foreign Minister Gromyko both warned of the dangers of rejecting the treaty or adding disabling amendments.

Indeed, the attention that the Kremlin paid to Congress was a mark of the Senate's potential power and of Moscow's appreciation of American constitutional politics. Soviet leaders courted senators, with Brezhnev and others meeting with legislative delegations in January, April, July, and August 1979. In the last of those meetings, Premier Alexi Kosygin gave additional assurances on Soviet restraint in building the "backfire" bomber.(170) There was even an improvement in the Soviets' Jewish emigration policy, and press reports cited Soviet sources in tying the move to improving relations in order to boost SALT II's chances. Scorn was also heaped on opponents, with <u>Pravda</u> assailing Senate foes as allies of the military-industrial complex.(171)

In Washington, an orchestrated campaign similar to, but even larger in scope than, the Panama Canal effort was mounted. Administration spokesmen fanned out across the country, and large numbers of local opinion leaders were invited to the Capitol to hear SALT II extolled.(172) There were also reports of deals made for SALT support, although, as usual, these were hotly denied by all parties. Senate Majority Leader Byrd, for example, was reported to have sought relaxation of environmental standards governing coal-fired plants as a sweetener to encourage his support of SALT.(173) More demonstrably, the Administration moved to buy the support of the Joint Chiefs of Staff and their defense minded Senate allies by increasing defense programs. Carter announced support of the MX missile racetrack system in early summer, and in the fall agreed to significant hikes in the military budget. Clearly the stops were out.

Yet the President was unsuccessful. His plans to add to his Camp David peacemaker image ran afoul of a number of internal factors sure to raise legislative hackles. Carter was also beset by a series of international misfortunes. Certainly, a substantial number of senators opposed to SALT on principle. The seeming lack of numerical parity between the respective nuclear arsenals and verification problems were the most troublesome. With only a handful of additional votes needed, however, the treaty might have been carried by a more skilled lobby effort and in a less tumultuous international environment.

Domestically, factors working against treaty ratification included changing Administration themes, senatorial resentment at attempts to stampede them, and anger over the Executive's attempts to end-run the constitutional process. Divisions within the Executive and electoral politics also weakened SALT's chances. The first factor, changing themes, made it more difficult for the Administration to wholeheartedly support its handiwork. Initially, President Carter and Secretary of State Vance had expressed a preference for an arms reduction treaty. When that became unattainable, they settled for a limitation on arms growth. Several liberal senators did not concur, however, and, in their disappointment, condemned SALT for not going far enough.

More significantly, negative reaction arose over a number of Carter's tactics. The most serious was the Administration's repeated assertion that it would honor SALT II as an executive agreement, even if it failed to win Senate ratification. In September 1977 when SALT I had expired, the Administration had announced it would continue to observe the terms of the treaty as long as the Soviets did likewise. However noble the purpose, it was an ill-advised move. Senate reaction was sharp and swift. Clifford Case condemned the ploy, Alan Cranston spoke of "constitutional excess," and Scoop Jackson dismissed the declaration as "contrary to established statutory and constitutional procedures." Even the liberal <u>New York Times</u> labeled the action an "evasive procedure" designed to "circumvent" the law.(174)

The Administration did not learn from its mistake. As the SALT II struggle grew, Carter repeatedly asserted it would go into effect regardless of its fate in the Senate.(175) In fact, there was an initial disposition in the White House not to present the treaty/agreement to the Senate at all. When the State Department labeled the pact a treaty despite White House objections, Vice President Mondale exploded that the "yahoos at the State Department [had] better learn the difference between a treaty and an agreement."(176) Majority Leader Byrd was moved to warn the White House of the negative impact of this tactic,(177) and, at a later date, of the attempts to paint the White House and Kremlin as institutions of peace and the Senate an institution of war.(178) In this case, the Administration picked up its cue and even cautioned its Soviet allies to tone down their condemnations.(179) The Senate's resentment of the attempt to force its hand was also aggravated by simple executive ineptitude. At one point, the Administration was caught creating a <u>post hoc</u> study to support its SALT position. The effort was described by a Senate aide as a "fabrication . . . an attempt to deceive Congress, . . . not just tendentious—but an outright lie."(180)

The Administration was also hampered by internal divisions. Dissenting executive factions regularly leaked information to allies in Congress and to the press.(181) As the treaty neared completion, bureaucratic sabotage became sharper and more overt. CIA Director Stansfield Turner was less than positive about the ability to verify Soviet compliance when he testified before the Senate.(182) Departing Ambassador to Moscow Malcolm Toon also worried publicly about possible Soviet cheating.(183) Most troublesome of all, the Joint Chiefs of Staff teetered on the edge of open opposition. Even after the Chiefs were brought formally on board by a combination of budget increase carrots and career threatening sticks, they were tepid in their endorsement. Admiral Thomas Hayward, for one, admitted "lack of raging enthusiasm" to Senate questioners. Defense-minded senators were not reassured.

As the time for treaty ratification and as the end of President Carter's term drew nearer, electoral politics also increasingly became a factor. Some analysts have argued that the President saw partisan advantage in SALT II as an issue that could help him and, by extension, congressional Democrats in 1980. Republicans also saw SALT II as a partisan issue, although with a different outcome. Republican leaders meeting at Easton, Maryland, in an electoral strategy session, resolved that bipartisanship should be abandoned and that Carter's "failure" to counter Soviet aggressiveness should be a campaign issue. Even moderate Republicans like Jacob Javits joined in. "Linkage," or Soviet action in general, was to be an important consideration in determining treaty ratification, Minority Leader Baker said.(184) Carter continued to worry that partisan politics would derail SALT II.(185) The Republicans kept up their attack on the Administration for being soft on communism and for its argument that SALT II should be decided on its merits and not linked to other aspects of Soviet international behavior.

In the end, the Republican's linkage stand prevailed. Whether, in more placid times SALT II would have been ratified, despite its domestic problems, is problematic. The fact is that, given the closeness of the issue, its fate was sealed by a series of international upheavals. In September 1979 revelation of the existence of a Soviet combat brigade in Cuba brewed up a tempest in a proverbial teapot and added ammunition to the armory of the linkage forces. In November, the American Embassy in Tehran was seized. The downfall of the Shah and the ensuing hostage crisis deprived the United States of important stations in Iran used to monitor the Soviet Union, and thus, verify SALT II compliance. It also heightened the sense of defensiveness and the related desire for strength in the country. Finally, the new year 1980 brought the Soviet seizure of Afghanistan.

The invasion tolled the death knell for SALT II in the Senate. Carter proclaimed his eyes opened to Soviet perfidy. Linkage reigned triumphant in the Senate. At first Carter said he hoped to proceed with the treaty in the Senate, but the advice of his staff and Senate supporters convinced him that the issue was lost. Within a week, he asked Congress to defer debate, and SALT went into limbo, being neither ratified nor rejected.

The fate of the treaty, however, cannot be completely counted as a congressional "victory" in the struggle over foreign policy. Indeed, SALT II is alive. Even as he asked for the deferral, Carter announced that, in accord with his initial predilections, SALT II would become a de facto executive agreement. The United States would abide by the provisions as long as the Soviet Union followed suit. Thus, the agreement went into effect, and the understanding was even continued by President Reagan who had earlier campaigned against it. Such twists make scorekeeping difficult.

## Congress and Personnel

The impact of Congress on the selection, confirmation, and continuance of foreign policy personnel remained much as it had been during the entire post-1945 period. In the immediate atmosphere of Vietnam and Watergate, legislative opposition altered a number of presidential preferences. G. McMurtrie Godley, for one, was rejected for the post of Assistant Secretary of East Asian Affairs. When the Army Chief-of-Staff died in September 1974, President Ford wanted to name Alexander Haig to that post, but, fearing a confirmation battle, chose to dispatch Haig to command NATO forces instead.(186)

There were also a number of instances of subtle legislative influence. Ford fired Secretary of Defense James Schlesinger, in part, because "he was obviously unsuccessful in dealing with Congress."(187) Following the same logic, Ford named Donald Rumsfeld as Schlesinger's successor because of Rumsfeld smooth relations with Congress.(188) Ford also had some difficulties getting George Bush confirmed as director of the CIA. Democrats did not want to boost the career of Bush, and Ford had to pledge that

Bush would not be his Vice Presidential running mate in 1976.
(189) President Carter also had to retreat on a few occasions.
For one, his nomination of Theodore Sorenson for CIA Director was
withdrawn after significant Senate opposition arose.

In the main, however, the presidents continued to succeed in
gaining confirmation of almost all their appointees. When, for
example, Nathaniel Davis, was put forward as Ambassador to
Angola, liberals were distressed because of his tenure in Chile
at the time of the assassination of President Salvadore Allende.
Still, Hubert Humphrey wrote a colleague, despite "strong reservation," the guiding principle remained that the President should
have "the widest latitude in staffing the Executive Branch, particularly ambassadors who will directly represent his policy."
(190)

The initial nominees of Ronald Reagan were generally treated
with equal senatorial deference. The idea of Alexander Haig as
Secretary of State distressed some liberals who remembered his
association with Vietnam and Watergate, and also some conservatives who connected Haig with the policy of détente. When
Reagan persisted, Haig was easily confirmed. Reagan's nomination
of Joseph Clark as Deputy Secretary of State caused a minor scan-
dal when it became obvious the man knew virtually nothing about
foreign policy. Yet, despite audible groans, even from Majority
Leader Baker, Clark was also confirmed.

When Reagan nominees did receive opposition, it came most
strongly from fellow conservatives. Senator Jesse Helms, the
arch conservative/moral majority guru, delayed the confirmations
of Chester Crocker, Myer Rashish, and Robert Hormats for ranking
Department of State slots. In the end, they were all confirmed,
but Helms was able to extract compensating appointments. The
Senator estimated that he had successfully sponsored some thirty
individuals for foreign policy posts, although he refused to
identify them "because they might get their heads cut off. It
would at least make it embarrassing for them."(191) Some of
Helms' choices could be identified, though, and included retired
Admiral James Nance, who became principal deputy to National
Security Advisor Richard Allen, and retired General Edward Rowny,
who was appointed chief arms negotiator.

The single major defeat of a Reagan nominee was the ill-fated
lot of Ernest Lefever, who had been named to the post of Assistant Secretary of State for Human Rights and Humanitarian Affairs. Lefever, who attracted liberal criticism for his amoral
approach to international human rights, might have survived had
he not been caught by a self-contradiction over his connection
with Nestles Corporation, which was accused of pushing infant
formula to the detriment of children in developing countries, and
by allegations that he viewed blacks as genetically inferior to
whites. Indeed, Lefever's views were so unpopular that even his
two brothers testified against him. Although the Administration
continued to support his nomination, it did so with waning enthusiasm. Howard Baker quietly asked Reagan to withdraw the nomination. Foreign Relations Committee Chairman Charles Percy
announced his opposition, and the Committee as a whole reported
the nomination unfavorably 13 to 4, with five Republican joining

all eight Democrats in opposition. Facing the inevitable, Lefever asked the President to withdraw his nomination.

Lefever's defeat was, however, a rather singular affair, as most overt rejections are. In the main, the Senate continued to defer to the President, but in the subtle process of sounding senators out on the potential nominees and in trying to accommodate legislative candidates for a variety of posts, congressional influence remained a factor in the appointment of personnel.


## A Pattern?

Overall, the pattern of congressional influence during the second term of Nixon, those of Ford and Carter, and in the early Reagan days represented both change and continuity. Spurred by a sense of acute institutional embarrassment, caught up in the chase to bring down the imperial presidency, faced with a series of systemically weakened or personally inept presidents, and urged on by an influx of less deferential members elected in the cynically turbulent aftermath of Vietnam and Watergate, Congress asserted itself. Numerous restrictions on unilateral executive action were passed. The War Powers Resolution and the legislative veto provisions of the Foreign Military Sales Act are the most prominent. Congress also used specific legislative actions to ban aid to Turkey, prevent intervention in Angola, and insist on human rights reforms in aid recipients. Congressional criticism also resulted in administration retreats from other anticipated actions. The down-grading of the American rhetorical and tangible commitment to El Salvador is but the most recent example.

Yet, these actions do not constitute a revolutionary change of legislative influence. Many have overestimated the change by underestimating Congress' past influence. That influence has been ever present. Congress surely often agreed with or deferred to the President, but the Executive also repeatedly took Congress' views into account. Would the United States' trauma in Vietnam have begun in 1954 instead of 1964 without the restraining impact of Congress? The answer is probably "yes." Would the rhetoric of the cold war have been so intense had Truman been able to institute the Truman Doctrine and Marshall Plan by fiat? The answer is probably "no." And what would have been the course of events in the Middle East if Congress had not been opposed to plans to aid Nassar's Egypt build the Aswan Dam? The answer is certainly "different."

Further, the factors which motivated Congress to action remained largely the same. Post war institutional ego reassertion, lack of foreign policy consensus, and a weak executive encouraged congressional activity in the late 1940s as they again did in the 1970s. Other motivating factors including partisanship, domestic economic considerations, and ethnic group pressure remained constant influences throughout the period.

Finally, the inherent constitutional and historical factors which caused the evolution of the Two Presidencies were not reversed in the 1970s, although they were at times temporarily

ignored. The phenomenon of presidential crisis leadership remained intact. So did doubts in the Executive, public, and
Congress about legislative ability to deal adequately with foreign policy. Legislative interest, information, and expertise in
the foreign policy field increased only marginally. The gap
between executive and legislative influence narrowed a bit, but
did not close.

The next question, then, is what will be the future of congressional influence? The answer, we shall see, is that the tide
has already begun to ebb, or perhaps the pendulum has begun its
reverse swing, and presidential power is again on the rise.

# 9
# The Future Is History

What are the future prospects of Congress in the foreign policy process? The basic response to that question is that Congress
will continue to play a significant, but secondary, role. The
theory of the Two Presidencies is alive and well in Washington.
Throughout the past three-and-a-half decades, Congress has played
an important, but fitful, role. Congress' bursts of assertiveness, contrasted to its normal posture of deference to the Executive, has been governed by a relatively constant group of factors. In turn, the Executive's responsiveness to congressional
concerns has also resulted from a related group of factors.
These have been discussed in terms of influence theory as set
forth originally by Lasswell and Kaplan, with both formal and
informal powers playing an important role.

The fluctuation in use of these means of influence, or swings
of the pendulum, if you will, has been less dramatic than characterized in other studies of foreign policy-making. At least
since the post 1930s isolationist period, and for perhaps longer,
the pendulum has remained in the executive quadrant. There have
been legislative-oriented movements, as in the mid and late 1940s
and again in the 1970s, but the basic fact of presidential dominance has remained constant. Further, those shifts have been
temporary. By the Eisenhower presidency, congressional activity
had abated somewhat, although it never reached the nadir pictured
by some. Congress is arguably the most significant part of a
president's domestic political environment, and it exercised
power through a variety of channels when actually or potentially
aroused.

The patterns established up to the present will continue to
characterize the legislative and executive foreign policy roles
and interactions in the future. Further, in terms of what
limited movement there has been in the recent past, congressional
activity has not only reached its high-water mark, it has already
begun to ebb. This reverse tide can be seen both in terms of the
opinions and in actions of various elements of the polity.

## Changing Perspectives

The Executive. The clearest change of tune is heard from the Executive. At times in the mid 1970s, executive officials attempted to assuage Congress by accepting enhanced legislative influence. Henry Kissinger proclaimed, with uncharacteristic deference, that "the decade-long struggle in this country over executive dominance is over . . . Congress is a coequal Branch of government . . . [and] foreign policy must be a shared enterprise."(1) Early in his term, President Carter echoed that line when he told an interviewer that, although the War Powers Resolution reduced his power, "I think it is an appropriate reduction." (2)

Such statements only reflected a short-term perspective. More recently, executive criticism of legislative "interference" has become increasingly common, as have attempts to repeal or amend some of the constraints on presidential discretionary power enacted only a few years before. Forecasting this trend, Vice President Nelson Rockefeller observed in 1975 that "the image of 536 individuals' hands on the tiller of the Ship of State does not inspire confidence that we will hold a steady course,"(3) Secretary of Defense James Schlesinger voiced similar sentiment that same year, quoting Tocqueville's observation that "it is especially in the conduct of foreign relations that democracies appear . . . decidedly inferior to other governments." Schlesinger added his own warning: "Let us be sure it is not an epithet."(4) In his memoirs, Secretary of State Kissinger has continued the attack on Congress. "In the Seventies," he wrote, "passion overwhelmed analysis." Further, he argued,

> Our system cannot function when Congress and the President have sharply conflicting goals or when the Congress attempts to prescribe day-to-day tactical decisions . . . When it has tried, the results have been unfortunate . . . The coalitions and power centers of Congress shift in response to the stimuli of various pressure groups. Foreign policy requires a constant view of the national interest.(5)

President Ford voiced similar sentiments. In his 1976 State of the Union message, Ford told the assembled Congress that, "as the framers of our Constitution knew from hard experience, the foreign relations of the United States can be conducted effectively only if there is strong central direction . . . That responsibility clearly rests with the President."(6)

This line of argument was continued in the Carter years. The President proclaimed his determination to "preserve presidential capacity to act in the national interest at a time of rapidly changing circumstances."(7) A bit less majestically, Assistant Secretary of State for Congressional Relations J. Brian Atwood criticized the Senate for its parochialism, observing that it "has its ear to the ground. That is not a good posture from which to exercise leadership."(8)

The Reagan Administration has continued the attack. In the wake of the Soviet invasion of Afghanistan, Carter asked Congress to ease some restrictions on his discretionary authority, especially in the area of granting military foreign aid.(9) Reagan has continued to press the point.(10) The two administrations not only presented a series of proposals (some of which succeeded) to Congress, but President Reagan ordered his Attorney General to challenge the constitutionality of legislative vetoes before the Supreme Court.(11) The Administration's attacks on congressional limits on presidential prerogatives reached a new rhetorical height during the AWACS debate. Veteran columnist Tom Wicker was so alarmed by the Administration's assertions that he wrote, "Life is being breathed once again into the Imperial Presidency that [argues that] . . . no matter how the President decides a foreign policy question . . . Congress and everyone else must accept it or his authority will be undermined."(12) Whatever its objective merits, however, Wicker's view is the exception to the general trend of comment.

The Galleries. Observers representing a variety of perspectives outside the government have also expressed concern with the new order of legislative activism. On the academic front, one analyst described the Executive as having been "emasculated" during the 1970s.(13) Another worried about Congress' ability to "unquestionably . . . foul up foreign policy."(14) Still others have found the practice of an enhanced legislative role unsettling. The drawback, one author commented, is that the new role "made positive foreign policy enormously difficult to carry out under any administration."(15) Yet another set of observers further concluded that "high expectations [are] not necessary for one to be disappointed in Congress."(16)

In the press, the small flurry of columns after the 1981 AWACS sale that fretted over the Reagan imperial juggernaut were atypical of the general trend of reporting and comment in recent years. Instead, articles entitled "War Powers Pendulum Swings Back--A Little,"(17) "A Return to Realism,"(18) and "Once Again, Power Pendulum Swings Toward the Executive Branch"(19) better represent the trend. The New York Times editorialized that the restrictions on the president needed to be examined because "they give too much comfort to the forces and movements hostile to the United States."(20) Summing up a growing consensus in the press, columnist David Broder wrote that, while "it is not popular . . . to suggest that there is danger in congressional dominance of foreign policy, . . . the caprice with which that power is now being exercised [by Congress] is full of foreboding."(21)

Public opinion has also begun to revert to its historical preference for strong presidential leadership. The image of Carter as "weak" was widely viewed as more important to his overwhelming defeat in 1980 than any individual issue. Reflecting on Congress' foreign policy role and the public desire for a strong president, a study by Holsti and Rosenau found that most "elites" felt that domestic constraints caused America's failure in Vietnam. Seventy-seven percent believed that Congress was one of the negatively contributing factors.(22) Another study similarly found that by 1978 mass public and elite support for a strong congressional role had declined since 1974.(23)

Foreign observers have also joined in and given a new currency to Theodore Lowi's old thesis that there is a need to make
"democracy safe for the world." Australian Prime Minister Malcolm Fraser reportedly told Chinese leaders in Peking that the
United States was unreliable because of the influence of Congress
on foreign policy.(24) On a visit to the United States, the
Prime Minister of Singapore toasted President Ford with the
thought that "no better service can be done to the non-Communist
governments the world over than to restore confidence that the
American government can and will act swiftly in tandem between
the Administration and Congress."(25) There have also been numerous reports that European leaders were troubled by divisions and
stalemates on the American domestic front.(26) A senior European
official deplored the fact that, in dealing with the United
States, "it isn't just the State Department or President any-
more. It's Congress now."(27) And in 1979 British Ambassador
Peter Jay asked Frank Church: "Senator, do you think it's time
for all of us to establish our embassies up on the Hill instead
of going indirectly through the State Department?"(28)

Even the Supreme Court has turned a deaf ear to Congress' reassertion of its constitutional prerogatives. During the Korean
War, Justice Robert Jackson observed that no "decision by this
Court can keep power in the hands of Congress if it is not wise
and timely in meeting its problems."(29) Echoing that philosophy, the Court recently rejected a suit brought by Barry Goldwater and others to block President Carter's decision to terminate the mutual security treaty with Taiwan. Speaking for the
majority, Justice William Rehnquist dismissed the suit as a political question. In a concurring opinion, Justice Lewis Powell
pointed out that Congress itself had made no legislative attempt
to join the issue with the President. "If Congress chooses not
to confront the President," Powell chided, "it is not our task to
do so."(30)

Congress. The most important factor in constraining presidential power, as Justices Jackson and Powell pointed out, is
Congress. Congress' future role in the foreign policy process,
therefore, depends on its attitudes and actions. At present,
Congress still generally favors an active role, and, as always,
presidential attempts to act unilaterally or "usurp" power tweak
the institution's ego. There was predictable grumbling about
steamroller tactics in the aftermath of the AWACS vote by a few
vanquished senators. In the face of Reagan's requests to ease
restrictions on military sales in other areas, Foreign Affairs
Committee Chairman Clement Zablocki declared, "I don't think
Congress will abdicate its rightful authority and responsibilities." His committee colleague, Stephen Solarz, also condemned
the president's proposals as a "frontal assault on the whole
fabric of congressionally adopted restraints on foreign policy
prerogatives of the executive."(31)

Despite such resolute statements, however, there are also a
growing number of voices in Congress expressing doubt about the
ability of Congress to achieve or exercise foreign policy "codetermination." Others question the wisdom of such a process

change, even if possible. William Fulbright's philosophical full
circle makes an interesting case in point. In 1954, referring to
the SEATO Treaty, Fulbright told his colleagues that he would not
support restrictions to the very same pact which, a decade later,
Lyndon Johnson would use to justify the war in Vietnam. "We can
only rely on our good sense," Fulbright ironically counseled,
"not to elect Presidents who are so unwise or arbitrary or uncivilized as to exercise arbitrary power."(32) By the mid-sixties, Fulbright had swung 180 degrees. In a speech before the
American Society of Newspaper Editors that could well have been
entitled, "Inefficiency in the Defense of Liberty is no Vice,"
Fulbright declared himself "not distressed by the charge that
Congress is not an up-to-date institution. In this age of the
SST, the ABM, the MIRV, and the Indochina War, being behind the
times is a mark of wisdom."(33) By the end of the decade, however, Fulbright was reevaluating once again and, despite his
protests to the contrary, completed a constitutional circum-
navigation. Calling his erstwhile brethren a "herd," the Senator
accused Congress of going "in the wrong direction, carping and
meddling in the service of special interests, but scarcely asserting itself through reflective deliberations on issues of national
interest."(34)

Other legislative leaders, both liberal and conservative,
have also had second thoughts. Hubert Humphrey wrote to former
CIA Director Richard Helms in 1976 that he was worried by the
"determined effort to undermine the power and the influence of
the presidency." Despite "some abuse" of power, Humphrey still
believed that "America needs a strong presidency . . . that has
the . . . authority to conduct the business of government."(35)
To Dean Rusk, Humphrey worried about the "awful toll" of Vietnam
and Watergate and about what "we Democrats are doing to the
office of the Presidency"(36)

On the conservative side, Barry Goldwater recently condemned
the War Powers Resolution as an "ill-advised attempt to limit"
the President and pronounced that office "the supreme architect
of American foreign policy" to which "the Congress plays a subordinate, supporting role."(37) Senate Armed Services Committee
Chairman John Tower has seconded that thought. He pictured the
pendulum as having "swung dangerously to the legislative side
. . ." "If the balance is not soon restored," Tower predicted,
"American foreign policy will not be able to meet the challenges
of the 1980s." The War Powers Resolution received particular
approbation as "the most potentially dangerous of the 1970s
legislation."(38)

Even supporters of the War Powers Resolution lost much of
their fervor. Clifford Case remembered having voted for it only
because of his affection for Senator Javits, and Frank Church
professed to have never really understood the measure.(39) Even
Javits, who considered his leadership in enacting the resolution
as one of the peaks of his career, gave way to frustration and
despair over Congress' ability to contribute responsibly to foreign policy. When the Senate failed in 1977 to join the President in extending the life of SALT I, Javits lamented:

> I have been in the Senate 21 years, and I have spent all
> that time trying to bring Congress into a real partnership
> with the President on foreign policy . . . Why have we not
> been successful? Precisely for this kind of performance It
> is unbelievable that 100 responsible men cannot do something
> on time, and it discredits us completely when we say we
> should be full partners in a foreign relations effort.(40)

In the aftermath of turmoil in Iran, Afghanistan, and Poland,
and faced with a new arms race with the Soviet Union, Congress'
attitudinal metamorphosis has continued its evolution in the late
Carter and early Reagan years. Regarding the President's request
for more discretional power, a House Foreign Affairs Committee
aide typically commented, "The general feeling is that the president is justified in asking for more flexibility."(41) Soon
after the Republican controlled Senate met in 1981, Democrat Paul
Tsongas pronounced the body not one "the White House will have to
worry about." "We don't have the votes to block anything now,"
Tsongas admitted.(42)


## Will Congress Put Up or . . . ?

It is tautological but true that the real test of influence
is in the actual determination of policy. Congress has certainly
enacted a variety of legislation designed to curb the Imperial
Presidency. U.S. policy in Turkey and Angola and on issues such
as human rights and arms limitations has certainly been influenced by Congress. These instances do not, however represent a
new era in the foreign policy process. Rather, they represent a
brief surge of activity based on traditional motivational factors
that have briefly enhanced Congress' influence but have not
changed the fundamentally executive-dominant character of the
process.

The War Powers Resolution in Practice. One important test
of Congress' ability to co-determine policy, or even come close,
is its role during international crises. The post-1945 era of
recurring crises, supersonic speed, and unfathomable destructive
power has been a key determinant of Congress' inferiority complex. Congress has not overcome its self-doubt. The bravely
passed War Powers Resolution has not proven an effective tool.
The question here is not whether that statute is constitutional,
although some scholars have expressed doubt.(43) Instead, the
issue is whether Congress will attempt to enforce its own mandate and, if necessary, confront the president.

In the years since passage of the War Powers Resolution,
presidents have unilaterally utilized the military on a number of
occasions which at least carried the potential of combat. Gerald
Ford dispatched the military to rescue American and friendly
foreign civilians from Danang, Phnom Penh and Saigon in April
1975. In 1976 he again used military forces to extract American
nationals from Lebanon. Jimmy Carter authorized Air Force planes
to carry French and Belgian troops to Zaire in May 1978, and in

June the Air Force flew Moroccan troops to Zaire. It can be argued, though, that the goal of the military in these instances was to avoid combat and, thus, they were only tangential tests of Congress' resolve.

The 1975 _Mayaguez_ incident leaves no such ambiguity. It is clear that executive-legislative relations during that crisis conformed to the normal pattern. Congress was, at best, informed rather than consulted by the President as required in the War Powers Resolution. Further, Congress displayed its traditional tendency to rally around the flag, to defer to and applaud the president, and to focus on the immediate conflict rather than on long range constitutional questions.

There is little doubt that time for consultation existed in May 1975. After the Executive learned of Cambodia's seizure of the merchantman _SS Mayaguez_, almost two and one-half days elapsed before Ford ordered the military into action. During the interim, he met four times with the National Security Council. The White House also informed numerous legislators of the situation and of its intention to use force to free the vessel's crew. Executive officials contended that these communications with Congress met the consultation requirement.(44) Monroe Leigh, Legal Advisor to the Department of State, later testified that "the congressional leadership was informed of the principal military operations prior to the commencement of those operations," and, further, "the congressional leadership did have an opportunity to express its views concerning the impending military operations.(45)

Congressional leaders viewed the situation quite differently. First, they contended that Congress was told what was going to be done, rather than asked what ought to be done. Senate Majority Leader Mansfield flatly asserted, "I was not consulted. I was notified after the fact about what the administration had already decided to do." House Speaker O'Neill, Senate President Pro Tempore Eastland, ranking Foreign Relations Committee member Case, and House Minority Leader Rhodes also did not consider themselves consulted--only informed.(46) During a post-mortem, War Powers Resolution progenitor Jacob Javits complained that "to a disturbing extent, consultation with Congress prior to the _Mayaguez_ incident resembled the old, discredited practice of informing selected members of Congress a few hours in advance of the implementation of decisions already taken within the Executive Branch."(47)

It is also clear that in the face of unilateral action which violated the spirit, if not the letter, of the War Powers Resolution, Congress did nothing to assert itself. To the contrary, the Foreign Relations Committee unanimously passed a resolution supporting President Ford. Scores of legislators hurried to add their individual endorsements. Senator Case, who had also been a sponsor of the War Powers Resolution, termed the move "justified" and a "police action," and Representative Morris Udall, an active opponent of the Vietnam involvement, pronounced himself "compelled to state . . . support for the limited military action taken by the President."(48) A few dissented. Senators Gaylord Nelson and Thomas Eagleton expressed concern over the lack of consultation, and George McGovern labeled the action "a spasm conducted by officials who want to prove their toughness."(49) Their voices were a tiny minority, however, and a strong tide of legislative and public opinion congratulated Ford and America. It was a clear victory for presidential power. The War Powers Resolution existed only in theory, not in practice.

The more recent attempt by President Carter to rescue American hostages in Iran is another case in point. Time for consultation was, again, clearly available--the raid was months in the planning. Also, the pro forma notification of Congress during the Mayaguez affair, which could at least be billed as "consultation," was totally absent. Congress was not informed until after the abortive attempt. Further and ironically, only hours before the action Senators Church and Javits dispatched a letter to Secretary of State Vance invoking the War Powers Resolution and demanding that, if any military action was taken in Iran, it be "a national decision entered into by the President and Congress." "Accordingly," the letter continued, "we hereby request that you inform the committee at an early date when consultation can begin."(50) That point had passed; military forces were already on the way to Iran.

Despite all of this, and even the raid's fiery failure, Carter's unilateral action met with only the mildest dissent. Senate Minority Leader Baker's "only criticism of the President" was that "he did not do this long ago."(51) What procedural criticism that did occur wilted under the rally around the flag syndrome, a spirited Administration defense of its prerogatives, and some careful presidential massaging of bruised congressional egos. Representative Zablocki, for instance, initially labeled the President as "stupid" for failing to consult with Congress. After an Oval Office meeting, however, Zablocki admitted, "No one criticized him for the actions taken," and candidly added, "He needs our support. If everything went in order without a hitch, we would all be applauding."(52)

## Statutory Reform--Shadow or Substance?

Veteran White House and Capitol Hill observer Bryce Harlow once pointed out that no statutory reform can supplant the need for congressional assertiveness.(53) The reaction of Congress to the Mayaguez and Iran actions attests to the wisdom of that observation. In the immediate aftermath of the War and in the very area of conflict that had spawned the War Powers Resolution, President Ford circumvented the statute with barely a dissenting murmur. Five years later, President Carter, who had earlier supported the principle of the resolution, ignored a specific congressional request for consultation and again received bouquets rather than brickbats.

The Legislative Veto in Practice. Those two events were the most dramatic examples of Congress' unwillingness to confront the president in order to enforce the restrictions it had enacted. Other examples certainly exist. Congress' utilization of restrictions on arms sales to influence policy in that area has been limited. The compromise achieved by Congress in 1978 that forbade the sale of advanced air-to-air missiles, bomb racks, and range enhancing fuel tanks to Saudi Arabia for its F-15's was overturned as part of the AWACS sale only three years later. And, of course, President Reagan's victory on the AWACS came in the face of ferocious counter-pressure by interest groups and against strongly negative opinion in both the House and Senate. The Senate wanted to be Israel's friend, but lacked the confidence and will power to insist on its view.

Other arms control measures have been equally limited in their effect. In 1975 Congress enacted a requirement that the Executive submit an Arms Control Impact Statement (ACIS) along with budget requests. The resulting ACIS reports have been so vague that the Congressional Research Service found that, "from the viewpoint of their completeness and analytical quality, it is difficult to understand how Congress could rely on them . . ." (54)

The 1978 Nuclear Non-Proliferation Act has also proven of limited effectiveness. That act forbade the export of nuclear fuel to countries which refuse to open their facilities to international inspection. It allows the president to waive the ban, but also includes a two-house legislative veto. The first test of the act came in 1980 over the sale of nuclear fuel to India. President Carter decided to sell thirty-eight tons of uranium to India, despite that country's refusal to allow international inspection. At first Carter suffered a series of setbacks. The Nuclear Regulatory Commission, the House of Representatives, and the Senate Foreign Relations Committee all went on record against the sale.

The issue then rested on the decision of the full Senate. The vote was close, 48-46, but in the end, the Senate balked at nay-saying the President. Part of that reluctance was based on what Senator Glenn described as "some of the heaviest lobbying I have ever seen."(55) A more important factor was Congress' traditional deference to executive authority. In the fall of 1980, détente with the Soviets rapidly faded in the aftermath of Afghanistan and in the face of turbulence in the Indian Ocean-Persian Gulf region, the revolution and hostage seizure in Iran, the Iran-Iraq war, and the rumors of Soviet activity, including troop movements in the area. In that tense, if not crisis, atmosphere, the Senate was not about to deny the country's Commander-in-Chief. "Do we want to dim the lights of Bombay and let the Russians turn them back on?" asked Charles Percy. "Is not the President entitled to the benefit of the doubt?" Frank Church asked his colleagues.(56) The answer, the majority concurred, was that, indeed, the President should be supported, whatever their reservations.

Early in the Reagan Administration, the spirit of non-proliferation continued to be eroded. The Administration succeeded in getting the Senate to repeal language in another act which forbade economic or military aid to any nation suspected of developing nuclear weapons. The Senate agreed to waive that restriction in the case of Pakistan, despite the near certainty that the

Pakistanis were developing a nuclear capability to match India's. Again, the long-term goal of avoiding nuclear weapons proliferation was swept aside by a perceived Soviet threat to Pakistan and the President's demand for flexibility in the face of the enemy. (57)

## The Record In Perspective

It is also important to remember that, in addition to those issues in which Congress has played some role, there have also been a wide variety of foreign policy initiatives taken by the Executive with either little reference to or dissent from Congress. The steady normalization of relations with China, Carter's alarm over—then his acceptance of—the Soviet brigade in Cuba, the reactions to Soviet intervention in Afghanistan and potential intervention in Poland, the Persian Gulf doctrine, Reagan's pledge to not allow "another Iran" in Saudi Arabia, and a variety of other actions and stances have all been accomplished unilaterally by the more powerful, foreign policy half of the two presidencies.

Analysis of the 1970s thus indicates that the distance of the pendulum's swing was less dramatic than was sometimes supposed. Congress was more active, but it was neither anywhere near dominant nor was its level of influence radically different than it was _ante_ _bellum_ _et_ _aqua_ _porta_. Further, the increased activity that has occurred has been an extension of the existing pattern of values, means, and scope. Rather than change, Congress' activism reflects the intensification and confluence of a number of factors (institutional ego, executive weakness, lack of consensus) which have long promoted enhanced legislative influence. But, foreign policy has continued to be basically devised and implemented by the Executive. For every legislative initiative (say Angola), several can be fielded in which the Executive acted alone (China), or in which Congress deferred, not even utilizing the "reform" powers it had itself enacted (_Mayaguez_, AWACS). The pendulum, then, while moving, did not swing as dramatically as some have imagined, nor did it ever approach passing into the legislative quadrant. It has remained firmly in the Executive's.

## Tomorrow and Tomorrow

Having considered both the recent and more distant past, a final, less certain, task is to gauge the future relationship of the Executive and Congress.

Recent events and current attitudes are persuasive that legislative influence will ebb from its minor high-water mark of the 1970s. A number of factors, some new, some renewed, and some continued, account for this. They include deference, organization, electoral politics, executive strength, and foreign policy opinion.

Deference: The reaction of Congress to pleas for support of the president on a number of recent decisions, including AWACS and non-proliferation, speak for themselves. So do the accolades accorded the president in the aftermath of the Mayaguez and Iran raids. The interlocking factors of congressional self-doubt in the supersonic nuclear age, the normal prestige of the president as head of state as well as head of government, and the "rally around the flag" and "politics should stop at the water's edge" values remain strong inhibitors of any significant, long-term congressional challenge to executive power in foreign policy.

The "wisdom" of Congress on Vietnam, the period of détente with the Soviet Union, normalization of relations with China, and the quasi-isolationist bent of opinion in the 1970s all muted congressional deference somewhat. The increase of tensions in the last Carter and first Reagan presidential years, however, has made Congress hesitant once again. The country faces increased Soviet-American hostility, energy dependency, the symbolic "window-of-vulnerability," increasing European independence from both superpowers, the shifting role of China, the Middle East quandary, leftist tendencies in South and Central America, and a host of other problems. It also seems that marked tension will continue in the foreseeable future. In that atmosphere, Congress will be reluctant to challenge the president and will be vulnerable to patriotic appeals to mute its views in the interest of unity during times of danger.

Organization. Congress' ability to organizationally deal with foreign policy has and continues to be an important internal determinant of its level of influence. Staff, leadership, and structure are the relevant sub-categories.

Staff - More But Still Not Enough. Increases in staff have been cited by a number of recent studies as enhancing legislative influence in the foreign policy process. (58) The basic idea is that increased staff breaks down the Executive's "cult of expertise." Staff is important to the legislative process.(59) The increse in staff levels of the foreign and defense subject matter committees during the 1970s, and the influence of individual staff members on policy questions(60) and more technical matters has been demonstrated.(61)

There are other factors, however, which tend to mitigate the impact of expanded staffs. The growth of staff has not created an infrastructure capable of rivaling the Executive's dominance of foreign policy information. The approximately two dozen staff members that the Senate and House Armed Services Committees each had in 1977 left them fourteenth of fifteen and thirteenth of twenty, respectively, among permanent committees in their chambers.(62) The Senate Foreign Relations Committee only had one person assigned to strategic arms control at that time. In contrast, the Defense Department had 333 people assigned to legislative liaison alone and thousands assigned to substantive matters. (63) The Foreign Affairs Committee, by the mid-seventies, had a staff of thirty-six, only half of whom were professionals. That left its staff tenth in size among House committees.(64)

The staff of the Foreign Relations Committee has grown to over fifty, but its impact has been limited by its fragmentation. Traditionally, the committee's staff was non-partisan and unitary. A number of changes, however, have split the staff between parties, allowed subcommittees to control their own staffs, and allowed members to include a personal staff member in the committee's work. The result is what one former staff director has termed "the Balkanization of the Committee."(65) Another observer has drawn a picture of "a staff of over 50 persons, in considerable disarray, split among four buildings and six locations, making communication difficult and devolution of responsibility awkward at best." His conclusion: "The role and stature of the CFR staff have been substantially diminished."(66) Thus, increases in the number of staff members, and even in the expertise of the staff in general, cannot be viewed as significant per se. The relative size of the staff and the scope of Congress' other informational resources vis-à-vis the Executive Branch is more the issue. And despite some improvements, a tremendous gap continues to exist. Further, the atomization of the staff of the Foreign Relations Committee leaves that body less able to muster and concentrate its resources than in the days of Carl Marcy's or Pat Holt's directorships.

A number of recent studies have also pointed to the increased outside expertise available to Congress. Others have noted that people are becoming more aware of interdependence and world impact on their domestic circumstances.(67) A variety of non-government organizations, ranging from educational groups to narrow interest groups, have also become increasingly active in foreign affairs.(68) This has led to an increase in the number of contacts and the level of expertise by groups and individuals bringing information to Congress through both formal and informal channels.(69) Such sources certainly add to Congress' ability to analyze foreign policy, but their existence is not new, even if their level of activity has increased. These private efforts are also not a totally positive factor. Congress is more subject than the Executive to interest groups, and the combination of the increase in perceived legislative influence and the increase of interest group activity on "intermestic" affairs has caused concern. Chairman Clement Zablocki, for example, has said, "Congress is too responsive to the lobbies of . . . special interests . . . to be able to take the lead in foreign policy-making without endangering the national interest."(70) Thus, non-governmental sources may be bringing more information, but there is some doubt as to the quality of that information or the desirability of intensive interest lobbying in the realm of foreign policy and the national interest.

Lack of Organization. Even if the staff and other informational resources were sufficient to fill the expertise gap, there is doubt about the ability of Congress to exercise the leadership needed to utilize the information it obtains. Observers generally agree that power in Congress has become highly fragmented in the last decade. Power has devolved from the committee to the

subcommittee level.  The old norms of apprenticeship and speciali-
zation have also decayed, particularly in the Senate.  These
changes have been partly responsible for the increase of legislative activity.  Operating from subcommittee bases and no longer
inhibited from speaking out on subjects outside their assigned
committee areas, more members have sought their places in the
political sun through foreign policy activity.  The further fragmentation of Congress has also compounded the turf battles that
have long scattered the substance of foreign policy widely
throughout the committee, and now subcommittee, substructure.
Finally, a number of troubles have beset the Foreign Affairs and
Relations Committees, leaving them unlikely to galvanize and lead
an alternatively balky and unbridled Congress.

A number of scholars and practitioners have written pieces
suggesting how Congress could consolidate and wisely exercise its
foreign policy power.  A common element found in nearly all these
studies has been a stress on the need to organize effectively.
(71)  Whatever the theoretical utility of such advice, the fact
is that Congress has not followed it.  In terms of leadership,
the limited role of the chambers' leaders or committee chairmen
has created a vacuum at the top.  To recall Dean Rusk's analogy,
there are no whales and many minnows in the current legislative
sea.  Whether it fitted neatly with democratic theory or not, the
likes of Vandenberg, Taft, Rayburn, Connally, George, and Johnson
could confidently speak for Congress.  The O'Neils, Bakers,
Byrds, Pells, and Percys of today have not yet demonstrated such
ability.  Congress may have become more democratic, but it has
also become more unmanageable and undirected.

Congress has also done little to consolidate oversight of
foreign policy.  Indeed, turf wars are endemic and raids common,
with the most recent feudal combat occurring between the Senate
Foreign Relations and Armed Services Committees over control of
military aid.(72)  Foreign trade is under the Ways and Means and
Finance Committees.  International monetary policy oversight is
shared with the Banking and Currency Committees.  Refugee issues
are handled by Judiciary in the Senate.  CIA operations come
under the Select Committee on Intelligence.  The Committees on
Agriculture, Commerce, Science and Technology, Armed Services,
Merchant Marine and Fisheries, and Government Operations, not to
mention the overarching Appropriations and Budget Committees, are
all active on foreign policy questions.  Further, the organizational fragmentation of Congress has meant that most of those
committees have, to some degree, divided into autonomous subcommittees.(73)

Finally, the traditional foci of foreign policy coordination
and leadership in Congress, the Foreign Relations and Foreign
Affairs Committees, have lost much of their prestige and effectiveness.  The attractiveness of the Foreign Affairs Committee as
an assignment has declined,(74) the committee has become highly
factionalized,(75) and attempts to substantially expand its
authority have been largely frustrated.

On the Senate side, the normally high-flying Foreign Relations Committee has also plummeted from its accustomed lofty
status.  Analysts attribute the decline in the committee's influ-

ence to several factors. One of these, ironically, was the
committee's own lead in the revolt against presidential dominance. This spurred wide-spread congressional activity which the
committee could not control. "The committee has been a victim of
its own successes," one observer commented.(76) The committee
has also been hurt by the increase in partisanship, culminating
with the split of the staff into majority and minority segments
in 1979.

The new Republican Chairman, Percy, is trying to restore
bipartisanship. The staff split has remained, but Percy re-
assigned some former Democratic appointees to the Republican
staff and hired Edward Sanders, previously with the Carter OMB,
as staff director. How successful Percy will be remains to be
seen. The committee contains a number of members from either
wing, including conservative Jesse Helmes and liberal Paul
Tsongas. The attitude of the Reagan Administration may also
inhibit bipartisanship. Reagan did appoint a few Democrats,
including United Nations Ambassador Jean Kirkpatrick, to foreign
policy posts, but the Administration's attitude toward bipartisanship has been cautious. When one official was asked whether the
Reagan Administration sought bipartisanship, he calculated that
"it depends on what you have to give up to get bipartisan support."(77)

Another factor in the Foreign Relations Committee's decline
was the laissez faire attitude of John Sparkman who chaired
the committee between Fulbright's 1974 primary defeat and his own
retirement in 1979. "There was a feeling that the committee fell
on hard times," a Senate aide recalled.(78) Under Sparkman, the
central direction that Fulbright had exercised declined. Subcommittees were strengthened and members were allowed to hire their
own staffs. Sparkman also did not believe in confronting the
president and, as one State Department official put it, "The
committee isn't significant in foreign policy--won't be seen as
such--unless there is a major issue to contest with the executive
branch."(79) Sparkman was followed as chairman by Frank Church
in 1979. But with only two years in that position, Church's
impact was marginal.

Senator Percy has given mixed signals in the early going. He
was, at first, generally perceived as in more of the Sparkman
than Fulbright mold. Administration figures were critical of his
reluctance to force action on nominees, despite Jesse Helms'
opposition. "There's a feeling we just can't rely on Chuck
Percy," a White House aide was quoted a saying. In the Senate,
Percy was similarly criticized as unassertive and, ironically,
chided for being too much the President's man. The Committee
swallowed the obviously uninformed William Clark as Deputy Secretary of State and acceded to many Reagan requests to ease restrictions on discretional presidential authority. Percy himself was
quoted as making statements such as "Who could support the President more than I have?"(80)

Before long, though, Percy tacked toward the independence he
needed to be the Senate's man and a strong chairman. He opposed
the nomination of Ernest Lefever, for example. "The Percy you
see today is different . . ." said Paul Tsongas. "He's a much

stronger person. He's carving out his independence from the Administration."(81) There is also some evidence that Percy's desire for an independent, bipartisan role may be shared by at least some of the committee's other members. Claiborne Pell, the ranking minority member, feels "the old system worked better," and would "like to see the committee play the same role as it did during the Vietnam era when . . . we played a major role in the country." Whether that will be is uncertain, but for the moment, as one foreign policy expert put it, the committee "is really a proverbial shadow of its former self."(82) Without its leadership, and in the absence of any other source of legislative leadership, Congress will be hard put to vie with the rejuvenated presidency that is emerging.

Executive Strength. The 1970s was a unique period in American political history. In rapid succession, we saw 1) the first de facto removal of a president from office, 2) the first president to come into office with no national constituency, and 3) a sort of "anti-pope" president, who was elected because of his disdain for and separation from the very political people and processes he needed to work with and master in order to govern effectively. Jimmy Carter told the nation, at one point, that there was a malaise loose in the land. He was correct, but the ennui emanated from the White House as much as any other source.

Whether one agrees with Ronald Reagan's programs or not, it would be difficult to dispute the general observation that he has revitalized strong executive leadership in the White House. In part, Reagan has been able to accomplish this because he has been tilling fertile ground. Both political elites and the mass continued to believe through the 1970s that the president was better suited than Congress to run foreign policy.(83) It is also generally acknowledged that the 1980 presidential election turned, in part, on the perceived weakness of Carter as a national and international leader. Concern with the "imperial presidency" has declined, and there has been a concomitant rise in expectation of presidential leadership by the media, academia, the public, the Executive, and even Congress. Reagan, then, has not forced firm executive direction on a resisting polity. Rather, he has moved with encouragement and applause and would have been roundly condemned had he vacilated.

Credit is also due to Reagan individually. Despite considerable bureaucratic bickering among members of his supporting cast, the President has maintained a high level of public confidence. His strong victory on the 1980 budget battle reflected strength and ability, and his snatch of AWACS from the jaws of Senate defeat both demonstrated and enhanced his political power. An exclamative Time cover, "AWACS: He Does It Again!" succinctly told the story.(84) If Reagan continues with anything like the firmness, assurance, and success he has managed in his first year, and does so without the excesses and hauteur that once imperialized and discredited the office, then it is likely that the pendulum will continue on its presidential swing. One of the primary causes of congressional activism on foreign policy, executive weakness, will have dissipated.

The Electoral Connection. David Mayhew has written convincingly of the electoral connection as a key motivator of Congress.(85)   That factor has been important through the nearly four decades covered in this study.  It has played two roles.  It has mostly resulted in parochialism.  Members concentrated on district-oriented issues likely to enhance their career prospects.  With elections normally dependent on domestic issues, members tended to leave the field of foreign policy to the Executive.

Countering that tendency were shorter term forces.  Individual members became active on foreign policy when it suited their particular needs.  The presidential "bug" motivated some.  Re-election activated others, such as Tunney in 1976.  Further, when public opinion did become foreign policy intensive, Congress responded.  Vietnam is the prime example.  In the Vietnam era, approximately forty percent of the public identified foreign affairs as the most important issue facing the country.(86)  The short-term activation of specific opinion groups, such as those centered around economic or ethnic issues, also activated Congress.

The future will see a continuation of this pattern.  In general terms, electoral considerations will enhance presidential power.  First, there is the basic public perception of the president as the rightful leader in foreign policy.  This normally makes it a losing issue on which to differ with the president. It is a factor which is multiplied many fold in times of tension and crisis.  Second, public concern with foreign policy plummeted after the U.S. withdrawal from Vietnam.  A forty percent identification of that area as a primary concern in early 1973 fell to ten percent in 1974 and remained basically in that range during the duration of the 1970s.  With a surge of concern over energy supplies and Soviet intentions, that figure increased in 1980-81, and has leveled off at a modest fifteen to twenty percent interest.(87)  Thus, foreign policy is no longer a prime factor in the electoral equation and will not normally appeal as an issue to careerist members of Congress.

Third, the defeat of Foreign Relations Chairman Frank Church in 1980 tends to give continued support to the feeling in Congress that foreign policy leadership is not only not career enhancing, but, indeed, dangerous to political fortunes. Church's name has been added to those of Connally, George, Fulbright, and others as proof of the theory.  The 1980 defeats of three other Foreign Relations Committee members (Jacob Javits, George McGovern, and Richard Stone) also gave credence to the story.

Electoral politics will continue to motivate members with presidential ambitions and on those issues which activate constituency-important support groups.  Overall, however, barring another Vietnam-level issue, foreign policy concerns will be perceived by members as a minor, even negative, factor on their electoral fortunes.  They will likely devote their energies to more fruitful issue areas.

Consensus.  The level of consensus on broad foreign policy

parameters has played an important role in the level of congressional activity. In the immediate post-World War II period, with the country searching for new direction and standards, Congress played a significant role in the origins of the cold war, anti-communist, containment consensus. That national accord lasted into the Vietnam period. The breakdown of the consensus in the 1970s and the neo-isolationist mood of the mass, and even some elites, helped spur renewed legislative participation in the policy process. Some have predicted that consensus would not be achieved in the near future, thus increasing the likelihood of continued congressional activism.(88)

It is still too early to be fully confident, but it may be that a new secular self-interest may be emerging to replace the semi-religious dogma of anti-communism. The Soviet Union will remain the chief villain, but in a more pragmatic, power politics guise. The American mood has turned more bellicose, favoring renewed emphasis on military strength and protection of world areas considered vital to the United States' economic and political well-being.(89) Surveys in the 1980-81 period found more than half of all Americans favoring increased military spending. Three-quarters favor defending Europe, and a majority would defend Japan, Pakistan, Israel, and other allies. Almost half would even favor defending China if it were attacked by the Soviet Union. All these figures represent major shifts of opinion since the mid-1970s.(90)

Concern with vital energy supplies has also militarized public opinion. Carter's "Persian Gulf doctrine" and Reagan's casual announcement that Saudi Arabia would be defended were met with hardly a murmur of dissent. Indeed, in 1981 seventy-five percent of respondents favored the defense of Persian Gulf oil supplies if threatened by the Soviets.(91)

Whether this interest-oriented consensus will have the staying power of anti-communism remains to be seen. In the short-run, however, it has achieved its purpose and, along with its attendant tension, plays into the hands of strengthened presidential leadership.


## Reciprocal Interest and Influence

Presidential influence is again on the rise from its modest and short-term retreat of the seventies. That is both normal and is likely to remain so. In drawing toward a synopsis of Congress in the foreign policy process, a series of short summary points can be made, based on the findings of this book.

A Tale of Two Theories. In the past, discussion of the role of Congress and the Executive in the foreign policy process has grouped around two symbolic standards. One was Wildavsky's Theory of Two Presidencies. According to this view, the modern Executive's power in the realm of foreign policy is so great, especially when compared to domestic policy, that, in effect, two presidencies exist. A competing conceptualization is based on Edwin Corwin's characterization of the Constitution as an "invitation to struggle" between the Congress and Executive over control of foreign policy. Adherents of that view have, at times, adopted the pendulum analogy to trace the movements of the median locus of power as first one then the other branch gained an advantage.(92)

This study leads to the conclusion that Wildavsky is essentially correct, but that the theory can be enhanced by a good measure of Corwinian struggle. The locus of power has remained in the Executive sphere since 1945. In terms of both constitutional and statutory power and informal authority, the president and his executive cast have dominated. Congress has played a secondary, but still important, role. The exact measure of the respective influence of the two branches has, however, varied within the confines of presidential primacy. In terms of stages or cycles, at least three can be identified. The Truman years were marked by significantly increased congressional activity. So were the seventies. Institutional ego, executive weakness, and lack of consensus were pronounced motivational factors in both periods. Partisan factors also played a major part in the late forties and early fifties. The middle period, the years of Eisenhower, Kennedy, Johnson, and Nixon's first term, saw a more quiescent Congress.

Congress did not control the first and third periods, however. Nor did the Executive hold unchallenged sway in the second. The Executive was in control, albeit less firmly so, in the earliest and most recent period. Congress, on the other hand, while more consensually compliant in the middle period, continued to exercise important, though more sporadic, influence.

Finally, yet another period seems to be in the offing in the eighties. The executive is reasserting itself. Congress' institutional ego has been assuaged. A tentative consensus on self-interested tension is emerging. These factors presage a return to an executive-legislative influence interrelationship akin to the fifties and sixties. The exact characteristics are as yet undetermined, but the presidential phoenix is again on ascendent wing.

A Multi-Dimensional Struggle: One way to picture the struggle for influence is as a two-dimensional struggle between Congress and the Executive. Both institutions are jealous of their prerogatives and defend them, apart from substantive issues. Also, the two branches operate from differing perspectives and motivations. In a recent and excellent study of foreign economic policy, Robert Pastor found that "in many of the policies analyzed . . . Congress and the Executive approached issues as coherent, unitary organizations with decided preferences and predispositions in each issue."(93)

Even more often, influence is a multi-dimensional phenomenon. Shifting coalitions and factions occur within Congress, within the Executive, and between various elements of the two branches. An element of executive strength is unity, and that is often absent. American intervention in Indochina in 1954, for example, was not blocked by Congress as such. Rather, it was stopped by a majority of the relevant legislative actors allied with such executive actors as the President and Army Chief-of-Staff in opposition to the Vice President, Secretary of State, the Chairman of the Joint Chiefs of Staff, and a minority congressional element, including the Senate Majority Leader.

Thus, the foreign policy process at times resembles conventional combat with the clearly defined congressional and executive sides arrayed against one another. In these instances, Pastor observes, "U.S. foreign policy, though theoretically . . . aimed abroad, will sometimes be pointed at the other end of Pennsylvania Avenue."(94) At other times, guerilla warfare, or even a free-for-all, seems a more apt analogy. There may be sides, but each has agents and elements of support in the other's camp. Both the bane and fascination of political analysis is that it is seldom neat.

Initiative or Impotence? Some earlier studies which gauged congressional influence in terms of initiative resulted in distortion.(95) It is certainly true that whoever initiates action or legislation also occupies the high ground. It is also surely the case that the Executive has by far the greater ability to take the initiative and to define situations. Both of these abilities are important elements in executive foreign policy strength. In most cases Congress' influence is reactive, but in that mode lies considerable potential. Often, in fact, Congress' influence does not have to be formally activated. Rather, it operates through Carl Friederich's rule of "anticipated reactions," with the Executive reacting to head off potential legislative criticism or statutory action. As Alton Frye aptly put it," The congressional impact on policy is more often indirect than direct, informal than formal, marginal than fundamental. Nevertheless, on complex issues of foreign policy the margins are frequently the vital edges, and Congress' ability to shape them is . . . real power." (96)


## Reciprocal Influence

A final task here is to return to where we started, to the theoretical influence base proposed by Lasswell and Kaplan. To review that in the briefest fashion, influence is dependent on "values." If you are valued by another or can affect something or someone valued by another, then you have influence. Therefore, where there is mutual influence, as in foreign policy, it is necessary to identify the values held by the two actors, Congress and the Executive, which can be affected. A second important factor is the Lasswell and Kaplan concept of "means" of influence. Means are the specific methods by which one actor affects the values of another actor and thus influences behavior. "Scope" is a third aspect of the Lasswell and Kaplan theory. Scope refers to the types of issues or policies in which actors' values are involved and which, therefore, stimulate the actor to utilize means to influence that policy.

Two other quick points should be made. First, influence is negative as well as positive. When Congress or the President is persuaded not to act or to stop acting, that is as valid an example of influence as initiating action. Second, the foreign policy process exhibits reciprocal influence. Thus, both Congress' influence on the Executive and the Executive's influence on Congress are relevant.

## The Rule of Congressional Deference--Values and Means

**Congressional Values:** Congressional values are those factors which deter Congress from asserting itself on foreign policy or which can be affected by the Executive in order to gain cooperation.

Parochialism. Congress values its electorally-motivated district orientation and is normally willing to leave foreign policy-making to the Executive. With most members concerned with reelection and with foreign policy usually a minor part of the electoral equation, congressmen generally find few benefits in specializing in foreign policy. Indeed, the fate of a number of highly placed foreign affairs specialists in the House and Senate demonstrate that a reputation as a foreign policy expert is more of a liability than a help when compaigning in the hustings.

Legitimacy. Another key cause of legislative diffidence is the widespread belief in Congress that the Executive legitimately occupies a preeminent place in the foreign policy process. Increasing the traditional lead of the Executive, the rapid and explosive nature of modern international politics have left Congress "mesmerized," according to Arthur Schlesinger, Jr., and with what John Manley has called an "inferiority complex."(97)
Even foreign policy leaders in Congress such as Arthur Vandenberg viewed the president as having "exclusive priorities in international relations."(98) The recent debate on the AWACS shows that Congress still remains persuaded that the President should lead and Congress should follow.

Consensus. Congress values consensus just as the Executive does. The normal emphasis on bipartisanship, rhetorical restraint at the "water's edge," and not "pulling the rug" out from under the president has been a strong and constant theme. Hubert Humphrey's comment at one point that "we gave the President authority that we are by no means agreed we want to do, and we did it all in the name of national unity," is typical.(99)
That urge toward consensus is strongest in time of tension. As William Fulbright noted, a "legislature which does not hesitate to defeat or override the executive on domestic legislation . . . . reverts to a kind of tribal loyalty when war is involved." (100)

Party Loyalty. The United States does not have anything like the party regularity found in a parliamentary system, yet party affiliation is an important index of congressional be-

havior. The president's partisan pull on members of his party in
Congress is based on similarity of views, by electoral interest,
and by pure party pride. Studies cited earlier showing partisan
orientations toward Republican and Democratic Secretaries of
State and patterns of party voting on foreign aid clearly demonstrate the existence of this value.

**Executive Means:**    Congress' normal disinclination to challenge
executive authority in foreign policy is part-
ly based on its values. It is also partially
a function of a variety of executive means.
The means directly or tangentially interact
with congressional values.

Invocation of Office. This method interfaces with the congressional values of executive legitimacy and unity in foreign
policy-making. When the president invokes the superior information and expertise of the Executive, and, in particular, when he
takes a symbolic stand as Commander-in-Chief, he will almost
certainly prevail over all but the most recalcitrant representative.

Ego Appeals. On a personal level, the president may flat-
ter members of Congress by a variety of techniques that play off
of the values of individual and institutional ego. The president, is, after all, the president, and personal calls, visits to
the Oval Office, first name intimacy, and even trading in pens,
cuff links, and other presidential paraphernalia have a powerful
ego massaging effect. The responsiveness of Arthur Vandenberg
and Everett Dirksen to such ministrations are classic examples.
Reagan's care and attention to Congress, both in general and
toward individuals on specific issues, is also an apt illustration of the benefits that accrue from the care and feeding of
congressional egos.

Political Support. The president can also sway members by
means which benefit their valued political self-interest. Patronage, favorable publicity, support for district-oriented projects,
and promises to support or not oppose a member's reelection have
all been repeatedly seen. Negative sanctions are rarer, but also
possible. Ordinarily this does not occur on a quid pro quo
basis, but direct trades do occur. The White House's hands-off
policy toward Arthur Vandenberg and Nixon's machinations against
Charles Goodell are good examples.

Partisan Appeal. A closely related means is presidential
appeal to the value of party loyalty. Eisenhower's repeated
remonstrations to Republicans that supporting him was not only to
be expected from good party members, but also vital to party prosperity is a case in point. A president must act with caution
though. Congressional bipartisanship and party loyalty represent
potentially competing values, and when a president appeals to
party loyalty, he risks making the issue a partisan cause and
diminishing his support on the other side of the aisle. It is a

high wire act which Eisenhower managed with great dexterity,
although not total success.

## The Exception of Congressional Activism--Scope, Means and Values

Executive dominance is clearly the rule in the foreign policy
process. Congressional activity is the exception, but hardly a
rare or insignificant occurrence. Just as the norm of deference
is based on an interacting pattern of congressional values and
executive means, legislative influence is similarly based on the
interface of a series of congressional and executive values and
congressional means in areas which tend to spark congressional
interest.

Scope:   The concept of scope reflects congressional values ex-
         pressed as policy typologies or issue-areas, which tend
         to activate that institution. The essential question
         is, what sub-set of issues within foreign policy motiv-
         ates Congress to contest executive dominance?

Domestic Resources. Issues involving domestic resources
activate Congress. The involvement of domestic resources is a
widely recognized basis of issue-area distinction. Inasmuch as
domestic economic factors are involved in many foreign policy
questions, a key factor is often a definitional struggle, with
the Executive gaining power if the question is perceived as a
foreign policy issue and losing power if it is seen as largely
domestic in nature.
Bearing out the principle in practice, legislative attitudes
toward the British Loan and Marshall Plan were initially negative, based, in part, on domestic economic considerations. But
they were reversed when the perceptual focus shifted to the international communist threat. Similarly, foreign aid is often
debated in terms of the domestic budget, its deficits, and priorities. Trade studies have also found the definitional question to
be important. In terms of the future, one of the strongest arguments for those seeing greater, long term legislative involvement
is the merging of domestic and international affairs to an "intermestic" unity.(101) That phenomenon certainly has a degree of
objective merit, but the real issue will continue to be definitional. It may be, however, that the definitional struggle will
be waged more often and that it will be resolved as a domestic
economic issue subject to legislative influence.

Innovative Policy. Another useful typological dichotomy
distinguishes innovative and incremental policies. The two most
pronounced periods of congressional activities, the late forties
and the seventies, both coincided with, and, indeed, were spurred
by, major reorientations of foreign policy. Congress helped
originate and then break down the cold war consensus. In the
fifties and sixties the existence of the anti-communist consensus
found Congress in agreement with the broad outline of American
policy and willing to allow the Executive to determine tactics

and incremental policy changes.

Subcultural Groups. Policy which stimulataes domestic sub-cultural groups is another which tends to motivate congressional activity. The Polish-Vandenberg connection in the forties, the Greek connection on Cyprus policy in the seventies, and the impact of the American-Jewish community on Mid East policy throughout the entire period are all excellent examples. Other illustrations involving Irish and Italian ethnic groups and even some evidence of racially motivated interest have also been identified.

Electoral Considerations. Issues involving electoral advan-tage also activate Congress. The parochial orientation of Congress tends to deter foreign policy interest, but, at times, the reverse is true. Both on individual and institutional levels, partisan concerns can motivate activity. On the general level, the Republicans' desire to drive Truman from office sig-nificantly added to their criticisms of Administation policy in the forties and early fifties. Truman was able to overcome opposition from the 80th Congress by playing on crisis and Vanden-berg's deep bipartisan beliefs. But in the fifties, with Vanden-berg gone, the Republicans turned the anti-communist hysteria around and effectively used it to capture both Congress and the White House. Policies that involve domestic economic and sub-cultural interest groups, as noted, also stimulate Congress as part of the electoral equation.

Even if these forces do not cause widespread interest, they may cause intense activity by some members whose districts and constituents are directly affected. Individual members are also activated by more general electoral concerns. John Tunney's attempt to use Angola to defuse his diletante image is one exam-ple.

Finally, individual members may be motivated by the strains of "Hail to the Chief." Henry Jackson's pursuit of the presiden-cy by posing as a friend of Soviet Jewry is by no means a unique example.

Institutional Pride. Issues involving institutional status activate Congress. Members of Congress value their individual and the institution's image. When they feel personally or collec-tively slighted, they react to reassert themselves. The question is one of form rather than substance.

Part of the "cycle" or observation that Congress is active in immediate post-war periods is based on the institution's image. War leaves Congress especially deferential, and it reacts once the crisis has passed to reestablish its "rightful" place. The events of the late forties illustrate this. So does the post-Vietnam period, when legislators were embarrassed by their seem-ing impotency to stop an unpopular war. In this vein, the War Powers Resolution and other such actions are better understood as symbols of Congress' status than as important to actual practice.

Failure to consult also causes a negative reaction in Con-gress. Acheson learned that was often the key to Vandenberg, and numerous other examples were noted throughout the period. In recent years, President Carter's liaison failures and the early difficulties of the Saudi AWACS deal in Congress continued to demonstrate the danger of denigrating Congress or leaving it to find the news in the Times and Post.

Executive Weakness: Issues that occur during times of executive weakness, or which cause executive division, activate Congress. The variety of advantages which the Executive has over Congress tends to be subverted by weakness in that branch. The congressional active periods in the late forties and seventies were both marked by general weakness in the presidency. Truman is now remembered as a strong president, but he was not perceived that way at the time. The shadow of Roosevelt and Truman's admitted inexperience saddled his first term with a caretaker image. After that, his professional and popular image improved somewhat, but he always remained the "little man from Missouri."

The unique combination of events and circumstances in the seventies again brought presidents and the presidency to a low point, and the resulting power vacuum temporarily enhanced legislative influence.

Another aspect of executive weakness is internal unity. Dissension in executive ranks helps break down the informational and expertise advantages enjoyed by that branch. As the military's reluctance to support SALT II shows, if the president cannot keep his house in order, it is more difficult to persuade Congress to follow his lead.

**Congressional Means**: On those issues on which Congress does assert itself, it possesses a formidable array of means. Many are formal, including appropriations, ratification, confirmation, and general statutory power. These may be applied directly or indirectly. Others means are informal and include investigation and criticism.

Formal Means. In theory, Congress' constitutional powers are impressive. Through the power of the purse, in particular, Congress could virtually seize control of foreign policy if it so chose. The history in the preceding chapters, though, demonstrates that the application of those powers was sporadic, at best. When statutory authority was needed or desired, Congress enacted the essential elements of the Executive's program.

One should not dismiss Congress' constitutional powers too lightly, however. They form a potential for action that has repeatedly seen the Executive amending its program or rationale in order to avoid or defuse opposition. Congress did not end the Vietnam War, but its power to do so and the growing probability that, in fact, it would do just that, helped hurry Nixon and Kissinger down the road to peace.

The actual use of Congress' constitutional authority also occurred often enough to keep the Executive mindful of its presence. Nominees were defeated or withdrawn in frustration. So

were treaties. Foreign aid was subjected to an annual pummel-
ling, and trade legislation underwent considerable metamorphosis
in Congress. The scoreboard may have counted the president's
initiative as "passed" by Congress, but the legislative stamp was
often strongly imprinted on the final form.

Informal Means. Congress also possesses the power to
generate information, debate, and dissent. Whatever one's view
of the activity, it is clear that the hearings held by Joseph
McCarthy in the fifties and William Fulbright in the Vietnam era
had an important impact on public opinion and foreign policy.
Dissent does not even have to occur within the formal confines of
Congress. The body serves as a status-conferring platform for
dissent. The Republican congressional clamor against Kennedy's
Cuban policy helped spur him to action and politically limited
his options. The emphasis that Eisenhower and Dulles put on
obtaining supporting resolutions and Johnson's morning reading of
the Congressional Record as well as his seeking the Tonkin Gulf
Resolution are also examples of the sensitivity about real or
potential congressional dissent.

**Executive Values:** The final pieces in the pattern of inter-
branch influence are the Executive's values.
They involve those desired conditions which
are subject to congressional modification and
which, therefore, make the Executive responsive to Congress.

Consensus. There can be little doubt that the Executive
values consensus. In Roger Hilsman's estimate, there is always a
"politician in a president" who "has as a need at times to postpone a decision until there is time to build consensus."(102) A
bit more tersely, Theodore Sorenson applied an old maxim, saying
that "in the White House, as elsewhere, the squeaky wheel gets
the grease."(103)

The message of Hilsman, Sorenson and others is that presidents desire congressional support of foreign policy whether
Congress can have a formal legislative impact or not. Congress
is perceived as part of the public opinion-building process,
partly echoing and partly determining that opinion. In either
case, the Executive takes heed. Presidents also believe that
domestic dissent will detract from their strength in diplomatic
negotiations.

Finally, one suspects that domestic acrimony takes away from
the president's self-image of national leader. It is hard to
imagine oneself the heroic leader of the pack when your own kind
are baying at your heels. Whether in direct or anticipatory
reaction, presidents have repeatedly modified, delayed, and, on
occasion, even abandoned preferred courses of action in the face
of real or potential criticism.

Examples of executive consensus-seeking were strongly evident
throughout the period. From Dean Acheson's hopeful recollection
of the barroom sign that pleaded, "Please Don't Shoot the Piano
Player," to the castigation Richard Nixon and Henry Kissinger

have leveled at Congress for its "aid and comfort" of the North Vietnamese enemy, the Franklinesque message of hanging together rather than separately has been clear.

Sanction Avoidance. A second cluster of Executive values centers on the desire to avoid legislative defeat, or in gaining victory, avoid risking later retaliation on other parts of the executive program. Neustadt's concept of professional reputation is a key here.(104) Washington politics is a mosaic. Defeats weaken and victories strengthen subsequent presidential power. Presidents also believe that domestic defeats will embarrass and weaken them abroad.

Where the president is committed to a goal, there is little evidence that the risk of defeat will deter him. AWACS is a good example. But where there is doubt, congressional opposition is often the decisive factor. Loan programs to the Soviet Union were dropped in the immediate post World War II period, in part, because of real or anticipated legislative difficulties. The loan to Egypt for the Aswan Dam suffered a similar fate. The 1960s Multilateral Force and the naval force proposal in the 1967 Arab-Israeli War are yet other examples. The continued status of the Genocide Convention in limbo and the withdrawal of the SALT II Treaty from the Senate serve as even more recent instances.

The "carom effect" can also come into play. Truman was forced to continue aid to the Nationalist Chinese in order to gain funds for Europe. There is also substantial evidence that in the 1960s the Kennedy and Johnson Administrations were inhibited from moving toward normalizing relations with Communist China and allowing its seating in the United Nations. Congress could not have directly blocked those actions. Nevertheless, the threat of McCarthyistic attacks on the foreign policy establishment, possible retaliation against the foreign aid program, or even a congressional-led drive for American withdrawal from the United Nations, effectively deterred any movement to regularize diplomatic relations.

Thus, because the Executive values its professional reputation and because it values its program and wishes to protect it from retaliation, it will at times amend, defer, or even delete preferred options. This is most likely to occur on issues of marginal importance to the Executive's program or on issues where there is ambivalence or division within the Executive.

# Notes

## Introduction

1. Harold D. Lasswell and Abraham Kaplan, Power and Society: A Framework for Political Inquiry (New Haven, Connecticut: Yale University Press, 1950), pp. 55-73, 86-102.

## Chapter 1

1. Vandenberg Diary, 5/13/45, Vandenberg Mss.

2. Aiken Oral History (Truman).

3. Lippmann to McCloy and reply, 11/14/45 and 11/18/45, Box 87, file 1393, Lippmann Mss.

4. Russell to Byrnes, 9/16/46, Byrnes Mss.

5. Joseph M. Jones, The Fifteen Weeks (February 21 - June 5, 1947) (New York: Viking Press, 1955), p. 89.

6. Vandenberg Diary, 5/13/45, Vandenberg Mss.

7. Arthur H. Vandenberg, Jr., ed. The Private Papers of Senator Vandenberg (Boston: Houghton Mifflin, 1952), pp. 224-225.

8. Ibid., p. 225.

9. For contrast see Representative John Taber, Chairman, House Appropriations Committee to Horace W. Whipple, 9/19/46, and Taber to M.L. Ross, 2/10/48, Taber Mss.

10. Alfred Steinberg, The Man From Missouri: The Life and Times of Harry S Truman (New York: G. P. Putnam's Sons, 1962), p. 79; Jonathan Daniels, The Man from Independence (Philadelphia: J. B. Lippencott, 1950), pp. 259-308; and Dean Acheson, Present at the Creation: My Years at the State Department (New York: W. W. Norton, 1969), p. 136.

11. Harry S. Truman. Year of Decisions (Garden City, New York: Doubleday, 1955), p. 546. For a contrasting view of the relationship, see Jerome L. Rodnitskly, "Two Men on a Horse: President Truman and Secretary of State Byrnes," International Review of History and Political Science, 7(1970), pp. 61-75.

12. William Hillman, Mr. President (New York: Farrar, Strauss, and Young, 1952), p. 122.

13. Truman, Year of Decisions, p. 97.

14. Harry S. Truman. Years of Trial and Hope (Garden City, New York: Doubleday, 1956), p. 101; Harold Smith Diary, 4/25/45, Smith Mss.

15. Forrestal Diary, 8/15/47, Forrestal Mss.

16. Truman, Years of Trial and Hope, p. 102.

17. Vandenberg to Dulles, 7/2/48, Vandenberg Mss. For a study of the continuing isolationist impulse in Congress see Justus D. Doenecke, The Old Isolationists in the Cold War Era (Lewisburg, Pennsylvania: Bucknell University Press, 1979), Chapter 3-9, pp. 55-188.

18. Byrnes to W. D. Sporberg, 1/5/46, Byrnes Mss.

19. Charles E. Bohlen, Witness to History, 1929-1969 (New York: W. W. Norton, 1973), p. 177.

20. Acheson, Present at the Creation, p. 97.

21. Memoranda of conversations between Dulles and Cohen, 10/15/45, and Dulles and Byrnes, 11/18/45, Dulles Mss.

22. Byrnes to Will Rogers, Jr., 10/26/46, Byrnes Mss. Also, see Marshall to Davies, 2/19/47, OF20(1947), Truman Mss.

23. Vandenberg to Hannegan, 10/28/46, Vandenberg Mss. Hannegan sent Vandenberg's letter to Byrnes, 11/1/46, Byrnes Mss.

24. Vorys is quoted in Susan Hartmann, Truman and the 80th Congress (Columbia, Missouri: University of Missouri Press, 1971), p. 9. On this theme, see Athan Theoharis, "The Rhetoric of Politics in the Truman Era, 1945-50," in Politics and Policies of the Truman Administration ed. by Barton J. Bernstein (Chicago: Quadrangle Books, 1970), p. 204. For contemporary concern, see memorandum of conversation between Forrestal and Representative John Lodge, Forrestal Diary, 6/28/47, Forrestal Mss.

25. Harold Smith Diary, 5/21/45 and 5/2/46, Smith Mss. Also, see Truman to Senator Estes Keafauver, 2/2/46, OF 419-C, Truman

Mss.

26. Forrestal Diary, 11/16/46, Forrestal Mss.

27. Hartmann, _Truman_, p. 16.

28. For Vandenberg's metamorphosis and his pre 1946 role see David Tompkins, _Senator Arthur H. Vandenberg: The Evolution of a Modern Republican, 1884-1945_ (Ann Arbor, Michigan: Michigan State University Press, 1970).

29. _E.g._, Senator Charles Tobey, Sr. to his son Charles, Jr., 7/20/45, Box 40, Tobey Mss.

30. Taber to Louis H. Folmer, 11/25/46, Taber Mss.

31. Dean Acheson, _Sketches From Life of Men I Have Known_ (New York: Harper & Row, 1956), p. 126; Acheson, _Present at the Creation_, p. 223.

32. Vandenberg to Eleanor Roosevelt, 1/9/47, Vandenberg Mss.

33. For a recent view of the significance of Vandenberg's role see, Daryl J. Hudson, "Vandenberg Reconsidered," _Diplomatic History_, 1(1977), pp. 46-63.

34. Louis L. Gerson, _The Hyphenate in Recent American History_ (Lawrence, Kansas: University of Kansas Press, 1964), p. 115; John L. Gaddis, _The United States and the Origins of the Cold War, 1941-1947_ (New York: Columbia University Press, 1972), p. 169.

35. Vandenberg to Frank Januszewski, 7/27/46, Vandenberg Mss. Emphasis in the original.

36. Memorandum of meeting between Truman and his advisors, 4/23/45, _FR_:1945, V, p. 255. The _FR_ designation refers to the title, year of coverage, and volume of the State Department's annual _Foreign Relations_ series. For a further discussion see Daniel Yergen, _Shuttered Peace: The Origins of the Cold War and the National Security State_ (Boston: Houghton Mifflin, 1977), pp. 69-86.

37. Extract from Stettinius Diary, 15-23 April 1945, _FR_:1945, I, p. 293.

38. Memorandum of conversation between Truman and his advisors, 4/20/45, _FR_:1945, V, Eden, and Molotov, 4/23/45, _ibid._, pp. 252-55. Gaddis, _Cold War_, pp. 198-206.

39. George C. Herring, Jr., "Lend-Lease to Russia and the Origins of the Cold War, 1944-1945," _The Journal of American History_, 61(1969), pp. 99-104.

40. George C. Herring, Jr. Aid to Russia, 1941-1946: Strategy, Diplomacy, and the Origins of the Cold War (New York: Columbia University Press, 1973), pp. 187-92; Gaddis, Cold War, pp. 194-97.

41. Stettinius to Harriman, 3/16/45, FR:1945, V, p. 988.

42. Harriman to Stettenius, 3/20/45, ibid.

43. Grew and Crowley to Roosevelt, 3/23/45, ibid., p. 991.

44. Truman, Year of Decisions, p. 98.

45. Herring, Aid to Russia, pp. 187-90, 203.

46. Truman, Year of Decisions, p. 98.

47. Representatives Robert Chippenfield, John Vorys, Karl Mundt, Bartel Jonkman, and Lawrence Smith to Truman, 5/31/45, and Truman's reply, 6/15/45, Box 13, Vorys Mss.

48. Grew to Harriman, 6/23/45, FR:1945, V, p. 1026.

49. Byrnes to John G. Winant, Ambassador to Great Britain, 8/19/45, ibid., p. 102.

50. Daniels, Man of Independence, p, 269; Minutes, 5th plenary meeting at Potsdam, 7/21/45, FR: Potsdam, II, p. 206; William D. Lahey, I Was There (New York: McGraw-Hill, 1950), p. 467.

51. Memorandum of conversation between Truman and Forrestal, 7/28/45, Forrestal Mss.

52. Truman, Year of Decisions, p. 227-29.

53. Acheson, Present at the Creation, p. 122.

54. Truman Diary, 7/17/45, quoted in Robert Farrell, Off the Record: The Private Papers of Harry S Truman (New York: Harper & Row, 1980), p. 53.

55. John Morton Blum, ed., The Price of Vision: The Diary of Henry A. Wallace, 1942-1946 (Boston: Houghton Mifflin, 1973), p. 490.

56. Lisle A. Rose, After Yalta (New York: Charles Scribner's Sons, 1973), p. 142.

57. Truman to Acheson, 3/15/57, quoted in Farrell, Off the Record, p. 348.

58. Davies Journal, 10/9/45, Box 22, Davies Mss.; Gaddis, Cold War, pp. 163-67, 275.

59. Memorandum of conversation between Byrnes and Molotov, 9/19/45, FR:1945, II, p. 243.

60. McCardle Oral History (Dulles), p. 17; John Foster Dulles, War and Peace (New York: MacMillan, 1957), p. 127.

61. Gaddis, Cold War, p. 290.

62. Patricia Dawson Ward, The Threat of Peace: James F. Byrnes and the Council of Ministers, 1945-1946 (Kent, Ohio: Kent State University Press, 1979), pp. 5, 173.

63. Truman Diary, 7/7/45, quoted in Farrell, Off the Record, p. 49.

64. Dulles, War and Peace, p. 127.

65. Vandenberg Diary, 5/11/46, Vandenberg Mss.

66. Vandenberg, Jr., Private Papers, p. 225.

67. Gaddis, Cold War, p. 292, n. 14.

68. Dulles memorandum, 8/23/45, CFM 1945-1950, Dulles Mss.

69. Forrestal Diary, 1/29/46, Forrestal Mss.

70. Dulles to Ferdinand H. Mayer, 10/15/45, Supplement, Council of Foreign Ministers, 1945-1950, Dulles Mss.

71. Memorandum of conversation between Dulles and Cohen, 10/15/45, Dulles Mss.

72. Memorandum of conversation between Dulles and Byrnes, 11/18/45, Dulles Mss.

73. Vandenberg, Jr., Private Papers, p. 237; Vandenberg to John W. Blodgett, 12/24/45, Vandenberg Mss.

74. Ward, The Threat of Peace, p. 49.

75. Gaddis, Cold War, p. 276.

76. Memorandum of conversation between Byrnes and Stalin, 12/23/45, FR:1945, II, pp. 752-56.

77. Kennan Diary, 12/19/45, quoted in George F. Kennan, Memoirs, 1925-1950 (Boston: Little, Brown, 1967) p. 287.

78. The Capehart and Martin quotations are from Gaddis, Cold War, p. 291.

79. Vandenberg to Luce, 5/28/46, Vandenberg Mss. For a discussion of the widening split between Truman and Byrnes see

Robert L. Messer, James F. Byrnes, Roosevelt, Truman, and the Origins of the Cold War (Chapel Hill, North Carolina: The University of North Carolina Press, 1982).

80. Byrnes Diary, 3/25/46, Box 23, Davies Mss.; Vandenberg to Dulles, 1/19/46, Dulles Mss., and Vandenberg to Senator Brien McMahon, 1/2/46, Vandenberg Mss.

81. Gaddis, Cold War, p. 294.

82. Eleanor Roosevelt to Bernard Baruch, 1/16/46, Selected Correspondence, Baruch Mss.

83. Stettinius calender notes, 3/1/46, quoted in Gaddis, Cold War, p. 294.

84. During early 1946 there was considerable tension between the United States and the Soviet Union over the latter's delay in ending its wartime occupation of northern Iran.

85. Byrnes' address can be found in The Department of State Bulletin, 14(3/10/46), pp. 355-58.

86. Vandenberg's address is in the Congressional Record, 2/27/46, 79th Cong., 2nd sess., XCII, pp. 1692-95.

87. Vandenberg to Hamilton Fish Armstrong, 4/2/46, Vandenberg Mss.

88. Gaddis, Cold War, p. 305.

89. Ibid., p. 306.

90. Byrnes to Senator Joseph Ball, 7/22/46, Byrnes Mss.

91. Vandenberg to Dulles, 4/15/46, Dulles Mss.

92. Tom Connally with Alfred Steinberg, My Name is Tom Connally (New York: Thomas Y. Crowell, 1954), p. 299.

93. Vandenberg Diary, 5/8/46 and 5/11/46, Vandenberg Mss.

94. Vandenberg to J. W. Blodgett, 8/23/46, to Hamilton Fish Armstrong, 4/2/46, and to Henry Luce, 5/28/46, all in Vandenberg Mss.

95. Vandenberg to Byrnes, 5/21/46, Vandenberg Mss.

## Chapter 2

1. Acheson to Mary Acheson Bundy, 7/19/45, quoted in Dean Acheson, Present at the Creation: My Years in the State Department (New York: W. W. Norton, 1969), p. 109.

2. Harry S. Truman, Year of Decisions (Garden City, New York: Doubleday, 1955), p. 272.

3. John Lewis Gaddis, The United States and the Origins of the Cold War, 1941-1947 (New York: Columbia University Press, 1972), pp. 28-30, 165; Archibald MacLeish to Acheson, 2/7/45, Box 1, MacLeish Mss.

4. Speech text can be found in the New York Times, 1/11/45, p. 16.

5. Arthur H. Vandenberg, Jr., ed., The Private Papers of Senator Vandenberg (Boston: Houghton Mifflin, 1952), p. 139.

6. Memorandum of conversation between Pasvolsky and Vandenberg, 3/20/45, Box 12, Pasvolsky Mss.; Vandenberg Diary, 3/20/45, Vandenberg Mss.

7. Vandenberg to Januszewski, 3/7/45, Vandenberg Mss.

8. Vandenberg, Jr., Private Papers, p. 155; Vandenberg to Warren Austin, 3/45, and Austin's reply 3/21/45, Box 24, Austin Mss.

9. Stettinius to Roosevelt, 3/16/45, FR:1945, VI, p. 125.

10. Vandenberg to Rt. Rev. Adalbert B. Zadala, President of the Council of American Priests of Polish Descent, 3/24/45, Vandenberg Mss.

11. Vandenberg Diary, 4/17/45, Vandenberg Mss.

12. Extract from Stettinius Diary, 15-23 April 1945, p. 293, and Minutes of 10th delegation meeting, 4/16/45, pp. 296-301, both in FR:1945, I. Also, Vandenberg Diary, 4/16/45 and 5/2/45, Vandenberg Mss.

13. Memorandum of conversation between Pasvolsky and Hull, 5/10/45, Box 4, Pasvolsky Mss.

14. Vandenberg Diary, 4/27/45 and 5/9/45, Vandenberg Mss.

15. Several articles, New York Times, 5/10/45-5/12/45.

16. Warren Austin to Harrison J. Conant, 5/16/45, Gen. Csp., Austin Mss.

17. Pasvolsky memorandum, 6/9/45, Box 1, Pasvolsky Mss; Vandenberg Diary, 6/6/45-6/8/45, Vandenberg Mss.

18. Vandenberg Diary, 3/23/45, 4/2/45, and 4/3/45, Vandenberg Mss.; Minutes of delegation meeting, 3/30/45, p. 170, and Stettinius to Roosevelt, 4/2/45, p. 180, both in FR:1945, I. Ironically, on Byrnes' advice, Roosevelt initially asked

adversely to the Soviets having three to the United State'
one. See, Charles E. Bohlen, Witness to History: 1929-1969
(New York: W. W. Norton, 1973), p. 195.

19. Durward V. Sandifer, "Regional Aspects of the Dumbarton Oaks
Proposals," Department of State Bulletin, 12 (1/28/45),
pp. 145-47.

20. Report of Nelson Rockefeller to the Senate Foreign Relations
Committee, Sen. 79A-F10, Tray 142, Conference of American
Foreign Ministers file, National Archives; David Green, "The
Cold War Comes to Latin America," in Politics and Policies
of the Truman Administration ed. by Barton J. Bernstein
(Chicago: Quadrangle Books, 1970), pp. 225-32.

21. Archibald MacLeish to Connally, 1/26/45, Sen 79A-F10, Tray
143, Inter-American Conference on Problems of War and Peace
file, National Archives; Stettinius to Grew, 3/1/45, pp. 132-
35, and 3/4/45, p. 139, both in FR:1945, IX.

22. Stettinius to Connally, 3/16/45, Sen 79A-F10, Tray 143,
Inter-American Conference on Problems of War and Peace file,
National Archives; Vandenberg to Austin, 3/45, Austin Mss.;
Vandenberg Diary, 5/7/45, Vandenberg Mss.; David Green, The
Containment of Latin America: A History of the Myths and
Realities of the Good Neighbor Policy (Chicago: Quadrangle
Books, 1971), pp. 225-32.

23. Vandenberg to Stettinius, 5/5/45, Vandenberg Mss.

24. Vandenberg Diary, May 5, 7, 9, 13, and 15, 1945, Vandenberg
Mss.; Green, "Latin America," p. 162.

25. Memorandum of conversation between Stettinius and Eden,
5/12/45, FR:1945, I, p. 698.

26. Vandenberg Diary, 5/13/45, Vandenberg Mss.

27. Ruth B. Russell, The United Nations and United States
Security Policy (Washington, D.C.: Brookings Institution,
1968), p. 571; Green, Containment of Latin America, p. 230.

28. Vandenberg Diary, 6/23/45, Vandenberg Mss.

29. Ibid., 4/30/45.

30. Green, Containment of Latin America, p. 253; Memorandum of
conversation between Acheson and Brazilian Chargé, 10/1/45.
FR:1945, IX, p. 160; Acheson, Present at the Creation, p.
188. Green notes that Assistant Secretary of State Adolf
Berle told him that the firing of Rockefeller was a public
relations move which did not reflect Administration policy
toward Argentina, Green, "Latin America," p. 192.

31. Green, Containment of Latin America, pp. 170-72; Vandenberg to Byrnes, 8/3/45, Vandenberg Mss.

32. Acheson, Present at the Creation, p. 189; Spruille Braden, Diplomats and Demagogues, (New Rochelle, New York: Arlington House, 1971), p. 358.

33. Vandenberg to Dulles, 7/2/48, Dulles Mss.

34. Marshall to Lovett, 8/6/47, FR: 1947, III, p. 35.

35. Memorandum of conversation between Marshall and Juan A. Bramuglia, Argentine Foreign Minister, 8/20/47, ibid., pp. 42-44.

36. Vandenberg to Dulles, 7/3/45, Dulles Mss.; Green, "Latin America," pp. 171, 193.

37. Minutes of meeting of the Secretary's Staff Committee, 7/24/45 and 7/25/45, Byrnes Mss.

38. Acheson to Mary Acheson Bundy, 7/28/45 in Acheson, Present at the Creation, p. 102.

39. Acheson to Mary Acheson Bundy, 7/19/45, ibid.

40. Margaret Truman, Harry S Truman (New York: William Morrow, 1973), p. 258.

41. Stimson to Truman, 9/11/45, FR:1945, II, pp. 40-44; Stimson Diary, 9/4/45, Stimson Mss.

42. Stimson Diary 9/12/45, 9/13/45, Stimson Mss.; Acheson, Present at the Creation, p. 14; Richard E. Hewlett and Oscar E. Anderson, A History of the United States Atomic Energy Commission, Vol. I, The New World, 1939/1946 (University Park, Pennsylvania: Pennsylvania State University Press, 1962), p. 419. Barton J. Bernstein feels Truman was only seeming to agree with Stimson because of the President's respect for the very senior and retiring Secretary of War. See Bernstein's "The Quest for Security: American Foreign Policy and International Control of Atomic Energy, 1942-1946," Journal of American History, 60(1974), p. 1017.

43. Acheson, Present at the Creation, pp. 123, 125.

44. Forrestal Diary, 9/21/45, Forrestal Mss.

45. H. D. Smith Diary, 10/5/45, Smith Mss.; Vandenberg to Representative Joseph W. Martin, 9/10/45, Vandenberg Mss.; Acheson, Present at the Creation, pp. 123-27; Hewlett and Anderson, New York, pp. 424-27.

46. Acheson to Truman, 9/25/45, FR:1945, II, pp. 48-50.

47. Acheson, Present at the Creation, p. 125.

48. Gaddis, Gold War, p. 267; Acheson, Present at the Creation, p. 125; Walter Millis and E. S. Duffield, The Forrestal Diaries (New York: Viking Press, 1951), p. 102. Byrnes had originally been opposed to atomic sharing, but then had shifted to supporting Stimson's way of thinking. See the Stimson Diary, 9/21/45, Stimson Mss.

49. Bush to Stimson, 9/23/45, Box 109, Bush Mss.

50. Hewlett and Anderson, New World, p. 469.

51. Gaddis, Cold War, p. 272.

52. Vandenberg, Jr., Private Papers, p. 227; Gaddis, Cold War, p. 278; Hewlett and Anderson, New World, p. 474.

53. Forrestal to Byrnes, 12/11/45, Box 2, Forrestal Mss.

54. Hewlett and Anderson, New World, p. 473.

55. Acheson, Present at the Creation, p. 135.

56. Vandenberg, Jr., Private Papers, p. 229. Emphasis is Vandenberg's (Sr.).

57. Tom Connally with Alfred Steinberg, My Name is Tom Connally (New York: Thomas Y. Crowell, 1954, p. 290; Truman, Year of Decisions, p. 549.

58. Acheson to Byrnes, 9/12/45 and Byrnes' reply, 12/17/45, FR:1945, II, pp. 609-10.

59. Acheson, Present at the Creation, p. 135.

60. Harry S. Truman, Years of Trial and Hope (Garden City, New York: Doubleday, 1956), pp. 7-10.

61. Memorandum, "Notes on Bernard Baruch," dated 1949, Box 58, Baruch Mss.; Hewlett and Anderson, New World, p. 556.

62. Byrnes to Baruch, 4/19/46, Box 58, Baruch Mss.

63. Baruch to Vandenberg, 7/30/47, Box 77, Baruch Mss.; Gaddis, Cold War, p. 334.

64. Harriman to Stettinius, 1/4/45 and 1/6/45, FR:1945, V, pp. 942-47; Gaddis, Cold War, p. 190; Herring, Aid to Russia, p. 148.

65. Memoranda by Collado, 1/4/45 and 1/7/45, FR:1945, V, pp. 398-40, 956-58.

321

66. Grew to Harriman, 1/26/45, ibid., p. 967. Thomas G. Paterson discounts the impact of Congress and public opinion in his Soviet-American Confrontation: Postwar Reconstruction and the Origins of the Cold War (Baltimore: The Johns Hopkins University Press, 1973), p. 42.

67. Harriman to Stettinius, 4/11/45, FR:1945, V, pp. 994-96.

68. Collado to Stettinius and Clayton, 4/19/45, ibid., p. 997. Gaddis, Cold War, p. 22 implies the political conditions to which Collado was referring were international. This author takes them to be domestic.

69. Memorandum of conversation between Truman and Molotov, 4/23/45, FR:1945, V, pp. 256-58.

70. H. D. Smith Diary, 5/21/45, Smith Mss.; Herring, Aid to Russia, p. 242.

71. Grew to Harriman, 6/2/45, FR:1945, V, p. 1011.

72. Harriman to Stettinius, 1/4/45, p. 945 and 3/20/45, p. 988, and Kennan to Stettinius, 5/18/45, p. 841, all in FR:1945, V.

73. Vinson's testimony is in U.S., Congress, Senate, Committee on Banking and Currency, Anglo-American Financial Agreement, Hearings, 79th Cong., 2nd sess. (1946), p. 68.

74. Baruch to Byrnes, 2/34/46, Box 68, Baruch Mss.; Herring, Aid to Russia, p. 253. Paterson, Soviet American Confrontation, p. 49 argues the Americans were stalling.

75. Kennan to Byrnes, 9/15/45, pp. 881-84, and 9/18/45, p. 1039, FR:1945, V.

76. Gaddis, Cold War, pp. 259-62.

77. Vandenberg to Dulles, 12/19/45, Dulles Mss.

78. Clayton to Harriman, 11/30/45, 13:1945, V, p. 1048.

79. Byrnes to Soviet Chargé, 2/21/46, p. 828 and 4/18/46, pp. 834-37, and Soviet Chargé to Byrnes, 3/15/46, p. 829 and 5/17/46, p. 841, all in FR:1946, VI.

80. Ibid., p. 839.

81. Memorandum from George Luthringer to Clayton, 7/23/46, ibid., p. 842; Richard M. Freeland, The Truman Doctrine and the Origins of McCarthyism: Foreign Policy Domestic Politics, and Internal Security, 1946-1948 (New York: Alfred A. Knopf, 1972), p. 69; Herring, Aid to Russia, pp. 257-66; Paterson, Soviet-American Confrontation, p. 53. Truman

indicated to Wallace as late as December 18, 1946 that he was ready to ask Congress for a loan to the U.S.S.R. Truman was being naive or insincere. See John Morton Blum, ed., The Price of Vision: The Diary of Henry A. Wallace, 1942-1946 Boston: Houghton Mifflin, 1973), p. 612.

82. Memorandum of conversation between Elbridge Durbrow, Chief, Division of East European Affairs and Polish Vice Premier Stanislaw Mikolajczyk, 11/8/45, FR:1946, VI, pp. 400-04; Lane to Marshall, 2/3/47, FR:1947, IV, p. 415; Memorandum of conversation between Llewellyn Thompson, Chief, Division of East European Affairs, and Polish Ambassador Jozef Winniewicz, 4/3/47, ibid., p. 423.

83. Memoranda from Acheson to Truman 5/1/46 and 5/27/46, OF 423, Truman Mss.

84. Smith to Austin, 2/6/47, Box 46, Austin Mss.

85. Byrnes to Representative Clarence Cannon and Senator Kenneth McKeller, 10/30/45, p. 1035, and UNRRA Director Herbert Lehman to McKeller, 11/1145, FR:1945, II.

86. LaGuardia to Byrnes, 78/13/46, Byrnes Mss.

87. Ibid.

88. Acheson, Present at the Creation, p, 201. Truman believed that Soviet intransigence was partly due to Congress' attitude on UNRRA. See, Forrestal Diary, 12/16/46, Forrestal Mss.

89. Memorandum of conversation between Byrnes and French Foreign Minister Georges Bidault, 8/23/45, FR:1945, IV, p. 711.

90. Freeland, Truman Doctrine, p. 69.

91. Joseph M. Jones, The Fifteen Weeks (February 21 - June 5, 1947) (New York: Viking Press, 1955), p. 96.

92. Gaddis, Cold War, p. 18; Jones, Fifteen Weeks, p. 94; Thomas G. Paterson, "The Quest for International Peace and Prosperity: International Trade, Communism and the Marshall Plan,: in Politics ed. by Bernstein, p. 83. H. Bradford Westerfield, Foreign Policy and Party Politics: Pearl Harbor to Korea (New Haven, Connecticut: Yale University Press, 1955), p. 58; Susan M. Hartmann, Truman and the 80th Congress (Columbia, Missouri: The University of Missouri Press, 1971), pp. 50, 179.

93. Grew to Winant, 3/5/45, FR:1945, VI, p. 26; Memorandum of Informal Discussions on Commercial and Financial Policy Between the United States and Canada, 7/9/45, ibid., p. 61.

94. Acheson to Mary Acheson Bundy, May 16, 22, 25 and 26, 1945 in Acheson, _Present at the Creation_, pp. 106-07; Truman to Rayburn, 5/25/45, OF275-A, Truman Mss. Truman's ability to invoke his personal prestige was still strong only six weeks into his presidency. It soon declined.

95. Senator Joseph C. O'Mahoney to Truman, 5/28/45, OF 275-A, Truman Mss.

96. Grew to Winant, 3/5/45, p. 27, Winant to Stettinius, 5/18/45, pp. 47-49, and Memorandum of Executive Committee on Multilateral Commercial Policy, 7/21/45, pp. 74-76, all in _FR_:1945, VI.

97. Memorandum of conversation between Winthrop Bow, Chief, Division of Commercial Policy, with Frank Lee, Member, British Treasury Delegation, 8/2/45, _ibid._, p. 78.

98. Memoranda of Informal Discussions of Commercial and Financial Policy Between the United States and Canada, 7/9/45, pp. 61-66, and undated, pp. 67-74, _ibid._

99. Gabriel Kolko, _The Limits of Power: The World and United States Foreign Policy, 1945-1954_ (New York: Harper & Row, 1972), pp. 86-90; Jones, _Fifteen Weeks_, pp. 91-93. Clayton is quoted in Hartmann, _Truman_, p. 50. The discussion in this and the following paragraphs dealing with trade in late 1946 and early 1947 is extensively based on Hartmann, pp. 50-53. The tactic of tying congressional action on a legislative measure to possible repercussions on the position of American negotiators at an international conference was not new, having been used by Truman to link Congress' action on the Bretton Woods Agreements to Potsdam. See Truman to Senate Majority Leader Alben Barkley, 7/15/45, and Henry Morgenthau, Jr. to Senator Robert Wagner, 7/5/45, both in Barkely Mss.

100. Jones, _Fifteen Weeks_, p. 98; Acheson, _Present at the Creation_, pp. 132, 200; Walter J. Hollis to Latta, 2/6/47, OF 275-A, Truman Mss.

101. Acheson, _Present at the Creation_, p. 133.

102. Lovett to Truman, 5/21/48, and George Elsey to Clifford, 5/26/48, both in Box 7, Clifford Mss.

103. Clark Clifford to Truman, 4/26/49 and Charles Murphy to Edwin Nourse, 4/28/49, both in _ibid._

104. Memorandum of conversation between Acheson and Senator Walter George, 2/7/49, Box 65, Acheson Mss.

105. Acheson to Truman, 11/20/50, _FR_:1950, I, pp. 782-86.

106. Notes of Cabinet meeting, 11/21/50, Box 65, Acheson Mss.

107. Ickes to Vandenberg, 5/14/48, Vandenberg Mss.

108. Vandenberg to Ickes, 5/17/48, Vandenberg Mss.

109. Ickes to Vandenberg, 5/21/48, Vandenberg Mss.

110. Acheson to Ickes, 7/5/45, p. 1519, and Acheson to Abraham Fortas, Acting Secretary of the Interior, 9/17/45, p. 1527, both in FR:1945, II. For Acheson's meeting with Connally, see ibid., note 77, p. 1527.

111. Acheson, Present at the Creation, p. 128.

112. Clayton to Byrnes, 8/18/45, FR:1945, VI, pp. 103–05; Clayton to Baruch, 4/26/46, in Freeland, Truman Doctrine, p. 48.

113. Vandenberg to Dulles, 12/19/45, Dulles Mss.

114. Minutes of Meeting of the United States Committee on the United Kingdom Loan, 11/7/45, pp. 157–62 and 11/8/45, p. 162 n., both in FR:1945, VI.

115. Diary of Hugh Dalton, pp. 254–55 quoted in D. C. Watt, Personalities and Policies: Studies in the Formulation of British Foreign Policy in the Twentieth Century (South Bend, Indiana: University of Notre Dame Press, 1965), p. 67.

116. Clayton to Vinson, 11/5/45, Box 38, Clayton Mss.; Winant to Byrnes, 1/1/46, FR:1945, VI, pp. 200–02; Edward Francis-Williams, A Prime Minister Remembers, The War and Post-War Memoirs of the Rt. Hon. Earl Attlee, Based on his Private Papers and a Series of Recorded Conversations (London: William Heinemann, Ltd., 1961), p. 133; Dalton Diary, p. 254 quoted in Watt, Personalities, p. 68.

117. Snyder to Dalton, 1/27/45, Box 34, Snyder Mss.

118. Dalton to Snyder, 2/4/47, ibid.

119. Vandenberg to Dulles, 12/19/45, Dulles Mss.

120. Dalton Diary, p. 254 in Watt, Personalities and Policies, p. 67.

121. Ibid. In addition to the Irish, Zionist groups opposed the loan because of British policy in Palestine.

122. Dalton Diary, p. 255 and Watt's own commentary in ibid., p. 68.

123. Byrnes to Judson W. Chapman, 2/6/46, Byrnes Mss.

124. See exchange between Acheson and Taft in Senate Banking and Currency Committee, Anglo-American Financial Agreement, p. 335.

125. Vandenberg remarks to the Senate in Congressional Record, XCII, 4/22/46, p. 4080. Contradicting Vandenberg and Taft, Senator William Fulbright claimed that at least twelve to fifteen senators were consulted and kept closely informed. He may have been mistakenly referring to consultations on legislative strategy once the agreement had been negotiated. See Congressional Record, 4/29/46, p. 4118.

126. On the administration position, see Memorandum of Executive Committee on Economic Foreign Policy, 9/7/45, FR:1945, VI, p. 120; Dean Acheson and Fred Vinson, "The British Loan and What It Means to Us," Department of State Bulletin, 16, No. 342 (January 20, 1946), pp. 51-56; Clair Wilcox, "The Significance of the British Loan," ibid., No. 343, pp. 96-100; Dean Acheson, "The Credit to Britain, the Key to Expanded Trade," ibid., No. 345, pp. 185-88; and James F. Byrnes, "U.S.-U.K. Economic and Financial Agreements," ibid., No. 347, pp. 267-71 (this is a transcript of Byrnes' major address on the subject to the Foreign Policy Association, 2/11/46). Also, see Senator E. H. Moore to Senator Theodore Green, 2/9/46, transmitting a letter from Acheson to Moore dated 1/21/46, Box 419, Green Mss.

127. Truman to Representative Brent Spense, 6/29/46, Box: Leg. A-M, Spense Mss.

128. Various letters from Senator Charles Tobey, ranking member, Banking and Currency Committee, to constituents, January-February, 1946, Box 34, Tobey Mss.; Rayburn to B. L. Ross, 12/19/45, Roll 18, Rayburn Mss.; Senator Barkley's opening address to the Senate, Congressional Record, XCII 4/17/46, pp. 3838-40.

129. Vardman to Truman regarding Eastland's call, 2/13/46, OF 212-A, Truman Mss.; Freeland, Truman Doctrine, pp. 63-66.

130. See Vory's address to House, Congressional Record, XCII, 7/11/46, p. 8725.

131. Ibid., 5/16/46, p. 4497.

132. Ibid., 5/3/46, p. 4373.

133. Ibid., 5/3/46, p. 4375.

134. Ibid., 5/8/46, p. 4600.

135. Ibid., 7/12/46, p. 8823.

136. Ibid., 7/9/46, pp. 8495-97.

137. Ibid., 7/9/46, p. 8512.

138. Ibid., 713/46, p. 8915.

139. Ibid., 7/13/46, p. 8913.

140. Taber's change of attitude can be traced through his letters to Rev. Frank Moore, 2/6/46 and to Robert Lockhart, 4/13/46, both in Box 76 and to Allen W. Dulles, 7/13/46, Box 77, all in Taber Mss.

141. Congressional Record, CXII, 7/13/46, p. 8925.

142. On confusion between British socialism and communism, see addresses by Senators McClellen, 5/9/46, p. 4713 and Stanfil, 4/18/46, pp. 3955-57 in ibid.. Also, Kirk Jeffery, "The Debate Over the British Loan, 1945-46," International Review of History and Political Science, 7(1970), p. 68.

143. Congressional Record, XCII, 4/19/46, pp. 4056-58.

144. Ibid., 5/3/46, pp. 4373-74.

145. Alsop's Washington Post article of 1/26/48 is in Freeland, Truman Doctrine, p. 68.

146. Harriman to Byrnes, 5/6/46, telegraph 4834, file 841.51.

## Chapter 3

1. Memorandum of Office of Near Eastern and African Affairs, 10/21/46, FR:1946, VII, pp. 240-45.

2. Memorandum of conversation between Byrnes and British Ambassador Lord Iverchapel, 1/4/47, FR:1947, V, p. 1; Acheson to Lincoln MacVeigh, Ambassador to Greece, FR:1946, VII, p. 284.

3. Susan Hartmann, Truman and the 80th Congress (Columbia, Missouri: University of Missouri Press, 1971), p. 55.

4. Acheson to Marshall, 2/2/47, FR:1947, V, pp. 29-31; Dean Acheson, Present at the Creation: My Years in the State Department (New York: W. W. Norton, 1969), p. 221.

5. Joseph M. Jones, The Fifteen Weeks (February 21 - June 5, 1947) (New York: Viking Press, 1955), p. 149.

6. Jones to Benton, 2/26/47, Box 1, Jones Mss.

7. Minutes of 1st Meeting of Special Committee to Study Special

Assistance to Greece and Turkey, 1/24/47, FR:1947, V, p. 45-47.

8. Acheson, Present at the Creation, p. 219; Jones, Fifteen Weeks, pp. 138-43. The following relies heavily on Jones, passim and Acheson, pp. 212-226.

9. Memorandum of Genesis of Truman Doctrine Speech by Donald Russell, Director, Office of Public Affairs, 3/17/47, FR: 1947, V, p. 121-23.

10. Henderson's position is recalled in an interview with J. Iselin, 6/5/61, as related in Chapter XI, p. 7 of Iselin's unpublished manuscript in Box 17, Elsey Mss.

11. George Kennan, Memoirs, 1925-1950 (New York: Bantam Books, 1969), p. 332.

12. Elsey to Clifford, 38/8/47, Box 17, Elsey Mss.

13. Charles E. Bohlen, The Transformation of American Foreign Policy (New York: W. W. Norton, 1969), p. 86.

14. Forrestal Diary, 3/7/47, Forrestal Mss.; Memorandum of Cabinet Meeting, 3/7/47, FR:1947, V, pp. 96-98.

15. Secretary of War Robert Patterson to Marshall, undated but written between March 5 and 10, 1947, ibid., pp. 105-107.

16. Acheson, Present at the Creation, p. 221.

17. Address is in Richard Freeland, The Truman Doctrine and the Origins of McCarthyism: Foreign Policy, Domestic Politics, and Internal Security 1946-1948 (New York: Alfred A. Knopf, 1972), p. 84.

18. For initial legislative reaction, see Acheson to Marshall, 3/15/47, p. 120 and Memorandum by Acting Legislative Counsel Durward Sandifer, 3/13/47, p. 114, both in FR:1947, V. Also, transcript of telephone conversation between Forrestal and James Reston, 3/13/47, Box 1, Jones Mss.

19. Smith Diary, 3/3/47, 4/8/47 and 4/23/47, H. A. Smith Mss.

20. Eaton to Patterson, 4/8/47, Box 19, Patterson Mss.

21. Vorys to Jim (Linton?), 3/29/47, Box 29, Vorys Mss.

22. Vandenberg to Bruce Barton, 3/24/47, Vandenberg Mss.

23. Flanders to members of the Senate, 4/14/47, Flanders Mss.

24. Case to Truman, 5/10/47, OF 426, Truman Mss.

25. Tobey to Daniel James, 5/2/47, and to Irma Otto, 4/21/47, both in Box 45, Tobey Mss.

26. Francis O. Wilcox, Congress, The Executive, and Foreign Policy (New York: Harper & Row, 1971), p. 126.

27. Schlesinger's and Williams' testimony are in U.S., Congress, House of Representatives, Committee on Foreign Affairs, The Cold War: Origins and Development, Hearings before the Sub-committee on Europe of the Committee on Foreign Affairs, 92nd Cong., 1st sess. (1971), pp. 7, 18.

28. Athan Theoharis, Seeds of Repression: Harry S. Truman and the Origins of McCarthyism (Chicago: Quadrangle Books, 1971), pp. 28-58. Freeland, Truman Doctrine, pp. 70-114.

29. J. Gary Clifford, "President Truman and Peter the Great's Will," Diplomatic History, 4(1980), pp. 216-23. Daniel Yergen, The Shuttered Peace (Boston: Houghton Mifflin, 1977), p. 10 argues most Administration figures saw the U.S.S.R. as an ideological revolutionary state rather than a national state.

30. Flanders to members of the Senate, 4/12/47, Flanders Mss.

31. Jones, Fifteen Weeks, p. 162.

32. Acheson to Patterson, 3/5/47, FR:1947, III, p. 197; Memorandum by Hildring, 3/17/47, ibid., p. 198; Jones Fifteen Weeks, 201-03. Acheson, Present at the Creation, p. 226.

33. Interview of Marshall by Harry B. Price, 10/30/52, Price Mss.; W. Averell Harriman, America and Russia in a Changing World: A Half Century of Personal Observation (Garden City, New York: Doubleday, 1971), p. 31.

34. Clayton to Acheson, 5/5/47 in Acheson, Present at the Creation, p. 226.

35. Jones, Fifteen Weeks, p. 211. Acheson's speech is on pp. 274-81.

36. Price interview with Kennan, 2/19/53, Price Mss.

37. Price interview with Marshall, 10/30/52, Price Mss.

38. Acheson's concerns are recalled in the Leonard Miall Oral History (Truman), p. 8. Also Acheson, Present at the Creation, p. 232.

39. Miall Oral History (Truman), p. 2.

40. Kennan, Memoirs, pp. 354-56.

41. Ben T. Moore to Clair Wilcox, 7/8/47, FR:1947, III, pp. 239-41; Price interview of Bohlen, 2/16/53, Price Mss.

42. Clayton to Marshall, 5/31/47, Box 42, Clayton Mss.

43. Kennan, Memoirs, pp. 354-56.

44. H. Van Der Beugel, From Marshall Aid to Atlantic Partnership: European Integration as a Concern of American Foreign Policy (Amsterdam, The Netherlands: Elsevier Publishing Company, 1966), p. 78.

45. Ibid., p. 65.

46. Price interview of Marshall, 10/30/42, Price Mss.

47. Lovett to Vandenberg, 9/30/47, FR:1947, IV, p. 591.

48. Smith to Marshall, 9/30/47, FR:1947, I, p. 79.

49. Kennan to Acheson, 5/23/47, FR:1947, III, pp. 225-29; Kennan, Memoirs, pp. 347-60.

50. Clayton to Marshall, 5/31/47, Box 42, Clayton Mss.

51. Forrestal Diary, 6/27/47 and 7/18/47, Forrestal Mss.

52. Price interview of Marshall, 2/19/53, Price Mss.; Acheson, Present at the Creation, p. 233; Bohlen, Transformation, p. 90.

53. Price interview of Bohlen, 2/16/53, Price Mss.

54. Byrnes to Thad Riker, 1/23/48, Byrnes Mss.; Jones, Fifteen Weeks, p. 252; Acheson, Present at the Creation, p. 232.

55. Series of dispatches and memoranda, 3/21/47 - 4/20/47, FR: 1947, IV, pp. 665-67 n.

56. Vandenberg to Bridges, 4/19/47, Bridges Mss.

57. Marshall to Vandenberg, RG 46, Box 7, Sen. 89A-79, National Archives.

58. Dulles to Eleanor Roosevelt, 5/26/47, Supplement, CFM 1945-50, Dulles Mss.

59. Vandenberg to Clark Eichelberger, 6/25/47, Vandenberg Mss.

60. Vorys to H.B. Burchinal, 7/27/47, Box 15, Vorys Mss.

61. Baruch to Daniels, 7/9/47, Box 73, Baruch Mss.

62. Jones, Fifteen Weeks, p. 252; Acheson, Present at the

Creation, p. 232; Forrestal Diary, 6/23/47, Forrestal Mss.; Bohlen, Witness to History, p. 264.

63. Quotation is from author's interview with Lewis Douglas, 10/30/72. Also, see Price interview with Averell Harriman, 10/1/42, Price Mss. Harriman felt that Molotov's withdrawal was stupid in that he could have killed the ERP by joining. Acheson, Present at the Creation, p. 234, relates that Bidault later told him that he had the impression that Molotov withdrew under orders from the Kremlin and that Molotov thought the instructions foolish.

64. Caffery to Marshall, 6/18/47, FR:1947, III, p. 258.

65. Georges Bidault, Resistance, trans. by Marianne Sinclair (New York: Frederick A. Praeger, 1965), p. 150.

66. Price interview with Harriman, 10/1/52, Price Mss.

67. James Reston, The Artillery of the Press: Its Influence on American Foreign Policy (New York: Harper & Row, 1966), p. 64.

68. Acheson, Present at the Creation, p. 230.

69. Ibid., p. 232; Acheson to Marshall, 5/28/47, FR:1947, III, 232.

70. Ross to Crider, 6/5/47, Of 419-A, Truman Mss.

71. Margaret Truman, Harry S. Truman (New York: William Morrow, 1973), p. 353. Senator Harley Kilgore attributed to name of the ERP similarly in Steinberg, Man from Missouri, p. 296.

72. Acheson, Present at the Creation, p. 215.

73. Bohlen, Witness to History, p. 270.

74. Miall Oral History (Truman), p. 9.

75. Hartmann, Truman, p. 108.

76. E.g., Lovett to Taber, 9/21/47, Box 128, Taber Mss.

77. Smith Diary, 10/10/47 and 10/15/47, H. A. Smith Mss.

78. Milton C. Renwinkel, U. S. Mission in Sofia, to Smith, 1/6/48 and J. D. Ravotto, U. S. Embassy in Rome, 12/1/47 to Smith, both in Box 96, H. A. Smith Mss.

79. H. Lawrence-Groves, U. S. Embassy in Athens, to Taber, 10/9/47, Box 128, Taber Mss.

80. For Republican thinking, see Representative Frederic Coudert to Taber, 11/6/47, Box 115 and Taber to Patterson, 12/2/47, Box 130, both in Taber Mss.

81. Truman to his daughter Margaret, 10/1/47 and to his sister Mary, 11/14/47, in Margaret Truman, Harry S.Truman, p.354.

82. Hatch to Truman, 10/6/47, Box 4, Clifford Mss.

83. Forrestal Diary, 6/28/47, Forrestal Mss.

84. Ibid., 7/14/47.

85. Quotation is from "Washington Wire," New Republic, in Hartmann, Truman, p. 112.

86. Frank McNaughton to Don Birmingham, File 80, Martin Mss.

87. Frank Southard and Thomas Lynch to John Snyder, 10/25/47, Box 8, Snyder Mss.

88. Elsey to Clifford, 9/22/47, Box 4, Clifford Mss.

89. Price interview of Marshall, 2/18/53, Price Mss.

90. Memorandum by Elsey on Truman's conference with congressional leaders, 9/29/47, Box 60, Elsey Mss.

91. Forrestal Diary, 9/29/47, Forrestal Mss.

92. Vandenberg to Taft, 10/8/47, Vandenberg Mss.

93. Lovett to Vandenberg, 9/21/47, Vandenberg Mss.; Lovett to Taber, 9/21/47, Box 128, Taber Mss.

94. Vandenberg to Floyd McGriff, 7/1/47, Vandenberg Mss.

95. Clifford To Truman, 10/3/47, Box 4, Clifford Mss.

96. U.S., Congress, Committee on Foreign Relations, European Interim Aid Act of 1947, Hearings of the Committee on Foreign Relations, 80th Cong., 1st sess. (1947), p. 20.

97. Marshall to Baruch, 11/19/47, Box 75, Baruch Mss.

98. Vandenberg, Jr., Private Papers, p. 380.

99. Coudert to Taber, 11/6/47, Box 115, Taber Mss.

100. James T. Patterson, Mr. Republican: A Biography of Robert A. Taft (Boston: Houghton Mifflin, 1972), p. 385.

101. Harold L. Hitchens, "Influences on the Congressional Decision to Pass the Marshall Plan," Western Political

332

Quarterly, 21(1968), pp. 52–55; Quenton L. Quade, "The Truman Administration and the Separation of Powers: The Case of the Marshall," The Review of Politics, 28(1965), passim; Memorandum by Leo Burnett, "Indian Summer in Washington," written after a White House conference, 11/3/47, OF 426, Truman Mss.

102. Vandenberg to Patterson, 12/10/47 and Patterson's reply, 12/11/47, Vandenberg Mss.

103. U. S., Congress, Senate, Committee on Foreign Relations, European Recovery Program, Hearings before the Committee on Foreign Relations, 80th Cong., 2nd sess. (1948), passim.

104. Ibid., p. 74.

105. Vandenberg to Marshall 3/24/48 and Marshall's reply, 3/25/48, Vandenberg Mss.

106. Acheson, Present at the Creation, p. 241. Vandenberg's veto of Clayton and Acheson as ERP Administrator was not the only case of Congressional influence on Presidential appointments in the foreign policy field at this time. In addition to Baruch's appointment as atomic energy negotiator, John Winant was appointed as Representative to the United Nations Economic and Social Council at the behest of Senator Robert Wagner; see Bernard Bellush, He Walked Alone: A Biography of John Gilbert Winant (The Hague, The Netherlands: Mouton & Company, 1968), p. 217. On Winant's resignation, Francis Biddle was to be appointed as his successor, but Vandenberg vetoed the idea. The basic reason for Republican opposition to Biddle, Vandenberg wrote Clayton, was that Biddle was, "looked upon by many Senators as a veritable symbol of the 'New Deal,' and they consider that they have a mandate from last November's election against the perpetuation of these symbols." Vandenberg to Clayton, 3/5/47, Vandenberg Mss. While he was at it, Vandenberg engineered the appointment of Herschel Johnson as ECOSOC representative; see ibid., and Vandenberg to Leon Henderson, 7/21/47, Vandenberg Mss. Republicans also blocked the appointment of Mark Etheridge to a United Nations post by threatening to fight his nomination; see Vandenberg to Ickes, 7/22/47, Vandenberg Mss.

107. Acheson, Present at the Creation, p. 233.

108. Price interview with Marshall, 2/18/53, Price Mss.

109. Gilbert Windham, "Developing Theories of Policy Making: A Case Study of Foreign Aid," Journal of Politics, 32(1970), pp. 41–70. Windham does a content analysis of administration and congressional statements for the Marshall Plan from May 1947 through April 1948.

110. Senate Committee on Foreign Relations, European Recovery Program, p. 2.

111. Freeland, Truman Doctrine, p. 263.

112. William Donovan to Vandenberg, 12/30/47 and Vandenberg's reply, 1/5/48, Sen. 80A-F9, Foreign Relations, Tray 182, European Recovery Program file, National Archives.

113. Arthur's interview with Lewis Douglas, 10/30/72; Lovett to Marshall, 12/4/47, FR:1947, III, p. 482.

114. Price interview with Kennan, 2/19/53, Price Mss.; Kennan, Memoirs, p. 427.

115. "Indian Summer in Washington," memorandum by Leo Burnett, 11/3/47, OF 426, Truman Mss.

116. Douglas to Lovett, 12/2/47, FR:1947, III, p. 807.

117. Caffery to Marshall, 11/3/47, p. 979, 11/29/47, p. 804, and 12/3/47, p. 810, all in ibid.

118. Author's interview with Lewis Douglas, 10/30/72.

119. Freeland, Truman Doctrine, pp. 262-64; Windham, "Developing Theories," p. 65

120. Kennan Diary, 1/23/48 quoted in his Memoirs, p. 428.

121. Ibid., pp. 421-27.

122. Millis and Duffield, Forrestal Diaries, p. 387. James Donovan claims that Clay's message came because Army Intelligence asked for something to persuade Congress to enlarge military appropriations. See Robert Donovan's Conflict and Crisis: The Presidency of Harry S. Truman 1945-1948 (New York: W. W. Norton, 197), p. 359.

123. Freeland, Truman Doctrine, p. 269.

124. Memorandum of the genesis of Truman's address to Congress, Box 20, Elsey Mss.

125. Quotations from headlines and Truman's speech are in Freeland, Truman Doctrine, p. 271.

126. Marshall to Marshall Carter, 7/22/46, and Carter's reply, 7/23/46, FR:1946, V, pp. 753-55; Truman to Marshall, 12/15/45, cited in Acheson, Present at the Creation, p. 744; John Carter Vincent to Byrnes, 11/6/50, Byrnes Mss.

127. Ross Y. Koen, The China Lobby in American Politics (New York: The MacMillan Company, 1960), p. 89; Hartmann,

Truman, pp. 162, 167; Acheson, Present at the Creation, p. 303.

128. Acheson, Present at the Creation, pp. 304-06.

129. E.q. Senator Harley Kilgore to Mme. Chiang 2/3/48, Kilgore Mss.

130. Author's interview with Lewis Douglas 10/30/72; Hartman, Truman, p. 167; Keon, China Lobby, pp. 227-32.

131. Tang Tsou, American's Failure in China, 1941-50 (Chicago: Quadrangle Books, 1971), p. 477.


Chapter 4


1. Ronald J. Stupak, The Shaping of Foreign Policy, The Role of the Secretary of State as Seen by Dean Acheson (n.p.: The Odyssey Press, 1969), pp.30-34. Quotation is from David S. McClellen, "The Operational Code Approach to the Study of Political Leaders: Dean Acheson's Philosophical and Instrumental Beliefs," Canadian Journal of Political Science, 4(1971), p. 56.

2. Acheson to Ferguson, 7/14/50, attached to a memorandum from George (Smith) to Bill (Reed), 7/15/50, Box 11, Reed file, G. Smith Mss. Smith and Reed were staff members of the Senate Republican Policy Committee.

3. Thomas G. Paterson, "Presidential Foreign Policy, Public Opinion, and Congress: The Truman Years," Diplomatic History, 3(1979), p. 17.

4. Washington Daily News, 1/6/50, p. 39, in Box 2 China file, Clifford Mss.

5. Memorandum of conversation between Lucas and Acheson, 1/19/50, Box 65, Acheson Mss.

6. Webb to Truman, 1/5/51, PSF 159, Secretary of State Misc. file, Truman Mss.

7. Memorandum of conversation between Benton and Acheson, 3/16/51, Box 66, Acheson Mss.

8. Heckler to George Elsey, 10/1/51, Box 102, Heckler file, Elsey Mss.

9. Heckler to Elsey, 10/16/51, ibid.

10. Memorandum of conversation between Lucas and Acheson, 12/7/50, Box 65, Acheson Mss.

11. Memorandum of conversation among Acheson, Connally, Francis Wilcox and Ernest Gross, 7/19/49, Box 64, Acheson Mss.

12. Acheson, _Present at the Creation:  My Years in the State Department_ (New York:  W. W. Norton, 1969), title of Chapter 39.

13. _Washington Daily News_, 1/6/50, in Box 2, China file, Clifford Mss.

14. Memorandum of conversation between Acheson and Vandenberg, 1/21/50, Box 65, Acheson Mss.

15. George Kennan to Acheson, 2/17/50, _FR_:1950, V, pp. 160-67.

16. Vandenberg to Acheson, 3/29/50, Box 65, Acheson Mss.

17. Vandenberg to Acheson, 3/31/50, _ibid._

18. Memorandum of conversation between Dulles and Truman, 4/28/50, _ibid._

19. Memorandum of conversation between Acheson and Wiley, 4/28/50, _ibid._

20. U. S., Congress, Senate, Committee on Foreign Relations, _Executive Sessions_, IX(1957), p. 20.

21. Notes on Cabinet meeting, 2/1/54, Anonymous Mss.

22. Notes on legislative leaders meeting, 2/1/55, _ibid._

23. Notes on Cabinet meeting, 5/14/55, _ibid._

24. Kern to Dulles, 3/14/54, Box 83, Dulles Mss.

25. E.q., Under Secretary of State Walter Bedell Smith interviewed on _American Week_, CBS Network, 4/11/54, published in _Department of State Bulletin_, 4/19/54, p. 539.

26. Radford to Eisenhower, 3/24/54, Box 32, Radford file, Administration Series, Eisenhower Mss.

27. An excellent contemporary account is Chalmers Roberts', "The Day We Didn't Go to War," _Reporter_, 9/14/54, pp. 31-35.

28. Radford to Eisenhower, 3/26/54, Box 32, Radford file, Administration Series, Eisenhower Mss.

29. Dulles to Embassies in Paris and London, 4/3/54, in U.S., Congress, House of Representatives, Committee on Armed Services, _United States-Vietnam Relations, 1945-1963_, (published 1971), Book 9, pp. 293-94.

30. Ibid., p. 298.

31. Telephone conversation between Dulles and Eisenhower, 4/5/54, Box 5, DDE Diary, Eisenhower Mss.

32. Diary Entry, 3/29/54, Box 1, Hagerty Mss.

33. U.S., President, Public Papers of the President of the United States, Dwight David Eisenhower, Press Conference of 3/21/54, p. 341.

34. Ibid., Press Conference of 3/17/54, p. 32.

35. Telephone conversation between Dulles and Eisenhower, 3/17/54, Box 4, DDE Diaries, Eisenhower Mss.

36. Joint Cabinet-legislative leader meeting, 1/4/54, Anonymous Mss.; telephone conversation between Eisenhower and Secretary of Defense Charles Wilson, 2/8/54, Box 4, DDE Diaries, Eisenhower Mss.

37. Stennis to Charles Wilson, 1/29/54, in House, Committee on Armed Services, United States-Vietnam Relations, Book 9, p. 239.

38. Notes on legislative leaders meeting, 2/15/54, Anonymous Mss.

39. Memorandum of meeting, 4/3/54, Reference Collection, misc. classified documents, Eisenhower Mss.

40. Handwritten notes of meeting by Senator Richard Russell, 4/3/54, XV, Red Line series, Special Presidents file, Russell Mss.

41. Richard Russell to Louis Wolfson, 1/4/66, I:J, Box 7, Vietnam 1964-1959 file; and Stennis to Russell, 2/8/68, 15:EE, Box 5, Letters to Save--1968 file, Russell Mss.

42. Conversation between Dulles and Eisenhower, 4/3/54, telephone transcripts, Box 10, Dulles Mss.

43. Dulles to Embassy in Paris, 4/5/54 in House, Committee on Armed Services, United States-Vietnam Relations, Book 9, p. 299.

44. Conversation between Dulles and Knowland, 4/3/54, telephone transcripts, Box 2, Dulles Mss.

45. Telephone conversation between Eisenhower and Dulles, 4/5/54, Box 5, DDE Diaries, Eisenhower Mss.

46. Dwight D. Eisenhower, Mandate for Change 1953-1956 (Garden City, New York: Doubleday, 1963), p. 463.

47. Telephone conversation among Eisenhower, Rayburn and Martin, 1/20/55, Box 9, DDE Diaries, Eisenhower Mss.

48. Telephone conversation between Eisenhower and Dulles, 1/20/55, _ibid._

49. Telephone conversation between Eisenhower and Dulles, 1/25/54, _ibid._

50. Conversation between Byrnes and Dulles, 1/26/55, telephone transcripts, Box 3, Dulles Mss.

51. Gary W. Richard, "Divisions and Dissent: Democrats and Foreign Policy, 1952-1956," _Political Science Quarterly_, 93(1978), p. 63.

52. Conversation between Dulles and Mansfield, 1/27/55, telephone transcripts, Box 3, Dulles Mss.

53. Smith to Dulles, 4/5/55, Box 120, H. A. Smith Mss.

54. Chester Bowles to Dean Rusk, 3/17/61, Box 300, file 0536, Bowles Mss.

55. Eisenhower to Dulles, 4/29/55, Box 9, Formosa (2) file, International Series, Eisenhower Mss.

56. _Ibid._

57. Townsend Hoopes, _The Devil and John Foster Dulles_ (Boston: Little, Brown, 1973), p. 283.

58. Meetings of 12/31/56 and 1/1/57, Box 2, Legislative Meetings Series, Eisenhower Mss.

59. Memorandum of meeting including Representatives Halleck and McCormack, Eisenhower, Herter, and Bryce Harlow, 3/26/59, Box 39, Staff Notes, March 1-15 file, DDE Diaries, Eisenhower Mss.

60. For a Democratic evaluation see Senator Stennis' remarks in John Stennis and J. W. Fulbright, _The Role of Congress in Foreign Policy_ (Washington, D.C.: American Enterprise Institute, 1971), p. 29.

61. Notes of meeting, 1/26/53, Legislative Meeting Series, Box 4, Eisenhower Mss.

62. Eisenhower to Martin, 12/21/53, Box 4, DDE Diaries, Eisenhower Mss.

63. Eisenhower to Halleck, 12/21/53, _ibid._

64. Notes of meeting, 11/17/54, Box 1, Legislative Meeting

Series, Eisenhower Mss.

65. Eisenhower to Secretary of State, Secretary of Defense, et al., 12/12/54, Box 8, DDE Diaries, Eisenhower Mss.

66. Telephone conversation between Eisenhower and Eden, 11/7/56, Box 8, Whitman Diary, Eisenhower Mss.

67. Hoopes, The Devil and John Foster Dulles, p. 42.

68. Bowie Oral History (Dulles), p. 37.

69. Nixon Oral History (Dulles), p. 11.

70. Dulles to Richards, 3/6/53, Box 74, Dulles Mss.

71. U. S., Congress, Senate, Committee on Foreign Relations, United States Foreign Policy, 86th Cong., 1st sess. (1959), p. 14.

72. Nixon Oral History (Dulles), p. 12.

73. Notes of meeting, 3/29/59, Box 37, Staff Notes, March 1-15, DDE Diaries, Eisenhower Mss.

74. Notes of Cabinet meeting, 3/23/56, Anonymous Mss.

75. Notes of joint meeting of Cabinet and Republican legislative leaders, 1/4/54, Anonymous Mss.

76. O'Connor Oral History (Dulles), p. 110

77. Martin Oral History (Dulles), p. 3.

78. Hickenlooper Oral History (Dulles), p. 13.

79. Aiken Oral History (Dulles), p. 2.

80. Dirksen Oral History (Dulles), p. 7.

81. Murphy To Dulles, 6/1/55 and McCardle to Dulles, 6/2/55, both in Box 95, Dulles Mss.

82. Conversation between Eisenhower and Dulles, 9/29/58, telephone transcripts, Box 13, Dulles Mss.

83. Lodge to Barbara Schulman, 3/29/56, Box 105, Dulles Mss.

84. Dulles To Eisenhower, 6/29/53 and 7/6/53, Box 1, Dulles-Herter Series, Eisenhower Mss.

85. Conversation between Dulles and Nixon, 10/17/55, telephone transcripts, Box 4, Dulles Mss. Also, conversation between Dulles and Attorney General Brownell, 10/17/55, ibid.

86. Walter Lippmann to Stevenson, 9/24/58 and Stevenson's reply, 9/25/58, Box 103, file 2003, Lippmann Mss.

87. Memorandum to Dulles regarding call from Robert Hill, 6/11/56, telephone transcripts, Box 5, Dulles Mss.; Conversation between Dulles and Eisenhower, 5/9/56, Box 15, DDE Diaries, Eisenhower Mss.

88. Conversation between Dulles and Eisenhower, 11/13/56, Box 6, Dulles-Herter Series, Eisenhower Mss.

89. Richards to Dulles, 11/26/55, Box 95. Dulles Mss.

90. Notes, Box 8, February 1956 file, Whitman Diary, Eisenhower Mss.

91. Conversation between Dulles and Representative Walter Judd, 12/18/53, and conversation between Dulles and Leonard Hall, 1/12/54, both in telephone transcripts, Box 2, Dulles Mss.

92. Conversation between Dulles and Byrnes, 3/16/53, telephone transcripts, Box 1, Dulles Mss.

93. Conversation between Dulles and Hickenlooper, 11/11/54, telephone transcripts, Box 2, Dulles Mss.

94. Notes of Cabinet meeting, 6/23/53, Anonymous Mss.

95. Conversation between Dulles and Hall, 1/12/54, telephone transcripts, Box 2, Dulles Mss.

96. Mundt to Laurie, 7/17/53, RG I, Box 206, file 7, Mundt Mss.

97. Hanes Oral History (Dulles), p. 18.

98. Conversation between Dulles and Leonard Hall, 1/12/54, telephone transcripts, Box 2, Dulles Mss.

99. Mundt to Bryton Barron, 7/22/53, RG I, Box 206, file 7, Mundt Mss.

100. McLeod to Mundt, 9/27/53, ibid.

101. Conversation between Dulles and Nixon, 1/21/58, telephone transcripts, Box 9, Dulles Mss.

102. Notes of meeting, 6/19/58, Box 2, Legislative Meeting Series, Eisenhower Mss.

103. Taber to Dulles, 7/15/53, Box 76, Dulles Mss.

104. Fulbright to Chester Bowles, 5/26/56, Box 233, file 0238, Bowles Mss.

105. Humphrey to Charles Turuk, 4/11/50, Box 628, McCarthy file, Humphrey Mss.

106. Humphrey to Charles Turuk, 4/21/55, Box 119, Foreign Policy-General file, Humphrey Mss.

107. MacComber Oral History (Dulles), pp. 46-48.

108. Conversation between Nixon and Eisenhower, 6/29/54, Box 2, Whitman Diary, Eisenhower Mss.

109. Hagerty Diary, 4/20/54, Box 1, Hagerty Mss.

110. Conversation between Dulles and Lodge, 11/29/55, telephone transcripts, Box 4, Dulles Mss.

111. Lodge To Eisenhower, 2/19/55, Box 27, Administration Series, Eisenhower Mss.

112. MacComber Oral History (Dulles), pp. 107-09.

113. Telephone conversation between Dulles and Eisenhower, 3/4/57, Box 22, DDE Diaries, Eisenhower Mss.

114. John Hanes to Dulles, 11/22/55, Box 4 and Dulles conversations with Brownell and Nixon, both on 1/28/57, Box 6, all in telephone transcripts, Dulles Mss.

115. George to Bowles, 10/21/55, Box 134, file 0250, Bowles Mss.

116. Johnson to Bowles, 10/15/55, Box 140, file 0349, Bowles Mss.

117. Fulbright to Bowles, 8/8/58, Box 133, file 0318, Bowles Mss.

118. Humphrey to Bowles, 8/22/57, Box 138, file 0318, Bowles Mss.

119. Dulles conversations with Brownell and with Nixon, 1/28/58, telephone transcripts, Box 6, Dulles Mss.

120. Eisenhower to Swede Hazlett, 7/22/57, Box 25, DDE Diaries, Eisenhower Mss.

121. Dulles to Eisenhower, 6/8/53, Box 1, Dulles-Herter Series, Eisenhower Mss.

122. Memorandum of conversation between Eisenhower and Senator H. A. Smith, 8/12/54, Box 3, Whitman Diary, Eisenhower Mss.

123. Harlow Oral History (Johnson).

124. Hagerty Diary, 4/19/54, Box 1, Hagerty Mss.

125. Conversation between Eisenhower and Brownell, 67/15/54, Box 2, Whitman Diary, Eisenhower Mss.

126. Hagerty to Eisenhower, 12/9/58, Box 9, The President-Memos file, Hagerty Mss.

127. Ibid.

128. Lodge to Eisenhower, 12/22/53, Box 26, Lodge file, Administration Series, Eisenhower Mss.

129. Eisenhower memorandum, 7/25/57, Box 9, Whitman Diary, Eisenhower Mss.

130. Notes of conversation between Eisenhower and Knowland, 11/24/54, Box 3, ibid.

131. Richard F. Fenno, Jr., Congressmen in Committees (Boston: Little, Brown, 1973), p. 30.

132. Telephone conversations between Eisenhower and Secretary of State Christian Herter, both on 3/9/59, Box 10, Presidential Calls file, Herter Mss.

133. Notes of Cabinet meeting, 2/1/54, Anonymous Mss.

134. Eisenhower to Lyndon Johnson, 6/25/59, Box 42, Staff Notes, June 16-30 (1), DDE Diaries, Eisenhower Mss.

135. Eisenhower to Senators Johnson, Russell, and Fulbright 6/29/59, ibid. Also, Eisenhower to Henry Jackson, 7/10/59, Bryce Harlow to Johnson, 7/11/59, and Johnson to Russell, 7/13/59, all in Series 15, Subseries EE, Box 19, Russell Mss.

136. P. F. Patterson to representative Harold Lowre, 4/23/54, RG III, Box 480, file 7, Mundt Mss.

137. Senator William Jenner to Herbert Hoover, 9/23/52, Post Presidential Files, Box 378, file 2996(2)-Jenner, Hoover Mss.

138. Eisenhower is quoted in the Hagerty Diary, 4/26/54, Box 1, Hagerty Mss. Also, see Eisenhower to Swede Hazlett, 7/22/57, Box 25; and Memorandum for the record, meeting of Eisenhower, McCormack, Halleck, Herter, and Harlow, 3/10/59 (dated 3/26), Box 39, both in DDE Diaries, Eisenhower Mss.

139. Undated Notes, Anonymous Mss.

140. George Smith to Taft, 8/23/52, Box 12, Taft (5) file, G. Smith Mss.

141. Jenner to Hoover, 9/23/52, Post Presidential Files, Box 378, file 2996(2)-Jenner, Hoover Mss.

142. Hoopes, The Devil and John Foster Dulles, p. 148.

143. Rod O'Connor to McQuaid, Memo on Secretary's testimony before the Senate Foreign Relations Committee, 3/3/53, Box 52, Liberation file, Dulles Mss.

144. Kennan Oral History (Dulles), p. 41.

145. For a discussion of the Bricker Amendment, see Stephen A. Garrett, "Foreign Policy and the American Constitution: The Bricker Amendment in Contemporary Perspective," International Studies, 16(1972), pp. 187-219.

146. Herman Phlager, Legal Advisor, Department of State, to John Heckerson, Assistant Secretary of State for United Nations Affairs, 2/18/53, FR:1952-1954, III, p. 1550. Also, Note 2, p. 555, ibid.; and Notes of Cabinet meeting, 2/20/53, Anonymous Mss.

147. Conversation between Dulles and Lodge, 10/21/53, telephone transcripts, Box 1, and Herman Phleger to Dulles, 3/30/53, Box 70, both in Dulles Mss.

148. Memorandum, Hickerson to Fisher, 2/12/52, FR:1952-1954, III, p. 1548.

149. Notes of Cabinet meeting, 2/20/53, Anonymous Mss.

150. Hughes Oral History (Dulles).

151. Notes on Joint Cabinet - legislative leaders meeting, 1/25/54, Anonymous Mss.

152. Eisenhower to Knowland, 1/25/54 and Notes of Cabinet meeting, 7/17/53, both in Anonymous Mss.

153. Notes of Cabinet meeting, 1/29/54, Anonymous Mss.

154. Memorandum of meeting between Eisenhower and Javits, 12/20/54, Box 1, Hagerty Mss.

155. Smith to Dulles, 7/16/56, Box 107, Bricker Amendment file, Dulles Mss.

156. Telephone conversation between Eisenhower and Smith, 1/28/54, Box 5, DDE Diaries, Eisenhower Mss.

157. Notes, 2/8/54, Anonymous Mss.

158. Telephone conversation between Eisenhower and Knowland, 1/29/54, Box 5, DDE Diaries, Eisenhower Mss.

159. Notes on Cabinet meeting, 1/11/54, Anonymous Mss.

160. Anonymous Mss.

161. Notes on Cabinet meeting, 1/11/54, Anonymous Mss.

162. E.g., telephone conversation between Eisenhower and Knowland, 2/1/54, Box 5, DDE Diaries, Eisenhower Mss.

163. Conversations between Dulles and Senator Wiley and Dulles and Senator Sparkman, both 1/9/54, telephone transcripts, Box 2. Dulles Mss.

164. Cabinet meeting, 7/17/53 quoted in Peter Lyon, Portrait of a Hero (Boston: Little, Brown, 1974), p.527.

165. Telephone conversation between Eisenhower and Dulles, 5/9/56, Box 15, DDE Diaries, Eisenhower Mss.

166. Telephone conversation between Dulles and Eisenhower, 1/20/54, Box 5, ibid.

167. Telephone conversations between Eisenhower and Knowland, 1/25/54, ibid.

168. Telephone conversation between Smith and Eisenhower, 1/28/54, ibid.

169. Dulles To Eisenhower, 2/3/59, Box 8, Dulles-Herter Series, Eisenhower Mss.

170. Kendell to Eisenhower, 2/9/59, ibid.

171. Carl Marcy to J. W. Fulbright, 4/8/59, BCN 146, file 7, Fulbright Mss.

172. Fulbright to Acting Secretary of State C. Douglas Dillon, 7/24/59, Box 6, Hickenlooper Mss.

173. Whitman To DDE, 11/14/60, Box 54, calls 11/1960, DDE Diary, Eisenhower Mss.

174. Kenneth Waltz, Foreign Policy and Democratic Politics, The American and British Experiences (Boston: Little, Brown and Company, 1967), p. 217; David Halberstram, The Best and the Brightest (New York: Random House, 1972), pp. 9-10.

175. Acheson Oral History (Kennedy), p. 7. Acheson suggested Republican John McCloy. Whitman memo (n. 173) on the Nixon-Kennedy conversation also implies Kennedy was not considering a Republican appointment.

176. Acheson Oral History (Kennedy), p. 8.

177. Halberstram, Best and the Brightest, p. 174.

178. Sorenson Oral History (Kennedy), p. 69.

179. Sorenson to Walter Lippmann, 10/5/61, Box 103, File 1977, Lippmann Mss.

180. Russell To Rev. James B. Sherwood, 10/25/63, Series 1, Sub-series C, Box 6, Foreign Relations 1958-1963 file, Russell Mss.

181. U. S., Congress, Senate, Committee on Government Operations, Administration of National Security, Hearings before the Subcommittee on National Security, 88th Cong., 1st and 2nd sess. (1963-1964), p. 1300.

182. Hickenlooper Oral History (Dulles), p. 16.

183. U. S., Congress, Senate, Committee on Foreign Relations, War Powers Legislation, Hearings, 91st Cong., 2nd sess. (1971), p. 425.

184. Neil MacNeil, Dirksen: Portrait of a Public Man (New York: World Publishing Company, 1973), pp. 188-93.

185. Ibid., p. 190.

186. On the impact of the right in these two crises, see Roger Hilsman, The Politics of Policy-Making in Defense and Foreign Affairs (New York: Harper & Row, 1971), p. 103.

187. Interview with Dean Rusk, 11/4/80.

188. Mansfield to Rusk, 3/22/61, Box 300, File 0536, Bowles Mss.

189. (Michael Gravel), The Senator Gravel Edition: The Pentagon Papers (Boston: Beacon Press, 1971), 5 vols., vol. 4, p. 42.

190. Theodore Sorenson, Kennedy (New York: Harper & Row, 1965), p. 644. There were also other inhibiting factors such as the Bay of Pigs disaster.

191. In another similarity, Eisenhower had been warned by Army Chief-of-Staff Matthew Ridgeway not to become involved in Vietnam. In April 1961, General of the Armies Douglas MacArthur advised Kennedy to avoid committing ground forces to Asia.

192. Author's interview with Dean Rusk, 11/4/80.

193. Sorenson, Kennedy, p. 654.

194. Ibid., p. 658.

195. Ibid., p. 657.

196. Robert F. Kennedy, Thirteen Days: A Memoir of the Cuban

<u>Missile Crisis</u> (New York:  W. W. Norton, 1969), p. 25.

197. Sorenson, <u>Kennedy</u>, p. 667.

198. Roger Hilsman, <u>To Move a Nation:  The Politics of Foreign Policy in the Administration of John F. Kennedy</u> (New York: Dell Publishing, 1964), p. 197.

199. <u>Ibid.</u>, p. 195.

200. Sorenson, <u>Kennedy</u>, p. 688.

201. Kenneth P. O'Donnell and David F. Powers, with Joe McCarthy, <u>Johnny, We Hardly Knew Ye</u> (New York:  Simon & Schuster, 1973), p. 359.

202. Sorenson Oral History (Kennedy), p.66.

203. Author's interview with Dean Rusk, 11/4/80; Fulbright to Angela T. Burr, 7/22/71, 48:13:39:3 Fulbright Mss.; Russell's handwritten notes, 10/23/62, XV, Red Line File, Special Presidential file, Russell Mss.

204. Sorenson Oral History (Kennedy), p. 59.

205. Kennedy, <u>Thirteen Days</u>, p. 67.

206. Emmet J. Hughes, <u>The Living Presidency</u> Baltimore:  Penguin Books, 1972), p. 258.

207. Doris Kearns, <u>Lyndon Johnson and the American Dream</u> (New York:  Harper & Row, 1976), pp. 349-50.

208. Lawrence F. O'Brien, <u>No Final Victories</u> (Garden City, New York:  Doubleday, 1974), p. 192.

209. Joseph Califano to LBJ transmitting Dirksen's voting record, 10/15/66, WHCF, Box 170, File:  LE5, 9/7/66-6/30/67; and Douglas Carter to LBJ transmitting Fulbright's voting record, 9/16/65, WHCF, Box 169, File:  LE 5/7/65-11/17/66; both in LBJ Mss.

210. Walt Rostow to LBJ, 10/5/66, NSF, Box 5, File:  Congressional Record Follow-up, LBJ Mss.

211. O'Brien, <u>No Final Victories</u>, p. 192.

212. Jack Valenti, <u>A Very Human President</u> (New York:  W. W. Norton, 1975), p. 224.

213. <u>Ibid.</u>, p. 230.

214. Church Oral History (Johnson), tape I, p. 22.

215. Ibid.

216. Naomi B. Lynn and Arthur F. McClure, The Fulbright Premise (Lewisburg, Pennsylvania: Bucknell University Press, 1973), p. 122.

217. Merle Miller, Lyndon: An Oral Biography (New York: G. P. Putnam's Sons, 1980), p. 460.

218. Halbertstram, The Best and the Brightest, p. 623. On Johnson's tendency to suspect the motives of others, see Kearns, Lyndon Johnson, p. 345. Church in his Oral History (Johnson) tape I, p. 20, even says Johnson "came to look upon those who disagreed with him as part of a sinister conspiracy - talked sometimes wildly about communist influence."

219. Valenti, A Very Human President, p. 193.

220. Author's interview with Dean Rusk, 11/4/80.

221. Miller, Lyndon, pp. 385, 203.

222. Meeting notes, 1/22/65, V. P. notes, late 1964-1965 file, Box 412, Humphrey Mss. Johnson's tactic was later endorsed by Henry Kissinger who conceded he wished the Nixon Administration had gotten a congressional resolution in 1969 to continue the war. See Henry Kissinger, Years of Upheaval (Boston: Little, Brown, 1982), p. 304.

223. Kearns, Lyndon Johnson, p. 143.

224. Ibid., pp. 143, 283.

225. Ibid., p. 143.

226. Ibid.

227. Author's interview with Dean Rusk, 11/4/80.

228. Eugene Rostow Oral History (Johnson), p. 15.

229. State Department memorandum on reasons against declaring war enclosed, in Pat Holt to Fulbright, 12/29/65, 48:17:43:1, Fulbright Mss.

230. Kearns, Lyndon Johnson, p. 341.

231. Ibid., p. 282.

232. Quoted in George C. Edwards III, Presidential Influence in Congress (San Francisco: W. H. Freeman, 1980), p. 87.

233. Halberstram, The Best and the Brightest, p.425.

234. "The Legislative-Executive Foreign Policy Relationship in the 90th Congress," _Congressional Digest_, 47 (10/68), p. 237.

235. Aiken Oral History (Johnson), p. 7; Church Oral History (Johnson), tape I, p. 20.

236. Charles Frankel, _High on Foggy Bottom_ (New York: Harper & Row, 1968), p. 41.

237. Memorandum of conversation between DDE and LBJ, 10/13/65, White House Famous Names, Box 2, Eisenhower file, Johnson Mss.

238. Jerome Stater, _Intervention and Negotiation: The United States an the Dominican Republic_ (Boston: Little Brown, 1968), p. 85.

239. Benjamin Reed, Executive Secretary of the Cabinet, to Walt Rostow, 7/7/67, NSF, Box 15, Table 1, Tab D, Johnson Mss.

240. Author's interview with Dean Rusk, 11/4/80.

241. Walt Rostow to Johnson, 7/12/67, NSF, Box 15, Table 1, Tab M, Johnson Mss.

242. Author's interview with Dean Rusk, 11/4/80.

243. DOS dispatch to Embassy in Congo, 7/10/67, NSF, Box 15, Table 2, Tab M, Johnson Mss.

244. Peter Dominick, _et al._ to Johnson, 7/27/67, Table 1, Tab M, _ibid._

245. Author's interview with Dean Rusk, 11/4/80.

246. Benjamin Reed to Humphrey transmitting DOS report, 8/1/67, Box 933, State Department - 1967 file, Humphrey Mss.

247. Notes on Cabinet meeting, 1/10/58, Anonymous Mss.

248. William Safire, _Before the Fall: An Inside View of the Pre-Watergate White House_ (Garden City, New York: Doubleday, 1975), p. 422.

249. Norvill Jones to Fulbright relaying Smith's comments, 10/21/69, 48:17:45:3, Fulbright Mss.

250. Scott to Kissinger, Klein, Harlow, Erlichman, Haldeman, Ziegler, Timmons, _et al._, 5/21/70, Box 65, White House 1970-76 folder, Scott Mss. The column was Richard Frank's "White House Kept Sen. Scott in Dark," _Philadelphia Bulletin_, 5/18/70.

251. Symington to Mansfield, 2/7/72, 48:17:46:3, Fulbright Mss.

252. U.S., Congress, Senate, Congressional Record, 7/12/73, p. 13198.

253. Richard M. Nixon, RN: The Memoirs of Richard Nixon (New York: Grosset and Dunlop, 1978), p. 351.

254. Safire, Before the Fall, p. 220-23.

255. Henry A. Kissinger, White House Years (Boston: Little, Brown, 1979), p. 1093.

256. Ibid., p. 969. Emphasis is Kissinger's.

257. Ibid., p. 513.

258. Ibid., p. 451.

259. Vernon Walters. Silent Missions (Garden City, New York: Doubleday, 1978), p. 517.

260. Kissinger, White House Years, pp. 1329, 1415.

261. Charles Bohlen, Witness to History: 1929-1969 (New York: W. W. Norton, 1973), p. 210.

262. Senate Foreign Relations Committee, War Powers, p. 436.

263. John Eisenhower to Dwight Eisenhower, 8/29/57, Box 9, The President-Memos file, Hagerty Mss.

264. Eisenhower to Whitman, 5/11/60, Box 50, DDE Diary, Eisenhower Mss. Several references to this appear in the DDE Diary series.

265. Hanes Oral History (Dulles), p. 18.

266. Bernard C. Cohen, The Public's Impact on Foreign Policy (Boston: Little, Brown, 1973), p. 114.

267. Bowles to Rusk, 2/21/63, Box 301, file 0538, Bowles Mss.

268. Bowles To Rusk, 5/19/61, file 0536, Bowles Mss.

269. Connell to Humphrey, 2/26/65, Box 41, FOA 7.3 Vietnam file, Humphrey Mss.

270. Connell to Humphrey including Gallup polls of 8/27/65 and 8/30/65, Box 41, Vietnam-Gen'l Csp 6/12/65 file, Humphrey Mss.

271. Connell to Humphrey, n.d., Box 4, American Dignitaries file, Humphrey Mss.

272. Humphrey to Johnson, 1/17/65, Box 924, Memos to the President-1965 file, Humphrey Mss.

273. Steven Neal, The Eisenhowers: Reluctant Dynasty (Garden City, New York: Doubleday, 1978), p. 380.

274. Lyndon B. Johnson, The Vantage Point: Perspective of the Presidency, 1963-1969 (New York: Holt, Rinehart, and Winston, 1971), p. 443.

275. Scammon to Ralph Duggan, 1/17/64 and Valenti to Walter (Rostow?), 1/23/64, both in WHCF - Countries, Box 27, E. Kennedy file, O'Brien papers, Johnson Mss.

276. O'Brien to Manatos, 6/4/65, Box 27, E. Kennedy File, White House Aides (O'Brien), Johnson Mss.

277. Edwards, Presidential Influence, p. 87.

278. Senate Committee on Government Operations, Administration of National Security, p. 625.

279. H. Schuyler Foster, "American Public Opinion and U.S. Foreign Policy," Department of State Bulletin, 41, p. 796.

280. Webb to Truman, 1/5/51, PSF, Box 159, Secretary of State-Misc. file, Truman Mss.

281. Senate Committee on Government Operations, Administration of National Security, p. 894.

282. Church Oral History (Johnson), tape I, p. 27.

283. Hilsman, To Move a Nation, p. 556.

## Chapter 5

1. Memorandum of conversation between Vandenberg and Lovett, 4/18/48, FR:1948, III, pp. 92-94.

2. George Marshall to Jefferson Caffery, 8/27/48, ibid., p. 22.

3. On Vandenberg's role, see ibid., pp. 1-353. Also, Dean Acheson, Present at the Creation: My Years in the State Department (New York: W. W. Norton, 1969), p. 266; and Susan Hartmann, Truman and the 80th Congress (Columbia, Missouri: University of Missouri Press, 1971), p. 172.

4. Acheson, Present at the Creation, p. 227. The following account of the NATO controversy relies heavily on Acheson.

5. Memorandum of conversation between Lovett and Vandenberg,

4/11/48, FR:1948, III, pp. 82-84. Memoranda of conversation among Acheson, Bohlen, Vandenberg, and Connally, 2/5/49 and 2/14/49, Box 64, Acheson Mss.

6. Minutes of 1st Meeting of Washington Exploratory Talks on Security, 7/16/48, FR:1948, III, pp. 148-55.

7. Memorandum of 10th meeting of Working Group Participating in Washington Exploratory Talks on Security, 8/12/48, ibid., p. 212. Also Secretary of State to Embassy in Norway, 2/13/49, FR:1949, IV, p. 102.

8. Acheson interview, 7/15-16/53, p. 14, Box 78, Acheson Mss.

9. Memorandum of meeting between Acheson and Truman, 2/28/49, memorandum of conversation among Acheson, Connally, George, and Vandenberg, 2/28/49, and memorandum of meeting between Acheson and Truman, 3/2/49; all in Box 64, Acheson Mss.

10. Memorandum of telephone conversation between Acheson and Truman, 4/26/49, ibid. Also, Acheson, Present at the Creation, p. 285.

11. Memorandum of conversation among Acheson, Connally, and Vandenberg, 6/24/49, Box 64, Acheson Mss.

12. Acheson to David Bruce, 7/26/49, ibid.

13. Acheson, Present at the Creation, p. 307; Memorandum of conversation between Acheson and Dulles, 7/26/49, Box 64, Acheson Mss.

14. Memorandum of conversation between Acheson and House leaders, 2/4/49, ibid.

15. Lippmann to Vandenberg, 8/8/49, Box 107, file 2145, Lippmann Mss.

16. Notes on conversations between Acheson and Matthew Connelly, Truman, Tom Connally, and Barkley all in single aide memorie, 8/3/49, Box 64, Acheson Mss.; Vandenberg to Lippmann, 8/9/49, Box 107, file 2145, Lippmann Mss.

17. Acheson, Present at the Creation, p. 313

18. Memorandum of conversation among Acheson, Attlee, and Foreign Secretary Aurin Bevin in London, 5/16/50, FR:1950, I, pp. 559-62.

19. Acheson, Present at the Creation, p. 484.

20. Ibid., p. 437.

21. Ibid., p. 495.

22. Mundt to L. H. Ickler, Jr., 4/21/51, and to Fred C. Christopherson, 4/6/51, both in RG III, box 480, file 1, Mundt Mss.

23. Coudert to Hoover, 1/25/51, Post-Presidential, Individual, Box 306, folder 2455, Hoover Mss.

24. Coudert to Vinson, 3/1/51, ibid.

25. Jenner to Herbert Hoover, 11/30/53, Box 378, file 2996-2, ibid.

26. E.g., Memorandum of telephone conversation between Acheson and Senator Henry Cabot Lodge, Jr., 1/16/51, Box 66, Acheson Mss.

27. Acheson, Present at the Creation, p. 496.

28. Memorandum of conversations between Acheson and Lovett, Harriman and Truman 4/3/51, Box 66, Acheson Mss.

29. Memorandum of conversation between Acheson and Joseph Pholien, 4/9/51/ ibid.

30. Acheson, Present at the Creation, p. 458.

31. Samuel F. Wells, Jr., "The Origins of Massive Retaliation," Political Science Quarterly, 96(1981), p. 32.

32. Acheson, Present at the Creation, pp. 436-40, 615-21, 648.

33. Assistant Secretary Livingston Merchant to Dean Rusk and George Ball, 2/7/64, NSF, Box 5, MLF file, Johnson Mss.

34. Reilly to Humphrey, 7/10/64, Box 722, MLF #2 file, Humphrey Mss.

35. Senators' letter, 9/7/674 and Representatives' letter, 12/7/64, both in MLF #1 file, ibid.

36. Dutton to McGeorge Bundy, 12/9/64, WHCF-Subject, Box 1, EX/ND 12/1/64 file, Johnson Mss.

37. McGeorge Bundy to Johnson, 12/9/64, ibid.

38. Reilly to Humphrey, 7/10/64, Box 722, MLF #2 file, Humphrey Mss.

39. Representative Chet Holifield to Johnson, 10/3/64, WHCF-Subject Box 1, EX/ND 5/6/64-11/30/64 file, Johnson Mss.; Holifield to Bowles, 1/7/65, Box 331, file 0102, Bowles Mss.

40. Holifield to Johnson, 10/3/64, Box 331, file 0102, Bowles Mss.

352

41. Author's interview with Dean Rusk, 11/4/80.

42. Quoted in Philip Geyelin, Lyndon B. Johnson and the World (New York: Frederick A. Praeger, 1966), p. 170. Also see, Johnson, Vantage Point, p. 477; Walt W. Rostow, The Diffusion of Power, an Essay in Recent History (New York: Macmillan, 1972), p. 393; and Annette Baker Fox, "NATO and Congress," Political Science Quarterly, 80(1965), p. 405.

43. E.g., Senator A. Willis Robertson to Lawrence O'Brien, 12/7/63, White House Aide Files (O'Brien), Box 29, Robertson file, Johnson Mss.

44. Gregory F. Treverton, Managing Alliances," in Report of the Commission on the Organization of Government for the Conduct of Foreign Policy (Murphy Commission), June, 1975, V. 4, p. 235-299. Mansfield to Johnson, 7/14/66, NSF-Names, Box 6, Mansfield file, Johnson Mss.

45. Henry Kissinger, The White House Years (Boston: Little, Brown, 1979), p. 935.

46. Ibid., p. 399 and Treverton, "Managing Alliances," p. 248.

47. Kissinger, White House Years, p. 940

48. Quoted in Jack Yochelson, "The American Military Presence in European: Current Debate in the United States," Orbis, 15(1971), p. 798. Also see Richard Moore to Walt Rostow, 1/26/67, NSF-Names, Box 6, Mansfield file, Johnson Mss.

49. Mike Manatos to Johnson, 7/24/65, WHCF-Country, Box 82, EX/CO 3/2 7/1/68-file, Johnson Mss.

50. Treverton, "Managing Alliances," p. 248.

51. Ibid.

52. Kissinger, White House Years, pp. 391-402. The quotation is from a briefing paper of 11/19/70, p. 402.

53. The above two paragraphs, including all quotations rely on ibid., pp. 938-49. On the continuation of pressure from Congress and its effect on European attitudes, see Henry Kissinger, Years of Upheaval (Boston: Little, Brown, 1982), pp.706-07, 1005-06.

54. E.g., Memorandum of conversation between Carl Marcy and Igor Bubnov, First Secretary of the Soviet Embassy, 10/19/66, Box 59, Foreign Relations-Marcy, Carl file, Hickenlooper Mss.

55. Kissinger, White House Years, p. 490. Kissinger attributes the Brezhnev speech to Soviet inflexibility, but agrees the Soviet loss of interest in the idea may have been partially a

result of the continued pressure by Congress.

56. Acheson, Present at the Creation, p. 204. Also see Tang Tsou, America's Failure in China, 1941-50 (Chicago: Quadrangle Books, 1971), p. 477; and Acheson interview, 7/22/53, reel 2, pp. 4-6, Box 79, Acheson Mss.

57. Acheson interview, 7/22/53, reel 2, pp. 4-6, Box 79, Acheson Mss.

58. Acheson's handwritten memoranda, 2/24/49 et seq., Box 64, Acheson Mss.

59. Acheson's memorandum, Item 4, 2/7/49 and NSC to S/S memorandum, 2/7/49 both in Box 64, Acheson Mss.

60. Acheson, Present at the Creation, p. 306.

61. Ibid.

62. E.g., memorandum of conversation between Acheson and Senators Knowland and H. A. Smith, 1/5/49, and memorandum of conversation between Acheson and Representative John Kee, Chairman, Foreign Affairs Committee, 1/4/50, both in Box 65, Acheson Mss.

63. Memorandum of conversation between Acheson and Truman, 11/17/49, Box 64, Acheson Mss.

64. Memorandum of conversation among Acheson, Connally, et al., 7/29/49, ibid.

65. E.g., Francis Wilcox, Chief of Staff, Foreign Relations Committee, to Senator H. A. Smith, 6/8/50, Box 100, H. A. Smith Mss.

66. Memorandum of conversation between Acheson and Senator H. A. Smith, 11/30/49, Box 64, Acheson Mss; Senator Knowland to Acheson, 5/15/50, Box 100, H. A. Smith Mss.

67. Acheson, Chapter 39, Present at the Creation, pp. 354-61.

68. Ibid., pp. 355-58.

69. Acheson to Bruce, 7/26/49, Box 64, Acheson Mss.

70. Acheson, Present at the Creation, p. 358.

71. Memorandum of conversation between Acheson and Vandenberg, 1/21/50, Box 65, Acheson Mss.

72. Acheson, Present at the Creation, p. 358.

73. Judd took credit for spawning the organization in his congres-

354

sional subcommittee. See Stanley D. Bachrack, The Committee of One Million: "China Lobby" Politics, 1953-1971 (New York: Columbia University Press, 1976), p. 66.

74. Memorandum on China Lobby by George Elsey, 6/8/51, and Truman to Attorney General, 6/11/51, both in Box 59, Foreign Relations, China Lobby file, Elsey Mss.

75. Elsey to Truman, 3/28/51, ibid.

76. Elsey to Tannenwald, 4/30/51, and Elsey memorandum on China Lobby, 6/8/51, both in ibid.

77. Acheson, Present at the Creation, p. 528.

78. Ross Y. Koen, The China Lobby in American Politics (New York: Macmillan, 1960), passim; William M. Bueler, U.S. China Policy and the Problem of Taiwan (Boulder, Colorado: Colorado Associated University Press, 1971), pp. 49, 88.

79. Acheson, Present at the Creation, pp. 369, 528.

80. Ibid., p. 364. Report of 7/20/51.

81. Ibid., p. 364.

82. Hughes Oral History (Dulles), p. 23.

83. Eleanor Lansing Dulles Oral History (Dulles), p. 38.

84. Murphy to Dulles, 1/18/54, Box 84, Dulles Mss.

85. Francis O. Wilcox, Congress, The Executive and Foreign Policy (New York: Harper & Row, 1971), p. 59.

86. Acheson, Present at the Creation, p. 100.

87. Acheson, A Citizen Looks at Congress (New York: Harper & Row, 1956), p. 65. Also, Oscar Perlmutter, "Acheson vs. Congress," Review of Politics, 22(1960), pp. 5-12.

88. Dwight D. Eisenhower, Mandate for Change, 1953-1956 (Garden City, New York: Doubleday, 1963), p. 215. A similar recollection is held by Bryce Harlow in his Oral History (Dulles), p. 16.

89. Bueler, U.S. China Policy, p. 37.

90. Quote is recalled in Beall Oral History (Dulles), p. 2. Also see Robert Bowie's testimony in Senate Committee on Government Operations, Administration of National Security, p. 909.

91. Notes on Cabinet meeting, 1/27/56, Anonymous Mss.

92. Senate Committee on Government Operations, <u>Administration of National Security</u>, p. 1283. Also see Edward Weintal and Charles Bartlett, <u>Facing the Brink: An Intimate Study of Crisis Diplomacy</u> (New York: Scribner, 1967), p. 153.

93. John Lehman, <u>The Executive, Congress, and Foreign Policy: Studies of the Nixon Administration</u> (New York: Praeger, 1976), pp. 115-65. Quotation is on p. 156.

94. Walter Pincus to Stuart Symington, 10/3/69, 48:6:24:1, Fulbright Mss.

95. Lynn and McClure, <u>The Fulbright Premise</u>, p. 152.

96. Acheson gives to detailed account of these events in <u>Present at the Creation</u>, p. 402-16. The discussion here relies heavily on the account.

97. Alfred Steinberg, <u>Sam Rayburn: A Biography</u> (New York: Hawthorn Books, 1975), p. 262.

98. Senator H. A. Smith to William Mylander, Publicity Director, Republican National Committee, 8/21/50 and 9/6/50, Box 100, H. A. Smith Mss.

99. Acheson interview, 7/15/53, Box 78, reading copy #1, p. 10.

100. <u>Ibid.</u>; and Acheson, <u>Present at the Creation</u>, p. 404.

101. Meeting at Blair House, 7/3/50, Box 65, Acheson Mss. This discussion here relies on the memorandum of conversation and, to a lesser degree this author's Rusk interview, 11/4/80.

102. Memorandum of DOS-JCS meeting, 4/11/51, p. 196, and Dulles to Marshall, 6/27/51, p. 221, both in <u>FR</u>:1951, VI.

103. Meeting of John Foster Dulles with Far Eastern Subcommittee of the Foreign Relations Committee, 3/19/51, <u>ibid.</u>, pp. 932-35.

104. Memorandum of conversation among Acheson, Yoshida, <u>et al.</u>, 9/3/51, Box 66, Acheson Mss.

105. Acheson, <u>Present at the Creation</u>, p. 603.

106. This letter is reproduced in <u>ibid.</u>, p. 759. For details of the Smith-Sparkman role, see Smith to William Castle, 1/3/52, Box 124, Dulles file, and memorandum of conversation between Smith and Dulles, 1/11/52, Box 107, both in H. A. Smith Mss.

107. Acheson, <u>Present at the Creation</u>, p. 698.

108. Notes of Special Legislative Conference, 8/2/53, Box 1,

Legislative Meeting Series, Eisenhower Mss. This can also be found in FR:1952-1954, III, p. 653. Also see Eisenhower, Mandate for Change, p. 215.

109. Eisenhower to Dulles, 6/2/53, p. 656, and memorandum of conversation between H. C.Lodge and the Danish foreign minister, 11/4/53, p. 325, both in FR:1952-1954, III.

110. Memorandum of conversation, 3/24/57, Box 114, China file, Dulles Mss.

111. Cabinet discussion on Korean War negotiations, n.d., Anonymous Mss.; Townsend Hoopes, The Devil and John Foster Dulles (Boston: Little, Brown, 1973), p. 187.

112. Jenner to Lodge, 7/16/54, FR:1952-1954, III, p. 360.

113. Memorandum of conversation between Assistant Secretary of State Robert Murphy and Richard Nixon,9/2/53, ibid., p. 350.

114. Memorandum of conversation between Dulles and Senator Bridges, 7/11/56, telephone transcripts, Box 5, Dulles Mss.

115. Hoopes, The Devil and John Foster Dulles, p. 419.

116. O'Connor Oral History (Dulles), pp. 44-46; Hanes Oral History (Dulles), p. 26.

117. Notes on Special Legislative Conference, 6/2/53, Box 1, Legislative Meeting Series, Eisenhower Mss.

118. Lodge to Eisenhower, 6/19/55 and Eisenhower to Herman Adams, 6/21/55, both in Box 27, Lodge 1955(3) file, Administration Series, Eisenhower Mss.

119. Estimate of Administration National Security Policy . . . . by Edwin Black, 7/11/56, Box 6, National Security Policy, FY 1958-60 file, Harlow Mss.

120. Robertson to Dulles, 6/22/57, Box 121, Dulles Mss.

121. Berding to Dulles, 6/18/57, Box 13, Adams file, Dulles Mss.

122. Quoted in Hoopes, The Devil and John Foster Dulles, p. 147.

123. Ibid., p. 146.

124. O'Connor Oral History (Dulles), p. 44; Hanes Oral History (Dulles), 36.

125. O'Connor Oral History (Dulles), p. 45.

126. Humphrey to F. W. Conrad, 2/12/55, Box 119, Formosa file, Humphrey Mss.

127. Humphrey to Jack (?), 3/16/60 and to Herb (?), 3/10/60, Box 185, Memos 1960 file, Humphrey Mss.

128. Fulbright to Marcy, 6/24/57, BCN 113:39, Fulbright Mss.

129. George Denney to Fulbright with a postscript by Marcy, 7/5/57, ibid. Also, Marcy to Fulbright, 4/8/59, BCN 146:7, Fulbright Mss.

130. Bowles to Kennedy, 6/8/62, Box 297, file 0498, Bowles Mss.

131. Bowles to Kennedy, 1/11/61, ibid.

132. Hilsman, To Move a Nation, pp. 307-10.

133. Ibid., pp. 305-07. Bridges is quoted on p. 306.

134. Ibid.

135. Alton Frye, A Responsible Congress: The Politics of National Security (New York: McGraw Hill, 1975), p. 156.

136. McGeorge Bundy Oral History (Johnson), tape 5, p. 24.

137. Pat Holt, Chief of Staff, Foreign Relations Committee to Fulbright and Aiken, 9/10/41, 48:11:36:5, Fulbright Mss.

138. National Journal, 5/29/76, p. 737.

139. Kissinger, White House Years, p. 785.

140. Ibid., p. 179.

141. W. Rostow to Johnson, 4/30/67, NSF-Names, Box 5, Mansfield file, Johnson Mss.

142. Kissinger, White House Years, p. 734.

143. Ibid., p. 1083.

144. Ibid., p. 1093.

145. Sherman Adams, First Hand Report (New York: Harper Bros., 1961), pp. 104, 176. Herbert S. Parmet, Eisenhower and the American Crusades (New York: Macmillan, 1972), pp. 295-315, 403.

146. Kefauver is quoted in Michael A. Guhin, John Foster Dulles: A Statesman and His Times (New York: Columbia University Press, 1972), p. 499. Also, memorandum of meeting between Eisenhower and Dulles, 7/20/54, Box 2, Whitman Diary,

358

Eisenhower Mss.

147. Summary record of NSC meeting #532, 5/15/64, NSF-Meeting, box 1, Johnson Mss.

148. Senator A. William Robertson to Lawrence O'Brien, 3/27/64, WHCF-Countries, Box 79, CO312, 11/22/63-6/14/64 file, Johnson Mss.

149. Summary notes of NSC meeting #538, 8/4/64, NSF-Meetings, Box 1, Johnson Mss.

150. McGeorge Bundy Oral History (Johnson), tape 1, p. 28; Hickenlooper Oral History (Johnson), p. 7; Sparkman Oral History (Johnson), p. 19. The records show that various members of Congress sat in on many NSC meetings during the late 1964-early 1965 period. See NSF-Meetings, Box 1, Johnson Mss.

151. Kwan Ha Yem, China and the United States (New York: Facts on File, 1972), p. 27.

152. Mansfield to Johnson, 6/9/65, NSF-Names, Box 6, Mansfield file, Johnson Mss.

153. Summary notes of NSC meeting #554, 8/5/65, NSF-Meetings, Box 1, Johnson Mss.

154. Summary notes of NSC meeting #545, 2/6/65, ibid.

155. Summary notes of NSC meeting (?), 4/2/65, ibid.

156. Charles Roche to Johnson, 7/6/66, Box 3, Memos to the President 1966 file, and Roche to Henry Wilson, and James Jones to Wilson, both 3/3/67, Box 11, Congressional Receptions file, all in White House Aides Files (Roche), Johnson Mss.

157. Robert L. Gallucci, "Bombing North Vietnam," Murphy Commission Report, p. 407. Also, O'Brien, No Final Victories, p. 213.

158. Summary notes of NSC meeting #547, 2/8/65, NSF-Meetings, Box 1, Johnson Mss.

159. Report of conversation with Symington, 12/13/67 attached to Jack Valenti to Marvin (Watson), 12/14/67, White House Aides Files (Watson), Box 32, Vietnam (2) file, Johnson Mss.

160. Handwritten notes of Foreign Relations Committee meeting by Senator Hugh Scott, 11/1/71, Box 180, Foreign Affairs-Foreign Aid (1) file, Scott Mss.

161. Mansfield to Johnson, 6/29/66, NSF-Names, Box 6, Mansfield file, Johnson Mss.

162. Lee Williams to Fulbright relating conversation with Hartke, 3/13/68, 48:17:45:1, Fulbright Mss.

163. Ibid.

164. Valenti to Johnson, 12/18/65, WHCF-Countries, Box 7, CO303 file, Johnson Mss.

165. Humphrey to Johnson, 2/17/65, Box 924, Memos to the President-1965 file, Humphrey Mss.

166. Reilly to Humphrey, n.d., Box 722, Humphrey Mss.

167. Roche to Johnson, 9/28/66, White House Aides Files (Watson), Box 29, Johnson Roche file, Johnson Mss.

168. Roche to Johnson, 7/20/66, White House Aides Files (Roche), Box 3, Memos to the President-1966 file, Johnson Mss.

169. Mundt to Robert H. Wagner, 11/27/65, RG III, Box 488, file 6, Mundt Mss.

170. Mundt to Javits, 11/15/67, RG III, Box 493, file 5, Mundt Mss.

171. Russell to Harvey J. Kennedy, 8/13/65, Series 1, Subseries C, Box 1, Political 1965-166 file, Russell Mss.

172. Valenti to Johnson, 3/2/65, WHCF Countries, Box 79, CO312 files, Johnson Mss.

173. Arthur Goldberg to Johnson plus attachment, 1/15/66, WHCF-Confidential, Box 71, ND19/CO312 file, Johnson Mss.

174. Mike Mantos to Johnson, 8/11/67, NSF-Names, Box 5, Manatos file, Johnson Mss.

175. Valenti to Johnson, 11/14/64, WHCF-Confidential, Box 12, CO312 file, Johnson Mss.

176. Johnson to Eisenhower, 3/5/65, WHCF-Central Name File, Box 2, Eisenhower-1967 file, Johnson Mss.

177. Kearns, Lyndon Johnson, p. 347.

178. Eugene Rostow Oral History (Johnson), p. 16.

179. Kearns, Lyndon Johnson, p. 347.

180. Fulbright to Johnson, 10/7/65, 1:1:3:2, Fulbright Mss.

181. Arthur Goldberg to Douglas MacArthur II, Assistant Secretary of State for Congressional Relations, 1/16/66, WHCF-Confidential, Box 71, ND19/CO312 file, Johnson Mss.

182. Eugene Rostow Oral History (Johnson), p. 39.

183. O'Brien, No Final Victories, p. 245.

184. Roche to Johnson, 12/4/67, White House Aides Files (Roche), Box 3, Memos to the President-1965, Johnson Mss.

185. E.g., Walt Rostow to Robert Kennedy, 5/5/66, NSF-Names, Box 3, Robert Kennedy file, Johnson Mss.

186. E.g., George Carroll to Bill Connell, 3/16/67, Box 930, Carroll 1966-67 file, Humphrey Mss.
187. Roche to Johnson, 4/18/67, White House Aides File (Watson), Box 29, Roche file, Johnson Mss.

187. Roche to Johnson, 4/18/67, White House Aides File (Watson), Box 29, Roche file, Johnson Mss.

188. Robert L. Peabody, Norman J. Orenstein, and David W. Rhode, "The United States Senate as a Presidential Incubator, Many Are Called But Few Are Chosen," Political Science Quarterly, 91(1976), p. 256.

189. Kearns, Lyndon Johnson, pp. 346-48 and passim; O'Brien, No Final Victories, Chapter 11 beginning on p. 212.

190. Kissinger, White House Years, Chapter 8 title, p. 226.

191. McCormack to colleagues, 10/17/68, WHCF-Subject, Box 170, LE5 1/13/68-file, Johnson Mss.

192. Kissinger, White House Years, p.215.

193. Ibid., p. 476.

194. Ibid., p. 481.

195. Ibid., p. 477.

196. Ibid., p. 245.

197. Ibid., pp. 483-513. The following discussion and quotations are drawn from these pages.

198. Ibid., p. 513.

199. Ibid., p. 969.

200. Sid Baily to Scott, 6/12/70, and Martin to Jim (members of Scott's staff), 5/12/70, both in Box 206, Vietnam-Cambodia Intervention file, Scott Mss.

201. Exchange of letters between Scott and Representative Donald Riegle, 4/1/71, Box 205, Vietnam (1) file, Scott Mss.

202. Bailey to Scott, 6/2/70, Box 206, Vietnam-Cambodia Intervention file, Scott Mss.

203. This and the following discussion relies on Kissinger White House Years, pp. 1012-24, 42.

204. Ibid., p. 1042.

205. Ibid., p. 1116.

206. Ibid., p. 1190.

207. Ibid., p. 1329.

208. Walters, Silent Missions, p. 517.

209. Nixon, RN, p. 724.

210. Kissinger, White House Years, p. 1330.

211. Ibid., p. 1453; Kissinger, Years of Upheaval, pp. 326-29, 337-38, 356-61.

212. Robert Sherrill, Why They Call It Politics (New York: Harcourt, Brace, Jovanovich, 1972), p. 21.

213. Kissinger, White House Years, p. 1464.

214. Acheson, Present at the Creation, p. 169-82.

215. Truman to David Niles, 5/13/47, PSF, Box 184, Palestine, 1945-1947 file, Truman Mss.

216. Memorandum of meeting, 5/12/48, Box 160, Palestine file, Elsey Mss.

217. E.g., Sol Bloom, ranking Democrat on Foreign Affairs Committee, to Truman, 8/3/48, PSF, Box 184, Palestine, 1948-1950 file, Truman Mss.

218. Memoranda of meetings between Acheson and Abraham Feinberg, 4/5/51 and 7/17/51, and memoranda of conversations between Truman and Acheson, 4/2/51 and 4/5/51, all in Box 66, Acheson Mss.

219. O'Connor Oral History (Dulles), p. 75.

220. Ibid., p. 117.

221. Javits Oral History (Dulles), p. 14.

222. Dulles conversation with Ives, 10/23/53, telephone transcripts, Box 1, Dulles Mss.

223. Dulles conversations with Brownell and Nixon, both 10/17/55, telephone transcripts, Box 4, Dulles Mss.

224. Dulles conversation with Henry Byroade, Ambassador to Egypt, 3/23/57, telephone transcripts, Box 1, Dulles Mss.

225. Dulles conversation with Eugene Black, 1/23/56, telephone transcripts, Box 5, Dulles Mss.

226. Adams First Hand Report, p. 248; Dwight D. Eisenhower, Waging Peace, p. 32; John Robinson Beal, John Foster Dulles, 1888-1959 (New York: Harper & Row, 1959), p.256; Guhin, John Foster Dulles, p. 272.

227. Dulles conversations with Roswell Barnes and Everett Dirksen, both 7/16/56, telephone transcripts, Box 5, Dulles Mss.

228. Dulles conversation with Knowland, 3/17/56, ibid.

229. Dulles to Eisenhower, 8/2/55, Dulles-Herter Series, Box 4, Eisenhower Mss.

230. Dewey to Dulles, 7/20/46, Box 102, Dulles Mss.

231. Eisenhower, Waging Peace, p. 31.

232. Dulles conversation with Knowland, 7/17/56, telephone transcripts, Box 5, Dulles Mss.

233. Dulles conversation with Allen Dulles, 7/19/56, ibid.; Hoopes, The Devil and John Foster Dulles, p. 341.

234. Dulles to Eisenhower, 9/15/56 quoted in Eisenhower, Waging Peace, p. 33.

235. Hoopes, The Devil and John Foster Dulles, p. 374.

236. Johnson to Bowles, Box 140, file 0349, Bowles Mss.

237. George to Bowles, 10/21/55, Box 134, file 0250, Bowles Mss.

238. Hanes to Dulles, 11/22/55, telephone transcripts, Box 4, Dulles Mss.

239. Ibid., margin notation.

240. Rabb to Hanes, 10/3/56, Box 108, Republican Presidential Campaign file, Dulles Mss.

241. Culter to Dulles, 10/26/56, ibid.

242. Dulles conversation with Nixon, 10/31/56, telephone transcripts, Box 5, Dulles Mss.

243. Hoopes, The Devil and John Foster Dulles, p. 394.

244. Memorandum of meeting between Eisenhower and representatives of Synagogue Council of America, 12/28/60, Box 55, Staff notes, 12/60 file, DDE Diary, Eisenhower Mss.

245. Dulles conversation with Luce, 2/11/57, telephone transcripts, Box 6, Dulles Mss.

246. Ibid.

247. Dulles conversation with Barnes, 2/19/56, ibid.

248. Lodge to Dulles, 3/7/57, Box 118, Dulles Mss.

249. Dulles conversation with Vorys, 2/13/57, telephone transcripts, Box 6, Dulles Mss.

250. Dulles conversation with Barnes, 2/19/57 and with Edward Elson, 2/22/57, both in ibid.

251. E.g., Vorys to Louis Berliner, 2/1/57, Box 124, Dulles Mss.

252. Johnson to Dulles, 2/11/57, Dulles-Herter Series, Box 6, Eisenhower Mss.

253. Sam Zagoria, A. A. to Senator Clifford Case, to William Macomber, Special Assistant to the Secretary of State, 2/18/57, Box 114, Case file, Dulles Mss.

254. E.g., Iowa's Bourke Hickenlooper's mail filled four file folders. See Box 23, Hickenlooper Mss. Examinations of legislative archival collections typically show that pro-Israel mail was often the most significant category of constituent mail on foreign policy.

255. Bipartisan Leadership Meeting, 2/20/57, Box 2, Legislative Series, Eisenhower Mss.

256. Dulles conversation with Vorys, 12/13/57, telephone transcripts, Box 6, Dulles Mss.

257. Dulles conversation with Knowland, 2/16/47, ibid..

258. Conversation between Dulles and Eisenhower, 3/4/57, Box 72, DDE Diary, Eisenhower Mss.

259. Conversation between Dulles and Lodge, 2/17/57, telephone transcripts, Box 6, Dulles Mss.

260. Conversation between Dulles and Lodge, 2/12/57, ibid.

261. Conversation between Dulles and Johnson, 2/25/57, ibid.

262. Legislative meeting, 2/20/57, Box 2, Legislative Meeting Series, Eisenhower Mss.

263. Conversation between Dulles and Lodge, 2/24/57, telephone transcripts, Box 6, Dulles Mss.

264. Ibid.

265. Conversation between Dulles and Lodge, 2/17/57, ibid.

266. Legislative meeting, 2/20/57, Box 2, Legislative Meeting Series, Eisenhower Mss. Also author's interview with Dean Rusk, 11/4/80.

267. Conversation between Herter and Richards, 5/1/47, Box 10, Herter Mss.

268. Herter to Eisenhower, 1/30/58, Box 29, Israel (2) file, International Series, Eisenhower Mss.; and Herter to Senator Green, 2/13/58 and Green to Senator Johnson, 4/25/58, Box 93, both in Hickenlooper Mss.

269. Eugene Rostow Oral History (Johnson), p. 17; Michael Brecher, Decisions in Israel's Foreign Policy (New Haven, Connecticut: Yale University Press, 1975), p. 399, note 3.

270. William B. Quandt, Decade of Decisions: American Policy Toward the Arab-Israeli Conflict, 1967-1976 (Berkeley, California: University of California Press, 1977), p. 44.

271. Notes of meeting, Box 930, Chronology, June 1967 file, Humphrey Mss.

272. Fred Panzer to Johnson, 6/2/67, WHCF-Confidential, ND19/CO1-6 file, Box 193, Johnson Mss.

273. Brecher, Decisions on Israel's Foreign Policy, p. 392; Quandt, Decade of Decisions, p. 45.

274. Brecher, Decisions on Israel's Foreign Policy, p. 391.

275. Ibid., p. 387 quoting an Israeli Foreign Ministry source.

276. Ibid., quoting an Israeli Foreign Ministry source. Also, see Abba Eban, Abba Eban, An Autobiography (New York: Random House, 1977), p. 350.

277. Brecher, Decisions on Israel's Foreign Policy, p. 391 quoting Evron's cable to Israeli government.

278. Quandt, Decade of Decisions, p. 52.

279. Eugene Rostow Oral History (Dulles), p. 18.

280. Brecher, Decisions on Israel's Foreign Policy, p. 400.

281. Quandt, Decade of Decisions, p. 47.

282. Eugene Rostow Oral History (Johnson), p. 18.

283. Johnson, Vantage Point, pp. 291-95. The Rusk-McNamara memorandum is on p. 295.

284. Rostow to Johnson, 6/1/67, WHCF-Confidential, Box 193, NO19/C01-6 file, Johnson Mss.

285. Manatos to Johnson, 7/5/67, ibid.

286. Peter Rosenblatt to Marvin Watson, 3/19/68, White House Aides Files (Watson), Box 24, Jewish Community file, Johnson Mss.

287. Eban is quoted in Valenti to Johnson, 11/4/67, WHCF-Countries, Box 42, EX/C0125 file, Johnson Mss.

288. Yitzak Rabin, The Rabin Memoirs (Boston: Little Brown, 1979), p.131; Barefoot Sanders to Johnson, 9/24/68, WHCF-Countries, Box 43, C0126 file, Johnson Mss.

289. Kissinger, White House Years, pp. 353, 363. On congressional pressure to resupply Israel during the 1973 war and the access of Israeli officials to Congress, see Kissinger, Years of Upheaval, pp. 495, 504.

290. Fulbright to Ambassador M. Kemmel, 12/28/70, 48:15:40:3, Fulbright Mss.

291. Fulbright to David G. Nes, 12/1/70, ibid.

292. Fulbright to the Rt. Rev. Ignatius Ghattus, 9/25/72, 48:15:40:4, Fulbright Mss.

293. Fulbright to Black, 8/6/71, 48:8:31:2, Fulbright Mss.

## Chapter 6

1. Raymond A. Bauer, Ithiel de Sola Pool, and Lewis Anthony Dexter, American Business and Public Policy: The Politics of Foreign Trade (New York: Atherton Press, 1963), pp. 33-39.

2. Robert A. Pastor, Congress and the Politics of U.S. Foreign Economic Policy, 1929-1976 (Berkeley, California: University of California Press, 1980), pp. 196-198.

3. Bauer, Pool, and Dexter, American Business and Public Policy, p. 33.

4. C. D. Jackson to Dulles, n.d. (circa early to mid 1954), Anonymous Mss.

5. Legislative leader meeting, 3/29/54, Box 1, Legislative Meeting Series, Eisenhower Mss.

6. Eisenhower conversation with Senator Homer Capehart, 3/30/54, Box 4, DDE Diaries, Eisenhower Mss.

7. Cabinet meeting, 8/18/54, Anonymous Mss. Also, John Emmet Hughes, The Ordeal of Power: A Political Memoir of the Eisenhower Years (New York: Antheneum, 1963), p. 177.

8. Legislative meeting, 12/13/54, Box 1, Legislative Meeting Series, Eisenhower Mss.

9. Bauer, Pool, and Dexter, American Business and Public Policy, pp. 50-73; Sherman Adams, First Hand Report (New York: Harper Bros., 1961), p. 392.

10. Pastor, Foreign Economic Policy, p. 190; I. M. Destler, Making Foreign Economic Policy (Washington, D.C.: Brookings Institution, 1980), p. 36.

11. Ibid., p. 333.

12. Robert A. Pastor, "Congress' Impact on Latin America: Is There Method in the Madness," in Murphy Commission Report, V, 3, p. 268.

13. Morton H. Halperin, Bureaucratic Politics and Foreign Policy (Washington, D.C.: The Brookings Institution, 1974), p. 71.

14. Pastor, Foreign Economic Policy, p. 333.

15. Ibid., pp. 191-93.

16. Lyndon Johnson, Vantage Point: Perspectives of the Presidency, 1963-1969 (New York: Holt, Rinehart, Winston, 1971), p. 39.

17. Fulbright to Humphrey, 9/2/65, Box 923, USSR-1965 file, Humphrey Mss. On the Consular Convention and East-West trade issues see Johnson, Vantage Point, p. 473; and Phillip Geyelin, Lyndon Johnson and the World (New York: Frederick A. Praeger, 1966), pp. 283-90.

18. Fulbright to Mansfield, 8/26/65, Box 923, USSR-1965 file, Humphrey Mss.

19. John Rielly to Humphrey, 10/26/65, ibid.

20. Edward Skloat, "The Decision to Send East-West Trade Legisla-

tion to Congress, 1965-1966 in Murphy Commission report. V.3, p. 79.

21. Fulbright to Johnson, 6/30/66, WHCF-Countries, Box 74, C0303 file, Johnson Mss.; and Robert Kertner, Secretary to the Cabinet, to Larry O'Brien, 6/29/66, WHCF-Subject, Box 169, LE5 5/18/66-8/31/66 file, Johnson Mss.

22. Fulbright to Mansfield, 6/17/66, Legislative Background Consular Treaty, Box 1, Johnson Mss.

23. MacArthur to Ledy, 9/26/66, ibid.

24. Unaddressed memorandum by Johnson, 7/7/66, and Bator to Johnson, 6/21/66, both in ibid.

25. John Rielly to Humphrey, 1/17/67, Box 931, East-West Trade file, Humphrey Mss.

26. Neil MacNeil, Dirksen: Portrait of a Public Man (New York: World Publishing, 1970) discusses Morton's role on pp. 293-95. The quotation is on p. 293.

27. Exchange of letters between Mundt and Hoover, 1/21/67 and 1/23/67, RG III, Box 505, file 1, Mundt Mss.

28. Mundt to Hickenlooper, 1/28/67, RG III, Box 492, ibid.

29. Memorandum of conversation between Carl Marcy, Chief of Staff, Foreign Relations Committee, and Igor Bubnov, First Secretary, Soviet Embassy, 10/19/66, Box 59, Hickenlooper Mss.

30. Hruska to Dirksen, 2/21/67, Working Papers, file 451, Dirksen Mss.

31. John Rielly to Humphrey, 2/4/67, Box 93, USSR-1967 file, Humphrey Mss.

32. DOS official to Charles McBride, aide to Senator Russell, ibid..

33. MacNeil, Dirksen, p. 294.

34. Ibid.

35. Nicholas deB Katzenbach, Under Secretary of State, to Dirksen, 2/2/67, and Rusk to Dirksen, 2/23/67, Working Papers, file 452, Dirksen Mss.

36. Mundt to Allan Ryskind, 2/9/67, RG III, Box 504, file 6, Mundt Mss.

37. Mundt to Donald B. Ward, 3/4/67, RG III, Box 492, file 4,

Mundt Mss.

38. Mundt to Eric L. Predonoff, 4/29/67, RG III, Box 493, file 3, Mundt Mss.

39. Johnson to Mundt, 6/8/67, RG III, Box 493, file 4, Mundt Mss.

40. Conversation among Humphrey, Irwin Miller, President, Cummings Engine Corp., and Anthony Solomon, Assistant Secretary of State for Economic Affairs, 3/16/67, Box 934, Miller and Solomon file, Humphrey Mss.

41. Mundt to Walter Miller, 7/19/67, RG III, Box 491, file 4, Mundt Mss.

42. Humphrey to Tom Watson, 10/4/67, Box 931, East-West Trade file, Humphrey Mss.; Geyelin, Lyndon Johnson, pp. 283-90.

43. Legislative meeting, 7/1/58, Box 2, Legislative Meeting Series, Eisenhower Mss.

44. E.g., conversation between Dulles and C. D. Jackson, 5/29/53, telephone transcripts, Box 1, Dulles Mss.

45. MacNeil, Dirksen, p. 137.

46. E.g. Herter conversation with Senator Saltonstall, 1/29/58, Box 11, Calls file, Herter Mss.

47. John D. Montgomery, Foreign Aid in International Politics (Englewood Cliffs, New Jersey: Prentice-Hall, 1967), p. 22; MIchael Kent O'Leary, The Politics of American Foreign Aid (New York: Atherton Press, 1967, p. 123.

48. Exchange of letters between Bowles and Senator A. S. Mike Monroney, 10/9/67 and 10/31/67, Box 334, file 152, Bowles Mss.

49. Fulbright to Bowles, 1/12/64, Box 334, file 0153, Bowles Mss.

50. Johnson to Hayden, 12/17/63, WHCF-Subject, Box 57, EX LE/FO3-2 file, Johnson Mss.

51. Benjamin Higgins, The United Nations and U.S. Foreign Economic Policy (Homewood, Illinois: Richard D. Irwin, 1972), p. 117.

52. U. S., Congress, Senate, Committee on Government Operations, Administration of National Security, Hearings by the Subcommittee on National Security, 88th Cong. (1963-1964), pp. 1183. Also, Kenneth Waltz, Foreign Policy and Democratic Politics, The American and British Experiences (Boston: Little, Brown, 1967), p. 199.

53. Waltz, Foreign Policy and Democratic Politics, p. 199.

54. Pastor, "Latin America," p. 267.

55. Ibid., p. 266.

56. W. E. Kuhn, "The Hickenlooper Amendment As a Determinant of the Outcome of Expropriations Disputes," Social Science, 14(1977), p. 71.

57. Henry Kissinger, White House Years (Boston: Little Brown, 1979), p. 651.

58. Daniel A. Sharp, "The Context of U.S. Policy for Peru," in U.S. Foreign Policy and Peru, ed. by Daniel A. Sharp (Austin, Texas: University of Texas Press, 1972), p. 13.

59. Pastor, Foreign Economic Policy, p. 298.

60. Richard P. Lillich, Requiem for Hickenlooper," American Journal of International Law, 69(1975), p. 97.

61. Remarks of Charles Halleck, 12/13/54, Box 1, Legislative Meeting Series, Eisenhower Mss.

62. Fulbright to Bowles, 8/19/63, Box 334, file 0153, and Fulbright to Bowles, 4/23/63, Box 330, file 0075, both in Bowles Mss.

63. Destler, Making Foreign Economic Policy, p. 28.

64. James A. Robinson, Congress and Foreign Policy-Making: A Study in Legislative Influence and Initiative (Homewood, Illinois: Dorsey Press, Rev. ed., 1967), p. 61. Alton Frye, A Responsible Congress: The Politics of National Security (New York: McGraw Hill, 1975), p. 172.

65. Conversation among Lovett, Truman, and Acheson, 8/6/51, Box 66, Acheson Mss.

66. Waltz, Foreign Policy and Democratic Politics, p. 200.

67. O'Leary, The Politics of American Foreign Aid, p. 117.

68. Mike Manatos to Larry O'Brien, 8/10/64, WHCF-Subject, Box 57, EX LE/FO3-2 file, Johnson Mss.

69. Harlow Oral History (Johnson), p. 42. Brackets in the original.

70. Waltz, Foreign Policy and Democratic Politics, p. 207.

71. David A. Baldwin, Foreign Aid an American Foreign Policy: A Documentary Analysis (New York: Frederick A. Praeger, Pub-

lishers, 1966), p.115. O'Leary, Politics, p. 101. David Allen Kay, "'Unconstitutional' Restrictions on the President of the United States in Foreign Aid Legislation, 1947-1967," in Columbia Essays in International Affairs, The Dean's Papers, 1965, ed. by Andrew S. Cordier (New York: Columbia University Press, 1966), passim. Many of the comments on foreign aid, particularly those relating to harassment of the Administration and budget cuts, but also indicating, overall progress, also apply to overseas information policy. See Ronald I. Ruben, The Objectives of the U.S. Information Agency: Controversies and Analysis (New York: Frederick A. Praeger, 1968), pp. 200-02; Robert E. Elder, The Information Machine: The United States Agency (New York: Frederick A. Praeger, 1969), pp. 36-40, 52, 221; and Thomas C. Sorenson, The World War: The Story of American Propaganda (New York: Harper & Row, Publishers, 1968), pp. 23-41.

72. George C. Edwards, III, Presidential Influence in Congress (San Francisco: W. H. Freeman, 1980), p. 26.

73. Vandenberg to Senator Clyde Reed, 1/12/49, Vandenberg Mss.

74. Bridges to Kissinger, 1/14/61, Box 299, file 0519, Bowles Mss.

75. Dean Acheson, Present at the Creation: My Years in the State Department (New York: W. W. Norton, s1969), p. 304.

76. Ibid., p. 711.

77. Ibid., p. 687. After the McCarthy era, Battle returned to the diplomatic service.

78. Memorandum of conversation between Acheson and Biddle, 5/3/49, Box 64, Acheson Mss.

79. Hanes Oral History (Dulles), p. 21.

80. Kennan Oral History (Dulles), p. 56.

81. Hughes Oral History (Dulles), p. 16.

82. Murphy to Dulles, 1/18/54, Box 84, Dulles Mss.

83. Letter to New York Times from Norman Armour, Robert Bliss Woods, Joseph C. Grew, William Phillips, and G. Howland Shaw, 1/17/54 quoted in Norman A. Graebner, The New Isolationism: A Study in Politics and Foreign Policy Since 1950 (New York: Ronald Press, 1956), p. 139.

84. Allen Dulles to Walter Lippmann, 8/7/53, Box 68, file 666, Lippmann Mss.

85. E.g., Bryce Harlow to Eisenhower, 7/14/53, Anonymous Mss.

86. See Senator Taft's comments at legislative leaders meeting, 3/9/53, Box 1, Legislative Meeting Series, Eisenhower Mss.

87. Senator Bourke Hickenlooper to Robert Mannheimer, 7/20/59, Box 3, Hickenlooper Mss.

88. Townsend Hoopes, The Devil and John Foster Dulles (Boston: Little, Brown, 1973), p. 160.

89. Conversation between Dulles and General Wilton Persons, 3/16/53, telephone transcripts, Box 1, Dulles Mss.

90. Conversation between Dulles and Taft, 3/16/53, ibid.

91. U.S., Congress, Senate, Committee on Foreign Relations, Executive Sessions-1953, V. II, part 2, 83rd Cong., 1st sess. (published, 1979). p. 382.

92. Eisenhower to Bohlen, 7/16/59, Box 43, DDE Dictation, DDE Diary, Eisenhower Mss.

93. Conversation between Dulles and Byrnes, 3/16/53, telephone transcripts, Box 1, Dulles Mss.

94. Hoopes, The Devil and John Foster Dulles, p. 160

95. Conversation between Dulles and Taft, 3/16/53, telephone transcripts, Box 1, Dulles Mss.

96. Conversation between Dulles and Knowland, 3/7/53, ibid.

97. Hoopes, The Devil and John Foster Dulles, p. 160

98. Hanes Oral History (Dulles), p. 22.

99. Adams, First Hand Report, p. 94; Graebner, The New Isolationism, pp. 134-39; and Hughes, Ordeal of Power, p. 121.

100. Vandenberg to Acheson, 3/29/50, Box 651, Acheson Mss.

101. Hoopes, The Devil and John Foster Dulles, p. 86.

102. Vandenberg to Acheson, 3/31/50, Box 65, Acheson Mss.

103. Memorandum of conversation between Acheson and Truman, 4/4/50, ibid.

104. Memorandum of conversation between Dulles and Acheson, 4/6/50, ibid.

105. Dulles to Acheson, 4/5/50, ibid.

106. Memorandum of conversation between Acheson and Lehman,

4/5/50, ibid.

107. Memorandum of conversation between Truman and Dulles, 4/28/50, ibid. On this episode, also see Louis L. Gerson, John Foster Dulles (New York: Cooper Square, 1967), pp. 57-61.

108. Pat Durand to Bowles, 2/28/61, Box 304, file 0579, Bowles Mss.

109. Eisenhower to Dulles, 7/22/57, Box 6, Dulles-Herter Series, Eisenhower Mss.

110. Senator Theodore Green to Dulles, 4/3/47, Box 125, Mid-East file, Dulles Mss.

111. Conversation between Dulles and Herter, 7/31/58, telephone transcripts, Box 9, Dulles Mss.

112. Conversation between Dulles and Halleck, 3/5/53, telephone transcripts, Box 1, Dulles Mss.

113. O'Connor Oral History (Dulles), p. 170.

114. Lodge to Eisenhower, 3/30/55, Box 27, Lodge, 1955(4) file, Administrative Series, Eisenhower Mss.

115. E.g., Robert Hill to Dulles regarding conversation with Senator George, 6/11/56, telephone transcripts, Box 5, Dulles Mss.

116. For an illustrative discussion of considerations, see conversation between Herter and Knowland, 6/20/57, Box 10, Herter Mss.

117. Dirksen Oral History (Dulles), p. 5.

118. Dirksen to Assistant Secretary of State Donald Lourie, 3/9/53, Box 69, Dulles Mss.

119. MacNeil, Dirksen, p. 350

120. Valenti, A Very Human President (New York: W. W. Norton, 1975), p. 183.

121. Memorandum of conversations between Acheson and Benton 3/16/52, Box 66, Acheson Mss.

122. Memorandum of Conversation between Herter and Adams, 6/22/57, Box 10, Herter Mss.

123. Bridges to Dulles, 7/18/53, Box 67, Dulles Mss.

124. Conversation between Herter and David Kendell, (mid-April

1959), Box 12, Herter Mss.

125. Hoopes, The Devil and John Foster Dulles, p. 148; Roger Hilsman, To Move a Nation: The Politics of Foreign Policy in the Administration of John F. Kennedy (New York: Dell Publishing, 1964), p. 299.

126. Charles Frankel, High on Foggy Bottom: An Outsider's Inside View of the Government (New York: Harper & Row, 1968), pp. 12-15, 46.

127. Carl Marcy to Senator Fulbright, 6/2/65, 48:4:19:1, Fulbright Mss.

128. Hoopes, The Devil and John Foster Dulles, p. 136.

129. Conversation between Dulles and Lodge, 11/10/54, telephone transcripts, Box 3, Dulles Mss.

130. O'Connor Oral History (Dulles), p. 57.

131. Richard Nixon, RN: The Memoirs of Richard Nixon (New York: Grosset and Dunlap, 1978), p. 339. Henry Kissinger argues that, as Roosevelt had chosen Truman as Vice President because of his standing with Congress, so Nixon, in a negative way, chose Gerald Ford as Vice President because of his lack of foreign policy expertise. According to Kissinger, Nixon chose Ford, in part, because "His selection would dampen desires to impeach [Nixon] because Congress would not want to run the risk of placing a supposedly inexperienced man in charge of foreign policy." Kissinger, Years of Upheaval, p. 514.

132. Diary entry, 8/19/47, Box 9, Whitman Diary, Eisenhower Mss.

133. Conversation between Dulles and Langer, n.d., telephone transcripts, Box 1, Dulles Mss.

134. Memorandum of conversation between Bricker and Eisenhower, 11/22/57, Box 24, May 1957-Staff Memos file, DDE Diaries, Eisenhower Mss.

135. Memorandum of conversation between Aiken and Eisenhower, 11/17/56, Box 8, Whitman Diary, Eisenhower Mss.

136. Claude Desaultes to Larry O'Brien, 9/30/64, Desaultes to O'Brien, 4/21/65, Mike Manatos to O'Brien, 7/8/65, and William Rice to John Marcy, 7/8/65, all White House Aides Files (O'Brien) Box 33, Morgan file, Johnson Mss.

137. Thomas C. Sorenson, The World War: The Story of American Propaganda (New York: Holt, Rinehart, 1968), pp. 29, 33, 40.

138. Mansfield to Richard Russell, 7/22/70, Series 9, Subseries AA, Box 1, Policy Committee-1970 file, Russell Mss.

139. Fulbright to Reuben Thomas, 8/1/73, 48:4:19:3, Fulbright Mss.

140. Sorenson, The World War, p. 94.

141. Eisenhower to Dulles, 4/28/58, Box 8, Dulles-Herter Series, Eisenhower Mss.

142. Diary entry, 4/28/59, Box 10, Whitman Diary, Eisenhower Mss. Claire Booth Luce to Karl Mundt, 6/5/59, RG III, Box 483, file 2, Mundt Mss. Eisenhower, Waging Peace, p. 391.

143. Henry Cabot Lodge, Jr., As It Was: An Inside View of Politics and Power in the '50's and '60's (New York: W. W. Norton, 1976), p.114.

144. Young to Fulbright, 9/15/70, Carl Marcy to Fulbright, 9/24/70, and Fulbright to Young, 9/24/70, all in 48:4:19:2, Fulbright Mss.

145. Conversation among Dulles and Capehart, Republican National Chairman Leonard Hall, and Sherman Adams, 7/24/53, and Dulles conversation with Hall and Adams, 7/27/53, all in telephone transcripts, Box 1, Dulles Mss.

146. Conversation between Dulles and Eisenhower, 8/19/54, telephone transcripts, Box 10, Dulles Mss.

147. Eisenhower to Dulles, 2/27/57, Box 6, Dulles-Herter Series, Eisenhower Mss. Dulles conversation with Sherman Adams, 7/28/54 and 8/5/54, telephone transcripts, Box 10, Dulles Mss.

148. Acheson, Present at the Creation, p. 575.

149. Doris Kearns, Lyndon Johnson and the American Dream (New York: Harper & Row, 1976), p. 184.

150. Bowles to Kennedy, 3/18/61, Box 297, file 0494, Bowles Mss.

151. Bowles to Rusk, 3/31/62, Box 301, file 0537, Bowles Mss.

152. Katherine Crane, Mr. Carr of State-Forty Seven Years in the Department of State (New York: St. Martins Press, 1967), p. 328.

153. Bowls Oral History (Kennedy), p. 103.

154. Melbourne L. Spector, "The Case of the Planning and Coordination Staff: Department of State," Murphy Commission Report, V. 6, p. 106.

155. Acheson interview, reading copy II, 7/8-9/53, p. 19, Box 78, Acheson Mss.

156. Senator Olin Johnson to Dulles, 3/15/55, and Representative John Phillips to Under Secretary of State Herbert Hoover, Jr., 3/19/55, both in Box 54, Francis Knight file, Dulles Mss.

157. Acheson interview, reading copy II, 7/8-9/53, p. 19, Box 78, Acheson Mss.

158. Stephen Gilbert, Soviet Images of America (New York: Crane, Russak, 1977), p. 75.

159. Memorandum of conversation between Fulbright and Herter, 7/31/58, Box 11, Herter Mss.

160. Memorandum of conversation between Igor Bubnov an Carl Marcy, 67/20/67, Box 59, Foreign Relations - Marcy, Carl file, Hickenlooper Mss.

161. Bader to Marcy, 6/13/67, ibid.

162. Bader to Marcy, 4/26/68, ibid.

163. Bader to Marcy, 7/18/678, ibid.

164. Holt to Fulbright, 12/23/71 with attached memorandum, and Holt file, 12/22/71, both in 48:13:39:3, Fulbright Mss.

165. John Rielly to Hubert Humphrey regarding meeting between Rielly and Yuri Babrakov, Soviet press attache, 12/14/66, Box 909, Yuri Bubrakov file, Humphrey Mss.

166. Foster Rhea Dulles, American Policy Toward Communist China, 1947-1969 (New York: Thomas Y. Crowell, 1972), p. 86; Ross Y. Koen, The China Lobby in American Politics (New York: Macmillan, 1960), p. 40.

167. Senate, Administration of National Security, p. 25.

168. Benjamin Reed, Executive Secretary of the Cabinet, to Humphrey sending State Department's Cabinet briefing paper, 9/8/67, Box 933, State Department - 1967 file, Humphrey Mss.

169. Kissinger, White House Years, p. 179.

170. Ibid., p. 811.

171. Ibid., p. 1020.

172. Nixon to Scott, 7/27/72, Box 205, Vietnam (2) file, Scott Mss.

173. Nixon to Mansfield, 8/3/73, ibid.

174. Kissinger, White House Years, p. 1170.

175. Nixon, RN, p. 888.

176. E.g., Thomas Hughes, Director of Intelligence and Research, State Department to Rusk, 4/2/64, NSF-Subject, Box 8, Fulbright speeches file, Johnson Mss.

177. Memorandum by Bohlen, 1/17/49, FR:1949, V, p. 558. Foy Kohler, Chargé in Moscow to Acheson, 3/19/49, ibid., p. 812.

178. Theodore Sorenson, Kennedy (New York: Harper & Row, 1965), p. 544.

179. David Detzer, The Brink: Cuban Missile Crisis, 1962 (New York: Thomas Y. Crowell, 1979), p. 53; Herbert S. Dinerstein, The Making of a Missile Crisis: October, 1962 (Baltimore: Johns Hopkins University Press, 1976), p. 200.

180. Arthur Schlesinger, Jr., A Thousand Days: John F. Kennedy in the White House (Greenwich, Connecticut: Fawcett Publications, 1965), p. 895.

181. Kissinger, White House Years, p. 545. This refers to the placement of an ABM system around Moscow, where it already was, and around Washington, which Congress was on record against. Why the option was presented to the Soviets anyway is a bureaucratic complexity detailed by Kissinger on pp. 534-44.

182. E.g., Memorandum of conversations between Acheson and Senator Vandenberg, Representative Kee, and Representative Eaton, 1/18/50, Box 65, Acheson Mss.

183. Culbertson to Acheson, 6/2/50, FR:1950, III, p. 1503.

184. Culbertson to Acheson, 9/6/50, ibid., p. 1573.

185. Theodore J. Lowi, Making Democracy Safe for the World," in Domestic Sources of Foreign Policy, ed. by James N. Rosenau (New York: Free Press, 1967.

186. Paper on Essential Elements of US-UK relations, 4/9/50, pp. 896-81, and Chargé in London to Secretary of State, 1/7/50, p. 1603, both in FR:1950, III.

187. Memorandum of conversation between Acheson and Wrong, 5/14/51, Box 66, Acheson Mss.

188. Memorandum of conversation among Smith, Gruenther, Francis Wilcox, and General Lauris Norstaad, 12/4/53, Box 10, trip

file, H. A. Smith Mss.

## Chapter 7

1. John F. Manley, "The Rise of Congress in Foreign Policy-Making," Annals of the American Academy of Political and Social Science, 397(1971), p. 69.

2. Doris Kearns, Lyndon Johnson and the American Dream (New York: Harper & Row, 1976), p. 140.

3. Macomber Oral History (Johnson), p. 8.

4. Conversation between Johnson and Herter, 5/18/60, Box 10, Pres. Calls files, Herter Mss.

5. Neil MacNeil, Dirksen: Portrait of a Public Man (New York: World Publishing, 1970), p. 192.

6. Hickenlooper Oral History (Johnson), p. 8.

7. J. William Fulbright, Old Myths and New Realities (New York: Random House, 1964), pp. vi-viii.

8. Samuel Huntington, The Common Defense (New York: Columbia University Press, 1961), p. 135.

9. MacNeil, Dirksen, p. 273.

10. Arthur M. Schlesinger, Jr., "Congress and the Making of American Foreign Policy," Foreign Affairs, 51(1972), p. 99.

11. Roger Hilsman, To Move a Nation: The Politics of Foreign Policy in the Administration of John F. Kennedy (New York: Dell Publishing, 1964), p. 79.

12. Edward Koledziej, "Congress and Foreign Policy: Through the Looking Glass," Virginia Quarterly Review, 42(1969), p. 13.

13. U.S., Congress, Senate, Committee on Government Operations, Administration of National Security, Hearings before the Subcommittee on National Security, 88th Cong. (1963-1964), p. 46.

14. Francis O. Wilcox and Richard A. Frank, eds., The Constitution and the Conduct of Foreign Policy (New York: Praeger, 1976), p. vii.

15. Richard F. Fenno, Jr., Congressmen in Committees (Boston: Little, Brown, 1973), p. 30.

16. Frederick Dutton to Carl Marcy, 5/19/66, attached to Marcy to Senator (Fulbright), 5/20/66, 48:4:19:1, Fulbright Mss.

17. Fulbright to Hickenlooper, 7/19/66, Box 46, Hickenlooper Mss.

18. Marcy to Fulbright, 5/16/66, 48:4:19:1, Fulbright Mss.

19. Mike Manatos to Larry O'Brien, 4/22/64, White House Aides Files (O'Brien), Box 27, Fulbright file, Johnson Mss.

20. U.S., Congress, Senate, Committee on Foreign Relations, Executive Sessions, VII, 84th Cong., 1st sess. (1955), (Published 1976), p. 57.

21. Ibid., p. 52.

22. Conference call among Eisenhower, Martin, and Rayburn, 1/20/55, Box 9, DDE Dairies, Eisenhower Mss.

23. Humphrey to Butler, 3/12/55, Box 119, Formosa Resolution file, Humphrey Mss.

24. Humphrey to Florence Fredrickson, 3/10/55, ibid.

25. Senate Committee on Foreign Relations, Executive Sessions, VIII, p. 101.

26. Ibid., p. 126.

27. Sherman Adams, First Hand Report (New York: Harper Bros., 1961), p. 9.

28. Morse is quoted in Kenneth Waltz, Foreign Policy and Democratic Politics, the British and American Experiences (Boston: Little, Brown, 1967), p. 114.

29. Meeting notes, 12/31/56 and 1/1/57, Box 2, Legislative Meeting Series, Eisenhower Mss.

30. Dulles to Truman, 1/14/57, Box 116, Eisenhower Doctrine file, Dulles Mss.

31. George To Humphrey, 12/12/56, Box 129, Humphrey file, and Humphrey to Green and reply, 12/18/56 and 12/20/56, Middle East file, all in Box 129, Humphrey Mss.

32. Humphrey to Green, 12/31/56, ibid.

33. Conversation between Dulles and Johnson, 1/14/57, telephone transcripts, Box 6, Dulles Mss. Russell's comments are in Senate, Committee on Foreign Relations, Executive Sessions, IX, p. 113. For estimate of support/opposition in the Senate see Assistant Secretary of State Robert Hill to Deputy Assistant to the President Wilton Persons, 2/5/57; Persons to Senator H. A. Smith and reply, 1/28/57 and 1/29/57; and Smith to Dulles, 1/28/57, all in Box 13, Mid East Resolution file, Harlow Mss.

34. Smith to Dulles, 1/17/57, Box 119, Smith Mss.

35. Dwight D. Eisenhower, Waging Peace, 1956-1961 (Garden City, New York: Doubleday, 1965), p. 179.

36. Senate, Committee on Foreign Relations, Executive Sessions, IX, p. 21.

37. Meeting notes, 3/26/59, Box 39, DDE Diaries, Eisenhower Mss.

38. Steve Neal, The Eisenhowers: Reluctant Dynasty (Garden City, New York: Doubleday, 1978), p. 402

39. Eisenhower, Waging Peace, p. 348.

40. Foster Rhea Dulles, American Policy Toward Communist China, 1949-1969 (New York: Thomas Y. Crowell, 1972), p. 154.

41. Norman A. Graebner, The New Isolationism: A Study in Politics and Foreign Policy Since 1950 (New York: Ronald Press, 1956), p. 203.

42. Lyndon B. Johnson, The Vantage Point: Perspectives of the Presidency, 1963-1969 (New York: Holt, Rinehart, and Winston, 1971), p. 195; Abraham F. Lowenthal, The Dominican Intervention (Cambridge, Massachusetts: Harvard University Press, 1972), p. 103; Theodore Draper, The Dominican Revolt: A Case Study in American Policy (New York: Commentary, 1968), pp. 206-09.

43. Aiken Oral History (Johnson), p. 11.

44. J. William Fulbright, The Crippled Giant: American Foreign Policy and Its Domestic Consequences (New York: Random House, 1972), p. 193.

45. Mundt to Clifford Hedberg, 3/7/66, RG III, Box 489, file 3, Mundt Mss.

46. Javits to Hickenlooper, 11/14/67, Box 84, Hickenlooper Mss.

47. Fulbright, Crippled Giant, p. 194.

48. Fulbright to Ralph Duggan, 7/25/66, 48:8:30:2, Fulbright Mss.

49. Naomi B. Lynn and Arthur F. McClure, The Fulbright Premise (Lewisberg, Pennsylvania: Bucknell University Press, 1973), p. 131.

50. Charles Frankel, High on Foggy Bottom, An Outsider's Inside View of the Government (New York: Harper & Row, 1968), p. 117.

51. Edward Laurence, "The Changing Role of Congress in Defense

Policy Making," Journal of Conflict Resolution, 20(1976), p. 217.

52. For a general view of this phenomenon relating to Vietnam, see Jayn Krishna Banal, The Pentagon and the Making of U.S. Foreign Policy: A Case Study of Vietnam, 1960-68 (Atlantic HIghlands, New Jersey: Humanities Press, 1978), pp. 234-97.

53. Henry L. Trewhitt, McNamara (New York: Harper & Row, 1971), p. 154.

54. Ibid., p. 118.

55. Richard A. Aliano, American Defence Policy From Eisenhower to Kennedy (Athens, Ohio: Ohio University Press, 1975), p. 205.

56. J. Ronald Fox. Arming America: How the U.S. Buys Weapons (Cambridge, Massachusetts: Harvard University Press, 1974), p. 125.

57. Morton Halperin, Bureaucratic Politics and Foreign Policy (Washington, D.C.: Brookings Institution, 1974), pp. 29, 231, 257.

58. Arnold Kanter, Defense Politics: A Budgetary Perspective (Chicago: University Chicago Press, 1979), p. 38.

59. Ibid., p. 119.

60. Henry Kissinger, White House Years (Boston: Little, Brown, 1979), p. 35.

61. Kanter, Defense Politics, pp. 47-49.

62. Kissinger, White House Years, p. 543.

63. Halperin, Bureaucratic Politics and Foreign Policy, p. 128.

64. Mundt to Al Clark, 2/5/66, RG III, Box 489, file 2, Mundt Mss.

65. Valenti to Johnson, 11/14/64 and Johnson's margin note, 11/21/64, WHCF-Confidential, Box 12, CO312 file, Johnson Mss.

66. Dean G. Acheson, Present at the Creation: My Years in the State Department (New York: W. W. Norton, 1969), pp. 358, 633-34.

67. On the aid program for FY 1956-1958 and Eisenhower's general lack of success in avoiding major cuts, see John D. Montgomery, Foreign Aid in International Politics (Englewood Cliffs, N.J.: Prentice-Hall, 1967), p. 209; Adams, First Hand Report, pp. 376-79; Andrew Westwood, Foreign Aid in a

Foreign Policy Framework (Washington, D.C.: Brookings Institution, 1966), pp. 62, 72, 160; H. Field Haviland, "Foreign Aid and the Policy Process," American Political Science Review, LII (1958), passim, and Peer A. Toma, The Politics of Food for Peace: Executive-Legislative Interaction (Tucson, Arizona: The University of Arizona Press, 1967), pp. 55-75.

68. Humphrey to Eugenie Anderson, 3/29/55, Box 120, Yalta file, Humphrey Mss.

69. Humphrey to Bowles, 8/22/57, Box 138, file 0318, Bowles Mss.

70. Fulbright to Krock, 7/16/58, BCN 125:7, Fulbright Mss.

71. Fulbright to Bowles, 8/18/58, Box 133, file 0238, Bowles Mss.

72. Eisenhower to Judd, 1/4/58, Box 7, Dulles-Herter Series, Eisenhower Mss.

73. For the aid bills in FY 1959 and FY 1961, see Westwood, Foreign Aid, p. 72; Montgomery, Politics of Foreign Aid, p. 202; and Michael Kent O'Leary, The Politics of American Foreign Aid (New York: Atherton Press, 1967), p. 127.

74. Herbert Feis, Foreign Aid and Foreign Policy (New York: St. Martins Press, 1964), p. 146. Uska Makajani, "Kennedy and the Strategy of Aid: The Clay Report and After: Western Political Quarterly, XVIII (1965), passim.

75. Fulbright to Bowles, 61/7/66, Box 330, file 0075, Bowles Mss.

76. Fulbright to William Benton, 7/29/65, 48:8:30:3, Fulbright Mss.

77. Bell to Johnson, 5/27/66, WHCF-Subject, Box 57, EX LE/FO 3-2 file, Johnson Mss.

78. Fulbright to Bowles, 7/23/66, Box 33, file 0142, Bowles Mss.

79. John E. Wiltz, From Isolationism to War, 1931-1941 (New York: Thomas Y. Crowell), p. 72.

80. Kearns, Lyndon Johnson, p. 236.

81. Martin B. Travis, "John F. Kennedy: Experiments with Power," in Power of the President in Foreign Affairs, 1945-1965, ed. by Edgar E. Robinson, Alexander DeConde, Raymond G. O'Connor, and Martin B. Travis (San Francisco: The Commonwealth Club of California, 1966), pp. 178-80. Abraham Holtzman, Legislative Liaison: Executive Leadership in Congress (Chicago: Rand McNally, 1970), pp. 272-83.

82. Edwards, Presidential Influence, p. 129.

83. Theodore Sorenson, Kennedy (New York: Harper & Row, 1965), p. 350.

84. Nathan Miller, "The Making of a Majority: Safeguard and the Senate," in Inside the System, 2nd ed., ed. by Charles Peters and John Rothchild (New York: Praeger, 1973), p. 118.

85. Richard M. Nixon, RN: The Memoirs of Richard Nixon (New York: Grosset and Dunlap, 1978), p. 218.

86. Edwards, Presidential Influence, p. 136.

87. Ibid., p. 142.

88. Lawrence F. O"Brien, No Final Victories (Garden City, New York: Doubleday, 1974), p. 120; John F. Manley, "Presidential Power and White House Lobbying, Political Science Quarterly, 93(1978), p. 264.

89. Sorenson, Kennedy, p. 350.

90. Notes, 7/25/57, Box 9, DDE Diary Series, Eisenhower Mss.

91. E.g., on Appropriations and Foreign Affairs assignments see Claude Desaultes to Henry Wilson, 12/31/64, White House Aides Files (Wilson), Box 7, Committee assignment file, Johnson Mss.; and Philander Craxton to Bryce Harlow, 1/28/58, Box 4, Mutual Security Part II file, Harlow Mss.

92. E.g., memorandum of conversation between Dean Acheson and Senator William Benton, 11/14/50, Box 65, Acheson Mss.

93. E.g., memoranda of calls between Herter and John McCormack, 1/3/58 and 1/7/58, and between Herter and Joseph Martin, 1/24/58, all in Box 11, Herter Mss.

94. Edwards, Presidential Influence, p. 80.

95. Sorenson Oral History (Kennedy), p. 110.

96. William Safire, Before the Fall: An Inside View of the Pre-Watergate White House (Garden City, New York: Doubleday, 1975), p. 319.

97. Lodge to Eisenhower, 12/22/53, Box 26, Lodge file, Administrative Series, Eisenhower Mss.

98. Dwight D. Eisenhower, Mandate for Change, 1953-1956 (Garden City, New York: Doubleday, 1963), p. 551.

99. Notes, June 6, 1956, Box 8, Whitman Series, Eisenhower Mss.

100. Safire, Before the Fall, p. 318.

101. E.g., Dairy, 2/19/54, Box 1, Hagerty Mss.

102. McCardle to Dulles, 5/18/56, and Keating to Dulles, 5/28/56, both in Box 104, McCardle file, Dulles Mss.

103. E.g., Hall to Dulles, 10/30/56, Box 103, Dulles Mss.

104. Goldwater to Dulles plus enclosure, 3/21/56, ibid.

105. Conversation between Dulles and Nixon, 10/7/58, telephone transcripts, Box 9, Dulles Mss.

106. Kissinger, White House Years, p. 552.

107. Ibid., p. 919.

108. Nixon, RN, p. 393; Kissinger, White House Years, p. 282.

109. Voight and Graebner, p. 38.

110. Kissinger, White House Years, p. 642.

111. Robert Peabody, Norman J. Ornstein, and David W. Rhode, "The United States Senate as a Presidential Incubator: Many are Called but Few are Chosen, " Political Science Quarterly, 91(1976), pp. 37-58.

112. McGovern to Mike Mansfield, 12/6/58, Series 9, Subseries CC, Box 2, Democratic Steering Committee-1968 file, Russell Mss.

113. Hugh Agor to Mundt, 11/27/62, Mundt to Agor, 11/22/66, and Max Greenwald to Mundt, 12/19/62, all in RG III, Box 485, file 2, Mundt Mss.

114. Meeting notes, 2/9/60, Box 3, Legislative Meeting Series, Eisenhower Mss.

115. Entry, 8/3/59, Box 11, Whitman Diary, Eisenhower Mss.

116. Ibid.

117. Meeting notes, 8/16/60, Box 3, Legislative Meeting Series, Eisenhower Mss.

118. William Gibbons to Henry Wilson, 5/18/65, White House Aides Files (O'Brien), Box 33, Morgan file, Johnson Mss.

119. Arthur H. Vandenberg, Jr., The Private Papers of Senator Vandenberg (Boston: Houghton Mifflin, 1952), p. 551.

120. Washington Daily News clipping, 1/6/50, Box 2, China file, Clifford Mss.

384

121. Vandenberg to Murrow, 11/24/50, in Vandenberg, Jr., _Private Papers_, p. 553.

122. Gary W. Reichard, "Divisions an Dissent: Democrats and Foreign Policy, 1952-1956," _Political Science Quarterly_, 93(1978), pp. 65-70.

123. Bowles to Johnson, 1/2/57, Box 140, file 0349, Bowles Mss.

124. Bowles to Humphrey, 8/16/55, Box 138, file 0318, Bowles Mss.

125. Humphrey To Bowles, 1/3/56, _ibid._

126. Humphrey to Bowles, 1/13/55, _ibid._

127. Humphrey to Senator Albert Gore, 12/17/56, Box 129, Middle and Near East file, Humphrey Mss.

128. Humphrey to Max (Kappleman?), 6/2/55, Box 185, Memos from the Senator file, Humphrey Mss.

129. See Reichard, "Divisions and Dissent," for a general discussion of this point.

130. Mansfield to Johnson, 6/29/66, NSF-Names, Box 6, Mansfield file, Johnson Mss.

131. _Ibid._

132. O'Brien, _No Final Victories_, p. 192.

133. _Ibid._, pp. 213-214.

134. MacNeil, _Dirksen_, p. 292.

135. Percy to Karl Mundt, 2/21/68, RG III, Box 494, file 1, Mundt Mss.

136. Riegle to Scott, 4/1/71, and Scott's reply, 4/7/71, Box 205, Vietnam (1) file, Scott Mss.

137. Kissinger, _White House Years_, p. 202.

138. Glenn R. Parker, "Some Themes in Congressional Unpopularity," _American Journal of Political Science_, 21(1977), p. 104.

139. James M. McCormick and Michael R. Coveyou, "Mass Political Imagery and the Salience of International Affairs," _American Political Quarterly_, 6(1978), p. 502.

140. Alan P. Balutis, "Congress, the President, and the Press," _Journalism Quarterly_ 53(1976), _passim_.

141. See Lee Sigelman, "The Dynamics of Presidential Support: An Overview of Research Findings," _Presidential Studies Quarterly_, 9(1979), _passim_. for a review of this phenomenon.

142. Vandenberg to Ferguson, 5/31/50 in Vandenberg, Jr., _Private Papers_, p. 551.

143. Reichard, "Divisions and Dissent," p. 69.

144. Humphrey to Rusk, 7/26/71, Box 4, American Dignitaries file, Humphrey Mss.

145. Paul Burnstein and William Freudenburg, "Changing Public Policy: The Impact of Public Opinion, Antiwar Demonstrations, and War Costs on Senate Voting on Vietnam War Motions," _American Journal of Sociology_, 84(1978), p. 116.

146. Kissinger, _White House Years_, p. 512; Nixon, _RN_, p. 410.

147. Robert McCaughey, A.A. to Senator Mundt to Bryce Harlow, 6/10/69, and Harlow's reply, 6/14/69, and Mundt to Harlow, 10/1/69, all in RG III, Box 497, files 5 and 2, respectively, Mundt Mss.

148. Colson to Scott, 5/11/72, Box 65, White House 1970-1976 file, Scott Mss.

149. MacGregor to Mundt, 1/18/72, RG I, Box 64, file 4, Mundt Mss.

150. Harlow to Fulbright, 11/5/69, 1:1:4:4, Fulbright Mss.

151. _E.g._, Norvill Jones to Fulbright, 4/23/65, 48:11:35:2, Fulbright Mss.

152. Acheson, _Present at the Creation_, p. 334.

153. Alfred O. Hero, Jr., _The Southerner and World Affairs_ (Baton Rouge, Louisiana: Louisiana State University Press, 1965), p. 8.

154. Eisenhower, _Waging Peace_, p.144.

155. Meeting notes, 2/16/60, Box 3, Legislative Meeting Series Eisenhower Mss.

156. _E.g._, Dulles to Eisenhower, 6/5/56, Box 102, Dulles Mss.

157. Meeting notes, 11/17/54, Box 1, Legislative Meeting Series, Eisenhower Mss.

158. Fulbright to Bowles, 2/12/64, Box 334, file 0153, Bowles Mss.

159. Marcy to Mansfield, 5/18/65, 48:8:30:4, Fulbright Mss.

160. Fenno, Congressmen in Committees, p. 141.

161. David B. Truman, "Functional Interdependence: The Elective Leaders, The White House, and the Congressional Party," in Aaron Wildavsky, ed., The Presidency (Boston: Little, Brown, 1969), pp. 454-76.

162. James N. Rosenau, "Private Preferences and Political Responsibilities: The Relative Potency of Individual and Role Variables in Behavior of U.S. Senators," in Quantitative International Politics: Insight and Evidence, ed. by J. David Singer (New York: Free Press, 1968), pp. 17-50. Also, Glen H. Stassen, "Individual Preferences Versus Role Constraints in Policy Making: Senatorial Response to Secretaries Acheson and Dulles," World Politics, 25(1972), pp. 98-119.

163. Stuart Gerry Brown, The American Presidency: Leadership, Partisanship, and Popularity (New York: Macmillan, 1966), p. 259.

164. Mark Kesselman, "Presidential Leadership in Congress on Foreign Policy," Midwest Journal of Political Science, 5(1961), pp. 284-89; and also his "Presidential Leadership in Congress on Foreign Policy: A Replication of a Hypothesis," Midwest Journal of Political Science, 9(1967), pp. 401-06.

165. Charles M. Tidmarch and Charles M. Sabatt, "Presidential Leadership Change and Foreign Policy Roll-Call Voting in the U.S. Senate," Western Political Quarterly, 25(1972), pp. 613-25.

166. Ibid.; Kesselman, "Presidential Leadership," passim; and Kesselman, "Presidential Leadership . . . A replication," passim.

167. Edwards, Presidential Influence, pp. 60-66, especially Tables 3.3 and 3.4.

168. Aage Clausen, How Congressmen Decide: A Policy Focus (New York: St. Martin's Press, 1973), Chapter 8; and Aage Clausen and Carl Van Horn, "The Congressional Response to a Decade of Change, 1963-1972," Journal of Politics, 39(1977), pp. 653; and Herbert Weisberg and Herbert Asher, "Voting Change in Congress, Some Dynamic Perspectives in an Evolutionary Process," American Journal of Political Science, 22(1978), pp. 409-16. These are discussed in Edwards, Presidential Influence, pp. 63-64.

169. Barbara Sinclair, "Agenda and Alignment Change, The House of Representatives, 1925-1978," In Congress Reconsidered, 2nd

ed., Lawrence C. Dodd and Bruce I. Oppenheimer, eds. (Washington, D.C.: Congressional Quarterly Press, 1980), pp. 236-38.

170. Meeting notes, 3/29/55, Anonymous Mss.

171. Fenno, Congressmen in Committees, p. 90.

172. Vandenberg to Lippmann, 1/19/50, Box 107, file 2145, Lippmann Mss.

173. Vandenberg, Jr., Private Papers, p. 498.

174. Diary entry, 7/18/58, Box 10, Whitman Diary, Eisenhower Mss.

175. Author's interview of Dean Rusk, 11/4/80.

176. McComber Oral History (Dulles), p. 1.

177. E.g., telephone conversation between Herter and Lyndon Johnson, 5/22/57, Box 10, Herter Mss.

178. MacNeil, Dirksen, p.272.

179. Ibid., p. 193.

180. Ibid., p. 282. Also, pp. 134-35, 188-93, 272.

181. Memorandum of conversation between Acheson and Anderson, 1/12/51, and calls log, 1/12/51, both in Box 66, Acheson Mss.

182. Lodge to Eisenhower, 7/1/55, Box 27, Lodge 1955 (2) file, Administration Series, Eisenhower Mss.

183. Lodge to Eisenhower with draft memorandum to department heads, 10/21/57, Box 27, Lodge 1957-58 (2) file, Administrative Series, Eisenhower Mss.

184. Harlow to Eisenhower, 8/27/57, Box 9, Whitman Diary, Eisenhower Mss.

185. E.g., Eisenhower to Lodge, 7/5/55, Box 27, Lodge 1955 (2) file, Administrative Series, Eisenhower Mss.

186. E.g., Notes on Cabinet meeting, 11/25/58, Anonymous Mss.

187. Meeting notes, 3/31/55, ibid.

188. Bowles to Kennedy, 5/22/61, Box 297, file 0494, Bowles Mss.

189. Valenti, A Very Human President, p. 63.

190. Manatos to O'Brien, 5/15/64, White House Aides Files

(O'Brien), Box 27, Hickenlooper file, Johnson Mss.

191. E.g., Memorandum of conversation between Hayes and Herter, 1/29/59, Box 10, Misc. Memos-1959 file, Herter Mss.

192. Charles Roche to Johnson, 1/25/68, White House Aides Files (Roche), Box 3, Johnson Mss.

193. Representative George Mahon to Johnson, 7/2/64, and Johnson to Representative Conte, 7/9/64, WHCF-Subject, Box 57, EX LE/FU 3-2 file, Johnson Mss.

194. Lynn and McClure, The Fulbright Premise, p. 105.

195. Johnson, Vantage Point, p. 33.

196. Sorenson, Kennedy, p. 736.

197. John D. Montgomery, The Politics of Foreign Aid: American Experience in South East Asia (New York: Frederick A. Praeger, 1962), pp. 221-24.

198. Hubert Humphrey to Phillip Monson, 2/4/57, Box 137, Dulles file, Humphrey Mss.

199. Kenneth Waltz, Foreign Policy and Democratic Politics, p. 79.

200. Scott to Harlow, 6/30/70, Box 65. White House, 1970-76 file, Scott Mss.

201. Henry Wilson to Johnson, 5/24/66, WHCF-Subject, Box 57, EX LE/FU 3-2 file, Johnson Mss.

202. Circular letter to Senate from Fulbright, 4/28/72, 48:8:33: 4, Fulbright Mss.

203. Sorenson, Kennedy, p. 736; William C. Foster, Director, U.S. Arms Control and Disarmament Agency, to Senator Hickenlooper, 5/6/63, Box 16, Hickenlooper Mss.

204. Phillip Geyelin, Lyndon B. Johnson and the World (New York: Frederick A. Praeger, 1966), p. 108.

205. John Yochelson, "The American Presence in Europe: Current Debate in the United States," Orbis, 15(1971), p. 798.

206. Byrd to Richard Russell, 11/6/69, Series IX, Subseries 1, Box 1, Foreign Relations 1969 file, Russell Mss.

207. Church to Russell, 6/16/69, ibid.

208. James N. Rosenau, "Foreign Policy as an Issue Area," in Domestic Sources of Foreign Policy, ed. by Rosenau, p. 14.

209. Lowi, "Making Democracy Safe for the World," _passim_.

210. Rosenau, "Foreign Policy as an Issue Area," p. 46; William Zimmerman, "Issue Area and the Foreign Policy Process," _American Political Science Review_, 67(1973), pp. 1204-13. For a good review of various typology approaches, see William C. Potter, "Issue Area and Foreign Policy Analysis," _International Organization_, 34(1980), pp. 405-28.

211. Stephen J. Cimbala, "Foreign Policy as an Issue Area: A Roll Call Analysis," _American Political Science Review_, 63(1969), pp. 748-56.

212. Robert H. Salisbury, "The Analysis of Public Policy: A Search for Theories and Roles," in _Political Science and Public Policy_, ed. by Austin Ranney (Chicago: Markham Publishing, 1968), p. 157.

213. Richard C. Snyder, H. W. Bruck, and Burton Sapin, _Decision Making as an Approach to the Study of International Politics_ (Princeton, New Jersey: Organizational Behavior Section, 1954), p. 35.

214. Toma, _The Politics of Food for Peace_, pp. 55-110 discusses P.L. 480.

215. Hubert Humphrey to staff members Herb and Tom, 6/4/57, Box 185, Memos from Senator file, Humphrey Mss.

216. Scott's handwritten notes of Foreign Relations Committee meeting, 11/1/71, Box 180, Foreign Aid (1) file, Scott Mss.

217. Aiken Oral History (Johnson), p. 21.

218. Herter to Eisenhower, 3/19/59, Box 40, Staff notes 3/15-31/59, Whitman Diary, Eisenhower Mss.

219. O'Leary, _The Politics of American Foreign Aid_, ps. 123.

220. Memorandum of conversation between Acheson and Fulbright, 2/29/52, Box 66, Acheson Mss.

221. Memorandum of conversation between Acheson and McMahon, 2/29/52, _ibid._

222. Eisenhower, _Mandate for Change_, p. 301; MacNeil, _Dirksen_, p. 136.

223. Bernstein and Freundenberg, "Changing Public Policy," p. 116.

224. Notes of meeting with legislative leaders, 1/9/67, Box 412, Humphrey Mss.

225. Fulbright to Bowles, 10/3/67, Box 330, file 0075, Bowles Mss.

226. Fulbright to J. W. Anderson, 5/25/69, 48:6:24:2, Fulbright Mss.

227. Hugh Scott's handwritten notes on Foreign Relations Committee meeting, 11/1/71, Box 180, Foreign Aid (1) file, Scott Mss.

228. Aiken Oral History (Johnson), p. 14.

229. Gerson, The Hyphenate, passim; Lawrence Fuchs, "Minority Groups and Foreign Policy," Political Science Quarterly, 74(1959), pp. 161-75.

230. Sid Bailey to Hugh Scott, 9/11/69, Box 118, Foreign Affairs-Israel file, Scott Mss.

231. Sid Bailey to Jerry Laughlin, 12/5/69, ibid.

232. Humphrey to Ken, 7/26/71, Box 168, Humphrey Mss.

233. Humphrey to Herb, 6/3/57, Box 185, Memos from the Senator file, Humphrey Mss.

234. Staff memorandum by David Lebedoff, 11/75, Box 68, Senate Caucus file, Humphrey Mss.

235. Holified to Johnson, 10/3/64, WHCF-Subject, Box 1, EX/ND file, Johnson Mss.

236. Rielly to Humphrey, 7/10/64, Box 722, MLF(2) file, Humphrey Mss.

237. Humphrey to himself, 5/3/61, Box 185, Staff File, Jan.-May 1961 file, Humphrey Mss.

238. E.g., Senator H. A. Smith to Dulles, 10/23/56, Box 124, Presidential Campaign file, Dulles Mss.

239. William Macomber to Dulles, 9/27/56, Box 108, ibid.

240. Stephen A. Garrett, "Eastern European Ethnic Groups and American Foreign Policy," Political Science Quarterly, 93(1978), pp. 301-24.

241. Conversation between Dulles and Herter, 1/13/59, telephone transcripts, Box 9, Dulles Mss; and Memo for Anne Whitman, 3/3/59, Box 39, Staff notes 3/1-15/59, Whitman Diary, Eisenhower Mss.

242. Charles W. Harris, "International Relations and the Disposition of Alien Enemy Property Seized by the United States

During World War II: A Case Study on German Properties," *Journal of Politics*, 23(1961), pp. 641-66.

243. Hubert Humphrey to Wynn, 5/18/61, Box 185, Humphrey Mss.

244. In addition to citations already noted, see WDH to President (Truman), 2/8/50, PSF, Box 181, Italy-Vatican file, Truman Mss.

245. Sinclair, "Agenda and Alignment Change," pp. 236-38.

246. Charles O. Lerche, "Southern Congressmen and the 'New Isolationism,'" *Political Science Quarterly*, 65(1960), pp. 321-37. Also his, *The Uncertain South: Its Changing Patterns of Politics in Foreign Policy* (Chicago: Quadrangle Books, 1964), pp. 68, 218-70. Hero, *The Southerner and World Affairs*, pp. 327, 430-32.

247. Hero, *The Southerner and World Affairs*, p. 64.

248. Robert E. Riggs, *U.S./U.N. Foreign Policy and International Organization* (New York: Appleton-Century-Crofts, 1971), pp. 215-17.

249. Memorandum of conversation between Acheson and Representative Daniel Flood, 1/29/52. Box 66, Acheson Mss.

250. *Ibid.*

251. Senator H. A. Smith to Senator Tom Connally, 1/16/51, Box 102, H. A. Smith Mss. Smith favored ratification

252. Senate, Committee on Foreign Relations, *Executive Sessions*, II, p. 399.

253. *Ibid.*, pp. 361-400, 643-54.

254. *Ibid.*, p. 653.

255. Herman Phleger to Dulles, 3/30/53, Box 70, Genocide file, Dulles Mss.

256. Dulles conversations with Lodge, 10/7/53 and 10/21/53 and with Phleger, 3/30/53, all in telephone transcripts, Box 1, Dulles Mss.

257. W. Rostow to Johnson, 9/22/66, WHCF-Subject, Box 10, EX/IT 42 file, Johnson Mss.

258. Fulbright to Oscar Fendler, 12/23/69, 48:5:22:5, and to Arthur Morse, 6/8/68, 48:5:22:4, both in Fulbright Mss.

259. W. Rostow to Johnson, 9/22/66, WHCF-Subject, Box 10, EX/IT 42 file, Johnson Mss.

260. The Lippmann quotation and his recollection of Kennedy's statement are in Lippmann Oral History (Kennedy), p. 16. Also, see Bowles Oral History (Kennedy), p. 95; and Lisagor Oral History (Kennedy), p. 46.

261. Conversation between Dulles and Fulbright 2/3/59, telephone transcripts, Box 9, Dulles Mss.

262. Lee to Senator, n.d., and attached Randolph to Fulbright, 6/22/67, 48:10:34:1, Fulbright Mss.

263. Lawrence Oral History (Kennedy), p. 18.

264. W. Rostow Oral History (Johnson), p. 39.

265. Salisbury, "The Analysis of Public Policy," p. 159.

266. James P. Lovell, Foreign Policy in Perspective: Strategy, Adaption, Decision Making (New York: Holt, Rinehart, Winston, 1970), p. 176.

267. Manley, "The Rise of Congress," p. 65.

268. H. Bradford Westerfield, "Congress and Closed Politics in National Security Affairs," Orbis, 10(1966), p. 750.

269. Johan Galtung, "Social Position, Party Identification, and Foreign Policy Orientation: A Norwegian Case Study," in Domestic Sources of Foreign Policy, ed. by Rosenau, pp. 161-93.

270. Louis D. Hayes, "The Relationship of Problem Perception to Policy Making for Members of the Senate Committee on Foreign Relations," International Review of History and Political Science, 4(1971), p. 116.

271. Werner Levi, "Ideology, Interests, and Foreign Policy," International Studies Quarterly, 14(1970), pp. 1-31.

272. Stanley Hoffmann, Gulliver's Troubles, Or The Setting of American Foreign Policy (New York: McGraw Hill, 1968), p. 258 takes this view.

273. Malcolm E. Jewell, Senatorial Politics and Foreign Policy (Lexington, Kentucky: University of Kentucky Press, 1962), pp. 160-63.

Chapter 8

1. Thomas M. Frank and Edward Weisband, Foreign Policy by Congress (New York: Oxford University Press, 1979), p. 3.

2. Cecil V. Crabb, Jr., and Pat M. Holt, Invitation to

*Struggle, Congress, the President, and Foreign Policy* (Washington, D.C.: Congressional Quarterly Press, 1980), p.3.

3. John Lehman, *The Executive, Congress and Foreign Policy: Studies of the Nixon Administration* (New York: Praeger Publishers, 1976), p. viii.

4. Doyle W. Buckwalter, "The Congressional Concurrent Resolution: A Search for Foreign Policy Influence," *Midwest Journal of Political Science*, 14(1970), pp. 434-58.

5. U.S., Comptroller General, General Accounting Office, "Executive-Legislative Communications and the Role of Congress During International Crises," A Report to the Congress (#ID-76-78), 9/3/76, p. 18.

6. Roger Majah, "Report of a Staff Survey of Congressional Views on the Organization of Government of Foreign Policy," p. 123, U.S., Commission on the Organization of the Government for the Conduct of Foreign Policy, Robert Murphy, Chairman, *Report*, 6/75 (Murphy Commission Report).

7. Both Fulbright quotations are in Frank and Weisband, *Foreign Policy by Congress*, p. 5.

8. Senators Mark Hatfield, George McGovern, Alan Cranston and Harold Hughes to colleagues, 1/21/71, Box 206, Vietnam (1) file, Scott Mss.

9. Humphrey to Editor, *Minneapolis Tribune*, -/23/71, Box 68, Pentagon Papers file, Humphrey Mss.

10. Frank and Weisband, *Foreign Policy by Congress*, p. 158.

11. Sid Bailey to Scott, 5/15/70, Box 206, Vietnam-Cambodia Intervention file, Scott Mss.

12. Bailey to Scott plus attachment, 6/12/70, *ibid.*

13. E.g., Barbara Hinkson Craig, "The President, Congress, and the War Powers Resolution: A Search for Comity," paper presented to the Southwestern Political Science Association, Dallas, Texas, 3/26/81, p. 2.

14. Alton Frye, *A Responsible Congress: The Politics of National Security* (New York: McGraw Hill, 1975), p. 215.

15. Thomas M. Frank, "After the Fall: A New Procedural Framework for Congressional Control Over the War Power," *American Journal of International Law*, 71(1977), p. 614.

16. Tristam Coffin to Frank Smith, 5/27/69, 48:8:33:4, Fulbright Mss.

17. Sid Bailey to Scott, 5/15/70, Box 206, Vietnam-Cambodia Intervention file, Scott Mss. Emphasis is Bailey's.

18. Frank and Weisband, Foreign Policy by Congress, p. 212.

19. Ibid., p. 16.

20. D. G. Henderson, "The Senate Foreign Relations Committee," The Washington Quarterly, 2(1979), pp. 4, 6.

21. Richard F. Fenno, Congressmen in Committees (Boston: Little, Brown, 1973), p. 108.

22. Fred M. Kaiser, "The House Committee on International Relations," Policy Studies Journal, 5(1977), pp. 144-46.

23. Henderson, "Senate Foreign Relations Committee," p. 8.

24. Richard C. Whittle, "Senate Foreign Relations Committee Searches for Renewed Glory," Congressional Quarterly Weekly, 3/4/81, p. 477.

25. Henry Kissinger, White House Years (Boston, Little, Brown, 1979), p. 513.

26. Speech of 4/16/71 quoted in Emmet J. Hughes, The Living Presidency (Baltimore, Maryland: Penguin Books, 1972), p. 286.

27. Frank and Weisband, Foreign Policy by Congress, p. 5.

28. James L. Sundquist, "The Crisis of Competence in Our National Government," Political Science Quarterly, 95(1980), pp. 183-208; Thomas E. Cronin, "A Resurgent Congress and the Imperial Presidency," Political Science Quarterly, 95(1980), pp. 209-38.

29. Frank and Weisband, Foreign Policy by Congress, p. 31.

30. Humphrey to Wilson, 1976, Box 4, Foreign Dignitaries file, Humphrey Mss.

31. Alton Frye and William D. Rogers, "Linkage Begins at Home," Foreign Policy, 35(1979), p. 55.

32. George C. Edwards III, Presidential Influence in Congress (San Francisco: W. H. Freeman, 1980), p. 173.

33. For details, see Eric L. Davis, "Legislative Liaison in the Carter Administration," Political Science Quarterly, 95(1979), pp. 287-302.

34. Cronin, "A Resurgent Congress," p. 210.

35. Arthur M. Schlesinger, Jr., The Imperial Presidency

(Boston: Houghton-Mifflin, 1973).

36. Alton Frey, A Responsible Congress: The Politics of National Security (New York: McGraw-Hill, 1975).

37. E.g., Bayless Manning, "The Congress, the Executive and Intermestic Affairs," Foreign Affairs, 57(1979), pp. 308-24.

38. Frans R. Bax, "The Legislative-Executive Relationship in Foreign Policy," Orbis, 20(1977), p. 882. Speech of 4/17/75.

39. Cronin, "A Resurgent Congress," p. 226.

40. Frank, "After the Fall,", p. 645.

41. James Chance, "Is a Foreign Policy Consensus Possible," Foreign Affairs, 57(1978), p. 1.

42. Crabb and Holt, An Invitation to Struggle, pp. 193-95.

43. Chance, "Foreign Policy Consensus," p. 16.

44. Case to Russell, 8/17/70, Series IX, Subseries 1, Box 1, Foreign Relations-1970 file, Russell Mss.

45. Loch Johnson and James M. McCormick, "Foreign Policy by Executive Fiat," Foreign Policy, 28(1977), pp. 129-131; "He Shall . . . Make Treaties," National Journal, 5/29/76, p. 735.

46. For an extensive discussion, see Richard F. Grimmett, "The Legislative Veto and U.S. Arms Sales," Congressional Research Service Report in U.S., Congress, House of Representatives, Committee on Rules, Studies on the Legislative Veto, 96th Cong., 2nd sess. (1980), pp. 248-320.

47. John Felton, "Congress Unlikely to Reject Sale of M-60 Tanks to Jordon," Congressional Quarterly Weekly, 8/2/80, p. 2232.

48. Hartford Courant, 6/21/80, p. 25. Unless otherwise noted, newspaper citations refer to the first section of the paper.

49. Ibid., 4/23/81, p. 3.

50. Time, 7/27/81, p. 23.

51. Hartford Courant, 4/18/81, p. 1.

52. Ibid., 4/17/81, p. 7, and 4/23/81, p. 3.

53. Ibid., 4/27/71, p. 1.

54. Ibid., 10/26/81, p. 1.

55. Ibid., 9/11/81, p. 1

56. New York Times, 10/28/81, p. 12.

57. Ibid., 10/18/81, p. 15.

58. The Nixon, Carter, and Ford quotations are from New York Times, 10/16/81, p. 35.

59. Ibid., 10/28/81, p. 1.

60. Ibid., 10/29/81, pp. B11 and 1.

61. Ibid.

62. Ibid., p. B11

63. Ibid., 10/16/81, p. 9.

64. Ibid., 10/18/81, p. D4

65. Ibid., 10/29/81, p. 1. Vote is on p. B11.

66. Ibid., 10/28/81, p. 13.

67. Ibid., 10/16/81, p. 9.

68. Charles McC. Mathias, Jr., "Ethnic Groups and Foreign Policy," Foreign Affairs, 59(1981), p. 993. Russell Warren Howe and Sarah Hays Trott, The Power Peddlers: How Lobbyists Mold America's Foreign Policy (Garden City, New York: Doubleday, 1977), p. 273.

69. Edward Sheehan, The Arabs, Israelis, and Kissinger (New York: Readers Digest, 1976), p. 176.

70. Mathias, "Ethnic Groups and Foreign Policy," p. 993.

71. William J. Lanquette, "The Many Faces of the Jewish Lobby in America," National Journal, 5/13/78, p. 748.

72. Robert H. Trice, "Congress and the Arab-Israeli Conflict: Support for Israel,in the U.S. Senate, 1970-1973," Political Science Quarterly, 92(1977), pp. 443-64. Trice does not reject the concept of a Jewish lobby as much as an electoral connection.

73. Fulbright to A. Ford Wolf, 12/16/69, 48:10:34:3, Fulbright Mss.

74. Fulbright to Erich Fromm, 11/6/73, 48:15:41:1, Fulbright Mss.

75. Lanquette, "Jewish Lobby," p. 748.

76. Mathias, Ethnic Groups and Foreign Policy, p. 993.

77. Howe and Trott, Power Peddlers, p. 283.

78. Frank and Weisband, Foreign Policy by Congress, p. 190.

79. Lanquette, "Jewish Lobby," p. 756.

80. Howe and Trott, Power Peddlers, p. 273.

81. Marvin C. Feuerwerger, Congress and Israel: Foreign Aid Decision-Making in the House of Representatives, 1969-1976 (Westport, Connecticut: Greenwood Press, 1979), p. 84.

82. Ibid., p. 85.

83. U.S., Congress, Senate, Committee on Foreign Relations, Proposed Sale of C-130's to Egypt, Hearings before the Subcommittee on Foreign Assistance, 94th Cong., 2nd sess. (1976), p. 108.

84. Mathias, "Ethnic Groups and Foreign Policy," 994.

85. Sallie M. Hicks and Theodore A. Couloumbis, "The 'Greek Lobby': Illusion or Reality," in Abdul Aziz Said, Ethnicity and U.S. Foreign Policy (New York: Praeger Publishers, 1977), p. 83-116.

86. Frank and Weisband, Foreign Policy by Congress, p. 38. Emphasis is their's.

87. Howe and Trott, Power Peddlers, pp. 444, 458.

88. Hicks and Coulombis, "The Greek Lobby," p. 86.

89. Howe and Trott, Power Peddlers, pp. 443-44.

90. R. Sean Randolph, "The Byrd Amendment: A Postmortem," World Affairs, 141(1978), pp. 57-70.

91. Anthony Lake, The "Tar Baby" Option: American Policy Toward Southern Rhodesia (New York: Columbia University Press, 1976), p. 118.

92. Dan to Humphrey, 8/12/74, and Humphrey to file, 8/14/74, Box 4 (shipment of 3/3/78), Kissinger file, Humphrey Mss; Lake, Tar Baby Option, pp. 217-21.

93. See the comments of Senators Jesse Helms and James Allen in U.S, Congress, Senate, Committee on Foreign Relations, Genocide Convention, Hearings, 95th Cong., 1st sess. (1977), pp. 106-08.

94. Crabb and Holt, An Invitation to Struggle, p. 180.

95. Richard J. Payne and Eddie Ganaway, "The Influence of Black Americans on U.S. Policy Towards South Africa," African Affairs, 79 (1980), pp. 585-98; Henschelle Sullivan Challenor, "The Influence of Black Americans on U.S. Foreign Policy Toward Africa," in Said, Ethnicity, pp. 139-74.

96. Howe and Trott, Power Peddlers, p. 183.

97. Hartford Courant, 10/2/81, p. 1.

98. U.S., Congress, Senate, Committee on Foreign Relations, Middle East Peace Process, Hearings before the Subcommittee on Near Eastern and South Asian Affairs, 95th Cong., 2nd sess, (1978), p. 28.

99. Howe and Trott, Power Peddlers, p. 316.

100. Frank and Weisband, Foreign Policy by Congress, p. 165.

101. Mathias, "Ethnic Groups and Foreign Policy," p. 997.

102. Manning, "Intermestic Affairs," passim; Harlan Cleveland, "The Domestication of International Affairs and Vice Versa," Annals of the American Academy o Political And Social Sciences, 442(1979), pp. 125-37.

103. Robert A. Pastor, Congress and the Politics of U.S. Foreign Economic Policy, 1929-1976 (Berkeley, California: University of California Press, 1980), p. 185.

104. I. M. Destler, Making Foreign Economic Policy (Washington, D.C.: Brookings Institution, 1980), p. 151.

105. Pastor, Foreign Economic Policy, p. 182. Emphasis his.

106. Destler, Making Foreign Economic Policy, p. 169.

107. Ibid., p. 170.

108. Ibid., pp. 188-90; Pastor, Foreign Economic Policy, Table 9, p. 183.

109. Destler, Making Foreign Economic Policy, p. 3.

110. Pastor, Foreign Economic Policy, p. 247.

111. Robert J. Samuelson, "The Big Business World of Washington's Foreign Agents," National Journal, 3/18/78, pp. 424-29.

112. Destler, Making Foreign Economic Policy, p. 148; Paula Stern, Water's Edge: Domestic Politics and the Making of American Foreign Policy (Westport, Connecticut: Greenwood

Press, 1979), p. 55.

113. Stern, Water's Edge, p. xiv.

114. Gerald R. Ford, A Time to Heal: The Autobiography of Gerald R. Ford (New York: Harper & Row, 1979), p. 139.

115. Stern, Water's Edge, p. 35.

116. Ibid.

117. Howe and Trott, Power Peddlers, p. 316

118. Stern, Water's Edge, p. 81.

119. James Buckley, If Men Were Angels: A View from the Senate (New York: G. P. Putnam's Sons, 1975), p. 205.

120. Stern, Water's Edge, pp. 63-69.

121. Ibid., p. 83. For Kissinger's description of Jackson-Vanik, see Henry Kissinger, Years of Upheaval (Boston: Little, Brown, 1982), pp. 250-55, 985-98.

122. Ford, A Time to Heal, p. 139

123. Ibid.

124. Ibid., p.225; Nixon, RN, p. 86.

125. Feueruerger, Congressional Israel, p. 60.

126. Congressional Quarterly Weekly, 10/25/80, p. 3214.

127. Feuerwerger, Congress and Israel, p. 60. Whitten became chairman of the Appropriations Committee, thus generally overseeing foreign aid appropriations.

128. Congressional Quarterly Weekly, 10/25/80, p. 3213.

129. Frank and Weisband, Foreign Policy by Congress, p. 273.

130. Lars Schoultz, Human Rights and United States Policy Toward Latin America (Princeton, New Jersey: Princeton University Press, manuscript in press), pp. 638-59.

131. New York Times, 9/25/81, p. 3.

132. Neil C. Livingstone and Manfred von Nordheim, "The United States Congress and the Angola Crisis," Strategic Review, 5(1977), pp. 35-36.

133. Frank and Weisband, Foreign Policy by Congress, p. 46.

134. Nathaniel Davis, "The Angola Decision of 1975: A Personal Memoir," Foreign Affairs, 57(1978), pp.110-16.

135. Livingstone and von Nordheim, "Congress and Angola," p. 42.

136. Frank and Weisband, Foreign Policy by Congress, p.52.

137. Livingstone and von Nordheim, "Congress and Angola," p. 37.

138. Ibid., p. 38; Frank and Weisband, Foreign Policy by Congress, pp. 51-52.

139. New York Times, 10/1/81, p. 9.

140. Ibid., 4/28/81, p. 3, and 5/14/81, p. 12.

141. Memorandum to files by George Pavlik, A. A. to Senator Hickenlooper, 7/5/67, Box 93, Panama Treaty file, Hicken-looper Mss.

142. Mundt to James Cameron, 2/22/68, RG III, Box 494, file 1, Mundt Mss.

143. McGee and Humphrey to Ford, 7/8/75, Second acquisition, Box 4, Gerald Ford file, and Dan to Humphrey, 7/2/75, Box 424, Panama file, HUmphrey, Mss.

144. U.S., Congress, Senate, Committee on Foreign Relations, Senate Debate on the Panama Canal Treaties: A Compendium of Major Statements, Documents, Record Votes, and Relevant Events, Report by the Congressional Research Service, 96th Cong. 1st sess. (1979), p. 75.

145. U.S., Congress, Senate, Committee on Foreign Relations, Panama Canal Treaties, Hearings, Part V, 95th Cong., 2nd sess, (1978), p. 17.

146. William J. Lanquette, "The Plight of the Uncommitted on the Panama Canal Treaties," National Journal, 3/11/78, p. 385.

147. Ibid., p. 387.

148. Crabb and Holt, Invitation to Struggle, p. 74.

149. I. M. Destler, "Treaty Troubles: Versailles in Reverse," Foreign Policy, 33(1979), p. 46. DeConcini's language allowed the United States to use military force to keep the canal open after the year 2000.

150. Frank and Weisband, Foreign Policy by Congress, p. 278.

151. Ibid., p. 279.

152. Crabb and Holt, Invitation to Struggle, pp. 74-75.

153. For a similar view, see ibid., p. 74.

154. Frank and Weisband, Foreign Policy by Congress, p. 278.

155. New York Times, 10/5/81, p. 12.

156. Congressional Quarterly Weekly, 3/3/79, p. 356.

157. Ibid., 2/10/79, p. 260

158. Ibid., 9/22/79, p. 2889.

159. Ibid., p. 2919

160. Ibid., 3/3/79, p. 354.

161. A. James Gregor, "The United States, The Republic of China, and the Taiwan Relations Act," Orbis, 24(1980), pp. 609-24.

162. Strobe Talbott, Endgame: The Inside Story of SALT II (New York: Harper and Row, 1979), p. 95; Alan Platt, The U.S. Senate and Strategic Arms Policy (Boulder, Colorado: Westview Press, 1978), p. 100.

163. Platt, Strategic Arms Policy, p. 100

164. Humphrey aide memoire, 3/9/77, second acquisition, Box 4, Carter file, Humphrey Mss; Destler, "Treaty Troubles," p. 48.

165. Peter J. Ognibene, Scoop: The Life and Politics of Henry M. Jackson (New York: Stein and Day, 1975), pp. 212-15; Talbott, Endgame, p. 140.

166. Frank and Weisband, Foreign Policy by Congress, p. 290.

167. E.g., New York Times, 5/14/79, p. 13.

168. Ibid., 7/20/79, p. 3.

169. Ibid., 5/28/79, p. 6.

170. Ibid., 8/31/79, p. 4.

171. Ibid., 5/21/79, p. 4.

172. Frank and Weisband, Foreign Policy by Congress, p. 291.

173. New York Times, 5/6/79, p. 27.

174. Frank and Weisband, Foreign Policy by Congress, p. 152.

175. New York Times, 1/5/79, p. 1, 2/24/79, p. 4, and 1/4/80,

p. 4.

176. Talbott, Endgame, p. 215.

177. New York Times, 2/25/79, p. 9.

178. Ibid., 5/14/79, p. 13, and 5/17/79, p. 3.

179. Ibid., 6/30/79, p. 3.

180. Talbott, Endgame, p. 136.

181. William J. Lanquette, "The Battle to Shape and Sell the New Arms Control Treaty," National Journal, 12/31/77, p. 1992.

182. Several articles in New York Times, 4/17/79-4/20/79.

183. Ibid., 6/23/79, p. 5.

184. Talbott, Endgame, p. 255; New York Times, 2/4/79, p. 1.

185. New York Times, 10/13/79, p. 3.

186. Ford, A Time to Heal, p. 185.

187. Ibid., p. 324

188. Ibid., pp. 324, 327.

189. Ibid., pp. 337-38.

190. Humphrey to Representative Charles Diggs, 3/26/75, Box 68, Africa file, Humphrey Mss.

191. Hartford Courant, 8/30/81, p. 6.


Chapter 9

1. Speech of 4/17/75 in Frans R. Bax, "The Legislative-Executive Relationship in Foreign Policy," Orbis, 20(1977), p. 882.

2. Thomas M. Frank, "After the Fall: A New Procedural Framework for Congressional Control Over the War Power," American Journal of International Law, 71(1977), p. 625.

3. U. S., Commission on the Organization of the Government for the Conduct of Foreign Policy, Robert Murphy, Chairman, Report, 6/75 (Murphy Commission Report), p. 236.

4. R. Gordon Hoxie, Command Decision and the Presidency (Pleasantville, New York: Readers Digest, 1977), p. 260.

5. Henry Kissinger, White House Years (Boston: Little, Brown, 1979), p. 940.

6. National Journal, 5/29/76, p. 736.

7. New York Times, 5/26/78, p. 10.

8. Address to the Conference on National Security, Center for the Study of the Presidency, Washington, D.C. 4/12/80.

9. Congressional Quarterly Weekly, 4/26/80, p. 1136.

10. New York Times, 3/22/81, p. D3.

11. Case is currently pending.

12. New York Times, 10/16/81, p. 35.

13. Hoxie, Command Decision, p. 322.

14. Cecil V. Crabb, Jr., and Pat M. Holt, Invitation to Struggle: Congress, the President and Foreign Policy (Washington,D.C.: Congressional Quarterly Press, 1980), p. 204.

15. I.M. Destler, "Congress as Boss?," Foreign Policy, 42(1981), p. 167.

16. Anthony Lake and Leslie Gelb, "Congress; Politics and Bad Policy," Foreign Policy, 20(1975), p. 232.

17. Time, 4/6/79, p. 37.

18. Washington Post, 4/22/78, p. 27.

19. New York Times, 3/22/81, IV, p. 3.

20. Ibid., 5/28/78, IV, p. 14.

21. Washington Post, 4/26/78, p. 27.

22. Ole R. Holsti and James N. Rosenau, "The Meaning of Vietnam: Belief Systems of American Leaders," International Journal, 32(1977), Table 6, p. 72.

23. John E. Rielly, "The American Mood: A Foreign Policy of Self Interest," Foreign Policy, 34(1979), p. 85.

24. William Olson, "The President, Congress, and American Foreign Policy," International Affairs, 52(1976), p. 567.

25. Murphy Commission, p. 236.

26. E.g., Olson, "The President," p. 567.

27. Kurt J. Lauk, "The European Perspective; <u>Congress and Arms Control</u>, ed. by Alan Platt and Lawrence D. Weiler (Boulder, Colorado: Westview Press, 1978), <u>passim</u>.

28. Thomas M. Frank and Edward Weisband, <u>Foreign Policy by Congress</u>, (New York: Oxford University Press, 1979), p. 45.

29. Youngstown Sheet and Tube Co. V. Sawyer (343 US 579), 1952.

30. Opinion is extracted in <u>Congressional Quarterly Weekly</u>, 9/22/79, p. 2919.

31. <u>New York Times</u>, 3/22/81, p. D3.

32. U. S., Congress, Senate, Committee on Foreign Relations, <u>Executive Sessions</u>, III (1954), p. 60.

33. Emmet J. Hughes, <u>The Living Presidency</u> (Baltimore, Maryland: Penguin Books, 1972), p. 286.

34. J. William Fulbright, "The Legislation as Educator," <u>Foreign Affairs</u>, 57(1979), p. 727.

35. Humphrey to Helms, 1/6/76, Box 191, H. H. Reading file, Humphrey Mss.

36. Humphrey to Rusk, 6/6/76, <u>ibid.</u>

37. Barry Goldwater, <u>With No Apologies:  The Personal and Political Memoirs of United States Senator Barry M. Goldwater</u> (New York:  William Morrow, 1979), p. 294.

38. John G. Tower, "Congress Versus the President:  The Formulation and Implementation of American Foreign Policy," <u>Foreign Affairs</u> 60(1982), pp. 230, 238.

39. Frank and Weisband, <u>Foreign Policy by Congress</u>, pp. 70-71.

40. <u>Ibid.</u>, p.154.

41. <u>Congressional Quarterly Weekly</u>, 4/26/80, p. 1136.

42. <u>New York times</u>, 3/22/81, p. E 3.

43. <u>E.g.</u>, Frank, "After the Fall," pp. 627-34.

44. <u>New York Times</u>, 5/15/75, p. 1.

45. U.S., Congress, House of Representatives, Committee on International Relations, <u>War Powers:  A Test of Compliance Relative to the Danang Sealift, the EVacuation of Phnbom Penh, the Evacuation of Saigon, and the Mayaguez Incident</u>, Hearings Before the Subcommittee on Internal Security and Scientific Affairs, 94th Cong., 1st sess. (1975), p. 80.

46. New York Times, 5/15/75, p. 1.

47. House, Committee on International Relations, War Powers, p. 67.

48. Frank, "After the Fall," pp. 617, 619.

49. John T. Rourke, "The Future is History: Congress and Foreign Policy," Presidential Studies Quarterly, 10(1979), p. 281.

50. New York Times, 4/25/81, p. 1.

51. Hartford Courant, 4/26/80, p. 10.

52. Ibid., p.1.

53. Hughes, The Living Presidency, p. 346.

54. U.S., Congress, Senate, Committee on Foreign Relations, and House of Representatives, Committee on International Relations, Analysis of Arms Control Impact Statements Submitted in Connection with Fiscal Year 1978 Budget Request, Report prepared by the Congressional Research Service, 95th Cong., 1st sess. (1977), p. 27. Also, see Robert L. Butterworth, "Bureaucratic Politics and Congress' Role in Weapons Development," Policy Studies Journal, 8(1979), pp. 76-83; and Alton Frye, "The Congressional Resource Problem" in Platt and Weiler, eds., Congress and Arms Control, p. 27.

55. Congressional Quarterly Weekly, 9/27/80, p. 2871.

56. Time, 10/6/80, p. 28.

57. New York Times, 10/22/81, p. 4.

58. E.g., Crabb and Holt, Invitation to Struggle, p. 192; and Lee H. Hamilton and Michael H. Van Dusen, "Making the Separation of Powers Work," Foreign Affairs, 57(1978), p. 227.

59. Harold L. Wolman and Dianne Miller Wolman, "The Role of the U.S. Senate Staff in the Opinion Linkage Process: Population Policy," Legislative Studies Quarterly, 2(1977), pp. 281-93.

60. E.g., Shawcross, Sideshow, p. 275 discusses SFRC staff activity in Indochina.

61. George Easterbrook, "The Most Powerful Nobody in Washington," Washington Monthly, 9/80, pp. 50-59 discusses the impact of the SFRC's William Johnson on foreign aid.

62. Thomas A. Dine, "Politics of the Purse," and Platt and Weiler, eds., Congress and Arms Control, p. 66.

63. Ibid.

64. Fred M. Kaiser, "Oversight and Foreign Policy," Legislative Studies Quarterly, 2(1977), p. 259.

65. Congressional Quarterly Weekly, 3/14/81, p. 479.

66. D. G. Henderson, The Senate Foreign Relations Committee," Washington Quarterly Report, (Spring, 1979), pp. 8-9.

67. Chadwick Alger, "The Foreign Policies of U.S. Publics," International Studies Quarterly, 21(1977), pp. 277-320.

68. Alfred Hero, "Non-Profit Organizations, Public Opinion and U.S. Foreign Policy," International Journal 33(1978), pp. 150-76.

69. Edward Laurence, "The Changing Role of Congress in Defense Policy-Making," Journal of Conflict Resolution 20(1976), p. 245; Alton Frye, A Responsible Congress: The Politics of National Security (New York: McGraw Hill, 1975), p. 106.

70. Frank and Weisband, Foreign Policy By Congress, p. 165.

71. Douglas Bennet, Jr., "Congress in Foreign Policy: Who Needs It?" Foreign Affairs, 57(1978), pp. 40-50; and Alton Frye, "Congressional Politics and Policy Analysis: Bridging the Gap," Policy Analysis, 2 (1976), p. 265-81.

72. New York Times, 9/29/81, p. 14.

73. Frank and Weisband, Foreign Policy By Congress, pp. 245-57.

74. Kaiser, "Oversight and Foreign Policy," p. 261.

75. Glenn R. Parker and Suzanne L. Parker, "Factions in Committees: The U.S. House of Representatives," American Political Science Review, 73 (1979), pp. 94-95.

76. Henderson, "Senate Foreign Relations Committee," p. 4.

77. Christopher Madison, "Percy Tests His Bipartisan Style at the Foreign Relations Committee," National Journal, 7/6/81, p. 1009.

78. Richard Whittle, "Foreign Relations Committee Searches for Renewed Glory," Congressional Quarterly Weekly, 3/4/81, p. 477.

79. Ibid.

80. Ibid.

81. Madison, "Percy," p. 1009.

82. Whittle, "Foreign Relations Committee," p. 479.

83. Frederick Paul Lee, "The Two Presidencies Revisited," _Presidential Studies Quarterly_, 10(1980), pp.620-28; Thomas E. Cronin, "A Resurgent Congress and the Imperial Presidency," _Political Science Quarterly_, 95(1980), pp. 210-211, especially Table 1.

84. _Time_, 11/9/81.

85. David R. Mayheu, _Congress: The Electoral Imperative_ (New Haven, Connecticut: Yale University Press, 1974).

86. Bruce Russett and Donald DeLuca, "Don't Tread on Me: Public Opinion and Foreign Policy in the Eighties," _Political Science Quarterly_, 96(1981), figure 6, p. 395.

87. _Ibid._

88. James Chance, "Is a Foreign Policy Consensus Possible," _Foreign Affairs_, 57(1978), pp. 1-16.

89. Rielly, "The American Mood," _passim_.

90. Russett and DeLuca, "Don't Tread on Me," Tables 2,3 and 4.

91. _Ibid._

92. For a five stage characterization, see Bax, "Legislative-Executive Relationship," pp.885-90.

93. Robert A. Pastor, _Congress and the Politics of U.S. Foreign Economic Policy, 1929-1976_ (Berkeley, California: University of California Press, 1980), p.345.

94. _Ibid._, p. 58.

95. James A. Robinson, _Congress and Foreign Policy-Making: A Study in Legislative Influence and Initiative_ (Homewood, Illinois: The Dorsey Press, 1967); and Robert A. Dahl, _Congress and Foreign Policy_ (New York: W. W. NOrton, 1964).

96. Frey, _A Responsible Congress_, p. 148.

97. Arthur M. Schlesinger, Jr., "Congress and the Making of American Foreign Policy," _Foreign Affairs_, 51(1972), p. 99; John F. Manley, "The Rise of Congress in Foreign Policy-Making," _Annals of the American Academy of Political and Social Science_, 397(1971), p. 69.

98. Vandenberg to Floyd McGriff, 7/1/47, Vandenberg Mss.

99. Norman Graebner, _The New Isolationism: A Study in Politics_

408

and Foreign Policy Since 1950 (New York: Ronald Press, 1956), p. 203.

100. J. William Fulbright, The Crippled Giant: American Foreign Policy and its Domestic Consequences (New York: Random House, 1972), p. 193.

101. Bayless Manning, "The Congress, the Executive, and Inter-mestic Affairs," Foreign Affairs, 57(1977), pp. 308-24.

102. Roger Hilsman, The Politics of Policy-Making in Defense and Foreign Affairs (New York: Harper & Row, 1971), p. 126.

103. Theodore Sorenson, Decision Making in the White House; The Olive Branch on the Arrows (New York: Columbia University Press, 1973), p.114.

104. Richard E. Neustadt, Presidential Power: The Politics of Leadership From FDR to Carter (New York: John Wiley & Sons, 1980), Chap. 4, pp. 44-63.

# Selected Bibliography

## Manuscript Collection

Dean Acheson Papers. Harry S. Truman Library. Independence, Missouri.

Anonymous Papers. By agreement with the subject, this collection was not for attribution.

Warren Austin Papers. University of Vermont Library. Burlington, Vermont.

Alben Barkley Papers. University of Kentucky Library. Lexington, Kentucky.

Bernard Baruch Papers. Princeton University Library. Princeton, New Jersey.

Chester Bowles Papers. Yale University Library. New Haven, Connecticut.

Styles Bridges Papers. New England College Library. Henniker, New Hampshire.

Vannevar Bush Papers. Library of Congress. Washington, D.C.

James F. Byrnes Papers. Robert M. Cooper Library. Clemson University. Clemson, South Carolina.

Arthur Capper Papers. Kansas State Historical Society. Topeka, Kansas.

William L. Clayton Papers. Harry S. Truman Library. Independence, Missouri.

Clark M. Cli}ford Papers. Harry S. Truman Library. Independence, Missouri.

Joseph Davis Papers. Library of Congress. Washington, D.C.

Everett Dirksen Papers. Everett M. Dirksen Research Center. Pekin, Illinois.

John Foster Dulles Papers. Princeton University Library. Princeton, New Jersey. N.B. The Dulles telephone transcripts are a separate collection. They are housed in the original at the Eisenhower Library in Abilene, Kansas with copies at Princeton.

Dwight D. Eisenhower Papers. Dwight D. Eisenhower Library. Abilene, Kansas.

George M. Elsey Papers. Harry S. Truman Library. Independence, Missouri.

Ralph Flanders Papers. George Arents Research Library. Syracuse

University.  Syracuse, New York.

James Forrestal Papers and Diary.  Princeton University Library. Princeton, New Jersey.

J. William Fulbright Papers.  University of Arkansas Library. Fayetteville, Arkansas.  N.B. The Fulbright papers citations are either for a Box Control Number (BCN) for the first acquisition or a four place number (e.g. 48:35:4: 2) which represents series, subseries, box, and file in the second acquisition.

Theodore Green Papers.  Library of Congress.  Washington, D.C.

James Hagerty Papers.  Dwight D. Eisenhower Library.  Abilene, Kansas.

Christian A. Herter Papers.  Dwight D. Eisenhower Library. Abilene, Kansas.

Bourke B. Hickenlooper Papers.  Herbert Hoover Library.  West Branch, Iowa.

Herbert Hoover Papers.  Herbert Hoover Library.  West Branch, Iowa.

Hubert H. Humphrey Papers.  Minnesota Historical Society.  St. Paul, Minnesota.

Joseph Jones Papers.  Harry S. Truman Library.  Independence, Missouri.

John F. Kennedy Papers.  John F. Kennedy Library.  Boston, Massachusetts.

Harley Kilgore Papers.  Franklin Delano Roosevelt Library.  Hyde Park, New York.

Lyndon B. Johnson Papers.  Lyndon B. Johnson Library.  Austin, Texas.

Walter Lippmann Papers.  Yale University Library.  New Haven, Connecticut.

Joseph Martin Papers.  Stonehill College Library.  North Easton, Massachusetts.

Karl Mundt Papers.  Karl Mundt Library.  Madison, South Dakota. N.B. "RG" citations stand for record group.

Edwin Nourse Papers.  Harry S. Truman Library.  Independence, Missouri.

Leo Pasvolsky Papers.  Library of Congress.  Washington, D.C.

Robert Patterson Papers.  Library of Congress.  Washington, D.C.

Harry Price Papers.  Harry S. Truman Library.  Independence, Missouri.

Sam Rayburn Papers.  Sam Rayburn Library.  Bonham, Texas.

Richard B. Russell Papers.  Richard B. Russell Library.  Athens, Georgia.

Hugh Scott Papers.  University of Virginia Library.  Charlottesville, Virginia.

George Smith Papers.  Yale University Library.  New Haven, Connecticut.

H. Alexander Smith Papers.  Princeton University Library.  Princeton, New Jersey.

Harold Smith Papers.  Franklin Delano Roosevelt Library.  Hyde Park, New York.

John Snyder Papers.  Harry S. Truman Library.  Independence, Missouri.

Brent Spense Papers.  University of Kentucky Library.  Lexington,

Kentucky.

Henry L. Stimson Papers. Yale University Library. New Haven, Connecticut.

Elbert Thomas Papers. Franklin Delano Roosevelt Library. Hyde Park, New York.

Charles Tobey Papers. Dartmouth College Library. Hanover, New Hampshire.

Harry S. Truman Papers. Harry S. Truman Library. Independence, Missouri.

Millard Tydings Papers. University of Maryland Library. College Park, Maryland.

United States Congress, Senate, Committee on Foreign Relations. Record Group 46, National Archives, Washington, D.C.

Arthur H. Vandenberg Papers. University of Michigan Library. Ann Arbor, Michigan.

John Vorys Papers. Ohio Historical Society. Columbus, Ohio.

Robert Wagner Papers. Georgetown University Library. Washington, D.C.

Alexander Wiley Papers. Wisconsin Historical Society. Madison, Wisconsin.

## Interviews

Lewis Douglas, October 30, 1972.
Dean Rusk, November 4, 1980.

## Oral History

Because several of those interviewed for oral histories have recorded their recollections in more than one collection, the citations indicate both the person interviewed and the collection. That is, Aiken Oral History (Truman) indicates Aiken's contribution to the Truman Library.

Acheson, Dean. Truman Oral History Collection.

Aiken, George. Truman, Kennedy, and Johnson Oral History Collections.

Bowie, Robert. Dulles Oral History Collection.

Bowles, Chester. Kennedy Oral History Collection.

Bundy, McGeorge. Johnson Oral History Collection

Church, Frank. Johnson Oral History Collection.

Dirksen, Everett. Dulles Oral History Collection.

Dulles, Eleanor Lansing. Dulles Oral History Collection.

Hanes, John. Dulles Oral History Collection.

Harlow, Bryce. Dulles, Eisenhower, and Johnson Oral History Collections.

Hickenlooper, Bourke. Dulles Oral History Collection.

Hughes, Emmet. Dulles Oral History Collection.

Kennan, George. Dulles Oral History Collection

Lawrence, David. Kennedy Oral History Collection

Lippmann, Walter. Kennedy Oral History Collection.

Lisagor, Peter. Kennedy Oral History Collection.

McCardle, Carl. Dulles Oral History Collection.

MacComber, William. Dulles Oral History Collection.

412

Markins, Roger.  Truman Oral History Collection.
Martin, Joseph.  Dulles Oral History Collection.
Miall, Leonard.  Truman Oral History Collection.
Nixon, Richard.  Dulles Oral History Collection
O'Connor, Rod.  Dulles Oral History Collection.
Rostow, Eugene.  Johnson Oral History Collection
Sorenson, Theodore.  Kennedy Oral History Collection.
Sparkman, John.  Johnson Oral History Collection.


## Public Documents

U. S. Comptroller General.  "Executive-Legislative Communications
     and the Role of Congress During International Crisis."  A
     Report to the Congress.  Report ID-76-78.  September 3,
     1976.
U. S. Congress. Congressional Record, 1945 - .
U. S. Congress. House of Representatives.  Committee on Armed
     Services.  United States-Vietnam Relations, 1945-1967.
     Book 9.  91st Cong., 1st sess. (1971).
_____.  Committee on Foreign Affairs.  Congress, the Presi-
     dent and the War Powers.  Hearings before the Subcommit-
     tee on National Security Policy and Scientific Develop-
     ments, 91st Cong., 2nd sess. (1970).
_____.  Committee on Foreign Affairs.  Implementation of the
     Taiwan Relations Act:  Issues and Concerns.  Hearings
     before the Subcommittee on Asian and Pacific Affairs,
     96th Cong., 1st sess. (1979).
_____.  Committee on Foreign Affairs.  The Cold War:  Origins
     and Developments.  Hearings, 92nd Cong., 1st sess.
     (1971).
_____.  Committee on International Relations.  Congress and
     Foreign Policy.  Hearings before the Special Subcommit-
     tee on Investigations.  94th Cong., 2nd sess. (1976).
U. S. Congress. House of Representatives.  Committee on Inter-
     national Relations.  War Powers:  A Test of Compliance
     Relative to the Danang Sealift, the Evacuation of Phnom
     Penh, the Evacuation of Saigon, and the Mayaguez Inci-
     dent.  Hearings before the Subcommittee on International
     Security and Scientific Affairs, 94th Cong., 1st sess.
     (1975).
_____.  Committee on Rules.  Studies on the Legislative
     Veto.  "The Legislative Veto and U.S. Arms Sales," by
     Richard F. Grimmett.  Congressional Research Service
     Report, 96th Cong., 2nd sess. (1980), pp. 248-320.
U. S. Congress. Senate.  Committee on Banking and Currency.
     Anglo-American Financial Agreement.  Hearings before
     the Committee on Banking and Currency, Senate, 79th
     Cong., 2nd. sess. (1946).
_____.  Committee on Foreign Relations.  "Analysis of Arms
     Control Impact Statements Submitted in Connection with
     the Fiscal Year 1978 Budget Request."  Report prepared by
     the Congressional Research Service, 95th Cong., 1st sess.
     (1977).

413

_____. Committee on Foreign Relations. European Interim Aid Act of 1947. Hearings, 80th Cong., 1st Sess. (1947).

_____. Committee on Foreign Relations. European Recovery Program. Hearings, 80th Cong., 2nd. sess. (1948).

_____. Committee on Foreign Relations. Executive Sessions of the Senate Foreign Relations Committee (1947-1951). 94th. Cong., 2nd sess. (1976).

_____. Committee on Foreign Relations. Genocide Convention. Hearings, 95th Cong., 1st sess. (1977).

_____. Committee on Foreign Relations. Middle East Peace Process. Hearings before the Subcommittee on Near Eastern and South Asian Affairs, 95th Cong., 2nd sess. (1978).

_____. Committee on Foreign Relations. Panama Canal Treaties. Hearings, 95th Cong., 2nd sess. (1978).

_____. Committee on Foreign Relations. Proposed Sale of C-130s to Egypt. Hearings before the Subcommittee on Foreign Assistance, 94th Cong., 2nd sess. (1978).

_____. Committee on Foreign Relations. Senate Debate on the Panama Canal Treaties: A Compendium of Major Statements, Documents, Record Votes, and Relevant Events. A Report by the Congressional Research Service, 96th Cong., 1st sess. (1979).

U. S. Congress. Senate. Committee on Foreign Relations. The Formulation and Administration of United States Foreign Policy, Study prepared by the Brookings Institution, 86th Cong., 2nd sess. (1960).

_____. Committee on Foreign Relations. The SALT II Treaty. Hearings, 96th Cong., 1st sess. (1979).

_____. Committee on Foreign Relations. Treaties of Peace with Italy, Rumania, Bulgaria, and Hungary, 80th Cong., 1st sess. (1947).

_____. Committee on Foreign Relations. United States Foreign Policy. Hearings, 86th Cong., 1st sess. (1959).

_____. Committee on Foreign Relations. War Powers Legislation. Hearings, 92nd Cong., 1st sess. (1971).

_____. Committee on Government Operations. Administration of National Security. Hearings by the Subcommittee on National Security, 88th Cong., (1963-1964).

U. S. Department of State. Foreign Relations of the United States. 1945-1951. A year by year, multivolumned publication.

U. S. Murphy Commission. Commission on the Organization of Government for the Conduct of Foreign Policy. Robert Murphy, Chairman. Report. June, 1975.

Books

Acheson, Dean. Present at the Creation: My Years in the State Department. New York: W. W. Norton & Company, Inc., 1969.

_____. A Citizen Looks at Congress. New York: Harper & Row, 1956.

_____. Sketches From Life of Men I have Known. New York: Harper & Row, 1956.

Adams, Sherman. First Hand Report. New York: Harper Bros., 1961.

Alino, Richard A. American Defense Policy from Eisenhower to Kennedy. Athens, Ohio: Ohio University Press, 1975.

Bachrach, Stanley D. The Committee of One Million: China Lobby Politics, 1953-1971. New York: Columbia University Press, 1976.

Baldwin, David A. Foreign Aid and American Foreign Policy: A Documentary Analysis. New York: Frederick A. Praeger, Publishers, 1966.

Banal, Jaya Ktishna. The Pentagon and the Making of U.S. Foreign Policy: A Case Study of Vietnam, 1960-68. Atlantic Highlands, New Jersey: Humanities Press, 1978.

Bauer, Raymond A.; Pool, Ithiel de Sola; and Dexter, Lewis Anthony. American Business and Public Policy: The Politics of Foreign Trade. New York: Atherton Press, 1963.

Beal, John Robinson. John Foster Dulles: 1888-1956. New York: Harper & Row, 1959.

Bellush, Bernard. He Walked Alone: A Biography of John Gilbert Winant. The Hague, The Netherlands: Mouton and Company, 1968.

Bernstein, Barton J., ed. Politics and Policies of the Truman Administration. Chicago: Quadrangle Books, 1970.

Betts, Richard. Soldiers, Statesmen, and Cold War Crises. Cambridge, Massachusetts: Harvard University Press.

Bidault, George. Resistance. Translated by Marianne Sinclair. New York: Frederick A. Praeger, 1965.

Blum, John Morton, ed. The Price of Vision: The Diary of Henry A. Wallace, 1942-1956. Boston: Houghton Mifflin Company, 1973.

Bohlen, Charles E. The Transformation of American Foreign Policy. New York: W. W. Norton & Company, 1969.

_____. Witness to History: 1929-1969. W. W. Norton & Company, 1973.

Braden, Spruille. Diplomats and Demagogues. New Rochelle, New York: Arlington House, 1971.

Brecher, Michael. Decisions in Israel's Foreign Policy. New Haven, Connecticut: Yale University Press, 1975.

Brown, Stuart Gerry. The American Presidency: Leadership, Partisanship, and Popularity. New York: The MacMillan Company, 1966.

Buckely, James. If Men Were Angels: A View from the Senate. New York: G. P. Putnam's Sons, 1975.

Bueler, William M. U.S. China Policy and the Problem of Taiwan. Boulder, Colorado: Colorado Associated University Press, 1971.

Carroll, Holbert N. The House of Representatives and Foreign Affairs. Boston: Little, Brown and Company, 1966.

Cheever, Daniel S. and Haviland, H. Field Jr. American Foreign Policy and the Separation of Powers. Cambridge, Massachusetts: Harvard University Press, 1952.

Cohen, Bernard C. The Political Process and Foreign Policy: The Making of the Japanese Peace Settlement. Princeton, New Jersey: Princeton University Press, 1957.

_____. The Press and Foreign Policy. Princeton, New Jersey: Princeton University Press, 1963.

_____. The Public's Impact on Foreign Policy. Boston: Little, Brown, 1973.

Connally, Tom with Steinber, Alfred. My Name is Tom Connally. New York: Thomas Y. Crowell Company, 1954.

Crabb, Cecil V., Jr. and Holt, Pat M. Invitation to Struggle: Congress, the President and Foreign Policy. Washington, D.C.: Congressional Quarterly Press, 1980.

Dahl, Robert A. Congress and Foreign Policy. 2nd ed. New York: W. W. Norton & Company, 1964.

Daniels, Jonathan. The Man of Independence. Philadelphia: J. B. Lippincott Company, 1950.

DeConde, Alexander. Half Bitter, Half Sweet: An American Excursion into Italian American History. New York: Charles Scribner's Sons, 1971.

Destler, I. M. Making Foreign Economic Policy. Washington, D.C.: the Brookings Institution, 1980.

_____. Presidents, Bureaucrats, and Foreign Policy. Princeton, New Jersey: Princeton University Press, 1972.

Detzer, David. The Brink: Cuban Missile Crisis, 1962. New York: Thomas Y. Crowell, 1979.

Dinerstein, Herbert S. The Making of a Missile Crisis: October 1962. Baltimore: The Johns Hopkins University Press, 1976.

Doenecke, Justus D. The Old Isolationists in the Cold War Era. Lewisburg, Pennsylvania: Bucknell University Press, 1979.

Donovan, Robert J. Conflict and Crisis: The Presidency of Harry S. Truman, 1945-1948. New York: W. W. Norton, 1977.

Draper, Theodore. The Dominican Revolt: A Case Study in American Policy. New York: Commentary, 1968.

Dulles, Foster Rhea. American Policy Toward Communist China, 1949-1969. New York: Thomas Y. Crowell Company, 1972.

Dulles, John Foster. War and Peace. New York: The MacMillan Company, 1957.

Edwards, George C., III. Presidential Influence in Congress. San Francisco: W. H. Freeman, 1980.

Eisenhower, Dwight David. The White House Years. Vol. I: Mandate for Change, 1953-1956. Vol. II: Waging Peace, 1956-1961. Garden City, New York: Doubleday & Company, 1963, 1965.

Etheridge, Lloyd S. A World of Men: The Private Sources of American Foreign Policy. Cambridge, Massachusetts: MIT Press, 1978.

Farnsworth, David N. The Senate Committee on Foreign Relations. Urbana, Illinois: The University of Illinois Press, 1961.

Feis, Herbert. Foreign Aid and Foreign Policy. New York: St. Martins Press, 1964.

416

Fenno, Richard F., Jr. Congressmen in Committees. Boston: Little, Brown, 1973.

Ferrell, Robert. Off the Record: The Private Papers of Harry S. Truman. New York: Harper & Row, 1980.

Feuerwerger, Marvin C. Congress and Israel: Foreign Aid Decision-Making in the House of Representatives, 1969-1976. Westport, Connecticut: Greenwood Press, 1979.

Ford, Gerald R. A Time of Heal: The Autobiography of Gerald R. Ford. New York: Harper & Row, 1979.

Fox, J. Ronald. Arming America: How the U.S. Buys Weapons. Cambridge, Massachusetts: Harvard University Press, 1974.

Francis-Williams, Edward. A Prime Minister Remembers: The War and Post-War Memoirs of the Rt. Hon. Earl Attlee, Based on his Private Papers and a Series of Recorded Conversations. London: William Heinemann, Ltd., 1961.

Frank, Thomas M. and Weisband, Edward. Foreign Policy By Congress. New York: Oxford University Press, 1979.

Frankel, Charles. High on Foggy Bottom, An Outsider's Inside View of the Government. New York: Harper & Row, Publishers, 1968.

Freeland, Richard M. The Truman Doctrine and the Origins of McCarthyism: Foreign Policy, Domestic Politics, and Internal Security, 1945-1948. New York: Alfred A. Knopf, 1972.

Friederich, Carl J. Constitutional Government and Democracy. Boston: Little, Brown and Company, 1949.

Frye, Alton. A Responsible Congress: The Politics of National Security. New York: McGraw Hill, 1975.

Fulbright, J. William. Old Myths and New Realities. New York: Random House, 1964.

_____. The Crippled Giant: American Foreign Policy and its Domestic Consequences. New York: Random House, 1972.

Gaddis, John Lewis. The United States and the Origins of the Cold War, 1941-1947. New York: Columbia University Press, 1972.

Gerson, Louis L. The Hyphenate in Recent American Politics and Diplomacy. Lawrence, Kansas: The University of Kansas Press, 1964.

_____. John Foster Dulles. New York: Cooper Square, 1967.

Gilbert, Stephen P. Soviet Images of America. New York: Crane, Russak, 1977.

Goldwater, Barry. With No Apologies: The Personal and Political Memoirs of United States Senator Barry M. Goldwater. New York: William Morrow, 1979.

Graebner, Norman A. The New Isolationism: A Study in Politics and Foreign Policy Since 1950. New York: The Ronald Press Company, 1956.

Gravel, Michael, ed. The Senator Gravel Edition: The Pentagon Papers. Boston: Beacon Press, 1971. 5 volumes.

Guhin, Michael A. John Foster Dulles: A Statesman and His Times. New York: Columbia University Press, 1972.

Halperin, Morton H. Bureaucratic Politics and Foreign Policy. Washington, D.C.: The Brookings Institution, 1974.

Harriman, W. Averell. America and Russia in a Changing World: A Half Century of Personal Observation. Garden City, New York: Doubleday & Company, 1971.

Herring, George C., Jr. Aid to Russia, 1941-1946: Strategy, Diplomacy, the Origins of the Cold War. New York: Columbia University Press, 1973.

Hero, Alfred O., Jr. The Southerner and World Affairs. Baton Rouge, Louisiana: Louisiana State University Press, 1965.

Hewlett, Richard E. and Anderson, Oscar E. A History of the United States Atomic Energy Commission. Vol. I: The Brave New World. 1939/1946. University Park, Pennsylvania: Pennsylvania State University Press, 1962.

Higgins, Benjamin. The United Nations and United States Foreign Economic Policy. Homewood, Illinois: Richard D. Irwin, Inc., 1962.

Hilsman, Roger. The Politics of Policy-Making in Defense and Foreign Affairs. New York: Harper & Row, 1971.

_____. To Move a Nation: The Politics of Foreign Policy in the Administration of John F. Kennedy. New York: Dell Publishing Company, 1964.

Hoffmann, Stanley. Gulliver's Troubles, Or the Setting of American Foreign Policy. New York: McGraw Hill Book Company, 1968.

Holtzman, Abraham. Legislative Liaison: Executive Leadership in Congress. Chicago: Rand McNally & Company, 1970.

Hoopes, Townsend. The Devil and John Foster Dulles. Boston: Little, Brown, 1973.

Howe, Russel Warren and Trott, Sarah Hays. The Power Peddlers: How Lobbyists Mold America's Foreign Policy. Garden City, New York: Doubleday, 1977.

Hoxie, R. Gordon. Command Decisions and the Presidency. Pleasantville, New York: Readers Digest, 1977.

Hughes, John Emmet. The Ordeal of Power: A Political Memoir of the Eisenhower Years. New York: Atheneum, 1963.

Hughes, Emmet J. The Living Presidency. Baltimore: Penguin Books, 1972.

Jewell, Malcolm E. Senatorial Politics and Foreign Policy. Lexington, Kentucky: University of Kentucky Press, 1962.

Johnson, Lyndon Baines. The Vantage Point: Perspectives of the Presidency, 1963-1969. New York: Holt, Rinehart, and Winston, 1971.

Jones, Joseph M. The Fifteen Weeks (February 21-June 5, 1947) New York: The Viking Press, 1955.

Kanter, Arnold. Defense Politics: A Budgetary Perspective. Chicago: University of Chicago Press, 1979.

Kearns, Doris. Lyndon Johnson and the American Dream. New York: Harper & Row, 1976.

Kissinger, Henry. White House Years. Boston: Little, Brown, 1979.

_____. Years of Upheaval. Boston: Little, Brown, 1982.

Koen, Ross Y. The China Lobby in American Politics. New York: The MacMillan Company, 1960.

Kolko, Gabriel. The Limits of Power: The World and United

States Foreign Policy, 1945-1954. New York: Harper & Row, 1972.

Korb, Lawrence, J. The Fall and Rise of the Pentagon: American Defense Policies in the 1970s. Westport, Connecticut: Greenwood Press, 1979.

Lake, Anthony. The "Tar Baby" Option: American Policy Toward Southern Rhodesia. New York: Columbia University Press, 1976.

Lasswell, Harold D. and Kaplan, Abraham. Power and Society: A Framework for Political Inquiry. New Haven, Connecticut: Yale University Press, 1950.

Leahy, William D. I Was There. New York: McGraw-Hill Book Company, 1950.

Lehman, John. The Executive, Congress, and Foreign Policy: Studies of the Nixon Administration. New York: Praeger, 1976.

Lerche, Charles O., Jr. The Uncertain South: Its Changing Patterns of Politics in Foreign Policy. Chicago: Quadrangle Books, 1964.

Levering, Ralph B. The Public and American Foreign Policy, 1918-1978. New York: William Morrow, 1978.

Liske, Craig and Rundquist, Barry. The Politics of Weapons Procurement: The Role of Congress. Denver, Colorado: The University of Denver Press, 1974.

Lodge, Henry Cabot. As It Was: An Inside View of Politics and Power in the '50s and 60s. New York: W. W. Norton, 1976.

Lovell, James P. Foreign Policy in Perspective: Strategy, Adaption, Decision Making. New York: Holt, Rinehart and Winston, 1970.

Lowenthal, Abraham F. The Dominican Intervention. Cambridge, Massachusetts: Harvard University Press, 1972.

Lynn, Naomi B. and McClure, Arthur F. The Fulbright Premise. Lewisburg, Pennsylvania: Bucknell University Press, 1973.

Lyon, Peter. Eisenhower: Portrait of the Hero. Boston: Little, Brown, 1974.

MacNeil, Neil. Dirksen: Portrait of a Public Man. New York: World Publishing, 1970.

Mayhew, David R. Congress: The Electoral Imperative. New Haven, Connecticut: Yale University Press, 1974.

Messer, Robert L. James F. Byrnes, Roosevelt, Truman and the Origins of the Cold War. Chapel Hill, North Carolina: The University of North Carolina Press, 1982.

Miller, Merle. Lyndon: An Oral Biography. New York: G. P. Putnam's Sons, 1980.

Millis, Walter and Duffield, E. S., eds. The Forrestal Diaries. New York: Viking Press, 1951.

Montgomery, John D. Foreign Aid in International Politics. Englewood Cliffs, New Jersey: PrenticeHall, 1967.

_____. The Politics of Foreign Aid: American Experience in Southeast Asia. New York: Frederick A. Praeger, 1962.

Neal, Steve. The Eisenhowers: Reluctant Dynasty. Garden City, New York: Doubleday, 1978.

Nixon, Richard. RN: The Memoirs of Richard Nixon. New York: Grosset and Dunlap, 1978.

O'Brien, Lawrence. No Final Victories. Garden City, New York: Doubleday, 1974.

O'Donnell, Kenneth P. and Powers, David. "Johnny, We Hardly Knew Ye": Memoirs of John Fitzgerald Kennedy. Boston: Little, Brown and Company, 1970.

Ognibene, Peer J. Scoop: The Life and Politics of Henry M. Jackson. New York: Stein and Day, 1975.

O'Leary, Michael Kent. The Politics of American Foreign Aid. New York: Atherton Press, 1967.

Pastor, Robert A. Congress and the Politics of U.S. Foreign Economic Policy, 1929-1976. Berkeley, California: University of California Press, 1980.

Patterson, James T. "Mr. Republican": A Biography of Robert A. Taft. Boston: Houghton Mifflin Company, 1972.

Peirre, Andrew, ed. Arms Transfers and American Foreign Policy. New York: New York University Press, 1979.

Platt, Alan. The U.S. Senate and Strategic Arms Policy. Boulder, Colorado: Westview Press, 1978.

_____ and Weiler, Lawrence D., eds. Congress and Arms Control. Boulder, Colorado: Westview Press, 1978.

Prochnau, William and Larsen, Richard W. A Certain Democrat: Senator Henry M. Jackson, A Political Biography. Englewood Cliffs, New Jersey: Prentice-Hall, 1972.

Quandt, William B. Decade of Decisions: American Policy Toward the Arab-Israeli Conflict, 1967-1976. Berkeley, California: University of California Press, 1977.

Rabin, Yitzak. The Rabin Memoirs.. Boston: Little, Brown, 1979.

Reston, James. The Artillery of the Press: Its Influence on American Foreign Policy. New York: Harper & Row, 1966.

Reiselbach, Leroy N. The Roots of Isolationism: Congressional Voting and Presidential Leadership in Foreign Policy. Indianapolis, Indiana: The Bobbs-Merrill Company, 1966.

Riggs, Robert E. U.S./U.N. Foreign Policy and International Organization. New York: Appleton-Century-Crofts, 1971.

Robinson, James A. Congress and Foreign Policy-Making: A Study in Legislative Influence and Initiative. Homewood, Illinois: The Dorsey Press, Rev. ed., 1967.

Rostow, Walter W. The Diffusion of Power, An Essay in Recent History. New York: The MacMillan Company, 1972.

Rourke, Francis. Bureaucracy and Foreign Policy. Baltimore: The Johns Hopkins University Press, 1972.

Russell, Ruth B. The United Nations and United States Security Policy. Washington, D.C.: the Brookings Institution, 1968.

Safire, William. Before the Fall: An Inside View of the Pre-Watergate White House. Garden City, New York: Doubleday, 1975.

Said, Abdul Aziz. Ethnicity and U.S. Foreign Policy. New York: Praeger, 1977.

Schlesinger, Arthur M., Jr. A Thousand Days: John F. Kennedy in the White House. Greenwich, Connecticut: Fawcett

Publications, 1956.

Schoultz, Lars. Human Rights and United States Policy Toward Latin America. Princeton, New Jersey: Princeton University Press, in press.

Sheehan, Edward. The Arabs, Israelis, and Kissinger. New York: Readers Digest, 1976.

Snetsinger, John. Truman, the Jewish Vote and the Creation of Israel. Stanford, California: Hoover Institution Press, 1974.

Snyder, Richard C., Bruck, H. W., and Sapin, Burton. Decision Making as an Approach to the Study of International Politics. Foreign Policy Analysis Series, Vol. 3. Princeton, New Jersey: Organizational Behavior Section, 1954.

Sofair, Abraham, D. War, Foreign Affairs and Constitutional Power: The Origins. Cambridge, Massachusetts: Ballinger Publishing, 1976.

Sorenson, Theodore. Kennedy. New York: Harper & Row, 1965.

_____. Decision-Making in the White House: The Olive Branch or the Arrows. New York: Columbia University Press, 1963.

Sorenson, Thomas C. The World War: The Story of American Propaganda. New York: Holt Rinehart, 1968.

Steinberg, Alfred. The Man From Missouri: The Life and Times of Harry S. Truman. New York: G. P. Putnam's Sons, 1962.

_____. Sam Rayburn: A Biography. New York: Hawthorn Books, 1975.

Stennis, John C. and Fulbright, J. William. The Role of Congress in Foreign Policy. Washington, D.C.: American Enterprise for Public Policy Research, 1971.

Stern, Paula. Water's Edge: Domestic Politics and the Making of American Foreign Policy. Westport, Connecticut: Greenwood Press, 1979.

Stupak, Ronald J. The Shaping of Foreign Policy, the Role of the Secretary of State as Seen by Dean Acheson. n.p.: The Odyssey Press, 1969.

Talbott, Strobe. Endgame: the Inside Story of SALT II. New York: Harper & Row, 1979.

Tang Tsou. America's Failure in China, 1941-1950. Chicago: The University of Chicago Press, 1963.

Theoharis, Athan. Seeds of Repression: Harry S. Truman and the Origins of McCarthyism. Chicago: Quadrangle Books, 1971.

_____. The Yalta Myths: An Issue in U.S. Politics, 1945-55. Columbia, Missouri: The University of Missouri Press, 1970.

Toma, Peter A. The Politics of Food for Peace: Executive-Legislative Interaction. Tucson, Arizona: The University of Arizona Press, 1967.

Tompkins, David. Senator Arthur H. Vandenberg: The Evolution of a Modern Republican, 1884-1945. Ann Arbor, Michigan: Michigan State University Press, 1970.

Trewhitt, Henry L. McNamara. New York: Harper & Row, 1971.

Truman, Harry S. Memoirs. Vol. I: Year of Decision, Vol.
II: Years of Trial and Hope. Garden City, New York:
Doubleday and Company, 1955, 1956.

Truman, Margaret. Harry S Truman. New York: William Morrow,
1973.

Valenti, Jack. A Very Human President. New York: W. W.
Norton, 1975.

Van Der Beugel, Ernest H. From Marshall Aid to Atlantic
Partnerships: European Integration as a Concern of
American Foreign Policy. Amsterdam, the Netherlands:
Elsevier Publishing Company, 1966.

Vandenberg, Arthur H., Jr., ed. The Private Papers of Senator
Vandenberg. Boston: Houghton Mifflin, 1952.

Wagner, R. Harrison. United States Policy Toward Latin America:
A Study in Domestic and International Politics.
Stanford, California: Stanford University Press, 1970.

Waltz, Kenneth. Foreign Policy and Democratic Politics, The
American and British Experiences. Boston: Little,
Brown and Company, 1967.

Ward, Patricia Dawson. The Threat of Peace: James F. Byrnes
and the Council of Ministers, 1945-1946. Kent, Ohio:
Kent State University Press, 1979.

Watt, D. C. Personalities and Policies: Studies in the
Formulation of British Foreign Policy in the Twentieth
Century. South Bend, Indiana: University of Notre Dam
Press, 1965.

Weintal, Edward and Bartlett, Charles. Facing the Brink: An
Intimate Study of Crisis in Diplomacy. New York:
Scribner, 1967.

Westerfield, H. Bradford. Foreign Policy and Party Politics:
Pearl Harbor to Korea. New Haven, Connecticut: Yale
University Press, 1955.

Westwood, Andrew F. Foreign Aid in a Foreign Policy Framework.
Washington, D.C.: The Brookings Institution, 1966.

Wilcox, Francis O. Congress, The Executive and Foreign Policy.
Published for the Council on Foreign Relations. New
York: Harper & Row, 1971.

_____ and Frank, Richard A. The Constitution and the Conduct
of Foreign Policy. New York: Praeger, 1976.

Yarmolinsky, Adam. The Military Establishment: Its Impact on
American Society. New York: Harper & Row, 1971.

Yergin, Daniel. Shattered Peace: The Origins of the Cold War
and the National Security State. Boston: Houghton
Mifflin, 1977.

## Articles

Acheson, Dean. "The Credit to Britain, the Key to Expanded
Trade." Department of State Bulletin. 14 (February
10, 1946), pp. 185-88.

Alger, Chadwick. "The Foreign Policy of U.S. Publics."
International Studies Quarterly. 21(1977), pp.
277-320.

422

Allison, Graham T. "Making War: The President and Congress." *Law and Contemporary Problems*. 40(1976), pp. 86-106.

Allsbrook, John W. "The Role of Congressional Staffs in Weapons Systems Acquisitions." *Defense Systems Management Review*. 1(1977), pp. 34-41.

Aspin, Les. "The Power of Procedure." *Congress and Arms Control*. Edited by Alan Platt and Lawrence D. Weiler. Boulder, Colorado: Westview Press, 1978.

Avery, William and Forsythe, David. "Human Rights, National Security and the U. S. Senate. *International Studies Quarterly*. 23(1979), pp. 303-20.

Baldwin, David A. "Congressional Initiative in Foreign Policy." *Journal of Politics*. 28 (1966), pp. 754-73.

Balutis, Alan P. "Congress, the President and the Press." *Journalism Quarterly*. 53(1976), pp. 509-15.

Bardis, Barbara and Oldinick, Robert. "Beyond Internationalism: A Case for Multiple Dimensions in the Structure of Foreign Policy Attitudes." *Social Science Quarterly*. 58(1978), pp. 496-508.

Bax, Frans R. "The Legislative-Executive Relationship in Foreign Policy." *Orbis*. 20(1977), p. 881-904.

Bennet, Douglas, Jr. "Congress in Foreign Policy: Who Needs It?" *Foreign Affairs*. 57(1978), pp. 40-50.

Bernstein, Barton J. "American Foreign Policy and the Cold War." *Politics and Policies of the Truman Administration*. Edited by Barton J. Bernstein. Chicago: Quadrangle Books, 1970.

Bernstein, Robert A. and Anthony, William. "The ABM Issue in the Senate, 1968-1970: The Importance of Ideology." *American Political Science Review*. 68(1974), pp. 1198-1206.

Bozeman, Barry and James, Thomas. "Toward a Comprehensive Model of Foreign Policy Voting in the Senate." *Western Political Quarterly*. 28(1975), pp. 477-95.

Brigg, Philip J. "Senator Vandenberg." *Mid America*. 60(1978), pp. 163-70.

Bundy, McGeorge. "Vietnam, Watergate, and Presidential Powers." *Foreign Affairs*. 58(1980), pp. 397-407.

Burnstein, Paul and Freudenburg, William. "Changing Public Policy: The Impact of Public Opinion, Antiwar Demonstrations, and War Costs on Senate Voting on Vietnam War Motions." *American Journal of Sociology*. 84(1978), pp. 99-122.

Butterworth, Robert L. "Bureaucratic Politics and Congress' Role in Weapons Development." *Policy Studies Journal*. 8(1979), pp. 76-83.

Byrnes, James F. "U.S.-U.K. Economic and Financial Agreements." *Department of State Bulletin*. 14 (February 24, 1946), pp. 267-71.

Buckwalter, Doyle W. "The Congressional Concurrent Resolution: A Search for Foreign Policy Influence." *Midwest Journal of Political Science*. 14 (1970), pp. 434-58.

Carey, George W. "Separation of Powers and the Madisonian Model: A Reply to the Critics." *American Political Science*

Review. 72(1978), pp. 151-64.

Caspary, William R. "The 'Mood Theory': A Study of Public Opinion and Foreign Policy." American Political Science Review. 64 (1970), pp. 536-47.

Challenor, Herschelle Sullivan. "The Influence of Black Americans on U.S. Foreign Policy Toward Africa." Ethnicity and U.S. Foreign Policy. Edited by Abdul Aziz Said. New York: Praeger, 1977.

Chance, James. "Is a Foreign Policy Consensus Possible." Foreign Affairs. 57(1978), pp. 1-16.

Cimbala, Stephen J. "Foreign Policy as an Issue Area: A Role Call Analysis." American Political Science Review. 63 (1969), pp. 148-56.

Cleveland, Halan. "The Domestication of International Affairs and Vice Versa." Annals of the American Academy of Political and Social Sciences. 442(1979), pp. 125-37.

Clifford, J. Garry, "President Truman and Peter the Great's Will." Diplomatic History. 4(1980), pp. 216-23.

Cronin, Thomas E. "A Resurgent Congress and the Imperial Presidency." Political Science Quarterly. 95(1980), pp. 209-24.

Davis, Eric L. "Legislative Liaison in the Carter Adminis-tration." Political Science Quarterly. 95(1980), pp. 287-302.

Davis, Nathaniel. "The Angola Decision of 1975: A Personal Memoir." Foreign Affairs. 57(1978), pp. 109-24.

Destler, I. M. "Congress as Boss?" Foreign Policy. 42(1981), pp. 167-80.

_____. "Treaty Troubles: Versailles in Reverse." Foreign Policy. 33(1979), pp. 45-65.

_____. "U. S. Food Policy, 1972-1976: Reconciling Domestic and International Objectives." International Organization. 32(1978), pp. 617-54.

Easterbrook, George. "The Most Powerful Nobody in Washington." Washington Monthly. September, 1980, pp. 50-59.

Entin, Kenneth. "Information Exchange in Congress: The Case of the House Armed Service Committee." Western Political Quarterly. 26(1973), pp. 427-39.

Etheridge, Lloyd S. "Personality Effects on American Foreign Policy, 1898-1968: A Test of Interpersonal Gen-eralization." American Political Science Review. 72(1978), pp. 434-51.

Foster, H. Schuyler. "American Public Opinion and U.S. Foreign Policy." Department of State Bulletin. 41 (1959), pp. 796-803.

Fox, Annette Baker. "NATO and Congress." Political Science Quarterly. 80 (1965), pp. 395-414.

Frank, Thomas M. "After the Fall: A New Procedural Frame-Work for Congressional Control Over the War Power." American Journal of International Law. 71(1977), pp. 605-41.

Fry, Alton. "Congress: The Virtues of Its Vices." Foreign Policy. No. 3 (Summer, 1971), pp. 108-29.

_____. "Congressional Politics and Policy Analysis: Bridging the Gap." Policy Analysis. 2(1976), pp. 265-81.

Fry, Alton and Rogers, William D. "Linkage Begins at Home." Foreign Policy. 35(1979), pp. 49-67.

Fuchs, Lawrence H. "Minority Groups and Foreign Policy." Political Science Quarterly. 74 (1959), pp. 161-175.

Fulbright, J. William. "The Legislator as Educator." Foreign Affairs. 57(1979), pp. 719-32.

Galtung, Johan. "Social Position, Party Identification, and Foreign Policy Orientation: A Norwegian Case Study." Domestic Sources of Foreign Policy. Edited by James Rosenau. New York: The Free Press, 1967.

Garnham, David. "Factors Influencing Congressional Support for Israel During the 93rd Congress." Jerusalem Journal of International Relations. 2(1977), pp. 23-45.

Garrett, Stephen A. "Foreign Policy and the American Constitution: The Bricker Amendment in Contemporary Perspective." International Studies Quarterly. 14 (1971), pp. 187-220.

_____. "Eastern European Ethnic Groups and American Foreign Policy." Political Science Quarterly. 93(1978), pp. 301-23.

Gazell, James A. "Arthur H. Vandenberg, Internationalism, and the United Nations." Political Science Quarterly. 88 (1973), pp. 375-94.

Gould, James W. "The Origins of the Senate Committee on Foreign Relations." Western Political Quarterly. 3(1959), pp. 678-32.

Green, David. "The Cold War Comes to Latin America." Politics and Policies of the Truman Administration. Edited by Barton J. Bernstein. Chicago: Quadrangle Books, Inc., 1970.

Gregor, A. James. "The United States, the Republic of China, and the Taiwan Relations Act." Orbis. 24(1980), pp. 609-24.

Hamilton, Lee H. and Van Dusen, Michael H. "Making the Separation of Powers Work." Foreign Affairs. 57(1979), pp. 17-39.

Hanrieder, Wolfram F. "Compatibility and Consensus: A Proposal for the Conceptual Linkage of External and Internal Dimensions of Foreign Policy." American Political Science Review 61 (1967), pp. 971-82.

Harris, Charles Wesley. "International Relations and the Disposition of Alien Enemy Property Seized by the United States During World War II: A Case Study on German Properties." Journal of Politics. 23 (1961), pp. 641-66.

Haviland, H. Field. "Foreign Aid and the Policy Process: 1957." American Political Science Review. 52 (1958), pp. 698-724.

Hayes, Louis D. "The Relationship of Problem Perception to Policy Making for Members of the Senate Committee on Foreign Relations." International Review of History and Political Science. 4 (1971), pp. 97-120.

Hero, Alfred. "Non-Profit Organizations, Public Opinion, and United States Foreign Policy." International Journal.

33(1978), pp. 150-76.

Herring, George C., Jr. "Lend-Lease to Russia and the Origins of the Cold War, 1944-1945." The Journal of American History. 56 (1969), pp. 93-114.

Herter, Christian A. "Relation of the House of Representatives to the Making and Implementation of Treaties." Proceedings of the American Society of International Law. 45 (1951), pp. 55-60.

Hitchens, Harold L. "Influences on the Congressional Decision to Pass the Marshall Plan." Western Political Quarterly. 21 (1968), pp. 51-68.

Holsti, Ole R. and Rosenau, James N. "The Meaning of Vietnam: Belief Systems of American Leaders." International Journal. 32(1977), pp. 452-74.

Hopkins, Raymond. "The International Role of Domestic Bureaucracy." International Organization. 30(1976), pp. 405-32.

Hoxie, R. Gordon. "The Not So Imperial Presidency: A Modest Proposal." Presidential Studies Quarterly. 10(1980), pp. 194-210.

_____. "Presidential Leadership and American Foreign Policy: Some Reflections on the Taiwan Issue, With Particular Considerations on Alexander Hamilton, Dwight Eisenhower, and Jimmy Carter." Presidential Studies Quarterly. 9(1979), pp. 131-43.

Hudson, Daryl J. "Vandenberg Reconsidered." Diplomatic History. 1(1977), pp. 46-63.

Humphrey, Hubert H. "The Senate in Foreign Policy." Foreign Affairs. XXXVII (1959), pp. 525-36.

Javits, Jacob. "The Congressional Presence in Foreign Relations." Foreign Affairs. XLVIII (1970), pp. 221-34.

Jeffery, Kirk. "The Debate Over the British Loan, 1945-46." International Review of History and Political Science. 7 (1973), pp. 63-80.

Johnson, Loch and McCormick, James M. "Foreign Policy by Executive Fiat." Foreign Policy. 28(1977), pp. 117-138.

Kaiser, Fred M. "The House Committee on International Relations." Policy Study Journal. 5(1977), pp. 433-49.

_____. "Oversight and Foreign Policy." Legislative Studies Quarterly. (1977), pp. 255-68.

Kay, David Allen. "Unconstitutional Restrictions on the President of the United States in Foreign Aid Legislation, 1947-1964." Columbia Essays in International Affairs, The Deans Papers, 1965. Edited by Andrew W. Cordier. New York: Columbia University Press, 1966.

Kesselman, Mark. "Presidential Leadership in Congress on Foreign Policy." Midwest Journal of Political Science. 5 (1961), pp. 284-89.

_____. "Presidential Leadership in Congress on Foreign Policy: A Replication of a Hypothesis." Midwest Journal of Political Science. 9 (1967), pp. 401-6.

Kohl, Wilfred, L. "Nuclear Sharing in NATO and the Multilateral Force." Political Science Quarterly. 80 (1965), pp.

426

88-109.

Koledziej, Edward A. "Congress and Foreign Policy: Through the Looking Glass." Virginia Quarterly Review. 43 (1966), pp. 12-27.

_____. "Foreign Policy and the Politics of Interdependence." Polity. 9(1976), pp. 121-57.

Korb, Lawrence J. "Congressional Impact on Defense Spending, 1962-1973." Naval War College Review. 26(1973), pp. 49-62.

Lake, Anthony and Gelb, Leslie H. "Congress: Politics and Bad Policy." Foreign Policy. 20(1975), pp. 232-38.

Lanquette, William J. "The Battle to Shape and Sell the New Arms Control Treaty." National Journal. January 31, 1977, pp. 1984-93.

_____. "The Many Faces of the Jewish Lobby in America." National Journal. May 13, 1978, pp. 748-56.

_____. "The Plight of the Uncommitted on the Panama Canal Treaties." National Journal. March 11, 1978, pp. 385-87.

Lauk, Kurt J. "The European Perspective." Congress and Arms Control. Edited by Alan Platt and Lawrence D. Weiler. Boulder, Colorado: Westview Press, 1978.

Laurence, Edward. "The Changing Roles of Congress in Defense Policy-Making." Journal of Conflict Resolution. 20(1976), pp. 213-53.

Lee, Frederick Paul. "The Two Presidencies Revisited." Presidential Studies Quarterly. 10(1980), pp. 620-28.

LeLoup, Lance T. and Schull, Steven A. "Congress v. the Executive: The Two Presidencies Reconsidered." Social Science Quarterly. 59(1979), pp. 704-19.

Lerche, Charles O., Jr. "Southern Congressmen and the 'New Isolationism'." Political Science Quarterly. 65 (1960), pp. 321-37.

Levi, Werner. "Ideology, Interests, and Foreign Policy." International Studies Quarterly. 14 (1970), pp. 1-31.

Lillich, Richard P. "Requiem for Hickenlooper." American Journal of International Law. 69(1975), pp. 97-101.

Livingstone, Neil C. and von Nordheim, Manfred. "The United States Congress and the Angola Crisis." Strategic Review. 5(1977), pp. 34-35.

Long, Clarence D. "Nuclear Proliferation Can Congress Act in Time." International Security. 1(1977), pp. 52-66.

Lowi, Theodore J. "Making Democracy Safe for the World." Domestic Sources of Foreign Policy. Edited by James N. Rosenau. New York: The Free Press, 1967.

Mahajani, Usha. "Kennedy and the Strategy of Aid: The Clay Report and After." Western Political Quarterly. 18 (1965), pp. 656-68.

Maning, Bayless. "The Congress, the Executive and Intermestic Affairs: Three Proposals." Foreign Affairs. 57(197), pp. 308-24.

Manley, John F. "The Rise of Congress in Foreign Policy-Making." Annals of the American Academy of Political and Social Science. 397 (1971), pp. 60-70.

Mathias, Charles, Jr. "Ethnic Groups and Foreign Policy." Foreign Affairs. 59(1981), pp. 975-98.

McClellen, David S. "The 'Operational Code' Approach to the Study of Political Leaders: Dean Acheson's Philosophical and Instrumental Beliefs." Canadian Journal of Political Science. 4 (1971), pp. 52-78.

Miller, Nathan. "The Making of a Majority: Safeguard and the Senate." Inside the System. Edited by Charles Peterson and John Rothchild. New York: Praeger, 1973.

Moe, Ronald C. and Teel, Steven C. "Congress as Policy-Maker: A Necessary Reappraisal." Political Science Quarterly. 85 (1970), pp. 443-470.

Morrow, William L. "Legislative Control of Administrative Discretion: The Case of Congress and Foreign Aid." Journal of Politics. 30 (1968), pp. 985-1011.

Nigro, Fleix A. "Senate Confirmation and Foreign Policy." Journal of Politics. 14 (1952), pp. 281-99.

Nelson, Randall H. "Legislative Participation in the Treaty and Agreement Making Process." Western Political Quarterly. 13 (1967), pp. 154-171.

Parker, Glenn R. "Some Themes in Congressional Unpopularity." American Journal of Political Science. 21(1977), pp. 93-106.

Parker, Glenn R. and Parker, Suzanne L. "Factions in Committees: The U.S. House of Representatives." American Political Science Review. 73(1979), pp. 85-102.

Paterson, Thomas G. "The Quest for Peace and Prosperity: International Trade, Communism, and the Marshall Plan." Politics and Policies of The Truman Administration. Edited by Barton J. Bernstein. Chicago: Quadrangle Books, 1970.

_____. The Abortive American Loan to Russia and the Origins of the Cold War, 1943-1946." The Journal of American History. 56 (1969), pp. 70-92.

_____. "Presidential Foreign Policy, Public Opinion, and Congress: The Truman Years." Diplomatic History. 3(1979), pp. 1-18.

Payne, Richard J. and Ganaway, Eddie. "The Influence of Black Americans on U.S. Policy Towards South Africa." African Affairs. 79(1980), pp. 58-98.

Perlmutter, Oscar William. "Acheson vs. Congress." Review of Politics. 22 (1960), pp. 5-44.

Potter, William C. "Issue Area and Foreign Policy Analysis." International Organization. 34(1980), pp. 405-28.

Quade, Quentin L. "The Truman Administration and the Separation of Powers: The Case of the Marshall Plan." Review of Politics. 26 (1965), pp. 58-77.

Randolph, R. Sean. "The Byrd Amendment: A Postmortem." World Affairs. 141(1978), pp. 57-74.

Reichard, Gary W. "Divisions and Dissent: Democrats and Foreign Policy, 1952-1956." Political Science Quarterly. 93(1978), pp. 51-72.

Reid, Ogden R. "Congress and Foreign Policy." We Propose: A Modern Congress, Selected Proposals by the House Republican Task

428

Force on Congressional Reform and Minority Staffing. James C. Cleveland, Chairman. Edited by Mary McInnis. New York: McGraw-Hill, 1966.

Rielly, John E. "The American Mood: A Foreign Policy of Self Interest." Foreign Policy. 34(1979), pp. 74-86.

Roberts, Chalmers M. "The Day We Didn't Go to War." The Reporter. October 14, 1954, pp. 31-35.

Rodnitsky, Jerome L. "Two Men on a Horse: President Truman and Secretary of State Byrnes." International Review of History and Politics. 7 (1970), pp. 61-75.

Rosenau, James. "Foreign Policy as an Issue-Area." Domestic Sources of Foreign Policy. Edited by James Roseanu. New York: The Free Press, 1967.

Russett, Bruce and DeLuca, Donald. "'Don't Tread on Me': Public Opinion and Foreign Policy in the Eighties." Political Science Quarterly. 96(1981), pp. 381-400.

Salisbury, Robert H. "The Analysis of Public Policy: A Search for Theories and Roles." Political Science and Public Policy. Edited by Austin Ranney. Chicago: Markham Publishing Company, 1968.

Sandifer, Durward V. "Regional Aspects of the Dumbarton Oaks Proposals." Department of State Bulletin. 12 (January 28, 1945), pp. 50-53.

Schlesinger, Arthur M., Jr. "Congress and the Making of American Foreign Policy." Foreign Affairs. 51 (1972), pp. 78-113.

Sigelman, Lee. "A Reassessment of the Two Presidencies Thesis." The Journal of Politics. 41(1979), pp. 1195-1205.

_____. "The Dynamics of Presidential Support: An Overview of Research Findings." Presidential Studies Quarterly. 9(1979), pp. 206-16.

Sinclair, Barbara. "Agenda and Alignment Change, The House of Representatives, 1925-1978." Congress Reconsidered. Edited by Lawrence C. Dodd and Bruce I. Oppenheimer. Washington, D.C.: Congressional Quarterly Press, 1980.

Stassen, Glen H. "Individual Preference versus Role-Constraint in Policy-Making: Senatorial Response to Secretaries Acheson and Dulles." World Politics. XXV (1972), pp. 98-119.

Stevens, Charles J. "The Use and Control of Executive Agreements." Orbis. 20(1977), pp. 905-32.

Stevenson, Adlai, E., III. "A Call for National Leadership." Presidential Studies Quarterly. 9(1979), pp. 8-10.

Sundquist, James L. "The Crisis of Competence in Our National Government." Political Science Quarterly. 95(1980), pp. 183-208.

Tidmarch, Charles M. and Sabatt, Charles M. "Presidential Leadership Change and Foreign Policy Role-Call Voting in the U.S. Senate." Western Political Quarterly. 25 (1972), pp. 613-25.

Travis, Martin B., Jr. "John F. Kennedy: Experiments with Power." Power of the President in Foreign Affairs, 1945-1965. Edited by Edgar E. Robinson, Alexander De Conde, Raymond G. O'Conner, and Martin B. Travis, Jr.

San Francisco: The Commonwealth Club of California, 1966.

Trice, Robert H. "Congress and the Arab-Israeli Conflict: Support for Israel in the U.S. Senate, 1970-1973." Political Science Quarterly. 92(1977), pp. 443-64.

Truman, David B. "Functional Interdependence: The Elective Leaders, the White House, and the Congressional Party." The Presidency. Edited by Aaron Wildavsky. Boston: Little, Brown and Company, 1969.

Wells, Samuel F., Jr. "The Origins of Massive Retaliation." Political Science Quarterly. 96(1981), pp. 31-52.

Whittle, Richard. "Foreign Relations Committee Searches for Renewed Glory." Congressional Quarterly Weekly. March 14, 1981, pp. 477-79.

Wolman, Harold L. and Wolman, Dianne Miller. "The Role of the U.S. Senate Staff in the Opinion Linkage Process: Population Policy." Legislative Studies Quarterly. 2(1977), pp. 281-93.

Yochelson, John. "The American Presence in Europe: Current Debate." Orbis. 15(1971), pp. 784-807.

Zeidenstein, Harvey G. "The Reassertion of Congressional Power: New Curbs on the President." Political Science Quarterly. 93(1978), pp. 394-405.

Zimmerman, William. "Issue Area and the Foreign Policy Process." American Political Science Review. 67(1973), pp. 1204-12.

# Index

ABM, 199-201, 218, 289

Acheson, Dean, 4, 7, 11, 13-14, 19, 26, 28-30, 32-33, 35, 38-43, 47, 50-52, 55-56, 59-63, 66, 69-70, 75, 80-83, 89, 94, 99, 103, 117, 122-126, 129-135, 137-140, 157, 180, 186-187, 189-190, 197, 201, 213, 226-227, 231, 242, 245, 307, 309

Administrative structure (congressional impact on), 38, 69, 173, 184-185, 211, 212, 267, 271

Afghanistan, 254, 281, 286, 290, 293-294

Aiken, George, 1, 90, 146, 150, 193, 209, 238-239

Allen, James, 251

Allen, Richard, 282

Allot, Gordon, 115, 155

Anderson, Clinton, 30, 231

Angola, 271-273, 283, 290, 294, 307

Anticipated reaction (by Executive), 35, 41, 50, 56-59, 61-62, 87, 139-140, 158, 167, 169, 172, 174-175, 187, 189, 193, 212, 257, 266-267, 277-278, 310

Anti-communist rhetoric (used by Executive), 46-54, 64, 70-74, 76-77, 180-181

Appeasement, 3, 5, 8, I3-14, 85, 134, 145, 187, 220

Appropriations, 9, 34-35, 37-38, 50, 60, 76, 85, 124, 126, 133, 139, 158, 180, 185, 196-198, 214-215, 233, 235, 270, 308

Arab-Israeli War (1967), 113, 164-169, 198, 310

Arends, Leslie, 211, 222

Argentina, 25-27, 271

Arms Control Impact Statement (1975), 293

Arms sales, 75, 168, 256-261, 264

Aswan Dam, 157-160, 164, 180, 310

Atomic energy, 14, 19, 28-34, 125

Attlee, Clement, 31-32, 125

Austin, Warren, 22, 37

Australia, 288

AWACS, 256-261, 265, 276, 287-288, 293-295, 299, 304, 308-310

Baker, Howard, 258, 280, 282, 292

Ball, George, 126, 196

Barkley, Alben, 46-47, 65, 206

Baruch, Bernard, 14, 33-34, 36, 60

Bator, Francis, 176

Begin, Menachem, 257-258, 260

Benton, William, 50, 81, 192

Berding, Andrew, 141

Berlin Crisis (1959), 88-90, 208, 215

Bevin, Ernest, 13, 15, 61

Bidault, Georges, 15, 61

Biddle, Francis, 187

Bidden, Joseph, 260

Bingham, Jonathan, 257

Bipartisanship, 2, 5-6, 12-13, 16, 20, 41, 51, 68, 79-83, 88-89, 91-92, 94-95, 102-103, 115-116, 126, 130, 132, 137, 145, 155, 158-160, 162-163, 166, 168, 189, 193, 220, 223, 225, 230, 234, 245, 280, 298-299, 304-305, 307
Bloom, Sol, 25, 27, 229
Bohlen, Charles, 4, 58, 63, 71, 116, 188-189, 197, 200
Boschwitz, Rudolph, 260
Bowles, Chester, 95, 117, 127, 142-143, 214, 216, 223, 226, 232, 239, 181, 186, 188, 190, 192, 196
Brademas, John, 263-264
Braden, Spruille, 26-27
Bradley, Omar, 138
Brezhnev Leonid, 129, 269, 278
Bricker, John, 100-103, 193, 243
Bricker Amendment, 94, 100-102, 193, 213, 219, 243, 255
Bridges, Styles, 59, 75, 92, 99, 132, 143, 186-189, 192, 230
Britain, see Great Britain
British Loan, 19, 41, 43-47, 49-50, 53-54, 80, 199, 238, 240, 242, 245, 306
Brown, Harold, 275
Brzezinski, Zbigniew 275
Buckley, James, 269
Bumpers, Dale, 260-261
Bundy, McGeorge, 103-104, 126-127, 143
Bunker, Ellsworth, 193
Bush, George, 281-282
Bush, Vannevar, 30-31
Butler, Paul, 207
Byrd Amendment, 155, 235, 264
Byrd, Harry, 115, 124, 155, 235, 245, 264
Byrd, Robert, 258, 274, 279-280
Byrnes, James F., 1-5, 11-17, 20, 28-29, 31-33, 36-37, 41, 45, 47, 86, 92, 188, 210

Cambodia, 152-155, 199-200, 250-251, 291
Caffery, Jefferson, 61, 63, 71-72

Capehart, Homer, 14, 47, 107-108, 195
Carney, Robert, 87
Carom effect, 41-42, 75, 100, 102-103, 124, 128, 132-133, 140, 143, 153, 163, 165-166, 173, 176, 178, 180, 185, 192-193, 195-197, 215-216, 234, 310
Carr, Wilber 196
Carter, Jimmy, 248, 252-254, 256-257, 259, 265, 270-271, 273, 275-282, 286-288, 290, 292-295, 298-299, 301, 308
Case, Clifford, 255, 265, 272, 279, 289, 291
Celler, Emmanuel 157, 168
Central Intelligence Agency, 103, 113, 187, 234
Chavez, Dennis, 211
Chiang Kai-shek, 74-75, 82, 87, 130-132, 138, 142, 186, 199, 213
Chile, 183, 271, 282
China, 68, 74-76, 82-86, 91, 112-113, 115, 117, 124, 130-134, 137-145, 155, 158, 178, 180-181, 186-187, 192, 197, 199, 211, 213, 222, 231, 250, 254, 277, 294-295, 301, 310
China Lobby 138-139, 141-142, 144
Church, Frank, 109-111, 119, 151-152, 154, 218, 221, 235, 252, 288-289, 292-293, 298, 300
Clark, Dick, 256, 272
Clark, Joseph, 176-177, 282
Clark, William, 298
Clay, Lucius, 73, 215
Clayton, William, 11, 35-36, 40-41, 43-45, 55, 57-58, 65, 69-70
Clifford, Clark, 6, 62, 67, 73
Cohen, Benjamin, 5, 13
Collado, Emilio, 35
Colmer, William, 36, 59
Colson, Charles, 226
Committee of One Million, 133, 142
Compton, James, 194
Confirmation, see Personnel
Congress, Foreign contacts by,

36, 63, 75, 89-90, 127, 181, 198-199, 201, 206, 260, 269, 274, 277-278; Foreign perceptions of, 21-22, 44, 57-58, 61, 123, 126, 129-130, 133, 136, 159-160, 163, 165, 168, 182-183, 197-202, 278-279, 288; Individual ego factor 7, 15-16, 82-83, 90-91, 104-105, 127, 144, 155, 178, 194-195, 222, 230-233, 275-276, 297 (also see Consultation); Institutional prerogative 12, 114, 122-126, 128, 173-174, 194, 214, 233-236, 276, 279-280, 288 (also see Consultation; Congress, Individual ego; Congress, Institutional pride); Institutional pride, 4-5, 9, 12-16, 19-20, 26, 65-66, 80-89, 114-116, 144-146, 194-195, 229-233, 247-251, 254, 259-260, 266, 268, 272, 275, 277, 307-308 (Also see Consultation; Congress, Institutional prerogative; Congress, Individual ego); Members as advisors, 12-13, 16-17, 24-25, 138, 173, 191; Staffing/Organization, 249, 270, 273, 295-299; Use of as negotiating device, 59, 106, 139, 144, 166-167, 182, 199-200

Connally, Tom, 13, 15-16, 19, 22-24, 26-28, 31-32, 42-43, 82, 102-103, 122-123, 137, 191, 196, 203, 226-227, 230-232, 297, 300

Connell, William, 118

Consensus (as Executive value), 85-87, 88-91, 103-116, 138, 166-167, 259, 309-310

Consensus (as congressional value), 53, 80, 85-86, 94-96, 150, 204, 209-210, 304

Consular Convention, 175-177, 179

Consultation (or lack of), 19, 24, 30-32, 45, 50, 53, 65-66, 80-83, 85-90, 95, 104, 106, 108-110, 113-117, 122, 129, 144-146, 154, 158-159,

163, 166, 178, 191, 196, 207-209, 233, 234, 258, 263, 291-292, 307-308

Coombs, Philip 196

Cooper, John Sherman 154, 250

Cooper-Church Amendment, 154, 250

Corwin, Edwin, 301-302

Coudert, Frederic, 68

Cranston, Alan, 273, 279

Crisis (impact on Congress), 52-53, 67-68, 73-74, 84-86, 124, 137-138, 146, 165-166, 206-210, 248-249, 290-292, 304

Criticism (as congressional means), 14-17, 20, 67, 85, 87, 94, 99-100, 104-105, 113-114, 116, 119, 132, 134, 138, 141-145, 147, 155

Crowley, Leo, 30, also see Lend-Lease

Cuba, 107-108, 119, 200, 209, 221, 229, 271, 281, 294, 309

Culberson, Paul, 201

Culver, John, 256, 261

Cutler, Robert 160

Cyprus, 241, 263, 307

Czech Crisis (1948), 55, 73, 198, 213

Davis, Nathaniel, 272, 282

DeConcini, Dennis 260, 275-276

Defense, 85, 113, 127, 129, 136, 153-154, 167, 211-212, 295

Deference (by Congress), 27, 53, 67, 81, 88, 146-147, 150, 163, 171-172, 186, 203-206, 216-217, 225, 236, 248-250, 273, 277, 282, 289-293, 295, 304

Destler, I.M., 266-267

Dewey, Thomas 74, 80, 101, 117, 159, 189, 245

Dillon, C. Douglas, 103, 107

Dirksen, Everett, 90, 104-105, 150, 168, 177-179, 181, 185, 191-192, 195, 197, 204-205, 219, 231, 233, 305

Dodd, Thomas, 241

Dole, Robert, 274, 276

Dominican Republic, 110, 113, 176, 205, 209

Douglas, Lewis, 57, 61, 63, 71, 75

Dulles, Allen, 46, 103, 159, 187

Dulles, John Foster, 5, 12-14, 16, 27-28, 59-60, 80, 82-84, 102, 104, 117, 134-135, 138-141, 145, 157-164, 172, 180, 187-191, 193, 195, 208, 214, 220, 226-227, 243, 309

Dutton, Fred, 127, 260

Eagleton, Thomas, 291

Eastland, James 45, 245?, 291

Eaton, "Doc", 25, 46, 68, 71

Eban, Abba 164, 166-168

Egypt 157-158, 161, 164-167, 185, 198, 257, 261-263, 283, 310

Eisenhower, Doctrine, 87, 208, 234

Eisenhoswer, Dwight, 80, 83-104, 110-111, 113-114, 116-117, 119, 126, 134-135, 138-140, 145-146, 148, 150, 157, 159-161, 163-166, 172-173, 178, 180, 185, 187-195, 202-208, 210, 214-215, 217-220, 222-223, 225-232, 234, 238-239, 242, 261, 267, 285, 302, 305-306, 309

Electoral connection, see Partisanship

El Salvador, 192, 283

Elsey, George, 51, 65

Ervin, Sam, 205, 256

European Recovery Program (ERP), 4, 56-58, 60-62, 66-73, 75, 213, 242, 266

Executive prerogative (as Executive value), 97-98, 108, 177, 286-287

Executive strength/weakness, 1-3, 6, 11, 25-26, 29-32, 40, 53-54, 56, 59, 62-63, 65-66, 74, 76, 87, 101-102, 114, 128-129, 131, 159, 172-173, 176-179, 210-217, 248, 252-254, 258, 263, 271, 273-274, 280, 299, 302-303, 308

Fascell, Dante, 174

Fenno, Richard, 227, 229, 251

Ferguson, Homer, 80, 188, 225

Flanders, Ralph, 53-54, 59

Ford, Gerald, 228, 232, 248, 252, 254, 261,263, 268-270, 273, 277, 281, 283, 286, 288, 290-292

Foreign Aid, 124, 180-185, 200-201, 214, 216, 218, 222, 226-227, 233, 238-239, 242, 261, 263, 272-273, 277, 283; To China (Taiwan), 74-77, 114, 131-133, 144, 175; To Egypt, 158-160; To Israel, 165-169, 180-185, 193-194; To Spain, 200-201, 213-217; To Soviets, 34-38; To Britain, 43-48; Truman Doctrine, 49-54; Marshall Plan, 54-72; See also Soviet Loan, British Loan, Marshall Plan, Truman Doctrine

Formosa, 86-87, 131-132, 139, 144-145, 156, 163, 206-209, 211

Forrestal, James V., 4, 6, 10-11, 13, 30, 32, 47, 55, 64-66

Foster, William, 103

France, 38, 57-58, 60-61, 65-66, 71-72, 84-85, 99, 105, 121, 125-127, 160-161, 168, 290

Fraser, Donald, 252

Fulbright, William, 93, 95, 98, 103-104, 108-111, 113, 127, 142-144, 148, 151-153, 163, 169, 176-177, 181, 184, 188, 192, 194-195, 200, 204-206, 208-210, 214-216, 222, 224-227, 230, 232, 234, 239, 243, 250, 252, 262, 289, 298, 300, 304, 309

Geneva, 41, 55, 105, 145

Genocide Treaty 100, 102, 242, 265, 310

George, Walter F., 26, 86-87, 90-91, 93, 95, 100-102, 122, 124, 158, 160, 191, 208-209, 226-227, 230, 242, 297, 300

Germany, 9, 17, 25, 34, 58, 71, 73, 100, 110, 125, 127, 129, 147, 241

Glenn, John, 259-260, 276, 293

Gonzales, Henry, 183

Godley, G. McMurtrie, 194, 281
Goldwater, Barry, 107, 112, 118, 145-146, 152, 178, 220, 273, 276-277, 288-289
Goodell, Charles, 219-220, 305
Gorton, Slade, 260
Grassley, Charles, 260
Gravel, Mike, 262
Great Britain, 19, 21, 23, 25, 30-31, 34, 37, 40-47, 49-50, 53-55, 57-58, 60-61, 63, 65, 80, 85, 89, 98, 105, 121, 125, 127, 138-140, 158-159, 160-161, 165, 180, 199, 201, 238, 240, 242, 245, 253, 263
Greece, 3, 45, 49-52, 54-55, 57-60, 62, 64, 241, 245, 263-264, 307
Green, Marshall, 144
Green, Theodore Francis, 95, 163, 208
Green, William, 257
Grew, Joseph, 9-11, 35
Gromyko, Andrei 23, 278
Gruening, Ernest, 147, 166
Griffin, Robert, 264

Hagerty, James 84, 94, 96-97, 222
Haig, Alexander, 258, 271, 281-282
Haldeman, Robert, 114
Hall, Leonard, 92, 220
Halleck, Charles 88, 191, 226
Hanes, John, 160
Harlow, Bryce, 96, 140, 185, 195, 222, 226, 230, 232, 234, 292
Harriman, Averell 6, 8-11, 22, 34-36, 46-47, 63, 68, 118, 137, 278
Hartke, Vance, 148
Hatch, Carl, 64, 67
Hatfield, Mark, 154, 260
Hayden, Carl, 181
Hayes, Wayne, 233
Hechler, Kenneth, 81
Helms, Jesee, 282, 298
Helms, Richard, 289
Helsinki Accords, 255
Henderson, Loy, 51
Herbert, F. Edward, 115
Herter, Christian, 66, 71, 88, 165, 204, 232, 238

Hickerson, John, 51, 100
Hickenlooper, Bourke, 90, 92, 104, 131, 182, 204, 232-234
Hickenlooper Amendment 182-183
Hilsman, Roger, 107, 119, 205, 309
Holifield, Chet 127, 154, 241
Holt, Pat, 198, 249, 296
Hoover, J. Edgar, 177-178
Hoover, Herbert, Jr. 193, 214
Hruska, Roman, 178
Hull, Cordell, 4-5, 13, 15, 20-21, 23, 39, 216
Human Rights Convention 100, 242
Humphrey, Hubert, 86-87, 93, 95, 115, 117-118, 127, 136, 142, 149, 151, 153, 159, 166, 168, 176, 179, 205, 207-209, 214, 221, 223, 225, 233, 240-241, 250, 253, 265, 273, 282, 289, 304
Hungary, 11, 37, 63, 100, 160, 241

Ickes, Harold, 42
India, 99, 105, 181, 184, 192-193, 293-294
Indochina, 84-86, 99, 102, 105, 145, 154-155, 165, 182, 194, 200, 206, 210-211, 217, 250, 255, 289, 302
Indonesia 85, 182
Information and expertise gap, 205-208, 210-211, 215, 249, 295-299
Inouye, Daniel, 261
Interest groups, Blacks, 243, 265; Economic, 41-43, 45, 69, 158-159, 171-174, 179, 183-184, 239, 260, 264, 267-268; German, 241; Irish, 44, 241, 263; Jewish, 127, 157-158, 160-162, 168, 240-241, 256-258, 260-263, 265, 268-270, 307; Polish, 7-8, 20-21, 188, 241; Miscellaneous, 133, 138-139, 141, 144, 268-270, 291; Other Domestic, 268-270, 296 (also see Committee of One Million)
Intermestic affairs (merging of international/domestic issue areas), 41-43, 45, 63, 66,

68-69, 122, 128, 148-149,
158-159, 171-182, 184, 215,
226-227, 236-239, 260, 266-
270, 296, 306 (also see Perceptual focus)
International Trade Organization, 41-42
Intra-House/intra-committee
rivalry, 124, 188, 251-252,
297
Investigations (as congressional means), 98, 119, 132,
134-136, 139, 142-143, 187-
188, 201-202, 208 (also see
McCarthyism)
Invoke office (as Executive
means), 88, 175, 208, 210,
259, 305
Iran, 15, 85, 248, 256, 258,
281, 290, 292-295
Isolationism, 3-6, 8, 41, 124-
126, 128, 149, 228, 254
Israel, 95, 112-113, 157-169,
180, 198, 240-241, 256-265,
270, 293, 301
Italy, 64-66, 71, 123, 127, 240
Ives, Irving, 157

Jackson, C.D., 172
Jackson, Henry, 98, 104, 115,
182, 219, 268-270, 278-279,
307
Jackson-Vanik Amendment, 265,
268-270
Japan, 82, 99, 130, 134, 138-
139, 142, 174, 199, 215,
233, 301
Javits, Jacob, 101, 143, 150,
157, 169, 209, 241, 250,
261, 269, 280, 289-292, 300
Jenkins, Thomas, 41
Jenner, William, 99, 125, 140,
195
Jepsen, Roger, 259
Johnson, Louis, 138
Johnson, Lyndon, 86, 91, 93,
95-96, 98, 104, 106, 108-
115, 117-119, 126-129, 142-
143, 145-152, 158, 160, 162-
163, 166-168, 175-179, 181,
185, 192, 194-195, 198, 203-
204, 206, 208-210, 212, 215-
218, 222-224, 226, 228, 230-
235, 239, 243, 248, 268,

289, 297, 302, 309-310
Joint-Chiefs-of-Staff, 84, 87,
131, 138, 147, 150, 211-212,
278-280, 303
Jones, Joseph, 50-51, 54
Jordan, 164-165, 167, 198, 256-
257
Judd, Walter, 75, 132-133, 141,
192, 199, 214-215, 219, 231

Keating, Kenneth, 107-108, 220,
241
Kefauver, Estes, 145
Kennedy, John, 103-108, 142,
145, 173, 175, 181-182, 190,
196, 200, 204, 215, 218-219,
221-222, 224, 227-228, 230-
233, 235, 238, 243, 267,
302, 309-310
Kennedy, Robert, 107-108, 143,
148, 151-152?, 198
Kern, Harry, 84
Kerr, Robert, 218
Khrushchev, Nikita 107, 200-
201, 204
Kennan, George, 14, 51, 56-58,
60, 71-72, 100, 182, 187
Kirkpatrick, Jeanne, 298
Kissinger, Henry, 114-116, 128-
129, 143-145, 152-156, 168-
169, 183, 186, 199-201, 212,
220-221, 225, 249, 252-254,
259, 261, 263, 269, 272,
275, 286, 308-309
Knight, Frances, 197
Knowland, William, 82, 85-86,
92-93, 96-97, 101-102, 132-
133, 141-142, 145, 158, 162,
189, 192, 207, 232
Korea, 57, 99, 111, 123-125,
130, 132-134, 136-137, 140,
145, 148-149, 180, 201, 206-
207, 209, 211, 213, 234,
251, 288
Kosygin, Alexi 198, 278
Krug, Julius, 63, 68

LaGuardia, Fiorello, 37-38
Laird, Melvin, 129, 153-154,
156, 192-193, 220
Laos, 105-106, 152, 155, 194
Larson, Arthur, 194
Latin America, 23-27, 174, 181-
183, 192, 194, 198

Lauche, Frank, 91
Laxault, Paul, 276
Leadership in Congress, 7, 41, 59, 66-68, 82-83, 86, 95, 98, 114, 132, 163, 177-178, 189, 203-204, 230-231, 251-252, 297, 298
Leahy, William, 10-11, 31
Lebanon, 164-165, 290
Legislative veto, see War power, National Commitments Resolution, AWACS, Nonproliferation
Lehman, Herbert, 86, 89, 189-190
Leigh, Monroe, 291
Lend-Lease, 8-11, 19, 34-36, 59
Lilienthal, David, 33
Lippmann, Walter, 1, 110, 124, 230, 243
Lodge, Henry Cabot, Jr., 91, 94, 97, 103, 131, 140, 149, 161, 163-164, 191, 193, 219, 232
London, 29, 31, 40, 46-47
London Conference (1945), 11-15, 31
Long, Russell, 259, 267, 269
Lovett, Robert A., 61, 63, 65-66, 69, 71-72, 103, 121-122, 184, 199
Lucas, Scott, 81-82, 138
Luce, Claire Booth, 194-195

MacArthur, Douglas, 133, 176, 201, 211
MacGregor, Clark, 226
Macmillan, Harold 98, 140
Macomber, William 93, 197, 204, 230
Mann, Thomas, 179
Manning, John, 266
Mansfield, Mike, 86-87, 105, 113-114, 127-129, 144, 146-148, 151, 153, 168, 176-177, 194, 199, 207, 209, 223, 227, 230, 234-235, 291
Mao Tse-tung, 130-131, 140, 186
Marcy, Carl, 142, 176, 198, 205, 226-227, 296
Marshall, George C., 3, 5, 8, 27, 41, 47, 50-53, 55-56, 58-75, 122, 126, 130, 134, 157, 245

Marshall Plan, 54, 64, 67-70, 72-75, 77, 180, 213, 216, 232, 238, 283, 306
Martin, Joseph, 14, 65, 71, 86, 88, 90, 194, 207, 211
Mathias, Charles, 128, 218, 235, 261-263, 265
Mayaguez, S.S. 291-292, 294-295
McCardle, Carl, 220
McCarran, Pat, 131
McCarthy, Eugene, 110, 151-152
McCarthy, Joseph, 83, 94, 98, 111, 133-135, 143, 186-187, 189, 194, 197, 202, 309
McCarthyism, 54, 83, 111-112, 134, 146, 150, 202, 213, 310
McClellan, John, 115, 166, 196, 232
McCloskey, Pete, 257, 264
McCloy, John, 1-2, 103, 193
McCone, John, 103, 146
McCormack, John, 39, 46-47, 65, 88, 90, 93, 153, 163, 192, 208, 230
McGee, Gale, 219, 265, 273
McGhee, George, 143
McGovern, George, 154, 221, 226, 263, 292, 300
McIntyre, Thomas, 274
McLeod, Scott, 92-93, 187, 189, 192, 197
McMahon, Brien, 81, 188
McMahon, George, 125, 239
McNamara, Robert, 103, 107, 109, 146-147, 149-150, 166-167, 211-212
Meany, George, 268, 269, 270, 272
Melcher, John, 260
Middle East, 51, 56-57, 84, 87-88, 91, 95-96, 121, 146, 156-169, 220, 240, 257, 261, 265, 268, 283, 295, 307
Middle East Crisis (1957), 83, 87, 160-164, 208-209
Middle East Crisis (1967), 164-169, 198, 209
Military-Congressional Relations, 147, 150, 211-212
Milliken, Eugene, 41, 99, 173
Mills, Wilber, 179
Molotov, V.V., 8-11, 13, 21, 26, 34-35, 58-59, 61
Mondale, Walter, 155, 260, 275,

280
Mongolia, 143, 271
Monroe Doctrine, 24
Monroney, A.S. Mike, 184
Morgan, Thomas "Doc", 193, 222
Morgenthau, Robert, 34
Morrow, Wright, 195-196
Morse, Wayne, 86-88, 95, 110,
    147, 166, 194, 199, 206, 208
Morton, Thurston, 177-178, 224
Moynihan, Patrick, 276
Multilateral Force (MLF), 113,
    241, 281, 310
Mundt, Karl, 50, 64, 92-93,
    125, 149-150, 175, 177-179,
    199, 209, 212, 221, 226, 273
Munich, 3, 17, 145
Murphy, Robert, 135, 187
Muskie, Edmund, 153, 199, 202,
    221

Nassar, Gamal Abdel, 158, 161,
    164-165, 167, 283
National Commitments Resolu-
    tion, 235, 255
National Security Council, 98,
    131, 146, 153, 291
Nelson, Gaylord, 291
New Deal, 5-6, 12, 45, 64, 69,
    99, 187
Nguyen Van Thieu, 156
Nitze, Paul, 189
Nixon, Richard, 84, 89-91, 94-
    96, 100, 103, 114-116, 121,
    128-129, 133-134, 143-145,
    147, 152-156, 161, 168, 174,
    183, 193, 199-200, 211, 218-
    221, 224-226, 228, 233, 238,
    240, 247-249, 251-254, 259,
    263, 265-266, 269, 277, 283,
    302, 305, 308-309
Northern Atlantic Treaty Organi-
    zation (NATO), 121-130, 139,
    161, 200, 202, 230, 235,
    264, 281
Nourse, Edwin G., 63, 68
Nuclear non-proliferation, 293

O'Brien, Lawrence, 109, 224
O'Connor, Roderick, 141
Olympics (1980), 254
O'Neill, Thomas "Tip", 291-297
Organization of American States
    (OAS), 122-123

Pace, Frank, 138
Packwood, Robert, 257-258, 260
Pakistan, 293-294, 301
Panama Canal, 24, 199, 235,
    273-276
Paris, 12, 16, 58, 60-61, 65,
    71, 84, 89, 156
Partisan appeal (as Executive
    means), 81, 94, 96-97, 99,
    149, 151, 153, 172, 220,
    305-306
Partisan politics (by Con-
    gress), 4-6, 13, 16, 41-42,
    64-65, 68-69, 74, 81-82, 92-
    98, 107-108, 112, 118, 127,
    137, 142, 147-148, 152-153,
    157, 160-163, 176, 179, 184,
    188, 195-196, 215, 221-228,
    240-241, 260, 268-270, 273-
    274, 280, 300, 304, 307
Partisan politics (by Execu-
    tive), 12, 13, 72-73, 81,
    91-98, 106-108, 112, 118,
    133, 140, 142, 149-151, 153,
    157, 160-161, 168, 174, 189-
    192, 219-221, 280
Party loyalty, 99-103, 224,
    227-229
Passman, Otto, 115, 185, 231
Pastor, Robert, 174, 182-183,
    266-267, 302-303
Pastore, John, 224
Pasvolsky, Leo 21-22
Patronage and Pork, 191, 193,
    217-219, 260, 270-271, 276,
    279
Patterson, Robert, 30, 42, 55,
    69
Pearson, James, 218
Pell, Clairborne, 297, 299
Pepper, Claude, 245
Perceptual focus (struggle over
    international/domestic
    focus), 46-47, 171, 174,
    180-181, 236-239, 259, 266-
    268, 306 (see also Intermes-
    tic affairs)
Percy, Charles, 224, 252, 262,
    282, 293, 297-299
Perle, Richard, 268
Personnel (congressional impact
    on), 26-27, 33, 69-70, 82,
    91-93, 103-115, 134-135,
    138-139, 141, 158, 172, 185-

197, 215, 281-283
Peru, 183
Poland, 7-8, 10, 15, 21-23, 37,
    100, 254, 290, 294, 307
Political support/sanction (by
    Executive), 5, 97, 110, 115,
    218-220, 243, 260, 281, 305,
    also see Partisanship
Potsdam, 7, 10-11
Pragmatic/innovative    policy,
    125, 244-246, 254, 306-307
Public Law 480, 184
Public Opinion 3-4, 14, 22, 58,
    66, 80-81, 98-99, 106, 116-
    119, 147-150, 153-156, 163,
    166, 224-227, 274-276, 279,
    287, 300-301, 309; Congress,
    impact on 37, 111, 112

Quemoy-Matsu, 85-87, 99, 165,
    209

Rabb, Maxwell, 160
Rabin, Yitzak, 168
Racism, 196, 210, 242-243
Radford, Arthur, 84-87
Randall, Clarence, 172-173
Randolph, Jennings, 274, 276
Rayburn, Sam, 39-40, 46-47, 65,
    86, 91, 93, 158, 163, 193,
    204, 207, 214, 230, 297
Reagan, Ronald, 118, 145, 248,
    257-260, 265, 271, 273, 281-
    283, 286-288, 290, 293-295,
    298-299, 301, 305
Reedy, George, 117
Reilly, John 127, 149
Reston, James, 12, 20, 32, 62
Rhodes, John, 291
Rhodesia, 196, 264
Ribicoff, Abraham, 269
Richards, James, 89-91, 124,
    127, 158, 165, 191, 226
Ridgeway, Matthew, 83
Riegle, Donald, 224
Robertson, Walter, 87, 141-142
Roche, Charles, 147, 149, 151
Rockefeller, Nelson, 23-26,
    265, 286
Rogers, William, 153-154, 193,
    197
Rooney, John, 93, 196-197, 231
Roosevelt, Eleanor, 7, 14
Roosevelt, Franklin, 1-2, 4, 7-

9, 12-13, 15, 19-20, 23, 28,
    34, 76, 116-117
Rosenau, James, 287
Rosenthal, Benjamin, 257
Rostow, Eugene, 167
Rostow, Walt, 105, 113, 126,
    178
Rowan, Carl, 196
Rowny, Edward, 278, 282
Rusk, Dean, 104-106, 109, 113-
    114, 117, 136, 138, 143,
    146-147, 149, 166-167, 178,
    182, 190, 196, 212, 225,
    230, 233, 289, 297
Russell, Richard, 86, 95-96,
    98, 100, 104, 108, 113, 115,
    124, 128, 150, 154, 163,
    177-178, 205, 208, 230, 232,
    235, 255
Rumania, 11, 13-14, 63

St. Lawrence Seaway, 42-43, 239
Saltonstall, Leverett, 85, 241
Sanction avoidance (by Execu-
    tive), 41-42, 75, 100, 108,
    124, 127, 139, 159, 176-177,
    258, 273, 310
Saudi Arabia, 257-260, 262,
    276, 293-294, 301, 308
Sarbanes, Paul, 263
Saxbe, William, 155-156, 224
Scammon, Richard, 118
Schlesinger, Arthur, Jr., 54,
    205, 253, 304
Schlesinger, James, 281, 286
Schultz, George, 269
Scott, Hugh, 114, 150, 155,
    199, 224, 226, 234, 238,
    240, 250-251
Smathers, George, 91
Smith, H. Alexander, 37, 52,
    63-64, 87, 91, 101, 137-139,
    163, 188, 202, 208, 242
Smith, Margaret Chase, 114, 134
Smith, Walter Bedell, 57-58,
    101-102
Sorenson, Theodore, 103, 106-
    108, 200, 218-219, 282, 309
South Africa, 253
South East Asia Treaty Organiza-
    tion (SEATO), 105, 123, 206,
    289
Soviet Loan, 19, 34-38, 59, 77
Soviet Union/Russia, 2-11, 13-

17, 19-24, 26, 29-37, 46-47, 49, 52-61, 64, 70-73, 76-77, 90, 104, 107-108, 112-114, 123-124, 129-131, 140, 143-144, 152, 155, 158-159, 161-162, 165, 175-179, 182, 198-201, 204, 208, 216, 220-221, 241-242, 245, 249, 254, 264, 266, 268-269, 271, 277-281, 293, 308

Spain, 75, 201

Sparkman, John, 139, 188-189, 191, 252, 272, 298

Stalin, Joseph, 2, 9-11, 13-14, 21, 23, 36

Stassen, Harold, 22, 25

State Department, 2-5, 9, 13, 19-22, 25, 28, 34-42, 49-50, 54, 57-58, 63, 65, 69-73, 81-82, 92-93, 102, 107, 114, 117, 119, 123, 127, 131-134, 136-138, 143-145, 157, 159, 165, 168, 171, 173-174, 177, 182-184, 186-187, 189, 192, 194, 196, 201, 204, 216, 229, 231, 238, 243, 251-252, 267, 271-273, 280

Stennis, John, 85, 113, 115, 154, 159, 166, 218, 251

Stettinus, Edward, 2, 8, 15, 19, 21-26, 35, 210

Stevenson, Adlai, 88, 91, 103, 158, 223

Stimson, Henry L., 8, 11, 17, 29-31, 33, 69

Stolarz, Henry, 288

Stone, Richard, 300

Strategic Arms Limitation Talks (SALT), 199, 201, 212, 249, 254

Supreme Court 277

Symington, Stuart, 114, 128, 136, 148, 221, 239, 252

Taber, John, 7, 46, 58, 60, 64, 68, 93,

Taft, Robert, 7, 9, 66, 68, 81, 92, 96, 99, 111, 118, 125, 132, 137-138, 189, 193, 199, 222, 230, 297

Taiwan Treaty, 273, 276-277, 288

Talmadge, Herman, 226, 269, 276

Taylor, Maxwell, 147, 149, 245

Teng Hsiao-ping, 277

Test Ban Treaty (1963), 200-201, 233, 235

Thurmond, Strom, 174

Trade, 38-43, 218, 234-235

Treaties 11, 138, 175-77, 233, 255, 256, 273-281; 1957 Peace, 13-14; U.N. Ratification, 19-23, 27-28; OAS, 27-28; Atomic Energy, 40-42; NATO 121-124; Panama, 235, 273-275; Genocide, 242; Taiwan, 275-77; SALT, 277-281

Tobey, Charles, 53, 232

Tower, John, 115, 260, 289

Truman, Harry, 1-6, 8-17, 19-21, 25, 28-33, 35-36, 41-43, 45, 49, 51-54, 58, 60, 62-70, 72-74, 76, 80-83, 91, 93, 98, 104, 108, 111-112, 115, 119, 121, 124, 126, 130-134, 136-140, 145-146, 157-158, 163, 181, 184, 186, 189-190, 194, 196, 203, 209-211, 213, 217, 222, 225, 227-228, 234, 239-240, 245, 252, 267, 283, 302, 307-308, 310

Truman-Attlee-King Accord, 31-32

Truman Doctrine, 2, 7, 49-56, 59-61, 70, 73, 75-76, 80, 180, 238, 283

Tsongas, Paul, 290, 298

Tunney, John, 273, 300, 307

Turner, Stansfield, 280

Turkey, 51-52, 54-55, 57-59, 62, 64, 241, 245, 263-264, 283, 290

Udall, Morris, 291

United Nations, 3, 7-8, 12, 14-15, 19-23, 25-28, 34-35, 57, 87, 91, 100, 133, 139-142, 144, 160-164, 166-167, 182, 190-191, 195, 237, 243, 264, 310

UNRRA, 34-38, 57, 61

U.S. Information Agency (USIA), 181, 196, 234

Valenti, Jack, 110, 148, 150, 212, 233

Vance, Cyrus, 275, 279, 292
Vandenberg, Arthur, 1-17, 18-28, 31-34, 36, 41-45, 47, 51-54, 59-63, 65-71, 73-75, 79-80, 82-83, 86, 111, 121-124, 130, 132, 178, 186, 189-191, 203, 219, 222, 225, 230-232, 241, 245, 249, 287, 289, 291, 297, 307
Van Der Beugel, Ernest, 57, 61
Vanik, Charles, 268-269
Vietnam, 84, 105-106, 110, 112, 114-116, 118, 127-130,135-136, 143-156, 166, 168-169, 176-181, 192, 198, 199-200, 206, 209-210, 212, 215-216, 219, 221, 223-226, 234, 239, 243, 247, 248, 249, 252, 254-255, 281-283, 295
Vincent, John Carter, 75, 186-187
Vinson, Carl, 125
Vinson, Fred, 30, 36, 43
Vorys, John, 5, 9, 53, 60, 71, 132, 162-163

Waggonner Joe, 115, 264

War Powers Resolution, 250, 254-255, 283, 286-287, 289-292, 301
Warnke, Paul, 278
Watergate, 210, 247, 249, 252, 266, 281, 282, 283
Watson, Marvin, 233
Webb, James, 81, 119, 189
Wheeler, Burton, 46-47
Wherry, Kenneth, 137-138
Wilcox, Francis 30, 53, 193, 301
Wiley, Alexander, 82-83, 89, 219
Wilson, Harold, 253
Wilson, Henry, 218

Yalta Conference, 2-3, 7-8, 11, 20, 22-23, 34, 116, 186, 188, 222
Yarton, Gus, 263
Yugoslavia, 182, 226
Young, Milton, 179
Young, Stephen, 195

Zablocki, Clement, 144, 265, 288, 292, 296
Zimbabwe, see Rhodesia
Zorinsky, Edward, 274, 276
Zaire, 113, 290-291